Liberty in Mexico

Liberty in

Mexico

Writings on Liberalism from the

Early Republican Period to the

Second Half of the Twentieth Century

Edited and with an Introduction by

JOSÉ ANTONIO AGUILAR RIVERA

Translated from the Spanish by

JANET M. BURKE and TED HUMPHREY

LIBERTY FUND

Indianapolis

Translations, introduction, editorial additions, and index © 2012 by Liberty Fund, Inc.

"La tradición liberal" (The Liberal Tradition), "La literatura y el estado" (Literature and the State), and "Poesía, mito, revolución" (Poetry, Myth, Revolution) are © Octavio Paz and are translated and reprinted here by permission of Marie Tramini de Paz.

Cover art: *Ceremony in Which Santa Anna Knights Manuel Lebrija to the New Order of Guadalupe*, by Edouard Pingret, CONACULTA-INAH-MEX. Reproduction authorized by the Instituto Nacional de Antropología e Historia, Mexico City.

Library of Congress Cataloging-in-Publication Data

Liberty in Mexico: writings on liberalism from the early republican period to the second half of the twentieth century/edited and with an introduction by José Antonio Aguilar Rivera; translated from the Spanish by Janet M. Burke and Ted Humphrey.
    p.   cm.
Includes bibliographical references and index.
ISBN 978-0-86597-841-6 (hardcover: alk. paper)
ISBN 978-0-86597-842-3 (pbk.: alk. paper)
1. Liberalism—Mexico—History—19th century.   2. Liberalism—Mexico—History—20th century.   I. Aguilar Rivera, José Antonio, 1968–   II. Burke, Janet, 1943–   III. Humphrey, Ted, 1941–
JC574.2.M6L56   2012
320.510972—dc23   2012005442

LIBERTY FUND, INC.
8335 Allison Pointe Trail, Suite 300
Indianapolis, Indiana 46250-1684

Contents

Introduction
Liberty and Liberalism in Mexico
by José Antonio Aguilar Rivera[1]

After their independence from Spain in the early nineteenth century, all of the new nations of Spanish America (except for
the brief and ill-fated Mexican Empire) adopted the same model of political organization: the liberal republic. At the beginning of the twenty-
first century all of these countries remain republics. Yet, at the same
time, the Latin American dictator became a hallmark of despotism and
brutality during the past century. This contradiction between ideal and
real has produced a vast body of literature. Historians, political scientists, and sociologists have tried to explain the pervasive authoritarian-
ism of Spanish America.

One key peculiarity of Latin America among developing and former
colonial regions is its liberal experience, the "ideas and institutions that
became established in this outpost of Atlantic civilization."[2] Yet, the failure of written constitutions to bring about the rule of law in that part
of the world is well documented. This skepticism has a long history. Indeed, on December 6, 1813, Thomas Jefferson wrote to his friend Baron
Alexander von Humboldt:

> I think it most fortunate that your travels in those countries were
> so timed as to make them known to the world in the moment they
> were about to become actors on its stage. That they will throw off
> their European dependence I have no doubt; but in what kind of
> government their revolution will end I am not so certain. History,
> I believe, furnishes no example of a priest-ridden people maintain-

1. The author wishes to thank Fabiola Ramírez and Roberto Mostajo for their assistance with suggestions for research.

2. Charles A. Hale, "The Reconstruction of Nineteenth-Century Politics in Spanish
America: A Case for the History of Ideas," *Latin American Research Review* 8 (summer
1973): 53–73.

ing a free civil government. This marks the lowest grade of ignorance, of which their civil as well as religious leaders will always
avail themselves for their own purposes. The vicinity of New Spain
to the United States, and their consequent intercourse, may furnish
schools for the higher, and example for the lower classes of their
citizens. And Mexico, where we learn from you that men of science
are not wanting, may revolutionize itself under better auspices than
the Southern provinces.[3] These last, I fear, must end in military
despotisms. The different casts of their inhabitants, their mutual
hatreds and jealousies, their profound ignorance and bigotry, will be
played off by cunning leaders, and each be made the instrument of
enslaving others.[4]

Likewise, an elderly John Adams wrote to James Lloyd in 1815:

The people of South America are the most ignorant, the most big-
oted, the most superstitious of all the Roman Catholics in Chris-
tendom. . . . No Catholics on earth were so abjectly devoted to their
priests, as blindly superstitious as themselves, and these priests
had the powers and apparatus of the Inquisition to seize every suspected person and suppress every rising motion. Was it probable,
was it possible, that such a plan as [Francisco] Miranda's, of a free
government, and a confederation of free governments, should be
introduced and established among such a people, over that vast continent, or any part of it? It appeared to me more extravagant than
the schemes of Condorcet and Brissot to establish a democracy in
France, schemes which had always appeared to me as absurd as similar plans would be to establish democracies among the birds, beasts,
and fishes.[5]

3. Alexander von Humboldt traveled in South and North America at the beginning
of the nineteenth century and wrote important books on the geography and society of
the nations he visited. Jefferson refers in this letter to his political essay on New Spain.
See Alexander von Humboldt, *Political Essay on the Kingdom of New Spain* (Norman: University of Oklahoma Press, 1988).

4. Thomas Jefferson to Alexander von Humboldt, in Thomas Jefferson, *Writings,* ed.
Merrill D. Peterson (New York: Library of America, 1984), p. 1311.

5. Letter to James Lloyd, March 27, 1815, in John Adams, *The Works of John Adams,*

The independence of Spanish America did not make Jefferson more optimistic regarding the future of those nations. On May 14, 1817, he wrote to the marquis de Lafayette:

> I wish I could give better hopes of our southern brethren. The achievement of their independence of Spain is no longer a question. But it is a very serious one, what will then become of them? Ignorance and bigotry, like other insanities, are incapable of self-government. They will fall under military despotism, and become the murderous tools of the ambition of their respective Bonapartes; and whether this will be for their greater happiness, the rule of one only has taught you to judge. No one, I hope, can doubt my wish to see them and all mankind exercising self-government, and capable of exercising it. But the question is not what we wish, but what is practicable? As their sincere friend and brother then, I do believe the best thing for them, would be for themselves to come to an accord with Spain, under the guarantee of France, Russia, Holland, and the United States, allowing to Spain a nominal supremacy, with authority only to keep the peace among them, leaving them otherwise all the powers of self-government, until their experience in them, their emancipation from their priests, and advancement in information, shall prepare them for complete independence.[6]

SPANISH AMERICA AND THE LIBERAL TRADITION

The importation of liberal constitutionalism into Spanish America has been the object of much political and scholarly debate. Much of the discussion has focused on the performance of institutions. As Charles Hale asserts:

Second President of the United States, comp. Charles Francis Adams, 10 vols. (Boston: Little, Brown, 1856), vol. 10, pp. 143–45. The key reason for Adams's skepticism regarding the possibilities of democracy in South America was the deleterious consequences of religious intolerance. "They [the people of South America] believe salvation to be confined to themselves and the Spaniards in Europe. They can scarcely allow it to the pope and his Italians, certainly not to the French; and as to England, English America, and all other Protestant nations, nothing could be expected or hoped for any of them, but a fearful looking for of eternal and unquenchable flames of fire and brimstone." Ibid.

6. Thomas Jefferson to the marquis de Lafayette, in Jefferson, *Writings,* pp. 1408–9.

Much of the skepticism about the liberal experience has focused on constitutionalism—the effort to guarantee individual liberty and limit central authority by the legal precepts of a written code. The strivings of liberal legislators to establish separation of powers, federalism, municipal autonomy, and even at times parliamentary supremacy or a plural executive typify the divergence between ideals and reality and between liberal institutional forms and political practice that is the hallmark of Latin American politics.[7]

As a result, Latin America was excluded from the liberal experience by many scholars. Liberalism, they contend, was only a disguise for traditional practices. One of the supporters of this view argues that "eighteenth-century political liberalism was almost uniformly and overwhelmingly rejected by Spanish America's first statesmen."[8] These authors assert that liberalism was a political tradition alien to the Spanish American nations. The British scholar Cecil Jane identified several contradictions within Spanish culture. Spaniards were idealistic extremists who sought both order and individual liberty in such perfect forms that politics went from one extreme (despotism) to the other (anarchy) rather than "finding stability in constitutional compromise between the two contending principles."[9] Conservatives in power carried the "pursuit of order" to such an extreme as to provoke a violent reaction in behalf of liberty. Likewise, when liberals enacted "standard western liberal protections of the individual," Spanish Americans did not use these liberties with the responsibility expected by the "Englishmen who had developed these liberties, but rather carried them to the extreme of anarchy."[10]

Richard Morse finds the key to understanding Spanish America in

7. Hale, "The Reconstruction," p. 55.

8. Glen Dealy, "Prolegomena on the Spanish American Political Tradition," *Hispanic American Review* 48 (February 1968): 43.

9. Lionel Cecil Jane, *Liberty and Despotism in Spanish America* (Oxford: Clarendon Press, 1929). I follow the critical review of cultural approaches of Safford. See Frank Safford, "Politics, Ideology, and Society in Post-Independence Spanish America," in Leslie Bethell, ed., *The Cambridge History of Latin America* (Cambridge: Cambridge University Press, 1995), vol. 3, pp. 414–17.

10. Ibid.

the Spanish patrimonial state.[11] The state was embodied in the patrimonial power of the king, who was the source of all patronage and the
ultimate arbiter of all disputes. Without the presence of the king the
system collapsed. According to Morse, Spanish American leaders in
the nineteenth century were constantly trying to reconstruct the patrimonial authority of the Spanish crown. One factor obstructing the reconstruction of authority along traditional Spanish lines, Morse argues,
was the meddling of Western constitutional ideas. Anglo-French liberal
constitutionalism — with its emphasis on the rule of law, the separation
of powers, constitutional checks on authority, and the efficacy of elections — stood as a contradiction to those traditional attitudes and modes
of behavior that lived in the marrow of Spanish Americans. Because
liberal constitutionalism was ill adapted to traditional Spanish American culture, "attempts to erect and maintain states according to liberal
principles invariably failed." The authority of imported liberal constitutional ideas, while insufficient to provide a viable alternative to the traditional political model, was often sufficient to undermine the legitimacy
of governments operating according to the traditional model.

These interpretations are wanting in several respects. For one thing,
they treat culture in an excessively static manner; and while it is true
that liberal constitutional ideas in Spanish America failed to gain the
hegemony that they enjoyed in other parts of the world, they did have a
significant effect on modes of political thought and became at least partially incorporated into the political rules.[12]

Never before were liberal constitutional procedures applied in so
many places at the same time as in the first thirty years of the nineteenth century. To assume that this fact says nothing about liberal constitutionalism is myopic at best. Until very recently, scholars had refused
to draw any lessons from the Latin American liberal experiment. While
it is true that many liberal principles flew in the face of Spanish politi-

11. See Richard Morse, "Toward a Theory of Spanish American Government," *Journal of the History of Ideas* 15 (1954): 71–93; Morse, "The Heritage of Latin America," in
Louis Hartz, ed., *The Founding of New Societies: Studies in the History of the United States,
Latin America, South Africa, Canada, and Australia* (New York: Harcourt, Brace & World,
1964); and Morse, *Soundings of the New World: Culture and Ideology in the Americas* (Balti-
more: Johns Hopkins University Press, 1989).

12. Safford, "Politics, Ideology, and Society," pp. 416–17.

cal traditions and the realities of Spanish America at the time, historians have not seized the opportunity to see Spanish America as the laboratory where liberal theories were put to the test. Until then, liberals had little empirical evidence to support their claims of universal applicability; the historical record was inconclusive at best.[13] Why was the evidence from Spanish America disregarded by liberal pundits? Embedded in the central propositions of liberalism, Joyce Appleby contends, "was the story of its own triumph, but it was a peculiarly ahistorical one."[14] The idea of progress helps to explain why, in the eyes of past and present liberals, the failure of liberalism in Spanish America was dismissed so easily. "Shining through the darkness that was the past," Appleby asserts, "were liberal triumphs to be recorded, examined, and celebrated. The rest of known history was useless to an enlightened present, its existence a reproach to the human spirit so long enshrouded in ignorance."[15] Since Latin America could not be celebrated as a liberal triumph it was repudiated from the liberal pantheon.

Yet, Spanish America constitutes the great postrevolutionary liberal constitutional experiment. After independence all of the revolutionary leaders moved quickly to write constitutions. As Frank Safford asserts, almost all of these constitutions "proclaimed the existence of inalienable natural rights (liberty, legal equality, security, property); many provided for freedom of the press and some attempted to establish jury trials. Almost all sought to protect these rights through the separation of powers and by making the executive branch relatively weaker than the legislature."[16] Within the first five years of the movement for independence in northern South America approximately twenty constitutions were drawn up in the provinces and capitals of the old viceroyalty of New Granada (present-day Ecuador, Colombia, Venezuela, and Panama). By the time Adams voiced his skepticism about the people of South America, Spanish America had already begun to experiment with

13. Even theoretically, the general applicability of the liberal constitutional model was problematic, as Montesquieu's small-republic theory evidenced.

14. Joyce Appleby, *Liberalism and Republicanism in the Historical Imagination* (Cambridge: Harvard University Press, 1992), p. 8.

15. Ibid.

16. Safford, "Politics, Ideology, and Society," p. 358.

the institutions of representative government, and highly competitive elections had taken place in New Spain in 1812. Recent historical studies on comparative elections in the early nineteenth century show that one of the peculiarities of Spanish America was the precocious adoption of modern forms of representation and universal suffrage when voting restrictions were predominant in Europe. Studies such as those of Richard Warren on popular participation in early elections in Mexico show that the selection of representatives by universal suffrage often had an impact on popular participation that challenges the usual depiction of elections as an exclusive and elite affair. Indeed, as both José María Luis Mora and Lucas Alamán argue in this book, one of their key political proposals in the 1830s was to *limit* broad popular participation in elections by restricting the vote to property holders. Moreover, even in countries where formal restrictions for voting applied, elections still had a significant effect on the process of democratization.[17]

The "liberal constitutional moment" denotes the moment, and the manner, in which liberal constitutionalism made its appearance in the Hispanic world at the dawn of the nineteenth century.[18] In Spain it can be traced back to 1808. In Rio de la Plata, New Granada, and Venezuela the moment fell between 1810 and 1827; in Bolivia it was concentrated in the 1820s; and in Mexico and Guatemala its peak occurred between 1820 and 1830.[19] As Frank Safford states, this "reformist burst" was followed almost everywhere by a period of pessimism and conservatism.

One of the main weaknesses of the intellectual history of the Iberian world has been its isolationism. Historians of Spanish America, Anthony Pagden asserts, "generally study Spanish America as if neither New France nor the Thirteen Colonies had ever existed." After all, America began as Europe transplanted: "The intellectual history of its early de-

17. See, particularly, Richard Warren, "Elections and Popular Political Participation in Mexico, 1808–1836," in Vincent C. Peloso and Barbara A. Tenenbaum, eds., *Liberals, Politics, and Power* (Athens: University of Georgia Press, 1996), pp. 30–59.

18. On the roots of Spanish liberalism, see Roberto Breña, *El primer liberalismo hispánico y los procesos de emancipación de América 1808–1824* (Mexico: El Colegio de México, 2006).

19. This periodization corresponds to Safford's phase of initial reform in Spanish America. See Safford, "Politics, Ideology, and Society," p. 353.

velopment is a history of transmission, and reinterpretation, a history of how traditional European arguments from classic texts were adapted to meet the challenges of new and unforeseen circumstances."[20]

One of the peculiarities of the liberal constitutional moment in the Hispanic world is that the sway of liberal ideas was, for the most part, uncontested.[21] Absolutism was more a practice than an ideology. Moreover, the Bourbon absolutism that preceded the liberal revolutions in Spain and its colonies was an enlightened despotism. There was a continuity between absolutist reform and liberal revolution: a confidence in the power of reason to order society. Moreover, liberalism found in Spain native support in the theoretical writings of Gaspar Melchor de Jovellanos and of schoolman Francisco Suárez.[22] For Spanish liberals, however, the "enlightened" character of the monarchy ceased when Charles IV

20. Anthony Pagden, *The Uncertainties of Empire: Essays in Iberian and Ibero-American Intellectual History* (Great Yarmouth: Variorum, 1994), p. x.

21. According to Guerra, in Mexico the liberal victory was complete. François-Xavier Guerra, *Mexico: Del antiguo régimen a la revolución* (Mexico: Fondo de Cultura Económica, 1991), vol. 1, p. 184.

22. Jovellanos was the "major intellectual figure" in Spain from 1780 to 1810. See Gaspar Melchor de Jovellanos, *Obras,* 2 vols. (Madrid: Atlas, 1951–52). On Jovellanos's arguments regarding the ancient constitution of Spain, property rights, and education, see Charles A. Hale, *El liberalismo mexicano en la época de Mora, 1821–1853* (Mexico: Siglo XXI, 1972), pp. 66–73. See also John R. Polt, *Jovellanos and His English Sources* (Philadelphia: American Philosophical Society, 1964). In the seventeenth century, the Jesuit Francisco Suárez was of the opinion that a monarchy—or rule "by one head"—afforded the best form of political government. Yet, the source of the king's power was an act of transfer on the part of the community as a whole, expressive of its "own consent." In transferring its power to a monarch, a community did not deliver itself into "despotic servitude." The transfer was made "under obligation, the condition under which the first king received the kingdom from the community." The monarch should rule "politically." One who ruled otherwise ruled tyrannically. In extreme circumstances such a ruler might lawfully be deposed. See Francisco Suárez, *Tractatus de Legibus ac Deo Legislatore* (Madrid: Consejo Superior de Investigaciones Científicas, 1971–81). Besides his *Tractatus de Legibus* (1610), Suárez's other influential works include *Defensio Fidei Catholicae et Apostolicae Adversus Anglicanae Sectae Errores* (1613) and *Opus de Triplici Virtute Theologico: Fide, Spe, et Charitate* (1621). See also J. H. Burns, ed., *The Cambridge History of Political Thought, 1450–1700* (Cambridge: Cambridge University Press, 1991), pp. 292–97.

and his favorite minister, Godoy, showed clear signs of political incompetence.[23]

Several developments prepared the ground for the uncontested predominance of liberalism in the early nineteenth century. First, there was no classical republican tradition to dispute the field; Spain had no equivalent of James Harrington. As the fifteenth-century debate between Leonardo Bruni and Alonso de Cartagena over the merits of Bruni's translation of the *Ethics* showed, the Italians saw Aristotle as an author whose texts had some literary and philosophical merit, while the Spaniards regarded him merely as "an exponent of natural virtue."[24] Although the impact of humanist Aristotelianism was felt in Spain at about the same time as it was in Italy, by the end of the sixteenth century Spain had reached the brink "of that desperate obscurantism so characteristic of the seventeenth and eighteenth centuries."[25] When Florentine political thought was flourishing in Italy, the School of Salamanca was instead devoted to new scholasticism and speculative thought.

The other historical development that proved crucial for Spanish liberalism was the French Revolution. Hispanic revolutionaries would have to perform two different tasks at the same time: on the one hand, to make the revolution, on the other, to avoid following the steps of France.[26] The terms "liberalism" and "liberal" were coined by the Spanish Cortes Generales[27] in Cádiz while drafting the 1812 Constitution.[28]

23. François-Xavier Guerra, *Modernidad e independencias: Ensayos sobre las revoluciones hispánicas* (Mexico: Fondo de Cultura Económica/MAPFRE, 1992), pp. 26–27.

24. Anthony Pagden, "The Diffusion of Aristotle's Moral Philosophy in Spain, ca. 1400–ca.1600," in *Uncertainties of Empire*, p. 305. See also Anthony Pagden, *Spanish Imperalism and the Political Imagination: Studies in European and Spanish-American Social and Political Theory 1513–1830* (New Haven: Yale University Press, 1990).

25. Pagden, *Uncertainties of Empire*, p. 312.

26. Guerra, *Modernidad e independencias*, p. 251.

27. The *cortes* were the legislatures in Spain.

28. For the Spanish origin of the term "liberal," see Vicente Llorens, "Sobre la aparición de *liberal*," in *Literatura, Historia, Política* (Madrid: n.p., 1967). "Liberal," as a political label, J. G. Merquior asserts, "was born in the Spanish Cortes of 1810, a parliament that was rebelling against absolutism." J. G. Merquior, *Liberalism Old and New* (Boston: Twayne, 1991), p. 2. Claudio Véliz asserts: "It is fair to add that its [the term "liberal"] international career was actually launched by the poet Robert Southey, who in 1816,

To recast the Spanish American revolutions as constitutive elements of the liberal experience it is necessary to assess the effectiveness of the institutional strategies designed to limit the power of absolute sovereigns in large states that are found at the core of the modern liberal republic.[29]

Before the American Revolution there was no historical precedent to predict where the application of the ideas of the Enlightenment would lead. Abstract thinking was much more important in the American and French cases than in the Iberian world. Furthermore, the impact of the French Revolution on Spanish elites was mainly negative. Spanish American revolutionaries knew, from the French experience, where the revolutionary logic could lead.[30] These fears were not without foundation: a large population of these countries consisted of oppressed Indians. The slave revolt of Santo Domingo reminded them of the dangers of a social revolution. Thus, the reactionary atmosphere of Europe "both reinforced these fears and also subjected Spanish American leaders to more conservative ideological influences than they had known before 1815."[31]

The most singular trait of the Spanish American revolutions is the absence of both modern popular mobilization and Jacobinism.[32] This assertion runs counter to a long-established tradition that considers the Spanish American revolutions as the ideological heirs of the 1789 revolution.[33] The "decisive" influence of Rousseau over Spanish Ameri-

---

used the Spanish form as a scornful epithet addressed to the British Whigs whom he described as 'British *liberales'* in an obvious reference to the Spanish political faction responsible for the disorderly and ultimately unsuccessful reforms initiated by the cortes of Cádiz in 1812." Claudio Véliz, *The New World of the Gothic Fox: Culture and Economy in English and Spanish America* (Berkeley: University of California Press, 1994), p. 130.

29. As Biancamaria Fontana asserts, the accent of the liberal republic was not so much on hereditary government as on "the limited, moderate character of the power that *any* government should be allowed to exercise." Biancamaria Fontana, "Introduction: The Invention of the Modern Republic," in Biancamaria Fontana, ed., *The Invention of the Modern Republic* (Cambridge: Cambridge University Press, 1994), pp. 1–5.

30. Guerra, *Modernidad e independencias,* p. 35.

31. Safford, "Politics, Ideology, and Society," p. 359.

32. Terror would preclude terror from happening in the ensuing revolutions. Guerra, *Modernidad e independencias,* p. 36.

33. See José Miranda, *Las ideas y las instituciones políticas mexicanas* (Mexico City: Universidad Nacional Autónoma de México, 1952); Solange Alberro, Alicia Hernández,

cans is, for many historians, an uncontested fact. Yet, this interpretation misses one of the most distinctive features of the Spanish American revolutions. Paraphrasing J. G. A. Pocock, the Spanish American revolutions can be seen less as the last political act of Jacobin radicalism than as the first political act of modern liberalism. Not Rousseau but Benjamin Constant would prove to be the most relevant influence for Spaniards and Spanish Americans in the early nineteenth century. The universal influence of Constant in the 1820s and 1830s, Safford states, "is only one indication of the hegemony of moderate European constitutional ideas among Spanish American intellectuals."[34] The influence of Constant is important because modern liberalism owes much to him.[35] Many of Constant's ideas, particularly those developed in response to the Terror and its Thermidorian aftermath (such as the limited nature of popular sovereignty, the freedom of the press, the inviolability of property, and the restrictions upon the military), became incorporated into the liberal theory that still informs many of the constitutions of democratic countries today.

Constant provided Spanish Americans with a practical guide to con-

------

and Elías Trabulse, eds., *La revolución francesa en México* (Mexico City: El Colegio de México, 1992); Leopoldo Zea, ed., *América Latina ante la revolución francesa* (Mexico City: Universidad Nacional Autónoma de México, 1993); and Jacqueline Covo, "La idea de la revolución francesa en el congreso constituyente de 1856–1857," *Historia Mexicana* 38 (July–September 1988), 69–79.

34. "[T]he three authors most frequently encountered were Montesquieu, Constant, and Bentham. Rousseau, of great help in justifying the establishment of revolutionary governments between 1810 and 1815, was decreasingly relevant to Spanish American concerns after 1820." Safford, "Politics, Ideology, and Society," p. 367. See also Ricardo Levene, *El mundo de las ideas y la revolución hispanoaméricana de 1810* (Santiago: Editorial Jurídica de Chile, 1956), pp. 179–218.

35. On Constant, see Benjamin Constant, *Political Writings* (Cambridge: Cambridge University Press, 1988); Constant, *Principles of Politics Applicable to All Governments,* trans. Dennis O'Keeffe, ed. Etienne Hofmann (Indianapolis: Liberty Fund, 2003); Guy H. Dodge, *Benjamin Constant's Philosophy of Liberalism: A Study in Politics and Religion* (Chapel Hill: University of North Carolina Press, 1980); Stephen Holmes, *Benjamin Constant and the Making of Modern Liberalism* (New Haven: Yale University Press, 1984); Etienne Hofmann, *Les "Principes de politique" de Benjamin Constant,* 2 vols. (Geneva: Droz, 1980); and Marcel Gauchet, ed., *Benjamin Constant: De la liberté chez les modernes* (Paris: Le Livre de Poche, 1980).

stitution making.[36] The political elite was interested, above all, in works devoted to the practical arts of government rather than in "abstract theoretical treatises on the foundation of sovereignty"; thus, Spanish Americans turned to Constant's *Curso de política* for its usefulness in constitution writing.[37] Constant was also popular among Spanish readers, Hale asserts, because they found themselves in a similar circumstance: José María Luis Mora and other liberals faced revolution and arbitrary power, just as Constant did in 1815. Therefore they shared the latter's urgency for establishing safeguards for individual liberty, an urgency that "was not felt in the Anglo-Saxon world."[38]

Despite the decades of factional struggle and cyclical outbursts of dictatorship that followed independence in many Latin American countries, the search for a constitution and the reform of the old order were the main motivations behind the different groups in dispute. Later on, as most countries entered a phase of increasing political stability by the mid-nineteenth century, the observance of constitutional norms and liberal values was also essential to understand crucial conflicts among the political elite.

LIBERTY AND LIBERALISM IN MEXICO

As political practice strayed from ideal, Mexican historians and politicians sought to reaffirm the country's liberal past. Many books and articles have attempted to show that liberalism was at the core of the founding of the republic in spite of authoritarian practices.[39] Liberal theories had to contend with traditional ideas and practices, such as the common negotiation among actors over the enforcement of laws, as well as long-established patron-client relations. For years, historians debated

---

36. Translations of Constant were readily available to Spanish-speaking readers. The standard translation was Benjamin Constant, *Curso de política constitucional,* trans. Marcial Antonio López (Madrid: Imprenta de la Compañía, 1820). In his translation, López suppressed the part of the book devoted to religious tolerance. He claimed that tolerance was irrelevant to Spanish Americans because the only religion practiced there was Roman Catholicism.

37. Safford, "Politics, Ideology, and Society," p. 367.

38. Hale, *Liberalismo mexicano,* p. 72.

39. This scholarship is epitomized by Jesús Reyes Heroles, *El liberalismo mexicano,* 3 vols. (Mexico: Fondo de Cultura Económica, 1988).

whether modernity had lost to tradition or vice versa. Daniel Cosío
Villegas, in his well-known *Historia moderna de México* (1955), claimed
that political practice after the Reforma and the República Restaurada
(the era of liberal dominance in the nineteenth century) had "betrayed"
the political constitution of the country.[40] Jesús Reyes Heroles, on the
contrary, proposed that liberalism had been successful in establishing
an alliance between the middle classes and the lower strata of the population. Whereas Cosío Villegas focused on the second half of the nineteenth century, Reyes Heroles's optimism was grounded in an analysis
of the first decades after independence.

In contemporary Mexico, nineteenth-century liberalism is not just a
historical phenomenon. It is, as Charles Hale states, an ideological land-
mark. The political relevance of liberalism has often obstructed sound
historical research.[41] National histories, as Appleby recognizes, rest on
a volatile mixture of the moral and the instrumental. Because they "aim
to establish order through shared sentiments, they seek consensus, but
because they partake in scholarly traditions inimicable to propaganda,
they encourage critical reasoning."[42] Until the late 1960s, the historiog-
raphy on liberalism reflected more the first trait than the second. Reyes
Heroles, a statesman, was far from a detached scholar.[43] His interpretation of liberalism was inevitably partisan.

The debate on liberalism in Mexico centers on the potency ascribed
to inherited intellectual traditions. Liberal historians, following the lead
of Cosío Villegas, have constructed an ideal picture of late-nineteenth-
century Mexico (1867-76). Under liberal rule, they contend, the country enjoyed unparalleled liberty, and individual rights flourished as they
had never before—or since. In order to establish the rule of law, the
country must look back to its liberal past, these historians claim. This
use of history by liberal intellectuals has been challenged. François-

40. Daniel Cosío Villegas, *Historia moderna de México,* 7 vols. (Mexico: Editorial
Hermes, 1955); and Cosío Villagas, *La Constitución de 1857 y sus críticos* (Mexico: Editorial Hermes, 1957).

41. Charles A. Hale, "Los mitos políticos de la nación mexicana: El liberalismo y la
revolución," *Historia Mexicana* 46, no. 4 (April-June 1997), p. 830.

42. Appleby, *Liberalism and Republicanism,* p. 31.

43. Jesús Reyes Heroles was minister of education as well as president of the ruling
party in Mexico, the PRI, in the 1960s and 1970s.

Xavier Guerra, Laurens Ballard Perry, and Fernando Escalante assert that the historical record does not support the rosy picture portrayed by Cosío Villegas and other sympathetic historians of the Restored Republic.[44] Echoing Morse, these three scholars claim that liberal institutions presupposed the existence of a body of citizens. In Mexico these were absent from the political scene: the relevant actors were not individuals but the corporations, the army, and the Church as well as the Indian communities. Traditional practices superimposed liberal forms. Escalante characterized liberal citizens in Mexico as "imaginary citizens,"[45] but other scholars have not given up the effort to establish historically the roots of limited and constitutional government in Mexico.[46]

Against the nationalistic "official" history Charles Hale provides a more objective overall view of liberalism in Mexico. His work still is

44. François-Xavier Guerra, *México: Del antiguo régimen a la revolución,* 2 vols. (Mexico: Fondo de Cultura Económica, 1991); Laurens Ballard Perry, *Juárez and Díaz: Machine Politics in Mexico* (DeKalb: Northern Illinois University Press, 1978); and Fernando Escalante, *Ciudadanos imaginarios* (Mexico: El Colegio de México, 1993).

45. Escalante, *Ciudadanos imaginarios,* pp. 13–20. For a survey on the current literature on liberalism in Mexico, see Alfredo Ávila, "Liberalismos decimonónicos: de la historia de las ideas a la historia cultural e intelectual," in Guillermo Palacios, coord., *Ensayos sobre la nueva historia política de América Latina* (Mexico: El Colegio de México, 2007), pp. 117–18.

46. One of the most interesting developments in the literature of nineteenth-century liberalism is the interpretation of how liberal innovations interacted with traditional political structures. Perhaps liberal institutions did not work as they were expected to, but they certainly changed the political scenario of the time. For instance, by mandating the formation of municipalities in territories containing more than one thousand persons, the liberal Spanish Cádiz Constitution changed radically the traditional structure of representation in Spanish America. A vast constellation of townships was created by this liberal reform. After independence, national leaders had to contend with a large number of newly created municipal governments that had been organized during the last years of Spanish rule and were reluctant to cede their power to a national state. See Antonio Annino, "El Jano bifronte mexicano: una aproximación tentativa," in Antonio Annino and Raymond Buve, eds., *El liberalismo en México* (Amsterdam: Asociación de Historiadores Latinoamericanistas Europeos, 1993), pp. 184–85. On representation, see François-Xavier Guerra, "The Spanish-American Tradition of Representation and Its European Roots," *Journal of Latin American Studies* 26 (1994): 1–35. More recently, see Alfredo Ávila, *En nombre de la nación: La formación del gobierno representativo en México* (Mexico: CIDE/Taurus, 1999).

the best and most authoritative account on the subject.[47] Prior to Hale's work, little comparative research had been undertaken.[48] Hale argued that

constitutionalism in Mexico took two forms, the doctrinaire and the historical or traditional. The doctrinaire tendency reflected a belief that rigid adherence to or imposition of the precepts of the written document, however general or abstract, could guarantee the realization of constitutional order. Doctrinaire constitutionalists often took a radical and democratic political stand, believing it was necessary to change society to conform to the constitution. Historical or traditional constitutionalists, arguing that a constitution should reflect social and historical reality, tried to change precepts they found abstract and unrealizable in Mexico. They tended to be politically moderate or conservative and socially elitist; historical constitutionalists called for "strong government," at the same time resisting personal presidential power. Historical constitutionalism in Mexico drew its inspiration from a current of French political thought that had its origins in Montesquieu and was put forth in the nineteenth century by Benjamin Constant, Alexis de Tocqueville, and Edouard de Laboulaye. French constitutionalists idealized Anglo-American institutions and made their point of departure a critique of the French Revolution and the egalitarian revolutionary tradition.[49]

47. Hale's three main works are *Mexican Liberalism in the Age of Mora, 1821–1853* (New Haven: Yale University Press, 1968) [The references are from the Spanish translation: Charles A. Hale, *El liberalismo mexicano en la época de Mora* (Mexico: Siglo XXI, 1972)]; *The Transformation of Liberalism in Late Nineteenth-Century Mexico* (Princeton: Princeton University Press, 1989); and *Emilio Rabasa and the Survival of Porfirian Liberalism* (Stanford: Stanford University Press, 2008).

48. A short article comparing Mexican and European liberalisms was published in 1959: José Miranda, "El liberalismo mexicano y el liberalismo europeo," *Historia Mexicana* 8 (1959): 512–23.

49. As Hale further develops: "By the mid-nineteenth century French historical constitutionalism was also receiving major influence from the German historical school of law, whose key figure was Frederic Charles de Savigny. Savigny's highly influential manifesto of 1814 rejected the tendency toward French-inspired legal codification in Germany and posited 'the spirit of the nation' as the only source for all law. Edouard

After 1857, the principal debates between doctrinaire and historical constitutionalists in Mexico

focused on the democratic and egalitarian provisions of the Constitution of 1857—the rights of man, universal male suffrage, a single chamber legislature, parliamentary government, a weakened executive, and popular election of judges. The debates emerged first in 1878 when historical constitutionalists, led by Justo Sierra and his colleagues in the newspaper *La Libertad,* attacked the "dogma of equality" that permeated the Constitution and called for conservative reforms. They did so in the name of "scientific politics," since by the 1870s the new scientific philosophy of positivism had melded with historical constitutionalism. They called themselves "new" or "conservative" liberals as opposed to "old" liberals, such as José María Vigil and Ignacio M. Altamirano, doctrinaire constitutionalists who defended the democratic and egalitarian provisions of the 1857 document. The debate resurfaced in 1893 over an effort by the historical constitutionalists, again led by Justo Sierra, to reform the Constitution to make judges irremovable, instead of being popularly and periodically elected, and thus subject to political manipulation. The measure was designed to limit the increasingly personal power of President Porfirio Díaz. They were again opposed by doctrinaire defenders of the pure Constitution (who did not necessarily support the personal power of Díaz). In the course of the debate the historical constitutionalists, or advocates of scientific politics, came to be labeled *"científicos"* and the doctrinaire constitutionalists "Jacobins," labels that became embedded in the political rhetoric of the next thirty years.[50]

---

de Laboulaye, who wrote an appreciation of Savigny in 1842, was to become an important guide for Mexican historical constitutionalists of the later nineteenth century." Charles A. Hale, "The Civil Law Tradition and Constitutionalism in Twentieth-Century Mexico: The Legacy of Emilio Rabasa," *Law and History Review* 18, no. 2 (2000), 4–7.

50. Ibid. According to Hale, "the nineteenth-century current of historical constitutionalism, infused with scientific politics or positivism, was perpetuated after 1906 by the jurist and historian Emilio Rabasa, a latter-day *científico.*"

As Hale asserts, the major enterprise of political liberalism in Mexico during the first ten years after independence was the construction of a constitutional system. Mexico experienced in the 1820s what Reyes Heroles termed a "constitutional euphoria." The constitution became a fetish, a magical object that would solve all the social and political ills of the country. In a way, this faith in written constitutions was new. The constitution was not considered as the safeguard of an ancient form of government (as the mixed constitution that preserved liberty by securing a proper equilibrium among the one, the few, and the many). It reflected not the ancient constitution but a whole new set of maxims and principles that would *create* a free civil state. The constitution was thus an instrument of the future, not of the past. In the midst of this "euphoria" some writers recommended "prudence" and argued that reformers should consider the "character" and the particular "needs" of the people. One pamphleteer argued that "it is undeniable that the safety of the people is the first law of societies, even prior to the best meditated constitution and even older than society itself."[51]

Mexican liberals followed the French model regarding a strict separation of powers. The American system of checks and balances was little known in Mexico when the first charters were drawn. The *Federalist Papers* was not translated or published until 1829.[52] It is thus not surprising that Mora, the leading liberal figure of the time, discovered that the "law" did not provide for adequate boundaries to the legislative branch. That "defect" was responsible, in his eyes, for all the "woes suffered by the peoples of Europe" who had adopted a representative system. In support of his ideas Mora cited the examples of Rome as well as those of the French and Spanish revolutions. Yet, when assessing the lack of effective restraints on legislative invasion, Mora failed to acknowledge that this was a deficiency of *a* particular constitutional model, not of *the* constitutional model itself. The weakness of the executive under a system of strict and functional separation would become one of the key

51. Juan Wenceslao Barquera, *La balanza de Astrea* (Mexico, 1820). Barquera, a local representative from Querétaro, argued that caution should be the fundamental rule of the liberal march. Cited by Reyes Heroles, *Liberalismo mexicano*, 1:61.

52. Ibid., pp. 200–203. In 1829 the liberal newspaper *El Atleta* translated selections of the *Federalist Papers*. Reyes Heroles, *Liberalismo mexicano*, vol. 3, p. 345.

issues in Mexico during the nineteenth century. This development was seen as a failure of "liberal constitutionalism," not as the shortcoming of a specific version of it.[53]

In 1857 the liberal faction drafted a new constitution. Although it followed the general tenets of liberal constitutionalism, the Constitution of 1857 was an original creation. The mix between a strong parliament and a presidential office followed the model of the French constitution of 1848, but the unicameral organization of the legislature in the context of a federal state broke with the models adopted by the vast majority of the constitutions at the time. Innovations also included the *juicio de amparo,* a form of judicial review, and the inclusion of emergency powers, which previous constitutions in Mexico omitted. The provisions of the constitution were designed to cope with specific political conditions: just as emergency powers were needed to deal with chronic political instability, the unicameral Congress was intended as a safeguard against the previous experience of executive despotism. These were perceived not as theoretical but as tailor-made solutions to real problems.

A central aspiration of the new constitution was the elimination of the traditional social order, which for Mexican liberals had its center in the corporate rights and special jurisdictions (*fueros*) of the military, the Catholic Church, economic guilds, and Indian communities. The most powerful of these corporations, particularly the military and the Church, soon became allies in the violent offensive initiated by the conservative opposition. Shortly after the enactment of the charter, the foes of the liberal regime issued the Plan Tacubaya in 1858. For three years, from January 1858 until January 1861, liberals and conservatives killed each other with unprecedented ferocity. The Reform War (or Three Years' War) ended when the conservatives were defeated in January 1861, yet the opposition had not been eliminated and its members sought other means to destroy the liberal regime. The conservatives attempted to reestablish monarchical rule in Mexico. Conservatives' pleas found an answer in Emperor Napoleon III of France, who wanted a Latin empire. Maximilian, an Austrian prince, made himself available for the adventure and was recruited by Mexican monarchists. Maximilian, however, had little more success than the dozens of *caudillos* before him. In Octo-

53. José Antonio Aguilar Rivera, *En pos de la quimera* (Mexico: FCE, 2000).

ber 1866, when Prussia became a threat to France, Napoleon recalled his troops from Mexico. Without foreign military support, the empire collapsed.

The fall of the empire implied the complete defeat of the conservative faction and, in a way, the end of the conservative-liberal cleavage in Mexico. The discrediting of conservatives (blamed for their alliance with a foreign power) inaugurated an era of liberal hegemony in which most ideological conflicts would take place within the general framework of the liberal project. The liberal reform became a reality. Laws that had been issued during the Reform War, such as the nationalization of Church property, separation of church and state, secularization of society, and the forced sale of corporate property, were now backed by a legitimate government acting in the name of the Constitution of 1857.

However, the experience of the civil war and foreign intervention deeply affected the perception of the liberal elite about the institutions that could finally stabilize the country. Toward the end of the French intervention it became increasingly clear to Mexican liberals that the strengthening of presidential power was a necessity. When the Republic was finally restored, in 1867, the problem of political order was far from settled. Political turmoil was widespread, and local bosses, road bandits, kidnappers, and small groups of rebels challenged the authority of the national government.

At the dawn of the twentieth century, Emilio Rabasa, a political historian and jurist, pointed out that by making governance impossible, the liberal Constitution of 1857 had condemned the country to a de facto dictatorship. Not surprisingly, Rabasa, unlike many others, was well acquainted with Anglo-American political thought.[54] Rabasa asserted that during the war, between 1863 and 1867, President Juárez de facto re-

---

54. Echoing Madison, Rabasa argued that it was not "sensible to pretend that the exercise of extraordinary virtues would in itself correct institutions, and to think at the same time that those institutions were wise, when they demanded from public officials superhuman qualities." He added, "since the physical existence of government is incompatible with the observance of the constitution, the superior law prevailed and the constitution was subordinated to the supreme necessity of survival." Rabasa explicitly cited Federalist 47 when he decried the rejection of the executive veto by the 1856 Constitutional Assembly. Emilio Rabasa, *La constitución y la dictadura: Estudio sobre la organización política de México* (Mexico City: Editorial Porrua, 1956), pp. 67, 112, 173–74.

placed Congress by appropriating for himself the power vested in Congress to enact laws, and he de facto replaced the voice of the people by extending his term in office without a popular election. While the amount of power concentrated in Juárez's hands had been unsurpassed, he used that power vigorously and successfully to fulfill his high purposes. The 1857 constitution, Rabasa asserted, "has never been observed because, had it been, it would have made the stability of government impossible."

As Hale indicates,[55] major political controversies during the long regime of Porfirio Díaz in Mexico (1876–1910) reversed the interpretation and application of the Constitution of 1857. While a fraction of the old liberal elite saw in the centralization of power under Díaz as a betrayal of the principles of the Constitution of 1857, "new," or "conservative," liberals defended the institutional changes of the regime as necessary to satisfy the demands of political order and economic progress.

The first half of the twentieth century was no more auspicious for liberalism in Mexico than it was in other parts of the world. While in other countries fascist and communist parties clashed against liberal parliamentary governments, in Mexico a revolutionary state existed that was neither socialist nor liberal. Mexico's regime after the revolution was eclectic in ideology. It did not oppose elections, but political legitimacy was not grounded on them. A single anticlerical, populist, and corporatist party ruled. The 1917 Constitution enacted by the revolutionaries embraced both individualism and collectivism. The Mexican regime was nationalistic and supported the intervention of the state in the economy. Through the years the government nationalized important foreign-owned industrial assets such as oil. While the Mexican regime shared some traits with several ideologies, it identified itself with none. For these reasons, the Mexican Revolution was a powerful source of illiberal inspiration for the rest of Latin America. While nineteenth-century liberalism became a founding myth of the official national history, liberal practices and ideas languished during the long period of postrevolutionary hegemony in Mexico (1929–2000). Since the 1930s a few lonely voices have voiced liberal ideas in an adverse ideological en-

55. Charles A. Hale, *The Transformation of Liberalism In Late Nineteenth-Century Mexico* (Princeton: Princeton University Press, 1989).

vironment. A few economists and some poets, historians, and philosophers have defended liberty against its many foes.[56]

This book presents sixty-four essays and writings on liberty and liberalism from the early republican period to the late twentieth century by key authors. The first period (1820–40) comprises the founding of the Republic and the early constitutional experiments. The most important authors in this creative and turbulent period were José María Luis Mora, Lorenzo de Zavala, Valentín Gómez Farías, and Lucas Alamán. During the era of liberal hegemony, in the second half of the century (1845–76), the most significant figures included Mariano Otero, Ignacio Ramírez, Francisco Zarco, Ignacio Manuel Altamirano, Guillermo Prieto, José María Lafragua, and Benito Juárez. The rule of Porfirio Díaz (1876–1912) provided lively debates over the nature of the liberal legacy. As noted above, the authors more relevant for this period were Justo Sierra, José María Vigil, and Emilio Rabasa. Important authors during the twentieth century (1930–90) include Jorge Cuesta, Antonio Caso, and Octavio Paz.

Unless otherwise noted, all footnotes in the texts are those of the authors.

Tepoztlán, Mexico, January 2010

---

56. Besides the authors featured in this book, a lone economist preached the gospel of the free market in the hostile environment of the 1960s and 1970s. See Gustavo R. Velasco, "A Program for a Liberal Party," in Friedrich August von Hayek, *Toward Liberty: Essays in Honor of Ludwig von Mises on the Occasion of His 90th Birthday, September 29, 1971*, vol. 1, ed. F. A. Hayek, Henry Hazlitt, Leonard R. Read, Gustavo Velasco, and F. A. Harper (Menlo Park: Institute for Humane Studies, 1971).

Acknowledgments

I would like to thank Emilio Pacheco for his
intellectual encouragement and continued criticism.
Several people made this book possible. Laura Goetz
provided valuable editorial insights. Janet M. Burke,
Arizona State University, and Ted Humphrey, Arizona
State University, were wonderful colleagues, and I was
fortunate to work with them because they are among
the very few persons able to proficiently translate
complex legal and political texts from the nineteenth
century. Also, I am indebted to Roberto Mostajo,
Fabiola Ramírez, and Esteban González for their
invaluable assistance in compiling, reviewing, and
editing this volume.

José Antonio Aguilar Rivera
Professor of Political Studies
Centro de Investigación y Docencia Económicas
(CIDE)
Mexico City

1

The Founding and Early Constitutional Experiments

1821–1840

JOSÉ MARÍA LUIS MORA

José María Luis Mora (1794–1850), the leading liberal thinker during the first federal republic (1824–53), was ordained as a priest and received a degree in theology. Later he studied law and became a lawyer. He was a member of the provincial deputation of Mexico and later was elected as a deputy to the constituent congress of the state of Mexico. He participated in the making of the state constitution and in the drafting of important laws.

Mora edited and published essays in newspapers such as *Semanario Político y Literario, El Indicador,* and *El Observador de la República Mexicana.* He played an important role as an adviser during the brief Gómez Farías administration (1833–34) when the government put in place the first reform policies against the privileges of the Catholic Church.

The essays gathered here were published as unsigned newspaper articles between 1821 and 1830. While Mora's positions were very close to those of Benjamin Constant at the beginning of his career, he later realized that fighting the privileges of the Church and the military required an active government. Two of the essays, "Discourse on Public Opinion and the General Will" (Discurso sobre la opinión pública y voluntad general) and "Discourse on the Nature of Factions" (Discurso sobre los carácteres de las facciones), have been attributed to the Spaniard Alberto Lista because they had appeared earlier in the Spanish daily Lista edited, *El Espectador Sevillano.* However, we decided to include the essays because they received prominent placement in *El Observador,* of which Mora was the editor and the arbiter as to what to include and where. Clearly, Mora believed the essays expressed important ideas with which he agreed and of which his readers should be aware. That is, he gave the essays his imprimatur, even to the point of allowing readers to assume that the essays expressed his own views, inasmuch as he did not attribute them to someone else or otherwise suggest that they were not his or that he disagreed with them. Furthermore, the views that the essays express are integral to Mora's overall argument on factions and on the proper conception of how public political and social opinion is to be formed and brought to action.

We present nine newspaper articles written between 1821 and 1827.

1

Discourse on the Independence of the Mexican Empire

The custom among civilized peoples, in making some substantial change to their government, has been to reveal and clarify before all other nations the reasons that justify those changes. Inasmuch as such change cannot be limited to the internal effects that constitutional alterations produce in a state, and inasmuch as such change is necessarily very important to foreign societies because of the established relationships that unite the peoples of the world and have more or less influence on their prosperity or decline, the right of self-preservation indisputably authorizes those other societies to inform themselves of the motives that drove their neighbors to establish the new constitution and also to remove the obstacles that the constitution might pose to their just aspirations.

The Mexican Empire, upon entering into the enjoyment of the rights that fall to it as an independent nation, could not feign ignorance of an obligation or consideration so important. It therefore endeavored to make clear to the world, through explanations and public declarations, the justifications that supported it in requesting and effecting its independence from the Spanish monarchy. To this end, its deputies have pursued independence with firmness and persistence in the cortes of Madrid, its writers have defended it in Mexico against the charge of treason and rebellion, and its soldiers have contended for it on the battlefield with arms in hand. But despite not having been able to give a solid and satisfactory response to the arguments that justify independence, despite having now proven itself by the force of arms, a necessary effect of the extent and rapidity with which the opinion that favors independence has spread, many consider that independence unjust and unlawful. Even the legislators of the [Iberian] Peninsula, those illustri-

Original title: "Discurso sobre la independencia del imperio mexicano." Source: *Semanario Político y Literario de México*, Mexico, November 21, 1821.

ous patriots who have known how to liberate their own country from the yoke that oppressed them, refusing to recognize the principles sanctioned in their Constitution and openly proclaimed to the world, cannot reconcile themselves to the fact that laws deduced immediately from those principles have their effective fulfillment on the American continent, which urgently demands they be observed.

Those heroes who have justly been admired by the nations of Europe for the great services they have rendered the cause of liberty; those wise men who have laid out the road and smoothed the path that leads to independence; those patriots, we repeat, are the ones who must be accused of inconsistency, because loving the cause, they detest and abominate the result; because establishing a principle, they reject its consequences; finally, because proclaiming liberty in their country with the greatest firmness, they sustain the slavery of Mexico with the same tenacity.

Indeed, without looking beyond the Spanish Constitution and without outside assistance from the works of the most celebrated writers on public law, the Constitution itself supplies us with enough to justify the independence of our empire. The Constitution firmly establishes, as an indisputable principle and as base of the entire constitutional system, the essential inalienable sovereignty of the nation, and the laws of that code proclaim and recognize this doctrine in the most legitimate way. Through those laws comes recognition of the incontestable right that all peoples have to establish the government most suitable to them, alter it, modify it, and abolish it completely when their happiness requires it. Through the Constitution, finally, comes the recognition that in the people of the nation lies the authority to dictate the fundamental laws that ought to rule the nation, to create magistrates that apply those laws to particular cases, settling the disputes that can originate in the opposing nature of interests and organizing a public force that makes effective the observance of the laws and the enforcement of judicial sentences. The consolidation of all these powers results in that supreme authority that exists in societies and that we know by the name of sovereignty. If, then, sovereignty, in those stated terms, is an essential and inherent power of all societies, how can it be denied to this totality of individuals that make up what we call the Mexican Empire? If the legislators of the Peninsula wish to act according to their principles, they will have to do one of two things: either acknowledge the right that helped us to effect independence, or deny that we have the capacity to create a strong government that can sustain that independence against external invasions, to enter into political and trade relations with external powers, and to combine those individual interests with the public interest in such a way that internal upheavals, the germ and origin of civil war and anarchy, are avoided. In a word, they will have to deny that our people can and should be understood in the sense that one ascribes to this word "society."

To proceed, then, with accuracy on such an important subject and to finish off the disputes between the Spanish and Mexican people from their origin at one stroke, we will attempt to put the question in its true perspective.

The independence proclaimed in Mexico can be considered either illegal for lack of authority in the society to alter its government or untimely because the individuals who make up this empire cannot yet be counted among the company of societies inasmuch as they do not possess the totality of conditions necessary to constitute a people. The first is notoriously opposed to the principles sanctioned in the Spanish Constitution, of which we have made mention, and contrary to the rights of all humankind, which the author of the universe did not create to be a patrimony of one or of many men or nations. So, then, the only possibility that remains to the Spaniards is to deny the status of people or nation to the inhabitants of these provinces. To argue persuasively against such an incorrect view, it will be enough to give an exact and precise definition of the ideas corresponding to these words and to apply them to the Mexican Empire in a way so clear and so obvious that no sensible man can deny recognizing in the totality of its individuals a legitimate and formally constituted people.

Those writers on public law who, to their great honor and the benefit of humanity, have supported and clarified the sovereignty of the people, placing the inalienable rights of nations within reach of even the least informed classes, have not taken equal care to determine the conditions essentially necessary to constitute a society. In our judgment, this lack of care is the reason why all the good effects that should be expected from this beneficent principle have not been perceived. Ignorant people, persuaded of their sovereignty but lacking precise ideas that determine in a fixed and exact way the sense of the word "nation," have believed that the entirety of the human species, without other qualities and circumstances, should be considered as "nation"—mistaken concepts that will surely foment discord and disunion and promote civil war!

What is it, then, that we understand by this word "nation," a "people" or a "society"? And what is the sense that writers on public law have given to the word "nation" when they confirm its sovereignty in those stated terms? It can be nothing other than the free and voluntary coming together of men who can and want, in a legitimately possessed land, to constitute themselves as a state independent from the rest. Nor is it credible that the nations recognized as sovereign and independent can allege rights other than the inherent power to constitute themselves as such and their determined intent to effect it. But which are these necessarily essential conditions under which a nation can constitute itself? Indispensable are: (1) The legitimate possession of the land it occupies. (2) The appropriate enlightenment and resolve to come to know the rights of the free man and to know how to sustain them against despotism's internal attacks and the external violence of invasion. Finally, a population sufficient to ensure, in a steady and stable way, the subsistence of the state by establishment of an armed force, which both avoids the internal convulsions produced by the discontent of the unruly disorderly elements and contains the hostile designs of ambitious foreign countries. In a word, a legitimately possessed land and the physical and moral force to sustain it are the essential components of any society.

From these luminous principles, whose palpable and manifest evidence must make a strong impression even on the most dubious man, one immediate and legitimate consequence is deduced: that the individuals of this empire are or should be recognized as a true people. They occupy a land whose possession cannot be disputed by any nation in the world; they have made clear to the world by explanations and public declarations that they know the rights of the free man and the justice of the cause they defend; finally, they have succeeded, by taking up arms, in achieving their independence with no assistance other than their own strength, destroying in the brief space of seven months the formidable power of an established government.

It remains for us to put each of these propositions to the test.

1. No nation in the world can dispute with us the land we occupy, because which nation would it be and which the rights that it could allege in support of its claims? Would it be Spain? This seems to be the only

one, and in effect no other nation seeks it. Let us examine, then, the titles to its dominion, and we will see that they appear to be unlawful. Neither the king, in particular, nor the people of the Spanish nation can revoke the right of property. The time passed when it was accepted as true that the king and some number of citizens were the wealthy proprietors with authority to dispossess the rest, for no other reason than their whim, from the land that the latter had made fruitful for cultivation through their hardships and personal labor. Since the fall of feudalism, every man has a sacred right not to be dispossessed of legally acquired land. How, then, does Spain claim to have rights over a territory that in no way belongs to it, that it gave away entirely in parceling it out among the colonists from whom the current owners descend, and who perhaps never possessed it legitimately?

Indeed, all the rights commonly alleged to justify this illegitimate possession appear unlawful as soon as they are examined. Everything Spain can allege in support of its claims consists in: the donation of Alexander VI; the cession of Moctezuma; the right of conquest; the preaching of the gospel; the establishment, defense, protection, and development of the colony; and, finally, the oath of loyalty.

To hold as legitimate the donation of Alexander, it is necessary to assume the Roman pontiff was the proprietor and universal lord of all the earth. Well, having no more reason to concede him this property in America than in Europe, Asia, and Africa, if his dominion is admitted in the first, it cannot be denied in the others. And what would be the result of such a doctrine, as absurd as it is monstrous? That the sacred right of property would be revoked; that nothing could be fixed or stable on this point, and that all the peoples and nations would exist at the discretion of a man who, with no other reason than his sovereignty and absolute will, could, as can any proprietor, dispossess them from the land they occupy; that is to say, he could exhaust the wellspring of wealth and dry up the fountains of public happiness. And would the wise and liberal legislators of the Peninsula let these antisocial doctrines stand? In no way; in the century of the Enlightenment and Spanish liberty, none of its sons thinks so absurdly and mistakenly.

The cession of Moctezuma is just like that of Fernando VII: It was snatched by force; it was declared null by the peoples of the empire, who took up arms to resist the usurpations of the invading army, which, like the French in Spain, tried to legitimate by violence a renunciation as unlawful as that of Bayonne. The Spanish censured this, and they cannot endorse something that is entirely similar to it.

The right of conquest is the right of the strongest, which can be and in fact has been suppressed by another, equal right.

The proclamation of the Gospel cannot be a legitimate entitlement for taking possession of the land of catechized peoples. Otherwise, the apostles in the first centuries of the church and the missionaries in the following centuries would be legitimate owners of the land of the converted faithful, and the sacerdotal monarchy, so justly censured in the catechists of Paraguay, could be realized.

The establishment, protection, and development of the colonies have always been the work of individuals, and the Spanish government has played no part in this except to impede by its prohibitive laws and exclusive commerce the progress of agriculture, violating nature in a land capable of producing everything and causing the misery and discouragement of its inhabitants. These inhabitants, because they were prohibited from freely exporting their surplus fruits and importing articles of luxury and comfort, did not make this most fertile land produce anything but what was necessary to sustain a paltry commerce or, better stated, monopoly, incapable of creating great wealth and therefore suitable only for holding back the progress of this nascent colony. And will it be possible that what has caused the unhappiness of Mexico be precisely what is alleged as a right to continue oppressing it? What person, who is not ignorant of the principles of natural equity, will be able to approve such tyrannical behavior? The facts expressed are constant, the consequences are legitimate. What argument, then, can stand up to so palpable a proof? Will it perhaps be the investment of wealth in the establishment and defense of the colony? But here one must note two things: first, that Mexico, although oppressed, has produced enough to cover its expenses, always deducting a surplus that, until the beginning of the insurrection, never has been less than five million duros, which Spain has arranged to its favor and, for this very reason, cannot be certain it has suffered any misappropriation of funds, inasmuch as it was utilized in the establishment of the colonies. The second is that this defense, purely imaginary, has been more harmful and noxious than useful and beneficial to the Mexican territory, whose ports and cities have suffered the horrors of an invasion and the violence of a sacking for no other reason than its dependence on the Peninsula, dependence contrary to the intent of nature, which did not create an entire world to subject it to following the fate of a small piece of Europe, the least extensive part of our antipodean hemisphere.

It remains for us only to make this illusion of a loyalty oath disappear, an oath that has been used so much to frighten the timid consciences and bewilder the minds of ignorant men. This oath is compulsory and necessarily conditional, that is to say, the people are obliged to obey the decisions of the government so long as they are beneficial to the community and fulfill their promise. If either of these two things is absent, the government's right to command and the peoples' obligation to obey terminate, and the social contract is dissolved. Every act emanating from a government that cannot or will not provide for the happiness of the people that has put its trust in it is null, unlawful, of no value, and, for this very reason, unworthy of being obeyed, and this is precisely the situation in which the Americas find themselves with respect to the Spanish government. Open the Constitution of the Spanish monarchy, and the slightest and most superficial examination will be enough to make clear the commitment of its authors to diminish American representation and obstruct the influence that the native born of those countries could and should have in the government established on the Peninsula. At each step, one comes across articles that confirm this truth, and this code, justly admired for the good judgment, common sense, and wisdom of all its measures in what pertains to Spain, does not lack for injustices, inconsistencies, and puerilities in what concerns America. But let us grant that the constitutional charter contains nothing contrary to the interests of America, that all and each one of the articles sanctioned in it are manifestly beneficial, and, if you wish, that they alone are capable of providing their happiness. It seems that no more can be conceded. Nonetheless, Spain's cause has not been improved by this. And why? Because despite the continuous and energetic demands that have been made to enforce their observance, nothing has been accomplished; our efforts have been useless, merit has been forgotten, virtue has been beaten down, incompetence positioned in high posts, and the outcries of a people reduced to misery disregarded. Well, now, either the Spanish government has tried to deceive us, observing a conduct entirely contrary to what is provided for in the text of the laws, or it has not had energy sufficient to see that they are observed. In either case we are absolved of the oath of loyalty because in neither have the conditions been fulfilled under which this oath was offered, conditions that are the bond of union between the people and the government, essentially embedded in the nature of these contracts and the fundamental principle of every social contract.

Given that neither Spain nor any other power has a right to the land we occupy, we must make clear that this right resides in the general body of the Mexican people; that is to say, in the individuals born and lawfully domiciled in the empire.

The right of the peoples to possess the land they occupy must necessarily originate in one of these three principles: origin, birth, or residence, because the donation or purchase, if it is of occupied land, can be made legal only by the will of the proprietors, and if the land is unoccupied, no right whatsoever authorizes the donor or seller to transmit to the purchaser or recipient a right it does not have.

A generally accepted truth is that the legitimate possessor of unencumbered assets can transfer the dominion he enjoys to his sons and constitute them lawful masters of the paternal inheritance, and this is what we understand by right of origin or filiation. In the same way, every individual human being has the right to live in the country where he was born and, if he submits to the laws established by the appropriate authority, to enjoy the comforts that the society occupying the land offers; and this is what we know as right of birth. Finally, every foreigner settled in a society, with the expressed or tacit consent of the individuals who constitute that society, can acquire property, enter into the enjoyment of all the comforts the citizens of the state enjoy, and acquire a right we call residency. Because the right of society to the land it occupies is not nor can be anything more than the sum of the individual rights, one unquestionable conclusion follows by deduction: that the citizens of the state, which consists of all of them together being its lawful proprietors, must have a true dominion over the occupied land. Well, now, the citizens who make up the Mexican Empire fall into three classes: the descendants of the old inhabitants, the children of foreign origin in the country, and the Spaniards and other foreigners all living together there. Each one of them is the lawful proprietor of a part of the land, and this the Spanish government has never questioned. So the empire, which represents the totality of all of them, is the owner and absolute master of the territory they possess.

2. But if the Mexican people, or what is the same, the people who make up Mexico, are the lawful masters of the land they occupy, it is no less certain that they are sufficiently enlightened to know their rights and the great benefits independence carries with it, and if there were no other evidence of this truth than the many and great sacrifices they made to achieve independence, these alone would make it clear in a conclusive and decisive way. Eleven years of espionage, prisons, scaffolds, and uninterrupted defeats demonstrate the difficulty of the endeavor and the perseverance of the Mexican people, which has known how to sacrifice its most precious interests in order to achieve liberty. And this immutable steadfastness, this invincible perseverance in confronting such powerful obstacles, are they not proofs guaranteeing that there exists in the general body of the nation an intimate conviction that everything must be sacrificed to the interests of liberty? Has their conduct not demonstrated that they prefer death to servitude and that they are firmly resolved to die free rather than live as slaves? But if, despite all this, even their enlightenment is doubted, peruse their writings published since the year 1810 in England, France, Spain, North America, in Mexico in the presence of masters, and not only will one find many documents that would do honor to some nations that pass for enlightened, but also a total and absolute uniformity with respect to the principal point; that is to say, each one cooperating, by the means in his grasp, in the great work of emancipating the Mexican Empire.

Take in your hands this precious code sanctioned amidst the noise and clamor of arms in the town of Apatzingán. Examine it impartially and you will find inscribed in it all the principles characteristic of the liberal system: sovereignty of the people, the division of powers, the appropriate jurisdiction of each of them, liberty of the press, mutual obligations between the people and the government, the rights of free man, and the means of defense that must be provided to the criminal. In a word, you will find, delimited with sufficient precision and accuracy, the limits of each established authority and, perfectly combined, the liberty of the citizen and the supreme power of the society. So we do not hesitate to affirm resolutely that this code, with some slight adjustments, would have produced our independence and liberty from the year 1815 if the insidious maneuvers of the Spanish government, calculated to divide us, had not produced the pernicious consequence of separating from the common interests a portion of citizens who, although very small compared with the rest, was the most necessary because it had taken up arms.

But the happy day arrived when the dawning light of citizenship broke throughout the land of Moctezuma, and the activity of this light penetrated the body of the Mexican army. The memorable twenty-fourth of February arrived, and the fields of Iguala repeated the echoes of the liberty pronounced by the immortal Iturbide. At that voice, the chains that bound our hemisphere and another were broken, and, free of them, we put into place, in the country of Anáhuac, a throne to the liberty that had been exiled from it for three centuries. This voice resounds in the provinces and spreads with the speed of light into all corners of the empire. The hero Negrete, as moderate in discussions as fearless on the battlefield, dispels the force of the tyrants with his presence alone and, at the head of his army, frees half the empire in two months. These generals, aided by the meritorious leaders Guerrero, Andrade, Bustamante, Echávarri, Herrera, Bravo, Barragán, Quintanar, Filisola, Santana, and others, make the Spanish domination disappear from this soil in the short space of six months, giving a new appearance to revolution, purging it of some stains contracted in the earlier era and, through moderation and concord, making it appear assured. How is it, then, that some men who have made the most deadly and destructive war against each other come together cordially to effect the liberty and independence of their country? How has it been possible that the voice of two generals in the short space of a few months united wills so discordant through a long eleven years that they would even wage a devastating war? This admirable phenomenon is the inevitable result of the rapid diffusion of the light, originating in the enlightenment that has made known to the people their true interests.

And for a people who knew how to gain their independence, destroying a formidable enemy that they harbored in their breast, will it be impossible to repel a foreign force? A people to whom the rights of liberty are so familiar and who have a more than sufficient knowledge of the eternal maxims of justice, will they be oppressed by an internal despotism? In no way. This outcome is contrary to the experience of all the centuries and does not cohere with natural reason. It is certain that the enemies of independence and liberty will make every effort, first, to compel us to enter the Spanish dominion and, second, to impede or make illusory the reforms consequent to the liberal system. But each of these until this day has a small following and, with passing time, no following, as is to be hoped from the liberty of the press and the enlightenment that characterizes the meritorious leaders who have led us to liberty.

3. To conclude this discourse, it remains only to make clear that to sustain the proclaimed independence, the physical force we have is sufficient. This physical force has as its base the population and the means of sustaining that population. With the population numerous and the state rich, there is everything necessary to raise an armed force capable of checking foreign invasions, especially when this armed force is inured to war by having been on campaign a considerable time.

Our population is much superior to that of various independent states of Europe and is indisputably double what the United States of America had when it pronounced itself independent, a force that made the British nation tremble and frustrated entirely all the plans of subjugation that Britain had with respect to its American colonies. This nation, whose maritime force is the greatest and most formidable the world has known, could not subject three million unarmed countrymen lacking in military knowledge and in a land that, as the least fertile of the entire continent, could not provide anything but the scarcest resources. And will Spain be able, threatened by foreign armies, shaken by internal upheavals, and with a navy in the most deplorable state, to reduce to its dominion the Mexican Empire, which has a population, according to the lowest estimate, of six million, an army inured to war, ready to sacrifice itself for the liberty of its *patria,* a fertile terrain, rich and abundant in every type of crop and, for this very reason, capable of raising and sustaining an army ten times greater than whatever the most formidable power of Europe can transport? It would be delirious to say so, and only a foolish man could enter into the ridiculous undertaking of supporting such a paradox.

Nor can the exigencies we have experienced in these days be avoided, for they are the inevitable consequences of the disorder that must emerge at the outset of a government that is starting to establish itself. Drain the water from the mines, establish freedom of trade, develop agriculture, and the state, by means of direct tax, without an excessive burden on individuals and without the espionage and fetters that the individual and system of customs carry with them, will have what is necessary for all the expenses of state, to cover its letters of credit and establish a public bank free, if possible, of taxes on individuals "for the extinction of the debt" or, at the least, noticeably diminish such taxes.

From the principles expressed so far and from the application that we have made of them to the Mexican Empire, one can deduce: that it is the legitimate owner of the land it has and currently occupies; that it has in its favor and in support of its sovereign decrees the requisite enlighten- ment, the necessary population—that is to say, the physical and moral power—to sustain them; that, for that very reason, it is and must be considered and recognized as a true nation; and that, by reason of such, it has an unquestionable right to alter, modify, and abolish totally the established forms of government, substituting for them those it judges suitable for achieving the ultimate goal of society, which is not nor can be anything other than the happiness of the individuals that make it up; and that for this very reason the Mexican people is not nor can be called rebellious for having pronounced itself independent of the Span- ish monarchy, for in this it has done nothing other than use the powers conceded by the author of nature to all societies to provide themselves with their happiness by the means they judge most adequate and con- ducive to this goal.

2

Discourse on the Limits of Civil Authority Deduced from Their Source

Surely few nations have been in such fortunate circumstances for creating constitutions with all possible human perfection as are the American nations, which a half century ago became independent of European powers: The enlightenment generally disseminated by the freedom of the press established in England, France, Spain, Portugal, and Naples; the spirit of liberty, rapidly diffused to all points of the globe; the enthusiasm with which liberal ideas and the rights of peoples, which have gone on to be the subject of a general discussion, have been proclaimed, maintained, and elevated to the highest state; the conviction, produced by the disasters of the most recent revolutions, that one cannot successfully implement certain theories, which, even though they present a store of speculative truths, cannot be realized in practice; and, finally, being entirely free of the obstacles naturally put in the way of any reform by a despotic government consolidated through hundreds of years on stale preconceived notions such as hereditary nobility, feudal domain, sovereignty of kings derived directly from God, and others of the same sort, which practically convinced peoples of the absurd and monstrous doctrine of natural inequality among the children of Adam and which have not permitted a total reform in the states of Europe through the slow but always progressive steps enlightenment has made in them. This lack of obstacles, we repeat, and this abundance of resources that at present make up the political situation of the American peoples, provide sufficient grounds for expecting, from the congresses established on their vast surface, constitutions much more perfect than those created in Europe.

In effect, the outcome has been completely what was to be expected. The Constitution of the United States of North America not only has

Original title: "Discurso sobre los límites de la autoridad civil deducidos de su origen." Source: *El Observador de la República Mexicana,* Mexico, December 19, 1827, p. 231.

been highly praised by the most celebrated writers of Europe, but has also created glory and prosperity, in a firm and stable way, in the freest people of the world, even putting that country almost at the level of England in its navy, and of France in its arts and manufacturing. It has done this in the short space of a half century, when those other nations have not been able to get to their current level of prosperity except after hundreds of years and terrible political oscillations and fluctuations. We, then, desirous that our country take advantage of the happy opportunity that has come within its reach to constitute itself with peace and tranquility, have proposed, and have already begun to carry out, placing before our fellow citizens the constitutions of the most notable peoples. At the end of all of them, in a separate discourse, we make the observations and reflections that seem most suitable to us. But before our proposal takes effect with respect to the Anglo-American and French constitutions that we have just published, it has seemed worthwhile to us to determine the general limits within which the authority of any government must be contained, without subjecting ourselves blindly to the doctrines of the European writers on public law, and keeping in mind only the goal of social institutions and the nature of the contract that unites peoples with governments.

Whatever might be the origin of societies, it is completely certain that these could not be established for any purpose other than fostering the happiness of the individuals who make them up, securing their persons, their interests, and their civil liberty, insofar as limiting these is not necessary to uphold the interests of the community. From this luminous principle are deduced all the consequences that constitute the science of government, and we will proceed to set them out. It follows, in the first place, that the authority of societies is not absolutely limitless as Rousseau believed, for such authority, wherever it might reside, is necessarily and essentially tyrannical. For what does it mean and what do we understand by unlimited authority, if not the power to do whatever one might wish? And cannot he who believes he has it, by virtue of this power, commit the greatest crimes, depriving an innocent person of life, divesting the legitimate owner of his property, and trampling on all the safeguards of liberty with no other motive than his whim? No, these are not the simple fears of an overexcited imagination. They are outcomes confirmed by experience, for, as the famous Constant observes, the horrifying crimes committed in the French Revolution against individual liberty and the rights of the citizen stemmed in great part from the vogue of this doctrine, which not only is not liberal, but rather is the fundamental principle of despotism. This principle does not consist, as many have convinced themselves, in the abuse the monarch makes of the authority entrusted to him or that he has usurped. In that case, it would be supremely easy to cure nations of their political ills by exiling the monarchs forever, and the popular government would always be justified in such a case. But reason and experience agree in disproving such an unfounded theory, showing us despotic peoples like those of France in its revolution and liberal monarchs like those of England and Spain. Despotism, then, is nothing more than the absolute and unlimited use of power, without subjection to any rule, no matter whose hands might be driving this formidable mass that makes all its weight felt on the individuals of the state. It follows that we can call despotic a measure that has been decreed only to satisfy the will of the one who commands. But if all government, considered in the scope of the three powers, must exercise its functions within prescribed limits, determining those limits with the greatest precision and exactitude is an absolute necessity to avoid the unfortunate consequences produced by the erroneous ideas of many writers regarding the rights of the people over the government and of the government over the people. Let us return, then, to the original source of societies. Let us examine the principles of the social contract with attentive impartiality and detailed reflective meditation, and with that effort alone we will discover the solution to this problem.

Men, in addition to the divine order to multiply, have in their nature strong drives for propagating their species and such inbred self-love that these do not disappear even in the least of their actions. Men do not enjoy except when their appetites and needs are satisfied; nor do they become sad and anguished except when they lack something that is necessary, or they believe is necessary, to satisfy their needs and to rest in that tranquility and repose that constitutes human happiness.

One of human nature's strongest inclinations is the one individuals have to preserve themselves in the state of natural liberty bestowed on them by the creator of all things and, thus, to obtain the enjoyments analogous to their natural inclinations; but in the few steps they made on this painful, difficult, and risky path, they became convinced that the happiness of each of them was not the act of a single man, but rather the result of common efforts. Surrounded everywhere by enemies, attacked by hunger and reptiles, pursued by ferocious beasts, and feeling the weakness of their strengths, they agreed to give each other aid under certain covenants or conditions. Here are both the first social contract in the world and the sovereignty of the people, which, in each one of the contracting parties, is nothing but the right one has over oneself to provide for one's happiness in accordance with the rules prescribed by sound reason and, in the association, the aggregate of individual rights organized to the same end. These agreements made, what came about was what should have been feared—that many of those who entered into the agreements received, with the help of the rest, the desired benefit, but, when it came to fulfilling the terms of the contract, they refused, either denying the agreement or resisting its taking effect or interpreting it in their own favor despite the protests of the others. In light of these drawbacks, the men, united as described, determined to clarify the established pacts by common agreement, making use of categorical and decisive phrases, and here is the origin of the laws. But despite the clarity of these laws, the insistence on exempting oneself from them, sustained by the spirit of caviling, rendered them empty and ineffectual, those who acknowledged their existence claiming that some individual cases were not comprehended by those laws, cases believed useful to some and prejudicial to others, so it was necessary to create a neutral power invested by the common authority to resolve definitively disagreements that arose, and this is the origin of the judicial power. Finally, men refused to carry out the intent of the laws and the declarations of the judges, and it was necessary for everyone to combine their physical forces to compel each one to fulfill the obligations entered into through the original pact, and what resulted was what we call the executive power. By this, we do not claim that those distinct powers were divided from the outset, conferring them on distinct persons or bodies, for it is clear that this was the work of time and reflective meditation. But we certainly want it to be understood that these powers, distinct in reality, and for that very reason separable, were acknowledged from the time societies were founded, although they were vested in a single person or body. For this very reason, the doctrine that informs this division is not a pure theory totally unrealizable in practice, as a writer of our day claims. But let us continue reflecting on this society that moves toward its perfection. When members of the society created these powers, it was necessary that they entrust the exercise of the functions typical of these powers to some individuals of the association who would dedicate themselves exclusively to their fulfillment. For this it was necessary to assist them with everything that their personal work was supposed to produce, and here is the origin of the posts of judges and executors of the laws. As for the legislators, who were themselves members of the association, they exercised the legislative power for themselves so long as society consisted of a small number of individuals; but the number of individuals later grew to such a degree that the personal attendance of all and each one of them at the national assembly was not possible, and he who could not [attend] entrusted his vote to someone who was ready to assist. But as these difficulties constantly increased, many began to entrust their votes to a small number of individuals, and sometimes to only one, so that, reflectively and maturely considering the interests of each, they might prescribe those measures that would be most advantageous to the maintenance of all, and this is the origin of national representation and legislative congresses. But it happened that, in exercising legislative functions, those empowered by the people did not express the will of their constituents but rather their individual wish or opinion, seeking to limit the natural liberty of the citizens more than was necessary to sustain the union. Then the individuals of the society declared that the representatives had violated the boundaries of the authority that had been entrusted to them, and the individuals of society wrote down in a solemn and positive way, in laws put before the entire public, the imprescriptible rights of man and citizen, working out the three acknowledged powers that seemed most useful for the preservation of the *liberty, property, security,* and *equality* of citizens, and here is the origin of these codes and collections of fundamental laws known by the name of constitutions.

By what has been expressed here so far, one sees clearly the origin, development, and present state of human institutions, the goal men have proposed in establishing them, and the primary reason for all their transactions, that is to say, the preservation of their rights to the extent that allows for the preservation of society. From this follows a general consequence, and it is that all authority, of whatever kind it may be, has limits to the exercise of its functions, within which it must be contained, and it is not lawful for either the people or their representatives to trample on the rights of individuals on the pretext of preserving society, given that men, in instituting society, had no other intent nor proposed any other goal than the preservation of their *liberty, security, equality,* and *property,* and not to relinquish those rights to a moral body that might fully and legally exercise the most despotic tyranny over those from whom it had received this immense and formidable power.

3

Discourse on the Freedom of Thought, Speech, and Writing

*Rara temporum felicitate ubi sentire
Quoe veils, equoe sentias dicere licet.*

An exceptionally happy time when
it is lawful to think as one wants
and to say what one thinks.

— Tacitus, *Histories,* book I

If, in the time of Tacitus, the ability to think as one wanted and to speak as one thought was an uncommon happiness, in our times it would be a consummate misfortune and a quite unfavorable mark on our nation and institutions should one try to place limits on freedom of thought, speech, and written expression. Tacitus and his fellow citizens were under the rule of a master, after all, whereas we are under the leadership of a government that owes its existence to such freedom, which can last only because of this freedom, and whose laws and institutions have given this freedom all possible expanse and breadth, sparing no means to guarantee citizens this precious and inestimable right.

In the same way that we have tried to demonstrate in our first issue the importance and necessity of the scrupulous, faithful, and prompt observance of the laws, let us make an effort in this issue to settle the entire and absolute freedom in opinions, for although those laws must be fulfilled completely, opinions must be free of all censure that precedes or follows publication of the laws, because one cannot justly demand that the laws be faithfully observed if the freedom of exposing their problems is not perfectly and totally guaranteed.

Original title: "Discurso sobre la libertad de pensar, hablar, y escribir." Source: *El Observador de la República Mexicana,* Mexico, June 13, 1827, p. 23.

It is not possible to place limits on the faculty of thought; it is not reasonable, just, or advisable to prevent one from expressing by word or in writing what one thinks.

Precisely because in the metaphysical order acts of understanding are necessary, they must be free of all force and coercion in the political order. Human understanding is a power as necessary as is sight; it does not actually have an ability to decide for this or for that doctrine, to keep from inferring legitimate or erroneous conclusions, or to adopt evident or false principles. It will be able, happily, to apply itself to examining objects with care and maturity, or with carelessness and negligence; to explore questions more or less and to consider them completely or only under one of their aspects; but the outcome of all these preliminaries must always be an action as necessary as is that of seeing clearly or vaguely, or with more or less perfection, the object held at a suitable distance. In effect, the analysis of the word "know" and that of the complete idea it indicates cannot do less than yield this result.

Knowledge in the soul is like sight in the body, and thus as each individual of the human species has, according to the different construction of his visual organs, a necessary manner of seeing things and does so without choice, so also, depending on the differences among intellectual faculties, he has a necessary manner of knowing to know them. It is true that both powers are subject to perfection and augmentation; it is true that their errors can be corrected or prevented, the sphere within which they operate can be extended, and the acts proper to them can be made more active or intense; not just one, but many and infinitely varied are the means of attaining them; one, many, or all can be put into action; they will, in their turn, give perfect, average, and sometimes no results, but it will always be certain that choice has not played any part in it, nor can it be counted among the means for achieving those results.

Men would be very happy, or at the least they would not be so unhappy, if the actions of their understanding were the product of free choice. Then, the bitter and sad memories of the past would not come to renew unhappinesses that no longer exist; nor would they arise from nothingness only to cause us pain. Then, forecasting the future would not bring forward for us a thousand sorrows, presenting us ahead of time persons, events, and circumstances that either will not come to exist, or if they do, give in advance an indefinite extent to our sufferings. Then, finally, we would not think about or explore through reflection the causes and circumstances of present unhappiness, nor would we worsen its intolerable weight with reflection. There is certainly not one single man who does not wish to separate from himself everything that can cause him annoyance and make him unhappy; and at the same time there is not, nor has been nor will be anyone who has not suffered a great deal because of such considerations. And what does this prove? That it is not possible for him to put limits on his thoughts; that he is led necessarily and irresistibly to knowledge of objects, good or bad, perfectly or inadequately grasped; that the immediate or distant choice has no part whatsoever in the actions of the mental faculties; and that, consequently, in the metaphysical order, the understanding is not free.

How, then, to impose rules on a power not susceptible to them? How to effect change in what is most independent in man, making use of violence and coercion? How, finally, to put order into the class of crimes and assign punishments to an act that by its essence is incapable of goodness and evil? Man will be capable of not conforming his actions and discourses to his opinions; he will be able to give the lie to his thoughts through his conduct or language, but it will be impossible for him to disregard or get rid of those thoughts because of external violence. This method is unsuitable and at the same time tyrannical and illegal.

Whenever one attempts to attain an end, no matter what its nature may be, prudence and natural reason dictate that the means one uses to attain it be naturally suitable to it. Otherwise, the plan will come to nothing, the nature of things being stronger than the caprice of the agent. Such would be the folly of the one who tries to attack firearms with water or prevent passage through a moat by filling it with grape shot. When, then, it comes to changing our ideas and thoughts, or inspiring new ones in us, and for this purpose one uses rules, prohibitions, and punishments, the natural effect is that those who suffer such violence adhere more tenaciously to their opinion and deny to their oppressor the satisfaction he might get with victory. Persecution gives an unfortunate character to opinions without destroying them, because destroying them is not possible. Human understanding is as noble in itself as it is miserable for the ease with which every kind of passion confuses it. The first principles undeniable for everyone are few in number, but the consequences that derive from them are as diverse as the multiplicand, because the way in which their relationships are grasped is infinitely varied. Habits and customs that education has inspired in us, the way of life we have adopted, the objects that surround us, and, above all, the persons with whom we interact, contribute, without our even being able to perceive it, to the formation of our judgments, modifying in a thousand ways the perception of objects and making them appear clothed in, perhaps, a thousand forms, with the exception of the natural and genuine perception. Thus, we see that what is for him obvious and simple is obscure and complex for others; that not all men can acquire or dedicate themselves to the same type of knowledge or excel in it; that some are fit for the sciences, others for scholarship, many for the humanities, and some for nothing; that with age the same person changes opinion, even holding as absurd what he previously deemed evident; and that no one, as long as he lives, is fixed and unwavering in his opinions, or in the concept he has formed of things. As the intellectual faculty of man does not have a precise and exact measure of the vitality with which it carries out its operations, neither does it have a measure of the amount of knowledge it needs for exercising them. To expect, then, that the majority be convinced by the judgment of some other person, even when this other person might be an authority, is to insist, says the famous Spedalieri, that they see and hear through another's eyes and ears. It is to oblige them to let themselves be carried blindly and with no more rationale than the force they cannot resist. It is, to put it succinctly, to dry up all the sources of public enlightenment and to destroy beforehand and radically the best sources they might have been able to develop over the course of time.

In effect, what would become of us and of the entire human race if the wishes of those who have wanted to place restraints on the understanding and limits on freedom of thought had been fulfilled? What would have been the progress of the arts and sciences, the improvements of governments, and the condition of men in the state of society? What, in particular, would be the fate of our nation? Thanks to the efforts of the extraordinary creative spirits that at all times have known how to throw off the chains that despots have sought to impose on thought, societies, although not having arrived at the highest level of perfection, have made considerable progress. Governments, excluding only a few that are called free, have always been alert to anything that could diminish their power and make clear their excesses. Therefore, they use every means to put thought in chains, making crimes of opinions that do not conform and calling those who profess them criminals. But have they had the right to do so? Have they proceeded legally when they have made use of these means? Or, rather, have they trod upon the sacred rights of man, assuming powers that no one could give them or that they could receive? This is the point we are going to examine.

Governments have been established precisely to preserve public order, ensuring to each individual the exercise of his rights and the possession of his goods in the way and form that have been prescribed by the laws, and not in any other manner. Their powers are necessarily determined in the pacts or agreements we call constitutional charters and are the result of the national will. Those who draw them up, and their constituents, cannot make provisions in them that, by the nature of things, are beyond their powers, such as the condemnation of an innocent person; making crimes of such truly praiseworthy acts as paternal love; much less subjecting to laws functions that by nature are incapable of morality, such as the circulation of the blood, the movement of the lungs, etc. From this, it follows that for a legislative, executive, or judicial measure to be just, legal, and equitable, it is not enough that it be pronounced by the competent authority, but it is also necessary that it be intrinsically possible and indispensable for preserving public order. Let us see, then, whether those measures that have been decreed or attempted against freedom of thought are of this type.

To this point we have shown that opinions are not free and consequently are not capable of morality; it remains only to show that they can never overthrow the public order, and especially not in the representative system. In effect, public order maintains itself by the prompt and faithful observance of the laws, which is entirely compatible with total and absolute freedom of opinions. Nothing is more common than seeing men who dislike laws and whose ideas are contrary to them, but who at the same time not only observe them religiously but are personally convinced of their necessity. To say this law is bad, it has this or that problem, is not to say that it will not be obeyed or carried out. The first is an opinion, the second is an action; the former is independent of all human power, the latter must be subject to the competent authority. Men have the right to mandate that something be done in this or that way, but not in order to make doctrines into dogmas, or to obligate others to their belief. This absurd right would suppose the necessity of a symbol or body of doctrine comprehensive of all truths, or the existence of an infallible authority by whose decisions one would have to abide. Nevertheless, nothing is more lacking in foundation than such suppositions.

But how could the first have been formed, or who would be so presumptuous and audacious that he would dare to appropriate the second to himself? "A body of doctrine," says the famous Daunou,[1] "supposes that human understanding has made all possible progress, opposes itself to all advancements that remain, draws a circle around all acquired understandings, inevitably includes many errors, opposes the development of the sciences, the arts, and all type of industry." And who would be capable of having formed it? Even if, for such an unattainable project, the most celebrated men of the universe had been gathered together, nothing would have been achieved. Should their writings be recorded anyway, they will be found full of errors in the midst of some truths they have contributed to public enlightenment. The daily and continuing improvement perceived in all human actions is demonstrable proof that the perfectibility of human mental powers has no limit and of how much would have been lost in holding back their advancement, had this been possible.

We are persuaded that none of the present governments will boast of their inability to err. They and the people entrusted to their leadership are too enlightened to be able to claim and grant such privileges, but if the governments are composed of men who are as fallible as others, through what principle of justice, or by what legal right, will they proceed to determine or prohibit doctrines? How would they dare determine for us those opinions we are to follow and those we are prohibited from professing? Is this not an act of aggression with an unattainable end, which nothing can justify? Without doubt. It, nonetheless, is common and almost always serves as a pretext for classifying citizens and immediately persecuting them. It makes men responsible for the opinions they hold or assume, and these are converted into a reason for hatred and loathing. In this way factions are perpetuated, given that the triumphant dogma will one day be toppled, and it then comes to be a crime to profess it. This is how nations become demoralized, and a forced traf-

1. Pierre Claude François Daunou, 1761–1840, was a politician, archivist, and French historian, and the lifetime secretary to the Académie des inscriptions et belles-lettres. (Editor's note)

fic in lies is established that compels the weak to conceal their ideas and makes those with strong spirits the targets of persecution.

Come, now, will it be lawful to express all opinions? Does not the authority have the right to prohibit the enunciation of some? Will many of them, inevitably mistaken, not be detrimental? Yes, but we assert resolutely that opinions about doctrines must be entirely free. No one doubts that the surest means, or, better said, the only means, to arrive at knowledge of the truth is examination that produces free discussion. Then not only one's own reflections are present but also those of others, and it has happened a thousand times that, upon criticism and perhaps error or someone's irrelevant observation, the fate of a nation has depended. No understanding, no matter how vast and universal one supposes it to be, can embrace everything or exhaust any subject matter. From this it follows that everyone, in all subject matters, especially those that treat of government, needs the help of everyone else, which they will certainly not obtain if freedom of speech and written expression is not assured, sheltering the opinions and their authors from all aggression that could be attempted against them by those who do not accept these opinions. The government, then, cannot proscribe or grant protection for any doctrine. This is beyond its jurisdiction; it is created only to observe and see that citizens observe the laws.

It is true that, among opinions, there are and must be many erroneous ones; it is equally true that all error, of whatever kind and under whatever aspect it is considered, is highly harmful. But it is not less true that prohibitions are not means of remedying error. The free circulation of ideas and the differences that result from counterviews constitute the only way to correct opinions. If the power to regulate opinions were conceded to some authority, this latter would very quickly abuse such power, and who would be charged with restraining us from error? He who is exempt from it? But governments do not find themselves in this category; very much the opposite. When one searches for causes that have most spread error and contributed to perpetuating error, they are always found in the prohibiting institutions. On the other hand, if governments were authorized to prohibit all errors and punish the foolish, the world would very soon be missing a large portion of humanity, the rest being reduced to eternal silence. We will be told that not all opinions have to be subject to the control of authority, but if one opinion is subject, the rest are not safe. Laws cannot make precise classification or exact enumeration of all opinions. Thus it is that such a power is necessarily arbitrary and, most of the time, will be converted into a reason for persecution. These are not unfounded suspicions. Look back at the barbarian centuries and it will be seen that the universities, the parliaments, the chancelleries, and the kings were determined to place proscriptions on the learned who were making physical discoveries and attacking the doctrines of Aristotle. Pedro Ramos Tritemio, Galileo, and innumerable others suffered what would not be believable if it were not made obvious to us beyond any doubt. And what was the fruit of such methods? Did the governments succeed in what they were attempting? Not in the least. Converts increased day by day, perhaps because of that very persecution.

In effect, if one wants to give credence to a doctrine, nothing else is needed but to forbid it. Men naturally suppose, and in this they do not deceive themselves, that a doctrine cannot be fought by reason when it is attacked by force. Strong spirits and courageous souls hold fast to forbidden doctrines, more for show than from conviction, because the spirit of novelty and making themselves the object of public excitement, attracting the attention of everyone, is so lively a passion, and as a final consequence an inappropriate remark that might have remained buried in the corner of a house degenerates into heresy that possibly undermines the supports of the social edifice because of the importance persecution bestows on it.

But does not discrediting the laws make them contemptible and inspire men to transgress them, depriving the laws of their stature? And is this not the outcome of the frank criticism that is made of them? When the laws have been dictated with calm and care, when they are the outcome of a free discussion, and when the spirit of partisanship and the fears that it instills in legislators have not contributed to their preparation, making the general interest subordinate to the private interest for reasons external to them, the fear of such outcomes is very remote; but to prevent it, governments must be very alert and not lose sight of public opinion, favoring it in everything. This is formed only by free discussion, which cannot be maintained when the government or some faction is granted the power of the press and condemns, with no sense of shame, those who either impugn the dogmas of the sect or throw light on its abuses of authority. On the contrary, when one proceeds without prejudice and in good faith, when one listens attentively and impartially, everything that is said or written in support of or against the laws is certainly on the road to being right. We never tire of repeating it: freedom of opinions regarding doctrine has never been disastrous for any people; but all the events of modern history prove with the greatest certainty the dangers and risks that nations have run when one faction has managed to take possession of the press, has dominated the government, and, availing itself of it, has silenced by terror those who could educate it.

But governments do not take warning despite such repeated examples. Always fixed in the present moment, they disregard the future. Their principal error consists in believing they can do anything, and it is enough to hint at its will for it to be promptly and faithfully obeyed. Perhaps they turn on themselves when there is no longer any remedy, when they have been discredited and have precipitated the nation into an abyss of evils. We conclude our reflections, then, recommending to the trustees of power that they be convinced that when they make crimes of opinions, they run the risk of punishing talents and virtues, of losing the idea, and of making famous the memory of their victims.

4 Discourse on the Means Ambition Uses to Destroy Liberty

Nothing is more important for a nation that has adopted the republican system, having just emerged from a despotic regime and having won its liberty by the force of arms, than to reduce the real or apparent reasons that might allow a great mass of authority and power to accumulate in the hands of a single man, giving him prestige and ascendency over all other citizens. The downfall of popular institutions has almost always originated in measures imprudently prescribed to preserve them, not because this preservation was not seriously and effectively attempted, but rather because the natural and consistent consequences of causes requisite to the downfall cannot be altered by the will of whoever sets them in motion.

The misfortune of republics consists now, and has always consisted, in the very limited moral and physical force entrusted to the depositaries of power. This necessity that naturally comes along with the system has, as with all human institutions, its advantages and disadvantages. These should be weighed faithfully before their adoption because, once accepted, it is necessary to consider the whole before making a change that, no matter how superficial it may be or may be imagined to be, opens the door to the total change of the system and is a shock that, although superficial, if repeated, slowly undermines the foundations of the social structure until it collapses. What is more attractive than being as far as possible from the control of authority and submitting one's own person and actions as little as possible to the vigilance and decrees of the agents of power? And in what system, if not the republican, is more space enjoyed and greater breadth given to such privileges? In none, certainly.

Well then, this inestimable good is in greater danger of being lost

Original title: "Discurso sobre los medios de que se vale la ambición para destruir la libertad." Source: *El Observador de la República Mexicana,* Mexico, June 20, 1827, p. 55.

than in any other type of government if free men are not very much on the alert to anticipate every kind of aspiration that tends, if only for a few moments, to reduce their liberty and to augment with these losses the power of the one who begins by directing them and will unfailingly end by dominating them.

The love of power, innate in man and always progressive in government, is much more terrible in republics than monarchies. The one who is sure he will always rule exerts himself little to increase his authority; but the one who sees, even from afar, the end of his greatness if the immense body of the nation and irresistible force of true public opinion do not curb him, always works indefatigably to occupy the highest office if he believes it within reach, or to prolong indefinitely its duration and expand its limits if he has managed to gain it.

The means one can put into play to arrive at this end are infinite, but among the most commonplace are making oneself popular to promote one's rise, presenting oneself as necessary so as to maintain oneself in the post, and suggesting, so as to destroy the Constitution, the impossibility or ineffectiveness of the fundamental laws.

Among a new people who because of their inexperience have never known liberty, demagogues have an immense field on which to exercise their intrigues, giving free rein to their ambition. Look for popular passions and, once found, flatter them immoderately; proclaim principles, exaggerating them to a degree that makes them odious; and arouse suspicion of all those who have not advanced this far and profess or propound principles of moderation. Here is the means of making oneself popular in a nation made up of men who, for the first time, tread the difficult and always dangerous path of liberty.

What has been done in England, in France, in Spain, and, finally, in all the former Spanish colonies, now independent nations of America? Consider carefully the first period of their revolutions. Follow, keeping in view all the steps of those who afterward have been their masters, and it will be seen, without exception, that they have owed to no other means the popularity that served as stepping-stones to the summit of power.

In fact, people who have lived under an oppressive regime do not believe themselves free when they shake off the chains that held them yoked to the cart of the despot. Rather, they want to break all the ties that unite them with authority and even the necessary dependence that brings with it inequality of classes, an inequality owing not to laws but to the various physical and moral faculties with which nature has endowed each man. Because of this they listen with enthusiasm and elevate to all the public offices those who preach that chimerical equality of fortunes, pleasures, and ability to be anything, and they become inflamed with passion against all those who try to cure them of this political fever, smearing them with the most denigrating nicknames, the most contemptuous insults, and the most barbarous persecutions, and forging, without noticing it, the chains that must once again reduce them to servitude.

Robespierre and Marat did not become masters of the destiny of France or spill so much blood by means other than these, and they were a thousand times more destructive than all the kings together whose lineage they overthrew. In the end they fell, as all those of their kind will fall, but leaving the way open for the rise of others who, although more quietly but with a happier outcome, manage for some more time to achieve their goals, placing themselves at the peak of power, violating all social guarantees, and perpetuating the misfortune of the people who, because of a prolonged cycle of miseries and calamities, return to the same point of slavery from which they had set out to embark upon the path of liberty.

The people, after a thousand oscillations and fluctuations, the terror of anarchy over, create a poor or mediocre constitution, and then another fate awaits them. Soon enough, those who, by chance, have owed their promotion to the rule of factions try to give themselves excessive importance, affecting public esteem by means of all the externalities with which such esteem appears to be in agreement, working to persuade others that the stability of the republic depends on the adverse or favorable fate of their personal existence. This error insinuates itself with extraordinary ease and has ready success, especially among people who have not known more of a *patria* than ground stained by servility and slavery, more rights than the gratuitous and mean concessions of a lord, or more laws than the vain and unstable caprices of an absolute master. From the moment it is believed or feigned to be believed that the fate of liberty and the existence of the republic depend on the political existence of one single man, they find themselves on the verge of ruin. Then he will be granted all manner of condescension; it will be attempted to put aside all the goals of the citizens, of the laws and national interests, to fix them to the ambitious person whose aggrandizement is sought; the sacred names of *patria* and liberty will be defiled, and the poisonous root will be cultivated, which, with the passing of time, will bear nothing but deadly fruit.

Yes, you peoples and nations that have adopted a system of government as beneficial as it is delicate, be very much on guard against that one who tries to make himself necessary and to assign himself greater importance than granted by those who occupy public posts, the Constitution, and the laws. He will begin by flattering you, promising everything, and will end by pushing you down into servitude, superimposing himself on the laws that guarantee public liberties and, if possible, ripping from your hearts all the generous sentiments that the independence of a truly free soul might have rooted in them. Plunge those detestable monsters, those disfigured children, into the abyss of nothingness, their odious memory, weighed down by the public curse, transmitted to posterity.

Having acquired an unmerited importance and the destiny of the *patria* entrusted to their direction, these men soon fix their intentions on expanding their power by putting themselves in a position to prolong it indefinitely. But what means do they use? How do they obtain this from a people that has enthusiastically adopted the institutions that destroy any arbitrary regime? Here enter all the tactics, all the skill and cunning of the despots of new designation and recent origin: the protectors, liberators, directors, etc.

There is no man so incautious that he endeavors at the outset to seduce an entire people or insult them openly by clear and manifest contempt for the duties to which he has just submitted himself. This would be the sure way to frustrate any plan, and ambitious persons proceed with greater circumspection. What is it, then, that they do? They try to create a large faction, accustom the public to the transgression of the laws, and feign or stir up conspiracies.

It is impossible that a man reduced to his individual strengths could acquire either the prestige or the power necessary to superimpose himself on an entire nation. His intentions and plans will always be mistrusted by the multitude, and they will never have any noteworthy success except with the help of an organized faction that is replicated everywhere, that seizes the voice of the nation, that attacks all who oppose its interests and reduces them to silence and inaction by stirring up feelings of fear in those who might take on the faction by the gathering of their forces and the legitimacy of their cause. So, then, the first necessity of an ambitious person is to create a party of this kind.

It is very easy to effect this plan after a revolution lasting many years, in which the belligerent sides have calamitously harassed each other. At that point, the elements necessary to carry out the plan successfully are spread everywhere, and bringing them together does not pose a major difficulty. Many men are left with neither fortune nor employment, and as the overbearing necessity for daily subsistence is greater than all political considerations, they will have no option but to sell themselves to the first one who might purchase them. The fear that all unjust persecution brings with it demoralizes a nation, then destroys the natural generosity of characters, obliges men to lie to themselves and others, to hide their feelings and suppress their ideas through a perpetual and constant contradiction in their speech, and abjectly prostrate themselves before all those from whom, in principle, they hope or fear something. A nation, then, that for many years has traveled this dangerous path and that, moreover, finds itself impoverished because of the accumulation of properties by a small number of citizens, because of its lack of industry and because of the multitude of jobs that encourage aspirationism,[1] is a field open to the intrigues of astute and enterprising ambition and offers a thousand means for the organization of audacious factions.

On these foundations, in fact, ambitious persons rise up and, going on from here, make the first attempts at arbitrariness on persons who are little known, and because of their obscurity do not attract public attention or focus the gaze of the multitude. Normally, such transgressors remain hidden, either because of the ignorance of those who tolerate them or because of the lack of means for exposing and denouncing them to public opinion. From the lowest class it goes, rising gradually, battering the resistance that might be opposed, taking breaks that inspire some confidence, make anxiety disappear, and make citizens conceive the possibility of their security being trampled without protests or in spite of them. Here is where the faction comes in to support the one who pays it. It makes accusations that it repeats ceaselessly, exempting itself from ever proving them, feigning ignorance of any response to them, and

---

1. *Aspirantismo,* for which there is no clear English equivalent, denotes anyone who is power- or money-hungry. (Editor's note)

suggesting gratuitously, although constantly, that those targets of per-secution are criminals. Sometimes it tramples those who demand social guarantees, punishing them for sedition. Other times it attacks with pro-hibited weapons, inserting itself even into the sacredness of the domes-tic sanctuary in order to make their weaknesses public and obvious. If they are not found there, it does not matter; they are suggested, and with this it gets out of its difficulty. In this way, public attention is distracted from the matter at hand; men of probity and merit are obliged to aban-don the field; terror imprints itself on almost all citizens, isolating them in their homes; the consolidation of efforts that would make factions tremble is impeded, and an entire people is dominated, as a whole prov-ince gives itself over to a gang of bandits. Thus is formed a phantom of public opinion, much clamor is put forward, a great noise is made, and new levels of power are acquired, which lead to the highest levels, and these to the desired end.

One of the means that ambition has most commonly employed and that has never lost its effectiveness despite the frequency with which it has been used is feigning conspiracies or stirring them up so that they serve as a pretext for the expansion and augmentation of the power it seeks. People who have obtained their liberty and independence at the price of blood are very easy to plunge once more into slavery by using their very desire to prevent those evils. Of course, it begins by making a pretext of the existence of powerful and terrible conspiracies. It makes great mystery of them, sparing no effort to make this conviction well known and popular. When this has been achieved, it ventures the dis-tinction between the good of the republic and observance of the laws. Then it goes on to maintain that the former should be preferred to the latter. It assures that the laws are *theories* insufficient to govern and ends by openly infringing them, seeking their total abolition as its outsized prize.

This insidious attack on public freedoms is the more terrible to the extent that one takes them as a pretext and hides behind the mask of their preservation. Almost never has it been done without the destruc-tion of the government or the republic. If the people allow themselves to be overtaken by fear of conspiracies and permit the system's principles to be destroyed in order to extinguish or prevent them, they have already fallen into the trap, and they themselves, with their tolerance or positive concessions, have advanced the evil for which they seek a remedy. The first thing sought by the one who tries to establish the arbitrary regime is to have the persons of citizens entirely at his disposal. Once attaining this, he moves without hindrance until he arrives at his goal. To achieve it, he suggests the need to increase the strength of the government by suspension of judicial forms, by laws of exception, and by establishment of tribunals that are all loyal to the power and are under his direction and influence. For this, the system of exaggerating risks and dangers serves admirably.

When Bonaparte disbanded the Consulate of France and destroyed the Directory, the talk in Paris was of an immense and intricate conspiracy in favor of royalism, which never existed except in the minds of the people of his faction. Iturbide, in the attacks he made on the national representation on the third of April and the nineteenth of May, when he fell upon some of its members and dissolved it, made no mention of anything other than the conspiracies he supposed had even penetrated the sanctuary of the laws. Nonetheless, time and subsequent events showed with the greatest clarity that the motive of both stratagems was not the good of the *patria,* or devotion to or concern for public safety, but rather the beginnings of ambition, of augmentation of power and personal aggrandizement.

It matters not at all whether this augmentation is obtained by force or by spontaneous concessions; the effect is always the same. Liberty is destroyed by events contrary to principles, whoever might be the agent to whom they owe their origin. Liberty is not a name empty and devoid of meaning that can be applied to any system of government. Liberty is itself the result of a conjunction of cautionary rules that the observation and experience of many centuries have taught men are necessary to avoid the abuses of the powerful and to secure the persons and goods of the members, not only from the oppressions of individuals, but also from those of the power. And although intended to protect them, many or most times the power degenerates into a malefactor, turning weapons against those who put them in its hands so that it might defend them.

Be convinced, then, citizens who have the happiness of belonging to a republic that has adopted free institutions for its rule—be convinced of the importance of putting a brake on a government that goes beyond or tries to go beyond the boundaries that limit its power; destroy by legal means all those who show aversion to the principles of the system and who have the audacity and brazenness to attack them; distrust all the demands relative to the augmentation or concession of powers that are extraconstitutional or contrary to the foundations of the system, no matter what their title or name might be, especially if to attain them the existence or fears of conspiracies is alleged; listen with the greatest distrust to those who speak to you about them for the purpose of provoking you into disposing of the common rules and established order; for if this should be carried out at some time, political crimes will be reproduced unceasingly and freedom will never be seated on its throne in a nation that is a theater of reactions and of persecution, composed of oppressors and oppressed, and that carries in itself the germ of its ruin and destruction.

Peoples and states that make up the Mexican Federation, take warning from France, from the new nations of America, and from the recent events of your history. Fear the power of the ambitious ones and of the factions they call to their assistance. Unite your efforts to destroy them, so will you be invincible; isolated, they will beat you bit by bit. May the law and the national will preside over your destinies and make dominion of factions, etc., cease.

5

Discourse on the Civil Liberties of the Citizen

Political liberty consists of security,
Or at least in the opinion one has of one's own security . . .
When the innocence of the citizens is not secure,
neither is liberty.
— Montesquieu, *The Spirit of Laws*, book XII, chapter 4

In a society that is well constituted and intends to destroy all the abuses that have perpetuated the existence of an arbitrary regime, it is necessary to accustom its members not to be enamored of insignificant voices and rather to concern themselves with the reality of things. The abuse of unspecified words, especially in political matters, has been, since the extinction of feudalism, the source of all the woes of peoples who emerge from the control of lords only to become slaves of governments. The word "liberty," which has been used so often for the destruction of its own meaning, has been the usual pretext for all the world's political revolutions. People have been moved just by hearing it pronounced and have reached out their hands to embrace the tutelary spirit of societies, which its leaders have made disappear like a phantom at the very moment it ceased being necessary for the attainment and successful outcome of their ambitious aims. Philosophical lovers of humanity have raised their voice in vain against such conduct. The people have been and will be frequently deceived if they are satisfied with forms of government and neglect to ensure the most important point of all free government, *the civil liberty of the citizen,* or, what is the same, the power to do without fear of being reprimanded or punished everything that the law does not expressly prohibit.

The precious right to do what does not harm another cannot, unfor-

Original title: "Discurso sobre la libertad civil del ciudadano." Source: *El Observador de la República Mexicana*, Mexico, July 25, 1827, p. 219.

tunately, be put into effect in the state of nature in which man, reduced to his individual strengths, would inevitably be despot or slave, depending on whether these strengths are adequate to suppress the rest or insufficient to resist their aggressions. Men, then, have regarded themselves as compelled to create societies and to organize a public force that, being superior to that of each individual, might check and contain the perpetrators of high-handed crime against helpless innocents. But before long, governments and the force put at their disposal, forgetting their origin and feigning ignorance of the purpose and ends for which they have been instituted, themselves commit those crimes that they were supposed to avoid or curb in individuals. It was necessary, therefore, to place limits on their power, to request and seek assurances that these limits would never be violated, that the authority could be exercised only in certain and specified cases and under fixed rules or conditions, which, when they have been well and religiously observed, have created in men such confidence that they can act as they please within legal boundaries without fear of being injured or disturbed and which we know by the name of individual security. Unfortunately, this open and honest conduct among the agents of power has been very rare, and its lack has led to a thousand disturbances because of the prolonged struggle between governments and the people, a struggle that depends on the diverse interests that drive different groups and are the reason for their different and contrary ways of acting.

It is in the nature of those who dominate, whatever might be their number and the name given to them, to seek to make the exercise of power as advantageous as possible for themselves, and it is equally in the nature of those who become subordinated to make domination a heavy burden for those who exercise it and the lightest it can be for those who endure it. Whatever may be the name of those who govern, the question for them is always the same. Whether they be called presidents, directors, emperors, or kings; be they five or be they three, whether there are two or only one; whether they be elected or hereditary, usurpers or legitimate, their interest is always the same: to have persons at their disposal in the most absolute way, to have no obstacle to the exercise of their authority, to shake off the grip of all responsibility or censure. To the contrary, those who are subject to power, whatever may be its form or name, are concerned to make themselves safe from all arbitrariness so that no one might make use of their persons without rule or measure.

They are equally concerned to become free and to remain so with respect to everything that does not infringe upon the right and security of another. From those two opposing tendencies results a conflict that must have as its ultimate end either the establishment of despotism, no matter what might be the form of government, or the destruction of all arbitrary power. There will be no rest among the people except when one of those outcomes has come to be so essential and inalterable that every hope of alteration or change has been extinguished in the heart of men.

There is no doubt that people will be free under any form of government if those who rule them, even if they are called kings and are perpetual, are truly powerless to make use of the person of the citizen at their whim and without subjection to any rule; and republican forms will be useless, even if the head of the nation is called president and serves for a fixed time, if the fate of the citizen depends on his omnipotent will.

The wise Montesquieu, who analyzed political powers and, making clear their driving and conserving principles placed the first stone of the edifice consecrated to civil liberty, does not hesitate to assert that, although the form of government has some influence on civil liberty's existence, it is not its true and essential component. In the judgment of this great man, the liberty of the citizen exists uniquely and exclusively in individual security and in the stillness, repose, and tranquility that the conviction of its existence produces in each of the members. In effect, all these words contain everything that a peaceful man, free of ambition, can desire and ask of society, and when one acts in good faith and with the spirit of doing the right thing, it is easy and simple enough to grant such assurances.

On what, then, are contingent the continuous and bitter complaints that are heard with such frequency against the agents of the power? Why are the terms "indifference," "indolence," "arbitrariness," "despotism," and "tyranny" applied with such frequency to the acts that emanate from the depositaries of the authority? How is it that they are accused by the very ones who have an extremely lively interest in the repression of crimes that are being committed or can be committed against the individual and public security? To resolve these questions with certainty, it is necessary to assert that all the depositaries of the authority, no matter what the political power may be, have the strictest obligation to prevent unjust aggressions among individuals and themselves refrain from committing them. Whenever the citizen suffers or endures any external violence without having infringed any law, or, what is the same, is innocent, the government must be responsible and know to make public amends, for, as nothing more than an agent of the nation, established precisely with the sole and unique objective of ensuring the exercise of public and private rights, to fail by aggression or omission in such duties, as sacred as they are important, is to commit a crime of lèse-nation. Thus it is when highwaymen and murderers have the support of the authority or, at the least, guilty tolerance; when libelers damage the reputation of the honorable citizen with impunity and lack the propriety due to public morality, feeding on and encouraging malicious defamation through publication of private defects, true or supposed, without the authority exercising any restraining methods whatsoever; finally, when the abuse with impunity of men who have no other crime than their birth or the opinions they profess is permitted or tolerated, it is evident that individual security does not exist and that a government that is indifferent to or colludes with such attackers is, at best, a useless burden for the nation that created it and onerous for the people that maintain it, without serving them at all. In effect, from the moment one or several members of society have just and well-founded reasons to fear that they cannot count on the protection of the government, and, so as not to provide that protection, the government shields itself with a lack of energy or with the ridiculous excuse that public opinion is against the persecuted ones and defying that opinion is imprudent, from this point, we repeat, individual security is at an end and the bases of authority are undermined.

This indolent inertia, or this partisan conduct, is not only destructive to those wretched who endure it, it is so for the persecutors themselves and, above all, the government. Nor will those who today attack the rights of others with impunity, riding roughshod over the reputation and persons of their opponents based on the fact that the authority, from complicity or fear that these opponents have instilled in it, cannot or will not curb their excesses, should their fortune be adverse tomorrow and should their misfortune make them a target of persecution, be able to expect, from the agents of power, that they will enjoy security and stability. For the same reasons that it has been a cold spectator to the crimes committed by a faction, it will simultaneously be a cold spectator to all crimes of other factions; and in its shadow the reign of force and anarchy will be forming, which sooner or later will topple the social edifice, enmeshing in its ruins the depositaries of the authority. France, in its revolution, provides us with conclusive evidence of this truth. From the installation of the Estates General, the spirit of persecution broke loose, which did not end even with the Restoration. In that nation, the destruction of a previously victorious party firmly dragged the government along with it. The constitutionalists banned the royalists; the republicans, the constitutionalists; the Girondists were banned by the committees of public health and public safety; those who made up these bodies went in succession to the guillotine by the orders of Danton and Robespierre. These famous cannibals fell at the stroke of the Thermadorians, and in all these convulsions France was flooded with blood, anarchy devastated everything, and the government, which did not know or did not want to make effective the guarantees protective of personal security, was always the victim of the rush of the factions.

Until now these have been and will always be the deplorable outcomes of the criminal indifference and abandonment with which those who are charged with curbing attacks on individual security view them. A government that deserves that name should shake off fear and not permit itself to be banished; it must remain firm and impassive among the factions. To abandon the principles of justice in order to seek the support of the dominant faction is to be lost, is to commit a crime that is more than atrocious, ineffective, and not conducive to the end it is endeavoring to attain. In effect, when the government does not think about governing, but rather about existing through criminal tolerance, it unfailingly reconciles the hatred of those who suffer with the scorn of those who persecute. The first cannot avoid becoming exceedingly irritated, especially on seeing that they are sacrificed to the existence of an authority that they created to protect their security. The second, inwardly convinced that they owe toleration only to the real or apparent strength of their faction and that tomorrow the same toleration will be owed by another, which at the very moment it replaces them, oppresses them, look with disdainful scorn on a power so debased that it loses the value of a just severity without escaping the odiousness of criminal toleration. Unhappy people entrusted to such a government! Public interests will be meanly sacrificed to the interests of the agents of the power, peaceful citizens will not have a moment of tranquility or rest, becoming obliged to seek in themselves and by preventive measures owing to their individual strengths, the security that cannot or will not be accorded to them by an authority that does not think about them except to deliver them defenseless to the voracity of their enemies. In vain will they invoke the principles of justice, the natural feelings of compassion for them and for their families, or the just compensation owed for their services. No other recourse remains to them but to endure their suffering and redouble their efforts to place at the proper time the sacred deposit of public liberties in more faithful hands and to entrust the reins of government to expert persons of known probity.

The people have another, much greater, woe to fear from governments, and it is that when these governments, emerging from their indifference, enter into such activity that they themselves commit the crimes they should prevent; to clarify, transforming themselves from protectors to aggressors, they attack individual security and turn against the citizens the same weapons they accepted for their defense. This abuse is the more terrible the more the very nature of the political powers gives way to frequent errors in such a delicate matter. The authority of the government, says the wise Bentham, is nothing but the exception to the general rule that individuals must observe. *You will not kill, you will not deprive anyone of his liberty:* this is the obligation of an individual. *The judge will condemn the murderer to death; he will imprison the criminal; the government will have the sentence executed:* here we have the powers of the authority. Although the primary benefit of society is providing individual security for us by curbing the aggressions of others, it is clearly possible to attain this only when the person of each citizen remains subject to the action of the public authority in the event of an attempt against the security of another. This act of submission is precisely where the risk is run. Here is where the government feigns acting as protector when it is actually turning into an aggressor; and as the dividing line between these two acts is so fine as, in general, to be scarcely perceptible to the majority of citizens, it is not strange that it continues to confuse them. So we strive to explain so important a subject through its effects and outcomes.

From the moment in which the government is empowered to arrange the fate of citizens without submission to any rule, all of them are its slaves. The citizen's state is that of governed, the slave's that of possessed, and the distance that separates such different conditions is immense. What is it, then, to be possessed? It is to be entirely and absolutely at the disposition of another and dependent on his will. And what is it to be governed? It is to be protected against all forms of aggression, reprimanded oneself when one commits them, and obliged to concur on the means of preventing them. Any other sacrifice that might be called for on the part of the citizen, and any other influence the government claims to have over his person, is an act of oppression and tyranny. A citizen, then, has no reason to complain when his imprisonment has been provoked by an act committed by him, an act declared criminal by an existing law that assigns a fixed penalty and when the trial directly follows the arrest. These methods can in no way be called undermining of individual security; on the contrary, they contribute to maintaining this precious right and are indispensably necessary to secure it. Such a procedure does not cause alarm or lack of confidence except for malefactors, and this, far from being an evil against which one should guard, is for a society a good for which legislators should always strive.

Those acts of the authority of which citizens complain, and with such justice call oppressive and tyrannical, are not of this class. They are those that spread mourning and consternation in the family of the peaceful citizen, of whose innocence the authority pretends ignorance; *they are judicial persecutions without regular judgments, when the public power arrests and imprisons anyone it pleases, prolongs detentions indefinitely, exiles, and, finally, disposes of persons according to its whim,* like a master over slaves he possesses and not like a leader over citizens he governs; they are, finally, those acts by which the authority itself commits an outrage against the security it has promised and is obliged to maintain, and by which it perpetrates the disorders it was supposed to curb.

The public authority in a nation that has changed institutions for the first time, passing from absolutism to liberty, is constantly reactionary; it has no other idea of government than what it could receive from the previous regime, nor is it persuaded that curbing crimes and taking precautions against the destruction of the state are possible by any means other than those that have been learned in the school of despotism. As the principles of this latter school are openly contrary to the new institutions, the complaints are not only frequent and repeated, but also just, well founded, and incontestable. The agents of the power, not finding a way to avoid the complaints, appeal to the *preservation of the Republic,* to this protective god of tyrants and oppressors, by which they try to persuade of the risk the government runs if it does not disregard individual security.

It is certain that the first necessity of a people is the existence of its government, but it is not equally so that this be incompatible with supporting such a sacred right as individual security.

It is not the interests of the authority, but rather those of the officials they are trying to secure; because what is it they understand as the interests of the government? Things not capable of feeling cannot have interests in anything. It is then clear that, when this expression is used, it signifies only the impotence of the agents of the power to give free rein to despicable and thieving passions, oppressing those who overshadow them or make evident their evil acts. Certainly, it would be as rare as it would be difficult to persuade those who neither occupy public posts nor can get any use of them that the arbitrary regime has been established precisely for their benefit, to have their persons at their disposal without submission to any rule. The truth is that it greatly pleases those who rule, whatever certain people may want to say, to constitute themselves into *masters* of the people who have been entrusted to its direction and to have the power to dispose of the members that make it up without the obligation of accounting to anybody or the fear of answering to anybody. All the unhappiness of which they complain is thus reduced to the fact that some do not rule everything they would like; but what is unhappiness for them is a great benefit to the other citizens who make up the society.

Let us openly confess, then, that illegal and arbitrary prisons push man down into slavery, and, at the same time, they prepare an interminable series of misfortunes for a people that, because of these acts, is in a permanent state of revolution.

The history of all times, both ancient and modern, shows with absolute certainty that the crimes of the arbitrary power inevitably end in public disorders. It will be useless to seek in these political oscillations the reestablishment of individual security; they will have had this as their aim, but it will not be achieved while they last. Sometimes ambition, other times hatred and vengeance, always the most violent passions take possession of and empower such movements, and in this violent whirlwind they are surrounded and stifled and successively become victors and vanquished. Then principles are abandoned and a throne is erected to the empire of circumstance. These necessities give the common pretext for destroying regular laws that could have stopped them, and in this way injustice and irregularity, which will be constantly demanded as a pledge of public security, will periodically renew themselves. See here, says a famous writer, how the generations contemporary to these catastrophes never gather anything but bitter fruit and how rare it is that the following generations inherit happier ones. Looking for security in the midst of convulsions is the grossest of errors, but an active and sensitive people is invincibly impelled toward it when oppression has drained its patience.

Any political system that allows arrest and exile without due process carries within itself the germ of disturbances that sooner or later will explode with a deafening noise.

So governments that try to argue that the means of containing the disturbances is to disregard individual security with protective methods deceive themselves and deceive others. Public indignation, which is the precursor of all disturbances, becomes stirred up in so indisputable a way that it can be hidden from no one. Among a moderately refined people, when it is suspected that an innocent person suffers, the liveliest interest is taken in this victim of arbitrariness, and the particular iniquities of the power are publicly and vigorously censured. When this happens, discontent and alarm spread rapidly through all members of society, who from this moment place themselves in open war with the government; very just war, but at the same time the most dangerous and harmful that can be undertaken, because through it the social bonds are completely destroyed and men are in the barbarian state of nature.

We never advise peoples to take such a step, but they move to adopt it, as if through instinct and without deliberation, when the crimes of the power have been multiplied to such a point that they have destroyed in the heart of men all hope of an alternative. Then hatred and revenge, driven strongly by the furor that oppression causes, inspire the most cowardly and place a dagger even in the hands of the weakest. The irresistible wrath of a rebellious people causes the most dreadful damage. It expresses itself in the sanctuary of the laws, hurling from it, as violently as ignominiously, both those who have usurped the most majestic power and the perfidious agents who, betraying their duties, have not given less thought to anything than maintaining the public liberties despicably sacrificed to the interests of a contemptible and criminal favorite, but also the honorable men, their faithful representatives, who have learned to sacrifice everything, including their existence and political reputation, to the public good, to the national good. The canopied throne of the king and the armchair of the president who cannot or do not wish to sustain the civil liberty of the citizen, or who attack his individual security, see them collapse, splattered all over with the blood spilled through hatred and national vengeance. The murderers who set themselves up in tribunals against the express will of the constitutive law, converting themselves into instruments of tyranny and oppressors of helpless innocence, expel their last breath in the hands of the furor, and their dreadful cadavers, covered with blood and wounds, are exhibited through the streets and placed in the public plazas, unless, to prevent this catastrophe, as unfortunate as it is horrible, the promises and assurances that their masters gave to those despicable and contemptible slaves had been effective. If only the criminals who instigated such excesses suffered, but, in the net's dangerous haul, innocents and even meritorious citizens are unfortunate victims of the power of anarchy.

Take warning, then, oh you who preside over the destinies of peoples. There is a moment in which their exhausted suffering makes them break up like an avalanche that tears to pieces, destroys, and drags along behind it everything that before contained its strength and reigned in its spirit. If you open some gap in the legal barriers, this immense mass will rush headlong through it and you will not be sufficient to resist it. The French Revolution is a practical and recent example that you should always keep in your sights. It teaches you that *the public authority has never attempted a crime against the rights of free men with impunity, and the first step taken against individual security is the unfailing harbinger of the destruction of the nation and the government.*

6

Discourse on Laws That Attack Individual Security

> In popular governments, laws of proscription
> have never saved a people.
> — Montesquieu, *Considerations concerning the Greatness and Decline of the Romans*

If one carefully seeks the causes of anger and discontent that one observes among peoples who have tried various systems of government, passing from the most absolute despotism to the most unrestrained democracy, one will find that always or almost always it is due to the obvious opposition and the continual conflict between the principles of the constitutive law and the character of secondary laws. When the first is given to them or they initiate it themselves, they receive and proclaim it with enthusiasm; they imagine the most agreeable prospects and they consider themselves free simply from the fact of having declared themselves so. But when experience makes them see that such declarations have been futile, that despite them the oppressor regime continues and what is most sacred and independent in man comes to be the patrimony of the authority, they are annoyed at the form of government they have adopted and tear apart the governing constitution to seek in another what they have failed to find in it. From here they sometimes remove those who hold power, substituting for them others with the same or a different denomination and at other times make elective what was hereditary. When it is a matter of shaking off the yoke of a king, all social bonds are loosened successively and gradually until ending in anarchy, but when one tries to get out of this anarchy, one runs the scale in an inverse order, and power proceeds to concentrate without interruption until it settles entirely and fully in the hands of a single person.

Original title: "Discurso sobre las leyes que atacan la seguridad individual." Source: *El Observador de la República Mexicana,* Mexico, August 8, 1827, p. 287.

At the extremes, as in the center, the same thing is always sought, that is to say, *liberty,* but always to no avail, for the set of declarations we call the Constitution is not what provides it, but rather the agreement secondary laws have with the Constitution. When this agreement is not sought, it will continually and without interruption rise and fall in the fathomless sea of political systems without being able to attach itself to any of them, but once obtained, public tranquility will acquire an unshakable firmness and solidity.

All constitutions, not excepting even those that have been calculated in support of the interests of the government, contain the sum of the essential principles of civil liberty, which serve as the base of the entire social order; but they are without doubt continually and frequently violated by secondary laws, which, far from being a consequence of their principles, are in open opposition to them, by virtue of which is destroyed with one hand what has been built with the other. Thus, then, freedom of the press, individual security, inviolability of property, and the division of powers are sanctioned in the Constitution. The legislative body will be prohibited from changing the constitutive law, the government will be prohibited from imposing any punishment for its own sake or usurping the functions of judges by having the citizen, directly or *indirectly* at their disposal, prescribing to the tribunals the rigorous observance of the formulas. All this and much more will be in the constitutive law. Afterward, however, will come other secondary laws through which the government remains invested with *extraordinary powers to move, from one point to another in the nation, anyone who seems to it suspicious; military commissions, war councils, and advisers will be created* that judge and prescribe as it appears to them and suits their interest; it will try to make them independent of the supreme judicial authorities, exempting them from responsibility and their verdicts from review. The greatest concern, however, will be that they are completely and absolutely under the influence of the government so that, through them and protecting itself with this phantom of *judicial power,* it can dispose of the persons who inconvenience it and whom it would outlaw with the show of a trial. It will authorize these tribunals of murderers, as a celebrated French legal expert calls them,[1] to hear exclusively the crimes of high treason, and it will exempt them from observing the formulas. They will serve the

---

1. Dupin, *Legislación Criminal.*

power, lending themselves as instruments of all the power's iniquities, and this power in its turn will support all their evil acts, rewarding them sometimes with promotions, pensions, and posts and exempting them other times from the responsibility and punishment with which they are threatened.

By this horrific picture the regime of the terror in France under the committees of *public health and public safety* will be recognized, influenced by the faction of *sans culottes*,[2] at whose head were Danton and Robespierre. It paints a portrait also of the empire of Napoleon and the state of other nations that, by paths as tortuous and misguided, move rapidly and with gigantic steps to their destruction and extermination.

When it is a matter, then, of preventing these evils, or solving them if they have already begun, one must seek their origin and cut their root, which in representative systems will always be found in the laws of exception through which civil liberty is made illusory, attacking individual security. The legislative bodies, a constitution assumed, lack powers to decree such laws and are truly aggressors when they lend themselves to doing it. Their method is unjust in itself because it tends to absolutism, it is illegal because it infringes on the constitution, and it is imprudent because it alarms the people, destroys confidence, and perpetuates the barbarous state of a disastrous revolution.

Despotism does not consist, as the majority of men who reflect little persuade themselves, in the rule of one only, or in the consolidation of powers, but rather in what is unlimited in each one or in all of them together. The laws of exception assume in one aspect the existence of such a power, and in another aspect they tend to strengthen it. In effect, as a constitution is nothing other than the declaration of the rights of man in society and the distribution of political powers with a view to the preservation of these very rights, the laws of exception, which consist in the total or partial suspension of this code, can do no less than deprive man of some right or of some of the means to make it actual. How is it possible to proceed in this way without sanctioning or supposing the omnipotence of deliberative bodies? What limits can be placed upon the action of a body that does not recognize these limits in individual

---

2. The *sans culottes* were extreme radical republicans at the time of the French Revolution. (Editor's note)

rights and believes itself authorized to deprive anyone of the means of maintaining them? If there are injustices in the world, without doubt this is the greatest of all.

The general will must not be a reason that justifies such ravaging; it cannot be unlimited, and its action must cease where the right of another begins. Where would we end up by asserting the principle that the general will can do everything and is sufficient by itself to legitimate doing so? The most repressive and tyrannical acts, the most barbarous proscriptions, and the most enormous crimes would need nothing to convert themselves into rights except a certain number of votes, which could not even be fixed, given that nations cannot consist of a precise and determinate number of persons. The death of Socrates and Phocian, the exile of Aristides and Miltiades, and a thousand other loathsome acts through the entire human lineage would remain fully justified by such an absurd and antisocial doctrine. In a word, the ignominious execution of Jesus of Nazareth, the most innocent, the most beneficent, the most virtuous, and to say it now, the greatest of the whole line among the children of men, would be nothing other than a lawful act and the exercise of a right essential to all society.

Nonetheless, there is no one who does not know and detest such injustices, and this is the most decisive proof that there does not exist on earth any unlimited power or authority, and even were the votes and opinions of the entire human race gathered, they would not be sufficient to justify what by itself and by its nature is necessarily unjust.

Well, now, if the gathering of all rational beings cannot bestow this character on certain acts, can some fractions of it, much less the very few called representatives, be invested with such power? It would be nonsense and the height of absurdity to maintain it.

But what rights are violated, it will be asked of us, by changing, through laws of exception in certain and determinate cases, the tribunals and forms of trials, omitting some proceedings when public safety is in danger? We do not have difficulty in asserting that many and almost all rights are violated, because either those tribunals and forms have been considered absolute and indispensably necessary to guarantee individual security and distinguish the innocent from the guilty, or not. If they are necessary, in no case can the tribunals be changed or the forms omitted without attacking the most sacred right of man, which consists of the independence of his person and in the free use of the indispensable means to make clear his innocence. If they are not necessary, the tribunals must not be established, nor the forms agreed to.

To clarify. When the ordinary tribunals were established they had to be constituted on such foundations that, at the same time they threatened crime they protected innocence, inspiring in this way confidence in the individuals and the government. They had to be, under one aspect, a bulwark of individual security and, under another, the maintainer of public tranquility. To attempt, then, to keep them from exercising their functions in certain cases is to expose the one or the other, and sometimes both, to being trampled and destroyed. There will be a reason, perhaps, to change their program and method of proceeding if experience proves in them some imperfections inseparable from human institutions, but it will be impossible, at any given time, to detect these imperfections in order to deny these tribunals jurisdiction over some crimes.

We say the same about judicial forms. They have been established as an essential means to make clear the innocence or guilt of an accused person. Thus it is that the achievement of this most important goal depends on their exact and faithful observance, and to abandon the goal is to be rendered absolutely and totally powerless to rule with certainty and obtain a happy outcome in so delicate a matter. There is no halfway. If the forms do not lead to making clear the truth of an accusation and the certainty of a crime, they should be dropped altogether; but if on the contrary they are considered necessary to the purpose, they must never be set aside.

Nor can the risk of threatened public security be given as an excuse sufficient to justify such provisions because, besides the fact that public security cannot be distinguished from individual security and he who attacks the interests of the first can hardly look after the second, we have already demonstrated that the tribunals and procedures in which one can have confidence in the punishment of some crimes should inspire confidence that the tribunals and procedures can curb them all.

Nothing, then, can exonerate laws of exception from the mark of injustice and the tendency to despotism; not the authority of the legislative bodies that receive that authority from the people, nor the authority of the people, because by its nature and essence that authority is necessarily limited by individual rights; nor public security, because public security can be provided through ordinary means; generally, public security is not at risk except when the civil liberty of the citizen is attacked, and fear of this ceases with the renunciation of extraconstitutional methods. A procedure of that kind remains, then, nothing more than an act of arbitrariness and despotism by legislative bodies, by means of which they overstep, without reason, the boundaries imposed by principles of natural justice, engraved with indelible characters in the hearts of all men. But it is not the only error from which these agreements that are incorrectly called laws suffer; illegality, disloyalty, and inconsistency are what constitute their distinctive character and make them more odious to all men in general because they grasp more clearly the contrast noted between promises set out in fundamental laws and the violations of these promises by laws of exception.

Any system in which one acts contrary to a compulsory law and through which a previously made commitment is ignored is called illegal and deceitful. These ideas are clear, precise, and widely accepted. The wise and the ignorant, the concerned and the impartial cannot help but know their truth. We come, then, to the application that can be made of them in the subject with which we are dealing.

If there is any universal and preferentially compulsory law in society, it is the fundamental code. A constitution is clearly nothing if it is not the law of all the others and if it does not obligate all the powers of a nation in the same way as those individuals who make it up. As soon as the subsidiary laws can withdraw from the rule of constitutive law, restrict it, violate it, or suspend it, it becomes reduced to a magnificent façade and an illusory monument behind which the chains of despotism are devised and forged. If the constitution is the only ineffective one among all the laws, and if it can do nothing against the other laws which can do anything against it; if it exists only to receive insults, what kind of obligation does one have to observe it, and how is one to understand that immutability that one ventures to grant it? An obligatory and immutable law is one that binds everyone and from whose observance no one is exempt. Its destruction begins from the moment any one of its literal provisions is disobeyed or thwarted, even by acts that are called legislative, and it remains without authority if, in any of its questions that have been resolved positively, any text other than it is consulted.

When legislators enter into the exercise of their august functions, they renew by a public and authentic act the commitment that, in the role of individuals, they contracted to observe it, and at the same time they assume another new commitment not to oppose it by acts that might destroy it. This solemn affirmation establishes a right in each one of the citizens to object not only to their nonobservance but also to their positive infraction. Those who dare to offer this proof of respect and obedience for the fundamental law, simply by confirming it, agree that they will consider null and illegal all acts that in any way might oppose it, and because among them must be counted the laws of exception, it is as clear as the light of midday that its provisions share in these judgments.

In effect, if the constitutional law of a nation is the statement of the rights that the entirety of citizens should enjoy and the exercise of these should be specified by the secondary laws, and if the first should proclaim the principles and the second ensure their being carried out, no people who obtain a fundamental code and a representative government could consider legal provisions that oppose these important ends. On the contrary, the social guarantees demanded in the name of the principles would be constantly violated or evaded, thanks to its exceptions; and this continual battle would make the fate of a nation more unfortunate than if it had remained subject to the arbitrariness of the absolute power, which, deprived of all the appearances of philanthropy in its principles and regularity in its action, would present a thousand flanks and weak points that could be attacked with success.

The endeavor, then, to legalize these acts, although quite natural to their perpetrators, can never be carried out or have a lasting and durable effect. The fraud in the long run cannot be hidden from anybody, and the contradiction and opposition that exist between the fundamental law and those that have as their goal undermining it, making it illusory, reveal naturally, and make clear even to the least sharp-eyed view, this fraudulent system. We cannot give another name to declarations, always repeated, of respect for individual rights, accompanied by the most insidious attacks that reduce these rights to absolute nothingness. This behavior would not be believable if it were not so well known in public officials, entrusted in a special way with the depository of public liberties. They proclaim and talk constantly about the most liberal principles, but in the excessive use of their powers they sometimes maintain, and other times prescribe and issue, decrees so barbarous that they could not pass even in governments branded as absolute. The inquisitorial system reestablishes itself from the moment when it suits their ambitious goals to outlaw a faction. Through acts they call laws, all those who make up the faction are delivered to military commissions; it compels them to be judged by people who have already irrevocably decided their sentence; and it subjects them to a barbaric and absolute code that permits prolonging arrests and solitary confinement indefinitely and delaying carrying out the verdict. It is true that all this is always in opposition to the fundamental law, but as it emanates from the *legislative body,* it is called *law,* and as the *circumstances* demand, it cannot be other than *legal.*

In this way the people and the laws are mocked by those whose position it is to sustain the laws and protect the people. This is how, through acts that they call *circumstantial laws,* they perpetuate the arbitrary regime and with it the germ of disturbances and riots, and thus they overpower social guarantees, seeking to deceive the people with a language that is fraudulent.

And will it be said of this behavior that it is wise? Inasmuch as it is not legal, does it offer security to the freedoms of the *patria?* Will it calm public disorders? Not in the least. It places institutions in danger, the spirit of persecution is perpetuated and takes root in nations, it destroys confidence in one's own security and provokes revolutions.

It is difficult to find a means less suitable for strengthening the institutions of a nation than that of violating them, and it would seem impossible that it might have occurred to anyone to use this means for the attainment of this end, if experience did not prove that the delusions of men can reach even this point. The simple explanation of the expressions will be sufficient to convince us that laws of exception are directed to this and nothing else. If one asks what is sought with them, it will be said that it is the salvation of the *patria.* As this is not distinct from the salvation of the fundamental laws, in the end we will come to deduce that putting these laws out of danger is what is intended. But if one asks again what a law of exception is, the only response can be that it is the deprivation of either a right or a means of sustaining it, both set out in the constitutional charter, and from this can be deduced, as in the last analysis, that what is sought is to save this charter by its own destruction. Once one constitutional article is violated, the rest are not safe. The guarantee of one is the guarantee of all the others, and no matter how pressing one might assume the reasons presented to demolish the first article, there will be no lack of other reasons that, in their turn, are considered pressing enough to attack the others. If the legislative body manages to provide this pernicious example, the government, the tribunals, and even individuals themselves will not be long in imitating it, and as everyone is prohibited from doing so, no one will have the right to reprimand the rest.

A constitution violated by the legislative body offers no security whatsoever, for as the transgressor is the supreme authority, it cannot be legally reprimanded, nor are there means to stop this aggression by punishing the guilty. The alarm, then, which lack of confidence follows is more lasting and permanent. As if individual security can have protection when the attack comes from the laws themselves. Men become inflamed in such cases upon seeing that they do not gain in society the equivalent of what they lose, for if one counts the value of the sacrifices, on the one hand, and the persecution that the laws cause them or the protection they do not provide them, on the other hand, the sum of woes comes out greater than that of the goods, or, better said, the latter disappear completely, and the former remain entirely.

But the effects of these abusive laws in the judicial order are worth closer scrutiny. When one wants to reduce to words empty of meaning the rights set down in a constitution, before corrupting ordinary judges put in place to defend those rights, one attempts to create special tribunals, whose very name is enough to imagine what must be expected from them. No one is unaware that such manner of administering justice does not have as its purpose the protection of innocence. Those who requested or dictated such laws hasten to make use of them to get rid of their enemies through the verdict of judges who are all at the disposal of whoever appointed them. Their decisions will be repeated and confirmed as if by an echo wherever they are brought. But public opinion censures them with a firm and unanimous voice that only their authors will have the misfortune not to hear, because lending an ear only to the voice of the man on whom they depend or of those he has at his service, they are concerned only with supporting a faction that might have disappeared much earlier from the heart of society. This regime, whatever might be the guise under which it attempts to present itself, is at its heart one of deception, shamelessness, and cruelty. In it, without any exception, all questions are decided, not by examining the facts, but rather on the basis of the views that they have regarding the political opinions of the accused. And when the most atrocious and entirely established abuses of authority remain unpunished, if the perpetrators belong to the faction classified as sound, the opinions contrary to it are considered unpardonable crimes. But the least of all the ills that laws of circumstance cause is the obstinacy that their authors show toward leaving the tortuous path down which they have begun, giving dangerous circumstances as their pretext, without wishing to understand that these dangerous circumstances become critical only when a constitution struggles with an arbitrary regime and when the securities promised by fundamental laws are evaded and remain without effect because of special laws. This is how the very principle of the ill that foments and perpetuates the sickness is applied as remedy.

Any moderately reflective man will be able to anticipate the conclusion of this fraudulent regime. It must end either in the total loss of individual security or in political fluctuations that do not offer individual security until too late. What is astonishing, says a celebrated publicist[3] in public law, is that such laws can reestablish themselves and that people enlightened enough to reclaim individual rights and strong enough to gain recognition for them take thoughtlessness and negligence to the point of allowing these rights to be reduced to puerile illusions. But who does not recognize the sway that words, formulas, and appearances exercise at the outset? Constitutional articles in which these rights are proclaimed, bodies constituted to defend them, representatives, voters, the apparatus, finally, of a representative system appear visible to everyone, calm the spirits, and discredit the first alarms of the small number of citizens it has not been able to seduce. The time required for public opinion to develop is used to employ all the means of usurpation and imposture in corrupting public agents, in depriving those who resist them of all influence, and in forming those habits and customs advantageous to a system of this kind among the various classes, until indiscretions and, what is worse, excesses bring setbacks that upset this system and storms that tear it from its moorings. Then its fall is as rapid as certain, because the first symptoms that announce it dissipate the illusions and return to public opinion its enlightenment, its liberty, and its power.

---

3. Berencer, *Justice Criminelle*.

7 Discourse on the Independence of Judicial Power

Ne quid nimis. Nothing in excess.
— Fedro

The inflamed frenzy that has been observed against the defeated dissenters and the excessive and sometimes immoderate determination with which their punishment is urged, seems to us to belong to the number of those excesses that, in general, are not subject to a noble principle, nor do they have favorable outcomes, especially when the judges are liable to lose an independence on which social order rests. The most august honor, the most noble privilege, and the most difficult assignment there can be among men in any government is being the arbiter among their equals, ending their differences, and being able to deprive them with a single word of their goods, honor, and even life. For this reason, in the first periods of the civilization of nations and in the infancy of societies, it was the supreme leader of the state who fulfilled such important functions, administering justice to the people. Once the machine of government became complicated and the attention of the rulers was distracted by many goals, it was necessary to dismember this branch of the sovereign authority and to entrust the judiciary to a particular class of magistrates. The government still reserved for itself their selection, the charge of overseeing them, the power to punish their breaches of trust, and the beneficent right of mitigating the severity of judicial verdicts.

Nonetheless, it was observed that the government, as the one that selected the judges and the one that rewarded their zeal or punished their negligence and intervened directly in judicial affairs to undo errors or mitigate the severity of sentences, exercised too much influence over

Original title: "Discurso sobre la necesidad de que sea efectiva la independencia del poder judicial." Source: *El Observador de la República Mexicana,* Mexico, May 26, 1830.

the judges and could abuse that influence to oppress innocence or make judgment tip from the side of passion. Since then it was sought in every good system of government to surround the judicial order with such guarantees that it should be assumed fundamentally that the judges, free of all dependence, would not listen to another voice than that of their conscience or have another regulator of their transactions than the law of which they are the instruments and ministers. In the nations, then, that are governed by the representative system, although the power to choose and name all the judges is left to the government, and it is charged with overseeing their conduct, it is not permitted to remove them from office at its will. Even for the selection itself, qualities and circumstances that persons must have in order to be named are set; and with these or similar precautions, what the writers in public law call the independence of judicial power is ensured in every country that might not be Constantinople or Morocco.

This independence is one of the primary and most important guarantees the fundamental law can and must accord the citizen so that his person and property might always be respected, because it serves a mere individual little to have a well-organized legislative body and very good laws or an executive power whose authority has been greatly curtailed if he has good reason to fear that, when one needs to defend his financial interests before civil tribunals or his innocence before criminal judges, it is not the law but the will, caprice, or passion of men that decides his fate and acquits or condemns him in his lawsuits. What do all the doctrines of the writers in public law on the division of powers and the balance of political forces matter to the individual of the society if, despite all of them, he is unjustly deprived of his goods or his life?

Life and the means of preserving and passing it in an agreeable manner; here is every man; here is everything that he requires and the only thing that interests him; and here is why the greatest benefit society can give him is that he never be deprived of existence or the things that can make it pleasant except when he has made himself unworthy, through his crimes, of life or things that make it desirable. But this benefit cannot exist if the constitution, the laws, and, above all, the vigor of the supreme government do not make impossible, insofar as it is given to human discretion, partiality in judgments or verdicts of the courts and tribunals. The constitution ensures honesty and impartiality in judges when, through the qualities that it requires to become one and the method of their selection, it can be hoped that this selection will fall equally to persons of education and probity, and when, through the unremovability that it bestows on them, it shelters them from arbitrary dismissal, the fear of which could make them instruments of the self-interested aims of the government. The laws augment these guarantees, assuring them appointments with which they can live without having to sell justice to silence the voice of poverty, a temptation so powerful that few resist it; threatening them with very serious penalties should they prostitute their august ministry; and specifying with great clarity the circumstances and ways of demanding responsibility from them in the event of breach of duty. The government, finally, completes this system of guarantees and independence, creating respect for the persons of judges, which are sacred during the time in which they exercise their judgeship, protecting them from any violence, insult, or threat that is intended to extract from them an unjust verdict or one contrary to their opinion in whatever the matter might be.

Here are the general and common doctrines on which all writers in public law agree, without a single one having expressed up to now a contrary opinion or having expressed the least doubt in even one of these protective principles; and what is more, here are some ideas that, in some way, can be called innate in the heart of man because, in effect, in it the instinct for his own preservation has written them with indelible characters. Who is the man who, led into the presence of the judge for his crimes, or perhaps only for the appearance of them, would wish a tumultuous multitude to be present in the audience and, with raised knife, shout out the interpretation of the law: condemn that wretch you are looking at, and if not, both of you will die by our hands? Well now, if no one, whether defendant or accused, would want the one who was to pronounce the terrifying verdict on which his life might depend threatened in this way, will it be just if someone dared to threaten judges to the same effect when they are about to pronounce in the trial of another? And will they be lovers of the *constitution,* friends of the laws, and adherents of *liberty,* those who, in a free government, threaten the judges to prejudice their verdict and do what would not be tolerated, not permitted, nor has ever been seen under an arbitrary regime? If such threats are overlooked, they will end in open violence, and if these go unpunished, they will be repeated, and then what will become of order and the rule of law? For what is it to speak of liberty, of enlightenment, or of philosophy? Has it not repeatedly been the case, and is it without doubt very certain that the aim of political constitutions and the effect of *enlightenment* and philosophy is that citizens live subject only to law and not to the whims or passions of men? For how can those who endeavor to substitute their will for what is predetermined in the laws and who command with threats the prophecies that have to be pronounced in the sanctuary of Themis be constitutionalists, philosophers, or lovers of liberty or the laws? We are fully persuaded that those who permit such sacrilegious crimes do so carried away by a zeal very laudable in itself but very unfortunate in its consequences, very foolish, and reprehensible, and for this very reason we advise them with confidence that once they know the error, they would be the first to detest it, to repent, and to be horrified.

Are those who request of the judges in this way that an accused be condemned to death sure that he is guilty of a capital offense? Have they fully examined the act of which he is accused? Is it legally proven that he is the perpetrator of that crime? Have they considered and weighed carefully all the circumstances of that deed? Are they fully convinced that no circumstance extenuates its maliciousness or excuses it in some manner? Is it as clear as the light of day that the law condemns him to death? Is his particular case decisively foreseen and defined in the penal code? We, they say, neither know nor care to know anything about these quibbles of a lawyer; the public voice says that the accused has committed a crime that *everyone* considers capital, and we want him executed, be the deed proven or not, and be there or not an express law that condemns him.

Well, now, is there a single man, not yet liberal, humane, and enlightened, but one who preserves in his soul some love, some respect for justice, who is not embarrassed by such a claim and by giving a response that one would not even find in the mouths of those who make up the most savage tribe? For this is, in sum, the behavior of those who demand the head of an accused person without knowing whether he is guilty because they have not studied his case, and the response they tacitly give when they are told that, because the constitution did not give them the right to apply the laws but rather gave it to the judges named by the government, they must leave those judges in full freedom so they might judge according to the circumstances of the trial and what their consciences tell them, and that to intimidate a judge with threats so that he would pronounce a verdict dictated to him is the greatest crime that can be committed against the constitution, for it tears down and destroys at a single blow the distribution, division, balance, and independence of the powers that have been established in it for the benefit of all.

But still they reply: And if the judge has been bribed to acquit a criminal or impose on him a more gentle punishment than the one he strictly deserves? The assumption, generally, is false and slanderous and almost always unfounded, but conceding that it might not be, the solution is very simple and delimited in the same laws: denounce such a scandalous and criminal breach of trust, judicially pursue that one or those who have sold justice, and ensure by legal means that a sensational example is made of them in order to dissuade all others who are in that situation from imitating their iniquity. But to threaten with taking justice into their own hands and killing the accused on the pretext that the judge has treated him with too much kindness, and to intimidate the tribunal that has not ruled to their satisfaction, more than being the greatest affront, the greatest insult that can be made to humanity, to reason, and to justice, is the surest way to put an end to the constitutional regime and the most infallible means of making even the name of liberty hateful.

In the first place, if such crimes are repeated, there would not be a single good man who would want to be a judge in a country in which he is threatened and the verdicts he is to pronounce are dictated to him, for no man of any probity wants to see himself reduced to the difficult choice of committing an injustice or being ridiculed and insulted. In the second place, what sensible man would want to live under a government which, were he to have the misfortune to be accused justly or unjustly of certain crimes, could not prevent his conviction, even when the tribunals recognized his innocence? Who would not hasten to flee from such a country of iniquity? Who would not blaspheme free institutions if they saw that, with this name, the upheaval of society, the subversion of all principles, and the violation of the most sacred rights were justified?

Among all injustices, the most odious, the least bearable, is that which is committed with judicial forms in the name of justice and by the very magistrates who were supposed to administer it. And if this is so, when the injustice is the result of the error or maliciousness of the judge, how much more horrific and terrible will the atrocity be when it is born of violence? Against the errors or personal arbitrariness of the judges, the

Constitution and the laws have provided us with a solution, authorizing appeals, and if these are not sufficient, means for annulment; but against the violence of threats or at gunpoint, what means will the unfortunate person have over whom this storm bursts? None, of course. Those who applaud, praise, or excuse at least the first crimes of this kind can now count on the most bitter fruits, for they serve as the text for the disrepute and slanders with which our enemies seek to discredit us in cultured, powerful, and civilized Europe.

It is time now that those who heretofore have proceeded in this way retrace their steps and consider that violating justice, trampling on the authority, so respectable, of the tribunals, and intimidating and threatening individuals is not a good way to guarantee and make amiable the present order of things. It will have served nothing to have removed and eliminated the power and favor that resurrected the notable extraordinary authorities, the weak influence they could have on tribunals and their decisions, if an influence much more direct, powerful, and terrible in criminal sentences is now usurped by a fraction of the people.

No good intention, no motive, however noble one might suppose it to be, can justify the threats that, in private conversations and gatherings and in some public papers, are poured on the judges and other constituted authorities because they do not venture to violate the forms, upset the order of trials, or apply capital punishment to those who, in their judgment, do not deserve it; on this point reason is in agreement with the Constitution and the laws. We sincerely desire to make those who are thus deluded know the truth, and for this, without insisting more on the incontrovertible truths that we have just urged, we will conclude our discourse with one single observation.

They say that they are lovers of justice and of the present order of things, that they see it perishing through the apathy and delay of the judges in accelerating cases and for their kindness in the application of punishments; arrange, then, the judges and tribunals in the desired way and, once this is done, let us ask what will happen when these judges acquit, as will happen many times, one or more persons accused of political crimes? Will they seek them out to take their lives because they have not ruled as they wanted? And who, after all this, would accept the honorable post of judge? And what would become of the liberty and independence that the law assures them in their deliberations and judgments if they do not have to perform according to their conscience, but rather at the whim of those who want everyone executed whom they suppose deserving of the ultimate punishment? We say that many of those accused of political crimes would be fully acquitted because, in the moment men see themselves invested with the august character of the judgeship, they become other than what they were before, and they see themselves placed under an obligation to follow the precise letter of the law. From this results that, not being able to get out of the case material anticipated in the law that serves as the basis for the accusation of guilt, and this many times not being the same as the law designates, they have to declare him not guilty of the crime of which he is accused; and as it is very difficult for the law to anticipate or precisely define all crimes, for some crimes it will inevitably come about, because of not being specified in the code, that it will be necessary to acquit the accused. We have many examples of this even in those tribunals disposed absolutely to condemn and universally recognized as barbarous and inhumane.

These detestable qualities cannot be denied in the revolutionary tribunal established in the very sad days of the French Convention and under the immediate influence of Robespierre; nonetheless, this tribunal, although in reality it was not a tribunal nor did it merit such a name simply because it had the appearance of one, sometimes did not satisfy the revolutionaries and absolved from the pain of death various persons accused of political crimes through the fury of the revolutionaries. One must, then, be convinced that it will not be possible to find a judge, even though deliberately sought, who would be sufficient to quench that rabid thirst for blood that rises in those moments immediately following the triumph of political factions, and that generally is due more to ignoble revenge than to impartial justice.

And will it be a great misfortune for society if the executioner has fewer occasions to exercise his odious and terrible ministry? If sound philosophy would like the bloody spectacle of an execution to be abolished, even for common atrocious crimes, will this show itself with more profusion and fewer formalities in political crimes that are only crimes in specific places? If those actions that generally depend on opinion going astray, on erroneous concepts and wrong ideas must be punished with the loss of life, what punishment, then, will be imposed on murderers, thieves, and the other vicious people whose crimes have their source in the heart's perversity? Yes, we insist that it be kept in mind that political crimes are among those in which some leniency is appropriate, because ordinarily they are born of an error in understanding and not of that malignancy of an incorrigible heart which, when a man has committed a series of atrocious crimes, makes it almost necessary to exterminate him like a wild animal from which society can expect nothing but injury.

Such a man is today the enemy of the present order of things, and he works to destroy it, and, corrected by an imprisonment or exile more or less extensive, will never return to take up the business of counterrevolution, because he does not contract the habit of plotting like the one who kills or robs. He who has been accustomed to being a thief does not easily let go of this vicious habit, but he who comes out badly in an attempted revolution generally remains forever taught by punishment. This rule can have exceptions, but it is fairly general.

If we did not observe in many of our fellow citizens that tendency to accelerate cases, trials of conspiracy, and to force and prejudice in a certain way the verdicts of judges, while, on the other hand, they do not show great insistence on the persecution of other crimes; if we do not recognize all this, we repeat, we would have exempted ourselves from fighting this inclination, which, if it begins to grow larger, can make itself excessively harmful to the system of tribunals and put social guarantees in great danger. We have suffered too much in the periods of our revolution, and it is now time for us to reestablish the reign of harmony, moderation, and justice in a shaking up that has taken as its motto *the constitution and the laws*.[1]

1. This essay was written in May 1830. Mora was referring to the motto ("Constitution and Laws") of the last successful rebellion. The government of Vicente Guerrero was toppled in 1830 by General Anastasio Bustamante. (Editor's note)

8 Discourse on Public Opinion and the General Will

Here are two phrases as often repeated in republics as silenced in absolute monarchies, perhaps because their *true meaning* constitutes the compelling strength of the first and is the implied censure and most constant threat against the existence of the second. But see at the same time two phrases humanity and philosophy will never pronounce without trembling, because in their name horrible crimes have been perpetrated in the world, and because they have been and will always be the cloak of demagogues, the deadly defense of factions and favorite watchword of all revolutionaries, similar to the comets, innocent stars like all the others, but which lent barbarism the occasion to cause, through impassioned imaginations, damages in which they did not take any part whatsoever. These phrases serve malice as a horrific weapon to get its way with their sacrilegious intentions, even when nothing corresponding to the phrases exists except sound devoid of all reality.

Just because the significance of these terms is so respectable, it is enough to pronounce them to make *absolute governments* tremble and fill with suspicious distrust and silence *popular governments* and make them lower their heads; but be careful, be careful with carrying that respect beyond its limits in such a way that it prevents us from approaching the intended object that must produce it (as almost always happens), for that way an illusion will generally intimidate us; we would worship a shadow instead of the divinity we imagine.

In no government is that examination more necessary than in the *popular,* and never more interesting than in times like, unfortunately, the present, in which diverse factions argue over the benefit of their opposing interests. As, then, each one of them defends his intentions with those

Original title: "Discurso sobre la opinión pública y voluntad general." Source: *El Observador de la República Mexicana,* Mexico, August 1, 1827.

respectable phrases, it is indispensible to know well their full value to determine if none, some, and which of the rivals possesses such treasure.

Let us attempt, then, to do for the government and the Mexican public a most interesting service, examining what those terms signify; if what they signify can exist and in which cases; if there will be sure indications to recognize their existence; and, finally, if it is assumed, whether there will always be an obligation to yield to their rule, or if one will be able to or even should resist it at some time.

These questions deserve all the attention and study of our fellow citizens, particularly the legislators and public officials, because on their erroneous resolution rest a thousand future woes of the *patria* and the noisy or silent undermining of the institutions on which it bases, with reason, its stability and its fate. Let us now get to the subject so that our reflections might contribute abundant material to whomever can speak with greater knowledge.

What do these phrases signify?

In *metaphysics, opinion* is adherence of the understanding to a proposition or propositions through *solid* foundations that one is convinced to be the *truth,* but not so clearly and evidently that they free it completely from the fear that it might be its contradiction. There are, for example, reasons for believing that the ebb and flow of the sea is the result of the attraction of the moon, but there are other, opposing reasons. He who on the basis of the first set of reasons decides to attribute such an effect to the moon without completely resolving the second is said to *embrace opinion.* Of him who repeats that proposition for no reason other than having heard it, what can be said with accuracy is that *he does not know,* and at most, that he *believes,* if his entire foundation for regarding the proposition as certain is the regard he has for the person from whom he heard it.

The significance of the word "opinion" does not change when it carries over into the *political.* There, the same as anywhere else, the term denotes *adopt, embrace* as *true* a proposition based on foundations that seem solid to the understanding, and more solid than those foundations that persuade of the opposite, although it cannot provide them a completely satisfactory response.

The word "will" is well understood by everyone; it always signifies the *attachment* of our soul to some object that the understanding has conceived as good. The *intensity* of love or desire is proportionate to the degrees of goodness that we apprehend in the object and those of the clarity with which the understanding presents that good to us.

These ideas are very clear; they are those that all philosophers assert and what all men experience. From them we deduce, then, the truths that pertain to our case.

To this point we are proceeding well, and we will not be contradicted. The difficulty begins with the adjectives in these phrases, because delving deeply into what "public" means in the first and "general" in the second, it is necessary that the spell vanish with which the unwary are deceived so as to make them blind instruments of destruction, who will, in their turn, be destroyed.

These phrases, "public opinion," and "general will," either signify nothing that can serve demagogic purposes, or they must denote the opinion and the will, at least, of the greater number of citizens who make up a republic, but not the absolute total, as it seems it should be.

Notice that the classical authors, when they use these phrases to establish their doctrines, seem not to give so much *latitude* to their meaning, but rather they understand by them the opinion and will more generalized among those who are capable of forming it with respect to each subject; but we, whose intention is to combat the frequent anarchic applications, give them *generally* the sense of *coincidence* of *opinions* and *desire of all,* or even the *considerable majority* of the *citizens regarding a specific object.* Having given this warning and the terms now defined, let us consider the second question.

Is there a subject regarding which a uniformity of opinions and the desire of the greater part of the citizens can be verified?

It has been said already that there is not desire or love with respect to objects that are not known, and that there is no *opinion* as long as the understanding has not settled on foundations whose solidity is sufficient to persuade it. So, therefore, there will not be *uniformity* in the thinking and desiring of the greater number of citizens of a republic, but rather only with respect to those objects that are within the reach of that *majority,* that is to say, in the reach of all men. How many objects of that class will there be? Will they exceed the number of fingers of the hands if we use them to count?

It can be established as a general rule that only certain experimental truths and simple first principles can be conceived uniformly by the majority; but at the moment when objects become complicated in their relationships, and in proportion to how these relationships multiply, how they get in the way of each other, and how the terms recede away to a greater distance, the impossibility of *uniformity* arises and grows. The majority abandon it, and their examination does not even occur to them, and the few who have an ability and dedicate themselves to the examination see them from different angles and, for that reason, establish on the basis of them very diverse and even, many times, contradictory principles.

All men have the same faculties, but perhaps no two apply them in the same way to their aims, from which grows such a multitude of passions, such a diversity of desires, and the infinite variety of concepts. Everyone experiences pleasures, but each in his own way; everyone suffers pain, but in how different a way, and how many times does the same object that provides pleasures to some, cause anguish and repugnance in others! So, about the only agreement we have is on the *vague and indefinite* desire to be happy, child of abstract, confused, and general understanding of happiness. But when it comes to realizing or satisfying that desire, each one goes by a very different road and believes himself able to find this treasure in objects very distant from one another. Let us agree, then, that if the truth is not *practical and experimental* or *exceedingly simple,* we waste time looking for it with respect to the *true opinion and will* of the greater number.

As societies and republics are nothing more than the consolidation of families, and these of individuals, it is necessary to acknowledge that *public opinion* and *general will,* if they exist, must have the same sources as individual opinion and will, and those can be verified only if the source of these others is identical. Well, now, let us examine the men, or better let each man examine himself, and tell us which were the sources of the opinions they embraced in their lives, which have produced *lasting* opinions and which transient, and all will respond that their opinions have arisen either from *education* or from *respectful habits* that they acquired from their education or from their *perceptions* or from their *reflective meditations and study;* that those which originate from this last source are generally readily changeable because, even when they are certain, they are accompanied by fear, because of the experience of other errors and mistakes; that those which originate in the other three primary sources create deep roots and, even should they be false, are set aside with difficulty.

Assuming this, and it being impossible that the greater part of the citizens dedicate themselves to *reflective meditation* and *study,* there only remains to us, as origins of public opinion, *general education, sensations, and respectful acquiescence,* repeating in regard to this last that it is more likely the source of *faith* than of *opinion* because, not providing us with direct foundations, it makes us defer to what the person or persons to whom we give credit present to us as certain.

Sensations provide us only with *experimental truths,* for example that the sun gives light, that fire burns; and so, putting these to one side, there can be *public opinion* only with respect to those objects that might have been subjects of *general education.*

From this, anyone will infer very correctly that, it being unfortunately undeniable, there has never been among us *popular education;* that the fruits of what is sown today will be gathered twelve or twenty years from now; that the majority of our people did not go to the few and bad schools; that those who went to them learned only and at most the catechism of Ripalda, badly explained most of the time; and that popular instruction has been relative only to religion — and would that they presented it in all its purity! — will infer, we repeat, that, besides the truths of *immediate experience,* there is among Mexican citizens *uniformity* of thoughts and desires only in matters of religion, because they drink it with mother's milk, and in *independence of all foreign domination,* because it is such a simple object, so perceptible, and because of its deprivation misfortunes came to us through all the senses. Excepted from this rule are neither the few that there may still be who have lost their sense of civic responsibility, longing for the sepulchral calm of the time of slavery, nor some who, for their misfortune and ours, detestable books have corrupted, which they read with neither principles nor criticism, and those books have made them waver in and even abjure the holy religion they professed.

The well-off class among our youth and the humblest and poorest among our citizens provide the confirmation of these truths. Observe the former carefully since our independence and you will note the yearning with which this class searches for works of the sciences whose names we did not previously know; the promptness with which it adopts the principles of each new work that arrives; the ease with which they are applied despite overrunning everything; and the equal ease with which they are abandoned with the arrival of another work that establishes different principles. From what does this changeability arise? From an excess of ingenuity and a lack of experience in scientific education. The desire to know and the necessity of governing ourselves make us devour whatever comes to our hands, and not being well rooted in the true principles, because they never gave them to us, nor did we learn them ourselves, we wander from theory to theory, and the same thing will happen to us until sufficient time has passed for reflective meditation and experience to root us in the solid truths which we still distrust. Therefore, for now we must not allege public opinion with such satisfaction and generality, not even in speaking of the well-to-do and studious class, because what we do not acquire in education only study and experience can give us, and those require a greater passage of time than what has passed since we have become free.

In the poorest class, which is incomparably the greater, the assertion is still more palpable: whoever goes out to deal with the people of the country or enters into artisan workshops to explore what they think about the innumerable questions of politics, economics, and morality that legislators must handle daily, will see that some respond only with the *smile of suspicion*, indicating that they fear one wants to make fun of them; and others, more simple, respond: *And what do I know of that?* There is no need to give this too much thought. Our people are almost uniquely *generally satisfied* with religion, with independence, with the desire to pay as little as possible in taxes or nothing if that is possible; with whatever will allow them to work and freely pursue their lives; that their personal security be stable; that they can enjoy their possessions in peace; and they become involved in nothing else, not even to inform themselves about *government* provisions; they respect their legislators, the government, and the subordinate authorities and let them do their work.

It seems very certain, then, and it is among us even if it might not be everywhere, that the only objects of common opinion are those that derive from popular education, those that come through the senses, that is to say *empirical* truths, or that are directly deduced from them, and those very few which, because of their simplicity and total lack of relational complication with other objects, are offered to the majority and are perceptible to everyone; but *speculative* truths, *complex and difficult* truths like those the science of government embraces, are neither objects of the opinion of the greater number, nor is there regarding them that *unifor-*

mity of the majority, except in the case in which they adopt them by *tradition*, instilled by three or four people who are referred to as entourage. Then, the majority *believes*, does not *opine*; is *incited* mechanically, does not *incite*; and thus their thought, as their desire, does not generally last longer than that of the voices with which those who have set themselves up as coryphaeuses urge them on.

The law, we will be told, *is the expression of the general will*; then how can there be so few objects of *public opinion* and consequently so few objects of that *will?* If that maxim, taken from Rousseau, were absolutely true, says the very profound Bentham,[1] "there is not a country that would have laws, for neither in Geneva nor in the small democratic cantons does the right of suffrage have that *universality*, nor is that right of suffrage of the true majority of the total number of inhabitants ever verified." If, through such a principle, one wants to indicate that those with responsibility for making the laws received from the people that very august investiture or that, given the law, the citizens accept it, those obligated to it by their social pacts, then, yes, it has a just and true meaning, and the will to carry out what the law prescribes is perfectly understood as the primitive will to observe what those whom the peoples elected for that very important end decree. Everything that is not this is neither *intelligible* nor philosophically *sustainable* and is the eternal breeding ground of anarchy and its consequent misfortunes.

It remains, then, to resolve the third question, and what has been said until now will shorten much of the road that we have to walk in examining

If there will be some fixed signs by which to recognize whether public opinion has been formed.

On this matter it is easier to say what is not than what is; the negative rules are very certain and, on the contrary, the positive ones are ambiguous, and generally their application to the practical can produce only probabilities.

It has been said that there is no *public opinion* if the question or proposition with which it deals is not *practical and experimental* or so simple as to be within the reach of the majority of people, and consequently there

---

1. Jeremy Bentham, *Tactique des assemblées législatives*, 2 vols. (Geneva and Paris, 1816).

is not public opinion except, as we will state later on, over propositions that, although *practical,* have complication of circumstances and aims that, in order to combine them, require more than *trivial attention* and some thorough reflective meditation, for it is clear that the generality of citizens is not capable of this.

In questions and propositions that are speculative, *complicated, and profound,* there can be no true public opinion unless these questions and propositions have been the object of popular, constant, and generalized education, in which case, although they come to be adopted *traditionally* and generally without proofs, the *way of thinking* is uniform, although it cannot strictly be called *opinion,* given what has just been said.

Self-love is the universal passion of all men, and in the judgment of even the great philosophers, all the other passions, to which are given different names according to the object to which it applies, are the very same. What is beyond doubt is that, if not every man is lascivious nor vindictive, etc. . . . every man loves himself and seeks his *well-being* wherever it may be and in all his actions, so that, although the objects of the application and reflective meditation of men might be infinitely varied, and although the exercise of study might be for so very few, there is no man at all for whom his individual interest does not require of him attention, deliberations, and frequent periods of thinking; and as meditation is a source of opinion, it follows that there can be public opinion on objects of common interest or utility.

The wise Bentham was, then, quite correct when, referring to legislation, he said *public utility was the surest criterion of public opinion,*[2] an expression that we convert into a negative maxim, saying: no measure whatsoever that is not in the common interest, immediate and readily perceptible, is a proper object of true public opinion.

Focus for a moment on the expression *immediate and readily perceptible* because there are innumerable measures that will surely produce general well-being and happiness; but because this has not been their immediate outcome nor has it yet been experienced, they do not have in their favor the majority of the people, for whom only experience is the foundation for believing and thinking, and for whom good and evil have either to enter through the senses or they enter them almost never.

2. Ibid.

Bayle[3] observed, before us, that it is almost natural in men not to think for themselves and that a quasi-innate apathy makes them form an idea of one or some individuals to allow them to know and hold for certain what those individuals tell them they have thought. Generally we pay that *respectful deference* to our parents, masters, and superiors, in whom we are accustomed to imagining more learning and talent. Thus, we experience, generally, that the opinion of the father is that of the sons, the opinion of the master that of his servants, and the opinion of a leader of a community, if he is well liked, that of those who are his subordinates. Besides these relationships, sources of opinion, there are others that, in order to distinguish them from those, we could call *artificial*. Among every people, individually if the people is not very numerous, one or some inhabitants acquire a following because of their generosity, because of their honesty, because of their beneficence, and even sometimes because of some reprehensible vice. Such as these also become sources of *beliefs and persuasions,* and their way of thinking spreads among their cronies, who by tradition embrace it. Opinions adopted and generalized in this way do not merit, as I have already repeated, the name of *opinion,* but it is appropriate to call them *belief* or *persuasion;* and we say that it can be taken as *common persuasion* what is felt to be so by the greater part of those individuals who have a following in their towns.

Nonetheless the previous rule is very open to ambiguities, principally in times of factions, for well known are the efforts that each one of them makes to win over those *popular coryphaeuses,* those who, won over by fairly well-known means repeat, many times against their conscience, the favorite axioms of the faction that won them. Their followers hear them, and they do the same thing. Be advised, however, that the voices are not diverse; it is one voice with *various echoes,* a very interesting observation, especially for legislators whom the situation always subjects to torments from which they will not emerge well except with rules that we will present in the fourth question, anticipating them now, the celebrated maxim and eternal truth of the immortal Bentham, "Good faith and justice are the most healthy politics and the most lasting."[4]

Neither of each individual alone, nor of all or most of them taken

---

3. Pierre Bayle, French philosopher and critic, founder of eighteenth-century rationalism. (Editor's note)
4. Bentham, op. cit.

together, can it be said that they have *opinion,* as long as understandings vacillate and wander uncertain over the truths under discussion. In order that there be *opinion* it is necessary that the understanding be decided, and not willfully, but because of foundations so solid that they must have compelled assent despite not having found a satisfactory response to the conflicting ones; and when the understanding has been settled for reasons of this nature, neither has it done so instantaneously, but rather by a *slow and reflective* process, nor *does it change opinion easily,* and so long as another reflective meditation, yet slower than the first, does not present new and more solid reasons in opposition.

One must understand that *constancy* is not the same as *invariability,* and thus when we establish as a rule that one cannot have public opinion without *constancy,* that is to say without the majority of the citizens being constantly advised of it (which is known either, first, when the same opinion is observed despite varying circumstances or, then, when it is being repeated notwithstanding the passage of time), we do not mean that the public cannot change its opinions, but rather that it has to change them in the same way it formed them, *slowly* and *gradually* and (the same as each individual) by this silent examination of the opposing foundations with which public opinion can sometimes be changed; but this is neither frequent nor the work of a moment, but rather worked out over a long time.

This reliable rule should allow us to give their legitimate value to those popular and tumultuous *surges,* principles of revolutions and exclusive work of ambitious demagogues. They will never be the mark of public opinion and the general will, because among other qualities they are lacking *stability and firmness;* they will be passing thoughts and desires, because always suggested by the depraved, but they will not be the public desire. A stirred up and deceived multitude will applaud the death of the Gracii in Rome; in Paris it will carry off to the guillotine the most enlightened and virtuous men; it will request, in Mexico, the elevation of a *caudillo* to the throne,[5] but none of these things will be the effect of *public opinion,* but rather "the echo of seduction, the cry of the scoundrels and whores who will climb higher, as a famous journalist explains, the better the coryphaeuses of the factions have paid them."[6]

5. This is a reference to Agustín de Iturbide's enthronement in 1824. (Editor's note)
6. *Espectador Sevillano,* no. 3.

The most essential character of public opinion is *liberty*. Human understanding is the power most jealous of its independence, it does not bear fetters; to want to put them on things that are subject to its ability is the greatest and most intolerable tyranny. This quality of public opinion is deduced from the definition of its essence in the same way as the previous one. Can there be opinion in the particular individual when he is not allowed to reflect and if he does not have all the freedom necessary to weigh the reasons that have to resolve it? Surely not; for his opinion must always be the fruit of a calm reflective meditation; and even regarding *faith,* although he cannot reflect on its immediate object, he should do so on the *foundations of credibility;* therefore if *public opinion* is nothing other than the coming together of individual opinions, it is necessary to acknowledge that there is not, nor can there be, *public opinion* when it does not exist, and about objects relative to which there is not liberty.

Infer from this that, in a time of bloody factions, during which not only is it not lawful to say what one thinks but not even to think in a way other than what suits the coryphaeus of the dominant faction; that when the sobriquets of *seditious, enemy of the patria,* and others of this sort that are maliciously invented on such occasions emerge with all the retinue of calumnies, abuses, and satires to stifle the voices that do not agree to be echoes of the powerful faction; and above all, that when the government declares itself for one of the factions, the allegation *public opinion* is to present an illusion beyond all reality. No, there is not such public opinion, because there has not been freedom to create it. On the contrary, true public opinion will be stifled; it will triumph in the long run, and the same people will take revenge for it on their oppressors; but in the meantime it does not exist, nor can it be alleged.

Well-known writers, particularly when they speak of the benefits of freedom of the press, consider *public papers* as a sure thermometer for knowing *public opinion,* and this is one of the benefits with which they most extol that institution. No, we will not deny an assertion so authoritative and rational; but unfortunate experiences cause us to assert that, to apply it without immediate fear of error, some criticism is needed.

Of course, public papers do not make law in the countries where the power to publish thoughts by means of printing is not free; but let us note that that is proven true not only where despotism subjects writers to prior censorship, but also where one hinders writing by *direct* or *in-*

direct means, unless it is in a specified way. What does it matter that the constitution of a country establishes freedom to publish ideas if a dominant faction will manage with certainty to ruin anyone who writes against its interest? What does it matter that that liberty is guaranteed, establishing that writings can be judged only by individuals chosen by the people, who, it is supposed, will vote for those of greater education and probity, if the spirit of faction alone manages to preside over the election, making it fall to the members most attached to it, and that as a consequence, they will let pass neither a statement nor a truth that hurts the faction? This happens few times in popular governments and in which the laws of election are well thought out, but it happens, and when the circumstance arises, freedom of the press is nominal. It *should* be able but *cannot* say what it thinks; the fear of persecution and punishments silences most of the citizens. Few are those who have all the courage necessary to speak the truth but almost never with impunity. We say, then, that when there is no true freedom of the press, be it in one way or another, public opinion cannot be deduced from public papers, which of course must express only the judgment of the tyrant, be this an absolute king, a vizier, or a popular faction. Public papers can be a thermometer of *public opinion* when they can produce it, should it not be formed, and when, of the qualities we have determined *public opinion* to have and to serve as a mark to recognize it when it does exist, are derived directly those that the papers must have in order to produce or show it. In truth, if public opinion must be and cannot be less than the free and spontaneous outcome of calm reflective meditation on the solid foundations that persuade one of a truth, almost always *practical* and generally *simple and perceptible,* papers will produce *public opinion* only if they were written in *complete freedom,* with *simplicity, impartiality, firmness, and circumspection,* showing what they are trying to prove, not threatening and forcing what is to be believed; letting reason speak through them and time mature their assertions, not presenting a scimitar to cut off heads that do not bow at their voice. When the writers of a nation, or the greater part of them, especially journalists, see themselves as respecting these qualities in what they produce, and they discover *uniformity* regarding some assertion, they can believe they will establish public opinion, and they can believe that they speak the truth if they announce that it now exists. On the other hand, if the nation is divided into bloody factions, villainous writers sell themselves, dipping their pens in blood and black bile, hurling sarcasms and threats, shamefully tearing away the always respectable veil of domestic mysteries, then neither is there public opinion, nor can the writers produce it, nor can it be known through the writings. "A writer," says the judicious journalist already cited,

> who provokes the struggle of the factions, who shows himself attached to one of them, who wants to tyrannize public opinion, lavishing insults on those who do not think as he, or silencing them by means of threats, is a man who presages despotic dispositions; he is a man unworthy of the esteem and confidence of a nation that aspires to liberty and that knows that the most sacred right is that of thought. Much more odious must be those who, in their writings, images of their atrocious souls, sow calumnies and satires against the virtuous citizen who is not of their faction and try to make those who differ from them in their public opinions look like enemies of the nation. . . . Where there are certain favorite errors of a dominant faction against which it is not lawful to speak, where it is not lawful to discuss even truths themselves, there is no *public opinion.*

We dwelled on this third question more than we intended, but its importance excuses us, and let us now proceed to gather the fruit in the resolution of the fourth.

Is there always an obligation to submit oneself to public opinion and the general will?

We have already indicated that, whenever there are existing parties, popular factions, an inability to base a measure or resolution that one desires in solid arguments and in the eternal principles of equity and justice, the defenders appeal to *public opinion;* they cry out as loud as they can, *the people want this, the people desire that,* and always the clamoring faction tries to identify with the generality of the nation, secure in obtaining its aims or, at least, of imposing them.

"Let us distinguish carefully the popular voice from public opinion: the first is formed with the same ease as the clouds of spring, but with the same ease it vanishes. It is produced by violence, terror, factions, ignorance, a thousand other accidental causes that can be destroyed by opposing interests. . . . [T]he cries of a people deceived or subdued by terror are not public opinion; they are their ephemeral and false images, invented by the power and perfidy to delude the nations."[7] In confirmation of truths so undeniable, we need nothing more than to remember the multitude of contradictory cries, unjust and of all manner that, with the greater appearance of *universal,* we have heard through the streets of Mexico since 1808 amidst the clamoring of the bells, the noisy din of artillery, etc., etc., demanding first . . . and then . . . Should we forget the history of our disgraces it will serve us only to repeat them at each step. Take care, much care, in believing and calling *public opinion and general will* what commanded and brazen bands implore on certain occasions.

It has already been understood that those difficult moments, as they do not contain *public opinion,* are not included in the present matter; nor do they need any principle other than *unwavering firmness* so as not to give in to the disorganizing torrents. It is equally understood that neither do we speak here of the multitude of occasions on which the application of the principles that we have established show that no opinion exists although it is alleged by the interested parties. Let us pass, then, to the case of the question at hand and we see what the obligation of a legislator is when there is *public opinion* or at least much probability that an opinion is generalized.

Those who argue for the obligation to yield to it and always to follow it appeal to the *sovereignty* of the nation because, they say, the people is sovereign, and the will of the sovereign must always be obeyed. We ask ourselves, where does sovereignty reside? Is it not true that it resides not in some, not in many, nor even in most, but rather in the *absolute totality* of the nation? Therefore, so that the alleged *will* might obligate as sovereign, it was necessary to show in each case that all and each one of the citizens wanted that thing. How will it be possible ever to provide such a proof and, much less, to deliberating bodies in whose very breast there are many representatives who oppose one another? Or is it only the will of the deputies that should be counted for nothing when the suppositions, perhaps imaginary and always indemonstrable from outside, count for so much?

Seeing the impossibility that there might be, and setting aside the impossibility of showing that *universal will,* one will perhaps appeal to the will of the majority, saying that the lesser number is obligated to

---

7. *Espectador Sevillano,* no. 3.

yield to the greater. If there is no more than this, we say that the mind of the *majority* alone, without other aggregates, cannot produce *obligation to yield.* In effect, no matter how much the defenders of those doctrines rack their brains, reason will never see in the *majority alone* anything but *force and power,* inasmuch as it is normal that the greater number can do more than the lesser. But is force alone, or does force give legitimate right? We believe that free republicans will not even have to grant it as a hypothesis; then if *right* and *obligation* are *correlative,* and in the majority *as such* there is no right to command, in the minority there is no obligation to submit.

Some considerations and circumstances can be attached to the preceding case that alter the question and its resolution; for example, when in a *rigorously democratic* government there has been an explicit social pact to submit everyone to the opinion and will of the majority. In this case there will be an obligation proceeding from the pact, but it will not be the case in question nor will it be ours. Perhaps it will happen that the will of the majority can be resisted only *violently* and by the *road of revolution,* and then the obligation to preserve social order and that of avoiding *truly* major woes can compel the minority to tolerate, endure, and acquiesce to the will of the majority. For this case *political moralists* give very good rules that are not to our present purpose, and those who would like will be able to see them in Locke, Paley, and others. We repeat, then, that the will of the majority, *for its mere sake,* cannot be obligatory.

This being so, someone will say, a representative of the general congress, a government, and a public agent are not bound, even when *opinion* and *generalized will* exist, which seems incompatible with the character of *mandataries of the people,* and no other rule of their conduct can be conceived if it is not that from which they always operate as they choose, which truly is a very clear despotism.

Before responding and determining the rules, we must dismiss a most unfortunate error that the *demagogues and anarchists* have spread and repeated without cease: they, ignoring the true essence of the *representative system,* believe, or feign to believe, that a representative is nothing more than a *mandatary of the people* that elects him; that he has to receive instructions, rules, and orders from them that he cannot violate; that the people can revoke his powers when they consider it wise; in a word, that he is a simple passive organ of the desires or caprices of his constituents. The famous Martinez Marina has given a motive for some of this. Martinez Marina who, completely conversant and steeped in all the old courts of Spain (where the agents of the cities who had a vote in them went not to deliberate but rather to present petitions of the city councils and to promote purely municipal interests, and at times as ridiculous as adding a figure to a coat of arms, etc., etc.), called deputies *mandataries* and wished to apply to them some of the attributes that civil jurisprudence gives to the common *mandate.*

It is neither the only nor the principal reason for the establishment of *deliberative congresses* and for the enthusiasm of the politicians in examining the representative system, justly regarding it as the most sublime endeavor of philosophy, that in which all the citizens of a society, many in number and spread over immense terrains, could not assemble and deliberate to decide, and it was necessary to adopt the expedient by which they would elect some from among themselves so that in the name of all and on their behalf, they would take part in the creation of laws and in systematizing all *public welfare.* The true origin of the modern representative system is the immense division of labors and occupations to which citizens now exclusively dedicate themselves for the civilization and progress of enlightenment of the people; each industry, each position, has been divided and subdivided into different branches, and each one of them is the sole occupation of a certain number of individuals who, dedicating all their attention to them, have raised the arts and sciences to the degree of perfection in which we see them. Since then, *philosophy, economics, and jurisprudence* also formed separate branches, whose intense study the multitude of citizens left to a very small number, and since then, there are few who acquire and have the capability to think through and work out the most difficult points of a civil government and to face up to public administration. Few, very few, are those who can have on their shoulders the charge of working out the laws, and of those, very few are the ones the people elect for the purpose of doing so, choosing not just *mouths* so that they go to express what their constituents suggest to them, but rather their *consciences and minds,* so that they might reflect on and understand what the constituents are not capable of understanding or even of giving it their attention, all of them employed in very different enterprises. Their *conscience and wisdom,* we repeat, are what peoples elect, so that without ever prostituting the first, and guided always by the second, they discover and decide what is best and most suitable for the common good, and everyone submits to the resolution and will of these *experts*. Here is the theory of the divine *representative system*, which we have fortunately adopted, for which the nations that have it are happy, and for which all those who lack it yearn.

The *democracy* of modern peoples has nothing to do with that of the ancients; they are of a very different nature. The latter was *barbarous*, filled with all the vices and defects, always degenerating into anarchy and involved in the disorders resulting from the *tumultuous* gathering of dull peoples in the plazas of Athens and Rome, where they all cast individual votes on matters of great seriousness. The *democracy* of the modern republics is now purged of all the defects that discredited it, even to the extent of showing it as horrible among the Greeks and Romans— Everyone a legislator! Everyone giving an opinion on matters over which they had never reflected and that require study by an ordinary man for his entire life! Let us distance ourselves for that reason from Greece, Rome, small cantons, always in uprising, always in disorder! A puzzling thing, very puzzling. If to a man of letters, merchant, etc. one proposes he make a statue or some other artifact, not only will he say without the least shame, *and what do I understand of that, when did I learn that job?* But he would even take it as an insult; and when it is a matter of *making laws,* the most sublime work of wisdom, everyone considers himself fit, and they would even show themselves offended if one said to them that they are not suitable to be legislators! Will perhaps a *bust* be more difficult than a *good law,* or will it require having had greater *apprenticeship?* Distinguished youth! May the famous *social contract* of the very profound Genevan not instill its errors in you, but rather its brilliant truths. Read, reread once and many times Book 2, chapter 7. Learn there what a *legislator* is and what is required to be one; and far from seeking, each one will tremble if the honorable misfortune of being elected deputy falls to him. But let us return to the subject.

The idea of *mandatary* and of *mandate* being false and dangerous applied to the representatives of a national congress (on which we could expound, drawing obvious terrible consequences, which perhaps we will do another time), it seems to us that if one wants to take from common jurisprudence some idea as the source of maxims and apply it, with less danger of absurdities, to modern congresses and their members, one should rather have laid one's hands on that idea of *independent arbiters* through whose judgment the parties to a lawsuit are obliged to pass than that of *mandataries and mandates.* Nor is this exact, but it is much less dangerous.

Let us listen, in corroboration of everything said, to one of the greatest politicians that a nation fertile with them has had, the immortal Burke, speaking to the electors of Bristol who had named him member of Parliament and wanted to give him instructions for his conduct:

> It is his [the representative's] to sacrifice his repose, his pleasures, his satisfactions, to theirs [constituent]; and above all, ever, and in all cases, to prefer their interests to his own. But, his *unbiassed opinion,* his *mature judgement,* his *enlightened conscience,* he ought not to sacrifice to you; to any man, or to any set of men living. These he does not derive from your pleasure; no, nor from the Law and the Constitution. They are a trust from Providence, for the abuse of which he is deeply answerable. . . . If Government were a matter of *Will* on any side, yours, without question, ought to be superior. But Government and Legislation are matters of *reason* and *judgement,* and not of *inclination;* and, what sort of reason is that, in which the determination precedes the discussion; in which one set of men *deliberate,* and another *decide;* and where those who form the *conclusion* are perhaps three hundred miles distant from those who hear the arguments?
>
> To deliver an opinion is the right of all men; that of *Constituents* is a weighty and respectable opinion, which a Representative ought always to rejoice to hear; and which he ought always most seriously to consider. But *authoritative* instructions; *Mandates* issued, which the Member is bound blindly and implicitly to obey, to vote, and to argue for, though contrary to the clearest conviction of his judgement and conscience—these are things utterly unknown to the laws of this land, and which arise from a fundamental mistake of the whole order and tenour of our Constitution.
>
> Parliament is not a *Congress of Ambassadors* from different and hostile interests; which interests each must maintain, as an *Agent* and *Advocate,* against other *Agents* and *Advocates;* but Parliament is a *deliberative Assembly of one Nation,* with *one* Interest, that of the whole; where, not local Purposes, not local Prejudices ought to guide, but the general Good, resulting from the general Reason of the whole. You choose a Member indeed; but when you have chosen

him, he is not Member of Bristol, but he is a Member of *Parliament*. If the local Constituent should have an Interest, or should form an hasty opinion, evidently opposite to the real good of the rest of the Community, the Member for that place ought to be as far, as any other, from any endeavour to give it Effect.

These truths assumed, and the pernicious error dismissed, let us proceed to give definite rules that might direct the legislator, whether it is a matter of adopting a *bad measure* in order to agree with the common opinion and desire, or of rejecting a *good measure* to go against it.

It is the first and principal rule that, even if it be possible that there is *true public opinion* on a measure *notoriously unjust and contrary* to the *eternal principles of equity and reason,* not only can the representative not submit to such *opinion* and vote for it, but rather he has a very strict obligation to oppose it, under pain of committing a crime before God and being a traitor to his own seduced constituents, who, sooner or later, will detest him and make him suffer the penalty of his criminal complaisance. This truth does not need much justification: God must be obeyed before men; no unjust command deserves the name of such, nor should it be obeyed. The *holy scriptures,* the priests, and moral and political philosophers are full of these and similar maxims. Well, if in unjust matters not even he who can mandate must be obeyed, how should *public opinion* be obeyed, which, as we have shown, must not be the *compulsory* rule of a representative? The preconceived notion, says Bentham, "can be an excuse for the common people but not for public men: it, at least, will not be justified when it might be the source or occasion for errors," and now this same profound politician warns what happens in those assertions of public opinion: "It even manages," he says, "to remove measures from examination; and what begins to demonstrate the bad faith is that they try to support them with all the power and influence of government."

The second very definite rule is that, if public opinion is for a measure which, although it might not be absolutely contrary to the *immutable principles* of reason and justice, the representative believes or knows will be detrimental to the nation in some way, he must not approve it but rather oppose it. For this he was elected; his obligation is to examine and decide only what can lead to the common good; he does not have to answer to God or to men for another's judgment, but only for his own; and he must say to those arguing the *contrary public opinion* what Valentiano said to the army that had just elected him emperor and required him to join with Valente in rule: *Vestrum fuit, o milites, cum imperator nullis esset, imperii mihi habens tradere, sed postquam illud suscepi meum deinceps, non vestrum est publicis rebus prospicere.*

The third maxim is from the same very profound Bentham: The representative, if he must never vote for a measure that he believes unjust, never for one he considers will cause public misfortunes, neither must he insist on the adoption of a measure that, although in his judgment *beneficial,* might be contrary to general opinion; in this case he should not give it up completely, but instead defer it to a better time. "Public opinion," says this learned man, "being only that of the greater number, without other evidence, is an argument without force: for the legislator it is not good reasoning, but rather respectable. It is not a reason to renounce the measure, but rather to defer it in order to enlighten minds, using legitimate means to combat the error, for the truth, daughter of time, secures it all from her father."[8]

To these three rules that include everything we will add now, only for light in dark matters of factions, two maxims from the same author repeated also by Paley and various others. "It is always boasting," he says, "to see *veracity* in politics as the morality of small minds and proof of simplicity and ignorance of the world; and men fearful of looking like fools adopt, relative to their conduct, public principles that they condemn in the ordinary actions of their life. A faction is, in some respects, a very vigilant and active guard; but if its principal aim is to seize power, it will be in its interest to perpetuate the abuses and will see them in advance as fruits of its victory."

We have concluded, if not with the dignity that the matter requires, or with the profundity with which we would like to have treated it, giving more than enough points so that true scholars and teachers of political science might be inspired to enlighten us in these very important questions. Neither the limits of the journal nor our competence permits us more; but what we have said is enough for those who reflect on our assertions with maturity, shedding preconceived notions and partialities unworthy of a philosopher.

8. Bentham, op. cit., *Sophismes,* pp. 71ff.

9 Discourse on the Nature of Factions

> The most perverse have the greatest power to stir up
> seditions and discords; peace and calm alone are conserved
> for the virtues.
> — Tacitus

Liberal institutions bring with them differences of opinion, because with each person making use of the precious right to express an opinion freely, it would be impossible that all members of society would agree on how to view issues. Thus, with reason it has been said that this division and balance of opinions is the life of a republic, supports the vigilance of some authorities over others and of the people over all authorities; it examines the truth closely, and enlightenment is advanced, through which the legislator and government discover appropriate means to carry out the high aims of their institution, and the craftiness and tortuousness of arbitrariness, natural enemy of free thought, cannot be hidden.

But is this liberty indefinite, or are there bounds within which it must be confined? If there are, by what signs will we know when these bounds have been crossed or when the disputes degenerate into dangerous factions? What will the consequences be? Such are the points we propose to elucidate at a time in which abuse of words, anarchical doctrines, and political absurdities are growing into an intense force to lead the incautious astray and justify enormous crimes.

In an already constituted society, the conflict of opinions can never be about the truly essential foundations of society, that is to say, about the agreements and laws that secure individual guarantees. For all men feel deeply embedded in their being the need to preserve, by all pos-

Original title: "Discurso sobre los carácteres de las facciones." Source: *El Observador de la República Mexicana,* Mexico, October 17, 1827.

sible means, their security, their liberty, their property, because they left the forests and formed societies only with this preeminent goal. The unanimity of this feeling is thus immutable, and dissent will be only the most offensive degradation or the most foolish ignorance. Thus, all opinion that openly or deceitfully attacks it is criminal by its nature.

Nor can there be differences over clearly constitutional laws, which are, according to Lanjuinais, "those which, created or agreed to by the representatives of the nation or by the nation itself, determine the nature, the extent, the limits of public powers, so that this code is truly the supreme law and has a special character of permanence that distinguishes it from ordinary laws." The permanence that must be an essential characteristic of the constitution is contrary to discussion that tends to change it, for otherwise society would never have that firm and permanent repose indispensable for achieving its goals, and the continual fluctuation would end in destroying society and making it the prisoner of tyranny.

Let us note that not all the articles of a constitution are constitutional, but rather only those that sanction national independence, the form of government, the division, limitation, and sphere of public powers. Such sanctions are a sanctuary where no one should go except to worship the protector deity of societies. Even when a better worked out constitution can be imagined, the one that exists, established by the vote and respect of the nation, will always be preferable, and the difficulties of the change can never be counterbalanced by whatever advantages are imagined, for a new constitution has been written only on the ruins and ashes of the nation that dictates it; and as long as the guarantees are respected, as long as the laws are observed and the constitution gives security to some and energy to others, the people are happy, they will live in tranquility, and they will not remember the terrible right of resistance, whose use should be so rare, it is even more unusual for altering the constitution, and so that resistance more often has restoration as its object than change. The classes that actually make up the nation will never risk their fate and well-being to the setbacks of an unfortunate commutation. Such desires are from those who, without industry or love of work, pursued relentlessly by poverty and provoked by fierce ambition, base their hopes on the upheaval and ruin of the *patria*.

The very broad field of combat is in the methods of administration; in the management, investment, and good use of public revenues; in the application of political economy to the needs of the nation; in the rules and procedures of justice; in the plans for education and national instruction; in the great and various matters that the legislative body examines; . . . the political subjects that, in a free system, can be clarified by public writings cannot be enumerated; in them each one can and must deploy the talents and knowledge that nature and his work have afforded him, keeping what is most useful and refuting the errors of his opponents. The beneficial truths are deepened and refined in these disputes; and if one wishes to give them the name of parties, these are necessary and advantageous for the people, for even those that are incorrect are useful at least occasionally so that the truth can be recognized and triumph. A good government does not remain indifferent amidst violence, and it makes good use of the enlightenment that is spread, impartially chooses the better, and stimulates the discussion necessary for success.

But going beyond this well-defined territory, and when heightened and base passions are substituted for the calm and sincerity of discussion, inasmuch as they cannot openly and impudently attack those primary and essential aims, they seek detours and tunnels to undermine them; they are not content with reasons; they take hold of seduction, convert error, the absurd, to practice; they set out as their sole aim that the inventions and cunning means of injustice take root. Then the old resentments are unearthed, the bitterness of the struggle is inflamed, hatred explodes like a volcano, vomits slanders and calumnies, intellectual darkness grows, and they do not consider the nature of the methods they use to destroy and annihilate the opponent. Unfortunate nation that carries in its breast these frenzied sons who, cutting each other to pieces, break and crush the nation. These are the true parties or factions of whom the dignified Hume justly says,

> As much as legislators and founders of states ought to be honoured and respected among men, as much ought the founders of sects and factions to be detested and hated; because the influence of faction is directly contrary to that of laws. Factions subvert government, render laws impotent, and beget the fiercest animosities among men of the same nation, who ought to give mutual assistance and protection to each other. And what should render the founders of parties more odious is, the difficulty of extirpating these weeds, when once they have taken root in any state. They naturally propagate them-

selves for many centuries, and seldom end but by the total dissolution of that government in which they are sown. They are, besides, plants which grow most plentifully in the richest soil; and though absolute governments be not wholly free from them, it must be confessed that they rise more easily and propagate themselves faster in free governments, where they always infect the legislature itself, which alone could be able, by the steady application of rewards and punishments, to eradicate them.

In truth, if, in a free government, the factions come to grow and progress to that extreme, one can infer that its agents are either imbeciles or depraved, because every constituted society has in its authorities, in its laws and tribunals, means that are quite sufficient to stifle at their outset and root out the factions that disrupt the order. No excuse can vindicate a government that sees and acquiesces to a faction that increases greatly because the government acquiesced to it, for if it had not, the faction would have perished when it was first arising.

But to what must this willingness to oblige be attributed? What interest can the government have in pretending not to notice destructive factions? This is clear to anyone who knows that in free governments there must be a persistent conflict between them and their subjects. The power exercised by men, no matter how broad it might be, always brings with it an irresistible drive to extend itself more and more, becomes annoyed with the obstacles that the law puts up against it, and, like a torrent, constantly pushes and hollows out the dikes in which the general will keeps it contained, always watchful and ready to invade if there is no resistance. As it cannot openly and clearly trample on the laws, it avoids them, glosses them in accord with its intentions, varnishes its transgressions with lovely names, hypocritically takes as a motto what society most esteems, that is, its independence and tranquility, pretends dangers, feigns or exaggerates conspiracies, and uses the vague and insignificant name of circumstances (when it is not possible to have them because of injustice) as a veil to hide its lies and as a weapon to destroy all social benefits.

But the personal interest of each member of society, spurred on by the danger that threatens it, claims offenses on the part of the authority, demands observance of the laws, cries out against abuses, criticizes the conduct of those who govern, and, with the weapons of reason and justice, encircles its guarantees against the assaults of the power, calls the nation to its aid, and because of this valiant resistance they end up thwarted.

It also happens that in their weakness, those who govern never believe it possible to advance by the well-worn path of the laws; they suppose that their powers are not sufficient for emergencies, all beneficial measures are paralyzed in their trembling hands; they do not dare uphold legal methods with vigor and integrity, fearful of everything and everyone, and in vacillation and uncertainty regarding all and everything, those who govern lose the favorable opportunity, squander the best elements; the edifice is worn away, and everything dies under their slow and collapsed administration, those being the first who are submerged in nothingness, where they should always hide themselves.

In both cases, which are common among recently constituted peoples, in which the public spirit has neither progressed nor formed customs, the government, not finding in itself means to triumph or resources not to die, casts its covetous eyes on the various classes that make up the nation; but the virtuous citizens are not capable of helping injustice triumph, and they are also very open in telling those imbeciles who govern that the only thing they have to do is entrust the post to whomever knows how to execute it. It is, then, a certain consequence that an evil or weak government will depend on factions composed of corrupt characters, those who, in exchange for commanding the government itself, lend themselves to the most iniquitous goals, and as a reward they immediately request and obtain jobs, pensions, wealth (all spoils of a sacrificed nation); as collaborators, they set themselves up as essential, they identify themselves with the government, one is their interest, the other their goal; disorder, injustice, oppression. In this case the agitators believe and consider themselves to be the government itself, and when the public voice cries out against their lies, they respond with insolence that doing so is to discredit the government, that *to attack them is to attack it,* as if the name of government could justify iniquities, or as if a government that has made itself factious would still merit respect and esteem, which in a republic is the reward for virtues. Meanwhile dull or perverse rulers degrade themselves, making themselves blind and passive instruments of their own and the general ruin. And here is the first and most terrible characteristic of a devastating faction.

The majority of a nation is always just and reasonable, for men, although they might individually be bad, gathered together or collectively are virtuous, according to Montesquieu's observation. Men gathered together inevitably identify themselves with what is useful to all, a clear instinct makes them sense that any injustice whatsoever redounds against them, and if they do the evil deed thinking they can escape its consequences, they never put into practice the evil deed that hangs over their heads.

Never, then, can disastrous projects be the work of any but a small group that, tenaciously pursuing its own prosperity, will impudently tread on the laws, do away with all barriers that oppose virtue, the most wicked methods costing it nothing so long as they lead to the venting of its revenge or the insatiable yearning of its ambition or avarice, it will defy public opinion and will abjure all decency. The agitators themselves will be amazed at having arrived where they did not foresee, for, drunken with their first triumphs, they will have embarked upon and achieved excesses that cannot have happened to anyone, except when that one is involved in enormous crimes that it is necessary to cover over with other, even more atrocious crimes. For them, morality (the only true politics) is an impediment that they have removed from their course, growing deaf to its clamors, and by force of combating it, they have managed to harden themselves against remorse and honor. What must be the fate of the unhappy nation whose destiny is in such hands? What fortunes will be enough to gratify the ravenous swarm of catilinarians? What laws, what equity, what rights will be respected by those who forsake order?

The difference between the methods of a faction and those of a sound part or majority of a people is palpable. This latter knows no other methods than guarantees, laws, justice, because these methods can never ever be contrary by their nature to the end to which they aspire; there are between them intimate relations that can hardly exist between injustice and benevolence, which is universal justice. How can those who violate the principles of justice, then, argue that they love the nation, that they promote the general good, the only foundation for justice? Are people so stupid that they come to believe that they can be saved only by trampling on the venerable principles of virtue? Will those who offend this essential principle and soul of the republic be republicans? Will the nation ever think that its situation is such that the political dogmas to which it has consecrated reason and experience of all the centuries have nothing to do with it? Has the nature of things changed? And so, if it suits a faction, must we abjure the most evident and holy truths and violate reason, this support and asylum of man? You who make a show of saving us by crushing the rights of humanity, know that if it were possible that our existence and honor were incompatible with justice, we would rather choose to die in disgrace. But it does not depend on you to change what is disinterested and eternal, and it is much easier to believe and even feel that your tricks and processes are what is incompatible with the good and honor of men; their future will depend on and be secured forever by justice. If you were fair you would say that ambition, vengeance, avarice . . . are the true motives for your conduct; give up fraud and histrionics that no one believes and everyone detests.

But despite everything, haughty with the experiment they have made of their power, they try to make good use of the moments, knowing that their fatal influence will last only until the nation, terrified by upheaval, deploys its irresistible resources against this handful of vipers that eat away at its core; so they try to lull the nation with deceitful snares and to intimidate and persecute those men who, with wisdom and character, can unmask them and make their crimes evident to the people, lead a reaction in support of the constitution and the laws, and oust them. From here emanates the spirit of intolerance and persecution, another innate characteristic of factions.

"Of all the proscriptions," says the famous Bignon,[1] "the most terrible are those stirred up by a minority. The majority, which knows its strengths, can be momentarily cruel; but neither is it for a long time, nor is it always. The minority, on the contrary, believes that it increases its number by multiplying its harsh acts. . . . Proscription has a frightening character when it attempts to repress the dominant spirit of nations, for inasmuch as it then originates from a fragment that wishes to subjugate the majority, it is inevitable that it be more violent and expansive. The nation as a whole needs fixed and constant laws, the minority has need of laws of exception."

In a free and civilized nation, it is not the same to seize power as to capture opinion; on the contrary, the seizing of power is always guarded against and opposed by those who fear (and that is everyone) the diminishment of their rights. A just government respects this guarding

---

1. Louis Pierre Edouard, Baron Bignon (1771—1847), French diplomat and historian.

and opposition for the advantages that redound to it; but a faction or a factious government that cannot bear the inspection of the public becomes irritated and enraged by its own conscience, for it knows that its errors and crimes are obvious to everyone, and in the inability to stifle the truth it furiously pronounces the maxim of tyrants: *Let them hate me, so long as they fear me.* Much better would be the love and respect of the people if they changed course. But what about the responsibility of the ministers? How is it possible that they resign themselves to giving up their posts and become objects of contempt and cursing? How to acknowledge themselves defeated in a struggle in which they have prostituted their consciences, sold their honor, assaulted what is most sacred? Will they not then reveal their dreadful secrets, and will there not come to light so many machinations, treacheries, depravities, atrocities . . . ?

Thus, they see themselves committed to continuing their maneuvers at any price, to trampling whatever crosses their path, to aiming their guns at whomever might have the courage and ability to oppose them. The first shots hit persons they carefully make loathsome beforehand, suggesting to people that they are their enemies, as the sans-culottes did in France with those they called aristocrats. Distorted equality was the popular idol, and as many as calumny had designated were sacrificed to it. With that name emphatically pronounced, several thousand were dragged to the scaffold, crushing the forms and all rights. It would be easy to cite other examples, but unfortunately we have among ourselves practiced worse trampling underfoot, for there is no proscription more barbarously unjust than that which besets an accidental quality that has no relation to the crime and is enough nonetheless to fulminate atrocious punishment with neither conviction nor any process against an industrious, honorable multitude, whose persecution is more harmful to the nation than to the ones proscribed.

By this the people are deceived, the most absurd calumnies breaking loose, but repeated by a thousand filthy and hired mouths. Blackening the purest reputation, they transform innocence and merit into guilt, for the immorality of the factions cannot pardon them; fantastic dangers are concocted and conspiracies revealed. In the workshop of the faction are created the instruments of death, and in the darkness of their dens are woven the cords in which one wishes to seize virtue. The victims pile up, they are denied all legal resources, they are deprived of all mercy, and the cruelty of their persecutors feeds their torment. Thus they intend to intimidate all those who are good. Madmen! They do not know that the human heart, raised by virtue, becomes enthusiastic in danger and is triumphant on the scaffold, that the majority of a nation can be calmed by flattery but never subdued by violence.

Fear is always cruel, and tyrants, always trembling from their injustices, stupidly believe they are diminishing their danger. Crowding tortures together, they wish to dominate, not over free men, who make them tremble, but rather over the cold tomb of a nation, so much do they desire its silence and inertia. But the exact opposite happens, because if the clemency and moderation of Caesar did not shield him from the dagger of Brutus, how could Caligula hope that his atrocities were more powerful to save him? To attack guarantees is to call to arms and to incite the indignation of the most gentle citizen; it is the same as saying to the nation, defend yourself from my aggressions; and who would dare say it to whom? A faction, a handful of miserable people, to the powerful and august gathering of millions of citizens who, led by the constitution and the laws, go forward majestically to their happiness, and who will trample those destructive insects who are trying ridiculously to frighten it.

Because a faction never can be made up of illustrious and distinguished men, the sensible, the property owners, never enlist under the tattered banner of demagoguery or band together against the common happiness of which their own is a part, and here we have the third characteristic of the factions. Vagrants who have not dedicated themselves to any industry; those who, fleeing from work and disdaining frugality, have not known how to acquire or preserve an honest fortune; those who have no other wealth than a mind capable of adapting itself to all the whims of the powerful; those who have no other resource than employment, wages of their infamy; those who, without any merit whatsoever, wish to be prominent and stand out; those who, consumed by envy, try to knock down and punish virtue; all of these seek in a faction the support and protection they cannot find in justice and order; the yearning to supplant and substitute themselves in all positions stirs them up; they can only and wish only to live from the substance of the nation. To achieve such patriotic ends, it is necessary to destroy the established system, turn it all upside down, stir up discord, and foment revolutions, whose result might be to leave them masters of the ungodly spoils of the *patria*.

Those who have produced, through their talents and probity, a merit acknowledged by the public; those who, dedicated to agriculture, the arts, business, have acquired a precious independence; those who truly make up the nation (for a famous author called the rest, with reason, tenants of the state); those who carry out public duties and actually sustain the government with part of their fortunes, acquired by means of zeal, risk, and frugality; those whose wealth cannot grow or be maintained except in the tranquility and security of public order; those, finally, who are the nerve, the hope, and the only power of the republic, will never be agitators, they will never want changes, always hazardous, they will never foster anything but the rule of the laws under whose protection they thrive and progress. The sources, the communication of public abundance that is in their hands, are blocked, are interrupted by disturbances; confidence disappears, and with it all the resources; burdens are increased and products are weakened. Everything redounds against the property owner, while the idlers view the ruin with the coolness of those who lose nothing, or with the complacency of those who see advancement in it.

For that reason, in times of danger, the *patria* always turns its eyes toward the property owners, who are those with effective means to save it, and it never counts on the egotistical vagrants who will sell themselves to whomever will pay them the most, and who bring their *patria* and all their duties into their personal interest. The property holders are one and the same with the *patria,* and thus in the crisis that it suffers they silence resentments, abandon personal aspirations, and emulation consists in looking at who will make the greatest sacrifices for the general happiness. This is patriotism, this the character of the truly free, this the public spirit that must always be generalized among us. Thus, one has seen at various times in England that the Tories and Whigs have alternately ceded their aims and their positions to their rivals when the *patria* has required it, and it would be for the *patria* a horrible crime to seize, out of spite, the ministerial seat because of an obstinacy as ridiculous as it is fierce and foolish. The laws in representative governments have prudently and justly anticipated that the destiny of the nation be entrusted only to property owners, whose progress is so intimately tied to it that the speculations of individual interests happily coincide with the general interest; the lack of these laws will frequently compromise us.

Finally, omitting other less important indicators, which can be reduced to those already expressed, the last is the impudence of violating all forms of legal equality. Neither the right and property of the professions, very effectively supported with clear reasons by Bentham, nor innocence and virtue will be free from violent plundering if persons have not bowed their heads to receive the seal of the horrible mysteries of the faction. Outstanding merit, the most distinguished service, is excluded inexorably from every position, if persons lack the shameful mark; but with it is obtained security to violate the most sacred laws; the impunity of the most atrocious crimes is a consequence of the installation, and, under this protection, the constitution, the public faith, whatever is respectable and holy is abused, not only without fear of punishment but instead certain of reward. The important jobs, the positions of trust, the revenues are concentrated in the hands of the agitators. The press is in their pay and at their service; anarchic writings are financed, bought, lavished profusely with public wealth; those who courageously support social rights are tenaciously pursued. In this way, they want to keep the nation chained in order to devour it in peace.

If factions are always harmful, they are much more so in a people who, just having emerged from slavery and devastated by it, need to see as evident the advantages of the new government in order to become enthusiastic about it and love it sincerely; but if instead of the magnificent promises that were made to them, they see only discord, injustices, maltreatment, disrepute (in a very great way we have fallen compared with all nations), burdens, and misery, results inseparable from the factions, it follows that a sense of emptiness and despair is engendered in spirits, which scorns a system that the unwise common man regards as the source of woes and which gives rise to the natural desire to change it, intending to improve it. So broken laws are viewed with disdain, the authorities, whose prestige consists entirely in observing them, become suspect and distrusted in their handling of things, obedience is undermined, impunity encourages insubordination, and as it progresses, there is not yet energy or resolve that might contain it. The contagion progresses rapidly, and the government, attacked on all sides, succumbs or, what is the same, makes concessions to the troublemakers, and the nation terrifyingly plunges into anarchy.

If the Mexican nation has an enemy that watches it, this is the moment that it awaited to clinch its chains and shackle it, perhaps forever, to its bloody cart. The people, plagued and aggravated by the greatest of misfortunes, which is anarchy, prefer to be victims of one despot and not of thousands; they prefer to fear one who can never do them as much harm as a swarm of demagogues who humiliate and destroy them in a thousand ways. Although one exhorts them then to take up arms and repel the invader, they will respond indignantly: "Execrable traitors of the *patria,* you have reduced us to the unhappy extreme of seeing despotism as a relief from the horrible ills with which your ambition and immorality have crushed and exhausted us. Will we consume the miserable scraps of our fortune that you have eradicated, and will we spill the blood that has escaped your cruelty to defend your power that you have used only to sacrifice us? What benefit could we expect from our efforts? That you surely continue your revenges and pillages, and that you will indefinitely prolong your exterminating rule! But you have not left us a glimmer of hope, and you have cruelly extirpated us and made the *patria* disappear. We no longer have it! And this is, barbarians, all the benefit we owe you. You are tranquil, and your decision is made: you will fly to meet the tyrant and, prostrated despicably, you will worship his footsteps; you will buy with the most ignominious prostitution a smile from the idol, and, infamous informers, you will top off all your crimes by slandering your brothers to ingratiate yourselves with your masters."

May the peoples of Anáhuac reflect on, confront, and apply these truths, may they look attentively at the terrifying aspect that the Republic presents in all its affairs; confidence has fled, and peace is about to flee a country that seeks it and roots out all of its supports. Already Europe, which had admired us, announces our downfall; and the complexity and clashes of our affairs and the scorn in which the laws are seen must hasten it. Our independence is threatened, our liberty abused, our property badly secured, and we sleep in a fatal confidence! But there is still time to save the *patria* that appeals forcefully to us. Let us not feign ignorance because time flies, and if we do not make the most vehement efforts and all the sacrifices it demands of us, a piercing regret will torment us much more than the loss of the precious goods of which we are going to be stripped.

LORENZO DE ZAVALA

Lorenzo de Zavala (1788–1836), a politician and historian, was born in Yucatán. He studied in the city of Mérida at the seminary of San Ildefonso. He became active in revolutionary politics, and in 1814 he was imprisoned by the Spanish authorities. Once released, Zavala returned to Yucatán, where he edited a newspaper. He was elected deputy for Yucatán to the Spanish Cortes[1] in 1820 and took his seat in 1821. However, he promptly returned to Mexico, where the military leader (and later emperor) Agustín de Iturbide (1783–1824) had won independence for Mexico after entering Mexico City with his troops on September 27, 1821.

Zavala was a member of the first constituent congress, in 1822, and was elected senator in 1825. He was active in the founding of the Lodge of York in Mexico. In 1827 Zavala was elected governor of the state of Mexico. In the 1828 election the *yorkino* candidate, General Vicente Guerrero (1782–1831), lost the election. Nevertheless, Zavala and others maneuvered to seat Guerrero in the presidential chair, and subsequently Guerrero appointed Zavala as a minister in his cabinet. When an opposing faction deposed Guerrero in 1830, Zavala went into exile in the United States and Europe. While in exile he wrote *Ensayo histórico de las revoluciones de México, desde 1808 hasta 1830.* A changing political situation allowed him to return to Mexico and reassume his office as governor in 1833.

Zavala worked with the reformist administration of Gómez Farías, and when the government was toppled at the end of 1833 went again into exile in Europe. Later, he returned to America and went to Texas, where he had land grants. There he sided with the colonists and supported Texas's independence from

---

1. The "cortes" were the legislatures in Spain.

Mexico. He signed the Texas declaration of independence and was elected vice president in 1836.

We present the introduction and conclusion of Zavala's *Ensayo histórico* as well as his individual vote in Congress regarding the separation of Guatemala from Mexico.

1 Introduction to *Historical Essay on the Mexican Revolutions from 1808 to 1830*

In undertaking the publication of *Ensayo histórico de la últimas revoluciones de México,* I intend to elucidate the character, customs, and different situation of the people involved rather than to create weary narratives in which, as Mr. Sismondi says so well, one encounters only a repetition of the same acts of cruelty, evil deeds, and baseness that fatigue the spirit, cause boredom in the reader, and, in a certain way, degrade the man who spends a large amount of time going over the horrors and havoc of parties and factions. "The history of peoples," says this same writer, "commences only with the beginning of life, with the spirit that animates nations." As the time prior to the events of 1808 is a period of silence, sleepiness, and monotony, with the exception of some glimmers that appear from time to time breathing liberty, the interesting history of Mexico truly commences only in that memorable year. But it is more advisable that readers, in order to begin reading this *Ensayo histórico* with understanding, be instructed about the customs of the inhabitants and of their condition before the referenced epoch.

The discovery of the Americas that Christopher Columbus made at the end of the fifteenth century and the conquest of those regions carried out a short time later are among those events that, to a large degree, have contributed to changing the political course of societies. My goal is not to speak of the influence these events have exercised on Europe, but rather of the course that political matters in the ancient empire of the Aztecs have taken, not in the time immediately subsequent to the conquest, regarding which various Spanish and foreign scholars have already written. In their writings, one can encounter repeated facts that will confirm those that form the picture I am going to present to my readers and which, perhaps, will shed more light on important political

Original title: "Introducción." Source: Lorenzo de Zavala, *Ensayo histórico de las revoluciones de México, desde 1808 hasta 1830,* vol. 1 (Paris: P. Dupont y Jaguionie, 1831).

questions which will doubtless recur successively in the course of the coming times. Is it not true that the heterogeneity of the elements that have made up European societies in different epochs has entered into the calculations and measures of their legislators and leaders in organizing their progress? The history of the middle age, of this period of grand vices and heroic virtues, of ignorance, energy, and universal upheaval, teaching statesmen what the basic parts that make up the nations they governed have been, showed them at the same time the different sources that are the basis of the rights or the aspirations of each class, of each hierarchy, of each family. In Spanish America, where there were no other foreign invaders, nor that tumultuous invasion of semisavage nations, we must assume that the conquistador laid down the law without conditions, and peaceably used the right of force with no restrictions except those to which he would subject himself.

The historians of the conquest of Mexico have given to their accounts an air of exaggeration that has been the origin of many ridiculous fables and amusing romances. The most judicious writers have not been able to protect themselves from giving credit to some entirely false and even absurd facts, which has led them into errors of great consequence. We can affirm that no history has been more adorned with illusions, hyperbole, romantic stories, and episodes than that of those far-off lands, the distance and isolation in which the policy of the Spanish government maintained them causing almost the same results as those the heroic times produced. Cortés himself, in his letters to Carlos V, paints pictures so flattering, so poetic and extraordinary of what he had seen and conquered with his fearless companions, that it was difficult not to believe oneself transported to a new world, to a land similar to and even superior to the imaginary Atlantis, or to those lands of gold, incense, and aromas of which Eastern writers speak. Magnificent palaces covered with gold and silver; kings and emperors richer than the most powerful potentates of Europe; temples comparable to those of ancient Greece; rivers that carried grains of the most precious metals and emeralds and diamonds instead of stones; extraordinary birds, monstrous quadrupeds; men of different physiognomy due to their features, color, lack of beard, and bristly hair; climates in which one breathes a fiery atmosphere or in which a perpetual spring represents the closest image of paradise. A religion made up of the most ridiculous and horrible ceremonies; a worship whose dogmas are a monstrous mix of everything that had been regarded as the most bizarre. All of this, partly true, waxing in the pens of writers, came to produce indelible impressions in Europe. But, how differently were these same things seen in those lands!

The Spanish conquest in America reduced the Indians to such a state of slavery that each white man considered himself to have the right to be served by the indigenous, without the indigenous having either courage to object or even the capacity to assert any right. Those who escaped the effects of the first slaughters were distributed among the conquistadors. In the beginning, there were only masters and servants. The authorities did not govern by laws, of which there were none, but rather in the name of the king. Later they were given those ordinances that they called the Laws of the Indies, which had as their goal moderating the tyranny of the descendants of the conquistadors and of the chieftains who left Spain to govern those lands. But inasmuch as the only ones who had those laws or royal decrees were those who were to execute them, in reality there did not exist anything but the will of the captains general, viceroys, or governors. Distributions of territories were in part converted into *encomiendas,* which had as its final result the payment of an annual tribute to the holders of the *encomiendas,* who were like the *borough mongers* in England. Later the kings reduced these privileged ones to receiving from the royal treasury the amount equal to the annual yield of the tributes they collected from the Indians who were their share in the original distributions, eliminating, in this way, much ill treatment produced by the method of collecting it, an abuse that later was adopted by the subdelegates and chief magistrates charged with collecting levies from the Indians, who were obligated to deliver them in *kind,* that is to say, in ordinary fabrics of cotton that their women wore or in other similar manufactured goods.

The Indians had their special laws, their judges, their attorneys and defense counsels that the government named for them because, legally, they were considered minors. The state of brutishness in which it kept them made them, in effect, unfit to demand any kind of rights or to enter into important contracts, which assumed the need for some complex ideas. Those who have tried to defend the policy of the Spanish government with respect to its colonies have cited the existence of this Code of the Indies that seems to have been formed as a bastion of protection on behalf of the Indians. But those who examine the questions from a philosophical point of view have considered this *institute* only as a system of slavery established on seemingly indestructible bases, and from whose effects those governments will continue to suffer for some centuries. In effect, those laws are nothing but a prescribed method of domination over the Indians. They take for granted, in the monarchs that issued them, rights over the *goods and lives* of the conquered ones, and consequently any act that was not absolutely an oppression was deemed in them a favor, a benefit from the legislator. There were laws that determined the weight with which they could be burdened, the distances they could go, what they had to be paid, etc. etc. So as to maintain this systematic order of oppression, it was necessary that the oppressed were never able to enter, so to speak, into the *rational world,* into the moral sphere in which other men live. In the majority of the provinces, they did not know, nor do they yet know, any language but their own, which is generally different from the others. The language (without excepting Mexican, which some novelists have pompously praised) is impoverished and lacks words to express abstract ideas. The speeches historians or poets imagine to have come from the mouths of the Jicotencales, Magiscatzines, and Colocolos are no more genuine than those that Homer, Virgil, and Livy attribute to the Agamemnons, Turnuses, or Scaevolas. Those Indian chiefs were as, or perhaps more barbarous than these Greek and Roman heroes, and their language could not lend itself to the beautiful oratories that a long sequence of centuries of civilization and regular governments assume.

It is certain that Spanish America before the conquest was more populated than today and that the Indians under their national governments began to develop some ideas. They had confused notions regarding the immortality of the soul, they had made a small number of observations, although highly imperfect, regarding the course of the stars, they were not completely lacking in the art of working metal. But such knowledge remained in its cradle, and now it is known how many centuries are necessary for peoples to attain the level of perfection that would allow them to deserve the title of civilized. The conquest destroyed entirely this movement that began to give flight to the spirit of invention among those indigenous peoples. A new worship as well as an unknown government substituted the bloody superstitions of Huitzilipoxtli and the patriarchal regimes of the Guatimocines and Moctezumas. The images of the saints and gods of the Roman Catholics were put in places that had previously been occupied by the horrible idols of the Aztecs; and the defenders of the conquistadors will not be able to deny, even if it is painful to admit it, that the Indians also had their martyrs, sacrificed because of the religious zeal of the Roman priests, because of the tenacious adherence of many of them to their ancient worship. But eventually force and terror triumphed over fanaticism for a religion that had against it the horrific dogma of demanding human victims. On the other hand, the Indians encountered much more perfect images than their monstrous idols, and the change was not very difficult, moving to our saints the ceremonies and tributes that they made to their gods. The assistance of miracles came about, and a multitude of celestial apparitions came in support of the new worship, because of which the astonished Indians could not but believe that their gods, along with their monarchs and rulers, had been defeated in a just war.

Missionaries dedicated themselves and, with the aid of troops, made wondrous conversions. The religious constructed their convents in high places like forts and gave those buildings all the solidity necessary to resist in case of attack. Very rare are the temples and houses of the clergymen that do not suggest the reasons that led the founders to make them works of fortification. They were together in them during the night, and by day they occupied themselves with gathering the Indians into settlements. It is clear that their sermons and preachings were not at first able to have any effect, because as they did not have the gift of languages, it was not easy to make their listeners understand dogmas, mysteries, and doctrines that assume many preliminary lessons. Catechisms and small books of rules were created in the languages of the land, not so the Indians could read them, because they didn't know how, but rather to repeat them in the pulpits and to make the people memorize them. There is not a single version of the sacred books in any language of the land; there is not a basic book that contains the fundamentals of the faith. But how could these works exist for the Indians, when their conquerors themselves could not read them? What I want to show by this is that the religion was not taught to those men, nor did they become convinced of its divine origin through proofs or reasoning; the entire foundation of their faith was the word of their missionaries, and the reasons for their belief, the bayonets of their conquerors. The Inquisition could not understand the motives of the Indians. Such was the Indians' state of degradation and so strong the idea that was held regarding their incapacity, that never could they be persuaded that an Indian was able to be the creator of some heresy, or even be the stubborn sectarian of any doctrine whatsoever. This exception came to be a protection, as a concession in favor of the Indians, owing to the judgment that had been formed of their stupidity.

Besides the tribute that the Indians paid to the royal treasury, or to their *encomenderos,* other ecclesiastical contributions with the name of *obvenciones* were created. They were exempted from the tithe and the parochial fees because their exploiters had carefully calculated that a man who possesses nothing, nor has more needs than the basics, could pay little of the tithe. The calculation was very correct, because in effect the Indians did not have territorial properties, or any kind of industry, generally speaking. They lived and live in huts covered with thatch or palm fronds, whose size is generally from fifteen to sixteen feet in length, by ten or twelve in width, oval in form. There, of course, are gathered the children, the domestic animals, and an altar on which are the saints or household gods. In the middle is a fire that serves to heat the water in which corn is cooked, their sole food, with few exceptions. There are not five among a hundred who have two garments, which are limited to one long shirt of ordinary cloth and some sandals; their women or daughters, dressed with equal simplicity or poverty, do not know that inclination so natural to their sex of looking good in front of others. In the same proportion referred to previously, there are not property owners, and they are content with gathering thirty-five or forty *fanegas* of maize per year, on which they live satisfactorily. When, because of some labor or day work, they have earned a small amount of money, they go to make some feast to the saint to whom they are devoted, and they expend their small personal money on fireworks, masses, feasts, and intoxicating drinks. The rest of the year they spend in idleness, sleeping many hours of the day in the warm lands, or in games of their liking in the delightful climates of the cordilleras. Two in a hundred learned to read; but today their situation has been greatly improved in this regard. In several provinces, the clergymen had such power and exercised such authority over the Indians that they ordered them whipped publicly when they did not pay the *obvenciones* on time or committed some act of disobedience. I have frequently seen many married Indians and their wives whipped at the doors of the temples for having missed mass on some Sunday or feast day, and this scandalous act was customarily authorized in my province!

Those who were whipped were obligated afterward to kiss the hand of the person who whipped them.

In speaking of the ecclesiastical influence in the land and of the moral situation of this privileged class, it is impossible not to collide with interests sustained by superstition and created by despotism. The principle of national sovereignty, recognized subsequently in those lands, might have uprooted prejudices destructive of liberty and made presumptions to blind obedience disappear if the declarations of abstract doctrines alone, even the most solemn, were sufficient. The force of habits created for three centuries will still remain an obstacle, so that at mid-century, enlightenment and philosophy have to triumph over this colossus after a terrible and hard battle. In those lands, the persons of the bishops were, without hyperbole, as reverenced as the person of the great Lama among the Tatars. When he went out into the street, the Indians knelt down and bowed their heads to receive his blessing. The friars in the towns and small villages distant from the capitals were the teachers of doctrine and the *masters* of common lands, in the large cities, directors of the conscience of landowners and women. The convents of the Dominicans and the Carmelites possessed and possess riches of great importance in rural and urban real estate. The convents of the religious in Mexico, especially the Conception, the Incarnation, and Saint Theresa, possess in property at least three quarters of the individual buildings of the capital, and the same happens proportionally in the other provinces. So one can be assured without exaggeration that the wealth that the clergymen and religious of both sexes possess amounts to the annual proceeds of three million in income. Put this revenue in the weight of the balance with respect to their influence, and one is able to calculate approximately what it will be among a poor population where properties are very badly distributed.

Now I enter into another delicate subject that can be considered one of the elements of discord in those countries and that will offer great obstacles to their legislators, depending on the degree to which they abandon infantile and frivolous questions and concern themselves more deeply with the true interests of their *patria*. I speak of the distribution of lands that the Spaniards made and the way those lands are divided today.

The Spanish government had to make concessions of lands to those persons who had contributed most to the conquest of that rich and beautiful territory. Naturally, the conquerors selected the best situated and most fertile plots of land in the order in which each one was believed to have the right or did have the right to receive this kind of compensation. The rich and considerable possessions of the Counts del Valle, de Santiago, San Miguel de Aguayo, the Marshall de Castilla, the Duke of Monteleone, and others occupy an immense and arable territory. The other rural farms that surround the towns and cities, which belong to the convents and pious establishments, have their source in royal concessions, others in testamentary bequests, gifts *inter vivos,* and some few come from contracts of purchase and sale. The third class of large landowners is that of families descended from rich Spaniards who bought, in distant times, lands from the government or from Indians when they had an extremely low price, and they were successively augmented until they formed haciendas that today are worth from a half-million pesos to two million, like those of the Reglas, Vivancos, Vicarios, Marquess del Jaral, Fagoagas, Alcaraces, and others. The fourth class is that of small landowners, who have rural farms whose value is not more than between six and fifteen thousand pesos, acquired by purchase or inheritance or other similar title. Here is how the greater part of the lands of the Mexican Republic were distributed, especially those that surround cities or great population centers. All these possessions are in the hands of Spaniards or their descendants and are cultivated by Indians who serve as day workers. Of the seven million inhabitants that will now occupy that immense territory, at least four are Indians or people of color, among whom nine-tenths are reduced to the state I have discussed before. Consequently, there does not exist in that land that gradation of fortunes that constitutes a common scale of comforts in social life, principle and foundation of the existence of civilized nations. It is an image of feudal Europe without the spirit of independence and the energetic force of those times.

During the three hundred years of colonial government, these classes, reduced to subsisting on their daily labor, had no notions whatsoever of a better condition of life, or at least did not even suspect they could be called to enter into the pleasures of any other kind of existence than the sad and mean one in which they remained. Their desires, on the other hand, were proportionate to their ideas, and these, as has been said, occupied a sphere so small that one could say with accuracy that they knew only the physical side of life. Those activities that put them in contact with white people, such as attendance at church and few, very rare, gatherings for some public act, were purely mechanical, and it was a phenomenon to hear a reasoned statement from the mouths of those degraded beings. Many travelers have said that the indigenous peoples of America are reserved and silent, mistaking what is only the effect of their ignorance for contemplation or not caring to speak. But if by some unknown caprice of nature a genius stood out, a notable character, at the moment he spoke to his companions with the language of desperation and, exhorting them to throw off their enslavement, he was sacrificed by the oppressors. Tupac-Amaro in Peru and Quisteil in Yucatán can be cited, among others.

"The equality or inequality among the different orders of citizens in a new and semisavage nation," says a famous writer, "depends essentially on the distribution of territorial property; because a nation that is not civilized does not have commerce, or accumulated capital, or manufacturing and arts; it cannot then possess other riches than those the earth produces. The earth is the only one that feeds men in a land without commerce and without accumulated riches, and men consistently obey the one who can, at his will, give them or take from them the means of living and enjoying. A nation," continues the same author,

sometimes without revolution and without conquest, acquires an imperfect degree of civilization, where lands are cultivated but commerce and the arts have not yet made any progress at all: then it is probable that the lands belonging to this nation were, at its beginning, divided among the citizens in more or less equal portions, or at least that none of them obtained from their compatriots permission to appropriate an amount of land extremely disproportionate to the abilities of the family to cultivate it. The haciendas can be more or less large, but never were they like provinces, and the inequality that existed in this case among individuals would not be such that it might place some necessarily in dependence on others. Citizens, unequal only in enjoyments, would not forget that they were equal by origin, and all were free. Such is the history of ancient Greece and ancient Italy, and here is where that idea originates that, from the most distant times, free governments are seen only in these regions. In our times, the distribution of fortunes in the colonies of North America retain some analogy with the early establishment of agricultural nations. The colonists give, it is true, a greater expanse to their haciendas than we give in Europe, but they are always proportional to the capacities of their families. Consequently, there exists among them a kind of *territorial balance,* as Harrington called it in his work, *Oceana,* a balance that *contributes to the preservation* of liberty in the United States of the North. For the rest, even without this balance, it might be able to have established that liberty; because the Americans have accumulated capital, have vast commerce and arts, the poor and the rich alike finding in their country abundant means to subsist with independence.

These doctrines, whose accuracy one cannot dispute, lend substance to very profound reflections, given the data I have noted in an orderly manner regarding the state of territorial riches in the Mexican Republic. What role will more than three million individuals, summoned suddenly to enjoy the broadest rights of citizenship from the state of the most ignominious enslavement, with no real property, no knowledge of any craft or office, neither commerce nor any industry, come to play in this society in which, appearing suddenly, they can be considered the progeny of Deucalion and Pirra? How are we to judge them, so detached from the desire to improve their fate that, having in their hands the ability to exercise their political rights in the assemblies and elective magistracies, they do not take advantage of their position? More to the point: What should the conquered families do, over whom ill treatment of all kinds has been exercised for three centuries, to become incorporated by the constitutions of the country into the great national family? How have the inexpert directors of those societies been able to forget or close their eyes to what has happened in all nations? Which have been the constant movements of the *radicals* in England, the liberals in continental Europe, and particularly in France, that laid the foundation for their revolution of '89 over the distribution of feudal properties? Is it perchance believed that the flight taken recently by the project of the *bill of reform* in England is in order to have a few more deputies or electors?

Every government has its principle of existence for which, once unsettled or distorted, another, analogous to the changes that have occurred in the country, must be substituted. The colonial system established by the Spanish government was founded: (1) On the *terror* produced by immediate punishment of the smallest actions that might lead to disobedience; that is to say, on the blindest passive obedience, without permitting the examination of what has been ordered nor by whom. (2) On the ignorance in which one must keep those inhabitants who could not learn more than what the government wanted, and only to the degree agreeable to it. (3) On religious education and, most of all, on the most despicable superstition. (4) On a Jewish isolation from all foreigners. (5) On monopoly in commerce, of territorial properties and of positions. (6) On a number of troops ready to carry out in a moment the orders of the mandarins, and who were more like gendarmes of the police than soldiers of the army, to defend the country.

After the Mexicans had secured their independence, the *terror* inspired by the Spanish authorities, maintained by custom passed down from fathers to sons, disappeared, and the broadest declarations of *liberty* and *equality* have been substituted. *Ignorance,* without having been able to disappear, has given place to a political charlatanism that takes possession of public dealings and leads the state to chaos and confusion. Popular superstition not ceasing, a large number of books have been introduced that corrupt the mores without enlightening the understanding. There is now no monopoly of commerce, positions, or territorial properties, and this item requires a long explanation.

Commerce has been opened to all foreigners, and speculators have taken out great profits, as was to be expected. Articles of merchandise conveyed by second, third, and fourth hand, passing from northern Europe to merchants in Cádiz, and from them to Veracruz in Mexico, had necessarily to arrive much more expensive, especially with no competition among the markets. In this area the fate of the country has improved a great deal, and many fewer destitute people are seen than in other times. But very few are the foreigners who, after having made great earnings, remain in the country and join with Mexican families. It appears that they see themselves in the country as in tents, ready to break camp as soon as they have concluded their business. On this point, one can expect much improvement with time. As for the monopoly of positions, it exists only among the factions that fight among themselves to attain them, but all are Mexicans. The territorial properties are among the great objects that will occupy the attention of those governments. On this, I have already said how it is enough to make known the difficult position of the directors of those towns, and I have not intended to make a treatise on insurrections. I reserve giving greater consideration to these ideas *in my memoirs* that should be published within a short time, and that I have at hand.

One of the greatest woes that will afflict those peoples for some time is that of the permanent troops, both for the useless expense they cause and because they work as organized masses under the direction of ambitious leaders, so the civil governments cannot offer resistance to them and are consequently their instruments or their victims. Ten or twelve colonels of regimental bodies and four or five generals, forming a united system, oppress the country, and, without altering the republican forms, everything proceeds under their inspirations. Foreign businessmen, who can have no other interests than their profits, which depend on the state of tranquility or slavery, favor this system to the extent they can unite with Spaniards who desire the same, and it is very common to see many liberals from Europe in Mexico enrolled in the ranks of the oppressors. This explains the mystery of why some newspapers, even those of the party of liberty in Europe, make apologies for the military governments of America. Receiving communication and news from overseas agents, and those agents always speaking in the sense of their profits and interests, it is clear that the military party must be considered most useful to their speculation.

But one must not lose sight of the principles I have set forth on the well-known facts to which I have also referred. The greatest and most dangerous errors of those who direct public affairs is not to think about the generations that will be following, nor about their advances and aspirations, and in no place is this error susceptible of easier realization than in the new states of America. From the year 1808 until 1830, that is to say, in the space of a generation, such is the change of ideas, opinions, factions and interests that has occurred, that it is enough to turn a respected and recognized form of government upside down and have seven million inhabitants pass from despotism and arbitrariness to the most liberal theories. Only the customs and habits are transmitted in all movements; actions and continuous examples have not been able to change, because how can abstract doctrines make the course of life suddenly change? Consequently we have in contradiction to the theoretical systems of established governments those powerful agents of human life, and the founders of republican forms will not be able to deny that they have only dressed, with the clothing of declarations of rights and principles, the old man, the same body or confluence of prejudices, the mass organized and shaped by previous institutions. What have they done to substitute usages and customs analogous to the new order of things?

There is, then, a continual clash among the doctrines that are professed, the institutions adopted, the principles established; and among the abuses sanctified, the customs that dominate, semifeudal rights that are respected; among the national sovereignty, equality of political rights, freedom of the press, popular government, and intervention of the armed force, laws of privilege, religious intolerance, and landowners of immense territories. Might the conserving principles of any social order whatsoever at least be made harmonious? If *a federal system,* which is what seems to me most suitable to those countries, is adopted by conviction, by rationality, by a judgment formed after profound reflection, not for that reason should the system of the neighbors of the North be copied exactly, nor, much less, literal articles from the Spanish Constitution. The height of absurdity and the absence of all good sense is the sanction of laws of privilege and privileges in a popular government. Let there be established an ecclesiastical, military, and civil aristocracy if one wants or believes it useful to the good of the country; let the republics of Genoa or Venice be imitated if it is possible; then might there be laws of privilege and privileged classes; might there be laws for each hierarchy or for each corporation or each person if it is judged suitable. But a constitution formed on the foundations of the broadest liberty, on the model of that of the North Americans, conserving a state religion without tolerance for another; privileged troops and military leaders in civil commands; convents of religious of both sexes instituted in conformity with the canons of the Roman Church; three million citizens with no property at all nor no known means of subsistence; half a million with political rights to vote in elections without knowing how to read or write; military tribunals judging certain privileged cases; finally, all the incentives of an unlimited liberty and the absence of all social guarantees, cannot fail to produce a perpetual war among such heterogeneous factions and such opposing interests. Make disappear that confluence of anomalies that mutually contradict each other. I will conclude this discourse presenting to the readers the state of income, expenses, and resources of New Spain, omitting minute details that form the object of my work.

2

Conclusion to *Historical Essay on the Revolutions of Mexico from 1808 to 1830*

I have completed the period I determined to examine in providing a theoretical basis for this little work. The reader will notice that, although I have passed rapidly over the events, I have not omitted any of the circumstances that can present them with clarity and from the genuine point of view. The passions at work, stirring up factions and men in a new nation where, by force of continuous shocks, the bonds of subordination, the greater part of the habits of order, and even, to a certain point, the social agreement by which the nation is maintained have disappeared together with the chains that were crushing it, cannot but offer for some time the spectacle of a chaos of successive episodes of liberty and slavery and of political problems that make the writers of Europe, who propose to resolve our great questions by abstract ideas and general principles without knowing our customs, prejudices, and circumstances, form absurd theories. I am going to venture some reflections about the principal considerations that will bear on the fate of our America for many years in the new republics, and where the intentions of those who might, in good faith, try to cut off their disagreements at its root the source should be directed. Of course, the fundamental objective of my observations is the Mexican Republic that I know, to which I owe the existence and fruit of all my work.

What does it mean that a country in which the sun is so brilliant and warm that fecundity spreads, the aspect of the mountains so varied and pleasant; where the fields are irrigated by abundant streams or by torrents that fall from the sky, and where nature offers, in its greater part, a soil covered by sumptuous vegetation; where the inhabitants receive at birth a lively and immediate imagination, susceptibility to impassioned

Original title: "Conclusión," from *Ensayo histórico de las revoluciones de México, desde 1808 hasta 1830*. Source: Lorenzo de Zavala, *Ensayo histórico de las revoluciones de México, desde 1808 hasta 1830,* vol. 2 (New York: Elliot and Palmer, 1832).

impressions, a disposition of the mind to comprehend easily, and a keen spirit, is populated for the most part with poor, ignorant people deprived of the social advantages and enjoyments that civilization provides? Why is it, in the very moment of entering into the great family of cultured peoples, they present a spectacle of interminable civil wars, acts of cruelty, and bloody scenes, instead of entering peacefully the road of liberty they have begun to travel and to which, with such heroism, they have given a beginning? No one can doubt that the principal causes of this situation involve the course this society followed, incompatible with the circumstances referred to and which for three hundred years blocked the beginnings of life and activity; hindered since the revolution of independence by a totally opposed policy that has called all progeny, so to speak, to renounce their old habits, customs, and prejudices to adopt others analogous in the new social system that the policy was trying to provide. Let us look at how this people was created, educated, and disciplined under colonial domination, and in the examination of this question we will see the origin of their calamities.

Four are the institutions that most essentially influence the fate of a society and that almost exclusively determine the character of the inhabitants of a nation: religion, education, legislation, and the ideas of honor that inspire it. Religion is, of all the moral forces to which man is subject, the one that can produce the greatest good or the greatest evil. All opinions that refer to interests superior to this world; all beliefs that have eternity as a goal; all sects that preach a religion, exercise a prodigious influence over moral sentiments and human character. None, nevertheless, penetrates more deeply into the heart of man, as a wise writer very well observes, than the Catholic religion, because none is more strongly organized; none has subordinated moral philosophy so completely; none has enslaved consciences; none has established, as it has, the tribunal of confession, which reduces all believers to the most absolute dependence on their clergy; none has, as it does, priests more isolated from the spirit of family or more intimately united by interest and esprit de corps. The unity of the faith, which can only be the result of the subjection of reason to belief and which, consequently, is not found in any other religion to the high degree as in the Catholic, tightly binds all members of this Church to accept the same dogmas, to submit to the same decisions, and to be formed on the same model of instruction. But its powerful influence has been exercised in various ways, according to whether the interests of its primary leaders have been more in agreement with the people or with the kings. During the centuries that preceded the reigns of Carlos V and Felipe II, from the beginnings of the tenth century, the immense moral force of pontifical power, then, was used to elevate the people and to place ideas of liberty and civilization in opposition to attempts by the emperors of Germany and the efforts of the Ghibellines who, under their protection, began to establish despotic principalities in Italy. Until then, says Mr. Sismondi, the popes had contracted a type of alliance with the people against the sovereigns; they had made conquests only over the kings. They owed their elevation and all the means of resistance to the power of the spirit as opposed to brutal force; and for policy, even more than for recognition, they had believed themselves obliged to expand this power of the spirit. They had made arise, directed, and called to their aid public opinion; they protected letters and philosophy, and they even permitted, with liberality, philosophers and poets to deviate sometimes from the narrow orthodox line. Finally, they proclaimed themselves protectors of liberty and they protected the republics. But as soon as half the Church, raising the standard of reform, shook off the yoke; as soon as that very philosophical enlightenment it had protected was turned against Rome, that spirit of liberty it had stimulated, that public opinion that escaped from it and that already had come to be a power in Europe, a feeling of profound terror made the popes determine to change their entire policy. Instead of remaining at the head of the opposition against the monarchs, they felt the need to make common cause with them in order to contain adversaries much more terrible than were they. They contracted the tightest alliances with the temporal princes, especially with Felipe II, the most despotic among all of them, and they occupied themselves only with subordinating consciences and enslaving the human spirit. In effect, they imposed a yoke on it, and at no time had it endured one so terrible.

This was the epoch of the discovery and conquest of America by the Spaniards. In establishing their power and domination among us, they brought with them the spirit of superstition, intolerance, and blind obedience that Don Fernando and Doña Isabel were trying to establish on the Peninsula, preparing the unfortunate days of Carlos I and his descendants. Hernando Cortés, brave *caudillo* but cruel and superstitious, impressed the conquered Indians so that they feared, honored, and obeyed him, by letting himself be whipped by a priest publicly in order to instill in the minds of those people the first seeds of spiritual power. On this base the Spaniards raised the edifice of the new society created in Spanish America. The power of arms and priestly influence bound the government, directed the morality, the sentiments, the character of the people. There was nothing outside this narrow circle, and the society moved like this in silence from generation to generation, without any other people hearing even the sound of its footsteps. But this degrading situation was necessary to imprint a deep seal of humility and slavery on all the inhabitants. The few ideas of all kinds that they had were lost; the colonies saw only through the eyes of their directors, and they understood or, better said, learned only what they taught them. The priests took control of public instruction; and moral philosophy, which is the patrimony most inherent to human happiness and which belongs to the domain of the conscience, passed entirely into the hands of religion, as happened in Spain. Theology took control of this science, which teaches men their rights and the reasons in which they are based, and the vital principles of society were perverted by the abuse that was made of it.

I do not in any way propose to deny that there is a close connection between religion and morality; and all good men must recognize that the most noble homage the mortal can render to his Creator is that of raising himself to the Creator by his virtues. But moral philosophy is an entirely distinct science from theology: it has its bases in reason and conscience; it carries with it proofs that produce our conviction; and, after having cut loose the spirit through investigation of its principles, it satisfies the heart by discovering what is truly beautiful, just, and fitting. The clergy took control of morality as a science exclusive to its rule; it substituted the authority of decrees of the councils and the Fathers for the enlightenment of reason and conscience, the study of the casuists for moral philosophy, and replaced the most noble exercise of the mind with a series of precepts that reduced its instruction to a servile routine.

But morality was perverted in this way in the hands of the casuists; it became like a foreign thing in the heart and understanding; vices were no longer judged by the evil consequences they produce, by the sufferings they carry with them, by the disregard in which they put vicious men into society, but rather uniquely under the province of divine laws. The foundation that nature had provided and put in the heart of all mortals was destroyed in order to substitute another, arbitrary and artificial. The difference between venial and mortal sins erased the difference that exists primordially in the conscience between the most serious offenses and the most pardonable; it appeared to place in a certain order, mixed among the crimes that cause the greatest horror, the faults that our weakness could hardly avoid. The casuists held up to execration among the most guilty men of the first category, heretics, schismatics, and blasphemers. See here the beginning of the hatred of South Americans for foreigners, hatred that will, for some time, be an obstacle to their prosperity. But this horror that was inspired against industrious, charitable, and moral men was the greatest misfortune that could have befallen national customs, as much because, seeing heretics practice good deeds they became accustomed to doubting the excellence of virtue, as because in their judgment it was less contagious dealing with the criminal and vicious men who were Catholics, heard mass, and recited the rosary than with people who had refined customs and a conduct beyond reproach but were not subject to the pope.

The doctrine of penance caused a new subversion of morality, continues Mr. Sismondi, now confused with the arbitrary distinction among sins. The pardon of heaven and the return to the path of virtue is, without doubt, a consoling doctrine; and this idea is so in accord with human needs and weaknesses that it has become an essential part of all religions. But the casuists have distorted this doctrine, imposing precise formulas for penance, confession, and absolution. A single act of faith and fervor was regarded as sufficient to erase a long list of crimes. Instead of holding out virtue now as a constant and perpetual obligation, it was nothing other than a settlement of accounts at the last moment prior to death. There was no sinner so obstinate that he would not have the plan of dedicating some days before dying to the care of his soul; but in the meantime, he gave free rein to all his passions, and those who preached against these doctrines were considered *Jansenists*. Another of the corrupting principles of morality were indulgences and the scandalous traffic in them. The kings of Spain obtained the bulls of dispensation, which were sold by force to Americans, who did not receive absolution if they did not purchase that document of infamy, ignominy, and superstition. The power attributed to contrition, to religious ceremonies, to indulgences, to the bulls all came together to convince people that eternal condemnation or salvation depended on the absolution of the priest, and this was perhaps the most lamentable blow dealt morality. Chance, not virtue, had to decide the eternal fate of the soul of the dying person. The most virtuous man, whose life might always have been pure, could be attacked unexpectedly by death in the moment when pain, anger, surprise might have made him utter one of those profane words that habit has made so common and that, according to the decisions of the councils, cannot be pronounced without incurring mortal sin. Then his eternal condemnation was inevitable, because there had not been present a priest to receive his penance and open for him the doors of heaven. On the other hand, the most perverse man, loaded down with crimes, could experience a moment of remorse and of transitory desire to make himself virtuous; with a good confession and communion, this man was assured of heaven. Thus, the morality taught to the people was a source of bad doctrine, because the enlightenment of reason and the constant inspirations of the conscience, which teach to distinguish always the good from the corrupted man, were contradicted by theological decisions, which condemned the first and beatified the second, only because of the unexpected chance of receiving absolution.

Yet more; in the catechisms of religious instruction, at the side of the great index of virtues and vices, whose understanding is universal and natural to man, was placed another index of the mandates of the Church, unsupported by a sanction so terrible as the mandates of the divinity; without making eternal salvation depend on their observance, they came to have the formality and power that the eternal laws of morality never managed to have. The murderer, still covered with the blood he had just spilt, did not eat meat on Friday no matter how much there was in the world; the prostitute placed the image of the virgin by her bed, before which she recited the rosary; the priest who got up from the gaming table or who committed crimes without scruple would not dare drink a glass of water before saying mass. It seemed that the more regularity man put into observing the precepts of the Church, the more he believed himself dispensed from observing natural law, to which depraved inclinations would have to be sacrificed. Meanwhile morality, properly speaking, never stopped being the object of the Church's preachings, but priestly interest has corrupted everything it has touched in Spain and its colonies. Mutual *benevolence* is the foundation of social virtues; the casuist, reducing it to a precept, has declared that it is a sin to speak badly of one's fellow being. With this he has impeded everyone from expressing the just judgment that should discern virtue from vice and has imposed silence on the language of truth. But becoming accustomed in this way to the fact that words do not express thought, he has done nothing but increase the secret distrust of each man with respect to others. *Charity* is the most excellent virtue in the Gospel, but the casuist has taught to give to the poor for the good of the soul, not to help his fellow creature; he has put into use alms without discernment, which stimulates vice and idleness; finally, he has taught to invest in the mendicant monk funds that should be destined for public charity. *Sobriety* and moderation are domestic virtues that maintain the faculties of individuals and ensure peace within families; the casuist has put in their place the observance of Fridays, fasts, discipline, the vows of chastity, and virginity. Nevertheless, at the side of these virtues and monastic vows, intemperance and libertinism could become rooted in the heart. *Modesty* is one of the most agreeable qualities of the better man; it does not exclude a just pride that serves as an aid against his own weaknesses and consoles him in adversity; the casuist has substituted *humility,* which allies with the most insulting contempt for others.

Such has been the inexplicable confusion in which the Jesuits put morality with works of casuistry, with which they flooded Spain and its colonies. They took exclusive control of the schools, which afterward passed to the hands of the friars. It was not permitted to do philosophical research that established moral rules on foundations other than theirs, nor enter into discussions regarding their first principles, nor appeal to human reason. Pascal, Malebranche, Locke had spoken as Christian philosophers, but their luminous doctrines could not penetrate among the inhabitants of Mexico. The entire store of ideas was in the hands of confessors and directors of consciences; the conscientious Mexican abdicated the power most essential to man, that is, to study and know his duties. How many times did he find himself burdened with difficult matters of life; whatever doubt occurred to him in complicated situations, he appealed to his spiritual guide. In this way the tests of adversity, which are those that elevate man, served to make him more subject. See here the reason why, as long as the interests of the clergy were in accord with dependence, people did not dare raise their voice against established laws preached and constantly inculcated as a dogma of blind obedience to the king and Roman pontiff. Let us now consider the kind of education that was given to Mexicans, and the reader will deduce the consequences of what can be expected in the future.

In some chapters I have spoken in passing of the type of instruction that was and still is given in many academies of the Mexican Republic. But in this chapter I am going to speak of the type of general education in order to proceed then to the public establishments. *Education* is one of the most powerful resources for the government of people. But those whom a bad *education* has harmed can be brought back to the noble sentiments of virtue and duty. Religion extends its healthy or unfortunate influence over the entire course of life; its power rests on the imagination of youth, on the enthusiastic tenderness of the weaker sex, on the terrors of old age; it accompanies man even to his most secret thoughts and is present even in the acts he can conceal from every human power. Nonetheless, the reciprocal influence of education over religion, and of the latter over the former, is so great that these two efficient causes can scarcely be separated from national characters.

Mexicans have received the same kind of physical, moral, and religious education as their Spanish conquerors. But as I have observed another time, three-fifths of the population was entirely abandoned to a type of purely animal life. This numerous class of that great society, without needs, without desires, without ambition, and without passions, was nothing more than the patrimony of priests and military authorities who put into action the physical forces of those people to pull out advantages, without even employing in their care, in their instruction, the careful solicitude that the owners of slaves do in countries where slavery is permitted. The education of the Indians was consequently nil, and there is very little one can say about a negative thing. The mental dispositions of these people have not even begun to develop since the new social amalgamation and their nominal incorporation into the great Mexican family. Their state of poverty, their dispersion into small population centers, the scanty incentive they have for their children to acquire notions about hopes inconceivable to them, or know their importance, and (I must say it even if it be shameful for us) the dereliction with which their education has been overseen by the directors of the new republics are the reasons why so few advances have still been observed in their social improvement. A very great accusation it will be for Mexicans, that of not dedicating special attention to the moral advancement of the Indians, whose education is today entrusted to their new governments. In Mexico there is an academy named San Gregorio, assigned to instruct a certain number of indigenous people, and in Puebla there was another such. But those establishments are useful only to their administrators and their teachers. In general, nothing is instructed or learned under the routine of a rector who only cares about the mass, the rosary, and the long vestments of his schoolboys. What is necessary, and I consider the foundation of society in the Mexican states, is that the schools of primary instruction be multiplied and in them be invested all the funds that were squandered on other things. Now I will move to making some reflections on the academies.

The contradiction in the United States of Mexico is very great between the methods of education adopted in its literary establishments and the kind of instruction young people must acquire to begin to carry out profitably the new posts to which they will be called under the present form of government. The same constitutions, drawn up by the bishops more than two centuries ago on royal orders and councils, created to provide clergymen who *learn in order to teach* the elements of blind obedience, renouncing all use of reason and submitting to the authority of the Holy Fathers, bulls, and councils, exist today in the seminaries of the Republic. Students are permitted only to acquire a certain kind of knowledge that teachers do not judge dangerous to the subversion of their routinist doctrines. All philosophy is subordinated to theology, which is the most general science; and with respect to other systems, nothing more is learned than the arguments with which theologians have refuted them. All moral philosophy is submitted to the decisions of the casuists, without it being permitted to seek in the heart principles other than those the authority of the casuists has pronounced. Political science, which was not known, has remained subordinated to those decisions that destroy all sentiment of individual independence, also becoming a science of formulas. In very few academies is history taught; but what sublime feeling can be aroused in the hearts of young people who receive only dry narratives, without being able to penetrate the profound resources that move the passions and the research into the great causes that produced past events? Can they know well history taught in collections of formulas, or at most through the jumbled compilations of Rollin or Segur, if they cannot research in the precious originals that ancients left us? Investigate Greek or Roman history, says Mr. La Harpe[1] to a young man who knows nothing but Rollin

1. Jean-François de La Harpe (1739–1803), French writer and critic. (Editor's note.)

and to another to whom the decades of Livy and the men of Plutarch have been given, and you will see the difference between the ideas and understandings of both. Eloquence, which in republican governments is the most necessary branch of instruction, is abandoned entirely, and very few are the teachers who can analyze for their pupils the orations of Cicero or the brilliant pages of Tacitus — what impression can poetry make when the religion of the ancients is constantly represented as a chaos of darkness and when the sentiments of an impassioned heart are explained by a man who has taken a vow of chastity? What interest can grow from the study of the laws, of the customs, of the uses and habits of antiquity when they are not compared to the abstract ideas of a truly free legislation, of a pure morality, and of habits that arise from the perfection of the social order? Thus it is that the study of antiquity, in the few establishments where it is taught, is nothing more than a science of facts and authorities, where reason and sentiment have no part and where one seeks only to make a display of memory.

Pious exercises occupy a considerable part of a student's hours. But they are limited to what they might do through the sound of their voice to make evident their presence in the chapel. The vast tautologies of daily prayers cannot fix their attention on what is being said. The same formula, repeated one hundred times, says nothing to their spirit or to their heart; and while a short exercise of devotion could serve to awaken religious sentiments in their conscience, rosaries, which are repeated many times, accustom them to separate completely their thoughts from the words they pronounce. This is rather an exercise in useless distraction or, what is worse, an act of hypocrisy. What instruction for young persons destined for the legal profession and the national court!

From the heart of these academies, nonetheless, men have been seen emerging who, having been educated by themselves, elevated themselves above their fellow citizens and have combated their errors, ridiculed their prejudices, and, confronting all kind of dangers, taught their fellow citizens the path of truth. This small number of privileged beings, sustained by the strength of their character and stirred by an inner feeling that they have a great mission to carry out, work without cease to obtain the triumph of liberty and enlightenment. The undertaking is arduous, their task difficult and filled with impediments that, at each step, *interest, egotism,* and power oppose. They encounter a youth *educated* under the old discipline, a people generally infected by habits of passive obedience, on the one hand, and by incitements to subversion, on the other. What can replace the primary education? Those who are currently present on the scene, launched into the labors of an active life, cannot possess that moral flexibility necessary to receive the culture they did not acquire earlier, and this is precisely when there is a double need to educate them. Because not being able to keep their desires inactive, it happens that when they do not move toward the good, that is to say toward *social progress,* left to themselves they will inevitably be directed toward *evil,* that is, toward *egoism.*

Our generation has been transported instantaneously into a kind of moral sphere distinct from that in which our fathers lived. Perhaps history presents no example of such a rapid change, if those in which the conquistadors compelled by force obedience to their rule and adoption of their institutions are excepted. But we must not make a mistake; the transformation is not complete, and there still remains much to do. With a little reflection, it will be noticed that the change that occurred is only in the most general order of FEELINGS and *interests,* and it will be only after much time, much labor, and successively that change in the order of *ideas, acts,* and thought will be fulfilled. Thus we have seen depart the generations that have been held up to us as suddenly converted, without being able for very long fully to realize the state of society that the principles they adopted create. The *rule of physical force,* principle, reason, and aim of the colonial administration will still be for some time what dominates, although it will be successively acquiring modifications more analogous to the progress of the moral education of the different classes into which the interest of that despotic government divided society. The *education of those* numerous *classes* and their complete amalgamation into the general mass is the great work that will surely lead to perfection, for which the true lovers of liberty yearn. It is true that one of the triumphs of the revolution has been to destroy the most *visible* classifications, and, getting rid of the shackles they had before, it has proclaimed the rights of equality so that each one can occupy the place for which he becomes worthy. But what has been done to give reality to that right? What has been done that is not purely negative? The obstacles have been removed, but there remain many to conquer. Without doubt it is thus, and *education,* without whose help the happiest circumstances are altogether sterile, is very far from being accessible without distinction to everyone. *Education* is still a privilege that depends on the fortune of the families; and fortune is a privilege that is very far from being proportional to the merit of the persons who have it. There is more; for the small number of citizens who can aspire to the benefits of education, nothing has yet been done so that it might be distributed by reason of their aptitudes and their vocation. In sum, despite the political triumph of philosophical ideas among Mexicans, proclaimed pompously in their constitutions and repeated even to boredom in their periodicals, *education* still remains inaccessible to the greater number, and as for the scant minority who receive it, unfortunately it is not adjusted to the institutions adopted; and on the contrary, it puts up open struggle against the momentum given to society by the solemn declarations of *liberty and equality*. I will not tire of repeating it, the essential object of *education* must be to place *sentiments, calculations, transactions* of each one in harmony with social needs.

Popular education has begun to take a new direction in the Mexican Republic. Liberty of the press, decisions by judges in matters of the press, the concurrence of discussions in the legislative chambers and assemblies, electoral councils, and other acts similarly originating in changes made since independence have had a considerable effect on diminishing the old inclinations to bullfights, to processions, to fiestas that were in another time the only spectacles presented to infancy, youth, and old age to distract the spirit of the inhabitants from every kind of serious responsibilities. In the ancient republics, each citizen, summoned to discuss in the public plaza the interests of the community and to take part in the enterprises that these interests made necessary, found himself called to conceive the relationship between his personal actions and the general interest. This situation has changed; our republics are not like Athens, Rome, Florence, and others, limited to the area of the city, and the people today could not be gathered in a public plaza where common interests can be discussed by or in the presence of everyone. But electoral councils, the representative form, the press, and patriotic societies, or orderly meetings of citizens to examine the resolutions of their governments and express peacefully their opinions, have more than adequately replaced those institutions. In England and the United States, the meetings or councils of citizens in public houses appointed for these purposes are ordinarily the organs of public opinion, whose repeated expressions come finally to triumph over the resistance that the interest or egoism of those who govern sometimes puts up.

Criminal legislation has not been reformed as should have been expected since the great changes occurred in the Mexican nation. The people, accustomed to seeing in their judges and courts instruments of tyranny, found the results that the salutary examples of justice should produce on morality almost extinguished. The series of cruel acts committed under judicial forms since the beginning of the revolution has produced an effect entirely the opposite. The Mexican coming before an authority which was not responsible for its actions, that was not subject to any law—and it was not rare to find some who did not even know honor—believed himself surrounded at all times by informers, spies, or agents provocateurs. Not being able to find a sufficient guarantee in the testimony of their consciences, the inhabitants felt obligated to acquire habits of covering up, adulation, and fawning. The punishment was no longer regarded as a consequence of the crime; torture came to be in their eyes like illnesses, a calamity inherent in nature, so the fear of suffering did not keep them from a career of crime. Without burdening myself further with these abuses under the rule of the factions, nor with those atrocious laws destructive of every social guarantee and of all morality which put in the hands of the victors the judgment of the vanquished, and limiting myself to the procedures in judgments of common crimes, penal legislation requires immediate and effective reforms. From the year 1826 I presented in the Senate a draft of a law establishing trial by jurors, and it was approved; but it has met resistance put up by those lawyers who find their elements of existence, their reputation, and their clientele in the defects of the laws.

Criminal jurisprudence is the part of legislation that most directly affects the liberty of the citizen; it is also that which can alter his character. In countries where trials are always public, every criminal trial is a great school of morality for those attending. The man of the people who many times has need of protection against the violent temptations that surround him and that arouse him to commit crimes learns in the debates before jurors and judges that the crime committed in the darkness of night far from any witness, with the precautions that prudence can suggest, comes, nonetheless, through a series of unforeseen circumstances to be discovered; that the perturbed conscience of the guilty one is his first accuser; and that these crimes have provided no enjoyment that seemed to fulfill the desires of their sad executors. The persons in attendance know that the authority who watches over the conservation of the social order is benevolent and active; that it is educated, that it never punishes except after having acknowledged the crime. They unite, they join together sincerely in the decision; and, convinced in this way of the justice and integrity of the judges, they abandon without regret the guilty person to the rigor of the laws.

But what happens among us, where that public openness is not known; where a judge of first instance shapes the process, examines the witnesses; where there is not that oral defense in the first trial; and where everything is done in the secrecy of the office? The people become accustomed to seeing in criminal justice only a persecuting and odious power; all join together to remove the guilty from the action of the laws, and they have secret associations whose purpose is to liberate, as they explain, the poor from the *clutches of justice.* A robbery committed publicly and murder committed in the public plaza do not generally encounter, in the people, that instinct that in free countries leads to seizing the delinquent; and there are many examples in which asylum is sought for them, other than the one churches offer. Witnesses interrogated about a crime committed in their presence believe they should not make the misfortune of the accused worse by telling the truth; the compassion for him is so lively, the distrust in the justice of the judge is so universal, that the courts many times fear clashing with this general feeling and fear defying, so to speak, public compassion with a sentence of death. The name of judge is among those labeled with a mark of infamy. This league against criminal justice is formed in many places of the Republic, and it has its origin in past injustices, in the lack of clarity with which criminals and the unfortunate ones who have belonged to a vanquished faction have been judged, in the secret manner of shaping trials, and in the scandalous delay in sentencing those guilty of the most atrocious crimes. The examples are very frequent of highwaymen and murderers who, held for three or four years in prisons, avoid with flight the delayed punishment that was reserved for them, and it is not rare to see reapprehended once or twice the same criminals who have committed new crimes since their escape. The great number of prisoners in the jails of Mexico City, which few times are under a thousand, is a melancholy proof, although obvious, of this assertion. Happily, many states of the federation are not infected with this epidemic to the same degree; and in some, the purity of customs, scarce contact with the vices of the capital, activity of their commerce with foreigners, and other circumstances have preserved them from the defects inherent in colonial education and the unfortunate influences of its laws. The states of which I speak, like Yucatán, Tamaulipas, Coahuila, Sonora, Sinaloa, and some others, are in the happy condition of shaping their codes as soon as their inhabitants acquire the habits of morality that the new institutions will bring. Mexico City, where all the judicial chicanery has been displayed; where the complexities of the court put up a barrier for many years against the simple action of the laws; and where gold, favor, intrigue, and power were employed by turns or at the same time to obscure justice and raise the rule of force over the ruin of the laws; in Mexico, I say, salutary reforms will come only with greater slowness and after violent clashes between the new generation and the past, between the *old man* and the *new man*.

The moral influence of *civil* legislation is not as powerful as the criminal, but it is more universal and no individual can avoid it. The totality of properties is distributed among citizens in accordance with civil laws. The law of the general congress in 1823 that abolished the entailed states and the laws of colonization that facilitated the distribution of lands are of greatest utility and influence for the progressive advance of national prosperity. But the shackles placed by subsequent provisions for the purpose of impeding the sale of real estate to foreigners will be the source of many issues and an inexhaustible fountain of lawsuits if they are not repealed. Civil legislation in the Mexican Republic finds itself tied up in an infinite number of contradictory conditions and with the innumerable multitude of laws, mandates, rules, decrees, royal ordinances, royal orders, records, and other rules that under different titles emanated from the *Institutes* of Justinian to the documents of Carlos IV. It is sad the picture the litigants present, consumed in the expenses of interminable trials; passing months and years in the sole exercise of moving their cases; running from the office of the lawyer to that of the solicitor, from there to that of the judge; and, moreover, debasing and degrading themselves by dint of repeated acts of submission on one side and contempt on the other. For these reasons the totality of rights seems unknown among the citizens; families inherit interminable trials from generation to generation. I have cited, at the beginning of the first volume, one that has continued more than one hundred years since it began. The more time runs between the beginning of a trial and its resolution, evidence becomes more difficult to obtain, presumption becomes less perceptible, wavers more, and each one, sustaining his interest, believes himself less exposed to the charge of bad faith. On the other hand, the prolongation of trials multiplies them with enormous damage to national unity. In a city where ten trials begin every year, if five end in six months, as happens in Geneva, not more than five are pending at a time. If they last ten years, as very commonly happens in Mexico, a hundred will be pending. At the same time, if they last thirty years, there will be three hundred. How many are those that, unfortunately, have this long duration! See here the reason why it is so common to see almost all families encumbered by some pending lawsuit, and why it is not now considered a stigma being occupied in litigation and continually speaking of lawsuits.

One of the great woes that befell the nation because the new legislators took their lessons in the school of Spanish reformers was being persuaded that the congresses were what the kings had been under absolute government. The abstract principle of national sovereignty was proclaimed; but instead of deriving the legitimate conclusion, by which the people, in delegating their powers to representatives gave only those faculties that were absolutely necessary to organize the new society in a manner *expeditious* to its needs and rights, the legislators appropriated to themselves the fullness of the selfsame sovereignty, and the congresses were considered arbiters of the fate of the Republic. This great error originated from the false idea that the nation transmitted all its faculties and powers to the congresses and from the habit it had of obeying a king who ruled unconditionally. From here have sprung those laws of exception, annulling equality among all classes of citizens; those retroactive laws, like those we have seen regarding sales to foreigners and that of the entailed estates, whose effects were made to go back two years. From this originates also that unfortunate ease with which extraordinary powers are conceded, especially to the governors of various states by their legislative assemblies; those declarations *outside the law* that destroy in their foundations every guarantee; those banishments and another multitude of arbitrary acts that must make the Mexicans wary of a future filled with hopes, although sown with dangers.

Another equally pernicious error has emanated from the same false principle. The general congress, which they rhetorically call *sovereign congress,* has arrogated to itself, or I will say more exactly has usurped the faculty of reforming, the laws of the states and that of interfering in the organization of their legislative assemblies. It has been seen with frequency that one or more deputies or senators who were not fond of the members who made up the legislature of a state, made a motion that elections be declared null, in part or in their totality, by virtue of protests made in the electoral councils; and both chambers have been seen to issue decrees which, interrupting the constitutional course of the states, annul the elections completely or in part. Why has this been tolerated? Because the assemblies of the states have been considered viceroys and the general congress the monarch!—Always the habits of the colonial system!

Mention would not have to be made of the *point of honor* among the great motives of the social compact in referring to the influences that have an effect in the Mexican Republic if this had not been one of the great Spanish prejudices most used to the detriment of the liberty and independence of the *patria*. I do not speak here of that type of honor Mr. Paley defines as "a system made up of rules by the people of rank calculated to facilitate their social commerce, and not for any other purpose." I speak of that honor converted by the Spanish government into one of the supports of its power and instilled so strongly in the highest classes of society, especially among the military. I speak of it also because, having changed government since independence, the education of Mexican politicians must tend to confuse it with public opinion and substitute this basic foundation of the democratic system for an isolated and abstract rule whose principles are as variable as undefined.

The traditional legislation of honor, as it was understood for some time in Europe, had its origin in chivalric times; it came to substitute the noble sentiments of liberty that animated the Greeks and Romans, when the spirit of individual independence was disappearing, to make way for courtly manners, which the monarchs, especially the Spanish kings, knew to put in its place. They converted this prejudice to their benefit, which replaced that inherent fondness of man for defending his rights and the other virtues that elevate the soul and lead it to great actions. But the law of honor readily allied itself with the corruption of manners and came to be, in certain respects, the basis for military despotism. Nonetheless, as it prescribed certain rules to the prince, certain respects among the social classes, a prominent consideration for the beautiful sex, and reciprocal politeness and civility, it was in a certain way, as Montesquieu observes, a brake on arbitrary power. But what a weak brake!

In conquered America, military honor and that of the other classes of society brought with them very few of the brilliant qualities of their native *patria*. Among the first became defending the rights of the kings of Spain, and the greatest glory of an official was to say: The king, *my master; I am servant of the king,* which was equivalent to acknowledging himself as the blind instrument of an unknown deity and the terror of society, the executioner of his fellow citizens. But these influences were profound; they were inherited and they were, moreover, sustained by religious doctrines. Point of *honor* in a military man was to sacrifice his father, his brother, and family if the greater service of the king demanded it; point of *honor* was to obey blindly the orders of the vice generals of the king, no matter how atrocious and cruel they might be. "Your *honor* is jeopardized," said the Spanish leaders to the American officials; "the greater service to His Majesty demands of you that with fire and sword you sustain his rights. The *honor* of the Mexicans must be immaculate." With these and other phrases he made our valiant military men enthusiastic to exterminate an entire generation. Today, the name of *military discipline* is used wrongly to commit the same acts of cruelty. But this is not the occasion to speak of this subject.

I have finished the history that comprehends the period from 1810 to 1830. I believe I have done a great service for the Mexicans, presenting them with events from the point of view from which they must be seen. No principle that can corrupt their customs; no doctrine that can compromise their liberty; no maxim that excuses tyranny; no axiom that does not have as its aim the advantage of the majority; no fact that offends decency; nothing, finally, has occupied a place in this work against the purpose that I have constantly proposed, and it was that of promoting the good of Mexicans, teaching them to know themselves and those who have directed their affairs, to compare them among themselves, to follow them in all their steps and judge them, not by proclamations of circumstance, or by pompous offers, or by appearances of virtue given the lie by facts, or by false modesty, or by a studied popularity, or by a prejudicial and dangerous charlatanism, *but rather by a series of positive acts of patriotism and of constant efforts for social improvement, enlightenment of the people, and propagation of enjoyment in the masses.* Anything that does not have these points as its aim is to deceive the people and want them to be content with words. Little has independence served the great part of the nation, because those who succeeded in commands and positions have believed that this was the good to which it aspired. But they were wrong. The people want *positive goods* and the *nourishment of the spirit.* Their instinct will always lead them to the attainment of this aim, and it will break the obstacles that egoism and interest put up against their progress.

3

Intervention Regarding the Independence of the Province of Guatemala

Mr. Zavala: Sir, the commission to draw up this judgment has found itself in major conflict because it dealt with a new question of public law, because it saw the gentlemen deputies of Guatemala divided, and because the resolution of this matter is of great importance.[1] It was not about a nation that was going, like Spanish America, to throw off the yoke for the first time after three hundred years of oppression; nor was it about American colonies established by commercial companies formed in different ways, which had carried on a terrible war. It is about a province or provinces that were joined to Mexico, we do not know whether by force of arms employed by General Iturbide or voluntarily. When this question was presented last year in Congress, the majority of the gentlemen deputies expressed a desire that the provinces of Guatemala establish a separate government, and many of the gentlemen who expressed this opinion now have changed from it, perhaps because the government changed; but I do not believe it is honorable for Congress to change its principles. The commission, I repeat, has found itself in the greatest difficulty because it had to deliberate about a matter of such importance. I will begin by replying to some objections that

Original title: "Sesión del día 18 de octubre de 1823. Intervención de Zavala sobre la independencia de Guatemala." Source: *Águila Mexicana,* vol. 2, nos. 189 and 190, Monday, October 20; and Tuesday, October 21, 1823.

1. The Capitanía de Guatemala (then encompassing the present republics of Honduras, Nicaragua, El Salvador, and Costa Rica) declared its independence from Spain on September 15, 1821, a day before Agustín de Iturbide issued the declaration of independence in Mexico. In January 1822 Guatemala voted to become part of the Mexican empire of Iturbide. However, when the emperor was toppled, in 1823, Guatemala peacefully decided to separate from Mexico and form a federal republic of its own: the Provincias Unidas de Centro América. The issue of separation was debated in the Mexican Congress, and Zavala, as a member of the congressional commission overseeing this issue, took an active part in that process. (Editor's note)

the gentleman minister has raised, and then I will pass to the gentlemen Terán and López Plata. The first bases what he says on the fact that the commission should not have begun judgment because it could have left this question for the coming Congress, this one being just about to close its sessions. The second reason, which has seemed stronger, is that if Congress declares that the province of Guatemala has a right to constitute itself into a free province, the government of Mexico forsakes those individuals who have shown themselves devoted to the union. Neither the one nor the other seems to me to have force. Not the first because this Congress, having expressed and even declared that the provinces of Guatemala had the right to constitute themselves, it was necessary that, having named a commission for this and presented its judgment, this matter is resolved; but if the reasons your honor has given regarding the effects on the government of Mexico have some force, Spain could say the same to America. Spain had many devoted people, and even has them still, and that was the pretext they gave for not absolutely abandoning America, because they said: We have there a large number of partisans that the new government will persecute everywhere. Vain subterfuge against the justice of our cause, but much less with respect to Guatemala because it has never belonged to the Mexican nation, and the right that Mexico has believed itself to have over Guatemala has been completely ephemeral and doubtful, as shown by the conduct of Congress and the government, which have given orders appropriate for the assembly of the Congress of Guatemala; and the government has ordered General Filisola to withdraw. So, then, what does the commission have to do? It could simply say: "The deputies who are here can withdraw."

Thus we have seen monstrously in the heart of this sovereign congress an individual who has the title of agent and deputy of Guatemala, something not found in any of the representative bodies. Consequently, the commission has believed it was the only road offered. Neither did it say that the independence of Guatemala be declared; it has said only that the deputies could withdraw and, once the Congress of that nation is convened, it could declare whether it was to unite with Mexico or not. The question that the previous gentleman speaker has proposed with respect to the difficulties Guatemala has in organizing its government has no force. For all new governments always experience these upheavals and suffer these difficulties. If these arguments were valid, Spain would have justice in claiming a right to intervene in our affairs, with the excuse that we are not succeeding in constituting ourselves. Buenos Aires has had twelve years to constitute itself and has not managed to do so. Why is this? Because revolution brings its difficulties. These are, sir, the reasons that the commission has had in saying that the deputies of Guatemala can withdraw. I go on to respond to Mr. López de la Plata. His honor asks what reason the commission had for including the province of Nicaragua in the judgment it has offered; I will say to his honor that the commission has included the province of Nicaragua because there is no other way of determining the will of peoples except through their representatives. The people of Nicaragua have already joined in the Congress of Guatemala, electors have been gathered, etc., and they have sent their deputies. Well, sir, if the Congress of Mexico itself, if all are of the view that this Congress represents those provinces, how can we have nothing to do with that representation? This is the reason why we have included the province of Nicaragua which has sent its deputies to the Congress of Guatemala. Now, his honor has said that the opinion of the deputies of his province in the Congress is different from the majority. But then the same can happen in Mexico and the rest of the congresses. Who knows what public opinion would be in this case; but what is certain is that the votes of the majority must always be followed. The commission could not do less than work for the same principles it has expounded, the same that have led Congress since last year. I agree, sir, that in the heart of this sovereign congress they were crying out strongly against the troops that were about to attack San Salvador; well, sir, why do we not respect the rights that were respected then? What right was there in Guatemala before to constitute a government and not now? I believe the same. Now it seems to me that the objections of the previous speakers are properly answered.

VALENTÍN GÓMEZ FARÍAS

Valentín Gómez Farías (1781–1858) was a liberal politician born in the city of Guadalajara. He studied medicine and became a prominent doctor in the city of Aguascalientes, where he started his political career. Gómez Farías supported Agustín de Iturbide after independence and was elected deputy to the First Constituent Congress in 1822. He soon became disaffected with the government, and after the regime fell supported the convocation to elect a new constituent congress under new rules.

Gómez Farías was a reformist and a federalist with radical ideas concerning education and the role of the Catholic Church. He was elected vice president in 1833, when General Antonio López de Santa Anna was elected president. Santa Anna soon requested a leave of absence from office and retired to his hacienda in Veracruz, leaving his vice president as head of the government. Gómez Farías launched several political reforms that were fiercely opposed by his political foes, such as closing the church-run university. He also challenged the privileges of the army. Later that year, Santa Anna, at the instigation of those who opposed Gómez Farías's liberal reforms, returned to office and terminated the brief reformist experiment. Gómez Farías was once again vice president, in 1846, and was elected deputy to the 1856–57 constituent congress, which drafted the 1857 Constitution.

We present an individual vote of deputy Gómez Farías regarding the need to summon a new constituent congress.

Individual Vote of Mr. Gómez Farías on the Issue of the Advisability of Convening a New Congress

Individual Vote of Mr. Gómez Farías,
As an individual of the special committee appointed by the Sovereign Congress to examine the question of whether or not a new Congress should be convened.

Sir:

The second day of this month, Mr. Muzquiz and I presented to Your Sovereignty[1] a motion reduced to these terms: We request that a notice of convocation be created for the meeting of another Congress, this Congress named before dissolving a permanent deputation, which, in agreement with the supreme executive power, would temporarily decide the urgent needs of the state.

This motion, heard by Your Sovereignty and declared urgent, was ordered passed to a committee of which I have the honor to be a member. In the first session we had, five deputies of the seven that make up the aforementioned committee were of the opinion that the notice of convocation should be prepared. Nevertheless, to proceed with greater success in so serious a matter and one of such importance, we agreed to summon the committee members who were in this capital and had been convened from [the city of] Puebla by a written communication dated last March 4, which the gentlemen the marquis of Vivanco, Don Pedro Celestino Negrete, and Don José Antonio de Echávarri directed to all

Original title: "Voto particular del Señor Valentín Gómez Farías, como individuo de la comisión especial nombrada por el soberano Congreso para examinar la cuestión de si se debe ó no convocar un nuevo Congreso," April 17, 1823. Source: Mexico, Imprenta Nacional (en Palacio), 1823.

1. Mexicans called their Congress "Sovereign Congress" as a consequence of the theory of legislative supremacy they adopted from the French and Spanish constitutions. (Editor's note)

the provincial deputations.[2] By virtue of this summons, those delegates from six provinces gathered, and everyone unanimously requested, in the name of those provinces, that the notice of convocation be created for the meeting of another Congress; others have subsequently said the same. I, on hearing that the provinces might wish that a new Congress be convened, hoped that the committee would stand more firmly in its opinion; it has not happened that way, and I attribute this fact to the arguments Mr. Tagle and Mr. Bustamante set out afterward in other sessions we had on the same matter. The brilliant learning of these gentlemen is much superior to mine; I respect it, but as I am not convinced of their arguments, I proceed to explain my individual opinion.

Everyone knows, sir, that the notice of convocation created by the provisionally governing junta was received in the provinces with displeasure and that it was generally considered, moreover, absurd. In effect, it restricted liberty, offended equality, and, consequently, was unjust. It restricted liberty, dividing the nation into classes and requiring the electors to get their representatives from each one of them.[3] It offended equality, adjusting the number of deputies by the number of municipalities [*partidos*], outlandish thought, which resulted in the province of Durango, which has, according to the last census, 177,400 inhabitants, being able to name twenty-two deputies, and Querétaro, which has almost the same population, being able to choose only one, monstrous inequality, which gave the first an unjust preponderance over the second, and which encumbered Durango with an enormous burden of taxes.

Nor was this the only attack that equality, so proclaimed among free and well-governed peoples, suffered. This political dogma also was destroyed by granting a vote to town councils because, by virtue of this concession, the parishes of the head municipalities, and the most important municipalities of the provinces, had as many electors as there were members of their municipal councils, and the subordinate parishes and

2. The provincial deputations (*diputaciones provinciales*) were local, representative bodies created by the 1812 Spanish Constitution. (Editor's note)

3. Gómez Farías was referring to the convocation of a constituent congress issued after independence by the Junta Provisional Gubernativa, presided over by Agustín de Iturbide in 1821. Representation by classes was provided in that *convocatoria*. (Editor's note)

municipalities did not have more than one. The unhappiness that the notice of convocation caused for the two reasons indicated was general, and it has been believed since then that it would be the source of complaints and dissensions.

With the national representation established on such unjust foundations, it could not unite the opinion of the people in its favor. The past government, which knew the defects of the notice of convocation and was perhaps their author, converted them into trouble for the Congress, whose destruction it meditated. Caustic writings promoted by the past government made the provinces' bad frame of mind worse; discontent increased everywhere, and as the people came to know of some misconduct of their deputies, lack of confidence grew. Opinion against the Congress prepared, the tyrant dissolved it.[4] This act was generally considered despotic; nonetheless, the people did not think of summoning their disbanded representation. They thought instead of taking advantage of the circumstances to improve it. So it cannot be certain that they were upset by this fact. I am sorry to say it, I am a member of this august assembly, justly interested in its honor.

Let us cast a rapid glance over the events that have occurred since that epoch.[5] On the second of December the city of Veracruz gave the memorable cry of liberty, proclaimed the Republic and the reestablishment of the Congress. The besieging army, no less zealous for glory and for the liberty of the *patria*, decided against the oppressor, but in the act of its military uprising, nothing was said about the reinstatement of the extinct Congress. On the contrary, the assembling of another new one was expressly requested. Its articles are clear, conclusive, and do not admit interpretation. Veracruz itself supported this act, and, after Veracruz, all the provinces. The nation, then, has decided for a new Congress, or has not adopted the Plan of Casa Mata. Some say the nation adopted the Plan of Casa Mata in the same way as the Plan of Iguala.[6] This is not

4. Emperor Iturbide. (Editor's note)

5. In December 1822 General Antonio López de Santa Anna rebelled against the government of Agustín de Iturbide in the city of Veracruz. General Echávarri, charged by the government with suppressing the rebellion, placed the city under siege but later changed sides, joining Santa Anna, and proclaimed the Plan of Casamata against Iturbide's empire on February 1, 1823. (Editor's note)

6. The Plan of Iguala, proclaimed in February 1822 by Iturbide, declared the inde-

because it requested a notice of convocation, but rather because it was a means to liberate itself from its new oppressor, focusing opinion. To these gentlemen I ask whether the Mexican nation, which desired to govern itself and made very costly sacrifices to achieve its emancipation, has given positive evidence after the cry of liberty that it wants the same Congress, as it expressed at another time in order to throw the Spanish yoke from its neck. Almost all the evidence demonstrates the contrary. Nonetheless, if it has given this evidence, let it be presented and the dispute come to an end; but if there is not proof, the Plan of Casa Mata, the rest of the acts, and other official documents are in force, whose content is supported by the printed pieces that are circulating and by the public voice. In light of these considerations, I do not understand on what basis one can be assured that the will of the nation has not been delivered in favor of the notice of convocation.

The army is not the nation, nor are the provincial juntas. A faction of aristocrats has taken possession of the towns and wishes to convince everyone that its voice is the general one; so I hear some explain it. Sir, the voice of the army is certainly not that of the nation; but will it be possible to say that the voice of the provincial capitals, the voice of the municipalities, and the voice of the subordinate towns are not the voice of the nation? In all these places, the bodies uniformly repeated the voice of the army, those bodies that were elected popularly, that are the depositories of public confidence. In all of them, the persons of greatest influence and opinion, and a part of the rest of the people openly joined its votes to theirs, without the other part of the rest of the people giving any evidence of resistance to its adherence. Moreover, sir, if the rapidity with which America separated itself from the [Iberian] Peninsula was owed in part to the desire everyone had to emancipate themselves, could not the marvelous speed and uniformity with which the act of Casa Mata was proclaimed be attributed to the fact that its articles conformed to the general will?

If what was expounded is not sufficient to know the expression of the people, tell me in what way should they have been explained, given their situation? What better means than the press? What organs more

---

pendence of Mexico. The country would remain a monarchy, and the throne was offered to Ferdinand VII or some other member of the royal family. The Spanish Constitution would remain in force until a new one was drafted. (Editor's note)

approximate to those of a representative system than town councils and deputations? Not for this reason have the latter already been raised up to the status of provincial congresses; they will take this step because, if I am not deceived, the progress of the Americas is inevitable. They, as Mr. de Pradt says, will be constituted into republics before a Europe divided into thrones. Just as the United States, that admirable model of government, that people who owe their prosperity and growth to their sublime institutions, has been a beacon for our brothers of the other America, it will also be so for us. In vain will forces develop to hold this event back for very long. From constitutional monarchy to the American government there is a distance easily traversed. What a beautiful perspective is offered to the imagination by an immense territory divided by nature itself into large parts, each one governed according to its interests without the others feeling oppressed, by men who know its needs and who merit its confidence, retaining separately its sovereignty, liberty, and independence, and all parts entering into a firm bond of reciprocal friendship for their common defense, the security of their liberty, and their mutual and general happiness. In an alliance of this nature society is not in danger, but rather the deep-rooted habit of dominating is! The provincialism of which one accuses Querétaro, Guanajuato, San Luis Potosí, Zacatecas, Guadalajara, Valladolid, etc., carefully analyzed, is, in the end, the very just desire to avoid such domination. Sometimes some province resents this aspiration. Maybe the aristocratic faction is in another part.

Considering the question in another way, I will ask, with Congress dissolved and the nation tied to the cart of absolute power, could the army and the people, without seeing the need to reestablish the extinguished national representation, create a courageous force to break the bonds of servitude, or could they not? If the first, why does one think they are obligated to recognize the dissolved Congress, having proclaimed the Plan of Casa Mata? Why will this sovereign nation and master of itself be considered bound to obey a body that it desires to replace with another? If the second, what greater despotism than supposing this same nation, facing the difficult choice of suffering the yoke of tyranny or of delivering itself to leaders whom they fear, will not honorably discharge their august functions? Is there no halfway for Mexicans between being slaves for Iturbide and restoring their representatives?

Sir, political bodies are like physical bodies. All of them die, not to

come back to life, and just as physical bodies, once dissolved or disorganized, do not return to life if not by a miracle of omnipotence, so
political bodies do not recover their political existence if not through
the power of public opinion. Do all deputies enjoy this public opinion?
Certainly not; for this reason, the provinces request at least exclusion[7]
or reform, a measure subject to very serious difficulties, which would
increase the inequality of representation in those provinces where some
deputies are excluded, or where it could make those provinces proceed
to new elections, a hateful measure that would not be sufficient to calm
the discontent resulting from the enormous inequality of representation and that would increase discontent in the situation if all the persons
charged were not to be excluded; a measure, finally, in which the judgment of Congress would be considered interested or partial. The best
way, then, of making the reform is through the notice of convocation;
this measure is the most discreet and decent that can be adopted. Draw
a veil over the misconduct of some men; it is not advisable to disturb the
pure pleasure that the enjoyment of liberty produces with the unpleas-
ant memory of offenses and evils. The triumph of reason and enlightenment should be marked with liberality of principles and moderation of
actions.

From motives like those I just explained and for other reasons deduced from the fundamentals of society, the provisional junta of Madrid
refrained from reinstating the Cortes of 1814. With the decree by Ferdinand VII issued, which called for the representative body of the nation
to gather, everyone knows that the junta itself proposed the following
doubt, to wit: Should the Cortes that were gathered in 1814 be summoned, or will it be necessary to go on to new elections? The junta decided for the latter, and its resolution was well received everywhere.
I will relate the passage because it is very analogous to the matter in
question.

The king of Spain dissolved the Cortes before they had concluded
their term of legislature; Iturbide destroyed the Mexican Congress before it completed its duties. The army demanded in the Peninsula the
constitutional regime; our troops here gave the cry that a congress
should be brought together that would constitute the nation. There, a
junta created during the last difficulties of the despotism produced the

7. Of some deputies. (Editor's note)

notice of convocation by order of the king; here, another junta, summoned by the generals of the liberating army and composed of persons of more popular representation, was destined to the same purpose. The former discharged its duty; the latter did not, because the very one [Iturbide] who dissolved the Congress ordered it reinstated. This measure hindered that of the generals; but leaving aside the history of this event, I will transcribe the arguments of public law on which the junta of Madrid determined not to reestablish the Cortes of 1814.

All men (say the members of that junta in their manifesto) who have studied the foundations of society know that the representative system is nothing other than a way to concentrate, in a certain number of individuals elected by the entire people, the right to vote the laws, which undeniably resides in each citizen, given the impossibility that all members of a large state be present in one place to make use of that right; so the ancient republics did not know this system, because the citizens, who resided in a single city, could come together and be present themselves at the assemblies. If this were feasible in the most perfect mechanism of modern nations, in which the parts, united with common laws and rights, form a large body equal and reciprocal in everything, it would doubtless be the one that the Spaniards have of assembling on the present occasion; but carrying this out not being possible, and delegating their powers to their representatives being inevitable, it is also evident that their will must be consulted and they must be allowed the exercise, which no one has the power of refusing them, of electing persons worthy of their confidence, whether they be those the system named before, or whether it be others because of their talent, their virtues, or the proofs that in six years of testing they have given of their unswerving character and their adherence to the constitutional system. And when, if not now, should the Spanish people make use of this precious right? Will we deprive them of exercising it at the moment in which the questions that most concern their future happiness are going to be aired? In the moment in which their representatives have to complete the political generation of the state? In this moment that perhaps they will not see return again for centuries, in which the eternal foundations of their greatness and their glory will be laid down, in which are fixed, perhaps forever, the destinies of entire generations?

Thus those learned Spaniards explained that they now had a constitution and they demanded nothing more than its observance. And we who are lacking a constitution, we who find ourselves in the situation of adopting the form of government that most suits the nation in its new political aspect, will we not be able to explain ourselves in the same way and with greater reason? Let us be fair, sir, and because we are free of the obligations under which the Plan of Iguala and the Treaty of Córdova placed us,[8] let us allow the nation to explain its will openly. Let us not ignore its desires; let us listen to its opinions. The provisional junta that preceded us certainly had no power to order the deputies to constitute the nation into a constitutional monarchy; nonetheless the peoples, although insulted by this limitation, obeyed it and named as representatives those whom they believed were capable of establishing with greater success the form of government that was prescribed to them. If, as it should have been, the convocation notice had been comprehensive, do I really believe that many elections would have devolved on other individuals? Would the people, fond of another form of government, have chosen as their deputies staunch monarchists? Consistent with the nature of the work, artifice is sought. Let us allow, then, sir, the nation to make use of a right that cannot be disputed, which is that of freely electing its representatives. The newly elected deputies will bring other powers and instructions that serve them as a guide in the very serious matters being prepared for deliberation and that we could not resolve without greatly risking going against the will of our constituents.

It is said that the nature of our mission demands absolute powers; this assertion is, at the least, very doubtful. Allow me to quote literally on this point the well-known Martinez Marina.

No one doubts (says this author) that it is an actual evil, although necessary in the representative system and a very costly sacrifice,

---

8. The Treaties of Córdova, signed by the Spanish viceroy, Juan de O'Donojú, and Agustín de Iturbide on August 24, 1821, recognized the independence of Mexico. (Editor's note)

that the citizens are obligated to entrust the authority to vote and enact relative to their most precious interests to a small number of individuals and be deprived of a right that nature itself has granted to each individual in society. As far as possible, by means of wise institutions, a good constitution should prevent those difficulties, at least the most dangerous ones: to reconcile the contradictions from which political philosophy is sown, and to organize the national representation in such a way that it does not harm the liberty of citizens, and not to demand more sacrifices of them than those that the essential order of society and the supreme law of the state, which is public utility, prescribes.

The citizens, then, obligated for reasons of common utility to sacrifice a part of their liberty and their rights for the benefit of the state, must freely elect representatives who carry their voice in the national Congress, commit themselves to them, and confer on them ample powers to deliberate in the Cortes and to decide in them whatever they judge suitable for the general good and particularly the good of the provinces they represent; I say ample powers, but not unlimited, absolute, and irrevocable. To demand of people that they grant letters of proxy with these exorbitant circumstances and characteristics is to deprive them of liberty, it is to dispossess them of an act of which they are the absolute owners, it is to upset the essential order of things. What use is the part of sovereignty that is their responsibility and the right to participate in the formation of the laws to the people if, after electing deputies, there is no other act for them than obeying? Is it believable that they would consent to extending the powers in such a way, if their will were examined? Who will be persuaded that citizens, knowledgeable about the extent and worth of their rights, would consent and want to transfer every act irrevocably to a deputy or agent, constitute him owner and absolute arbiter of their fortune and their fate and their most precious interests, and deliver blindly to his will the destinies of the man and the state? Has anyone ever seen that some great property owner, businessman, or merchant has granted to his agents or deputies absolute and irrevocable powers to execute in their name whatever he might want, without asking them to share at least the state of their interests and the course of the business and that they con-sult them on doubts, on difficult matters, and matters of great importance?

I acknowledge that, once the citizens can elect deputies to the Cortes to their satisfaction and freely, the election and appointment done with appropriate good judgment and prudence, it is just and proper to trust them and rely on the credence of their patriotism and talents. Nonetheless, there is no doubt that it would be very risky and hazardous and highly dangerous for a people to surrender without any reserve or precaution at all to a proxy or deputy, whatever might be his standing and reputation, granting him absolute authority to do whatever he might like regarding matters of the greatest interest, and obligating themselves at the same time to obey blindly and fulfill without objection what their agent might execute and order. A people that appreciates its liberty and its rights must make use of prudent management in granting powers, especially because it just fortunately threw off the yoke of despotism, to show a certain caution and distrust and take certain measures so that ignorance or malice, intrigue or the spirit of faction can never decide the fate of men.

The deputies from the provinces authorized with absolute powers, as soon as they are gathered in the Cortes, can work and proceed with total independence from the citizens, establish laws without their consent and approval, and decide with sovereign authority the interests of the citizen and the state. And how many times will it happen that the deputies, abusing the confidence of their principals, will vote against their opinions and rights? And would this not be a more horrifying despotism than that of our old government? I will say nothing of the intrigues and negotiations of the interested and ambitious ones to surprise and attract the unwary to their opinion. Nothing of the justified fear that parties bought by powerful agents of the executive power might develop. Nothing of the danger, as fatal as inevitable, that a total vote on matters of the greatest consequence might be lost by a small number of deputies, either ignorant of or unfaithful to their ministry, or won over by the government. Nothing, finally, of the ease with which the contaminated air of the assembly can corrupt the virtue of the deputies if some preventative against this pestilence is not used. Will society not be able to apply a prompt remedy and take precautionary measures to avoid some ills that naturally conflict with national liberty and aim at the destruction and dissolution of the state?

It is a very much repeated thought that the deputies are representatives of the whole nation, not proxies or agents of specific provinces. Is this a truth? In order to respond, it seems to me that a constituted nation must be distinguished from one that is not. A constituted nation has already established, by means of its deputies, the rules of the social pact with which the constituent parts have been bound, rules that include everyone equally and that are directed to their mutual and common happiness; in this constituted nation, the deputies represent everyone and proportionately each one of the contracting parties. In the nonconstituted nation they represent only the provinces that send them and elected them from their midst, or outside of it on condition always that they be natives or residents for some time in the province so they know their interests, have greater fondness for them, and, consequently, defend them and promote them with greater efficacy and success. This is the situation in which we find ourselves; we are at absolute liberty to constitute ourselves but we have not yet settled the foundations of our union.

I will finish, sir, my opinion, saying to Your Sovereignty that, because the notice of convocation was so faulty, because the nation has altered its political situation, and because the provinces have declared themselves in favor of a new Congress, without regretting having suffered privations, sarcasms, and other misfortunes for having defended liberty and the imprescriptible rights of men, let us resolve immediately to vacate the seats of this sanctuary of the laws and return to our houses and our fates, ready always to serve the *patria* when it summons us. If Your Sovereignty adopts this measure, it will give greater proof of personal disinterest, obedience, and respect for the sovereign people; it will silence the critics and leave the discontented ones expectant; on the contrary, if you resolve to continue, the anger that has been manifested will increase, and that war that is feared if you do not continue will perhaps take place if you do not dissolve. Sir, let us not give occasion to what some bold spirits might say: *that Congress is occupied in constituting us and should not do so; if it had limited itself to working on what was necessary, on what the order of society and its conservation require, while another congress comes together, which, with broader powers and instructions creates the great charter of our pact, then it would merit our gratitude, but stepping over those boundaries, as we see, this very Congress forces us to disobey it.* In this case, our situation would become worse, because the sources of public wealth are obstructed, the course of affairs paralyzed, confidence is lacking, everything is lifeless, and this sad picture that, in my opinion, cannot be enlivened with the continuation of this Congress, would turn out more gloomy if you continue your sessions. So I fear it, and for this very reason I insist on the motion that Mr. Muzquiz and I present to Your Sovereignty.

Mexico, April 17, 1823

LUCAS ALAMÁN

Lucas Alamán (1792–1853), born in the state of Guanajuato, was a leading politician and a historian during the first half of the nineteenth century. His best-known work is his five-volume *Historia de Méjico* (1849–52), published toward the end of his life. Until the 1840s Alamán shared with Mora and other liberals many of their ideas. Alamán was a deputy to the Cádiz Cortes before independence in 1821. During his life he served three times as minister in the cabinet. Alamán was minister of internal and external relations in the administration of General Anastasio Bustamante (1830–32). During his tenure in office he endeavored to check the military revolts in the country. A military coup staged by Santa Anna deposed Bustamante, however, and Alamán and other members of the government were charged with various crimes by the new government. Falsely accused of hiring the murderer of former independence hero Vicente Guerrero, Alamán went into hiding to avoid arrest.

While he remained underground he wrote a legal brief as his defense as well as an essay, a critical examination of the Bustamante administration, which we present here. In this text Alamán discusses the institutional flaws of the 1824 charter. After the 1847 Mexican-American War of Independence Alamán became more reactionary, and in 1849 he founded the Conservative party.

Impartial Examination of the Administration of General Vice President Don Anastasio Bustamante

I have little to recommend my opinions but long observation and much impartiality. They come from one who has been no tool of power, no flatterer of greatness; and who in his last acts does not wish to belie the tenor of his life. They come from one almost the whole of whose public exertion has been a struggle for the liberty of others; from one in whose breast no anger, durable or vehement, has ever been kindled by what he considers as tyranny; they come from one who desires honors, distinctions, and emoluments but little, and who expects them not at all; who has no contempt for fame, and no fear of obloquy; who shuns contention, though he will hazard an opinion; from one who wishes to preserve consistency, but who would preserve consistency by varying his means to secure the unity of his end, and, when the equipoise of the vessel in which he sails may be endangered by overloading upon one side, is desirous of carrying the small weight of his reasons to that which may preserve its equipoise.
— Edmund Burke, *Reflections on the French Revolution*

If, in all things, past experience is the surest guide for what is to come, in political matters it is almost the only rule that can be adopted with confidence, because the science of government, being a practical science by its nature and destined for practical ends accord-

Original title: "Examen imparcial de la administración de General Vicepresidente D. Anastasio Bustamante, con observaciones generales sobre el estado presente de la República y consecuencias que éste debe producir." Source: Lucas Alamán, *Documentos diversos (inéditos y muy raros)*, vol. 3, comp. Rafael Aguayo Spencer (Mexico: Jus, 1946), pp. 235–75.

ing to one of the primary experts in public law in our era,[1] cannot be learned a priori, being not only a subject that requires experience, but even more experience than a person can acquire in the entire course of his life; for this, the profound study of history will always be indispensable, not only for those who take upon themselves the difficult business of governing people, but for the people themselves who, in the lessons history teaches them, learn to recognize what suits them and what harms them and to judge with impartiality those who have directed them. This study is even more beneficial when it devolves upon events closest to us and that interest us more from being close by, whether because they are about our own country and our days, or because they belong to peoples and nations that have greater similarity to our present circumstances. From all these points of view, an impartial examination of an administration that has existed in the Republic for two and one-half years must seem very important; an administration that gave luster and splendor to the nation, rendering it esteemed and respected in foreign countries; that affirmed and increased its credit in those countries; that mended internal finances in a way that had not been seen since independence; that developed industry and created hope for a lasting prosperity, which nonetheless disappeared with the very administration that produced it, like those luminous meteors that shine in the obscurity of night for a few moments and then return to the same darkness from which they emerged. This administration, atrociously calumnied and cruelly persecuted by its adversaries, has been defended many times with anger and sometimes with skill by various writers, but never has it been judged with the calm of reason and the impartial seriousness of justice, considering the totality of all its operations and the basic foundations of its conduct. Neither could this impartial judgment truly develop in the midst of the fervor of the passions and the tumultuous cry of persecution, nor for this reason have I previously undertaken the writing of this paper, waiting to enter into this examination not that of the revolutionary spirit, which unfortunately has put down such profound roots among us, might have been calmed, but rather that it might have changed course, which happens with sufficient frequency, for, similar to the vapid rich of Rome, who, as Horace describes with such elegance

1. Burke.

(*diruit aedificat; repetit quod imper omisit*), today destroys the edifice that it raised up yesterday and tomorrow praises publicly the same individual who, a short time before, was the object of a terrible persecution. Now that it is already clear that the administration of General Bustamante has been only the pretext and not the cause of the revolution, that the men who prepared it have for the most part been forgotten, his conduct can be judged with neither hatred nor love, completely setting aside his people in the examination we are going to make of his political administration, in order to keep in view only his actions and to determine from these what the principles have been that drove them, to what point these can be justified, what the consequence of the success, of the error, of the circumstances, or of the crime might be.[2]

To judge impartially the conduct not only of a government but also of an individual, whether he be in the sphere of a public committee or in the more limited sphere of a private post, it is necessary to focus on these essential points: what was the nature of the assignment entrusted to him, in what circumstances, what means were given him to carry it out, and, given these, to what point did he learn to make use of them to fulfill the objectives of his committee. Without giving its true weight to each one of these points, any judgment that might be formed would be precipitate or arbitrary, and therefore I will be excused for entering at some length into the examination of each of them, combining them at times when their contact might be so intimate that it might not be possible to deal with them separately without confusion.

The Republic, after a series of almost uninterrupted disturbances since the year 1826, found itself weary of this continuous motion in which the factions had kept it: its forces had been drained, its treasury was not only exhausted but also overloaded with obligations, its foreign credit destroyed, and commerce and industry weakened, inevitable outcomes as much from these very disturbances as from the legislative mea-

---

2. On December 4, 1829, the reserve army of the city of Jalapa, commanded by the vice president, General Anastasio Bustamante, revolted against the government of Vicente Guerrero. In a little less than a month, Bustamante ousted Guerrero and seized power. Lucas Alamán was then appointed minister of internal and external relations in the new administration. The role played by Alamán was so central in the government that people came to call it the "Alamán administration." (Editor's note)

sures the general Congress felt compelled to dictate because of them. Of the old parties that had divided the Republic, the one had remained entirely disorganized and destroyed by the events of Tulancingo,[3] the other had been internally divided on the occasion of the election of the president; one part of it, united to the remnants of the crushed party, had formed a new party that, supported by a very pronounced but inactive general opinion and because of the very effective strength of the army, gathered in Jalapa, produced a revolution that was generally desired; the other part of that same party, tarnished by the blemish of the triumph that it obtained in the Acordada,[4] found itself detested in public opinion and judgment but had in its support the Chamber of Deputies, composed largely of individuals from that party and various congresses of the states. Others of these congresses and the Senate were loyal to the plan promulgated in Jalapa and very quickly generalized to the entire Republic. The general discontent had begun to show itself before the proclamation of this plan, and, seeking the remedy for public woes in an essential change in the Constitution, some individuals in Jalisco had proclaimed the centralized form of government; in Yucatán a more important movement had taken place with the same objective.

Such was the state of things when General Bustamante took the reins of government in his hands on January 1, 1830; a few days later he named his cabinet, and the appointments were generally well received. Public confidence was reestablished almost immediately just with the reputation of the individuals who made up the new administration, and for the nation a new epoch of prosperity seemed to begin from that moment.

As the revolution had not changed the Constitution and established

3. The "old parties" were the Scottish (considered aristocratic) and the Yorkist (considered more popular), both with origins in the Masonic lodges. On January 6, 1828, the leader of the Scottish party, General Nicolás Bravo, who rebelled against the government of President Guadalupe Victoria, was defeated in the town of Tulancingo by troops loyal to the government commanded by the Yorkist Vicente Guerrero. (Editor's note)

4. The Scottish candidate, Manuel Gómez Pedraza, won the 1828 presidential elections and defeated the Yorkist candidate, Vicente Guerrero, whose supporters refused to acknowledge the results and revolted in several cities. In Mexico City a pro-Guerrero mob stormed the Acordada prison, a colonial building. The popular riots forced Gómez Pedraza to flee the country, and Guerrero became president. (Editor's note)

laws in any way, the observance of and compliance with the one and the others had to be the objective of the new government, and the means it had to fulfill their duties were solely those that this Constitution and these laws in current force provided. The desire and most urgent necessity of the nation was the preservation of peace, and any fundamental innovation whatsoever could produce nothing other than new and more disastrous convulsions; therefore duty, suitability, and public opinion equally compelled the government to submit to conserving and consolidating what existed.

If it has been possible to state briefly what the objective was of the office entrusted to the new administration and to present at a glance what the state of the nation was in the epoch of its installation, it is not equally possible to explain briefly the means that were placed in its hands for this, because those involve very extensive considerations on the exercise of constitutional powers and require a more specific examination of the moral, political, and physical state in which the Republic found itself than what is presented by the picture that I have only outlined with a few light strokes. If the length that might be necessary to give to these considerations seems excessive, thinking men capable of understanding fully the importance of this subject matter will readily pardon what will seem prolix to the less reflective person, and in order not to depend solely on my own opinion, I will be permitted also to support myself with the opinion of the man who has been able to comprehend better the tendency and outcomes of political movements in our era. This man, Edmund Burke, in his profound reflections on the revolution in France, has announced, with a spirit that might be called prophetic, the entire series of events that we have seen in our country and in foreign countries, and, as his observations are so relevant to our circumstances, what I take from his brilliant pen will enrich and support this paper.

The entire force of government, all the means that are in its hands to conserve public order, suppress and contain unsettled and seditious persons, prevent the misappropriation of national wealth, and, in short, carry out the necessary functions of an authority that must be active, vigilant, and foresightful are derived from the division of powers that the Constitution established and from the powers that in this division are settled on the executive. The model that was in mind for the writing of our federal Constitution was the Constitution of the United States of the North, but it is a mistake to believe that the executive of our Republic is constituted in the same way as that of the United States, and another still greater mistake to think that that Constitution, even were it copied exactly, would produce the same results operating over dissimilar elements.

The United States of the North were independently formed in the beginning because of the different migrations of English colonists who, for different reasons—some political, some religious—felt they had to abandon their country and settled on the coasts of America, giving to each colony a particular constitution, modeled generally on the principles adopted in England. These colonies not only did not mix and blend with the natives of the country, but rather they expelled them from their settlements to the point of wiping them out. They all depended on the English government, and the authority constituted by it was the bond that united them to each other and to the metropolis. When independence came to break this bond, all the legislators had to do was substitute a national union for this common bond of foreign rule, and this is what was done with the federal Constitution. This did not alter in any way the particular existence of the states, it did not change their individual constitutions, and these constitutions to which the English colonists were habituated from their *patria* were, rather than written codes, the habitual customs, the ordinary way of life of all individuals; and as they were derived from that of England, they had established on the experience of England the division and balance of powers with neither shock nor collision among them. Independence, then, did not change anything in that Republic except a nonessential property, but it left existing everything that constituted the essence of the original constitution. From this it follows that, since the era of its independence, the United States have moved forward every day without impediment on the path of their prosperity. They did not have more than one single difficulty to overcome to constitute themselves as a nation, and this difficulty is the most minor for a people, which is to shake off the rule of a distant nation, no matter how powerful it might be.

Our fate in this regard has been different: independence came by means very different from that of the United States, and while the United States were constituted from the very moment they found themselves free, we, destroying everything that existed before, found ourselves independent and in anarchy. We congratulated ourselves for the liberty we had acquired, much more when the Plan of Casa Mata[5] opened the field for the establishment of institutions absolutely different, or rather entirely opposite to everything that was known and had existed until then. We began to count the epoch of liberty from that event, but we should not have congratulated ourselves on it "until [we were] informed how it had been combined with government, with public force, with the discipline and obedience of armies, with the collection of an effective and well-distributed revenue, with morality and religion, with the solidity of property, with peace and order, with civil and social manners. All these (in their way) are good things, too, and without them liberty is not a benefit whilst it lasts, and is not likely to continue long."[6] All these delicate but necessary combinations had to be the objective of the Constitution, and the results we continually see prove clearly that these important objectives have not been fulfilled with the Constitution.

The model that was taken to constitute the nation, as I have said above, was the United States, but one hardly had any slight knowledge of this model, and what one had seen practiced in some way was the Spanish Constitution, which in itself was nothing other than an imitation of the Constituent Assembly of France, and this latter the result of all the metaphysical errors of the speculative philosophers of the last century. Thus it is that, without noticing it, the entire spirit of the Spanish Constitution was transmitted into our federal Constitution, which had the structure of the Constitution of the United States, and this influence was yet more characterized in the constitutions of some states. The constitution that the Constituent Assembly gave to France and that the Cortes of Cádiz servilely copied not only did not properly distinguish the powers, not only did not establish a suitable balance between them, but rather weakened the executive excessively, transferred all authority to the legislature, creating, in place of the absolute power of the monarch, a power as absolute as the monarch but entirely arbitrary, without any of the brakes to contain it that could in some way restrain

5. On February 1, 1823, Santa Anna issued the Plan of Casa Mata, which called for the reinstatement of the constituent congress disbanded by Emperor Iturbide. The rebellion extended throughout the country and was the beginning of the end for the short-lived first Mexican empire. (Editor's note)

6. Burke.

the arbitrariness of the monarchs. France and Spain, through similar constitutions, did nothing more than pass from the tyranny of one to the infinitely more unbearable tyranny of many, and among us we have seen the same results. To this principle and not to any other must be attributed the excesses that we have recently seen in Zacatecas: a Congress that declares war on the general government, that enters into relations with the congresses of other states, that condemns to exile its deputies in the general Congress because they have not supported these errors, is an institution most opposite to the idea that all the theories have us form of a representative body, and, on the contrary, an institution most similar to those oligarchic corporations which, in the Italian republics of the sixteenth century, exercised the most horrible tyranny alternately with the despots who from time to time dismissed them to concentrate authority in themselves. This imperfect division of powers, or rather this monstrous accumulation of power in bodies called legislative, is that much more prejudicial when these bodies in some state, like the already cited Zacatecas, are composed of only one chamber made up of a small number of individuals and do not even have a time limitation in the exercise of their omnipotence, so their sessions last the entire year. Thus, we have seen the Zacatecan oligarchy dominated by two active intriguers followed blindly by nine simple men who, with the sincerest intention in the world, have let those two evil spirits precipitate their state into all the misfortunes of war and stir up those misfortunes of anarchy in the rest of the Republic.

There is a very serious circumstance that increases even more disproportionately the power of the general Congress and, in its proper proportion, that power of the state legislatures, and it reduces the executive to the greatest nullity, and it is the following that I see has never been given proper attention. The Constituent Congress believed it had finished its work with dividing the Republic into states and establishing two chambers and a president, and it said pompously on taking its leave: *I have given you a Constitution;* but it did not reflect that this Constitution it had written, infusing the form of the United States Constitution with the complete spirit of the Constitution of the Cortes of Cádiz, destroying at their roots everything that existed, did nothing more than put the form of government in contradiction with all the sound legislation of the nation, and because this sound legislation was coherent with the nation's habits and customs, the application of that very Constitution came to present great difficulties. The constituents without doubt believed this work would be carried out by their successors, but they did not consider that it was absolutely impossible for an ordinary Congress, overloaded with the duties that the Constitution imposes on it, to dedicate itself to the giant work of revising all the old legislation to adapt it to the new form that had been given to the nation. Thus it is that such a work has not been undertaken, and a few other isolated measures have done nothing more than make the state of things worse, and the nation remains with a legislation totally contrary to its institutions, which not only causes supreme difficulty in the administration of justice and in public finance, but also subjugates the exercise of executive power even more to legislative authority.

In effect this contradiction between the laws and the Constitution encountered at every step in the political and judicial administration necessitates frequent consultations to Congress, even regarding those points that according to the Constitution pertain to the executive. Procrastination in attending to these questions infinitely delays tending to matters, and, at times, resolutions suffer from legislative omnipotence. Thus, for example, in the noisy matter of General Inclán,[7] as it was very clear that there was no existing law for such a case inasmuch as the law established by the Cortes of Spain could not be applied among us, Congress declared, at the very time it made a new law, that this law had always been in force and was made a crime of the government because, lacking prophetic spirit, the administration had not executed the law before it existed.

In the Constitution, certain powers and many duties are in fact assigned to the government, but this demarcation of obligations has been made without calculating at all whether, in order to carry them out, the powers with which it was vested were sufficient, and this is another very essential point of difference between the organization of our executive and that of the United States, in spite of the claim that ours has

7. General Ignacio Inclán, commander of the Guadalajara garrison, abused his powers as military commander and was dismissed from his command by Bustamante in December 1831 but was not prosecuted. The government claimed that there was no law under which to charge and convict Inclán. He was considered a centralist and a loyal supporter of the administration by the Yorkist opposition. The opposition accused the government of unduly protecting him. (Editor's note)

been modeled on that one. One power alone, with which the president of the United States of the North is vested and which the president of the United States of Mexico lacks, is sufficient to constitute an authority of so different a kind that a comparison of one with the other is not possible. The president of the United States of the North can dismiss by his will alone, without cause or even having to state the reason, all military, political, and financial employees of the federation, with the sole exception of the judges, without granting them any pension or retirement; and he can use this power however and whenever it seems best to him. Imagine for a moment an executive power armed with this important authority. What would its influence not be? From the moment this authority is conceded to it, all employees depend exclusively on the president. They become as many supports as he can have to sustain his authority; but this authority, being exercised with the discretion with which it has been used in the United States—only the present president, General Andrew Jackson, has been accused of any arbitrariness—is enough to avoid the disloyalty or extravagance of the employee in finance, to impose respect and fear in the military, and to instill in everyone a sense of regard toward that person on whose will they absolutely depend; while among us, the president wonders who the official of the ministry is, who is selling government secrets to the intriguers and rebellious persons. He knows positively, although without proofs that can be presented judicially, who the employee of the customs office is who allows contraband, without being able to do anything other than take the ridiculous and useless measure of suspending that employee for up to three months, leaving him with half his salary. Thus it is that the government can do nothing to correct the woes it sees as self-evident and, instead of being an object of regard and respect, is nothing more than an object of derision and scorn, even to its most immediate subordinates.

If, then, the president of the United States of the North is considered vested with this power and, moreover, exercising his authority by virtue of a Constitution incorporating all the habits and customs of the country, which could be described as innate in the country, entirely in accord with the civil and criminal legislation, which therefore presents almost no impediment to the fulfillment of the Constitution, one will see how different his power is from that with which the first magistrate of our Republic is vested; but there are still other differences no less im-

portant. The president of the United States of the North has the power
to commute or pardon completely penalties imposed by tribunals except in the case of high treason against the nation. How much confusion, how many difficulties would be avoided among us if our Constitution had given this power to the president! And, in fact, there is no part
of our political organization more defective. The constituent congress,
blindly following the theoretical principles of the speculative philosophers, believed that only the one who makes the law can reform it, even
in cases when the law could establish the manner of granting individual
pardons, and under this principle it reserved to Congress the power to
grant this kind of pardon. It did not keep in mind that, in this way, those
condemned to death during the recess had to suffer this punishment ir-
remediably whatever the merits that their cases might show to commute
the sentences, and that, on the contrary, none of those sentenced during the sessions, no matter how atrocious their crimes might be, would
have to suffer the punishment because of the excessive ease with which
the collegial and unaccountable bodies grant this type of pardon; for
although, through a law, the restriction was set by which only the requests that the government informs and supports could be taken into
consideration, this law has been eluded completely by means of a subtle
distinction based in the unlimited right of initiative and the omnipotence of the legislative body. The consequences have been what might
have been expected and no less unfortunate in what is moral than in
what is political: there is not a criminal who does not hope for pardon
up to the very moment of execution when he has seen that it is enough
that the porter in the Chamber of Deputies can scribble a motion for
pardon, collecting signatures that, for this and other things, are given
with blameworthy ease; and so if the execution takes place, the criminal who suffers it has not been sufficiently prepared and presents himself before the Tribunal of the Eternal Judge where things do not go as
lightly as in our congresses, not carrying in his heart the penitence that
must save him, but rather, perhaps, the despair that causes him to presume that he has suffered for lack of sufficient resources. This is how the
most solemn and fitting act for the exercise of national power has come
to be a kind of legerdemain, and the life or death of men depends on
mere chance. On the great occasions in which a reprieve or general amnesty can save a nation from the horrors of civil war with an opportune
and well-arranged stroke, the harm in this way of proceeding is even

greater. Sometimes a member of either chamber, ignorant of the state of things or because it suits the faction to which he belongs, inopportunely grants a general pardon and occasionally, when the government puts it forward, the Congress lets pass the opportunity of granting it to its advantage with useless or awkward discussions that lessen the value of the pardon when it has been agreed to and that, when it is granted, influence crimes to multiply with the probability of obtaining the pardon.

If the Constitution of our neighbors differs so essentially from ours in the two great powers it grants to the government to suspend positions and grant pardons, it differs even more in the methods it provides for the success of its workings. Our Constitution leaves the government entirely isolated, with no one to advise its decisions or inform it on the points of fact and law in the serious pieces of business that must apply to it frequently for its decision. In the United States, just as in England, there is a type of adviser with the title of attorneys of the nation or of the crown, with whom ministers discuss their measures, and these can be issued not based on the rough report of the officer of a board, but rather based on the considered opinion of a lawyer, to whom theoretical and practical knowledge must lead correctly. In this part, the constitution of these states moved away absolutely from its two models, that of the United States of the North and the Spanish, and produced its own creation, the *Council of the government,* and in truth this original invention does not do the greatest honor to the creative genius of its authors. This Council is composed of one-half of the Senate; it exists in the interval between the ordinary sessions and, by an erroneous interpretation of the Constitution, also ceases during the extraordinary sessions, and among its duties are advising the government in whatever the government discusses with it. It will be noticed very quickly that this Council is entirely inadequate to fulfill the objectives of a consultative body. The act of consulting a person or corporation supposes necessarily, on the part of the one who consults, confidence in the knowledge and sincerity of the one consulted. In order to have this, it is necessary that the one who consults have had at least some part in the selection of the consultant; this is how, even in the Spanish Constitution, which is the one that has set forth the greatest restrictions on the selection of the consultative body of government, the Cortes presented on a short list the advisers of the state, but the king could freely select among these short-listed persons. Here, the government finds itself in the situation of consulting persons who are perfect strangers to it, who many times will be indifferent to its successes, and when the majority of that Council consists of individuals from what is called the opposition, their consultants will be positively interested in ruining it with their counsel, for among us opposition and sedition are entirely synonymous. Must, then, the government seek counsel from someone who will either give advice with indifference or might give it with malice? And this last case is so far from being hypothetical that, inasmuch as following the opinion of the Council does not in any way preclude the responsibility of the minister, the Council, governed by self-interest in holding the government accountable, will not let the opportunity pass to lay a trap. But, supposing that nothing of this happens and the government can count on the integrity and learning of its counselors, will the need it has of its counselors be limited only to some months of the year and not continue in the time in which the most important business of the nation must be debated in the chambers? One must agree that this part of the Council of the government and its operation in the meeting of extraordinary sessions is what was least thought out in the Constitution.

We maintain, then, through the examination and comparison we have made of the executive of the United States of the North with ours in the Constitution, that the latter is infinitely weaker than the former in its vested powers and, moreover, is deprived of that kind of counsel that among our neighbors contributes to the success and prestige of their operations, and so, accumulating weakness upon weakness, our government has all the weaknesses inherent in the nature of an elective government and all the weaknesses that come from the restrictions and ties with which the somber and distrustful legislators of Cádiz bound and restrained the phantom of the king they created in their Constitution. Is it, then, a wonder that a government so weakly organized cannot fulfill the objective of its creation, suppressing the wicked, protecting the good and peaceful, ensuring order, strengthening military discipline, and enabling the nation to enjoy the benefits of society, primordial objective of all human institutions? And is it a wonder that the government of Sr. Esteva[8] should have endeavored to place itself at the head of a faction to

8. The government is called "the government of Mr. Esteva" and not "the government of General Victoria" because it is known how small a role Victoria played in what was done in his name and that everything was the doing of that minister.

be, in this way, what it could not be by means of the laws because, among us, the government can do nothing and the factions can do everything? Is it a wonder that the minister of war, Gómez Pedraza, should want all the leaders of the army to be provisional and as if on assignment, so they might thus remain necessarily dependent on the government?[9] When the hands of the government are so tied that it cannot move them in any direction, it should not seem strange that it seeks some means to make these ties somehow looser.

This habitual weakness of the government, although always harmful to the interests of the nation, would be less so if it existed only in ordinary and tranquil times, giving way in times of danger and revolution to greater energy. This is why in England, despite the fact that the authority of the government is in all times greater than among us, as much because of its form as for its powers, it is still not judged sufficient in times of public unrest, during which those laws protective of personal security known by the name of "law of habeas corpus" are suspended. This is also why in modern France, constituted according to all the enlightenment of the century, it has been necessary very quickly to have recourse to empowering its government with a dreadful military law, which it puts into use when the frequent unrest of its not very peaceful subjects requires it. But the Constitution not only did not foresee anything of this, but it also would be very doubtful or, better said, very clear to a person of rigorous principle that, in accord with the Constitution, it might not have had recourse to the expedient of which it has made use already on more than one occasion, of vesting the government with extraordinary powers in urgent cases. These powers, because they carry this mark of extraordinary, already have the stamp of odiousness in addition to the impediment of the untimeliness with which they are usually granted, in accord with the general order of our political upheavals, which is the following: any ambitious person whatsoever, as soon as he can become the leader of some faction or take possession of some stronghold, raises the banner of rebellion under whatever pretext, but always proclaiming something very different from what constitutes the true aim of his movement; of course, conferences between the government and its rebellious subject are entered into, and mean-

9. Alamán is referring to cabinet politics during the administration of General Guadalupe Victoria (1824–28). (Editor's note)

while, more precious time to act is lost; in the meantime, the revolution grows, the forces of the government weaken, in Congress various laws of circumstance are discussed, each more inadequate than the others; and, finally, extraordinary powers are resorted to when the opportunity has passed for granting them and when they are already becoming useless. If, on the contrary, it were established by a general rule in the Constitution or by subsequent laws what must be done in the not rare instances of public disturbances, the government could make use, at the appropriate occasion, of an amplitude of powers that would come to be ordinary, although applicable only in determinate times and circumstances, and revolutions would cease to be so frequent and dangerous, having a strong hand, ready and always armed with a power sufficient to curb them. Because of this large and notable void in our legislation, each revolution requires a series of partial and ineffective provisions, and conspiring has come to be a true joke inasmuch as all the advantages and no risk are on the side of those who conspire. We see them calmly taking walks and putting all their plans to work in the middle of the population centers where, although everybody knows them, the hand of the weak authority can never get to them.

In modern institutions, it has almost always passed from one extreme to the other: the abuses of the absolute power made people believe that restraining the powers of those who until then had been depositaries of that power was enough to ensure liberty, but these restraints have been carried so far that all power has been reduced to the inability to do any good and many times to the need to do evil by indirect means, while, because of one of those contradictions so frequent in the administrators of systems, at the same time that accumulation of power that constituted absolutism in the hands of one individual was destroyed, this same absolutism was transferred to the collegial bodies, in which its exercise came to be much more dangerous. Liberty came, then, to be lost by the same road by which it tried to become secure, and with it has also been lost public order, security of property, personal security, and all the goods that society should produce and that had been enjoyed in the old order of things.

In the United States of the North, this power of the Congress is far from being absolute. It has necessary limitations not only in the text of the Constitution, which are always illusory when the same one who is subject to them has the liberty of interpreting them, but principally in the short duration of its sessions, there being not more than one single instance since the epoch of independence in which extraordinary powers have been given to it; in the greater power of the executive; and, above all, in the organization and functions of the Supreme Court of Justice. The members of this court, unlike the one that has been established among us, are named by the president as are all other employees of the federation, and in all matters of right, one appeals to this court the acts of the general Congress, which, acting simply as a party, appoints its lawyers and agents and, in an opposing action, is going to defend its resolutions against whoever has filed a lawsuit against it; and in almost all the cases that have occurred until now, Congress has been rebuffed. Among us it was believed better to leave the selection of the individuals who should make up this supreme tribunal to the congresses of the states, being based also in the principle that, because those individuals would have to judge the ministers, these ministers should not have any part in their appointment. In the United States of the North, they have believed that this last objection was overcome more than enough by the removability of ministers[10] and the perpetuity of judges, and they did not fear entrusting to magistrates named by the president the power of judging the president himself who, in that Republic, is personally responsible in many more matters than in ours, although in order to make effective that responsibility, the complete unanimity of the House of Representatives is needed. But it is not only in matters of responsibility that the Supreme Court of Justice has to judge the government, but just as one appeals to it the decisions of Congress in matters of right, the same is done in cases involving decisions of the executive; and with this executive having to act as a party, that tribunal has had frequent occasion to show its integrity, pronouncing judgment on the very one to whom some of its members owe their appointment. In this way it has been confirmed by experience that the partiality of judges in favor of the government that named them was not to be feared, and the wisdom of the appointment has been proven, just as appointments have always fallen to the men most respectable for their knowledge and virtues, and I find that more is always to be expected from this method of selection than from the one adopted among us, according to which the congresses of the states have to be guided by rudimentary knowledge gathered about

10. By Congress. (Editor's note)

persons whom they do not know and by recommendations sent to them from the capital.

How different must then be the power of a congress that in some matters, and unfortunately among us and in the rather frequent times of disturbances, has to submit many of its actions to the judgment of an immovable tribunal and, for this very reason, one less sensitive to the shocks of the moment! If this practice existed among us, would we have seen those decrees of expatriation of individuals and families without their being heard or judged, those measures of sequestration, those resolutions of confiscation, one more shameful than the other? The law, as impartial toward corporations, whatever might be their title, as toward individuals, would have sheltered those individuals from the fire of the passions of the corporations, and an impartial verdict would have honored the Mexican magistrates as it has made the reputation so many times of the magistrates of the States, our neighbors. I have said if this practice existed among us because, in substance in the text of the Constitution, not only is there nothing that conflicts with it but rather quite a bit that supports it; but this idea that the Congress is sovereign and that nothing but the weak obstacle of the very limited veto of the president can provide resistance to their absolute wills, would cause an outcry to rise to the clouds if a judicial body tried to put shackles, although working very much in the sphere of its powers, on their resolutions of whatever type. The new sovereigns have taken from the old even the habit of adulation, and thus we see that they accept without embarrassment, and are given without reserve, the treatment of sovereignty, which belongs to them only to the degree that it belongs to any other constituted authority who exercises by virtue of the Constitution a part of the national sovereignty that resides only in the total body of the nation and whose sole sovereign act has been to issue a Constitution. Because of these same bizarre and fawning ideas of sovereignty, it will not be surprising that they take these observations badly, although in the depths of his heart, each one finds them justified, and it might be considered a crime the way some parts of the Constitution have been critiqued, because, through another of the strange contradictions of the human spirit, in the very epoch in which the infallibility of the pope is most ridiculed, the principle of the infallibility of congresses has been consecrated, and when the greatest scope is given to liberty of the press, permitting the exercise of a purulent criticism on everything that existed and produced the wisdom of the past centuries, any doubt shown about what the learning of our century has produced is least tolerated. Inevitable result of the pride of self-love that, sustained by ignorance and presumption, it cannot bear any contradiction at all nor criticism, no matter how restrained it might be, regarding what it believes to be a masterpiece of its knowledge and profound understandings.

Everything that has been expressed until now shows not only what kind of authority was placed in the hands of General Bustamante and what the means were by which the Constitution equipped him to provide for the happiness of the people, but also that it is extensive and equally applicable to the governments that preceded it and to the one that has followed it. For this reason I have expanded somewhat on this matter, and I will also do so in some of the considerations that will follow, for it seems important to me that those who read this understand fully the true situation of their government, and that, knowing the very narrow limitation of its powers and the dependence for all its actions on the legislative power, they might demand less of those who can do little and be more disposed to look with compassion than to incriminate those who, vested with an authority almost null, find themselves charged with an immense responsibility. Moreover, those who are inclined to believe that a change of system would be the good fortune of the Republic, understanding by this change replacing the one that presently rules[11] for central government, might become convinced that evil does not exactly consist in what they believe it to consist, but rather in a much more effective and profound cause, which works as much in the general government as in the governments of the individual states, and that as long as one does not attend to this cause, any other change would be useless. This cause is nothing other than the impotence of the executive to fulfill the obligations necessary for all government and, if at some time Mexicans, tired of the misfortunes of anarchy which necessarily increase every day, might think seriously of remedying them, the first step they should take is to invigorate the government, give energy and strength where now there is nothing but languor and weakness, in sum that there be a government, because they now have nothing more than a shadow or illusory appearance of it.

Inasmuch as, following the error committed by the Spanish legisla-

---

11. Federalism. (Editor's note)

tors who created the Constitution of Cádiz, absolute power was transferred from individuals to corporations, it seems that the most foresighted measures should have been taken so that the composition of these corporations would be such that they would provide the greatest assurances for success and so that the method of exercising this terrible power might guard against the abuse that could be made of it. When a power is very extensive, the good or bad use made of it can depend only on the personal qualities of the men in whom it is deposited, for, especially when these men are gathered in a numerous corporation, nothing on earth can contain their misconduct: "Besides, they are less under responsibility to one of the greatest controlling powers on the earth, the sense of fame and estimation. The share of infamy that is like to fall to the lot of each individual in public acts is small indeed, the operation of opinion being in the reverse ratio to the number of those who abuse power. Their own approbation of their own acts has to them the appearance of a public judgment in their favor. A perfect democracy is, therefore, the most shameless thing in the world. As it is the most shameless, it also the most fearless. No man apprehends in his person that he can be made subject to punishment. *Quidquid multis peccatur inultum est.*[12] It is therefore of infinite importance that they should not be suffered to imagine that their will, any more than that of kings is the standard of right and wrong."

The only positive quality that can exist in a democracy and that can most ensure the restrained exercise of such a gigantic power is property, yet certainly nothing is less in accord with modern theories, for if political society is nothing more than a conventional company, each individual must represent in this association whatever the capital is that he might have brought into it. Against the soundness of this principle is frequently opposed the claimed ignorance of the propertied class, which presents them as unsuited to carry out a charge that also requires learning, and we have recently seen these arguments expressed in a very bitter manner in the tribunal of the Senate in a discussion over jurors. But these arguments are very far from being established to the fullest extent that one has wanted them to be given, and, in truth, if we relinquish for one moment the intolerable presumption that has us continually calling ourselves a very learned nation, perhaps because in our saying it,

---

12. "The sin of thousands always goes unpunished," Lucan, *Civil War.*

the rest, who are far from giving us that praise, might believe it of us, and if we examine with impartiality who makes up the small number of men who possess general understandings and the even smaller number who have demonstrated the necessary aptitude for business, whether in the court, whether in the office, we will see that the propertied class is not inferior to the rest because "let those large proprietors be what they will—and they have their chance of being amongst the best—they are, at the very worst, the ballast in the vessel in the commonwealth." On the contrary, if we have seen men of property distinguish themselves by their talents and aptitude in the management of businesses, we have, unfortunately, seen by the hundreds those who, filled with pretensions of knowing and scorn toward that class, have committed the most horrendous blunders and, with them, have submerged us in an abyss of misfortunes. If errors and ignorance were definitely the lot of the propertied class, the law that regulates relations between masters and servants in the state of Tamaulipas and some other laws of that state would be sufficient to persuade one that that legislature is made up of millionaires, and this same could be justly thought of some other legislatures when what in fact happened was that everything that sounded like property was persistently excluded from them.

It should not be understood by this that one is trying here to close the door of legislative bodies to all who are not property owners. Nothing less than that.

> There is no qualification for government but virtue and wisdom, actual or presumptive. Wherever they are actually found, they have, in whatever state, condition, profession, or trade, the passport of heaven to human place and honor. Woe to the country which would madly and impiously reject the service of the talents and virtues, civil, military, or religious, that are given to grace and to serve it, and would condemn to obscurity everything formed to diffuse luster and glory around a state. Woe to that country, too, that, passing into the opposite extreme, considers a low education, a mean contracted view of things, a sordid, mercenary occupation as a preferable title to command.
>
> Nothing is a due and adequate representation of a state that does not represent its ability as well as its property. But as ability is a vigorous and active principle, and as property is sluggish, inert, and

timid, it never can be safe from the invasion of ability unless it be, out of all proportion, predominant in the representation. [It must be represented, too, in great masses of accumulation, or it is not rightly protected.][13] The characteristic essence of property, formed out of the combined principles of its acquisition and conservation, is to be unequal. The great masses, therefore, which excite envy and tempt rapacity, must be put out of the possibility of danger. Then they form a natural rampart that naturally protects the lesser properties in all their gradations.[14]

I have expanded on these principles not only to demonstrate how insufficient are the scant restrictions that the Constitution establishes for the composition of our legislative bodies, but also to show the need to give property, above all landed, which is the most stable and the most closely related to the prosperity of the nation, a direct influence on legislation, which has not seemed to me a superfluous concern in circumstances where, because of very prejudicial concerns, in some states above all, a war to the death has been declared on property. It will be said perhaps, and it is an objection I must foresee, that Burke wrote according to the principles of a monarchy and that these cannot be adaptable to a republic, but the form of the executive is nothing more than an accident in a constitution, and the bases on which the stability of society is supported is the same in all countries and in all systems, for it is based on the inclinations, emotions, and interests of men that arise from their hearts, which are not moved by systems of convention established for their government. These principles are those of all centuries, and in them alone can be established the stability, peace, calm, order, and prosperity of political societies; but as we will be seeing in the course of this paper, these principles are not the benefits to which the instigators of public unrest aspire, but rather to the privation and lack of them all.

These precautions against the abuse of a power as extensive as the one our legislative bodies have, that can come only from the individual qualities of their members, the Constitution has claimed to establish through

13. The bracketed passage is found in Burke's original text but was omitted by Alamán. (Translators' note)

14. From Edmund Burke's "Speech to the Electors of Bristol," November 3, 1774. We have used the original English text for this passage. (Editor's note)

the division of the general Congress into two chambers, but this division can never fulfill this objective as long as those two chambers differ only in the method of their selection and by some accident in the length of their term but do not represent essentially distinct interests whose combination must produce the general utility of the laws. Thus it is that two chambers can at most represent only two different opinions, and as opinions, unlike the positive interests of society, they soon move to become political parties or factions with all their ardor and acrimony, and from this we have seen our two chambers almost constantly transformed into two enemy fortresses occupied by opposing belligerents and taking shots that are that much more constant the more the dependence of the two chambers on each other is no longer essential, as we will see further on. By the order in which these ideas have been expounded, one will be able to see clearly, of course, the supreme preponderance of legislative power over the other powers, the consequent incapacity or impotence of the executive, and the insufficiency of the restrictions that the Constitution establishes for the composition of this legislative power itself, so that in the final outcome everything depends on the judgment of the electors who concur with their votes on its makeup, and on the will of the individuals to whom this election falls. This gives greatest importance to the functions of the electors, and therefore we must look attentively at how these functions are carried out.

Nothing requires such generally broad learning and such a well-formed public spirit as exercising the right of election, and these two qualities should work with that much more effectiveness the fewer the restrictions the Constitution sets out regarding the persons to whom the election can fall. It is necessary that the elector be in a position to formulate an exact idea of the political state of his country and that, knowing the opinions, integrity, and education of the individual or individuals to whom he is going to give his vote, he would give the first impetus to the decisions of Congress through the men for whom he opens the door of this Sanctuary of the Laws. From this, the inevitable preventive measures originate that various nations have set out limiting the right of suffrage to property holders according to the sum they verify having paid in full as direct taxes. These or other restrictions never seem to be more necessary than when, passing from one system in which there is not the least idea regarding popular elections to another in which everything depends on them, such an important right is going to be given to a people who have not formed any concept whatsoever of the purpose of elections, of their consequences, or of the very importance of that power. In the civil order more than in the natural, everything is graduated, because the civil order is nothing other than the natural order modified by movements of yet slower effect such as religion, morality, and enlightenment. Never do we see nature work by sudden movements; the only things in it that are momentary are earthquakes and storms, and those are not means of creation but rather of destruction. To avoid this problem and continue to save the metaphysical fiction of the general will, the artifice has been appealed to that elections are not to be direct, but instead, through diverse graduations and reelections, the appointment of the deputies comes to be the work of few persons; but as no conditions have been established regarding these persons, the problem remains at its feet and is made much greater by the intrigue that is easily exercised among few persons, but that perhaps would not have the opportunity among many persons. This right of suffrage, then, is exercised in the first place by a mass of people who give their vote to certain individuals without knowing who they are nor for what it designates them and, then, for other individuals who many times have no knowledge of the persons whom they elect, toward whom all resources of intrigue are put into play, stimulated by interest in the salaries that provide an easy and relaxed way of living for many who do not have any other. Solely to this principle of the electors' ignorance, whether it be of the personal character and opinions of the elected ones or whether it be of the importance of the functions they are going to perform, can be attributed the singular discord that is found in the behavior of deputies from the same state appointed by the same electoral council; or if the electors know the personal character and opinions and are informed about the importance of the functions, one would have to say they are betraying their consciences, casting into the heart of Congress all the elements of discord to make a plaything of the contrary opinions of their deputies and amuse themselves with the disputes of the Jansenist and the Jesuit, the exalted philosopher and the man of judgment, the impious one and the moral and religious man to whom they have indiscriminately given a vote. If I were permitted to designate the persons by name in this writing, with the lists of deputies of some states in hand, it would be very easy for me to prove the truth of what has been said so far. What opinion, then, should we have of electors who behave in this way? The kindest, certainly, is that they frequently appoint without knowing whom, or, not having any idea about the workings of a Congress, they do not try to give, as they should, the first impetus to opinion through the elections. Among the people, it is no surprise that they do not view elections with commitment, not knowing their importance, and thus we see the indifference they have toward taking part in them, this being noted most obviously in all places where, in some way, elections have been regularized in a way that ensures individual casting of the vote, for when this was not the case and a considerable number of votes appeared, it was not because there really was that number of votes, but rather because the factions, making the cruelest mockery of this solemn act, had thousands of lists presented for some few persons and had many entire infantry and cavalry regiments vote as a body.

Chosen in this entirely casual manner, the workings of the congresses finally depend solely on the disposition of their members because of the breadth of power the Constitution gives them. Even the fetter that the division into two chambers and the sanction of the executive establishes for the general Congress comes to be illusory, for as has been said before, this dependency of the two on each other and on the president is not absolute. It is sufficient that in one chamber two-thirds of the individuals are united even if they are not in the other, because those two-thirds can constitute the legislative body, and if the president, because of weakness or some other motive, joins with them, they exercise the most despotic power that has ever been known on earth. They, without the agreement of the other chamber, can make anything they want pass as law. If the president does not accede to their wills, they can deprive him of the service of his ministers by an arbitrary declaration of responsibility; they can subject members of the Supreme Court of Justice and even members of the other chamber to the same action of responsibility, and, in sum, they can shatter society to its foundations, without there being a human power that can prevent it. If, to this terrible power that the majority of one chamber can exercise without any dependence at all on the other chamber or on the president, one adds the not-insignificant power that each chamber can exercise individually with the name of economic powers and to which an unlimited breadth has been given without any dependence on anyone, there will result a body, in its totality or in its parts, vested with an authority such as the most despotic institutions have never constituted. If, moreover, there are two-thirds in the other chamber in accord with those in the first, the very person of the president can be removed by an arbitrary declaration of ineptitude or of whatever physical or moral impediment. The Constitution seemed to have required the concurrence of three elements for the creation of laws and created these three elements, but immediately it destroyed its own work, reducing the practice of legislation to the cooperation of only two of these elements, and in order to give greater range to arbitrariness, these two elements can concur by chance, whether it be the president with two-thirds of one chamber alone against the other chamber, or whether two-thirds of the two chambers against the president, who is in this case compelled to execute what is contrary to his opinion or conscience and to which he has made formal opposition, negating his approval.

In the United States of the North, one does not see this very powerful and independent influence of one Chamber over the other in any possible event, and this circumstance, together with the other differences we have been noting between that Constitution and ours, is sufficient to make them so different, the one from the other, that there does not remain in their most essential parts even a shadow of similarity. The Constitution of the Constituent Assembly of France was the first that established the independence of operations of the legislative power from the veto of the executive; the legislators of Cádiz followed this model with certain restrictions and, as implemented, having been the tacit but very effective model of ours, it received even greater breadth, establishing the independence not only of the legislative power with respect to the executive, but also of the two branches of the legislative from each other, with fewer restrictions than those that in their case the Spanish constitutors made necessary. This is how everything the Constitution puts in place to safeguard persons, properties, and everything dear to man and society, everything that constitutes the harmony and even the existence of this society, can disappear at the voice of a factious majority of one single chamber, very easily formed through an election in which, because it is almost accidental, the factions have such room; this is how that complexity of institutions intended to protect the rights of man in society falls in a moment as a result of the abuse of the theories that contributed to forming the institutions; and this is how, fleeing from despotism, society will fall directly into it. A sententious verse of Horace might literally be relevant to this case, although without intending to offend the learning and persons of the authors of the Constitution, *Dum vitant stulti vitia, in contraria currunt.* Wishing foolishly to avoid one extreme, one comes to fall directly into the opposite one.

For this reason, the advantage that the chamber in which a *law or decree* is initiated (two things that it seems should be different but that the Constitution has nonetheless not distinguished) has over the reviewing chamber as well as the function attached to the right of initiative that both chambers have equally and of which all their members have unrestricted benefit, gives way to competition among both in which that spirit of schoolboy prank is fully exercised that, unfortunately, is preserved among us even in the most serious functions. Those who carry the banner of the party which dominates in one or the other chamber are spying on one another to take advantage of an opportune time, a carelessness of the opposition, to launch a proposal which, adopted quickly by a sufficient majority, could put the other chamber in a bind, for which, if there is no other recourse, it appeals to the same miserable tricks to prevent them from having a quorum, by separating on whatever pretext such or such individual from the committee, by speeding up or delaying discussion depending on the hopes or fears of the moment and by it win the selection of president at the time of renewal, all this creating a spirit of miserable and base intrigue inherited and learned from the Cortes of Cádiz in Madrid, capable of degrading I do not say an assembly of legislators, but rather a social gathering of vapid dandies. The august act of lawmaking is many times the work of these improper dealings, and the more important and transcendent the subjects of which they deal, the more they customarily are so. Is it surprising that laws created in this way are what so many times we have seen they are?

If the supreme importance of the functions of Congress and the breadth of its power require much circumspection in the use of this power, the multiplicity of those same functions demands hard work and continuous application. With the congresses transformed into efficient elements from which everything arises, thus reversing the nature of legislative bodies, which is not nor can be other than the nature of conservative masses and resistance, the entire time of ordinary sessions, even extended for the thirty working days that the Constitution permits, can barely suffice for the dispatch of even those extraordinary and nonetheless very frequent matters to which, as we have seen, what is incomplete and contradictory in the Constitution gives way every day, but even for the dispatch of matters that constitute the periodic and ordinary operations. It was then necessary that the committees persistently work to instruct and prepare the pieces of business in such a way that, directed perfectly by the committees, the discussion might be facilitated and abbreviated; it was necessary that, in the sessions, not a moment be lost and that the members of both chambers, considering their duties as sacred, carry them out with that respect and attention that the fate of the nation or thousands of individuals who depend on their vote deserve. Unfortunately, none of this happens. The pieces of business pass to the committees, where they remain an eternity; these committees have difficulty getting together, everything is seen quickly in them during some little time that is stolen from presence at the session, and very commonly allowing only one of the members to assert his authority on the matter, and with the opinion rendered, the rest swear *in verba magistri,* or, if someone dissents from the opinion, he frequently creates the scandal of saying he was not summoned and did not agree with the committee, this sometimes being one of the miserable snares employed to delay a piece of business which is being dealt with in that moment and that does not suit the faction to which the *protester* against the committee belongs. The sessions never open at the hour that the regulations anticipate, but this is certainly observed punctually for the hour of closing the session, thus defrauding the public of very many hours of work that the same public pays for in excess. During the session, few are the men earnest about fulfilling their duty who are present at the session with reflective meditation, with the desire to inform themselves about matters in order to vote correctly. Most of them pass the entire time of the debate outside, and the greater number of members is always found in the recreation halls of both chambers, and when the hour for voting arrives, in vain the unfortunate president rings the bell with the greatest violence he can; in vain he assigns one after another of the porters and secretaries to gather some members; some answer that they are busy, as if at that hour they should have any other business than being present at the session, the others are waiting to finish smoking, and some, more bold, respond that they do not want to go in; those who do go in enter asking those who are with them what has been discussed or what is being voted. And without instruction and without background and sometimes without knowing what they are speaking of, they toss off, without remorse of conscience, a hasty vote on which perhaps depends the fate of hundreds of families or very serious interests of the nation. If ministers, out of zeal to ful-fill an obligation or from some other motive, get worked up about some matter, they have to turn themselves into brokers and go around beg-ging as a personal favor that the committee gather and that it take under consideration this or that action; and if, on the contrary, they want to delay some piece of business, and they do not know how to dispose of it in another way, they do not have to do anything but, with whatever of the frequent motives or pretexts that lends complication to legislation, send it for consultation to Congress, secure in knowing that, but for some rare accident, it is going to be buried eternally in the committee to which it is passed. This is how the expression "it is necessary to con-sult Congress" has come to be, in every office, the terror of the people in those offices who have matters pending; this is how matters of busi-ness have been accumulating more and more every day with no hope whatsoever of expediting them. In this way the most serious matters are discussed and voted, and this is how this immense power that the Con-stitution has entrusted to the Congress is exercised, proving that classic verse, *Nec color inperii, nec frons erat ulla Senatus.*[15]

Do not say that this is an exaggerated harangue against the body that exercises almost absolute power in the nation. It would have been desir-able not to have to show these defects, but there is not one of the many who have assembled in Congress, whether as members of it or as spec-tators, who does not know the truth of what has been said, and many members of both.

15. Neither the dignity of the supreme command nor some appearance of Congress was seen. [This is Alamán's note, and his translation into Spanish of the Latin phrase. Editor's note.]

2 Liberty in the Liberal Republic
1845–1876

POLEMIC BETWEEN *EL UNIVERSAL, EL SIGLO XIX,* AND *EL MONITOR REPUBLICANO,* 1848–1849

After the war with the United States (1846–48) and the loss of more than half of the country, Mexicans became increasingly pessimistic regarding the future. As they searched for the causes of the problems that had plagued their nation since independence, some conservatives argued that liberalism and representative government were out of touch with the realities of the people. Between 1848 and 1849 the conservative newspaper *El Universal* wrote strong editorials criticizing such ideas as popular sovereignty, equality before the law, individual rights, and modern natural right in general. The paper argued not just for the establishment of monarchical rule in Mexico but also against limited, modern constitutional government. The liberals answered these arguments in articles in their own dailies, *El Monitor Republicano* and *El Siglo XIX*. The polemic raged in the press for more than a year and comprised dozens of editorial articles.

We present a sample of this exchange. *El Universal* (1848–55) was established in 1848 by the Catalan editor Rafael de Rafael y Vilá. It was the principal conservative daily of the Santa Anna era (1853–55), representing the values of aristocratic and centralist factions. Favoring the imposition of monarchy, *El Universal* supported the Santa Anna regime and engaged in heated debates with its contemporaries, especially *El Siglo XIX* and *El Monitor Republicano*. *El Universal* ceased publication in August 1855, when the conservative regime was defeated. First published on December 22, 1844, *El Monitor Republicano* (1846–95) was founded and directed by Vicente García Torres under the original title *El Monitor Constitucional.* The name was changed in 1846 to align the paper more closely with republican principles. Liberal in stance, *El Monitor* strove to defend the laws revoked by General Santa Anna and conserve the integrity of the state of the Republic. *El Siglo XIX* (1841–96) was founded on October 8, 1841, by Ignacio Cumplido and overseen by Mariano Otero and Juan Bautista Morales. Although publication was suspended twice, the newspaper continued until 1896. From 1848 to 1856 it was led by Francisco Zarco. During this period the paper was characterized by its moderate liberalism. It was also one of the first and principal opposition newspapers of its era.

1

What Might Be the Causes of Our Ills, Part 1

El Siglo XIX entitled its lead article of the twenty-first of this month in this way [What Might Be the Causes of Our Ills], and we congratulate ourselves that periodicals, even those that, like *El Monitor* and *El Siglo,* show themselves fierce defenders of a system now instinctively censured by our people, lower themselves to serious and impartial analysis of the cause of our ills, because the duration of these ills can be determined only by the time we delay in understanding the origin and true source that produces them, if, as is to be hoped, such understanding inspires in us all the sincere desire to remedy the ills; because with our forces united, we will remove all obstacles, and the difficulties that vile interests and despicable passions place in opposition will yield to the united force of the true lovers of our unfortunate *patria.*

Our colleagues fashion the first paragraphs of their editorial with comic sentences, ironic phrases, ambiguous expressions, and false imputations about our writings, without reflecting that, even if we deserved all that, it was in the interest of their honor to conceal it, at least when it came to attacking us, because otherwise they snatch from their triumph, if they obtain it, the glory they might have acquired, and they prepare greater confusion and shame for their defeat if some mischance of the war leads them to it. *The most beautiful ideas of human genius* can gather no glory from *reducing to dust the products of the creative intellect of writers* who, by comparison with them, *are less significant than an atom.* Encouraged, then, by the very humble position in which our adversaries place us, let us continue with greater delight our efforts to defend the doctrines and principles we have expressed; for when the enemy with whom one fights is powerful and strong, if in the end one succumbs,

Original title: "Polémica entre *El Universal, El Siglo XIX,* y *El Monitor Republicano,* entre 1848 y 1849: 'Cual sea la causa de nuestros males'" [primer artículo]. Source: *El Universal,* Mexico, January 24, 1849.

it is not as shameful as when one fights with greater or equal strength. Therefore, in return for this advantageous position, we gladly pass by whatever neither concerns nor directly affects the essence and substance of the question.

The gentlemen of *El Siglo* say that we of *El Universal,* inquiring into the causes of our ills, have believed we found them in the adoption of the system that governs us today. This is true, and now we add that, even if we had neither said it nor even imagined it, reading the editorial that engages our attention now, we would have thought it immediately, and we would say it and defend it with all the force of which we are capable. For that reason, we insert next the greater part of that writing, for it seems to us that all of our writings together do not throw half the light on the question that is shed by that editorial alone, without it being necessary to add more than a few simple and minor reflections to provide an absolute and total conviction. It says:

1. When our *patria* was the colony and property of Spain, the ideas that for a long time prevailed on the old continent were completely unknown in our country. Those ideas, above all those of liberty and independence, had an epoch of general excitement; all their renown was necessary to liberate the world from the domination of a daring conqueror whom fortune seemed to have taken under its special protection. The cry of liberty that resounded in all Europe had echoes in our *patria;* valiant men rose to liberate it from Spanish domination; at the end of eleven years they were successful, and since then the nation has occupied a place among independent peoples.

Here a historical error of our colleagues slipped out. In the first place, the cry of Dolores[1] was not an echo of the cry of liberty that resounded in all Europe; the mother *patria* was invaded by the foreigner, and it was feared that the domination might be extended to the colonies. It was said then: Let the sovereign establish his throne in the colonies.[2] This is how

1. On September 16, 1810, the local priest of the town of Dolores, Miguel Hidalgo, called on the people to revolt against the colonial authorities in the name of the deposed Spanish king, Ferdinand VII. (Editor's note)

2. It is certainly lamentable how ignorant we, the majority of Mexicans, still are of the principal and most important events of our own history. The cry of Dolores was not

the people were aroused and thrown into revolution; and it would not be groundless to believe, because of the tenaciousness and invincible resistance the nation put up when that pretext disappeared, that without that pretext, the nation could not possibly have been moved with only the goal of independence and with no other prop. Contemporary history reveals to us, and our eyes see that, of the brave men who rose up,

––––––

only not the echo of liberty as we have said, but moreover it was enabled and spread in our country because Ferdinand VII was proclaimed in it, the fiction being carried to the extreme that the leader of that uprising, when he entered into Guadalajara, drove in his car an unknown person who was said to be Ferdinand himself. The manifesto to the Europeans by the person commissioned by the junta of Zitácuaro, Don José María de Cos, delivered in the Real de Sultepec March 16, 1812, says in paragraph 12: "You have had the temerity to claim the supreme power, unjustly and in the august name of the king, to rule haughtily and despotically over a free people *who do not recognize any sovereign but Ferdinand VII.*"

Articles 1 and 4 of the plan that accompanied this proclamation say the following:

Art. 1. That the Europeans yield the command and armed force to a national and independent congress of Spain, *representative of Ferdinand VII,* which affirms his rights in these domains.

Art. 4. That with independence declared and sanctioned, all past grievances and incidents are forgotten everywhere, taking the most energetic measures toward this end; and all the inhabitants of that soil, creoles as well as Europeans, constitute without distinction a nation of American citizens, *vassals of Ferdinand VII,* pledged to promote public happiness.

Article 2 of the plan of war that accompanies the same proclamation is as follows:

Art. 2. The belligerent factions *recognize Ferdinand VII.* The Americans have given obvious proofs of this, swearing allegiance to him and proclaiming him everywhere, raising his portrait as a standard, invoking his name in their patents and judgments, stamping it on their coins and currency. *On this supposition was based everybody's enthusiasm, and on this foundation the party of insurrection has always operated.* (*Cuadro histórico* of Don Carlos María Bustamante, 2nd ed. vol. 1, pp. 393ff.)

It can be seen by those documents how flippantly our adversaries proceed to set down the facts from which their strongest arguments come. To avoid this and a thousand other errors of that type, which have brought and are causing woes of the greatest gravity and importance, we would like Sr. Alamán to hasten publication of his history of the war of independence, even if the preliminary essays that he has offered should be postponed. We believe that by doing this he would perform a service of the highest importance to the nation, and therefore we encourage him to carry this out. (Original editors' note) only some did it to free our *patria* from Spanish domination. The few of those very men who remain speak about this, and they escaped the personal vigilance of those called patriots with more difficulty than they did the persecution of the viceregal government. At the end of eleven years, independence was, in fact, achieved; but one must not forget that it was achieved thanks to a plan, whose principal basis was bringing to America Ferdinand or another of the individuals from the ruling house in Spain.

2. We see now what was to be expected in the new order of things, given the state of political education among the people. The Spanish domination, which had as its objective enriching the peninsula with the products of our soil, completely neglected the education of the people, both morally and politically. There was lacking, then, in the immense majority of the nation, public habits that formed their character and knowledge of the simplest social principles. Because Mexicans were accustomed to obeying blindly the orders of a mysterious and terrible power, far from any participation in government and public affairs, habituated to suffering the hatred and scorn of the Spaniards, whose ideas of nobility and superiority had hindered the moral fusion of the two races, it was to be expected that their feelings and ideas would go astray. The division between Mexicans and Spaniards had also exerted the same kind of influence among the former; that is to say, Mexicans, instead of forming a compact and unified people through the bonds of feeling, habits, and interests, formed only a people whose unity was based exclusively on the power they all obeyed. However, such a bond was by its nature violent, and it was to be expected that at the same time it failed, the many dissolving elements that had germinated in silence during a period of several years would have their effect.

In the preceding paragraph, historical impartiality was certainly lacking where it is asserted that the Spanish government neglected moral education; *we are speaking of Catholic morality.* Let us appeal to the judgment of those who, witnesses to the uses and customs of those times, might even be witnesses to ours.

It was to be expected that, at the same time the unity based exclusively on the UNITY of the power failed in our people, the many dissolving elements that had germinated in silence during a period of several years would have their effect.

Gentlemen editors, what greater proof can we adduce to justify that the cause of our ills is the federal system than those words of yours? It was "to be expected," you say with much discernment and good sense, that the *unity* of power failing, the unity of our people fails, because they have no other bonds of union than the bond of obedience. Well, how do you even fight against such a conviction! Neither you nor any person who might have even a slight notion of social science has denied, nor will ever be able to deny, the necessity of bonds that link the peoples of a nation to each other to be able to form a truly sovereign and independent body that figures among the nations of the globe. Without forming such bodies, these nations would not distinguish themselves from one another. Otherwise, it would be necessary to conclude that all the nations spread over the vast surface of the earth are nothing more than a single nation, groups of men scattered here and there without any relationships, without uniformity, unity, or agreement, that is to say, without any bonds that tie and join them to each other; either they do nothing at all or all the nations of the globe are only one nation.

But such arguments offend simple common sense; and without insulting the learning and knowledge of our adversaries, it would not be becoming to push to the limit all the consequences deduced from them. The gentlemen editors of *El Siglo* know very well, or perhaps better than we, that the entire science of a wise legislation, of a patriotic and just government, consists in conserving, developing, and creating by all possible means the bonds, the relationships most suitable and best for binding the individuals who form families to the families who make up the towns and to the towns that constitute nations. Take a look over the history of all the centuries, and you will see confirmed in all areas and in all times that the rise and decline of empires and republics is proportional to the increase and decrease of such bonds. The barbarians came down from the north and took over the great and cultured nations of Europe because they came united; a handful of adventurers conquered the greatest of the empires, but it was a divided empire; the bonds of the Mexicans, broken and shattered by fanaticism, tyranny, and barbarity, presented to the Spaniards, instead of a nation, only a large countryside, which confirms the truth of what we are saying. The Anglo-Saxon phalanx came to write it down in the pages of our own history only a few days ago.

Mexico, then, independent of Spain and independent in seven months (prematurely) because of the irresistible strength that the bonds established by the Plan of Iguala imparted to it; Mexico, we say, the great work of its emancipation completed, had to endeavor before everything else, in order to figure among the independent and sovereign nations, to tighten the bonds among its members and find out how much they might bind them to form a compact and homogeneous people capable of resisting the vicissitudes to which, for the first time, its elevated position exposed it.

Well then, according to our adversaries, the Mexicans were united only by obedience based in the unity of the power, and our colleagues did not hesitate to state that, lacking such unity, "it was to be expected that the many dissolving elements that had germinated in silence during a period of several years would have their effect."

And will it be possible to doubt, will it be possible to attribute to any other cause but the representative and federal system we have adopted, all the ills that weigh us down? Only one bond tied the Mexicans together, *unity* of power; one single thing is lacking in the representative, federal republican system, unity of power. What had to happen? That the nation would turn into a country whose inhabitants were strangers to one another because no ties, no bonds, link them to each other to form a compact body; that as a consequence they would fall prey to the factions, plaything of the parties, victims sacrificed to the whim, the ignorance, the ambition of the presumptuous and wicked ones and, the unity of power unraveled, absolutely broken, "the dissolving elements that had germinated in silence" developed completely; that once those elements that the unity of power would have suffocated in their germ developed, there will hardly be a human power that can suppress them; that, finally, once those elements had developed, strongly and noisily clashing with each other, the absolute division in which we find ourselves would be produced. The federation, then, is not only the cause of our ills, but rather the precise, inevitable, and inexcusable cause of all our misfortunes, because it destroyed by its very nature the one bond of union that linked Mexicans, if it is certain, as *El Siglo* assures, that it was founded uniquely in the unity of power.

3. Independence completed, the nation was told: "You are free, you can constitute yourselves in the way that most pleases you; the laws that from now on will govern you will be solely the expression of the national will. From today on, the odious distinctions will cease between nobles and plebeians, between masters and slaves; there will be a single law to govern the actions of all; the same rights will be protected by that law; there will be a single legitimate and just authority to decide disputes, punish infractions, and defend citizens in the exercise of their rights. And you, all of you born on this soil, you will form a single family, a family of brothers who, united by tight bonds, will labor in unison on the great work of public happiness, of national happiness." Well, now, is the nation, the immense majority of citizens, disposed to appreciate the true value of this language? Surely not. Only education, experience, and the practical understanding of events are capable of valorizing those principles, principles that, when they have not put down deep roots in an innermost conviction, serve only to dazzle the imagination and carry off the spirit. This is why the nation, removed from the orbit in which it had moved for so long and placed on a path totally unknown but glittering and captivating, began to move uncertainly, developing along its path the many elements of dissolution accumulated over a long time.

That is to say, the *unity* of power in which was based the only bond of *union* that existed among Mexicans was broken; but if, instead of saying to the nation: "You are free, you can constitute yourself in the way that most pleases you," etc., it had been said, "You are independent"; but this event, however glorious, does not instill the aptitude and knowledge necessary to appreciate the republican form properly; "only education, experience and the practical understanding of events are capable of valorizing those principles, principles that, when they have not put down deep roots in an innermost conviction, serve only to dazzle the imagination and carry off the spirit"; you must not, then, go out "from the orbit in which for so long" you have moved, nor enter "on a path totally unknown," no matter how glittering and captivating it might be, because you will move uncertainly, and "the many elements of dissolution accumulated over a long time" will develop. If the nation had been spoken to of this fate, we say, "the Mexicans, accustomed to obeying blindly the orders of the power," not because "mysterious and terrible," for the physical force in which it was based was in its greater part that of Mexicans, but rather because of the moral force that gave it its unity, they would have conserved that same obedience, strengthened with the love of independence, acquired in seven months (prematurely) by the *unity* produced by the bonds that so properly established the memorable Plan of Iguala. To think, then, as the gentlemen of *El Siglo* think, that whatever might have been the political system adopted after independence was completed would have produced the same ills that we are lamenting, is, it seems to us, the same as thinking that an infant, when it begins to walk, left without any support in its freedom of action and decision on broken and slippery ground, will suffer the same falls as when sustained by the hand of its wet nurse.

2

What Might Be the Causes of Our Ills, Conclusion

4. Because Mexicans were accustomed to not having any influence at all in public administration — continues *El Siglo* — once the doors of the magistracy, the offices, and the army were open to all ambitions, mania for public office spread its fatal influence, public posts were stormed by persons scarcely worthy of them, offices were filled with useless and burdensome people, and in the army promotions multiplied astonishingly, until those promotions came to the state of sad degradation in which we find them.

All of that better proves the inappropriateness of the federal representative system for Mexico and explains in a more satisfactory way the ills that are lamented even today. Who opened wide to Mexicans the doors of public administration, the magistracy, the offices, and the army? It was certainly not independence, but rather the systems; but among systems, none opens the path more to public administration, the magistracy, the offices, and even the army than the federal representative system, for that characteristic is precisely the quality that has earned it the preference of liberals. It must, then, be foreseen that the mania for public office would extend its fatal influence, that public posts would be stormed by persons scarcely worthy of them, that offices would be filled with useless and burdensome people, and that in the army promotions would be multiplied astonishingly. All that was very easy to foresee, recognizing the principle of popular sovereignty, equality of rights, removability of authorities, absolute liberty of the press, the division of powers, of elections, etc., on which the system is based, recognizing

Original title: "Polémica entre *El Universal, El Siglo XIX,* y *El Monitor Republicano,* entre 1848 y 1849: 'Cual sea la causa de nuestros males'" [concluye]. Source: *El Universal,* Mexico, January 25, 1849.

at the same time the lack of education, experience, and unifying bonds from which we Mexicans suffered.

> 5. Accustomed to seeing power in the hands of foreign authorities and of considering the law as an expression of the will of a despotic and absolute power, they acquired the habit of obeying both but with a passive obedience, child of terror. When they were told, then, that in the future the authority that had to rule the destinies of the country should come from their own hearts and should govern with laws that the national will dictated, the prestige that terror gave to the authorities was lacking, passive obedience to the laws was lacking, and moral obedience based in innermost conviction did not and could not replace it. From this has come, then, the little regard for men who have successively governed us; from this also the discredit of the laws, powerful only with the weak, impotent with the strong.

Although we do not understand how the *habit* of obedience comes from "seeing power in the hands of foreign authorities and of considering the law as an expression of the will of a despotic and absolute power," because this consideration and that view are biting and violent and consequently make it difficult for them to produce in man the docility and indifference that the *habit* of obeying requires, the gentlemen of *El Siglo* tender their reasons for believing it so, and that point does not interest us now. It is enough for us to know that there was a *habit of obedience* in Mexicans and that they broke this *habit* the moment it was said to them "that in the future the *authority* that had to rule the destinies of the country should come from *their own hearts* and should govern with laws *the national will dictated.*" And this you say, this you acknowledge so explicitly, expressly, and formally, you gentlemen editors of *El Siglo,* you the same ones who sometimes mocked, other times became irritated and even became infuriated with us because we have proclaimed and maintained that the principles of popular sovereignty, equality of rights, etc., are as absurd as they are *disastrous?* What is it, then, that we have done to you, what profound insult have we inflicted on you so that you fight us even against your own convictions? Well, put aside your scowl, let that hand of friendship extend; let us arrive at the place where it was necessary to join together; look now at the usefulness of the discussion when one lets oneself guide reason by the light of truth to an examination of the facts. *El Siglo* and *El Universal* now have a point of contact, a principle will now be the same point of departure for both combatants: "popular sovereignty is a DISASTROUS maxim." Yes, indubitably, disastrous and a thousand times detestable, given that just the announcement that the authority that in the future should rule the destinies of a people, the most docile and gentle of peoples, just the announcement, we say, that *the authority* would proceed from their own hearts was enough to break and rend, instantly, the *habit of obedience* it had acquired so that insubordination might occupy that place, so that impudence, rebellion, tumult, and restlessness were from then on its insignia and character. Disastrous and a thousand times detestable, loaded down with the execration and curses of thousands of victims whose blood has dyed our fields, turned our lakes red, stained our buildings, violated even our churches, at just the announcement that the laws the *national will* dictated would govern. Let our adversaries now judge if we are going off the road when we affirm that the adoption of the system that today rules the nation is the cause of our ills, given that the soul, the foundation of that system, is *popular sovereignty.*

6. It was said to Mexicans that all were equal, that as citizens all had equal duties and identical rights; the defenders of the new ideas raised their voices against stale statutes granted to the privileged classes; they did more, they carried their boldness even to open the doors of the monasteries of the religious and tried to destroy the monastic institutions. What has been the result? We all feel it; society divided into enemy classes, one against the others; dismal division, which has been the source of so many ills in the country!

And who told Mexicans *that all were equal, that as citizens all had equal duties and identical rights?* Was it independence or the federal system? And if, as cannot be denied, it was the latter and not the former that made such unfortunate remarks, and if, as *El Siglo,* unimpeachable witness, maintains here, the unfortunate consequences to which *El Siglo* refers with great exactitude come from this, to what, if not the federation, must the cause be attributed? But as interesting as that so necessary conclusion might be for our opinions and doctrines, it is more than interesting, it warms our heart, because it reveals that the desirability of the dogma of equality enjoys as much standing in the convictions of the gentlemen editors of *El Siglo* as it does in the convictions of the editors of *El Universal,* and consequently, when reason speaks they are not so opposed as they are when interest takes possession of ideas.

7. Finally, so as not to increase the number of such observations like those that go before, seeing the state of notable backwardness in which the nation found itself at the beginning of its political existence, one wanted to give it a violent push, one wanted to place it at the level of the civilized European nations; but our nation was not ready to respond to that movement, and in attempting to launch itself along the new path, a new element of dissolution was created. 8. From all this we infer that the multitude of ills that the nation has suffered during twenty-eight years is an inevitable consequence of the state in which it found itself on beginning the new march of its political existence. When our *patria* abandoned the name of colony to take that of independent nation, it could not change habits and customs as it had changed its name; the ground was not prepared to receive the new seeds that were required to make it bear fruit; they sprouted, perhaps, but the underbrush with which they mixed when they came up quickly weakened them.

We fear that our subscribers might believe that the two previous paragraphs are unauthentic; for that we ask that they compare them with the original and be persuaded that, although the language in which they are conceived is the same as that of *El Universal,* it is none other than *El Siglo* that has pronounced them.

9. Might one infer from all this that independence has been detrimental to us? Will we be accused of having made a lamentable gift to the brave men who toiled so hard to give us *patria* and died in honor of our liberty? No, certainly, in no way. Independence was achieved and had to be achieved because it was inevitable, because it was just, because it had to be beneficent.

Might one infer from all of this—ask our colleagues—that independence has been detrimental to us? To answer this question, we will first transcribe the conclusion of the article that concerns us.

Whatever might have been, say those gentlemen then, the system that the nation might have adopted for its government, the results would have been the same, the same disorder, the same confusion, the same upheavals; because these ills are not the particular result of *a certain system, but rather the inevitable consequence* of the antecedents we have related; and *it is probable* that under another system the damages *might have been worse.*

Well then, under the assumption that our present misfortunes are "the *inevitable* consequence" of the related antecedents; under the assumption that these misfortunes are the lightest that we might experience, given that with other systems *it is probable that they would have been worse,* under these assumptions, we repeat, assumptions that are not ours, but rather those of the gentlemen of *El Siglo,* we do not hesitate to respond to their question — "Does one infer from all this that independence has been detrimental to us?" — stating openly that, yes, because the conclusion seems correct to us. In our language we call "detrimental" what is damaging and causes ruin and discredit. It is thus that independence has damaged us, has ruined and discredited us; so independence has been damaging to us. That we have been damaged, ruined, and discredited is a proposition that does not require proof, because we are all in agreement with it; even *El Siglo* notes the following in its antepenultimate paragraph:

One will ask us: "In what, then, are the benefits resulting from that independence? Compare the year 1810, which excites such sad memories in the minds of liberals, with the year 1849 in which we live, and tell us frankly if such a comparison is favorable to the era called one of liberty and progress . . ." It is certain, we acknowledge, we have said it repeatedly: from independence until today, everything has been a chain of ills that, following one after the other without interruption, have exhausted, have beaten down the youthful vigor of the Republic.

Now, that independence is the reason we have been damaged, ruined, and discredited, *El Siglo* itself proves, if it is certain, as it assures us, that our ills have been the inevitable consequence of our antecedents and not the particular outcome *of a certain system.* For if under *whatever system* we had to have been damaged, ruined, and discredited after independence, "independence has been damaging to us indubitably." Our weak minds do not follow, then, why *independence was sought* and why *it had to be achieved;* what was the necessity that compelled us to worsen our condition; *why was it just,* and how *had it to be beneficent* if there was not a system in the world that could avoid our miseries.

Such is, to our way of thinking, the consequence that one deduces from the propositions of *El Siglo,* and, as shameful to reason as denigrating to the authors of independence, the extreme to which it drags along the caprice of denying that the federation is the cause of our ills. If the blind partisans of that system considered how much more is lost in attributing to independence rather than to their favorite system the misfortunes of the *patria,* we believe they would abandon their theme and would work with us in restoring good principles, thus preparing the nation for fundamental reforms, but peaceful and gradual ones, which might restore its *youthful vigor.*

Independence, say what you might, is a good, and a precious good that we know how to respect in all its worth; we are therefore very sensitive to the fact that fanaticism for a certain system of government blinds the understanding in such a way that it makes the understanding see in independence the origin of all our misfortunes. What would become of the system itself if such an opinion were generalized? Is it not enough to have destroyed the unity of power in which obedience was based, the sole bond that linked Mexicans, but do we also have to dispel the spirit of independence, stirring up common prejudices that only a crass ignorance has been able to introduce, breaking in this way the connection of union that might provide that bond? It will not be *El Universal* that does this! It will paint the misfortunes of the *patria,* yes, but it will never look for their cause in independence, but rather in the bad choice of principles, in the disastrous adoption of the means to enjoy the true and precious good of our independence.

3

What Might Be the Causes of Our Ills, Second Article

Regretful, like every good Mexican, for the series of calamities that have afflicted the country since the time of our political emancipation, wishing to ascertain the causes that have provoked those ills, and, most of all, anxious to dam up so much disaster, attacking the illness at its source, we proposed, in our editorial of January 21, to ascertain the causes of the ills we have suffered, and to do that we tried to analyze the facts and delineate the state in which the country found itself at the beginning of its new course as an independent nation. Our article has suffered the severe censure of our *illustrious* antagonists, the gentlemen editors of *El Universal*. These gentlemen have done us the honor of believing our observations just but have judged as spurious our arguments; they have agreed on the facts but not on the consequences we deduced from them. We pursue this question because it seems to us of vital importance and because we are not yet convinced of the truth of our adversaries' opinions; and one should not understand by this that we gainsay the *persuasive eloquence* that reigns in their *luminous writings;* no, sir, we are not yet convinced, because . . . what is one to do? . . . Our concerns, the obligations to our ideas, and who knows how many other motives hinder our desire to get to the truth, which, finally and at last, we will have to acknowledge when we come to understand the lamentable error writers on topics of public interest have made with the strange notion of believing and saying that civil societies have had the social pact as their original foundation. But let us get to our topic.

We will begin by frankly demonstrating to our adversaries that we refuse to believe they have so poor an opinion of us when they ascribe to us lamentable ignorance regarding the principal and most important

Original title: "Polémica entre *El Universal, El Siglo XIX,* y *El Monitor Republicano,* entre 1848 y 1849: 'Cual sea la causa de nuestros males'" [segundo artículo]. Source: *El Universal,* Mexico, February 3, 1849.

facts of our own history. We said, and we repeat today, that the cry of liberty that resounded throughout Europe had echoes in our *patria;* but we do not say with assurance, nor do we think of saying with assurance, that the masses that arose at the voice of the parish priest of Dolores were moved by that cry, which they neither heard nor could understand. We know, at least as well as our *illustrious antagonists,* that not the name of liberty, but others very different, among them that of the Virgin of Guadalupe, were the ones invoked the memorable night of September 15, 1810. We know equally well that if the *caudillos* of that glorious revolution, in declaring war on the Spanish power, had thrown forth the names of liberty and independence, they probably would have achieved nothing; those watchwords would have died without finding echoes in the multitude for which they had no significance whatsoever. We know, lastly, that the revolution was completed thanks to the Plan of Iguala, one of whose bases was the transfer to America of Ferdinand or other individuals of the reigning house; but we know also that the leaders of the revolution, in its first and last epoch, used the watchwords they invoked only to move the multitude. We know as well that the merit of the famous Plan of Iguala, whose realization is the holy grail of our *very esteemed compatriots* and colleagues, the gentlemen of *El Universal,* did not consist in its intrinsic goodness, but rather in having been the most convenient, the most suitable to the circumstances, because only by unifying the opposing interests that divided public opinion could one direct this public opinion to a single end. This the author of the above-mentioned plan tried, and he attained it, as was to be expected. But it will not appear that we have known all this after the gentlemen of *El Universal* undertook the enormous task of digging up the documents of the history of our country to throw in our faces the lamentable ignorance in which we find ourselves with respect to the most important facts of history. We will explain, then, in what sense we said that the cry of liberty that resounded throughout all Europe had echoes in our *patria.*

When the Peninsula struggled with the French troops that had invaded it, the writings, proclamations, manifestos, etc., multiplied there, in which were invoked the eternal principles of liberty and independence of nations. A portion of those writings found their way to us, and some Mexicans had, by this means, the first news of the doctrines that establish equality, sovereignty, and independence of peoples. These were the first germs of the new ideas, and this made some of our compatriots think about justice and the possibility that Mexico had to become an independent people, a project that the priest Hidalgo began in Dolores and that Iturbide completed eleven years after that first event. For this reason, then, we said that the cry of liberty throughout all Europe had had echoes among us. But we feel we have expounded excessively on this matter when the discussion calls us to a more worthy and comprehensive field.

We stated that the Mexicans, in the epoch when independence was achieved, did not form a compact people united by bonds of feeling, habits, and interests, but rather a people whose *unity* was exclusively based on that of the *power* everybody obeyed; we said also that such a bond was by its nature violent, and that once it was lacking, the dissolving elements that had germinated over some years had to produce their natural outcome. Gentlemen editors, in order to succeed in making you understand us, we will explain ourselves by means of a little example. Let us suppose a bad father of a family, despotic and absolute with his own children, as the Spanish power was with the unfortunate children of this soil. Let us suppose, then, that such a man directs the business of his house and sometimes uses his children as passive instruments. Let us suppose furthermore that such a one has completely neglected the education of his family to such an extent that no feeling, no interest, no bond unites its members. Nonetheless, the business of the house goes on with regularity; everyone obeys the leader, not because they are convinced they have to do so, but because at the slightest mistake the whip falls on them, and, intimidated and made brutish, they tremble at the sight of the one they see as an insufferable tyrant.

Well, when that man is missing, what will happen to the supposed family? Will the members continue united? Will they labor on into the future for the common good? Surely not. Should we then counsel the family that, to avoid the new ills that irremissibly threaten it, it search for another man, no less despotic and tyrannical than the first, so that everything continues as before? Or do we advise it that it manage itself by itself, that it not be frightened by the ills that might befall it, that it try to create and tighten bonds that unite its different members, that it profit by the experience, that inevitably events will afford it, and that in this way, despite the difficulties over which it stumbled at first, it will come to be at some time rich and happy? And so, how does this comparison seem to you, gentlemen of *El Universal?* It is very poor, very weak with respect to the picture the Mexican nation presents under Spanish domination. The unity of power the nation obeyed is not the unity that is sought and that must form the foundation of any type of government. That obedience was not based on a moral conviction, but on terror; there were not citizens who obeyed, but rather slaves made brutish and degraded who submissively lowered their heads on hearing pronounced the name of the king. When it was said, then, to the Mexicans that that tyrannical power no longer existed, that they were free and brothers, that New Spain had disappeared to give way to the free and independent Mexican nation, the difficulties, the stumblings, the setbacks were inevitable. Yet these ills had to produce the beneficial effect of experience. Thanks to it, the nation that at first had to encounter difficulties of every kind in its path, had to emerge with time from these difficulties, advance with order and regularity, and at some time come to be as rich, as powerful, and as happy as the magnificent elements that nature put at its disposal promised. But instead of profiting from the experience, instead of developing the natural elements, it appears that we pledged ourselves to follow fatally the course of apathy, disorder, waste, demoralization, in short, what we have followed until now. It appears we pledged ourselves to extinguish completely our powerful elements of wealth. For this reason, the Republic presents everywhere the sad picture of a rich and fertile nature struggling with a poor and aged society because of disorders.

Our colleagues at *El Universal* make a charge against us that we must not pass over in silence. They say that, fanatically pledged to the defense of the federal system, we have attributed the cause of our ills to the independence of the nation, and they cannot conceive how we said later with assurance that this had to be, because it was just, because it was necessary, because it had to be beneficent. Gentlemen of *El Universal,* we know how to appreciate the independence of the Republic as much as or more than you. We have not accused independence of having produced our ills. We said, and we repeat it today, that the state in which the nation found itself, thanks to the stupid policies of the kings of Spain, had to produce great upheavals at the time when the nation, abandoning the ancient yoke, would appear among free peoples. This change alone had to produce great upheavals, whatever might be the system the nation adopted. For that reason, we said it had indeed been a very great inanity to believe that the nation would be happy just by adopting the federal system; it is no less an inanity to attribute the cause of our ills to the adoption of that system.

4

What Might Be the Causes of Our Ills, Third Article

In our editorial of the third, we replied to some of the observations the gentlemen of *El Universal* made regarding the first article we published with the title at the head of this one; today we go on with our task, and we will explain our ideas about the causes that have contributed secondarily to the development of the ills Mexican society has suffered in the short period it has existed.

We have said that the ills the Republic has suffered are owed principally to the state in which the Republic found itself upon achieving independence; this glorious change, which elevated the old colony to the status of independent and sovereign nation, was not, nonetheless, enough to make it happy, although it must be considered the first step it had to take on the path to happiness. The gentlemen of *El Universal* have insulted us, an injustice we do not accept; nor can we pass over it in silence, and for this reason we will insist today on our ideas, reproducing without fear what we have said other times. They have asserted that we accused independence of having caused all our ills, and with this motive they declare emphatically that *El Universal* would not do such a thing! You, gentlemen editors, you who long so much for the year 1810, you who defend so much the system of the Spaniards when they ruled these countries, you who mocked the liberty, sovereignty, and independence of the nation, you say with assurance, seemingly filled with a prideful satisfaction, that independence "is a precious good that you know how to value in all its worth." We do not know how to reconcile such an explicit acknowledgment with what you assert in the same article, correspondent to January 25, when responding to our question, "might it be inferred from all this that independence has been harmful to us,"

Original title: "Polémica entre *El Universal, El Siglo XIX*, y *El Monitor Republicano*, entre 1848 y 1849: 'Cual sea la causa de nuestros males'" [tercer artículo]. Source: *El Universal*, Mexico, February 7, 1849.

you do not hesitate to say frankly, yes. There it said independence had harmed us, had ruined and discredited us, and consequently has been detrimental to us; and we, gentlemen editors, we have not asserted such things. We said that the upheavals the country has suffered were an inevitable consequence not of independence, but rather of the state in which the country found itself in achieving independence, of the defective education the Spaniards provided to our fathers, of the ignorance, of the brutalization to which the masses had been condemned by the viceregal power; those are the facts to which we allude when we assert that the ills that have overwhelmed the country were a powerful consequence of the aforementioned antecedents. Thus, then, independence, producing such an important change in our situation, placing the Republic on a new and little-known path, put us in a difficult position from which only some men of noble sentiments and uncommon abilities could have saved us. Unfortunately, such men were lacking, and difficulties, obstacles, and upheavals marked the first steps of the Republic in its halting advance. But this does not mean that our ills are the inevitable consequence of independence; if it were so, they would last as long as independence did; and reason, the experience of what has happened among other peoples of the world, the natural order of things, assure us that more or less quickly they must end, that more or less quickly the Republic has to occupy, among the free and happy people of the earth, the place that providence has designated for it. The seriousness of this matter, the injustice with which the gentlemen of *El Universal* have accused us of being enemies of our independence, have compelled us to deal with it in this article, despite having explained our ideas already in the correspondent of the third of this month. We will continue, then, the task we began.

After having achieved independence, the men who had contributed to it tried to find recompense for their efforts in the public posts the new order of things made accessible to all legitimate ambitions. Unfortunately, the men were few, very few, who, like the liberator of the North American republic, were happy with enjoying the sweetness of private life, the most beautiful recompense for good actions, which the man who is truly great and virtuous finds in the testimony of his conscience. Very much to the contrary, our men wanted to appear on the public stage, and as there was no competent judge who could designate for each one the place he merited according to his shareholdings, the result was that, so many private ambitions not being satisfied even if legitimate, they did not for that reason cease being detrimental, emulation was converted into envy, and, once the torrent of private passions ran wild, the public good served as pretext and powerful lever for sustaining mean interests.

This was the start of the general demoralization in which all classes of society found themselves submerged. Ambitions had no end, those who had ambitions threw themselves into revolution to satisfy them, and the first triumph of the revolutionaries expanded the field of ambition; and since then all those who have wanted to prosper at little cost have had to do no more work than hoist a revolutionary standard. This system continuing for twenty-eight years, we have seen the country constantly involved in internal wars; changes have followed one another without interruption, barely have some men taken possession of public posts, dispossessing from them those who occupied them, when others in turn have ousted and replaced them; these latter have ceded their place to those who have come after, and in this interminable chain of changes, in this continual series of revolutions, the country has not only not been able to prosper, but it has not even been able to remain stationary. In our history of disorders there is a fact we must note, and it is the following: generally, a minority, an insignificant faction, has managed to take possession of the public posts, holding them against the opinions of the majority of the nation. Nonetheless, there is nothing strange in this fact, and in order to recognize it, it is enough to analyze, although superficially, the history of our disorders and consider the effects that these would inevitably produce.

In that continual change of persons, of principles, and of systems, the nation has not seen any positive good; on the contrary. Today, as a consequence of a change of system, great goods are promised the nation, it came to conceive brilliant hopes for improvements, and tomorrow everything continues the same: the same system, the same abuses, the same waste in the administration, the same lack of morality in the functionaries. For this reason, all the principles, all the systems, have been brought into disrepute; for this reason the proclamations of many generals, the manifestos and programs of our governments, are considered ridiculous documents in which no one believes. This disrepute, which began through persons but then continued through principles and systems, has contaminated, in the end, the laws themselves, making them impotent and ridiculous. And this terrible ill that our legislators have not even been able to foresee has developed the most complete demoralization in all classes of society, loosening the most powerful social bonds. The result has been that the majority of the nation, which has seen itself sacrificed a thousand times to the interests of the ambitious ones, that has seen mocked the most agreeable hopes, the most brilliant promises, has lost its faith in all the constitutions, has suffered with indifference all the changes, and a miserable minority, taking advantage of that political indifference, has played at its whim with the destinies of the country.

We could expand upon this particular matter a great deal, but the fatal results of our revolutions are clear to everybody. For that reason, one voice alone, one single cry, is to be heard throughout the entire Republic: everyone clamors for peace; commerce wants peace; agriculture demands peace, industry needs peace, the entire Republic, finally, calls for peace to ensure its existence, to prevent the ills with which our past disorders threaten us still.

MARIANO OTERO

Mariano Otero (1817–50), born in Guadalajara, Jalisco, was a lawyer and a liberal politician. Otero was editor of the newspaper *El Siglo XIX* and a firm believer in liberal reform. He played a prominent role as a constitution maker in the 1840s.

The writings of Alexis de Tocqueville influenced Otero's thinking regarding the role of the judiciary, federalism, and particularly judicial review. Otero proposed in Mexico a legal recourse to protect individual rights against the state called *juicio de amparo.* Otero was acutely aware of some of the institutional flaws of the 1824 federal Constitution. When, in 1847, the liberal faction in Congress considered restoring the Constitution, Otero, a deputy, wrote a dissenting vote in which he elaborated on the reforms that were necessary to amend that charter. Otero's individual vote so influenced the deputies in Congress that when the 1824 Constitution was finally restored, an "act of reforms" (basically Otero's recommendations) was attached to it. He served as minister of internal and external relations under President Herrera in 1848. His untimely death from cholera at thirty-three years of age prevented him from participating in the 1856–57 Constituent Congress, which drafted the 1857 liberal charter. We present Otero's individual vote submitted to Congress on April 5, 1847.

Individual Vote
in the Constituent
Congress

Sir:

When I received from Congress the difficult assignment of taking part in shaping the constitution project, I did not think I would find myself in the painful situation in which I am, required, unfortunately for me, to provide my individual opinion in disagreement with the considerable majority of the commission. I hoped, on the contrary, that all of us, agreeing on the principles regarding the work that had been entrusted to us, would understand each other perfectly and, after discussing the form and details rather than the cardinal points, we would be able to present to Congress a report that, corrected by its wisdom, might fulfill the principal objective for which Congress was convened. The conservation of the federal system, the establishment of the liberal and philosophical principles that belong to our century, and the rapid and sure development of democracy are and have always been unanimously accepted in Congress. Because of the press of circumstances, the sad results of our past discords, the various opinions, inevitable in matters equally as difficult as they are important, they have not managed to come to an agreement on any differences other than the ones relative to the best means of making those principles triumph and those that consist in some questions of a secondary and even a transitory nature.

My hopes, nonetheless, have not been realized: our division, for which some incidents beyond the subject of my report were the reason, became inevitable and has put me in the disadvantageous position of entrusting to my powers alone the support of an opinion that is sensitive because of the matter with which it deals and much more so by reason of the circumstances.

But precisely because of the circumstances, it is in my judgment, sir,

Original title: "Voto particular presentado al congreso constituyente en la sesión de 5 de abril de 1847." Source: *El Republicano*, Mexico, nos. 105 and 106, April 15 and 16, 1847.

extremely advisable that as soon as possible the political organization of the country be settled definitively by means of the fundamental code. The advisability of adopting the code of 1824 with reforms cannot be disputed. The points of improvement that the security and progress of our institutions demand are clear; and to decree them there are, in the patriotism of the Congress and in the true state of public affairs, the elements required to fulfill our assignment honorably. But with the very tight deadline that has been set for us, and distracted by other very urgent assignments, I scarcely have time to indicate the reasons on which I base my opinion. I am consoled that my desire, more than registering an individual opinion, is explaining my convictions without any presumption that they would be approved.

That the present state of the Republic urgently demands the definitive establishment of the constitutional order is a truth one sees to be self-evident just by contemplating that very state. A war in which Mexico struggles for nothing less than its existence, half its territory occupied by its enemy, which already has seven states in its power, our primary maritime city having just yielded, and even our capital itself seriously threatened, nothing would be better than the existence of some political organization that, avoiding internal difficulties, leaves for later the debate over fundamental principles. But this organization does not exist, and to carry that very war through to its conclusion it is necessary as soon as possible to end the complications that stand in its way. In war, with even more reason than in peace, a people cannot live and resist except when they have the use of all elements of their power, and inasmuch as their political organization is the only one that unites, directs, and regulates them, it is not possible for the people to survive if they are maintained under an entirely defective organization. It is not our fault, but rather a consequence of the past, that the complexity of circumstances is as great as it is. The weakness of what exists is obvious, and there is no reason to hope otherwise.

Nothing is solid and organized. Everything we have is from yesterday: it was the difficult work of a movement that, as national as it might have been, could not produce the security that time and order do. The federal government has just organized itself, and already it is struggling with a thousand difficulties: with the violence of every type of reaction, the lack of means to command, the inexperience of an almost new system, the spirit of foreboding so characteristic of these moments, the alarm of all those who, seeing their fate linked to the institutions, do not know whether their interests will be sacrificed or respected. The states test their power with lack of confidence; the center sees that it is not as respected as it should be; and the revolution has just taken possession of the most beautiful of all our hopes, the Guard,[1] which in a moment of dizziness has given an example that the lovers of institutions hope will not repeat itself again. In short, we have today a public power overwhelmed with the difficulties of a necessary war and with the difficulties of an organization in which everything is transitory, in which no power has consciousness of its stability, in which are noted very alarming tendencies toward disunion, in which certain conditions of order are lacking, and all this when the civil war has been a fact, when it still is, perhaps, a threat.

In view, then, of so dangerous a situation, I have believed that every transitory state, just because it is such, would not have the necessary force to dominate the circumstances and that the best of all remedies would be to resolve the problem at once, take direction of affairs with a firm hand, adopt the reforms that are clamored for, provide institutions with the power they need, and make the nation enter, without the least delay and with all haste, the tranquil path of a constitutional system, which, not threatened by change, might give all social interests order, quiet, and security.

I am confirmed in this judgment that much more when I see that the revolution of August[2] and public opinion have preceded us in indicating the most appropriate means to attain that end. Because, in effect, it is necessary to consider that that movement has not been so solemnly accepted, except because it effected two great goods: it put an end to an order of things that conspired against republican forms, and it returned to Mexico the only institutions with which the Republic and liberty could be a reality among us. Thus, the reestablishment of the federation, decreed simply as a provisional organization and submitted to the decision of this Congress, has been confirmed and exists as a consummated and unassailable fact. The old states of the federation have again exer-

---

1. The National Guard. On February 27, 1847, the National Guard revolted against the national government in Mexico City. (Editor's note)

2. In August the federalist faction managed to gain power, restored the federation, and reenacted the 1824 federal Constitution. (Editor's note)

cised their sovereignty, have recovered the full exercise of that right, according to the express declaration of some and the way of operating of all of them, it being evident that no one is trying to oppose that fact and that nothing today would be so useless as to set out to demonstrate the need for and appropriateness of the federal system. Why, then, not end by recognizing that fact, sheltering the federal institutions from the dangers that its apparent state of near provisionality brings with it? The manner of doing it seems to me perfectly indicated by the press, the legislatures, and the considerable number of gentlemen deputies who have requested "the reestablishment of the Constitution of 1824 with the appropriate reforms."

The only idea from this proposal that might be able to divide us, the determination to make a new federal constitution or alter that one substantially, is a gratifying but lamentable idea, a temptation seductive to self-love but whose dangers should dissuade us. Since 1835,[3] with the Republic dominated by the force of a revolution, the crime was committed of destroying a constitution whose legitimacy has never been questioned and which had the immeasurable advantage of being the first and having lasted eleven years. How many who have wanted to construct another one on the ruins of that edifice have received the saddest disappointment? The discussion of fundamental laws, most productive amidst dangers, has come to be our normal state. All who had the illusion of believing that they were going to settle the question by means of their respective systems have seen in very little time their works ripped from their foundations by the torrent of revolutions. Before this, and without considering that the Constitutional Congresses have been ceaselessly occupied with discussing reforms, four constituent assemblies have been gathered in only twelve years without advancing a single step down the road of our reorganization and placing us, at the end of this time, in the same situation we were in 1835, but with the sad fruits of that disorder, with the territory dismembered, civil war converted into a habit, society being dissolved by corruption.

Is this not a vivid and indelible lesson on the respect with which the original institutions of a people should be regarded? If we yield today to the temptation of forming a new code in order to offer, in its literary

3. In 1835 the Constitution of 1824 was annulled; a new centralist constitution known as the Seven Laws was enacted in 1836. (Editor's note)

and scientific point of view, advantages that are very obvious over the Constitution of 1824, who would assure us that this work, child of our sad circumstances, published in the midst of civil discords and exposed to the judgment of so many opinions, to the clash of so many interests, could rise above that habit of contempt, of inconstancy and destruction that respects nothing? What hope could we have that it would not pass into oblivion like the earlier ones, after a short and tempestuous reign, during which neither were its principles popularized nor the practical advantages of its application felt? The first condition of life for fundamental laws, after their suitability, is the people's love and veneration.

But this condition does not come to the people from the Constitution's scientific and literary perfection, because there are few judges of that and these are divided on so controversial a subject, but rather from the memories that are aroused, from the opinions that are transmitted about it from fathers to sons. In this regard, duration is in itself a recommendation; and the best code that might be drawn up by us today could not compete with respect to those advantages with the code of 1824, superior to all in veneration and legitimacy. In the epoch of its formation no one contested the powers of deputies elected in the midst of a profound peace; all the states concurred on that solemn pact, and it was also confirmed in the midst of the emotions of a people who had just won their independence and who surrendered their most happy future to dreams. The entire nation accepted the code of 1824 as the reward for its past sacrifices, as the symbol of its future hopes, and retained such a love for it that deception and oppression were necessary to wrench it from the nation's hands, and it has never stopped fighting for that code. On the other hand, the memory of that Constitution is linked to the establishment of the Republic and the representative system, for which that Constitution became the security; to local liberties, so beloved by the nation; to our respectability abroad, which remained inviolable during its reign; to the only tranquil and happy days we have ever enjoyed. The most cursory examination of our present circumstances should convince us that we are very far from being able to have such favorable omens; it should persuade us that nothing today will be as patriotic as organizing the fundamental laws of the Republic under the protection of all those positive influences.

In order to understand the complete importance of this observation, it is necessary to remember that peoples are governed by habits and beliefs, by imagination and customs. From the point of view of a skillful plan and a brilliant exposition, the constitutions of revolutionary France will always serve as admirable models. There the principles were expressed with energy and concision, the ideas developed in all their details, the most profound and ingenious plans followed with mastery; and nonetheless, one after another was passed without taking hold of society, while, despite its unfavorable origin, the Constitution of 1815 has lasted thirty years simply because it came to be regarded as the compromise between the old and new states, simply because it made the influences of the past serve the realization of hopes for the future. The example of England is still more obvious. That nation, cradle of representative institutions, has for two centuries maintained its Constitution disseminated among a multitude of laws, many of them obscure and badly written, and, nonetheless, such is the love of all English citizens for their institutions that reforms are initiated only around special items that require improvement and that if one were to announce a project to reduce those original foundations to a code as perfect as that wise nation would so easily be able to do, all parties would unite against the unhappy instigator of the perfection. The Constitution of the United States itself is very far from being a finished work. In large part it has a relation to the social customs of that people, and precisely because it is in perfect harmony with them, it has presided over the most admirable advance recorded in ancient and modern history. From this it follows that an intelligent legislator will always prefer a constitution in which the people see their glory, their nationality, and their liberty symbolized, although it might not be perfect compared with another that might be but lacks memories and influences.

Finally, and to express with loyalty to the Congress the motives that have made me decide in favor of the continuation of the Constitution of 1824, I will say that I consider the advantage of its legitimacy invaluable, which seems of little importance to some others. Earlier I stated that the result of the destruction of our original pact was to proclaim that the society was not constituted and so to abandon it to the turbulent struggle of all those who believed they possessed the secret of securing its stable organization on various foundations. And to end this lamentable movement, what means would be better than returning to the starting point, recognizing that the nation has been and is constituted, condemning the results of a crime in which we would appear equally complicit by adopting its outcomes, announcing solemnly on behalf of the Union that in Mexico there are no rights other than those created by the Constitution of 1824, and requiring of everybody the fulfilling of correlative obligations? Only in that way will we be able to say that we have returned respectability to the laws, and this type of renunciation of the omnipotence of constituent power before the legitimacy of our original pact would be an example as useful for the Republic as it would be honorable for the Congress.

I insist, then, on the opinion I have declared other times, that we ourselves must limit our powers and our task only to making, in the Constitution of 1824, the reforms that its own stability requires, and this for reasons that are in the grasp of everyone and are, to my way of thinking, incontestable.

The necessity of reforming the Constitution of 1824 has been as generally recognized as its legitimacy and appropriateness. Regarding it, all learned men of the Republic have been in agreement, and they corroborated the strength of the best arguments with the irresistible evidence of the facts. Who, remembering that under that Constitution our civil discords began and that it was so impotent against the disorder that, instead of suppressing it and governing society, the Constitution had to yield in the face of the disorder, will be able to doubt that the Constitution contained within itself the causes of its weakness and the elements of dissolution that undermined its existence? And if this is so, then, as it is in fact, will it be a good for our country to establish that Constitution with no more strength or force than it had before, so that its name again becomes only an illusion? Would not reestablishing the federal system under the same conditions with which experience has demonstrated it cannot exist decree its ruin, and precisely today when much more unfavorable conditions exist than those that were enough to destroy it? Nor can the situation of the Republic now endure any longer an uncertain and provisional state. The seriousness of its ills, the force with which events are rushing toward us, demand prompt and effective remedy; and because this remedy consists in establishing the constitutional order, no less than in the appropriateness and solidity of the way it is resolved, it seems totally beyond doubt that it is completely necessary to proceed immediately to the reforms.

In days much less unfortunate, reforms were the constant desire of the nation, expressed through all the legitimate means of which it usually makes use to enunciate its will. Never, from 1834 until now, has the restoration of the federal system been proclaimed without requesting as a necessary condition, in order to give stability to the federative principle and to bring its consequences into line, important reforms in the old Constitution. No one has advocated that it should once again govern in the country and remain intact contrary to the indications of experience. On this point, I understand for this very reason that the fullness of our powers works in all its force. Thus, wanting nothing to do with refuting an opinion that does not have partisans, I am going to show Congress what might be, from my point of view, the indispensable and most urgent modifications our situation requires and the best means of facilitating other new modifications for later when we arrive at that degree of perfection that present circumstances do not permit us to attempt, but whose attainment will also be credited to us if we know to prepare for it, starting now, with the foresight, prudence, and insight that must distinguish legislators of nations. For the rest, time does not permit me to be excessive. I propose passing over each point with only simple suggestions, and what I am going to say about the proposed reforms will prove they cannot be deferred, neither for another epoch nor another Congress, no matter what its proximity might be.

In 1832 it began to be observed that the federal Constitution had to put the exercise of citizens' rights in order, and I have believed that this must be the first of the reforms, persuaded as I am that it is on this point that the principle of the form of governments is characterized and guaranteed, depending on how those rights are extended or limited. For that, it has been said with reason that "in the popular states the laws that establish the right of suffrage are fundamental and as important as those that in monarchies establish who is the monarch";[4] and the Constitution must never leave to secondary laws the power to destroy them. The method copied from the institutions of the north, and adopted by ours of 1824, of leaving that arrangement to each one of the states seems to me dangerous and of little import: dangerous because in this way an objective as essential as the very form of government is abandoned by the federal power to other outside powers and exposes the Republic to a very terrible irregularity, from which only its customs have been able to preserve the Americans; and of little import by reason of which (and this

4. [Montesquieu 1748], *Spirit of the Laws,* book 2, chapter 2.

is the principal one) the federal system in its final state of perfection, as we wanted to adopt it, is not as it was earlier—a simple society of societies—but rather, through the most admirable political mechanism, the citizens of a state form a perfect society among themselves for the matter of their internal administration, and united with those of the other states themselves form, but without the intervening of its local powers, another nation, no less perfect, whose government is general; the result of which is that the action of the citizen on the government and of the government on the citizen in everything relative to the Union is exercised directly without any intervention whatsoever from the authority of the states. This principle, marvelous step forward of social science, is observed in comparing the mechanism of the American Constitution with the weak confederations of old, which succumbed perhaps because of this defect, and surely dominated the thought of the authors of that Constitution when they promulgated it in the name of the people of the United States. Well then, once this truth is established and once the fact demonstrated that the government of the Union is, from a certain point of view, a truly national government, and once it is characterized through its form as a popular representative republic, it is necessary to agree that to it, and only to it, belongs the responsibility of preserving this character and regularizing its own organization through the fundamental law.

Once the rule on this point is introduced, Congress will see that it could not be more liberal. Granting the right of citizenship to every Mexican who has reached the age of twenty, who has not been sentenced in a legal process to any shameful punishment and has an honest means of living, the democratic principle is established and guaranteed in all the states of the Union in the most open way that could be desired. The idea of requiring a certain income as necessary to enjoy the rights of the citizen, an idea recommended by some writers of reputable liberalism and also adopted in some of our constitutional laws, does not seem appropriate to me, because never can a reason be given that justifies one amount over another; and principally because estimating that amount as a guarantee of morality and independence in order for it to be just, it would be necessary to vary it with respect to the diverse professions and the different localities of the Republic, which would be so difficult as to be impossible. Apart from this, so that this right has the importance due it, and so that its exercise would be the fundamental foundation of public order, it is indispensable that a secondary law regulate the procedure by which it should be guaranteed, exercised, and suspended.

In my judgment, in the Constitution, once the foundation is established, only the privileges inherent in that quality remain to be determined; and Article 2 that I propose establishes that the right of citizenship carry with it the right to vote in popular elections, the right to exercise the right of petition, the right to gather in order to discuss public affairs, and finally the right of belonging to the National Guard, all in accordance with the laws. No mention had been made in any of our earlier constitutions of these three last privileges, and nonetheless they are of the greatest importance. If the entire theory of representative democracy were reduced to summoning the people one day in order to elect their mandataries and relinquish to them afterward the direction of their affairs, it would be certain, as some writers claim, that the representative system had not been able to replace the old procedures, whereas leaving to the people constant participation in and direction of public affairs through peaceful discussions places the representatives under the influence of their own constituents, business affairs under the power of public opinion; and in this way the peaceful and reasoned action of the people is substituted, with a thousand advantages, for the sudden rush of passions of the multitude, deceived in the forum by the intrigues of ambition or the spellbinding eloquence of political speakers. Even under monarchical governments, where the democratic element is subject to a thousand hindrances and subordinated to other adverse authorities, one admires how the majority, supported by those powerful resources, comes to take direction of affairs and advances every day in greatness and power. These means are the essence of the representative system. The National Guard is the most solid guarantee of republics, and this guarantee must also be set down in the fundamental code.

Congress, called to establish these principles that by themselves alone amount to an enormous advance, cannot disregard them because the first attempts are naturally weak and imperfect. This is the natural progress of all human affairs. It matters not at all that the right of petition is exercised under the direction of the passions of our epoch, that the first popular gatherings do not offer all the interest of their great purpose, or that the National Guard, still limited to much less than it should be, displays some defects. In the wise combination of all these peaceful methods of government there is an excellent intensity of advancement: that once public affairs are taken from the field of riots to deliver them to democratic institutions, these institutions will come to prevail, even more because it is true in our country they do not encounter those obstacles that have made violent upheavals and bloody revolutions necessary in other places. To depict the defects of the attempt in order to make the institution hateful is the sophism of the hidden enemies of liberty; but history rejects this sophism. "Even the Roman people," says a profound writer, "this model of all free people, was not capable of governing itself when it emerged from the oppression of the Tarquins. Degraded by the slavery and ignominious labors the Tarquins had imposed, the people, in the beginning, were no more than a stupid rabble, which had to be flattered and governed with the greatest wisdom so that, accustoming themselves little by little to breathing the salubrious air of liberty, these souls weakened, or more correctly brutalized under tyranny, might gradually acquire that austerity of customs and that noble and indomitable pride that made it, in the end, the most respectable of all peoples."[5]

In most of the known constitutions, not only are the principles relative to the organization of public powers fixed, but also the foundations of individual guarantees are established, probably because the social condition of the members is the original objective of the institutions and one of the most distinctive characteristics of the true nature of governments; and notwithstanding the fact that these guarantees, in the reality of things, depend on the individual measures of the states, our federal constitution declared that the nation was obligated to protect the rights of the citizen by wise and just laws; and, in imitation of the code of the United States, in various of its articles are found truly philosophical provisions directed to that very end. I have not yet found a solid argument against this means of putting the guarantees of man under the protection of the general power, and those that should have convinced me in their favor are not few. On this point, the lack of precision in constitutional declarations does not present any disadvantage, because the principles dictated by reason are the same in all countries and under all climates. But without them, how could the general government protect those rights or strengthen the reality of democratic institutions in all the

5. J. J. Rousseau, in his *The Government of Poland* (Indianapolis: Hackett Publishing Company, 1985).

states; how could it make effective the principles of liberty? It is, on the other hand, incontestable that, in the present state of our civilization, such an interesting arrangement could not be left to the absolute discretion of the states. Consequently, I understand that the present constitution must establish individual guarantees, and on foundations so stable that no man who inhabits any part of the territory of the Republic, without distinction between citizens and foreigners, would have on this point anything to ask of the best laws of the land.

Swayed by this thought, I propose that the constitution specify the individual rights and ensure their inviolability, leaving to a subsequent law, but general and of a lofty character, to specify them in detail. Because the gentlemen deputies will have already observed in this matter that, even being reduced to fundamental principles, it is necessary to give them a breadth little suited to the limits and character, so to speak, essential to the constitution; and if one authority had to proclaim the principle in its vague and abstract generality, and another authority had to specify the details on which its reality depends, the former will have done nothing. In order to recognize in this matter the inadequacy of general principles, it is enough to choose some point, as if at random; for example, security: all our constitutions established a certain length of time between detention and formal imprisonment, anticipating that in this period of time the statement of the accused might be taken; and all, forgetting the instance of the apprehension of the confirmed criminal in a site different from that of its judge, have allowed an exception in which the infraction of the law becomes inevitable. The same can be observed with respect to property: the broadest declarations have not been sufficient to stop the system of forced loans and taking possession of beasts of burden, which are nothing more than crimes against property. A more extensive law that sets forth the principles exactly, that recognizes the exception and, above all, establishes the means of making them effective, is the only way it will be able to fulfill this very important need. In the constitution, I propose that only the general principle be stated, that its inviolability be declared, and the only situation in which the guarantees can be suspended be set forth, not all the guarantees, but only those respective to the detention of the accused and the searching of homes. If, with more tranquil times coming, Congress could concern itself with the creation of that law, seemingly a work for it alone, it would raise a monument of very agreeable recognition to its memory.

Passing from these matters to the organization of the federal powers, primary object of the Constitution, the legislative function is presented as carried out by a Congress composed of two chambers. The one, popular and numerous, represents the citizenry and expresses the democratic principle in all its energy. The other, smaller and slower, has a very difficult double character, because it represents at the same time the political bodies considered equal, and it comes to fulfill the urgent need that every social organization of a body has, storehouse of wisdom and sound judgment that moderates the impetuousness of unthinking democracy and, in the incessant personnel change of popular institutions, preserves the science of government, the memory of traditions—the treasure, so to speak, of a national policy. On this point, more than on any other, I feel the lack of the possibility to work out my ideas calmly and to express thoroughly to Congress the reasons for the reform I am proposing.

With respect to the popular chamber, having set firmly as a principle that it should represent individuals, there remain only three objects of reform: its number, the conditions of eligibility, and the form of election.

Regarding the first, the Constitution of 1824, setting the base of one deputy for each eighty thousand inhabitants, established a less numerous popular chamber than we have had, and in this it must be reformed. The chamber of deputies in the best constitutional countries has a growing number of individuals, because only in this way does it manifest the democratic element, unite great quantity of learning, represent all interests, all opinions, and is not exposed to some few rising to the top and the will of this minority ruling it without difficulty. A chamber elected on the same base on which our current Congress has been, even in a country where the general business might not be less important for each individual, where the public functions might not be held in little regard, could scarcely bring together one hundred representatives, with the consequence that the law might come to have only fifty-one votes among the democratic representation.

With regard to conditions of eligibility, my opinion is very clear: I consider them a very sad measure of good sense. I believe that the paramount condition is to obtain the confidence of the people and that, in this matter, there cannot be guarantees more important than the organization of the electorate. In effect, all the desired conditions of eligibility should be set down; a mature age, a respectable profession, a comfortable income, residence or birth in a specified place. By chance, will everyone who has these qualities be good as deputies? And will the people have elected them because they have them? No. A distinguished writer in public law[6] observes that "elections fall to specific persons precisely because they have qualities that are lacking in the greater part of those who have the legal qualities"; and experience teaches us that, although the law speaks of age, income, and residence, the elector looks for the opinion he believes patriotic, the interest he estimates as national, and the capability most suitable for making those very opinions and those very interests triumph. The law does not surpass customs or have an effect on facts; in a word, it is useless.

Nor can it prevent persons little worthy from entering into the sanctuary of the laws, because the abilities it requires will never be more than probable, and remotely probable with respect to certain qualities; and when the misguided electoral body makes a bad choice, all those stipulations will be powerless, because there will always be individuals who meet the requirements the law establishes as a measure without having the qualities it seeks; this makes for a bad choice. Who does not know that frenzied demagogues can be found with all the strictest requirements of eligibility, just as men of order among enthusiastic youth without resources? In Rome the tribunes of the people were patricians, and in the Convention the highest nobility concurred in destroying the monarchy and putting the king to death. There is still more: just as there are, among those the law admits, some who are not worthy of suffrage, some are found among the excluded ones who are more than worthy of it. The result is that the system I oppose either keeps capable men from the matters of business or contravenes the law approving invalid elections. Of this, the greater part, if not all our chambers, has given an example; and in England it is known that Pitt and Fox entered Parliament only by means of a deceitful supposition that mocked the law. The best is, then, that we separate ourselves from the routine and recognize the truth. Later I will talk about the arrangement of the electoral power.

Moving on to deal with the organization of the Senate, no man moderately educated in these matters is ignorant of the fact that this is the most difficult and, at the same time, the most important point of republican constitutions. "Each day we must be more convinced," says one of

6. Pinhetro Ferreira, *Curso de derecho público.*

the most illustrious thinkers of the century, "that the ancient peoples understood infinitely better than we liberty and the nature of free governments . . . above all, they entrusted the sacred cult of the *patria,* the priesthood of liberty, the spirit of life and durability, the guardianship of traditions, of glory and the fate of the nation, the constant foresight of the future to a senate in which they make an effort to concentrate everything that is good and great of the aristocracies, rejecting at the same time whatever there is in them of the defective."[7] Villemain,[8] analyzing the Roman Constitution, attributes all the glory and liberty of the first republic of ancient times to the organization of the Senate, which, gathering together all the eminent men, governed, through centuries, the pieces of business with the greatest wisdom. In the United States, observes the author of *Democracy in America,* that "Senate gathers together the most distinguished men, ensuring that all the words that go out of that body would do honor to the greatest parliamentary debates of Europe."

In our country, the need for this kind of body has made itself felt in such a way that the organization of the senate is precisely where our constitutional efforts have been most varied, and where, whenever it has been a matter of reforms, the greater number of plans has been presented; the idea of summoning there the landowning class enjoying, finally, neither a small nor insignificant favor. But is this idea really fair? Permit me, sir, to say no, because we seek by other measures that institution we need so urgently. It seems to me that in a republic, the representation of certain classes that do not have political privileges lacks the foundation with which it exists in other institutions and sacrifices all the other eminent conditions of wisdom and patriotism required in the conservative body to one condition only, a certain love of order. If there were no landowners, in a country where the public path produces misfortunes and sometimes misery rather than probity, if the Constitution summons to the Senate the most capable and meritorious men, these men will contribute to public order, to the stability of the laws, and to the respect for the legitimate interests of minorities, which it is necessary neither to eliminate nor damage, but rather to make effective those guarantees sought with the summoning of certain classes, in the

7. Sismonde de Sismondi, *Ensayo* . . .
8. In his discourse on the Republic of Cicero.

sense of the general good; and, moreover, they will unite in themselves ardent love of the *patria,* worship of liberty, and the science of public affairs that the simple assets of fortune do not give and that are absolutely indispensible in that elevated post, leaving this path of honor open also to the propertied class, and more readily than to any of the other classes if it combines those very abilities without which it can have no right to govern its country.

To support this opinion, since it is not given to me to expound to the chamber some observations about the influence that the organization of property has in the political order, because this would take us to the most abstract and broadest theories of social science, let me be permitted to observe that in the first and most brilliant of the modern aristocracies, that of the English Constitution, this prerogative has been possible only inasmuch as the public path has been the primary preoccupation of the British nobility because it constantly provided the most eminent men for the administration, for Parliament, and for the profession of arms, and because, like the patrician rank of Rome, it has always been eager to be honored, admitting into its breast all great men who arose from the people. The idea that property owners, simply for being such, would be devoted to the administration of public affairs seems to me neither just nor appropriate. The only aristocracy in democracies is the aristocracy of knowledge, of virtue, of service; and if this is not improvised nor can be found readily in a nation that, assailed by revolutions, has seen immorality corrupt everything, neither are constitutions works of a single generation; it is necessary to create, from this moment, what must exist someday.

Without ceasing to appreciate the difficulty that this reform presents, I understand, sir, that preserving the representation of the confederated bodies in the Senate as a whole, the problem can be resolved by simple methods, as are all those of the better-arranged institutions we know. If the term of office of this chamber is longer than that of the other bodies and the other authorities of the state, with this we will have ensured that its action is the most permanent and regularized. If, besides participating in the legislative power, its functions can be extended to other equally interesting purposes, if it is permitted to be, in part or as a whole, a consultative body so that it is always available to the great affairs of interior and exterior policy, it will also become the power of greatest influence. If it is replaced partially, always leaving a considerable majority, it will have no difficulty in preserving a national policy. If a prior public career is required to belong to it, which supposes expertise in public affairs, the Senate will be made up of experienced men, and it will be considered the honorable end of a civil career. Finally, if, after having made it in that way the most important, the most influential, lasting, and respectable body of the state, for the success of the election it has recourse to that admirable means that democratic institutions include and both ancient and modern writers on public matters extol, and if, in a fixed period in each state, public spirit is moved and produces the decisive electoral moment for no other reason than to select a very high magistrate, then only a distinguished reputation will be able to win the votes of the majority of citizens. Trusting, then, in these means, I have the hope of believing that, without denaturing democracy, with neither hateful exclusions nor unmerited privileges, we will have succeeded with the principal point of our political organization.

Consistent with these ideas, I propose that the Senate be composed of a number three times the number of states in the federation, so that, having sixty-nine senators, they might have a quorum with thirty-five, and resolutions might have at least eighteen votes; I propose as well that every two years a third be replaced; I request a prior public career as advisable, as easy to be certified without danger of fraud; and meanwhile, so that the direct election of senators might enter into our constitutional practices and be perfected by them, I recognize the need for each one of the states electing two, thereby guaranteeing the federal principle, another third being named by the authorities most appropriate to summon eminent men to the management of public affairs. Giving the right to put forward this third to the executive, the Senate itself, and the Chamber of Deputies, and to this last the right of selecting definitively, a very substantial step occurs; because this chamber is the pure expression of democracy and of the federation, it has great guarantees of success, and it takes from the Senate the formidable right of electing its members, a right that, forgetting the doctrine of a profound writer on public affairs,[9] was conferred on the Senate by one of our constitutions. So, in only three articles, I expressed as many reforms as seemed to me appropriate for the organization of the legislative power.

In measures of the federal Constitution relative to the creation of

9. Montesquieu, in *Spirit of the Laws,* book 2, chapter 3.

laws, much attention is called to what is needed for a resolution to become law, the vote of two-thirds of the initiating chamber combined
with the vote of a little more than one-third of the reviewing chamber, because in this way the advisable equilibrium in both bodies is
destroyed; and even further attention is called to the fact that in this
situation, the objections of the government might not require a greater
number of votes to reproduce this outcome, as happens when the majority of the two chambers has approved it. An example perfectly clari-
fies the contradiction in this inexplicable theory: suppose a resolution
comes out of Congress with all the votes of one chamber and a majority
of the other, if the government makes objections to it and the same vote
is reproduced, it is not yet law, because there is not two-thirds of the
vote in both chambers; and if that same resolution had had fewer votes
in its favor, that is to say fewer guarantees of success, if its approval,
instead of unanimous, had been by those two-thirds of the initiating
chamber, and not by the majority of the reviewing chamber, but rather
only by a little more than a third, then, despite the objections of the executive, it would have become law.[10] To avoid this unfortunate circumstance, which can be serious, one article of the reforms sets forth that
the approval of the majority in both chambers is necessary for all laws.

With respect to the executive, the reforms that seem necessary to
me are few but very obvious ones. Nowhere does the Constitution of
1824 appear as defective as in the part that established the post of vice
president of the Republic. It has been said many times now, and without argument, that placing over against the supreme magistrate another
standing magistrate, one who has the right to succeed him in whatever
situation, was a creation only a people like those of the United States
could adopt, where respect for the decisions of the law is the primary
and strongest of all customs, where the progress of constitutional order

---

10. Permit me a calculation that makes that contradiction even more palpable. Let us
suppose that the Senate consists of 30 individuals and the Chamber of Deputies of 75: if
a resolution initiated in the Chamber of Deputies has in its favor, in the first and second
discussion, the vote of 75 deputies and 19 senators, it takes only the vote of the executive
for it not to become law; if the same resolution, initiated in the Chamber of Senators,
had in its favor the vote of 20 and of 26 deputies, it would be law despite the objections
of the executive; in the first case, the law that is not passed has 94 votes in favor and 11
against; in the second case, the law that is passed had 46 votes in favor, 59 against.

during more than sixty years has not been disturbed by a single revolution, but completely inadequate for a country where political questions have always been decided by revolutions and not by the peaceful methods of the representative system, in which possession of the supreme command has been the first motive of all disputes, the reality of all changes. And when one observes that the electoral method was settled in the Constitution of [1]824 in such a way that the votes were not cast separately for president and vice, but rather it was agreed to confer this latter post on the one who had fewer votes, declaring in that way that the vice president of the Republic would be the vanquished rival of the president, one must be astonished that such an unfortunate combination would be allowed. Thus, it has had an effect on not a few of our dissensions and civil wars and has generalized the opinion that the post should be eliminated. I have been of the belief that this reform was one of the most necessary because it was essential to free our first and next constitutional periods from this danger, leaving for later other improvements that I do not consider to be absolutely indispensable. I also advise reform in the vital area of responsibility.

In this area I consider essential resolving a multitude of difficult questions and settling the true moral character of the chief of the executive power, declaring him inviolable as long as he acted through a responsible minister, who would be responsible for any infraction of the law, whether it consist of acts of commission or mere omission. With respect to procedure, according to the federal Constitution, either of the chambers could hear the accusation as two-thirds of the grand jury was necessary to decide on bringing the lawsuit, the matter then passing to the Supreme Court of Justice. This system has made responsibility illusory. To the Chamber of Deputies, because more impassioned in its love for the institutions, must belong the pronouncement of whether or not there is cause for bringing the case, and for this a simple majority should suffice, because the respect owed to the laws and the interests of society, directly affected in the cases of responsibility of public functionaries, demand that acts or omissions of these functionaries be examined whenever any doubt might be raised with respect to the infraction; they require that a lawsuit then be heard, and this step is the only result of that pronouncement. It falls to the Senate, which will combine justice with the love of institutions, to give a verdict on the matter, because political crimes, by their very nature, must be judged differently from common crimes: in them, the procedures require less waiting and greater reputations and scope of action in the judges; innocence is guaranteed by requiring three-fifths for censure; and determination of the punishment is left to the judicial power, or the entire lawsuit in common crimes. All these reforms are contained in three articles. I must, finally, warn the chamber that, in this matter, I have differed from some of my fellow committee members, who wanted to establish an impeachment procedure, not only for the crimes designated by the law, but also in general to remove the president and his ministers from office because of ineptitude or bad conduct and declare them unfit for other employment, basing my opinion on two arguments. In the first place, I do not believe that one should treat those high functionaries from a state inferior to that of the least man, violating in their case the principle of natural justice, according to which no one can be punished for a deed if this deed has not been defined precisely beforehand and prohibited as a crime. In the second place, it seems to me that that arbitrary power would be a tremendous weapon in the hands of the factions, one more hindrance that will keep honorable men without ambition from power and will be a seed of incessant convulsions. In a nation where there have been so many crimes and no punishment, we congratulate ourselves if we succeed in ensuring that those crimes that have been clearly defined do not go unpunished.

The reforms I propose in the judicial power will be better explained further on. For now I will only say something about the electoral system.

I have already said that, in my judgment, the electoral system is the foundation and guarantee of every constitution, and most especially of democratic constitutions, which make all the powers of the state derive from election, because whether public functionaries are good or bad, whether they represent the entire nation or only a more or less numerous, vanquishing, and exclusive faction depends on elections. But as this final outcome depends not only on the general statement that establishes who has the right of suffrage, but also on all the measures that regulate the way suffrage is exercised, all the details are of interest, and from this it follows that in this matter, as in that of individual guarantees, not everything can be reduced to fundamental principles, sole property of the constitution, and that only an extensive and well-worked-out law can bring about the longed-for reform.

Unfortunately, in this matter, our constitutional right is beginning to weaken from the most lamentable backwardness. We have barely made any progress with respect to the flawed system adopted by the Spanish Cortes, which was the one through which we came to understand the representative system; and I dare maintain that, to the extent we do not correct that part of our Constitution, major reforms regarding the rest will be useless, because the indispensable condition for realizing all those reforms will be lacking, electing the most worthy citizens to carry out public functions.

Because of a defect in our laws, the primary elections, whether they are as tumultuous as when all the votes are admitted without demanding any previous requirement, votes that, to ensure victory, the multitude repeats as many times as it wants, or whether it be more regulated through previous distribution of ballots, they are always verified without citizens coming together as a body and with only a simple majority of votes. Passing these elections through two further levels, then, in which an absolute majority for the formation of the electoral college and the appointment of the elector or deputy are now required, we have in this way made our elections indirect at the third level, without taking into account moral causes that contribute so powerfully to producing very bad results; and submitting this procedure to a very simple calculation, it comes out that a deputy can represent, as a vote of the majority, the vote of two out of one hundred or, at most, three votes out of the same number, a very favorable and extraordinary supposition.[11]

---

11. As dry as this calculation is, the importance of this matter obligates me to express it here, because the force of its demonstration seems incontestable to me. Given the procedure of the elections, any number can be taken to work with, 12,001 for example; if, then, only the relative majority is needed, supposing that the primary election is decided by a third, without counting omitted votes or dispersed votes, that is to say by 4,001, is not to calculate too low, which number represents the primary elector; but as all of them are never united, and the majority is sufficient, an electorate that represents 2,001 citizens can elect also, by simple absolute majority of those present, a secondary elector who does not represent more than 1,001. In its turn, and for the same reasons, the secondary electorate, with a majority that represents only 501, can elect a deputy who represents 251 citizens from among 12,001, which is the ratio of 2,998/12,001 to 100. The simple possibility of this case is sufficient to impugn and discard such an absurd system. But I do not want to go to extremes, and so that one sees what such a system of indirect election at three levels and absolute majority is in its best combinations, I am going to suppose a very favorable case, in which the primary election was decided by two-thirds, and in which in all the electoral bodies and all the elections two-thirds of electors and votes

So dreadful is the progression of the calculation in this fatal system; so much is the true national will led astray and falsified by the will of factions and personal aspirations passing through each one of those levels. Here the numeric observations, the theories of writers on public matters, and all examples, including the example of the very nation that left us that system, concur in showing us that we must take another road, much more so when experience now convinces us that this has produced the worst consequences in our country. We have all seen elections, and we have all contemplated with pain that, in each one of them, public spirit has appeared less energetic, that sanctions and incentives have not brought to the electoral booths citizens whose fate was at stake in them, and thus what occurs is very natural. "Among a well-run city," says an eminent thinker, "each one flies to the assemblies; under a bad government, no one takes a step to go to them, because no one takes an interest in what happens, because everyone anticipates that the general Will will not prevail, and domestic concerns absorb everything. Good laws bring others better; bad laws produce others worse."[12] Among us the imperfection of the electoral system has made the representative system illusory. Because of it, minorities have taken the name of majorities, and because of it, instead of Congresses having represented the nation with all its opinions and interests, they have frequently represented only a fraction, and, leaving the rest without legal action and without influence, they have hastened them into revolution.

However much it might be wished, sir, this last misfortune is of grave importance. The need to summon all the interests to be represented is today a truth so universally recognized that only through ignorance of the present state of the science [of government] can the hard and absolute rule of the majority without the balance of minority representation be proclaimed. "We believe," says Sismondi, "that the representative

---

always come together. The calculation is the following: of 12,001 citizens, 8,001 elect the primary elector; two-thirds of the primary electors gather together, the electoral college represents 5,534 citizens, and the secondary elector, who obtains two-thirds of the votes, represents 3,556 citizens. Then the last college, composed of two-thirds, represents 2,371 citizens, and if the deputy elected by a series of such considerable majorities obtains the votes of two-thirds, he represents only 1,581 citizens out of 12,001, which is a ratio of 132,087/12,001 to 100.

12. [Jean-Jacques Rousseau] *Social Contract,* book 3, chapter 15.

system is a happy creation, because it brings eminent men to the fore, gives them opportunities to win and, above all, to earn the confidence of the people, and it leads them to the goal of controlling the rudder of state. And we understand that it is an institution still happier because it puts some interests, sentiments, and opinions before all others, providing the means for discussing those opinions and of rectifying those sentiments, of balancing those interests, of uniting, finally, the opinions, interests, and sentiments of all citizens in a single center that can be considered the intelligence, interests, and sentiment of the nation . . . and we believe that skillful measures, although difficult, can, with the aid of representative government, protect all localities, all opinions, all classes of citizens, and all interests." Examining, in the development of European civilization, the all-powerful influence of the institutions and admiring the English Constitution, Guizot has said: "Only in the exercise of all rights, the expression of all opinions, the free development of all forces and all interests is there permanence and life: the legal existence of all the elements and systems ensures that no element dominates exclusively, that no single system arises to destroy the rest, that free examination redounds to everyone's benefit and advantage." Simple, natural reason tells us that the representative system is better the more closely the body of representatives resembles the nation represented. The theory of the representation of minorities is nothing but a consequence of universal suffrage, because it matters not at all that no one is excluded from the right to vote if many remain without representation, which is the objective of the suffrage.

Congress will pardon me for placing emphasis on a point whose interest seems to me above all the others, and that to strengthen the force of my suggestions I sought authorities, never so necessary as when one is introducing something new. As for the means of ameliorating the flaws I have attacked, I would set out what seems to me most suitable, if, on emerging from the adopted system, we were to write the new system into the Constitution, which in my opinion would be very dangerous. Because, in fact, whether Congress adopts the means agreed to in [1]842 for the representation of all interests, or whether it might prefer some other method, it is obvious that we are going to enter onto the road of innovation, that there will be trials, and this is enough for me to opine that we not affirm those means in the Constitution but rather through a law. Because I believe firmly, sir, and this can be applied to many other points, that the Constitution, in order that it be respectable and lasting—that is to say, so that it have a solid existence—must contain very few principles only, all fundamental, and if possible, none disputable. With the principle safeguarded in the Constitution that elections must necessarily be popular, if, in seeking the best among the measures that this foundation specifies, we come upon this law, which will be a most precious adoption for the Republic, it will come to be as immutable and respected as the fundamental code itself because of its practical effectiveness. If, on the contrary, successive changes and improvements must be made in it, this will not open anew the discussion of the Constitution nor hasten its destruction. For these reasons, I propose to Congress that it leave to a law the regulation of the electoral system and the designation of the way in which, on constitutional foundations, elections of president, senators, deputies, and ministers of the Court of Justice must be carried out.

But as this law, the law of guarantees, the law of responsibility, and the rest of the laws that regulate the action of the supreme powers should not be equal, but rather superior to all other secondary laws, it is established that they are characterized and distinguished by the special term "constitutional" and that they not be amended except when a period of six months has elapsed between the presentation of the report that proposes it and its discussion. This measure will free laws of such interest from the ill effects of haste and will provide Congress the assistance of a thorough discussion through the press and all organs of the public will. Would that similar measures could be adopted for all laws!

Having explained what seems to me essential to change in the Constitution, it seems necessary to be concerned with another very interesting point omitted in the Constitution, or at least treated very superficially. What are the respective limits of the general power and the power of the states? And once these limits are known, what are the best ways to take precautions against reciprocal invasion, so that neither does the central power attack the sovereignty of the states nor do the states dissolve the Union, not understanding its powers or usurping them? No other matter, sir, seems to me today more urgent than this one because we have the evil before us, and it is so serious an evil that it threatens the institutions with death. At one time we saw the general Congress converted into arbiter of the factions of the states to decide the most important questions of their internal administration; and now, with the federation scarcely reestablished, we see already symptoms of the dissolution because of the opposite extreme. Some legislatures have suspended the laws of this Congress, another has declared expressly that in its territory no general law will be obeyed that has as its objective altering the current state of certain goods; one state announced that it was going to reassume the sovereignty of which it had been divested; with the best intentions a coalition is being formed that will establish one federation within another, and we have just been informed of the law by which a state, in certain circumstances, would confer the power of the entire Union on the deputies of that coalition; and perhaps attempts even more disorganized and criminal are being pondered. With such principles, federation is unattainable, it is absurd, and for that reason those of us who have constantly defended it, those of us who see encoded in it the hopes of our country, raise our voices to warn of the danger. And, in view of this danger, will there still be anyone who maintains that it is not urgent to expedite the constitution? Or that we can wait for it until the conclusion of a war as long as the one we now endure? Or rather that we will have finished by publishing, in isolation and without reforms, a Constitution that does not contain in it any remedy for this misfortune, and that, perhaps for this reason, has yet again succumbed, yielding to the force of some incomparably less powerful elements? No, these facts clearly demonstrate the imperative necessity that we settle the fate of our country, decree the reforms, whatever might be the dangers, so long as it is physically possible for us to do so.

And this duty is that much more sacred the more obvious are the means to fulfill it, because to tell the truth, these unfortunate symptoms of dissolution that are already being observed have been able to appear only because the true principles that should be generally known are forgotten. Article 14 of the draft of reform, establishing the maxim that the powers of the Union are exceptional powers and limited only to the purposes expressly designated in the Constitution, gives to the sovereignty of the states all the breadth and security that might be desired. But for this very reason, and because of the fundamental theory I already pointed out in expressing the reasons by which it fell to the general power to establish the rights of the citizen, it is also necessary to declare that none of the states has power over the goals agreed to by all the states of the Union, and that not being in this regard more than parts of a constituted whole, members of a great Republic, in no instance can they by themselves, in exercising their individual sovereignty, make any resolution regarding those goals nor provide for their regulation except through federal powers, nor demand more than the fulfillment of the exemptions the Constitution grants them. Given these assertions, it remains only to establish the means of making them effective, and for this it is necessary to distinguish the abuses that can be committed according to whether they affect the rights of persons or the authority of public powers.

For this last contingency, it is indispensable to give the Congress of the Union the right to declare null those laws of the states that amount to a violation of the federal pact or that might be contrary to the general laws, because otherwise the power of a state would be superior to that of the Union, and the power of the Union would become a mere mockery. But to avoid making imprudent declarations, it is advisable that these laws be initiated only in the Senate, which represents the federative system in all its strength and provides the greatest guarantees of calm and circumspection; moreover, it is established that the majority of the legislatures of the states have the right in every case to decide whether the resolutions of the general Congress are or are not unconstitutional. In this way, each state individually is subject to the Union, and the totality of all will be the supreme arbiter of our differences and the true conserving power of institutions. If there is yet another more effective means of strengthening the federative principle, if another better guarantee of the liberties of the confederated bodies is known, I do not propose it because I do not know it.

The attacks made by the powers of the states and by the same powers of the federation on individuals have among us, unfortunately, numerous models, so it might not be urgent beyond measure to accompany the reestablishment of the federation with a guarantee sufficient to ensure that those attacks will not be repeated. This guarantee can be found only in the judicial power, inherent protector of the rights of individuals and, for this reason, the only suitable one. Even in absolute monarchies, liberty, having taken refuge in the precincts of tribunals, has forced justice to find there a support when political guarantees have been lacking. A profound writer has observed that the breadth and respectability of the judicial power was the surest sign of the liberty of a people, and for this reason I have not wavered in proposing to Congress that it greatly elevate the judicial power of the federation, giving it the right to protect all the inhabitants of the Republic in the enjoyment of the rights that the Constitution and constitutional laws assure them against all incursions of the executive or the legislative, whether of the states or of the Union. In North America this saving power originated in the Constitution and has produced the greatest results. There the judge has to subject his verdicts above all to the Constitution; and from this results that when he finds it in conflict with a secondary law, he applies the former and not the latter, so, without making himself superior to the law or putting himself in opposition to the legislative power or disparaging its resolutions, in each individual case in which it would have caused harm, he declares it null. Such an institution is completely necessary among us, and as it requires that the federal tribunals be organized in a corresponding way, the proposed reforms leave to the constitutional laws the determination of this point. Concerning it, finally, I will show that, also in my judgment, it is necessary to extend a bit more the action of the federal power of the Union, very imperfectly organized in the federal Constitution, and, above all, to raise the status and ensure the independence of a tribunal called to represent in the political body so important a role as that of supreme judicial power.

With these reforms proposed, it only remains for me now to speak to the Congress about one single reform, the one relative to the method that should be adopted to provide constant improvement of the institutions. On this point, no one doubts that the effectiveness of a fundamental code essentially consists in its being the best possible for the circumstances in which it is issued and that it contain, furthermore, the most adequate means for advancing the society and the consequent perfection of its institutions. The difficulty of the problem consists in reconciling the respect owed to those institutions with the possibility of legitimately making the necessary changes that experience indicates; and, because this alone manages to distinguish in the institutions the fundamental from the secondary, I think that every general rule is bad. To declare, as the Bases Orgánicas[13] did, that the entire Constitution can be reformed at any time, although this is a matter without danger when speaking of a constitution as solid as England's, among us it would be to proclaim that the country must remain eternally unconstituted, that the change of society's primary principles should be the subject of discus-

---

13. A centralist constitution enacted in 1843. (Editor's note)

sion and the constant work of the Mexican people, and with this supposition peace is impossible. On the other extreme, to subject the least
important and minute detail to the same impediments as a fundamental
principle is to hinder the reform even to the extreme of fearing that the
obstacle might lead to destruction. Guided by these observations, I distinguish three parts of the Constitution. With respect to the primordial
principles and those prior to the Constitution, like the independence
of the nation, its form of federal, popular, representative, republican
government, and the consequent division of powers, principles that are
identified with the very existence of the nation, reform is not appropriate, and they must be declared permanent. For what has to do with the
limits of the general power and the sovereignty of the states, it is unquestionable that some modifications can be made; but in this event, besides
the vote of two-thirds of each chamber or the consecutive ratification
of a reform by two legislatures, I require the consent of the majority of
these legislatures for the purpose of giving all imaginable guarantees
to local liberties. On all other points I permit reforms provided that
two-thirds of both chambers or the simple majority of two consecutive Congresses consent, providing also to the constitutional reforms
the guarantee of calm and reflective meditation established by laws of
that kind. This last method of reform was that established by the Constitution of 1824, and its preservation seems to me that much more appropriate the more we avoid in this way all dispute over its legitimacy;
because finally, if the nation does not want them or desires others, we
always leave in the hands of its representatives the same power they had
before to serve its will. There is no reason to mistrust the future. Those
who might come after us will not give up good intentions, and under
auspices less destructive and with the elements we have now left them,
they will progress a great deal in the perfection and consolidation of our
noble institutions.

For now, sir, I have completed my arduous task. What I expressed,
and even more the plan with which I conclude, will show Congress the
way in which, in my judgment, the great question that has shaken our
country for thirteen years should be resolved. Quite convinced of the
difficulties of the undertaking, I am very far from having feelings of
intolerance or fanaticism for my ideas, and I deliver them to the judgment of the chamber with that much greater lack of confidence, the
more the constraints of time have compelled me to present them with-

out having reviewed them beforehand and without being able to correct
them afterward; nonetheless, Congress, in its wisdom, will examine the
articles more than their foundations, will consider my observations despite the lack of method and style. I only request for them an act of justice in the moment in which I leave them to the monumental judgment
of thinking men, to the intense and impassioned opinion of the factions.
If I deceive myself in believing that my plan has been eminently democratic and federal, there is no doubt that these ideas are the ones I have
always maintained in the good as well as in the bad days of the federation. In this Congress I myself proposed them to the committee well
before the terrible circumstances of last month arose. The plan is not
my work alone, although today I might have no other support than my
isolated signature and my feeble voice. I formed it during very extended
discussions with another of the gentlemen of the committee (Mr. Car-
doso), whose vast knowledge of this subject matter is well known, and
who today differs from this vote only with respect to the question of its
timeliness, and Mr. Espinosa de los Monteros, whose very name is authority, discussed and corrected it. The work having been concluded
about two months ago, I do nothing more than present it to Congress
just as it was conceived earlier, so that it might be seen that in some way
it can be called a work of circumstance, and for this reason I even leave
for later the article regarding the regulation of the territory.

Above all, I say it would be disgraceful to compromise the sacred
interests of the *patria*. My intention, sir, is ending the crisis in which we
find ourselves. I desire that Congress bring the difficulties under control
and that, putting a stop to the disorder, it constitute the Republic, determining the improvements that its institutions might require, and which
are, to my way of thinking, encompassed in the few articles to which I
have referred. Everything warns us that this need is more urgent each
day and that neither our internal unrest nor our foreign war can justify
delay. We cannot wait until circumstances improve, because it is a question of Congress making the circumstances change promptly; nor would
it be honest and patriotic that, losing hope in the fate of our country,
we abandon it to the struggle of all the elements of anarchy, which, if
they present and strengthen themselves, it is only because everything is
provisional and nothing stable, because doubt and uncertainty drain the
strength from the power and its restorative hopes from the future; and
this we would do if we set aside our work until a time when there might

not be any more difficulties. The difficulties of today are at least known to us; who might foresee those of tomorrow? Who, above all, does not tremble just at the idea of exposing the fate of the country and the institutions to the fickle and drawn-out outcome of the war? Ah, sir, perhaps now the only days are drawing to a close during which, for some time, we will have had the power to constitute our country and save the institutions. Let it be thus, that preference be given to whatever bears on the war, and that Congress continue working on it with the courage, perseverance, and good faith that have so much honored it and through which it will do justice by us; but that if the fulfillment of the principal objective of our mission is still possible, we not abandon it from this moment on or delay it more, because this is equivalent to renouncing it and leaving our ills without remedy, with so much less excuse, given that we do not need to undertake a new labor, but rather that discussing fifteen or twenty articles of reform will suffice. Let us remember that, in the opening of the Cortes of Cádiz, the noise of foreign cannonballs was mixed with the pomp of the oaths that solemnized that act, and that that Congress in a few months gave the monarchy a complete constitution. The confidence of the people in the solemn days of their misery imposes on us the duty of struggling with the difficulties even to the furthest extreme. With pleasure, I dispense with showing why we have sufficient liberty for our labors; on this each consults his own conscience. For me, I do not have difficulty dealing with all the questions, and so I will do it whenever Congress wishes to occupy itself with these matters.

And so today I must give Congress only an account of the labors I undertook by its order and explain my dissenting vote on the propositions and initiatives regarding which the definitive reestablishment of the Constitution of 1824 has been requested; I do it submitting to your enlightened deliberation the following:

PLAN
IN THE NAME OF GOD, CREATOR AND preserver of societies, the Extraordinary Constituent Congress, considering: THAT the Mexican states, by a spontaneous act of their own and individual sovereignty, and in order to consolidate their independence, secure their liberty, provide for the common defense, establish peace, and seek the good, confederated themselves in 1823 and constituted afterward in 1824 a political system of union for their general government under the form of popular

representative republic and on the preexisting foundation of their natural and reciprocal independence; THAT that pact of alliance, source of the first Constitution and only legitimate source of the supreme power of the Republic, endures in its original vigor and is and had to be the first principle of every fundamental institution; THAT that same constitutive principle of the federal Union, if a superior force has been able to oppose it, has neither been able nor is able to be altered by a new constitution; and THAT in order to consolidate it further and make it effective, the reforms that experience has demonstrated to be necessary in the Constitution of 1824 are urgent, has DECLARED and DECREED and, using its comprehensive powers, DECLARES AND DECREES:

1. That the states that make up the Mexican Union have regained the independence and sovereignty that, for their internal administration, are reserved in the Constitution.

2. That said states continue associated in accordance with the pact that once constituted the mode of political existence of the people of the United Mexican States.

3. That the Constitutive Act and the federal Constitution, sanctioned on January 31 and October 24 of 1824, form the only political Constitution of the Republic.

4. That besides those codes, the following must be observed:

ACT OF REFORM

Art. 1. Every Mexican, through birth or through naturalization, who has arrived at the age of twenty, who has an honest means of living, and who has not been condemned in a legal action to a shameful punishment, is a citizen of the United States of Mexico.

Art. 2. It is the right of citizens to vote in popular elections, exercise the right of petition, gather to discuss public affairs, and belong to the National Guard, all in accordance with the laws.

Art. 3. The exercise of the rights of a citizen is suspended for being habitually intoxicated, or a gambler by profession, or a vagrant, because of religious status, because of the status of legal interdiction, by virtue of trial on those crimes by which the attribute of citizen is lost, and for refusing to serve the public duties of popular appointment. By means of a law the exercise of these rights, the manner of proving possession of the attribute of a citizen and the procedures suitable for declaring its loss or suspension will be regulated.

Art. 4. To ensure the rights of man that the Constitution recognizes, a law will set forth the guarantees of liberty, security, property, and equality, which all the inhabitants of the Republic enjoy, and it will establish the means of making them effective.

These guarantees are inviolable, and only in the case of a foreign invasion or an internal rebellion will the legislative power be able to suspend the established procedures for the apprehension and detention of individuals and searching of homes, and this for a specified time.

Any assault on these guarantees is an occasion for liability, and neither exemption nor amnesty nor any other measure will be able to fall to the favor of the guilty, even should it emanate from the legislative power, which removes it from the tribunals or prevents the punishment from being effective.

Art. 5. For every fifty thousand souls, or for a fraction that passes twenty-five thousand, a deputy will be elected to the general Congress. To do so, he is required only to be twenty-five years old, be in exercise of the rights of the citizen, and not be included at the time of the election in the exceptions of Article 23 of the Constitution.

Art. 6. Besides the two senators each state elects, a number equal to the number of states will be chosen by nomination of the Chamber of Deputies voting by deputations, of the Senate, and of the executive. The persons who garner these three votes will be elected, and the Chamber of Deputies, voting as persons, will name those that lack the three from among the other candidates.

A third of the Senate will be replaced every two years.

Art. 7. To be a senator one must be thirty years old, have the other characteristics required to be a deputy, and in addition must have been constitutional president or vice president of the Republic, or for more than six months secretary of the department or governor of state, or member of the chambers, or twice of a legislature, or for more than five years diplomatic envoy, or minister of the Supreme Court of Justice, or for six years judge or magistrate.

Art. 8. It belongs exclusively to the Chamber of Deputies to establish itself as a grand jury in order to declare, by a simple majority of votes, whether it has reason or not to indict the high functionaries to whom the Constitution or the laws grant this privilege.

Art. 9. The Chamber of Deputies, having declared that it has reason for building the case, if the crime is general, it will move to the dossier of the Supreme Court; if it is prosecuted *de oficio*,[14] the Senate will be established as the jury of verdict and will be limited to declaring whether the defendant is or is not guilty. For this declaration the vote of three-fifths of the current members is needed. This declaration made, the Supreme Court will determine the punishment according to what the law advises.

Art. 10. For every law the approval of the majority of the current members of both chambers is needed.

Art. 11. The articles of the Constitution that established the office of vice president of the Republic are repealed, and the temporary absence of the president will be covered in the way the Constitution establishes for the situation in which both functionaries are absent.

Art. 12. The president is liable for the public crimes he commits during the exercise of his position and even those that are prosecuted of its own initiative (*de oficio*), excluded by the Constitution, provided that the action involved is not authorized by the signature of the responsible minister.

Ministers answer for all the infractions of the law they commit, whether they consist of acts of commission or pure omission.

Art. 13. The elections of deputies, senators, president of the Republic, and ministers of the Supreme Court of Justice will be regulated by laws, adoption of direct election allowed, the only exception being the third of the Senate that Article 6 of this act establishes. The law will also establish and organize the courts of first and second instance, which must hear matters reserved to the judicial power of the federation.

Art. 14. All powers of the Union are derived from the Constitution and are limited only to the exercise of the faculty expressly designated in the Constitution itself, without other faculties understood to be permitted through absence of an expressed restriction.

Art. 15. No state has rights over the aims subordinated to the power of the Union, other than those expressly set forth in the Constitution, or any legitimate way of taking control of them other than the way established by the general powers of the Constitution. The Constitution alone recognizes as legitimate, among all or some of the states, the relationship that their federation constituted and currently constitutes.

Art. 16. Every law of the states that attacks the Constitution or the

14. *De oficio* refers to crimes, such as murder, that are prosecuted by the authority even without a plaintiff. (Editor's note)

general laws will be declared null by the Congress; but only the Senate will be able to initiate this declaration.

Art. 17. If, within a month of publication of a law of the general Congress, it is protested as unconstitutional either by the president in agreement with his ministry or by ten deputies or six senators or three legislatures, the Supreme Court before which the objection will be made will submit the law to the examination of the legislatures, which, within three months and precisely on the same day, will issue their vote.

The declarations will be remitted to the Supreme Court, and this court will publish the result, the resolution being what the majority of the legislatures say.

Art. 18. In the matter of the two previous articles, the general Congress and the legislatures, in their turn, will decide *solely* whether the law whose invalidity they are discussing *is or is not unconstitutional;* and in every affirmative declaration, the words of the annulled law and the text of the Constitution or general law to which it is opposed will be inserted.

Art. 19. In the exercise and preservation of the rights that this Constitution and the constitutional laws grant, the tribunals of the federation will protect any inhabitant of the Republic against every attack by the legislative and executive powers, whether of the federation or the states, said tribunals being limited to giving their protection to the particular case with which the process deals, without making any general declaration at all regarding the law or the act that might motivate it.

Art. 20. The laws of which Articles 3, 4, and 13 of this act speak, that of liberty of the press, the organic law of the National Guard, and all the laws that regulate the general measures of the Constitution and of this act, are constitutional laws and cannot be altered or repealed without a period of six months intervening between the presentation of the decree and its discussion.

Art. 21. The articles of the Constitution can be reformed at any time, provided that two-thirds of both chambers or the simple majority of two distinct and consecutive Congresses agree to it. The reforms that limit in some way the extension of the powers of the states need, moreover, the approval of the majority of the legislatures. But in no case can there be alteration to the primordial principles and those antecedent to the Constitution, which established the independence of the nation, its form of federal, popular, representative, republican government, and the division both of the general powers and of the states. In every plan of reform the intervening period established in the previous article will be observed.

Art. 22. With this act of reforms published, all public powers will be regulated by it. The general legislative power will continue entrusted in the current Congress until the chambers meet. The states will continue observing their individual constitutions and, according to them, will replace their powers within the time periods and terms they designate.

Mexico, April 5, 1847.—M. Otero

IGNACIO RAMÍREZ

Ignacio Ramírez (1818–79), born in Guanajuato, was a writer, poet, journalist, lawyer, and politician. Along with Guillermo Prieto, he founded the newspaper *Don Simplicio* in 1845. Ramírez's pen name was El Nigromante (the necromancer). Early in his life he was imprisoned because of his satirical writings. A formidable orator, Ramírez was elected deputy to the 1856–57 Constituent Congress and became part of the radical wing of the liberal party. Ramírez struggled to end the privileged status of the Catholic Church and the army. He contributed to the drafting of the reform laws, which separated church and state, forced the church to sell its property, secularized public services such as marriage, and established the civil registry.

When the conservative faction was temporarily defeated at the end of the Three Years' War (1857–61), President Benito Juárez (1806–72) appointed Ramírez secretary of justice and public instruction. During his term Ramírez established the National Library and reorganized primary education. Ramírez fought against the imperial armies in the state of Sinaloa during the French intervention and was exiled to the United States. He returned to Mexico before the fall of the empire and was imprisoned. After the fall of Emperor Maximilian, Congress appointed him to the Supreme Court, and he served a long tenure there.

We present two of his writings from the Constituent Congress period: the poem "The National Representation" (La representación nacional) (1845) and a speech delivered to the Constituent Congress on July 7, 1856. Also, we present a letter to Guillermo Prieto ("Fidel") written at the time of the French intervention, between 1863 and 1865.

1 | The National Representation

Representative, open your books,
And say if the *patria* mercantile be,
Industrial or agricultural.
   — Agricultural Mexico is,
The matter decided a long time ago;
— But will urban dwellers be wise
When a city so populous is,
If they plant the rooftops and streets
And close every one of their ports?
   Friend deputy do not believe it,
For the good of the country I beg you,
Seek industry where you see houses.
   — Deputy, doctor of Tampico am I.
I've not seen the port, but from letters I've read
From my niece I know it is not very rich.
If the port had been closed, foreign hordes,
Who from Paris and Europe have come with stuffed bags,
Would not make us soup and a suit,
And their boats would not carry our gold
Nor our eyes nor our feet nor our teeth 'fore the wind.
   The Tampico forum is silent, their fault;
And no one plants olive or wheat,
Although the fertile ground is a treasure.
   Nor on the beach is there any maize field;
But here is a part of a mule load they left,
And there is a barrel, and luckily some fish.
The town, very poor, scarcely a third will be ours;

Original title: "La representación nacional." Source: *Don Simplicio, periódico crítico, burlesco y filosófico*, vol. 1, no. 1, p. 6, 1845.

My niece closed her shop
And a new business has.
Someone who customs duty can get
Is the only one with daily bread guaranteed.
The foreigner, I repeat, the reason for such ruin is.
　　—All that news I had yesterday
From Blas, your muleteer. And I have known
From that very same Blas what I'm talking about.
　　—What! Is a representative thus so informed
About the country that he represents?
—What more can I know? —Your pardon I beg.
Exact account should you have
Of the farms and their crops,
Of the people who feed themselves there,
And in the same way you should know
Something of workshops, and even for sure
What the poor small shops do spend.
　　How many ships there are in the port, not only if ships there be.
—Come on, do you want that a deputy be
An expert in statistics of sorts?
　　Yes, that and in other things. —I have faded away
As a jurist, but as statistician I've not:
To know all to what mortal is it given?
But then if a sophistical orator
A challenge to me from the rostrum should give,
The syllogistic system to me matters more,
The bar and the royal decrees,
Than the ranches, the ships, and the shops
That in my district might be.
To create wise and marvelous laws,
Is it not sufficient for me, and by a wide margin, the maneuver,
that might get me two revered tassels?
　　—To formulate laws platonic, more than enough do you have;
But to formulate laws that produce genuine wealth,
You must learn them from people, and no other work.
　　—Responsibility for general laws lies with Congress
And your theory we study in immortal works.
　　In Tocqueville, knowledge easy and cheap we can find,

In Montesquieu, and in Ferrier,
And followed by every person these days.
— Of Solons, we thus have a bunch,
But the people consumptive become
Because Congress's system so philosophical is,
　Studying politics as if it were physics,
It learned with thermometers painted,
And metaphysics without seeing any objects.
　What can speeches as sermons prepared generate
In the rostrum? Decrees not begot but aborted.
Among the people they do well, it's true,
To the extent that the people sovereign be called,
They applaud and ask not if the king might be fasting.
　Haughty Fraud, in a salon, rises up from her knees
And with poetic style maintains
That man is immortal and that gold is vain;
But dying she fears and gold she has,
And at the end of her discourse, with "Happy they make you,
Patria, your mines," comes Don Maimed Mummy to us,
　Who dares not to speak, even in his defense,
If he has not a text
To close his most tiresome sermon:
　In all the sessions Don Bothersome
Just one impertinence blasts,
In an endless, indigestible sermon;
　President they make him to silence him,
A post he occupies with his voice and his pen.
Fool arrives, swears, a leave of absence requests.
　He allows Dog his knowledge consumed
In a law the president orders
To use Moctezuma's costume and name.
　Don Schemer in great misery is,
For to manage his wealth he knew not,
And the treasury he wanted in his very hands,
　Don Gut the just means recommends
So to both parties he can belong
And ascend with the one who ascends.
　In his speeches are always two meanings,

And he makes of the just means a ball
To play with and punish the losers.
    Fool, in order to speak, does not logic exhaust.
"The sixth of December it was; to cast off the government
In vain you attempt," he says and he votes;
And always on all fours he says this,
With his hands on the railing, his feet on the ground,
Whether of contracts one speaks or bulls from the pope.
    Stupidity, how much can there be in one room!
The parties are growing each day;
But the people lose only in war.
    The parties increase, still
The stake has its friends, despotism:
Federation for despotism heresy is.
    And freemasonry the *juri* for that.
Joe saw in Paris constitution and kings,
And in Mexico he might want the same.
    Another would like to revive Spanish laws,
And I indignantly Imams demand
As well as Janissaries and beys.
    What is our liberty? It is pure lie.
—Are you seeking the cause? The man pointed to you;
But as a slave of the law he looks upon you.
    —A syringe with a different cylinder is the law
That enslaves instead of the man,
For me, the evil is being a slave.
    Is there some rational being who does not astound
Seeing in revolution the crowd
To change of their woes only the name?
    The light of the law is not always pure;
To sacrifice helots as lambs,
A law gave to Eurotas the custom.
    To the Romans, cultured and strict,
The law of property power did give
To feed breeding grounds with their serfs.
    And the law the cursed fire ignited
That fanaticism three centuries might nourish
With Iberian and American blood.

Do we not know the banishment laws
And many others of tax?
About centralism the Seven Laws[1] were.
   —Your arguments nothing but sophisms are:
The place constitutions will give to reproach
at every step I know well.
   But law plunders not for the carriage,
Nor has a mistress of it been seen,
Nor even for this does it haphazardly choose.
   —What does it matter if the law has not life?
—The birth of knowledge it is. —I confess
I would like to see the multitude as one brought to life.
   Laughter is caused by the source of a congress;
To name wise electors, intelligence
I have, but for deputies not:
   And the electors, they give no assurance
Of voting for only those unblemished men
Who might be trustees of my good.
   —The ballot box you want to make useless
And the registration list too? —At the hour designated
I run to vote, but only a chair
For the commission is taken:
Ten and twelve strikes the clock, and three only have gathered,
And at five there were four and after, no more.
   But the members of the junta we've had
Are feeling burdened I would suppose;
And more than one cannot read or write.
   —Whether a woman, a servant, a boy,
A ballot box makes them annoyed;
The council shuts up until drunk.
   And then what enthusiasm reigns!
Secondary elections follow this path;
Their usefulness I do not fathom.
   —Ah! So pigheaded are they, these can be so essential,
A thousand intrigues they avoid. But I see before

1. Ramírez refers to the 1836 centralist constitution known as the Seven Laws. (Editor's note)

Intrigues secondary, and primary intrigues as well.
　　If the masses could elect, which is what I desire,
The election would much more be pleasing to them,
And success there would be, I firmly believe.
　　—Illusions and systems! What kind of man
Tries to put saddles on donkeys instead of a horse?
The multitude doesn't know who obeys it.
　　Give boots to an Indian and you just give him corns,
As if the doctor would patiently hear
From his water bearer verdicts judicial.
　　Ixtacalco would scarcely be seen
With a theater, and goodbye to its gardens that float
It would say, and to its roses and cabbages too.
　　It will barter its boats for engravings.
—That would be a sign it was rich;
And the doctor, learned traps he'd not fear;
　　For though never a holy judge will be seen,
But the justice that you now despise,
From a water bearer might not cost so much.
　　The multitude you deprecate
You flattered so as a deputy to be.
—For its own good it was deceived—it was you who did the deceiving!
　　You are like Joe, who from soldier to general went,
But not on campaign;
Finding himself mocked by his friends,
　　For being faithful to the standards of Spain.
It is true, he responded: but also I ran,
Against the Iberian I used this trick.
　　If more philosophy you had
And your Gómez you forgot and your laws
And you descended one day to the earth,
　　You will find ten rich men like kings,
A thousand leagues under their rule,
But ten maguey plants a thousand Indians have.
　　With what right? Given it by the theft
Of the conquest.—The conquest is the original way of such acquisition.
Venio you should read.

—The Indian pulls pulque and maize from the mud;
The rich not a footprint they make on the soil;
Nothing does the former enjoy, but the latter everything does.

    To protect agriculture with jealousy
And to deliver to four feeble men the earth,
Is to wish that Satan to heaven would carry us.

    The poor man makes war on the thieves:
What do the poor have to lose? Them I prefer
To a farmer who goes and locks himself up

    In the city, and because he was heir,
Without even knowing his ranch or its place on the map,
Floods of money from it he pulls.

    His cloak he doesn't remove in the streets,
Without risking confronting all classes:
Without risking, a successor gets what's not his.

    —With your blasphemies you now pass from here,
Oh Nigromante of Jacobinism!
Property is one of the foundations.

    —Unfortunately it is true; but likewise to live
is another foundation with which the first I attack;
And the government does the same.

    From us does it not collect taxes? Does it not snatch away
Tobacco from all the old women? Does it not use notes promissory
And from us a cigarette in each tlaco[2] take?

    —You only think of material goods,
And the Congress only to glory aspires.
—Well such congresses like church councils would be.

    To every junta that knowledge might breathe
The tumultuous juntas of Rome I prefer,
And with adornment, and it is not a lie.

    On a dusty plaza the people so proud
Deliberated, loudly it's true,
But among arid voices the kernel it came.

    And also there the kings it dethroned,
And their existence to combat delivered;

2. Ancient Mexican coin. (Editor's note)

But rich plunder it did enjoy.
    Never to science was it sacrificed
Which a nation sparingly creates,
Nor showing a terrible omnipotence
Did it remain satisfied beating a drum.

The Necromancer

2

Speech to the Constituent Congress, July 7, 1856

Gentlemen:

The project of Constitution, submitted to the enlightenment of your sovereignty today, reveals in its authors a not insignificant understanding of the political systems of our century, but at the same time an inconceivable neglect of the positive needs of our *patria*. Inexperienced politician and unknown orator, I make such serious charges to the committee not because I foolishly claim to instruct it, but because I wish to hear its lucid responses; perhaps in them I will find that, because of my confusion, my reasonings reduce themselves to some solemn admissions of my ignorance.

The social pact that has been proposed to us is based in a fiction; here is how it begins: "In the name of God . . . the representatives of the different states that make up the Republic of Mexico . . . fulfill their lofty charge . . ."

With these words the committee elevates us to the priesthood; and, placing us in the sanctuary, whether we set forth the rights of the citizen, whether we organize the exercise of public powers, it obliges us to move from inspiration to inspiration until turning an organic law into a genuine dogma. It would be very gratifying for me to announce, like a prophet, or rather playing the role of augur, the good news to the peoples who have entrusted their destinies to us that on the fourth of July some gentlemen of the committee discharged their duty with considerable skill; but in the century of the disillusioned ones, our humble mission is to discover the truth and apply to our ills the most mundane remedies. I know well what there is of the fictitious, the symbolic, and the poetic in

Original title: "Discurso ante el Congreso Constituyente del 7 de julio de 1856." Source: Francisco Zarco, *Historia del Congreso Extraordinario Constituyente (1856-1857), Estracto de todas sus sesiones y documentos parlamentarios de la época,* vol. 2 (Mexico: Imprenta de Ignacio Cumplido, 1857).

known legislation; some of this legislation has lacked nothing to remove it from reality, not even the meter; but I judge it is more dangerous than ridiculous to suppose ourselves interpreters of the Divinity and, without a mask, to parody Acmapichtli,[1] Mohammed, Moses, and the Sibyls. The name of God has produced divine right everywhere, and the history of divine right is written by the hand of the oppressors with the sweat and blood of the peoples; and we, who presume ourselves free and enlightened, are we not still struggling against divine right? Do we not tremble like children when it is said to us that a phalanx of petty women will assault us in discussing tolerance of worship, all of them armed with divine right? If a revolution casts us from the rostrum, it will be divine right that drags us to the prisons, to exile, and to the scaffolds. Leaning on divine right, man has divided the heaven and the earth and has said—I am absolute owner of this land; and he has said—I have a star, and if he has not monopolized the light of the upper spheres, it is because no speculator has been able to soar to the stars. Divine right has invented public punishment and the executioner. Shielding himself in divine right, man has considered his brother a commercial object and has sold him. Gentlemen, for my part, I declare that I have not come to this spot prepared by raptures or revelations; the only mission I carry out, not as a mystic but as a profane, is in my credential, you have seen it, it has not been written like the tables of the law on the crest of Sinai amidst lightning and thunder. The task of creating a constitution is very worthy, so I begin it by deceiving.

Why did the committee, from the sublime heights to which it has been able to raise itself, not direct a quick glance toward our troubled territory? One of its members has said that the territorial division is not a panacea; oh! certainly, in politics, in the same way as in medicine, the *cure-all* has not been discovered; but that is no reason for the physician not to be vain about his discoveries, as the politician is with his: the inventor of vaccine and the inventor of penitentiaries have equal glory. What misfortunes come to us—it has been asked—from the fact that populations are still distributed in the way the Plan of Ayutla[2] found them? It has gone as far as denying the need for a new organization of

1. A pre-Hispanic deity. (Editor's note)

2. The Plan of Ayutla in 1854 called for the overthrow of the regime of General Antonio López de Santa Anna. The revolt was successful. (Editor's note)

local public offices based on the demands of nature. The committee, finally, judges that the discontented peoples do not know their interests, and the reason it gives is convincing because it does not know them either.

Whether I take men as my basis or the lands they inhabit, with my humble intelligence I can see that a new territorial division is a pressing necessity. The physical elements of our soil are distributed in such a way that they by themselves bid the nation to divide in large sections with very marked characteristic features. That Yucatán Peninsula, connected to the continent by a narrow and unpopulated strip of land, has the independence that the high mountains, the deserts, and the seas offer. From the Isthmus of Tehuantepec to the borders of Guatemala, we have a division drawn by nature. From the vicinity of the isthmus to the frontier of the United States, three strips, one temperate and two hot, suggest to us three different series of territorial combinations. In the Pacific Ocean we have another peninsula. On the coasts of the Gulf of Mexico I can see a vast land irrigated by fast-flowing rivers and extensive lakes; the abundance of navigable water moves closer to and jumbles together its populations. Where nature formed a single people, we form fractions of five others? Between Tuxpan and Tampico we can improvise a bridge of vapor; but if I am not deceived, we have already given Tuxpan to Puebla instead of Tlaxcala. And that island lost in an ocean of savages, that northern frontier, does it not demand from us in the name of humanity the unity of its government? Why preserve in Chihuahua and Durango populations separated from their capitals by a dangerous desert and an impassable mountain range, and more when their separation is a genuine theft of Sonora and Sinaloa? And why not extend the limits of Colima? And why is the state of the Valles not established in the old Anáhuac? The state of Querétaro is reduced to a single population center of the many that are sown throughout the fertile Bajío.

The territorial division appears still more interesting considering it in relation to the inhabitants of the Republic. Among the many illusions with which we sustain ourselves, one of them, not the least unfortunate, is the one that originates by supposing in our *patria* a homogeneous population. Let us lift that light veil from the mixed race that spreads out everywhere, and we will find a hundred nations that in vain we attempt today to put together into one only, because that undertaking is assigned to the constant and energetic labor of individuals and well-worked-out institutions. Many of those peoples still preserve the traditions of a diverse origin and of an independent and glorious nationality.

The Tlaxcaltecan shows with pride the fields that the wall separating him from Mexico oppressed. The Yucatecan can ask the Otomi if his ancestors left monuments as admirable as those preserved in Uxmal. And near us, gentlemen, that sublime cathedral that makes us arrogant reveals less knowledge and less talent than the humble stone preserving the calendar of the Aztecs that seeks a support in the cathedral. Those races still preserve their nationality, protected by the domestic hearth and by the language. Marriages between them are very rare, between them and the mixed races occur less frequently every day; the means of facilitating their bonds with foreigners has not been found. In the end, love preserves the territorial division from before the conquest.

Also the diversity of languages will make any amalgamation fictitious and unrealizable for a long time. The American languages consist of significant roots, not in the eyes of science but rather in common usage; these roots, genuine parts of the sentence, never or rarely are presented alone and with a consistent form as in the languages of the Old World; thus it is that the American, instead of detached words, has sentences. From this comes the notable phenomenon that, in constructing a term, the new element is put by preference in the center through a proper interposition of organic bodies, while in the languages of the other hemisphere, the new element is placed by juxtaposition, a character peculiar to inorganic combinations. In these languages, where the least member of the word palpitates with a life of its own, the loving heart and the ardent imagination cannot manifest themselves except with the lively and seductive forms of poetry. But these treasures each nation enjoys as a family, hidden by fear, decayed through ignorance, the last hieroglyphics that Bishop Zumárraga cannot burn nor the sword of the conquistadors destroy.[3] Enclosed in his hut and in his language, the indigenous person does not communicate with the other indigenous tribes or with the mixed race except through the Castilian language. And in this, to what are his thoughts reduced? To the sterile formulas for the thought of a mean mercantile usage and to the odious expressions that are exchanged between the tycoons and their servants. Do you want to

3. Juan de Zumárraga (1468–1548) was a Spanish bishop during early colonial times. As Protector of the Indians he ordered pagan religious artifacts burned. (Editor's note)

form a stable territorial division with the elements the nation possesses? Elevate the indigenous people to the sphere of citizen, give them a direct interposition in public affairs, but begin dividing them by languages, otherwise your sovereignty will only distribute two million free men and six million slaves.

If what I have expressed says nothing to the committee, at least direct your gaze at the unrest in which the Republic finds itself. Cuernavaca and Morelos want to belong to the state of Guerrero, and against their wishes the interests of a hundred feudal proprietors are prevailing. The Valley of Mexico has been working to organize itself for many years. La Huasteca has suffered plundering for having requested its local independence. Tabasco is requesting possession of its territory, presenting legal titles. Sinaloa claims Tamazula. And the frontier calls us weak in order not to call us traitors. To all these demands of the peoples we answer:—now is not the time. It is not time yet!—The peoples will answer us tomorrow, if we want finally to accommodate their desires in order to contain the horrors of anarchy.

The most serious of the charges that I make to the committee is having preserved the servitude of day workers. The day worker is a man who, by force of painful and continuous labor, pulls from the earth, now the wheat that nourishes, now the silk and gold that adorn the people; in his creative hand the rude instrument is converted into a machine, and he shapes stone into magnificent palaces. The prodigious inventions of industry are owed to a small number of learned men and to millions of day laborers. Wherever there might exist value, there is found the sovereign effigy of work.

Well then, the day worker is a slave. Originally he was a slave of the man; he was reduced to this condition by the right of war, terrible sanction of divine right. As a slave, nothing belongs to him, neither his family nor his existence; and nourishment is not a right for the man-machine, rather an obligation to preserve himself for the service of owners. In different epochs the laboring man, emancipating himself from the persons who lived off the income from their investments or real estate, continued subject to the service of the earth; the feudalism of the Middle Ages, of Russia, and of tropical lands are well known enough that it is not necessary to paint their horrors. The laborer succeeded also in breaking the chains that tied him to the land as a product of nature; and today he finds himself a slave of capital, which, requiring only brief hours of his life, speculates even with his very nourishment. Before, the serf was the tree cultivated in order to produce abundant fruits; today the laborer is the sugar cane that is squeezed dry and abandoned. Thus it is that the great, the true, social problem is to emancipate day laborers from capitalists; the resolution is very simple and comes down to converting work into capital. This operation, urgently demanded by justice, will assure the day laborer not only the salary appropriate for his subsistence, but a right to divide the profits proportionally with every businessman. The economic school is correct in claiming that capital in hard cash must produce a return like capital in mercantile assets and in real estate. The economists will complete their work, moving forward to the aspirations of socialism, the day they concede the unquestionable rights to an income from work-capital.

Learned economists of the committee, in vain you proclaim the sovereignty of the people so long as you deprive each day laborer all the fruit of his work, you oblige him to use up his capital, and in return you put a ridiculous crown on his brow. As long as the laborer consumes his funds in the form of a salary and yields his income with all the profits of the business to the capitalist associate, the savings bank is an illusion, the bank of the people is a metaphor, the direct producer of all the wealth will not enjoy any mercantile credit in the market, he will not be able to exercise the rights of citizenship, he will not be able to become educated, he will not be able to educate his family, he will perish of misery in his old age and in his illnesses. In this lack of social elements you will find the real secret why your municipal system is a chimera.

I have dispelled the illusions to which the committee has given itself over; no scruple plagues me. I know well that, despite deceit and oppression, many nations have raised their reputation to a glittering sphere; but today the people do not desire either the glittering throne of Napoleon swimming in blood or the rich booty, won by pirates and conserved by slaves, that the United States divides each year. They do not want, no, the splendor of their masters, but rather a modest well-being spread among all individuals. The instinct for personal conservation that moves the lips of the child seeking nourishment is the last plunder we deliver to death; here is the base of the social edifice.

The Mexican nation cannot be organized with the elements of the old political science, because they are the expression of slavery and worries; it needs a constitution that organizes progress for it, that puts order in motion. To what is this Constitution reduced, which establishes order in absolute immobility? It is a tomb prepared for a living corpse. Gentlemen, we bring to mind with enthusiasm a privilege that introduces a breed of horses or creates a deadly weapon; let us create a constitution that is founded in the privilege of the needy, of the ignorant, of the weak, so that in this way we can improve our race and so that public power will not be anything other than organized beneficence.

3

Letter to Fidel

Ures, March 1865

Dear Fidel:

Do you remember that in one of my last letters I spoke to you of a woman of some years, but of much talent and a well-preserved beauty? Well, she knows you and has insisted on writing to you; I enclose her letter. As ever yours. — The Necromancer

Señor Fidel: — You were so gallant to me when I was in Mexico that, without fear of bothering you, I take the liberty of asking some news of you, because your friend, the Necromancer, does not answer my questions without caricaturing the persons who deserve from me the liveliest and most affectionate compliments.

Is Mr. X still a specialist in history? Does he still preserve, among his Mexican antiquities, the ring of Acatempan?

Why have some rectors and professors around you become so enamored when they abandoned the studious youth?

From Mexico to Chihuahua you have acted as a Tyrtaeus;[1] do you believe that the brave ones who accompany you will be enthusiastic to the point of fighting after arriving at the Paso del Norte, not having done it before?[2]

Two years ago, with deputies and other functionaries, you were more than a thousand, you who represented the nation; now there

---

Original title: "Carta a Fidel [Guillermo Prieto], marzo de 1865." Source: *El Semanario Ilustrado,* vol. 1, September 25, 1868, pp. 341–42.

1. Tyrtaeus of Sparta was a poet who composed elegies to courageous warriors. (Editor's note)

2. Ramírez was at the time traveling with the Juárez republican government in its march to the north, withdrawing as imperial troops closed on them. (Editor's note)

are not even thirty, counting Romero,[3] who is helping out so much in the United States so that the states of the South might be ruled by those of the North; what would become of both republics without our diplomacy? Do you believe, my sweet friend, that eight million Mexicans are well represented in a foreign war by thirty persons who play, make love, and intrigue when they are not running?

These questions will surprise you when you do not know what I am going to confide in you: Have I become an imperialist? Only the love of my sex has committed me to this change; you see how I reason.

The great caprice of Mexicans, which has been such a misfortune for them, consists of the adoption of that system they call representative. They, who make a war to the death on the clergy, have delivered themselves body and soul to a theocratic system! Do not laugh or feel scandalized. Who does the pope represent? God. Who does the lord bishop represent? The pope. Who do the priests represent? The lord bishop. Who do the sextons represent? The priests. And that whole hierarchic machine, who does it represent? God and the Christian people. God is the law; the people are the beneficiaries. But in reality, neither does the people gain anything nor is God obeyed. If God and the people understood each other directly, our affairs would go better, and I would ask him for the eternal youth of Chavito and those eloquent words with which you charmed me.

Who does Don Benito represent? (I say the same of the other powers when there are some.) The states. Who do the states represent? The prefectures and municipalities. And those? The electors. And that whole representative retinue? The Constitution and the sovereign people. The result is that you are organized like the Church; you have done nothing more than parody it; and you treat the law and the people as the others do God and the Christians. I would like to represent myself myself, because in doing that it interests and amuses me so much more, no one can humanly represent me, not the priest, not the deputy, not my own husband.

Both systems of social organization can exist only under this sup-

3. Matías Romero, President Juárez's ambassador to the United States at the time of the French intervention. (Editor's note)

position: *some individuals were born to represent and others to be represented.* But what does it mean to represent? It is to play the role of another; it is to pretend to be another person; it is to substitute the mask for the face. And can a system that is necessarily based in the lie be successful? Between a Congress and a Council there is no difference; if the Holy Spirit in whichever of the two bodies was not sold to the pope or to Don Benito, it would be relegated to the minority and excluded from great affairs, and would be prosecuted by the law against conspirators and plagiarists.[4]

I do not know if you have come to put that famous representative system into effect, but I believe it impossible in Sonora, and not because representatives are lacking, but because in no constitution are those who represent the majority here recognized. Tell me, my life, in what law have you seen the following proclamation? In Sonora, Gándara represents his relatives; Tánori his tribe; the Chato Almada half of Alamos; Tomasito half of Guaymas; the cacique of the Yaqui the yaquis; and the greater part of the young women their boyfriends. Such is the situation of our state, despite the fact that divine and human laws say something else.

And since I have touched on a point that interests me, I can do no less than show you that perhaps I would tolerate such a representative system if women could figure as representatives. Why exclude us? I think of it in terms of the ancient drama, when among the Greeks and Romans, as later in the academies, men played the parts of women. I do not tolerate it now that both sexes appear on the stage. And since I can play with applause the role of Elizabeth of England or Catherine of Russia, I do not see why I could not play the Mayos and the Ópatas[5] in that theater you call the temple of the laws. Temple! No doubt to remember its monkish origin.

You know me very well, Fidel; tell me, what do all of you do that is not within my grasp? Above all, the ministerial majority, what secrets does it have that some time ago I might not have discovered? Does it have some weaknesses? I have mine. Does it chat about all matters? You see how I chat. And in matters of finance, they will

---

4. A contentious criminal law passed earlier by the republican government. (Editor's note)

5. Mayos and Ópatas were Indian tribes from the state of Sonora. (Editor's note)

not leave the taxpayers as content as I. The adoption of my idea would bring with it the advantage that many deputies would accustom themselves to representation by women, leaving them free for carrying out the rest of the household matters.

These convictions that I hold have helped me compare your system with that of Maxmilian. The Austrian also represents the nation, but in his way; he shares power with his wife, and as long as she lives, a favorable star will shed its light on him. The ladies in waiting are thus as close to power as their husbands.

Nonetheless, from the North an arm will reach out to save you, in the same way someone pulls out by the tail a dog that has fallen in the fountain, and return you to the capital of the Republic. Then you will return, adding to your lyre the string of pure patriotism. Poet, you could not do for the nation more than sing the battles and the glory; and you have sung, making each verse sparkle before enemy eyes like an avenging sword. You are called to be the first of the pure ones; your influence is guaranteed. To it I appeal so that you might initiate and defend the women's cause in the coming council of representatives.

I will go back to being republican and always yours. — *A Sonoran*[6] *woman.*

To Fidel:

I have seen the letter that our friend wrote to you; we have lost everything, for the women lavish their sarcasm on us. Let us not lose heart; faith in representative system; and I do not know for the present who represents us legally in Chihuahua; but would you believe that Rosales, of his own accord, has proposed himself to represent us once again on the fields of battle? If he lives and we once again come to be deputies, we will grant him a pardon.

For the present, we have lost the port of Guaymas; soon I will write you the details. Your very affectionate — *Necromancer.*

6. From the state of Sonora. (Editor's note)

FRANCISCO ZARCO

Francisco Zarco (1829–69) was a liberal politician and writer born in the state of Durango. He was the editor in chief of the liberal newspaper *El Siglo XIX*. Zarco was considered one of the most important liberal writers of his time, writing on many subjects, not only politics, and agitating for reform in his articles.

In 1856 he was elected deputy to the Constituent Congress. As a deputy Zarco not only participated in the parliamentary debates but also wrote and published chronicles of its sessions from which he composed a history of the 1856–57 Constituent Congress that was published in 1857.

After the enactment of the Constitution, President Ignacio Comonfort was sworn into office, but he ultimately decided not to enforce the charter. This coup started the Three Years' War. Zarco opposed the Comonfort government and was imprisoned until the victory of the liberal faction in 1861 brought Juárez into power. Juárez appointed Zarco as a minister in his cabinet. During the French intervention Zarco was exiled to the United States.

We present six of Zarco's articles published in *El Siglo XIX* between 1856 and 1867, the period in which the Constituent Congress met.

1 The Question of the Veto

Having been the first to call public attention to the need for resolving conclusively the question of the veto, which arose when the Ministry of War objected to the decree of Congress that declared null the articles of the law of Santa Anna regarding rewards for services lent in the war with the United States, we have little wanted to provoke a conflict between the government and the Congress or try to humiliate one of the two powers. Our intention has been only that a question of order be resolved, that the assembly preserve intact its prerogatives, and that serious difficulties be avoided that hereafter might present themselves.

We have always been convinced that public order consists not in one power holding the rest subservient, but rather in each one being limited to its functions without overstepping them or encroaching on the functions of the rest. In the same way we oppose enlarging the powers of the executive and extending them even to having the veto; we would be opposed to the constituent body appropriating to itself legislative power that the people did not grant it.

There are no other means, no matter how hard one looks for them, to preserve equilibrium among the powers and to maintain peace, than the assiduous and precise observation of the law to which each authority owes its origin and which at the same time designates its functions. From the moment in which an authority aspires to enlarge its powers, it violates the legal title of its existence and takes the first step toward subversion of the very principles that might be able to serve it as support.

We have said a thousand times, and we do not tire of repeating it, that at the present time there is no cause for disagreement between the government and the congress, and that the Plan of Ayutla, instead of desiring perpetual antagonism between the two powers, wanted on the

Original title: "La cuestión del veto." Source: *El Siglo XIX,* Mexico, June 28, 1856.

contrary to establish between them the most perfect harmony, so that in this way the promises of the revolution might be fulfilled and the hopes of the people realized. Whatever the difficulty, the slightest disagreement paralyzes the forward movement of the administration, which must be active, intelligent, and progressive, and holds back the work of the congress, which must be about redress, justice, and morality in exercising its power of oversight, and about liberty, reform, and civilization in drawing up the fundamental code. In periods of transition and revolution, which is essentially what we are going through, to waste time is to go backward, and it is an incontestable truth that revolutions that go backward are distorted, denatured, and lost, and they lose the people with them.

This conviction, which is very dear and sincere to our mind, is what makes us ardently desire the rapid and satisfactory settlement of all questions created by lack of foresight or imprudence, and that if it is necessary, even at the cost of mutual sacrifices, the liberal union be maintained and the accord between the government and Congress.

The conservative press, which was despicably at the mercy of the oppressors of the country and which does not understand that the friends of a government can have sufficient loyalty and good faith to tell it the truth; the conservative press, which persisted in calling us ministerial and in attributing to our newspaper a semiofficial character, accusing us of defending a government that professes our same principles, jumps with joy announcing that we have had differences with the ministry, that we have passed to the ranks of the opposition, that our aims are ignoble and self-interested, and, taking for granted that we are attacking the cabinet, begins its defense, forgetting that we have been among those who have defended it with the greatest ardor from the unwarranted accusations of that reactionary and inconsistent press, which does not even have the virtue of giving the names of its writers, who always hide behind a despicable professional who will sign anything.

With respect to the question of the veto, they have said that we want the omnipotence of Congress, the dictatorship of the assembly, a coup d'état against the cabinet, the tutelage of the government to the caprices of the parliamentary majority. Not at all. What we want is simply that no one leave the orbit of his power; that the Plan of Ayutla be observed as the sole political law of the country; and that the government and the Congress, each in its sphere, can fulfill the mission appropriate to them.

If the Congress, going beyond its powers, produced common laws, assuming powers that only the president of the Republic has today, we would be the first to condemn such an act of usurpation. In the same way, and without giving such a harsh assessment of the government's undertakings, it is our duty to oppose them, because as revolutionary as is the present order of things, it is based in genuine and clear principles of legality.

We will not pause to refute the exaggerated laments of the absolutist press, which is talking nonsense dreaming of a coup d'état without understanding that the *caudillo* who today exercises the supreme magistracy of the nation is the steadfast supporter of the representative system and the democratic cause.

In vain those writers called him bandit and partisan of larceny when in the fields of battle he faced death in order to liberate their *patria* from the conservative yoke, in vain they will seek to lead him astray now with their vain adulations; the sincere voice of the truth in his spirit has to be worth more. They very much wanted to flatter him when he ascended to the presidency so that he would nullify the reforms that the administration of General Álvarez completed; they did not achieve anything, and Mr. Comonfort was somewhat later the power and force of the liberal party in suppressing the reaction. It is a wasted effort by those who want to separate him from the Constituent Congress and remove him from the liberal party, which has faith in his oaths and which expects from his administration splendid and positive political, social, and economic reforms.

But in the liberal press it has been said vaguely and without adducing the slightest argument that it is prudent to grant to the government the power of raising objections, that the executive in other countries has such a function, and that our executive has had it in institutional times. Those who reflect in this way have very good intentions; but the government itself, through the gentleman minister of war, has declared in the heart of Congress that it does not believe it has the right to raise objections to the decrees of the assembly, and when this has happened, we have only to warn some of our colleagues that it is neither prudent nor wise to be more royalist than the king nor more papist than the pope.

But it will be said, "If the government itself declares that it does not have powers to raise objections, what need is there for Congress to deliver an opinion on the same matter?" To this we answer that although we have the greatest confidence in the declarations of the worthy minister of war because we know his honorable record, his sincerity, and his political consistency on this question, considerations of public interest must be worth more than purely personal considerations, and as the real and actual fact is that the executive has not published a decree of Congress, it is indispensible that Congress be jealous of its own prerogatives so that this does not occur in the future and so as to overcome every difficulty. If public questions had to be treated like purely private ones, the declaration of the gentleman minister of war would be more than sufficient for calling this matter finished, but when it is about principles, when it is about ensuring public order and the permanence of legality, there is no precaution that is excessive, and it is necessary to arrive at definitive results.

In defense of the veto, until now, it has been contended only that other governments have it, that some constitutions grant it. But this very fact proves that there are great differences between a constitutional and a transitory order in which the constituent power exists.

Constitutions, more or less democratic, more or less based on distrust, can limit the legislative power, can enlarge the executive, can give to this latter a part in the formation of laws and even authorize him to terminate assemblies, as happens in some moderate monarchies; they can also give him the power of raising objections to the laws and establishing certain conditions so that the project, once voted, can become law despite the resistance of the executive, as happens in the United States and as happened among us when the Charter of 1824 was in force. But all these rules arise from the written law, arise from the Constitution that demarcates the functions of all the powers, and we are certain that there cannot be cited a single example of a constituent assembly subject to the absolute or suspensive veto.

It is as absurd to expect today that the government have this function as it would be to impose on it any of the shackles our constitutional governments have had, like not being able to decree taxes and the president not being able to put himself at the head of the army without prior authorization from Congress. What would one respond to those who maintain such expectations? Simply that there is no constitution in force, and the Plan of Ayutla, which is today the only rule of our public law, has conferred discretionary powers on the head of state. Well, we answer the same to the defenders of the veto; there is no constitution in force, and the Plan of Ayutla does not put the slightest restriction on the resolutions of the assembly.

It is necessary to observe that where the veto exists, it is based precisely on the fact that the government is the executor of the law and, for that reason, can know better than anyone its difficulties, and in the fact that the legislative power resides in the representatives of the people. In monarchies there is another reason for the existence of the veto, and it is that the legislative power resides at one and the same time in the crown and in the *cortes* and that the suspension is the direct means the throne has to nullify laws that seem to it to be in error.

From this observation, which can be proven by examining all the constitutions and studying their commentaries, it follows that such rules are not nor can be applicable to our present situation, because here the government is not executor of the law, but rather a true legislator, and Congress does not have the legislative power but rather the constituent, which it cannot divide with any other power, and the oversight power to examine the acts of the past and present government. If the veto, according to its defenders, has as its objective to restrain the inclination of the assemblies to overstep and to avoid the misconduct of the legislative power, then according to this theory, which is that of the writers of public law of all the schools, who today in Mexico should be subject to the veto? The government or Congress? The second is not the legislative power. Indeed, the first is; this one is the one that should have some limitation. And the roles reversed, as it is said, the Plan of Ayutla, by establishing the oversight, established in truth a type of veto for the acts of the executive, absolute veto, veto with no more guide than public advisability, veto that perhaps is more consistent with democratic principles, given that it is not the power that is opposed to parliamentary decrees but rather the people who reject the impolitic or mistaken acts of the government.

The present question is not a question of party; it is not a struggle between the government and Congress; it is rather a theoretical question that must be examined with calm and circumspection, according to democratic principles and according to the legal order that, however provisional, established the Plan of Ayutla.

It is not a matter, then, of crushing the dignity of the government, but rather of setting properly the functions of the powers that exist today, with no other intention than to make possible the fulfillment of the principles that the democratic revolution proclaimed.

The day after tomorrow is the day designated for the discussion of this matter in Congress, and we hope it agrees upon a resolution as prudent as proper, as suitable to its dignity as consistent with the principles of democracy.

2 | The Constitutional Order

We have already said the issuing of the fundamental code is the strongest blow the reactionary party has suffered in its defeat, because it ends all pretext for continuing to promote the civil war. If the reaction is the work of some political party, if this party has a program, if this program can be shown openly to the nation in order to seek converts, such a party should give up its weapons, should stop the crimes committed by those who are active under its banner, direct itself to opinion, seek support in the electoral college, and, once in power, if it is favorable to the majority, carry out the reforms that constitute the symbol of its faith. For us, and we believe for the entire Republic, what the conservative party wants and does not want is a mystery. We have asked it many times in vain. When, however, it has been triumphant, it has answered with fines and threats. When it has been victorious, it has always been conspiratorial, and neither the acts of its statesmen, nor the expression of its periodicals, nor its banner of religion and privileges, nor its government of General Paredes, nor its famous Seven Laws shed light on its program or its inclinations.

Talking incessantly of religion, of order, of the family, and of property, it sometimes defends the principle of authority without saying from where it should be derived; other times it seems to long for Spanish domination or something like it; other times it dreams of erecting a throne for a foreign prince; and other times, finally, it implores the protectorate of foreign powers. If its doctrines, if its aspirations, leave its program shrouded in mystery, there is nonetheless reliable information for knowing it and for appraising what it is worth as a party of government and morality. This action, which it cannot deny, is the recent dictatorship of Santa Anna, based on perjury, treason, and perfidy, sup-

Original title: "El orden constitucional." Source: *El Siglo XIX*, Mexico, February 14, 1857.

ported by brutal force, sustained by atrocity and barbarism, grandiose action in which the conservative party took pleasure, for it could then calmly carry out all its intentions and managed to establish the Order of Guadalupe as an institution only amidst streams of blood, and it amused itself by legislating incessantly over liveries, uniforms, and court ceremonies. That unforgettable state of affairs, with its odor of sacristy, guardroom, and gambling den, concealed in its cloaks, its embroideries, and its fiestas a den of malefactors. In the middle of its carnival pageantry there was something of corruption, immorality, and rottenness that recalled the decadent epoch of the late [Roman] empire. That order of business sensed that it was tottering, and so it thought of the protectorate, or it sought Swiss armies, and so also the party of the authority principle, the party that calls to the silent people, that party, in order to perpetuate itself in power, in order to prolong the harvest time of its notables, that party had no shame in appealing to the parody of universal suffrage to say that the autocratic power of His Serene Highness[1] was derived from the will of the people.

If the restoration of that dictatorship is the desire of the reactionary party, it is right in accepting the legal order because the will of the Mexican people can never tolerate infamy, insult, and servitude; but it is now time that it consider that it will not achieve anything with the rebellion other than ruining and uselessly making Mexican blood run.

The party that created and supported the tyranny of twenty-seven months[2] cannot accept the constitutional order, and this does not surprise us because in this order it is not possible for speculators, bad priests, treasonous soldiers, and riffraff to succeed as an organized party, obscene assemblage that gives itself the title of aristocracy.

But if there is a party that from respect for the traditions of the past believes in good faith that our people is not yet ready for liberty or for the free discussion of its affairs, if there is a party that would like to strengthen the power, restrict local liberties, and limit certain rights, that party will enthusiastically accept the constitutional order; it will appeal to legal weapons, to the press, to elections, to the floor to defend and disseminate its ideas with openness and loyalty.

---

1. *Alteza serenísima* (serene highness) was the title Santa Anna gave himself. (Editor's note)

2. Santa Anna's rule. (Editor's note)

It is necessary to reiterate that the new constitution does not exclude any party, any opinion, any creed, but rather that it calls all of them to the legal sphere, without any condition other than submitting themselves to the will of the majority. Getting to be the majority depends on the morality and the ability of each party. And this constitution has over the earlier ones an advantage that makes it acceptable to all political convictions. Its authors have not declared themselves infallible, they do not present their work as perfect, they do not establish a status quo that one can leave only through rebellion. Far from this, it opens the doors to reform in every sense; there is not a single constitutional article that is not subject to official notice[3] if the national will wishes it so. And for reform, they do not establish long procedures or great obstacles. In few months, the most substantial innovation can be carried out. Given this ease, no party can reject the constitutional order, but rather can embrace it in good faith as the only way to put its principles into practice in a legal and peaceful manner without having to resort to civil war and bloodshed.

Those who do not accept the new constitution declare themselves outside the law, confess their impotence before public opinion, turn themselves into enemies of peace, and admit that they can achieve power only through upheavals and rebellion, that is, through harassment, surprise, violence, and not through the will of their fellow citizens.

When the constitution excludes no one, when it delivers power to the people so the people govern themselves, there is no pretext for not accepting the new legal order. In it fit all programs, all legitimate aspirations, and in it is possible the struggle of all men who, partially yielding their political principles, do not forget that they are compatriots and brothers and that the vanquished today can be the victors tomorrow, without defiling themselves with hatreds, atrocities, or persecutions.

We do not believe in the merging of parties, nor do we desire it, because if it were possible it would put a halt to all spirit of progress and innovation. The fundamental charter cannot produce the never-before-seen phenomenon in which all parties are fused into only one; but it certainly can give to their discussions, to their differences and even their struggles, a character of temperance and moderation that could maintain the public peace, might avoid civil war, and could revive in everyone the

3. Debated and amended. (Editor's note)

feeling of nationality. This is as far as it can go; to think of other mergers is to pursue one-sided agreements, accept humiliating conditions, and have faith in the kiss of Judas.

The constitutional order is acceptable for all men who love their country and wish to see it free of upheavals. Our convictions would be lacking and we would be inconsistent if we said that the constitution is a perfect work when many of its measures have been openly and vigorously attacked by us in the press and in the rostrum. We have said that the new constitution is not the symbol of the progressive party; we believed that the time had come to put into practice all the principles of democracy with all their consequences. We made mistakes; there were still compromises, obstacles, delays, and half measures. We must bow respectfully before the majority; we accept the new constitution as the source of legality and as a means by which one day progressive ideas might triumph, because the future belongs to them.

We insist on the idea that the new fundamental charter not exclude any political faith, and this noble conduct of the liberal party offers a notable contrast with the one the conservatives always observe. The Revolution of Jalisco,[4] which they distorted, proclaimed the existence of the federal system and the reform of the Charter of 1824 by means of a congress elected by the people. The conservatives, holders of the power thanks to the most indecent intrigues, evaded all the promises and arrived at the dictatorship for life of Santa Anna, giving liberals only jail cells and exile. The revolution of Ayutla promised a democratic constitution, and this promise has been faithfully kept, and the new legal order does not depend on party denominations but rather calls to all Mexicans.

Up to now, no one has attacked the new constitution directly. When the debates in Congress have had the greatest publicity, there are periodicals that feign not to know what it is about and await news as if they had to consider events in Peking or Ispahan. Other periodicals ask if there is liberty to express opinions freely about the new fundamental code. And there is no lack of those who insist on expressing the opinion that the constitution will not be promulgated, and they advise that it

---

4. José María Blancarte revolted in Guadalajara, Jalisco, against the government of Mariano Arista in July 1852. (Editor's note)

be published only as a curious document so that the approval it finds in public opinion and the reforms that it needs can be understood.

The press should truly act with greater openness. No one in the country can be ignorant of what the new constitution is. The law does not prohibit its free examination by the press, and the writer who makes evident the imperfections from which it suffers will do a service to the country and has nothing to fear. Because the constitution has been sworn by the president of the Republic, doubting whether it will be promulgated is to insult this magistrate. To those who are gratified by stirring up these doubts, we can assure them that the constitution has already been sanctioned by the executive and will be published very soon. As for reforms, the country can make them, but in a legal manner, and if public opinion longs for certain modifications, it can achieve them immediately, sending to the first congress and the legislatures of the states men who vote those reforms.

From now on, the press can judge very well with ample freedom the new constitution, which, despite its imperfections, is accepted by the country as the end of the dictatorship and of arbitrariness, as the end of the civil war, and as the foundation of the legal order.

3 | Elections

Before long the battle among the parties on the electoral field for the selection of the constitutional powers must begin. With the representative system established and the decision regarding sovereignty delegated to the general powers and the states, no other action but the elections remains for the people to exercise their sovereignty for themselves. For this very reason they must watch the elections with the greatest interest, understanding that on their votes depend the organization of the government, success in the public administration, and the fate of the country. If, because of a lamentable abandonment, the majority of our fellow citizens had not almost always regarded the elections with indifference, abandoning them to turbulent factions that, as masters of the terrain, distorted the national will, it is evident that the country would have been saved many errors, many mistakes, and many crimes, that it would have lacked pretext for many rebellions, and that the governments deriving from the people would have found support among the same people.

This abandonment, this indifference that we lament, are not inexplicable phenomena. In order for the election to be of interest and to attract the citizens, it is necessary that the citizen feels, perceives, that his vote has some influence on the fate of the country, that his will counts as much as that of each of his compatriots, and that if the majority of them participate, the men who deserve their confidence can be elevated to high offices. Explaining our thinking with more precision, we will say that the indifference with which the people regard electoral acts results from having adopted the system of indirect election, of the progressive delegation of the suffrage, which can never produce as an outcome the legitimate expression of public opinion.

What faith, what interest, can the people have in naming electors

Original title: "Elecciones." Source: *El Siglo XIX*, Mexico, February 15, 1857.

who have to name other new electors, who have still to go to select a new electoral body? What faith can the people have in all these operations, whose outcome they cannot even predict and that, as experience teaches, will be the most unexpected, if not the most contrary to their desires? To proclaim popular sovereignty, to recognize that all power derives from the people, and to appeal to indirect election, which distorts, corrupts, and denaturalizes the suffrage, is to fall into a monstrous inconsistency that immediately produces the evil of distracting citizens from public affairs, putting public affairs at the mercy of the audacity and intrigue of small factions and imprudent candidates.

We are supporters of direct and universal suffrage because, when we accept a principle, we conform to all its consequences without vacillation and timidity; we cannot approve the indirect system that the new constitution establishes, nor much less the severe restriction that the circle of eligible ones has undergone thanks to the triumph of the mean spirit of provincialism over the democratic principle and over the sentiment of national unity and the fraternity of all Mexicans.

We recognize nonetheless that, in the constitution, a step has been taken toward progress, reducing the stages of indirect election, and it seems to us that the division of the country into electoral districts will make the expression of the will of the people more genuine and will keep away official influences and the intrigues of factions.

Having one single stage of election, the naming of high functionaries moves closer to the people, who can become more interested in the electoral struggle.

If the people wish to conserve their liberty, if they wish to maintain order, if they wish to have morality and intelligence in public posts, they must take an active part in elections without letting themselves be led by any guide other than their conscience.

The electoral struggle is appropriate so that all parties that accept the legal order carefully measure and organize their strengths, which should consist of the moral influence they exercise on public opinion. We would look with pleasure at our adversaries being disposed to enter into the electoral dispute with no weapons other than their program and their principles and openly proclaiming their candidacies.

Leaving elections to chance is one of the most unfortunate errors of people. To think only about the electors is to be left in the middle of the road. Above all, opinion must seek which citizens are worthy of rising to legislative seats, the highest magistracies, and the presidency of the Republic. Otherwise, one would see what has already happened, that a party that believes it has won the primary elections loses the elections of the deputies. So as not to move blindly, at least in what concerns our political communion, we believe that the labors on behalf of the elections should have the greatest publicity, that before one decides for certain men, it is necessary to take their records into account and be assured of the resoluteness of their convictions. And as there is no one who does not fear some inconsistency, it seems to us indispensable that the progressive party should demand of its candidates clear and explicit programs in order to be able to reproach turncoats for their defections and to have a pledge that places the honor of the elected ones under an obligation not to abandon democratic principles.

Without a program there cannot be candidacies or nominations who inspire confidence. It will be said that what we want clashes a bit with our customs, that here there is a false modesty that dissuades the citizen from acknowledging that he aspires to public posts. We know this difficulty, but we believe that the open, public, sincere aspiration, the complete commitment of the man of honor to a party, is worth much more than the shameful intrigue of one who begs for votes, of one who gets them by wicked means and, in order to obtain them, lavishes promises with the most conflicting meanings.

The man who longs to serve his country cannot be ashamed of acknowledging it; his aspiration is noble and patriotic, and eligibility is one of the rights of the citizen. The deserters, the ones that resist change, the timid, the fickle, those who always want to serve circumstances, are those who can remain aloof from formulating a program, from entering into a solid commitment. It is the majority of these men who almost always have been elevated to regions of power; when each administration has taken power the greatest uncertainty about its policy has predominated, and afterward this policy has been uncertain and as changeable as the seasons. From this comes that unfortunate system of governments consecrated to the thankless task of Penelope; from this comes that habit of weaving and unweaving and of retracing steps on the path of reform and progress.

The same when the legislative assemblies have appeared. The puff of ministerial favor, the threat of presidential ire, and reasons perhaps more disgraceful have been sufficient to make the majority today become the minority tomorrow, and, with scandal, one has sometimes seen that the principles that form the creed of an entire party can scarcely be sustained by a few individuals, because men of the same communion turn their backs on those principles and cover their desertion with the outward show of prudence and good judgment, pronouncing, "it is not time," the eternal refrain that is always on the lips of the timid and inconsistent.

So that this political immorality might stop, so that there might be men of firm principles, it is necessary that there be the greatest openness in elections and that the people demand strict programs from the candidates. For the deserters, for the obstinate ones, for those who abandon their cause in the supreme hour of misfortune, there is not a punishment in the written codes; they are not subject to review before ordinary courts, but on them must fall the verdict and anathema of public opinion, which will be limited to leaving them in the obscurity of private life, from which they should never have emerged.

A sad experience dictates to us these words that we wish the progressive party would accept. Trusting in past history, in private promises, in declarations that seemed sincere, we have more than once loaned our support to some candidacies, and when they have triumphed, we have almost always received some bitter disappointment, and we have had to condemn terrible attacks on our principles by the very ones who feigned to profess them. And as there was not a solemn commitment before public opinion, we have not been able to throw their disgraceful inconsistencies in the faces of those men.

Taught by experience to take warning from the lessons of the past, we will be more cautious in the future, and from now on we declare that in the next elections, no candidate will have our support so long as he does not formulate a program whereby he enters into solemn contracts with the progressive party. Otherwise, we will always proceed by chance, and in the electoral campaign we will always proceed in the dark and as though delivered to the whims of a game of chance.

We venture to provoke our coreligionists in the press to adopt the same behavior we propose to follow, because we believe it suitable to the public interest in the cause of democracy.

If there are other candidacies that stand without a program, we will examine them with the greatest impartiality, turning our eyes always to the records of the public life of all the candidates. And if we find inconsistencies and defections, we will not be silent about them, because in electoral times it is appropriate that the country know its public men. We will be, then, more severe with those who call themselves progressives than with those who present themselves as our adversaries, because in these latter there will be more openness and fewer vacillations.

Soon there will be elections of deputies to the constituent legislatures of the states, bodies that have to carry out an arduous and difficult mission, that of working out the interior rule of the localities in such a way that they enjoy all the privileges the constitution grants them without going against the foundations of the federal pact in the slightest way.

Following them are the elections for the general Congress, which has to develop the principles of the constitution, drawing up the organic laws that the constituent assembly cannot issue. Those elected by the people must represent, in the first constituent congress, the opinion of the country regarding the new constitution and the reforms it needs, which can be initiated immediately. These are circumstances that make it indispensable that men whose political ideas are not a mystery to their fellow citizens come to the assembly.

The people have also to elect the seven magistrates of the Supreme Court and the president of the Republic. In conferring such lofty positions, it must be remembered that it is not a matter of rewarding them for their services, but of seeking the best and most worthy servants of the country for their patriotism, for their morality, and for their ability.

We sincerely desire that the people, being persuaded that the happiness of the country depends on the success of the elections, take the appropriate part in them without abandoning them to the intrigues of a few candidates.

The press is within its right, attempting to guide and enlighten the public spirit in the electoral struggle, and we believe that the progressive press, for the interest of its principles and for the public good, must refrain from making spontaneous nominations and from supporting candidacies when it does not have evidence of what the cause of democracy has to expect from each candidate, for which it is necessary that the candidate have very clear and very definite programs.

That is, at least, the conduct we propose to follow, advised by the lessons of a sad experience.

4 | Progress and Innovation

The *Eco Nacional* has published a lead article with this title to complete the refutation of our ideas in opposition to the amalgamation of parties.

Our colleague agrees that our society cannot remain static and recognizes that the need for movement, the tendency to perfect oneself and to improve conditions, is inherent in man, whom God endowed with all the powers necessary to elevate his destiny. It pleases us beyond measure to be entirely in agreement with the view of our colleague, and that need for movement, that necessity to improve conditions, being obvious and insuperable, we think that in order to develop it, to make it beneficial, and not to misdirect it, it is necessary that laws, institutions, and governments do not become an obstacle to the progressive movement of society, and that it is thus appropriate to leave human activity free, to trust individual liberty, not to be alarmed by the right of association, and to free industry, commerce, and agriculture from all shackles to make possible the material progress of the people. For this we believe it appropriate that the most extensive liberty for all opinions should exist in the legal order, and we do not judge it necessary that the political parties sacrifice their principles with base compromises.

Material progress cannot be considered to be independent of political institutions. Liberty creates new needs, and liberty facilitates the means of satisfying them. If trade and exchange are not subject to absurd restrictions, the need for new ways of communication will be felt, and if the spirits of association and enterprise do not encounter obstacles because of the distrust of authority or because of administrative centralization, opening pathways will be easier. The same analogy we have just indicated can always be found between material progress and political

Original title: "Progreso e innovación." Source: *El Siglo XIX,* Mexico, February 26, 1857.

institutions. For there to be progress, it seems to us that the best system consists in what the economists have called *laissez faire*. We do not know up to what point the *Eco* will share these ideas; but for us there is no doubt that the excessive expansion of authority, its distrustful vigilance felt everywhere, the restrictive system with its passports and prohibitions and fiscal investigations, etc., constitute the most unfortunate hindrance to all progress. Where no one can move without the permission of the authority, where the spirit of enterprise encounters barriers in everything and for everything, material improvements come to be impossible, and in our country it is well known which party it is that, in order to maintain itself in control, has resorted to the most absurd restrictions.

So, *laissez faire*. We agree with the *Eco* in that the peace and stability of governments are the principal elements for achieving material progress. This peace and this stability will be found in the legal order and in the peaceful struggle of parties, not in their impossible mergers. The same can be said of intellectual progress and of every type of progress, that is to say, they are impossible without the broadest, the most complete liberty; and as for the dissemination of public instruction, it will be easier with the freedom of instruction and with administrative decentralization, for in that way instruction without cost will be provided from the municipal school up to the great national establishments.

Our colleague believes that enlightened men are in agreement on this point, without difference of opinions, and he reminds us that to the party we consider the enemy of progress is owed the restoration of the Academia de Nobles Artes, the institution of the College of Agriculture, and the creation of the Ministry of Economic Development, and he adds that the laws that have been decreed in matters of instruction by men who are not of the progressive party demonstrate that they are not indifferent to public instruction, although they believe that it must be regulated in a suitable manner.

We recognize that the restoration of the Academia, the creation of the School of Agriculture and that of the Ministry of Economic Development are from the time of the conservatives; but we can say that the Academia de Nobles Artes has been protected by all governments, that the School of Agriculture has received very important improvements from the present government, that the Ministry of Economic Development was created at the request of many men of the liberal party, and that its creation was opposed only by the most recognized organ of the conservatives, by the old *Universal*, which feared the increase of candidates for state ministries.

In the laws and rules of the conservatives, there was a great deal of restrictive spirit and of tendencies not to disseminate instruction. The plan of studies of Lares put shackles on instruction and drove a large part of the youth away from literary careers. Although it is certain that, through the Ministry of Economic Development, some measures were generally decreed in support of instruction in this capital alone, the *Eco* cannot deny that to the conservative domination of the twenty-seven months were owed: the abolition of the National College of San Gregorio, which was devoted to the education of the indigenous race and which was replaced with a house of Jesuits, but we do not know whether it has rendered services to public instruction or to the poor classes of society; the closing of the School of Medicine of Puebla, which compelled many students to abandon their career; the closing of the Instituto Literario of Toluca, where young people from all the municipalities of the state of Mexico were instructed; the closing of the Liceo and of the Instituto de Guadalajara, which was carried out even though the professors offered to continue serving without pay; the closing of the Instituto de Ciencias of Oaxaca, out of hatred for its reformer and director, Don Benito Juárez; the closing of the Instituto de Zacatecas; the closing of the college of Durango. This was the appropriate way of regulating instruction that the conservatives had: eliminate it.

Many of these establishments were converted to barracks, and the physics and chemistry laboratories were destroyed by an uncontrolled army rabble that recalled the day of the most horrifying barbarism.

And the lack of trust was such that when the literary academy of San Juan de Letrán came together to prepare the apotheosis of the distinguished Ruiz de Alarcón, it could not examine poetic compositions except in the presence of a guard sent by the authority.

The organ of the dominant party maintained then that the people could not be given any instruction or code other than the catechism of Father Ripalda.

If this is what secondary instruction owed to conservative domination, we must say that, under the rule of the liberals, all the establishments that the dictatorship closed have been restored. The contrast does not need commentary.

Primary instruction did not come out any better. With the municipal power destroyed and the people's funds in the possession of the military commanders, the councils totally eliminated in some parts and named by the government in the large population centers, they could do nothing. The great rage for regulating instruction in an appropriate manner inspired that very famous decree on primary schools that, among other things, limited the materials of instruction in private establishments; fixed the invariable time limit of two and a half years to teach reading, writing, and the four primary rules of arithmetic; imposed fines on teachers who taught anything more; and prepared for the catechism to be recited one hour daily by the pupils while they were in the school. The conservatives limited and held back instruction, magnifying the restrictions and showing themselves to be entirely ignorant.

Apart from this, closing schools was the order of the day, and those of Tabasco and the other states were closed because the government ordered that all municipal funds be used for the passage of troops and for the transfer of replacements, the levy forcibly plucked from industry and agriculture.

More than enough reason for us, then, in view of the notorious facts, to consider the conservative faction as the enemy of intellectual progress and to believe, based on experience, that such progress is impossible with limitations and restrictions. We said before that the colleges the conservatives closed have been restored by the progressive party, and we believe that the liberty of instruction the constitution establishes is the best way to facilitate intellectual progress.

Our colleague is occupied continuously with moral progress, which he describes as superior to all the rest, and whose sole source he finds in the gospel dogma; he asks us if what we want is to destroy religious unity, to attack Catholicism in its dogmas, in the persons of its ministers, in the regulations and laws of its church, and to introduce religious anarchy by allowing all sects. The question of freedom of worship in the fundamental code forgotten, the gentlemen of *Eco* must be proud of the triumph of intolerance. Nonetheless, we say to them that the progressive party does not wish to destroy a religious unity that does not exist where a Protestant, foreign population lives, and where, according to what some bishops say, entire towns of idolators exist; that the progressive party does not attack Catholicism in its dogmas, or in its ministers, or in the regulations and laws of the church; and that it only wants those ministers to fulfill their duty and not to confuse dogmas with matters of simple discipline. The progressive party does not believe that the society where different forms of worship exist is demoralized, and it bases its belief on the fact that the Roman pontiff, the visible head of the Church, most interested as he is in maintaining Catholic unity, does not find it inappropriate as temporal sovereign to permit in his states the free exercise of Protestant and Jewish worship.

Our colleague tells us, and in this he does very well, what services the moral progress of the country owes to the conservative party; our colleague is very enlightened in presenting himself as satisfied with the recitation of the catechism in the schools and believing that this compensates for the excessive immorality of the government of twenty-seven months. Neither morality nor religion was served by those who degraded the priest, converting parish priests into police agents; those who passed judgment on the ones who ate meat during holy week; those who in Chiapas imposed fines on the ones who did not hear mass or did not go to confession. This pharisaical spirit of persecution and espionage is not the spirit of the sublime law of Christianity; it was the hypocritical cloak with which the men of the reactionary faction wanted to cover their wretchedness, their perjuries, and their iniquities. Those who persecuted the innocent, those who sold men, those who breathed hatred and vengeance, those who established the compulsory denunciation as a point of moral progress, carried us back to the times of the Inquisition. Moral progress, like all progress, is derived from liberty, and the authority with its restrictive laws can invent, if it wants, new crimes; but it cannot change the indelible ideas of good and evil engraved in the hearts of all men.

Our colleague rants continuously against demoralization, decadence, misery, the ruins of the epoch; he makes fun of the word "philanthropy" and misses the past, decrying the fact that theaters are being built and railways designed and the development of commerce, industry, and the arts secured; that, finally, what is referred to as the material order and the intellectual culture is being urged on, without anything being done in what the jeremiad of our colleague refers to as true instruction. But if religious instruction is neglected, the charge is not against the progressive party, and the *Eco* must direct it where it belongs, to that faction that invokes the august name of religion to stir up civil war, commit murders like that of the priest of Tuto and robberies like that of

the two hundred forty thousand pesos of San Luis Potosí; to some misguided priests, who leave the modest parish priesthood in order to become leaders of factions; to the sincere part of the clergy that does not
roundly condemn these excesses. With such examples, it is not strange
that, among an innocent and simple people, religious and moral instruction goes astray.

The *Eco* declares itself finally a partisan of progress, but of a progress
organized under a prudent and wise direction and within the bounds
that order, justice, and morality demarcate. We believe that true progress
is incompatible with disorder, with injustice and immorality, and we are
persuaded that it results from the combination of order with liberty.

Progress must be the work of the people; it must be the work of all
the spirits, of all the intelligence, of all the aspirations; it must satisfy
all needs; it is possible within the legal order when in it one encounters
neither shackles nor restrictions. And we do not know from where, if
not from the people themselves and the force of society itself, must come
that prudent and wise direction that orders, that regulates progress.

Always enigmas, always rules. Progress is in liberty; it is necessary not
to oppose useful innovations with barriers, and the appropriate system
is *laissez faire.*

5

Laws and Customs

The laws must conform to customs, and not customs to laws. Such is the maxim the gentlemen of the *Eco Nacional* have established in the most absolute terms in order to say afterward that in Mexico the liberal party wants social customs to conform to the laws, from which it can only follow that the political and religious opinions of the great majority of citizens are opposed to its work, and that consequently it finds invincible resistance everywhere.

Of course, for our colleague the new constitution is in conflict with the social customs of the Mexican people, above all in two main points, namely, the reestablishment of the federal system and the incomplete resolution of the question relative to freedom of worship.

Without denying the principle our colleague establishes, that the laws must conform to customs, but also not admitting it in an absolute, invariable, and general way, we permit ourselves to observe that, for the solution to questions of political science, the most gifted talents have not been able, nor will be able, to find maxims that in legislation are equivalent to algebraic formulas that serve, in all countries in all epochs, for the same problem. The day when such formulas are found, politics would be converted into a simple mechanical art, ceasing to be a science of observation and experimental science susceptible to improvement and progress. If the unknown everywhere is the well-being and prosperity of societies, the means of facilitating the attainment of that aspiration to perfectibility, aspiration in which our colleagues and with them the greatest philosophers of the world, have recognized to be the

---

Original title: "Las leyes y las costumbres: La federación y la libertad de cultos."
Source: *El Siglo XIX,* Mexico, March 30, 1857.

seal of divinity in man; the day when, to explain this unknown, one encounters an $x = a + b$ or some other formula, all social questions would cease to be that, and humanity would have arrived at the height of its perfection. But should there be anyone who believes in such an unrealizable dream and a country that seeks it in practice, the most probable would be the reign of the status quo and the hindrance of all progress. People would suffer the torment of that tyrant of whom the pagan myths speak, who compelled men of all types to accommodate themselves to a bed [lecho] of fixed dimensions.

There are not, then, in our opinion, political maxims invariably applicable to all countries and all ages. Although those maxims seem to contain great truths and, as they say, adages of men of state, when one probes them deeply — and for theories the best examination is the practical — one sees very often that it is necessary to depart from them.

The laws must conform to customs. It would be well and good if this meant that the legislator must not clash openly with the customs of the people or try to transform them as if by magic or resorting to violence. But not for this should the legislator renounce all major innovation, all progress, and much less have a worship blind to customs or yield to the most absurd fears.

The lesson of history says more about this than all arguments. There is not a legislator, a founder of nations, one of those men who has personified the vital forces of humanity, who has been held back by the *status quo*. If they had behaved in that way, they would not be the glories of humanity and the world would still be immersed in barbarism. Moses makes of a mob of Pharaoh's slaves a strong people, warlike and filled with faith in God, going against the customs of captivity and idolatry. Solon imprinted his spirit on the republic of Athens, radically modifying the established customs that he found. Lycurgus, the Spartan, respects[1] the customs that make people effeminate. Of all the advances, of all the innovations, of all the great revolutions of the human spirit, the most extraordinary, the most admirable without a doubt is Christianity. Well then, the law of the Messiah, the law of grace, is the one that most departs from the rule that laws must conform to customs, and so it had to be, because to overthrow paganism and idolatry with all their

1. Disrespects, most likely. (Editor's note)

errors, it was necessary to combat them at their foundations and not come to terms with them.

The idea of national unity supported much later in various European countries could triumph only by attacking the customs that gave strength to feudalism.

The French Revolution would not have had such influence on humanity if there had not been the tremendous struggle of progress and reform against tradition and custom.

The emancipation of all the Americas fought against the custom of centuries.

It will be said to us, perhaps, that it is a matter of laws and not revolutions. We answer that, for us, there are no greater revolutions than those that come about by virtue of the laws.

It seems to be a law of history that all progress finds existence in the traditions of the past, in that force of inertia that one wants to make venerable by calling it custom. But it is also a law of history that the new triumphs over the old and that custom changes, modifies itself, and perfects itself in a progressive sense, never resisting the law of the consummate action.

These are observations based not only in the history of politics, of legislation, and of revolutions, but also in the history of philosophy and science. When the pagan world heard for the first time talk of the unity of God, this truth upset it so much in its institutions, in its beliefs, and in its manner of being that it wanted to kill the new idea, making the man who had favored it finish off the hemlock at one draught. But ideas do not die, and polytheism, even with the force of custom, had to succumb to truth.

When a man who speaks in the name of God confounds the doctors of the law, pulling the mask from their hypocrisy; calls to the children, thus preferring candor and innocence to the splendors of the world; teaches the love of all men, the forgiveness of enemies, humility, charity, disdain for riches; when he emancipates the woman, raising her to the status of companion to man; when he throws the merchants from the temple; when he teaches the separation between the mean interests of the earth and the future destinies of heaven, all those ideas, all those lessons supported by example, clash in such a way with tradition, with custom, that the conservative spirit, that spirit of immutable laws, that spirit that wants the perfect alliance of law and custom to protect the past, sacrifices the innovator in torment—and this innovator was Christ! The redemption that struggled with custom, is there any doubt that it was the great revolution in morality and philosophy?

Centuries later, tradition and custom want our planet to be the center of the universe and condemn as criminal the one who has explored the mystery of creation; but the cry of Galileo, *E pur si muove!,* is the cry of humanity against errors of the past and oppression by custom.

Custom also, commanding with the apparatus of theology and flowing with the authority of Saint Augustine, denies the curvature of the earth and declares Columbus crazy because he divines the existence of this continent. The discovery of America is for custom, for tradition, for the beliefs of the past, a mortal blow that should have reduced them to perpetual silence.

And understand well, there is no physical, moral, intellectual, political, economic, social progress that has not come about through open war against custom. The plow, social life, matrimony, free inquiry, all the sciences, political freedom, commerce, industry, steam, the railroad, the telegraph, the press, the abolition of slavery, poorhouses, vaccination, the penitentiary—in a word, everything great, everything useful, everything beautiful—has been the triumph of progress over custom. And it had to be so because God, in bestowing intelligence and free will on man, wanted that man might travel toward his perfection himself.

To want custom to be the up-to-now of the law is to want, Oh holy God! that the sun not give light at the hour of dawn because it must respect the custom of the shadows of the night.

See, then, that if laws must always conform to customs, any progress, any improvement, would be impossible, and human societies would be failing to keep the divine law of unceasingly working for their perfection.

The gentlemen of the *Eco* who want the law always and forever to adapt itself to custom bring upon themselves a palpable contradiction, no matter who might be the author they use to support themselves, claiming that if the people are apathetic and weak of character, the constitution must carry stamped and printed a seal of life and energy that neutralizes that character, and that if the people are bellicose and irascible, the constitution must breathe calm and gentleness. Our colleague, in wishing stimulants for the listless and phlegmatic and sedatives for the sanguine, moves himself away from his own maxim and agrees that, at times, the laws can fight a little, not only with the customs but with the character of the people.

Assuming that the new constitution fights to a certain degree with our customs, this would not be sufficient reason to describe as great nonsense the plan of the constituents, accusing them of having been ignorant of the differences that matters of government, race, traditions, customs, and even geographic situation and physical configuration of countries occasion.

Our colleague did not examine the constitution deeply, he does not specify which are the measures that do not conform to customs, and he limits himself only to federation and the freedom to worship, feigning not to know about the bill of rights that is opposed to certain customs everyone describes as abuses.

The federation does not fight with customs because, of all the forms of government, it is the one that has been in force for the most time in the country and the one that has allowed it to enjoy the greatest prosperity, which explains why, as our colleague noted another time, it might have left welcome memories in a great number of Mexicans.

The *Eco* repeats that appreciation of differences between the origins of Mexico and the United States, appreciation answered many times in this old polemic.

The federation of Mexico is not the breaking up but rather, on the contrary, the bond of unity that leaves appropriate administrative freedom to the localities. The federation is necessary precisely if it attends to the geographic situation and the configuration of the country, and it has to its credit the contrast between it and the central form of government, this latter being powerless with respect to the good of the people although always oppressive.

The federation has the prestige of the Charter of 1824, a prestige that our colleague has recognized, and, practiced in the country for many years, it cannot be said that it is in conflict with our customs; much less in accord with our customs were the attempts to centralize everything, the crazy eagerness to improvise aristocratic classes and knightly orders, and the sad insistence on dividing Mexicans into more or less privileged castes when here equality is the child of custom and tradition, and when those who as colonists were equal cannot stop being so with the formation of an independent nation.

With respect to liberty of worship, comparison between Mexico and the United States is unnecessary; every attack on the new constitution is unnecessary because it does not establish such liberty. The exercise of this liberty guaranteed by political institutions would surely be an innovation in the Republic. But on this point the *Eco Nacional* must, at least, recognize that the law conformed strictly to custom without offending it in the slightest way. When the assembly and the government recoil before this innovation, it is the height of injustice to accuse them of being innovators. We do not find, then, the least motive that justifies the fear that the new constitution is in conflict with the customs of the Mexican people. It does, indeed, authorize some innovations that tend to correct lamentable abuses and affirm liberty.

The constitution is very far from being an empirical work, for it accommodates itself to the needs of the people, and if perhaps it does not satisfy all of them, it leaves open the door to reform without committing the most serious error of setting tradition and custom against true progress, that is to say, the satisfaction of social needs.

6

Manifesto as Preamble to the Constitution of 1857

Mexico, February 5, 1857

Mexicans:

Today the great promise of the regenerative Revolution of Ayutla to return the country to the constitutional order is fulfilled. This noble demand of the people, so energetically expressed by them when they rose up to break the yoke of the most menacing despotism, is satisfied. Amidst all the misfortunes that tyranny made them suffer, they knew that people who lack institutions that are the legitimate expression of their will, the invariable rule of their mandataries, are exposed to continual upheavals and the harshest servitude. The will of the entire people cried out for a constitution that would ensure the guarantees of man, the rights of the citizen, the regular order of society. To this sincere, innermost wish of the brave people who, in better days, won their independence; to this aspiration of people who, in the violent shipwreck of their liberties, anxiously sought some plank that might save them from death and something worse, infamy; to this will, to this aspiration, the Revolution of Ayutla owed its triumph, and from this victory of the people over their oppressors, of right over brute force, was derived the meeting of the Congress called to bring about the burning hope of the Republic: a political code adequate to its needs and to the rapid progress that, despite its misfortunes, it has made on the path of civilization.

Divine providence, blessing the noble efforts that have been made on behalf of liberty, has allowed Congress to end its work and today offer the country the promised Constitution, awaited like the good news to

Original title: "Manifiesto formulado por Francisco Zarco como preámbulo de la Constitución de 1857." Source: Francisco Zarco, *Historia del Congreso Extraordinario Constituyente (1856-1857). Estracto de todas sus sesiones y documentos parlamentarios de la época,* vol. 2 (Mexico: Imprenta de Ignacio Cumplido, 1857).

reassure agitated souls, calm the uneasiness of spirits, heal the wounds of the Republic, be the peacemaker, the symbol of reconciliation among our brothers, and put an end to that painful uncertainty that always characterizes difficult periods of transition.

The Congress that you freely chose, in concluding the arduous task you entrusted to it, understands the duty, feels the necessity of addressing the word to you, not to extol the fruit of its deliberations but to exhort you to union, to harmony, and so that you yourselves might be the ones who perfect your institutions without abandoning the legitimate pathways from which the Republic should never have departed.

Your representatives have passed through the most critical and difficult circumstances, have seen the agitation of society, have heard the deafening noise of fratricidal war, have contemplated liberty threatened, and in such a situation, in order not to lose hope in the future, their faith in God has inspired them, in God who protects neither iniquity nor injustice, and nonetheless they have had to make a supreme effort to obey humbly the mandates of the people, to resign themselves to every type of sacrifice in order to persevere in the work of constituting the country.

They took public opinion as guide, made good use of the bitter lessons of experience to avoid the stumbling blocks of the past, and the hope of improving the future of the country has smiled tenderly on them.

For that reason, instead of restoring the only legitimate charter that the United States of Mexico had previously had, instead of reviving the institutions of 1824, venerable work of our fathers, they undertook the formation of a new fundamental code that would not have the unfortunate seeds that, in days of sad memory, proscribed liberty in our country, and that would correspond to the visible progress achieved through the spirit of the century since that time.

Congress regarded national unity as the foundation of all prosperity, of all enhancement, and therefore it has endeavored to make the institutions serve as a bond of fraternity, a sure means of arriving at stable harmonies, and has tried to remove whatever might produce clashes and resistance, collisions, and conflicts.

Congress, persuaded that for society to be just, without which it could not be lasting, it must respect the rights granted to man by his Creator, and convinced that the most brilliant and dazzling political theories are clumsy delusions, bitter derision, when they do not ensure those rights, when civil liberty is not enjoyed, has defined clearly and precisely individual guarantees, sheltering them from every arbitrary attack. The bill of rights that stands at the head of the Constitution is an homage honoring, in your name, by your legislators, those imprescriptible rights of humanity. You are, then, free; use all the powers you have received from the Supreme Being for the development of your intelligence, for the achievement of your well-being.

Moreover, from today, equality will be the great law of the Republic: there will be no greater merit than that of the virtues; slavery, the disgrace of human history, will not defile the national territory; the home will be sacred; property inviolable; work and industry free; the expression of thought with no other fetters than respect and morality, public peace and private life; transit, movement without difficulties; commerce, agriculture without obstacles; the affairs of state examined by all citizens: there will not be retroactive laws, or monopolies, or arbitrary prisons, or special judges, or confiscation of wealth, or opprobrious punishments; nor will justice be paid for, nor will correspondence be violated; and in Mexico, for its glory before God and before the world, the inviolability of human life will be a practical truth as soon as the penitentiary system can achieve the repentance and rehabilitation of the man whom crime has led astray.

Such are, fellow citizens, the guarantees that Congress believed must be fixed firmly in the Constitution in order to make equality effective, in order that no right will be violated, so that institutions reach down by themselves and beneficently to the most destitute and unfortunate classes to pull them from their dejection, to carry the light of truth to them, to enliven them with knowledge of their rights. Thus will their spirit awake, which servitude made lethargic; thus will their activity be stimulated, which abjection paralyzed; thus will they enter into the social community, and, ceasing to be miserable serfs, redeemed, emancipated, they will bring new energy, new strength to the Republic.

Not for an instant could Congress waver with respect to the form of government that the nation was yearning to be given. Clear were the manifestations of the opinion, evident the needs of the country, certain the traditions of legitimacy, and eloquently persuasive the lessons of experience. The country wanted the federal system, because it is the only one suitable to its population, spread over a vast territory; it alone is adequate to so many differences in products, climates, customs, needs;

it alone can extend the life, the movement, the wealth, the prosperity to all the borders; and it is the one that, distributing the exercise of sovereignty, is the most suitable for making the rule of liberty permanent and for providing zealous defenders for it.

The federation, banner of those who have struggled against tyranny, reminder of happy eras, strength of the Republic to sustain its independence, symbol of democratic principles, is the only form of government that in Mexico has the love of the people, the prestige of legitimacy, the respect of the republican tradition. Congress, then, had to recognize the free and sovereign states as preexistent; it proclaimed their local liberties, and, concerning itself with its limits, it made no changes other than those urgently demanded by public opinion or for public convenience so as to improve the administration of the people. Desiring that in a democracy there not be people subjected to tutelage, it recognized the legitimate right of different localities to enjoy their own life as states of the federation.

Congress loudly proclaimed the doctrine of the sovereignty of the people and wanted the entire constitutional system to be a logical consequence of this brilliant and incontrovertible truth. All powers are derived from the people. The people are governed by the people. The people legislate. It is up to the people to reform, to change their institutions. But, it being necessary, given the organization, given the size of modern societies, to resort to the representative system, in Mexico no one could exercise authority except through the vote, the trust, the explicit consent of the people.

The states, enjoying very extensive liberty in their internal rule and tightly united by the federal bond, the powers that must represent the federation before the world retain the capabilities necessary to sustain independence, to take care of all general necessities; but they will never be an alien entity that conflicts with the states unless, on the contrary, they will be the creature of all the states. The electoral field is open to all aspirations, to all intelligences, to all parties; the suffrage has no restrictions other than those that were believed absolutely necessary for the genuine and true representation of all localities and the independence of electoral bodies. But the Congress of the Union will be the country through its delegates; the Court of Justice, whose lofty functions are directed to maintaining harmony and preserving right, will be instituted by the people; and the president of the Republic will be the one chosen by Mexican citizens. There is not, then, any possible antagonism between the center and the states, and the Constitution establishes the peaceful and conciliatory method for resolving difficulties that might arise in practice.

One seeks harmony, agreement, fraternity, all means of reconciling liberty with order, a happy combination from which true progress springs.

In the midst of the turbulence, hatreds, and resentments that have imprinted such a sad character on contemporary events, Congress can boast of having elevated itself to the height of its grand and sublime mission. It has not paid attention to these or those political epithets; it has not let itself be pulled along by the impetuous whirlwind of the passions; it has not seen only Mexicans, brothers, in all the children of the Republic. It has not created a Constitution for a party, but rather a Constitution for an entire people. It has not tried to pass judgment on behalf of whomever is responsible for the errors, the mistakes of the past; it has tried to avoid repeating them in the future; clearly, it has opened the gates of legitimacy for all men who wish to serve the *patria* loyally. No exclusivity, no proscriptions, no hatreds: peace, union, liberty for everyone; this is the spirit of the new Constitution.

Public discussion, the press, the rostrum, are for all opinions. The electoral field is the terrain on which the parties must struggle, and thus the Constitution will be the banner of the Republic in whose preservation all citizens take an interest.

The great proof that Congress has not nourished resentments, that it has wished to be the echo of magnanimity of the people of Mexico, is that it has sanctioned the abolition of the penalty of death for political crimes. Your representatives, who have suffered the persecutions of tyranny, have pronounced the pardon of their enemies.

The work of the Constitution must naturally, Congress knows it, be weakened by the hazardous circumstances in which it has been created and can also contain errors that might have escaped the perceptiveness of the assembly. Congress knows very well that in the present century there is no barrier that can keep a people static, that the current of the spirit does not stagnate, that immutable laws are a weak barricade against the progress of societies, that it is a vain undertaking to want to legislate for future ages, and that the human species advances day by day necessitating continual innovation in its mode of political and social being.

For this it has left the road clear to reform of the political code without any precaution other than the certainty that the changes be demanded and accepted by the people. Reform being so easy to satisfy the needs of the country, why resort to new upheavals, why devour ourselves in civil war if the legal means neither cost blood nor destroy the Republic, nor dishonor it, nor put its liberties and existence as a sovereign nation in danger? Be persuaded, Mexicans, that peace is the first of all goods and that your liberty and your happiness depend on the respect, on the love, with which you maintain your institutions.

If you want liberties more extensive than those the fundamental code grants you, you can obtain them by legal and peaceful means. If you believe, on the other hand, that the power of the authority needs greater extension and robustness, you can also arrive at this outcome peacefully.

The Mexican people who had heroic strength to overthrow Spanish domination and join the sovereign powers; the Mexican people who have vanquished all tyrannies, who always yearn for liberty and constitutional order, now have a code that is the full recognition of their rights and that does not hold them back, but rather encourages them on the road of progress and reform, of civilization and liberty.

On the path of revolutions there are deep and dark precipices, despotism, anarchy. The people who constitute themselves on the foundations of liberty and justice rise above those abysses. They do not have them before their eyes, neither in reform nor in progress. They leave them behind, they leave them in the past.

It falls to the Mexican people to maintain their precious rights and improve the work of the constituent assembly, which relies on the assistance that will be lent it, without doubt, by the legislatures of the states so that their particular institutions might strengthen national unity and produce an admirable completeness of harmony, strength, fraternity among all the parts of the Republic.

The great promise of the Plan of Ayutla is fulfilled. The United States of Mexico returns to constitutional life. Congress has sanctioned the most democratic constitution the Republic has had, has proclaimed the rights of man, has worked for liberty, has been faithful to the spirit of the epoch, to the inspirations radiating from Christianity, to the political and social revolution to which it owed its origin; it has built on the doctrine of the sovereignty of the people, and not so that they will be excited by it, but rather to leave to the people the full exercise of their sovereignty. May the Supreme Regulator of societies make the new Constitution acceptable to the Mexican people and, acceding to the humble prayers of this assembly, put an end to the misfortunes of the Republic and dispense to it with a generous hand the benefits of peace, justice, and liberty!

These are the wishes of your representatives as they return to private life to mix with their fellow citizens. They hope that their errors will be forgotten and that a day might shine when the Constitution of 1857, as the banner of liberty, might do justice to their patriotic intentions.

IGNACIO MANUEL ALTAMIRANO

Ignacio Manuel Altamirano (1834–93), a liberal politician, writer, lawyer, teacher, and noted orator, was born in the state of Guerrero, of humble origins. Altamirano was a student of Ignacio Ramírez at the Instituto Literario de Toluca and taught at several schools and institutes. With Ramírez and Guillermo Prieto he started a newspaper, *El Correo de México.*

Altamirano joined the liberal faction and fought against the conservatives in the Three Years' War, and after the triumph of the liberals was elected a deputy to Congress. During the French intervention Altamirano became a colonel in the republican army that fought against the empire. His military career ended in 1867, when the Republic was restored. Later, Altamirano was elected to Congress on three occasions. He also served as attorney general, chief justice of the Supreme Court, and consul in the foreign service. Altamirano was a writer in the Romantic literary style and devoted much effort to his literary pursuits. He wrote several novels, including *El Zarco,* and essays on a wide variety of topics.

We include two of his speeches on the civil war from the 1860s and an article published in 1880.

1 Against Amnesty. Speech before the Second Constitutional Congress, July 10, 1861

Sir:

With the full conscience of a pure man, with the full heart of a liberal, with the just energy of the representative of an outraged nation, I here raise my voice to request that the chamber reject the report in which the decree of amnesty for the reactionary party is proposed.[1]

And I request this because I judge that this decree would today be too untimely and highly impolitic.

Let me begin by saying that I very much respect the virtues of the gentlemen deputies who have endorsed the report, that I recognize in them excellent hearts, filled with sensitivity and mercy; but I believe that they have erred in believing that the nation should pardon its enemies with the same ease that these gentlemen, because of their magnanimous nature, pardon theirs. That is to say, they have confused their individual selves with the entire nation, and in that lies the error, in my opinion.

With this duty fulfilled that my openness imposed on me, I am now going to broach the question.

I have said that the decree would be untimely and impolitic. Here are my reasons:

It would be untimely because mercy, like all virtues, has its hour. Beyond that, mercy has no good outcome, or speaking in all truth, it produces the opposite of what might be desired.

Original title: "Contra la amnistía" [intervención en la Cámara de Diputados durante la sesión del 10 de julio de 1861]. Source: Felipe Buenrostro, *Historia del Segundo Congreso Constitucional de la República Mexicana, que funcionó en los años de 1861, 62 y 63. Extracto de todas las sesiones y documentos relativos de la época*, vol. 1 (Mexico: Impresa Políglota, 1875).

1. The Three Years' War between liberals and conservatives had just ended with the victory of the liberal faction. (Editor's note)

Amnesty, sir, is the completion of victory, but it must follow victory immediately. The history of all nations tells us this, and it is in the nature of these very things.

A victor who has just defeated his enemies, who still holds in his hands the bloody sword of battle, whom one supposes is still enraged and thirsty for vengeance, and whom one sees suddenly put aside the terrible expression on his face, throw away that threatening sword, open his arms to embrace against his chest his humiliated enemies, trembling with fright, this man, I say, is to be admired and loved.

The greatness of soul captivates, because the human heart instinctively admires everything that is great and sublime. Gaius Caesar won more sympathy with his generosity in Rome than with his sword in Pharsalia, and the Romans, intoxicated with enthusiasm and gratitude, dedicated the temple of clemency in his honor.

Henry IV, the Huguenot, made himself loved by his old enemies with his *general pardon.*

But Caesar and Henry IV were timely.

Because in effect, sir, amnesty is forgetting the past completely, it is an absolute pardon. Amnesty must be granted as a gift of mercy, as a concession that strength makes to weakness; it is rage that absolves repentance. But we, are we in the time for pardoning? Here is the question. And it can it be answered with equal precision:

"Now is not the time or it is still not time."

If after the triumph of Calpulalpan the government had come out with a word of amnesty, if it had opened its arms to the enemies of public peace, this would have been immoral, but perhaps it would have been successful, because I am sure that two roads were open then to the liberal government, that of absolute, open amnesty, or terrorism, that is to say, righteous power.

The government did not take either of those paths, but rather, wavering in its steps, uncertain in its decisions, adherent to routine in its methods, was half magnanimous and half severe, with the result that it made everyone discontent and it came to be censured by opposing factions.

Never let it be said that I slander: the nation knows it; Mexico has seen it. When plain and firm justice was expected, the government exiled bishops instead of hanging them, as these apostles of iniquity deserved; it fired some employees and others no, of those who had served the reaction; it pardoned Díaz, whose skull should now be white on the pillory; it had Trejo shot because, although he was guilty, he belonged to the rabble; and it pardoned the murderer Casanova because he was *respectable* and had someone who interceded for him; it absolved Chacón; it tolerated Caamaño; it was Montaño's plaything; it was going to employ Ismael Piña; and finally, it has the guilt that many of those bandits might have gone with Márquez;[2] and it has shown sufficiently that it has neither the gift of opportunity nor the merit of justice.

The result you are now seeing, legislators; I will not say anything to you about it. Well then, what was not done after Calpulalpan is now impossible.

The government with its errors caused the revolution not to end definitively at that time; it caused it to lose more in six months than it lost in three years, because the constitutional vessel that has traveled so serenely in the time of storms is close to sinking as it reaches port. Yes, sir, today it lies heavy on the optimists. We find ourselves in full revolution; we have suffered serious setbacks; the reaction is imposing; it will not win, but it battles with a terrible ferocity; the great victory is not very close, the reactionaries who are not in the field provide every kind of resource to those who are; *those unhappy ones who groan in hiding places,* as Señor Montes says, conspire from there in a thousand ways; the hopes of this cursed faction are reborn; the bevies of Márquez have just visited the streets of the capital and . . . is now when we are to offer amnesty?

A beautiful opportunity, to be sure!

Amnesty now would not be the word of pardon; it would not be the caress of a victorious force to conquered weakness; it would be . . . a shameful capitulation, a parachute, a miserable cowardice.

No, the national representation will not abandon its dignity in that way, it will not go on its knees to put its law in the hands of the bandits, it will not surrender those pariahs to the Moloch of the clergy.

If such should happen, I would curse the hour in which the people have named me their representative.

Think about it, legislators. If today we decree the amnesty, the reactionary party would say, and with reason: "They are afraid of us and they flatter us." "The Congress fixes its gaze with terror on the gloomy Mount of the Crosses and on the scaffold of Ocampo, and it fears for

2. Leonardo Márquez, conservative general. (Editor's note)

itself." And no, by God! the Congress does not fear, because the Congress is the nation, and the nation that has struggled for so long against great hosts of these outlaws would not come now to tremble before just one.

You now see, then, that the occasion is not right, and for that reason the decree would be untimely.

I have said that it would also be impolitic because everything that does not lead to public happiness, everything that does not extend to the good government of the people, is impolitic.

Until now, sir, it has been believed in Mexico that politics consists of shameful compromise with all acts of treason, with all crimes; until now the motto of the greater part of our governments has been *today for you, tomorrow for me*. Well then, sir, that is disgusting, that will be a form of politics but a misleading and contemptible form of politics.

We belong to the liberal party, which is the party of the nation, and we must not here imitate the old sea god, taking different forms and disguises; here we must take our own color and follow our own program honestly. Enough of these political Proteuses influencing opinion.

Either we are liberals or we are liberticides; either we are legislators or we are rebels; either judges or defense counsel.

The nation has not sent us to preach union with criminals but to punish them.

The opposite would be to pull it down into an abyss of afflictions and horrors.

Pardoning the conservative party in Mexico has never produced good results; it would be impolitic, then, to pardon it again.

Clemency in theory is very beautiful, I agree; but in practice it has always been fatal for us. It will be enough for us to cast a retrospective eye on our last years. I will relate individual deeds to you, and I will relate them because personal deeds characterize the collective individual, because they are the result of the program of a faction.

After the Revolution of Ayutla, the celebrated general Alvarez decided to pardon all the followers of Santa Anna, who, not being able to vanquish Alvarez, carried conflagration and murder to the poor peoples of the South. Never had clemency been carried to such a degree of selflessness. Being in Cuernavaca he called Don Severo del Castillo, and this gentleman of the Middle Ages, *this model of military delicacy,* responded to the call after a thousand requests and orders. General Alvarez reminded him of the infamous deed of having burned his modest country farm. Trembling, Castillo begged pardon; then the general said to him that in return for that action he entrusted to him the command of his old battalion of sappers. Castillo, moved or feigning to be moved by this noble action, went to prostrate himself at the feet of the old *caudillo* when this latter held him back, saying to him that these acts, which degraded men and debased soldiers, did not please him.

Castillo, grateful, swore eternal faithfulness to the government of Ayutla, and what happened? You already know. In a few days, with the brigade that Comonfort had entrusted to him, he pronounced himself against the government.

And Osollo pardoned and shamefully indulged by Comonfort? And Miramón pardoned also? And Gutiérrez, and a long list of others, what have they done? They believed clemency was weakness and bit the hand that was extended to them. I have referred a while ago to Chacón, to Caamaño, to Montaño, and to others who are with Márquez, and I should still add, what did the prisoners do whom González Ortega saved in Silao? Did he perhaps not meet them again in Calpulalpan? Sir, ingratitude characterizes the reactionary party, and to be generous to ingrates is to sow on rocks, here and among all peoples.

I said that Caesar and Henry IV had been timely, and despite this, ingratitude, not love of their country, armed Brutus and Cassius against their benefactor, who had pardoned them and honored them with a praetorship; and fanaticism put a dagger in the hands of Ravaillac. Well then, here we meet precisely with ingratitude and fanaticism.

And do we go, without even chastising, to offer the enemies of the nation the opportunity to do harm to us?

Above all, sir, is it about pardoning trivial political offenses? No. It is about pardoning a crime, the greatest one of all, high treason.

The Mexican Republic has been constituted; it has elected its government by popular and voluntary vote, and it has been given a fundamental law. Well then, these men have attempted a crime against that government and against that law, and they have attempted a crime, filling the entire nation with sorrow, desolation, and blood. There is not a place in the Republic not marked with the savage trace of that rebellious faction. There is not a crime it has not committed. Will it be necessary to bring to mind the murderers of Tacubaya, of Cocula, and of the *Esperanza?* Will it be necessary to invoke the bloody images of Larios, of Ocampo, of Degollado, and of Valle? Will it be necessary for you to see the destroyed properties, the devastated fields, the people dying of misery, bankruptcy in the treasury, and our entire soil stained with the blood of our brothers? And observe that, in all this, not only the leader who commands has the blame, but also the subordinate who obeys, because all are wheels and parts of that horrible machine of destruction.

And are we going to pardon those men? Are we not going to notice the national indignation?

Is it that we do not know what justice is?

No, let us for once be honorable; let us for once be just. Enough now of compromises and of sterile generosity. Justice and not clemency!

It is shameful, sir. Many criminals are being acquitted in our presence, and we are not raising our voice. Isidro Díaz, Casanova, and many of those accused are still alive. Their cause seems to have no end. National justice cries out for their punishment. The executioner should have finished them off some time ago, and one might believe that, far from suffering the deserved punishment, within a short time they might go strolling through Paris if you will not encounter them one day in those streets.

This is disgusting. Finally, does the national majesty have to continue being the king of mockery of all rogues? Is there no respect here for virtue and hatred of crime? Is the murderer of a man, a horse thief, punished, but not a punishment for the one who sets fire to entire villages, for one who robs the public coffers, for one who spills torrents of Mexican blood?

Instead of organic laws, instead of prompt punishments, instead of raising the guillotine for the traitors, a timid law of amnesty is presented to us.

And this in moments of seeing the bodies of our distinguished men with their skulls cut to pieces, with the horrible ecchymoses that the cord with which they were hanged produced?

Oh manes[3] of our sacrificed friends . . . ask vengeance of God . . . ! We think of pardoning your executioners and the friends of your executioners!

I know well that expressing myself thus with this frank and fervent energy displeases certain people. I know that these are not the feelings

3. Mythological spirits of death. (Editor's note)

of those armchair politicians who stood there indifferent during the struggle, taking no pity on the anguish of the *patria* but taking pleasure in the horrors occurring outside the capital.

But I do not like compromises; I am a child of the mountains of the South and descend from those men of iron who have always preferred eating roots and living among wild beasts to bowing their heads before tyrants and embracing traitors.

Yes, I belong to that phalanx of partisans who can be called, without fear and without blemish, "the Bayards of liberalism."[4]

Since I left the coasts to come to this post I have been stoically resigned to not knowing how to act, and while I may not have my head very securely on my shoulders, I do not have to grant a single pardon to the executioners of my brothers. I have not come to compromise with any reactionary or to weaken myself with the softness of the capital, and I understand that if all the deputies seated on these benches do not decide to risk their lives in defense of the national majesty, we have nothing good to do.

But I believe the Congress will know how to show the nation that it is at the high level of its desires and that it understands its holy mission. I believe that the legislative will say frequently to the executive, in the presence of each evildoer, what Marius said to Cinna in the presence of each enemy: "He must die."

We must have a principle in place of a heart. I have many reactionary acquaintances; with some I cultivated friendly relations in another time, but I declare that the day they fall into my hands, I would have their heads cut off, because before friendship comes the *patria;* before feeling comes the idea; before compassion comes justice.

And what! . . . Señor Ocampo, one man alone, would have the greatness of soul to say, "I break but I do not bend." And the Congress, that is to say the entire nation, would now say: "I do indeed break, and I do bend and I do lower myself"?

It is an insult to the national representation to suppose so.

I beg you legislators to put your hand on your heart and tell me: Can there be any friendship between the liberal party and the reactionary

4. Pierre Terrail, seigneur de Bayard, was a French military hero known for his fearlessness and chivalry in the Italian campaigns of Charles VII, Louis XII, and Francis I. A cavalier "without fear and without blemish." (Editor's note)

party? Will the men of the fifteenth century be joined with the men of the nineteenth century? Men and wild beasts?

No. We or they; there is no middle ground.

If you think that party is weak, you are wrong; certainly it lacks moral force, but it has physical force. They have taken the wealth from the clergy but they cannot take from them their hopes; and, above all, those bandits that Márquez leads, having just chewed on the last bread of the clergy, hurl themselves now over the property of the citizens, and you see what future awaits Mexico for some years to come if the terrible hand of an energetic and powerful government does not come to save the situation.

No, censure that opinion; to pardon would be to make oneself an accomplice. Jesus Christ pardoned his executioners on his scaffold, but he was dealing with personal offenses and not those of an unhappy nation ... Do not imitate that noble martyr, because you are not in his situation, and with your exaggerated evangelism you would lose the Republic. Rise up just, severe, terrible, and say to the rebels what God said through the mouth of the prophet: you used the sword ... and the sword will fall on you!

2 | Martyrs of Tacubaya

Today, April 11, 1880, makes twenty-one years since the clerical party committed a great crime that horrified the Republic and drew down on itself the condemnation of the people and the anathema of history.

The savage and infamous murder committed on the persons of young physicians and prisoners at the very gates of Mexico City, far from instilling terror, made the liberals, worked up by indignation, acquire new spirit, and alienated from the murderers the sympathies of all people who value honor and generosity in anything.

Since the eleventh of April 1859, the clerical reactionaries have only traveled a road of hatred and curses. In vain they appealed to extreme means; in vain they armed phalanx after phalanx, compelling by force the unfortunate ones they snatched from the workshops and fields to train them to fight against the soldiers of Liberty; in vain the bishops and friars exhausted the resources of their churches to pay the highwaymen of fanaticism; in vain they stirred up the frenzy from the pulpit, preaching a ferocious crusade against the Constitution of '57 and the men who supported it; in vain the factions, which called themselves government here, compromised the national honor, throwing themselves on the money of the English Legation to equip new expeditions; in vain, finally, they infuriated society with their levies and their outrages, and they carried everywhere the standard of the Cross stained with blood and presiding over killing and extermination.

They were condemned to fall vanquished, and eight months later were thrown out in Calpulalpan by the blast of the avenging people and disappeared from this city, which they had infested with their presence for three years.

Original title: "Los mártires de Tacubaya." Source: *La República,* Mexico, April 11, 1880.

Since that time also, the torment of Tacubaya has been held up to the eyes of the nation as a constant reproach, as a stain of eternal ignominy for the enemies of public liberties, as a protest of an outraged humanity against those who did not learn to respect science, philanthropy, and youth.

The picture of that abominable killing still presents itself to our memory with all its frightening reality.

It was the tenth of April 1859. The famous *caudillo* Don Santos Degollado, so constant in the struggle for the Reform but so unfortunate in it, had brought a new army, reorganized after ten defeats, to threaten Mexico, which had a limited garrison at that time because Miramón[1] had marched to Veracruz with the cream of the reactionary army to besiege that stronghold where the constitutional government was.

Señor Degollado, always unlucky in his measures and his plans, had remained inactive in Tacubaya, letting the troops of Callejo and Mejía, which had come to reinforce the garrison, enter freely into Mexico. Moreover, he did not intend anything serious against the stronghold, be it because the number of his forces was insufficient, be it for their lack of discipline, or be it, finally, because his sole mission was reduced to distracting the attention of the enemy, attracting the army of Miramón to the center of its military action, which was Mexico.

This last was accomplished fully. Miramón besieged in vain the stronghold of Veracruz, aided by a squadron under the command of Marín, who tried to block the port and deprive it of the resources it could receive by sea. With this squadron destroyed and seized in a heroic combat in which the valiant generals La Llave and Juan José de la Garza commanded the boarding, Miramón, despite his persevering efforts by land, had no recourse but to retreat confused and make his way to Mexico in haste, threatened as this stronghold was by the liberal troops under the command of Degollado.

As soon as he arrived, the best forces of the garrison, under the orders of Márquez and Mejía, seeing the inaction of the liberals, resolved to attack them on their field of Tacubaya itself.

The rest is well known. The reactionary columns, ready to march from the night of the tenth, began the attack on the morning of the

1. Miguel Miramón, conservative general who fought for Maximilian and was shot in June 1867 after the defeat of the imperial troops in Querétaro. (Editor's note)

eleventh, and although they encountered a stubborn resistance, they were victorious and entered Tacubaya a little after noon. The troops of Señor Degollado retreated in disorder following a rout, leaving their artillery, their baggage, their wounded, and a great number of prisoners in the hands of the enemy.

That was the moment of carnage and blind ferocity. The reactionary leaders exemplified cruelty and lack of restraint. It seemed as if the hatred of the clerical faction had let loose over Tacubaya all its Maenads, frenetic and eager to kill.

Among the prisoners had fallen General Lazcano, who belonged to the old army, and some other officers and leaders such as Dionisio Bello, and a young lawyer who had the position of military adviser, Manuel Mateos.

Manuel Mateos was an arrogant young man of twenty-seven and the incarnation of liberal youth of that era. Gifted with a great talent, a poetic and enthusiastic imagination, and an exalted liberal faith, he had taken part as a writer and as a soldier in all the fights that had opened the great drama of the Reform since the time of Comonfort. Profound and elegant writer, even before finishing his career as lawyer, he had already been noted in the journalistic press for his impassioned writings, in which the fire of a young and ardent heart was felt. Poet, he had played his lyre not so much to sing about love, the noble passion of his age, but rather to extol the glories of the *patria* and to arouse the people to the fight for Liberty. Gifted, moreover, with a majestic stature, a Dantonian face, and a robust and sonorous voice, he had appeared many times in the popular tribunal as a conventional orator, thundering against tyranny and preaching the rights of man. Finally, understanding that in a time of Reform the writer, the poet, the tribune must become the armed champion, Mateos had worn the sword when he left Mexico in 1857 with Juárez, Ocampo, Prieto, Guzmán, and Ruiz, and had formed with Leandro Valle and other spirited young men the first guard of that government, which was called to make the Decalogue of the Constitution and the Reform triumph amidst the tempests of war.

But Manuel Mateos, although an ardent partisan of these great ideas and of the law, had never stained his hands with blood. He had not made himself responsible for those acts that carry reprisal as a consequence. In sum, he was a brave and noble partisan.

After these shackles, others were ordered. On soldiers? No, on doctors. Some young men accompanied the liberal army as doctors, and as such they were tending to the wounded; they did not think about running when they learned of the rout. They understood that their duty was beside the beds of the wounded. They knew moreover that their profession was a priesthood, that it was respected in the entire civilized world as a holy thing, and that for this very reason they could not even anticipate a crime against them. Duval, Portugal, and Sánchez were those three friends of Humanity. To them was added Juan Díaz Covarrubias, a young student of medicine, who had also come from Mexico with the objective of lending his humanitarian services to the liberal army, believing that the number of men of his profession would be scarce.

Juan Díaz was a gentle and melancholy poet whose verses had shown simultaneously, from very early on, an ardent and sad inspiration, an excellent organization, and a spirit enamored of the ideal. Ay! Who would have said a few days before, on seeing that young student pass through the streets, dreaming and gentle, inoffensive and agreeable, that he was going to be sacrificed like a terrible evildoer by a stupid army rabble precisely because, moved by his fine sentiments, he had gone to help suffering humanity!

The young physicians tended the wounded and occupied themselves with the philanthropic chores of military surgery beside the beds of the dying.

From there the brutal claw of the executioners of Márquez seized him to enclose him in barracks, incommunicado with the other prisoners of war, in the same way the licenciado Juáregi was seized from the domestic hearth.

Miramón had just arrived in Mexico, and, still covered with the dust of the road from Veracruz, presented himself on the field of the bloody victory. He was furious with indignation, and to him the triumph of Tacubaya seemed barely a weak compensation for the rout of Veracruz.

Márquez gave him an account of the battle and requested orders from him regarding the fate of the prisoners. Miramón conferred a moment with Mejía and then gave the order to execute them all by shooting. Miramón was brave but he was never magnanimous, and he was still driven by an implacable hatred of the liberal party, without understanding well, because he was of very middling intelligence, the ideas the liberals defended and he opposed.

The order was carried out, the night already gloomy. The rabble of murderers pulled the prisoners from their prison and led them in single file to the outskirts of Tacubaya. The prisoners believed, at first, that they were leading them to Mexico; but when they saw that they were taking them by out-of-the-way paths in the countryside between the ravines that wound through the hills where Tacubaya is situated, they no longer doubted their fate. They were going to be killed! Then they asked to write, to give a final goodbye to their families, to speak to some friend. Everything was denied to them. It was necessary that mystery and shadow completely cover the crime; it was necessary that the clamp of silence close the mouths of those martyrs; it was indispensable that it have the appearance of an ambush and not the glory of the political gallows. Be quiet and die! That was the fate of the enemies of clerical tyranny. The inquisition still had the show of the auto-da-fé; the gallows of the viceroyalty still had the testimony of the notary and of the mob. The cruelty of the clerical party went much further; it bit, like rabid dogs, in silence. It is not known exactly what happened at that frightful scene. It is known only that the squad formed itself around the victims. Dionisio Bello has recounted that he escaped, slipping away into the depth of a ravine, and that he was not seen thanks to the darkness of the night that the torches scarcely rent. It is known also that O'Horan and Daza Argüelles ordered the execution, that Ángel Buenabad created the list of those to be shot, that Manuel Mateos gave the word to the soldiers in a clear voice, that Díaz Covarrubias embraced Sánchez and that he wanted to die like that, and then . . . that were heard various continuous explosions and that the hired killers returned to Tacubaya, now in the early morning hours, bringing the shattered bodies of the victims, and that they threw them in the great hall *De profundis* of the San Diego convent. Some were thrown completely nude onto the patio.

There we saw them on day twelve when, mixed in with the crowd, we could look for our friends who could scarcely be recognized, torn to pieces as they were by the bullets. Mateos had his skull cut to pieces and the right eye bulging out; Díaz Covarrubias also with his skull and eye and part of a cheek mangled, and a hand in shreds. The heads of the rest were a shapeless combination of dust and blood.

Next to those bodies, the soldiers drank and smoked indifferently, and the disgusting camp followers, accustomed to those spectacles, laughed and frolicked like a band of harpies.

At noon, some soldiers, assisted by various disguised students, took the bodies on stretchers to the small and humble church of San Pedro in the south of Tacubaya, almost in the countryside. There, a long and shallow ditch was dug in which the bodies were placed, one next to the other, covering them with a light layer of earth. A reactionary leader in a white jacket watched the labors with repugnance and surliness.

Later, the army of Márquez prepared to make its triumphal entry into Mexico, parading by, in fact, in a few minutes and entering into the great city at four in the afternoon.

And then began the clerical orgy, the saturnalia of blood, the dance of the scalps, frenetically danced in duet by the uniforms and the cassocks.

The Catholic churches, beginning with the holy cathedral, were bedecked for a fiesta; enormous red draperies hung from the towers and belfries; the bells dazed the city with a thundering, senseless ringing; the *aristocratic* families threw flowers and garlands from the balconies to Márquez and his companions, who passed by self-satisfied on their battle steeds, and to the troops that had vanquished the heretics.

The escaped prisoners, among whom came our friend, today General Chavarría, wounded but saved by a friendly intervention, marched among the ranks with the sad but not beaten down aspect of the liberal soldiers. The crowd silently watched pass by this army of bloodthirsty soldiers, for whom there was no sympathy whatsoever in the town.

Thus ended this unfortunate day.

. . . .

The eye of the historian could not absorb the details of the tremendous crime, but the eye of the people who sympathized with the victims took note of the names of the executioners and, implacable as Fate, have now punished them one by one.

Popular justice is slow at times, but it is certain and terrible.

A few months from that day, Daza Argüelles fell into the hands of Carbajal's soldiers in Tulancingo, and his body was dragged over the stones of the streets and trampled by maddened horses. That was one!

Later, in 1867, Buenabad was run through by republican bullets while going over the Mount of the Crosses with the troops of the traitor Tavera, beaten by the soldiers of Riva Palacio. And Buenabad died devoured by worms and regrets a few days later. And that was two!

In June of the same year, Miramón, the one who ordered the killings, was executed on the Hill of the Bells and atoned for the long series of his crimes in that place in which national justice gleamed with all its august majesty. And that was three!

And Mejía, the one who had helped with the decision made in Tacubaya, fell also in the same place. And that was four!

O'Horan, the executor, fell a few days later in Mexico at the hands of General Díaz, and the small plaza of Mixcalco saw the expiation of the crime of Tacubaya. And that was five!

One remains, he who has borne the entire burden of the hatred produced by the atrocious event. The truth is that Márquez only obeyed Miramón's order. Nonetheless, the entire nation has given him the dreadful name Hyena of Tacubaya, a name that follows him everywhere like a curse.

He has escaped punishment, but he has not escaped from the hatred, from the dishonor; from the hatred even of his party, which calls him traitor because he abandoned Maximilian in Querétaro; from the dishonor, because he is a pariah condemned to drag out, in a foreign land, a life of nostalgia, tedium, and self-contempt, condemned to the punishment of Tantalus of second-guessing, of feeling the beaches of the *patria* very close without ever being able to touch them, and of seeing in every wave that arrives, impelled by the current from our coasts, an unending curse.

The execrable old man has thus arrived at a septuagenarian age, devouring the bitter bread of the usury to which he has had to appeal so as not to die of hunger, and he slithers along like an old reptile amidst the mire to die devoured by the ants of humiliation and of misery. What worse punishment?

Such is the justice of the People! Another would say, "Such is the justice of God!"

For us, the eleventh of April 1859 is the great reason for being implacable with the clerical faction and for having given justification to the tremendous punishments imposed on their *caudillos,* who were executioners and enemies of humanity.

Later, we have pardoned it en masse, even despite the treason to the *patria.* But to pardon is not the same as to forget.

The great liberal party must understand it always. Between pardoning and forgetting exists an abyss. Pardoning puts the sword in the sheath, but remembering must keep the sword ready to pull out on the least occasion.

3

Speech by Citizen Manuel Ignacio Altamirano on the Occasion of the Anniversary of Independence, September 15, 1861

Citizens:

You have called me to the rostrum on this solemn night, and I thank you for it. You have esteemed my poor talent too kindly; but you have done justice to my patriotism, and I will never forget so distinguished an honor.

We have, then, gathered here to celebrate our great family holiday. It is here that the divine star of 1810 reappears in our heavens, today dark and cloud covered. But its light dissipates the shadows and makes the space shine; but its appearance counsels us in our sorrows, if only for a moment, and even the thousand hecatombs in which the blood of our patricians still smolders seem to us today so many other altars offered to the God of free peoples.

Yes, this memory of our old glories is sweet, whether it be that it surprises us on the fields of battle or on foreign beaches, whether it be that the shackles of our tyrants oppress us or the errors of our friends sadden us, or whether it be that the weight of our setbacks afflicts us or the sterility of our victories disillusions us.

Yes, in whatever situation fate places us, all of us turn our eyes to our glorious year '10 to revive our political faith, just as the Persians turned theirs to the east to revive their religious faith.

And who does not forget in this moment his misery and animosities to give one another a brotherly embrace? Who does not acknowledge his smallness before the majesty of our fathers? Who does not glorify those who gave us *patria* at the cost of their lives?

Only the clergy and its party do not share our happiness, and they have reason. They are the last expression of Spanish tyranny in our

Original title: "Discurso pronunciado en el Teatro Nacional de México la noche del 15 de septiembre de 1861 por el ciudadano Ignacio M. Altamirano." Source: *El Monitor Republicano,* Mexico, September 20, 1861.

country. Thanks to God that they withdraw from our national holidays, some with somber faces, others brandishing the fratricidal dagger. Their spite and their rage are for us new reasons for elation, and one day we will make them cry in vain, from foreign soil, for this *patria* that they wanted to see enslaved and that today they view with so much rancor because it is free.

As for us, liberals, today we give each other a cordial handshake, today we present ourselves closely united, today we forget our disappointments in order to make room only for hopes; today we should gather together filled with veneration around the glorious standard of Dolores; it does not matter which hand grasps it so long as it be the hand of a democrat, because only the hand of a democrat is worthy of hoisting it.

Yes, Mexicans, today it is not a matter of praising this or that political method, this or that small personality; here the great principle of national sovereignty is to be extolled, and "as diverse as might be our opinions in politics, the love of the *patria,* of national honor, of independence, and of the freedom of the country, is a general sentiment for which everyone is ready to sacrifice up to the last drop of blood," as said Kossuth, the great Hungarian patriot, on July 11, 1848, in the Assembly of Pest.

This is a sacred night, fellow citizens, a sacred night because in it, the tribunes of the people not only have the mission of recounting the glorious epic of our insurrection, like the ancient rhapsodists and the troubadours of the Middle Ages, but rather principally the mission of speaking in the name of that very people, of setting forth their sorrows, of giving an account of their sacrifices, and of being placed at the summit of their desires.

Thus, the orators who the Greek people named to offer the panegyric of their heroes would understand this priesthood.

Thus will I also speak to you; I will make myself here the faithful interpreter of that poor people whose affection is bought with promises and whose blood is repaid with excuses.

I can speak in their name because I identify with them, because I carry in my heart all their pains, all their disillusions, all their indignation, all the feeling of their power. Because I am a true man of the people, descending from twenty unfortunate races that have bequeathed me, together with their love of liberty, all the sorrows of their ancient humiliation.

What the people have suffered! You know it. The martyrology of Mexican democracy is very long. Before the Spanish adventurers brought us their friars and their executioners, the Mexican people had already suffered the oppression of their autocratic kings and their bloodthirsty *teopixquis*. The conquest, making colonists of the Mexicans, made their slavery more bitter; but Moctezuma had been the worthy predecessor of Charles V.

The poor people changed masters. The *encomenderos* were the successors to the caciques, the friars to the Indian pontiffs, the bonfire of the Inquisition replaced the stone of sacrifices, the bloody cross that Father Olmedo planted atop a pile of cadavers and ashes was the successor to the bloody Huitzilopoxtli.

What civilization did they have to bring, those who had in Spain a Jiménez de Cisneros,[1] who had the scientific riches of the Arabs burned, those who had in Mexico a Zumárraga who had the scientific riches of the Aztecs burned!

What humanitarian idea did they have to make germinate, those who raised a scaffold in Spain for the courageous Padilla, those who burned a pyre in Mexico for the heroic Cualpopoca!

But it will be said to me: and liberty? and democracy? From where did they come? By chance, did those ideas not arrive incubated in the religious ideas of our conquistadores?

Oh, liberty! . . . But liberty is prior to Christianity, because liberty was born with man, because the love of liberty lives in the heart of the human species, and there it stirs, continually boiling, like the fire at the center of the earth.

This is how liberty has exploded among our people, this is how we owe our liberty only to God, who ignited in the human soul that flash of his infinite Being.

We were free finally, but now you see, before being so other martyrs were still needed, because that is the fatalism that accompanies the defenders of liberty, like all initiators of a magnificent idea: martyrdom!

As for democracy, it has done nothing more than transmigrate. Exhausted in Greece, prostituted in Rome, suffocated in the Italian republics of the Middle Ages, it seemed to have been extinguished forever

---

1. Francisco Jiménez de Cisneros (1436–1517) was a Spanish cardinal and inquisitor. (Editor's note)

because the age of kings came to take possession of the world when it appeared suddenly and shamefaced in Holland and Switzerland, terrible although fleeting in England, tempestuous and omnipotent in France, and young, vigorous, and restless in the New World.

And that is the destiny, that the tendency of civilization, that the future of humanity: Democracy!

But wishing to be democratic, I repeat, how much have the Mexican people suffered!

What sacrifices yours!

The people have sacrificed their sovereign dignity for many centuries, the burning tears of their shame, and then their most precious interests and their most heroic sons.

From the great men of independence who almost all ascended to the gallows or fell dead on the fields of battle to the obscure martyrs of San Martin whom the murderer Gutierrez hanged not many days ago.

The people have now passed half a century amidst streams of blood, amidst conflagration and misery; is this not sacrifice enough?

And why so long a struggle? Because in all the countries of the world, and also in ours, the tyrannical and theocratic elements have been in conflict with the liberal element, with as much stubbornness and persistence as the gods of good and the gods of evil of the ancient Manicheans.

Political tyranny and religious fanaticism in monstrous alliance have wielded against the people the double weapons of iron and anathema in such a way that they attacked man in his heart and in his conscience. Never was any war so cruel or so costly.

And we have the proof in our ancient history and in our contemporary history. The viceroys allied themselves with the bishops to combat the insurgents.

Independence was won, the Spaniards were cast from our soil; but on leaving our shores they directed at us a gaze of angry satisfaction, a look that said, "We are going, but you are left with the clergy."

And they were right. The clergy has avenged them of their defeat from 1821 until now.

The clergy made a despot of a hero; it erected an imperial throne to convert it into a scaffold; the clergy slipped in a traitorous hand in order to write in the constitution of '24; the clergy through Alamán, the cowardly murderer whom the conservative party so much glorifies, erected another scaffold for the great insurgent of the South and treacherously led him to it; the clergy deified Santa Anna and corrupted the miserable Comonfort; the clergy, finally, supplying arms and money to the young rogues who were put in high positions in Mexico in 1858, has made the soil of the *patria* overflow with blood.

The clergy, accumulating riches with the insatiable voraciousness of the she-wolf that Dante encountered in his inferno, has been able to be a political force . . . until, exasperated, the people, taking the bandage from their eyes, have fought with fierceness and resolution against their oppressors and have attained victory.

The clergy! The conservative party! Watch those miserable titans wanting to ascend to the heaven of liberty!

And they are still moving, and they still fight; but the people have not yet thrown their last thunderbolts . . . Beware! Not all times have to be like these; the chalice of popular patience overflows and . . . The people, irate, will be able someday to go to the old cathedrals to trample on their pagan idols and to stab their traitorous pontiffs.

The nineteenth century is not the fifteenth century. France showed us the way in [17]93, and its example is still affecting the world. The people make the pope in the Vatican tremble; the old Catholicism of the friars is in the throes of death.

Soon evangelical democracy will prevail in all its fullness . . . Yes, we will realize the pure, the holy, the divine religious liberalism, such as the virtuous Son of the Carpenter of Nazareth conceived it.

But . . . I fail to speak to you of what the people desire.

The people desire that the promises of their leaders not be like the mirages of the African deserts, always promising but always deceiving. The people suffer, the people fight, the people triumph, and then? . . . Then, after their victories, they have to go, like Belisarius,[2] saying, "Give me a small contribution, because after having aged in the war, I do not see and I am dying of hunger."

What does the reform, until now placed in a plan, mean for the people? The humiliation of the clergy, it is true; but the clergy could

2. Flavius Belisarius was one of the greatest generals of the Byzantine Empire. Justinian is said to have ordered Belisarius's eyes to be put out and to have made him a beggar near a gate of Rome, condemning him to ask passersby to give him an obolus. (Editor's note)

have been destroyed and pauperism alleviated, that ulcer that eats away at us and annihilates us.

The great Lerdo died when his thought had been half-developed. What a shame! And who will complete the great end that was proposed? Probably no one. We have many owners of books but few economists.

In this way, what is being called reform is nothing but pure destruction. Destruction of monastic buildings, destruction of the estates of the clergy. Nonetheless, when I consider that this destruction takes away a weapon from the enemies of humanity, when I consider that this destruction was a few years ago a utopia that was anathematized, I admire those demolishers, I canonize those who have seized the wealth of the clergy, because at least they are gambling their heads for liberty.

I continue. The people desire that their anger no longer be played with, as until now. Tremble that upon awakening, they will say some day what the populace of Aristophanes said, "What? . . . they treat me thus and I had not noticed it!"

Franklin played with lightning, but he dressed in silk. Those who play with the anger of the people, what do you dress in to dare so much? Consider that it is dangerous to abuse the weapons of God.

But meanwhile, on this sublime night, anniversary of that night in which our emancipation was begun, the Mexican people make fervent vows for the liberty of all peoples.

Yes, today we the sons of Mexico pray to God that he permit you to be free . . . oh! you, unfortunate Magyars on whom is avenged the glory of Attila, you who still tremble with the holy words of Kossuth and with the sublime poems of Petofi!

Oh you, poor sons of Koskiusco, who cry when comparing the feats of Sobieski with the "*Finis Poloniae*" that your tyrants decreed, who today the Russian despotism prohibits from even the drink of your *patria*!

Oh you, valiant Cubans, who, without trembling at the disaster of López, are soon to explode against your Spanish executioners!

Oh French Republicans, you who have seen with sadness your dreams of '48 eclipsed by the imperial shadow of a soldier of fortune!

Oh sons of Cato and Spartacus, whom the tyranny of a crowned hermit still oppresses!

Also you, magnanimous Spaniards, whom the first smile of liberty has now touched lightly in the gallows of Loja.

All you on the earth who suffer from despots and await the blessed hour in which, face to face, you can pull the sword of free men from the monarchs and say to it, like the Almovogares, *"Iron, wake up!"*

Oh! do not despair; have faith that the sweet, the beautiful, the holy liberty will come!

And as for you, Mexicans, I will repeat to you the words that Pericles addressed to the Athenians: "And you also, follow in the footsteps of your ancestors, convinced happiness is in liberty, liberty in valor, and do not be afraid to confront the dangers of war." —I HAVE SPOKEN.

GUILLERMO PRIETO

Guillermo Prieto (1818–97) was born in Mexico City. He was a liberal politician and a poet, and he worked with Valentín Gómez Farías and Anastasio Bustamante in the 1830s. In 1838 Prieto enlisted in the National Guard. He wrote literary criticism for *El Siglo XIX* and served as secretary of the treasury and in the administration of President Benito Juárez during the Three Years' War. In the latter capacity he helped to draft the reform laws.

At the end of the civil war Prieto was elected to Congress for the period 1861–63. At the time of the French intervention (1863), French and imperial troops held most of the country and forced the republican government, including Prieto, to flee to the north. When his term as president expired in 1866, in the midst of the war, Juárez decided to stay in office because of the extraordinary circumstances. Prieto, however, thought that Juárez should step down and let the chief justice become president. As a result of this disagreement with Juárez, Prieto went into exile in the United States.

When the Republic was restored in 1867, Prieto returned to Mexico and served for ten years in Congress. Later, during the era of Porfirio Díaz, he was again elected to Congress for sixteen years (1880–96). He continued publishing articles in the daily press at the same time.

We present some of his parliamentary speeches and one article from the period 1857–74.

1 | In Favor of the Abolition of Internal Duties and Customs. Report on the Speech before Congress on January 28–31, 1857 (excerpt)

Mr. Prieto says that, although the committee does not respond to those who oppose it, he has the duty of sustaining an appeal, because he has been working tirelessly for many years and he will strive to have it written down in the Constitution.

The abolition of the internal customs [*alcabalas*][1] will be an improvement, it will be a victory for liberty, it will also be the fulfillment of one of the promises of the Revolution of Ayutla. Agriculture, commerce, and industry believed in that gratifying promise. The Revolution was economic, as it was social, as it was political, and the principle of freedom of commerce cannot be a point neglected in a Constitution that is derived from the Plan of Ayutla and that is the testament to democracy, the proclamation of all its principles.

The federation will be impossible if state-to-state rivalries must exist and if all of them must wage the war of taxes that reduces them to misery in atonement for their errors. If the salts of San Luis must find the markets of Zacatecas closed, if the pigs of Morelia cannot enter Toluca, if the struggle between the prohibitive system and that of the free-trader must be perpetuated between Puebla and Veracruz, unfortunate germs of discord will remain, finally, which will sooner or later put an end to institutions.

The committee resolves nothing. It limits itself to saying that before destroying one must build, and it does not see that it is easy to replace the duty with the direct tax.

A tax is untenable that weighs heavily on the necessities of the poor, that falls on consumption, that introduces inequality into commerce

---

Original title: "En favor de la abolición de las alcabalas y aduanas interiores" [extracto; pronunciado durante el Congreso Extraordinario Constituyente en la sesión permanente del 28 al 31 de enero 1857]. Source: *El Siglo XIX*, Mexico, February 3, 1857.

1. *Alcabalas* were internal duties merchants paid for transporting their merchandise from one part of the country to another. (Editor's note)

and is accompanied by denunciation, espionage, and the most odious and absurd obstacles.

It is necessary to understand that revolutions are the expression of the aspirations of the people, and that, if their hopes are thwarted, it throws them into incessant upheavals.

The danger in which national unity remains, the principles of true liberty, the irrelevance of feudal institutions in a democracy, the injustice, the wickedness of the tax, all lead to the idea that the principle must remain written down in the Constitution. The abolition of internal customs is worth more than other principles to which great importance has been given. It is worth more to give bread and clothes to the people than to offer them dazzling theories. [...]

Mr. Prieto says it is not certain that the internal customs is established everywhere and that this unevenness gives a more odious character to and makes more serious the inequality of rates of exchange and municipal excise duties.

As Mr. Gamboa has said that the decree issued by the speaker when he was minister of finance did not have the desired effect, to respond to this inaccuracy it is sufficient to refer to what happened in the states of México, Jalisco, and some others. If one had persisted in the measure, the good would have been achieved without harming the treasury.

Internal customs, by their very nature, offer more difficulties of collection and require the greatest number of employees. From this comes the fact that the greater part of their profit is put into administrative expenses, and this fact should be kept in mind by the gentlemen deputies.

It has been said that this is a matter of fulfilling a solemn promise of the Revolution and truly that the realization of the Plan of Ayutla concerns the honor and morality of the liberal party. To await the gathering of data and information is to delay the reform by more than forty [sic], as those who know the difficulty of creating fiscal statistics understand, and as the fact that the fiscal statistics of France are still imperfect despite the most persevering and enlightened efforts of its economists and statesmen confirms.

If the committee finds reasons for doing so, it should extend the time limit, but under no circumstances should it avoid the question.

He concludes by requesting that, in so serious a matter, the debate be extended so that reasons that might lead to a correct resolution might be heard.

2

Freedom of Commerce. Report on the Speech before Congress on January 6, 1869 (excerpt)

Citizen Prieto, in a passionate speech, lamented with pain that the educated youth, of whom the citizen mayor is one, supports restrictive views on freedom of trade and industry, views that not even Don Lucas Alamán himself, some of whose paragraphs he read, was ever the champion.

To the definition of the value of articles of merchandise that the citizen mayor gave, Mr. Prieto answered that the asking price, the offer, and their market circulation constituted the value of things.

With respect to wealth, he said that its value is relative.

Sonora is filled with rich veins of gold that are worth nothing because that wealth is abandoned and does not circulate. That glass of water that costs nothing in the city will be worth a great deal in the desert. A savage exchanges sums of gold for a little bit of powder.

This demonstrates that the value of things depends on many circumstances.

That metals go out and return only in cash is not a loss; it is an exchange, because money is an article of merchandise like any other.

The commission is accused of wanting to protect individual interests. What the commission wants is to put into practice truly progressive economic principles and, in doing so, give life to an industry that is today dead. A mine worked, whose products enter into vast circulation, will make agriculture and other branches of human industry progress, and the benefits are for all the people; while if its products are, as now, unprofitable, paralysis dominates all the rest.

Original title: "Durante la consideración de las medidas restrictivas a la libertad de comercio" [pronunciado en el Cuarto Congreso Constitucional, durante la sesión del 6 de enero de 1869]. Source: Pantaleón Tovar, *Historia parlamentaria del Cuarto Congreso Constitucional,* vol. 3 (Mexico: Imprenta de Ignacio Cumplido, 1874).

We are not a manufacturing or agricultural country; we are a mining country, and we must give expansion and flight to the wealth of our soil.

It is said that the benefit will be for foreigners. When one speaks of political economy, there are not Mexicans, there are not foreigners, there are numbers; it amounts to the same here as in France and England.

Moreover, if the benefit is for foreigners, the truth is that they are the ones who have spent immense sums to work our mines and that many have been ruined in that speculation.

The speaker concluded by showing that export of precious stones is not profitable and by requesting that Congress approve the project under discussion.

3

On the Laws of Reform.
Report on the Speech before
Congress on April 28, 1873

DEBATING THE REPORT TO ELEVATE THE
LAWS OF REFORM TO THE STATUS OF
CONSTITUTIONAL PRECEPTS

Citizen Prieto: Sir, I am certainly surprised to see that the discussion has gone awry and that it is desired to determine, with respect to this article and the committee's addition, whether this matter is special or if it is a regulatory law. As some references to history are made and other circumstances brought forward that demonstrate the zeal of some representatives in favor of the interests of the states, all this makes me call the attention of the chamber to the fact that this is not one of those ordinary pieces of business; this is not a piece of business with which one can deal by means of special circumstances and in accordance with constitutional laws, but rather by means of how it came about historically and so that Congress understands what the nation desires. The historical conditions are as follows: With the Constitution proclaimed in the year 1857, including within it the declaration of the political rights of the nation, a problem of the highest importance lurked in the shadows; the issues denominated Reform remained, as though asleep under the burden of the administration that found itself then facing the destinies of the country, going down a road of transitions. The leader of the power himself, intimidated before the great work that presented itself to him, went along a path of difficulties and dangers whose only results were half-concessions, words of double meaning, social errors that since then had to be accounted for to the nation after having cost torrents of blood. The Constitution of 1857 has very serious flaws because it was

Original title: "Al debatirse el dictamen para elevar al rasgo de preceptos constitucionales las Leyes de Reforma" [pronunciado en el Sexto Congreso Constitucional, durante la sesión del 28 de abril de 1873]. Source: *Diario de los debates. Sexto Congreso Constitucional*, vol. 2 (Mexico: Imprenta F. Díaz de León y Santiago White, 1872).

simultaneously an exhortation of the rule, the doctrine, and the axiom; it was the consecration of the historical antecedent; it was the consecration of the innermost conviction of the representatives of the people. For that reason there is much ill-defined, much generalization in the way the constitutional articles were drawn up, very few precepts that have the character of absolute imperative as a code should contain. The country progressing thus, much had been won, but the political revolution was scarcely completed. The national party had a symbol; there was not yet room for the sad lament that the liberal party had no symbol and that we were progressing without a compass amidst shadows and fanaticism, nor that we found ourselves without direction in the difficult consideration of the fate of the country in relation to its future fortunes. This symbolic program had been achieved. In the Constitution of 1857 the political matter was to a large degree dealt with, but as for the clerical matter, attention was riveted on this mistake, on this unfortunate mistake of immense importance. The wealth of the nation was the property of certain individuals, but only those individuals could enjoy their own property. These concessions to individuals, in moments when the famous gentleman Don Miguel Lerdo was at the head of the ministry, made the Reform die, so to speak. They made it stumble, it remained in impossible contradiction and produced all the irregularities that some call the inconsistencies of the Revolution of 1857. The social needs were others. The social needs required the proclamation of a gospel for humanity in which civil marriage might be instituted, in which the ecclesiastical bodies had no wealth, in a word, the heightening of civil power, the elevation of human dignity, so that the immense horizon of progress might open before the eyes of the *patria*. This was the Reform, and this Reform, by the nature of things, was proclaimed on the fields of battle at the sound of an arsenal, a gun carriage serving many times as a rostrum. And it was in fact proclaimed by the will of the nation; it was a law as great as the Constitution, as venerated as it, as dogmatic as it, and as much considered the will of the nation as it.

Establishing a parallel between the two, so as to determine to which of the two preference is to be given, would be to work in an inconsistent way. The Constitution of 1857 has the revolutionary tradition and the will of the people. The Laws of Reform have the revolutionary tradition and the will of the entire nation. The one has the laurel crown of the parliamentary triumphs, and the other has the palm crown of the martyrs of our independence. All these contradictions, all these particularities, and these thousand trifles that are weighing us down have the grandeur of the will of the nation, and on this point of departure we should stand. To set the Constitution against the Laws of Reform, to seek this contraposition in this childish game of the governing articles of secondary laws, is to want what is already done to be done. And it was done by a supreme authority that we represent and to which we cannot be opposed; this is as if to wish that we might have the logic of the school but not the logic of statesmen. The Laws of Reform have a loftiness as great as the Constitution; the Laws of Reform, by the very nature of things, have been embedded in the Constitution, have been made a permanent part of it. They have become inviolable and great in such a way that we cannot make changes in them unless it is with the danger of resurrecting the civil war.

For these reasons, when Mr. Lemus has asked that the Laws of Reform form part of the fundamental code, he has not necessarily wanted them to figure into all and each one of the governing articles of these Laws of Reform. He has not wanted it because, in scholastic terms, it would produce a deformity, because one is the political code and the others are the secondary provisions. The legal disposition provides the rule, and the secondary provision develops the idea. The constitutional disposition must be the political axiom, and all the details the development of these original ideas. It is from this that, by the nature of things, Mr. Lemus wanted in this sixth section [of a constitutional article] that the governing laws and the complementary provisions of the constitutional articles form part of the Constitution as organic laws. This was consistent with history, this was consistent with political principles, this was the rigorous logical deduction from those antecedents; it was to stand in the true path, having nothing to do with the governing particularities and the scholastic discussions that have since arisen.

What was the political rationale Mr. Lemus had in mind to support these provisions and to regard them as an article of our code? Having said this, by drawing this comparison, I intend to bring to the chamber the true assessment, the comparison, so that it might see what the likeness was, what the resemblance was, what the symmetry of soundness, and what the reason was. The reason cannot be found in any way in the artifices of the subterfuges of the laws. The reason must be sought in a great political question that has the authority of history, the historic consecration it might contain. What was the reason? The argument is very obvious. These declarations [the Laws of Reform] have been made on the field of battle and by the men who attained the palm of martyr-dom in the struggle of the [war of] Reform. They had come to create laws that were no longer discussed or disputed and that the will of the entire nation had already set down. These laws could be defective in their details, some others in their form; but they were embedded in the sentiment of the people in such a way, they lived with the affection and tenderness of the entire nation in such a way, that the will of the nation and not ours is what makes them prevail. To its loftiness and its sublimity, and in no way to our aspirations and to our wishes, did they owe it this kind of fanaticism, this kind of monumental existence that determined historic facts must have and that is considered, so to speak, the genealogy of the glories of a nation. Thus, by the consent of the en-tire nation the Laws of Reform have remained undamaged. These laws, without trampling on any right, without violating any guarantee, with the consent of the men who sealed the Reform with their blood, are now set down unharmed in the fundamental code. These laws, sir, are the history of the sentiments of all nations; this is the history of the most profound sacrifices; this is the generation of ideas that arose in a myste-rious and undefined manner in the heart of man that end up as the goal to which all their aspirations are directed; this constitutes, if one will, the mysterious, indefinable reservoir that is creating the great fountain of the nationality of a people that respects itself, that grows, and that strives for its future.

What would we say tomorrow if we were to say to the Spaniards, break up your tree of Guernica, destroy that rotten and dry trunk, that rigid cadaver of the desert, as Calderon says. They will tell us no, be-cause here is our glory, our liberty. What would we say if we were told that one of our towns is more beautiful than another: Tacubaya has more fertility, for example, has more parks, more mansions than the humble town of Dolores where we celebrate our independence; so blot out the name of Dolores. No, sir, no, because there lies the cradle of our inde-pendence, and with its crooked streets, with its shapeless nature, with all this it constitutes a greatness, a glory, a poetry, it is the poetry of the nation, and however much might be said in its greater good, it is the beacon that illuminates the nation's future. In dealing with the Laws of Reform we can no longer change anything because it is no longer

debatable, because they were sealed with the blood of our martyrs, because when one deals with them there appears the bravery of León, the
heart of Ocampo, the brilliant oratory of Arriaga, the invincible spirit
of Degollado, the irreproachable probity of Zamora, because we have
in the Laws of Reform the genealogy of the greatest events of our history, because we feel ourselves being stirred by the glory of the men of
1857. (*Applause*) To take this away, destroy it, break it, humiliate it, are
matters of chicanery. (*Applause*) No, by God, let us not touch the sac-
rosanct Laws of Reform, which are the glory of our *patria*. (*Frenetic applause*) [. . .] .

Sir, I will be brief in what I am going to explain to Congress, and I
cannot have a better introduction, because the chamber is very tired.
The gentleman who was the previous speaker has said that the Laws of
Reform cannot be considered constitutional and cannot be included in
the Constitution. Neither the committee nor those of us who have defended its report want them to be included in the Constitution. We do
not want to add them to the Constitution, nor do we want to create a
code of a thousand and some articles; we want only that they appear in
the Constitution as constitutional laws. No constitutional law forms part
of the Constitution. The Constitution contains the political principles
necessary for the public powers to function, marking their orbits and
keeping them from clashing with each other. The others are the secondary laws, the unfolding of the precepts the Constitution contains, and
they do not form part of it, they are not indivisible. So I do not believe
that the learned Mr. García de la Cadena in presenting this distortion
has judged, in a consistent way, either the sentiments of the committee
or the defense that those of us who are in agreement with its ideas have
made.

Mr. García de la Cadena has said: "If these laws are set down by the
people, why should we make an innovation that could become dangerous?" This innovation is made, sir, because once the Laws of Reform are
declared constitutional, because once written down in the code, it is an
inevitable consequence that these Laws of Reform will have to run the
same fate as the Constitution. Being superimposed on it, being made
more powerful than the Constitution itself, they will have been constituted not in an uncertain situation, but as a social complement to the
political code.

For this reason the Laws of Reform must run the same course. This is the powerful reason why the individuals who have sought the consecration of the principles of reform have wanted that the governing part of these articles not be subject to vicissitudes, leaving them in the category of secondary laws. What has happened, sir, in fact? That in defending the prerogatives of the states, the Laws of Reform have been thwarted. What has happened to the alienation of the lands that were for the Indians? What would happen to public worship entrusted to specified authorities? Believing it would be a matter of their jurisdiction, they would destroy the security of the principles of reform. These principles could be terminated or completely rejected, and we have to be most cautious on this point, because it is a matter that, having proclaimed tolerance, we must respect the manifestation of this tolerance, but we must take care always that they do not fight against us and take our sword by the fist to wound the heart of the institutions we have wished to save. Why, sir? Because it is not possible that, once a specific liberty is proclaimed, we seek the thousand ways that the beliefs have to work with specific political aspirations; it is not possible for us to establish a policy of the confessional; it is not possible that we carry our gaze to the interior of consciences; it is not possible that we put specific preachings that are in conformity with the interests of the clergy in harmony with the principles of Reform that proclaim the guarantees of all opinion.

To detach the constitutional principles already accepted by the committee from the laws that establish regulations for them was to repudiate the success of the Reform with the pretext of the states, regaining the liberty the Constitution gives them. The states would make of the Constitution an instrument to destroy the Reform. Here is why, sir, those who have defended the report and the gentlemen of the committee have wanted to make indivisible the constitutional principles and the regulatory matter, marking in a perfect way what was constitutional precept and what was governing matter.

To make synonyms of the word "Constitution" and the word "regulating" seems to me to seek deliberately a reason to distort the matter.

These reasons seem to me so conclusive that they will remove every one of Mr. García de la Cadena's scruples. Mr. García de la Cadena has said that we are going to put into the fundamental code a thousand and some articles that the Laws of Reform contain. This is not true; what we have wanted is that they be officially recorded as governing articles of the constitutional law. We have not wanted even the explanatory parts that the Laws of Reform contain to be declared constitutional articles. Neither have we wanted complete laws to come to form part of the Constitution, because this was divergent from the Constitution; it was to pass over the Constitution without taking it into account on a subject approved and deliberated by the revolutionary matter. This was what Mr. García de la Cadena should have kept in mind.

Whether there were many or few articles, we have to pass by them because it would be a subterfuge of bad law to discuss them now. To approach the matter of the Laws of Reform, it is necessary to think about how delicate this subject is, because in this matter of rights and liberties, we are constantly conspiring against these very liberties. We in the powers of the states see a conspiracy against the Laws of Reform; under the pretext of specific rights for specific classes we are accepting a permanent conspiracy in our own bosom against the declarations the liberal party has made. We are placing the flag of Reform in contraposition to the principles of liberty, and we have absolutely no means to defend ourselves, and we are suckling that terrible social hydra, that terrible hydra that tomorrow we would have to drown once more in blood, and this against all these trifles that are being placed on us. We are seeing the resurrection of fanaticism, of backward movement and evils without number, still sheltered by the altar and clerical prerogatives. We are seeing the attempt of the terrible reaction, the reaction that strives toward infamy as a final outcome. The clerical party believes that it still lives, the clerical party believes that it still can dominate the liberal party, the clerical party wants us to bow before the crisis to see if they could sacrifice us. One is the political issue of the country and the other is the clear and final issue; one is the pharisaical and formulaic issue, and the other is the philosophical issue; one is the dishonest and ridiculous issue, and the other is the issue of the future of the *patria*. Those who want this future, those who seek its well-being, should vote for the article under discussion.

4

On Reforms to the Law of Public Instruction. Report on the Speech before Congress on January 2, 1874

Citizen Prieto: In such moments of necessity as the present, a discussion is begun that positively concerns the future of the Republic and that in all countries of the world has been the object of attention of parliaments in order to achieve the future prosperity of the nation. The present matter is of the highest importance, and I could not have been more surprised to hear the argument that one of the previous speakers has given, declaring that the committee had no reason whatsoever for having submitted its new report once certain foundations were in agreement with the opinion of the executive.

This is not true. In sections VI and VII of Article 70 of the Constitution, it says that if a project is contested completely or in part, a new report subject to discussion might be drafted with the objective of seeking all the wisdom, all the study, that is indispensable when he who has knowledge of the facts, he who has a definite awareness of how the law was brought about, must be brought into agreement so that the law might have every probability of success. So it will not be strange that the committee enters into the discussion of articles that have not been impugned by the executive and of some other articles that, without having been challenged by the executive, come up in the report. A sad and painful experience has opened our eyes to the direction the law of public instruction might follow regarding the plans we have proposed in directing the fate of the youth.

It seems to me that the first foundation affirms the victory that the Constitution wanted to make, that of instruction being free.

Everyone has the ability to teach, everyone that of learning, so the

Original title: "Sobre reformas a la Ley de Instrucción Pública" [pronunciado en el Séptimo Congreso Constitucional, durante la sesión del 2 de enero de 1874]. Source: *Diario de los debates, Séptimo Congreso Constitucional,* vol. 1 (Mexico: Imprenta F. Díaz de León y Santiago White, 1874).

business of public instruction should not be a business of determinate persons. Public instruction is a religion of conscience, this is the unanimous view in all nations, it does not belong to any person, it does not belong to determinate individuals, it is strictly a matter of humanity in which the fate of the *patria* takes interest.

It is the right of the child, which we have the duty to demand at this rostrum; it is the highest, the most sublime of the social matters that can be presented for our scrutiny.

I would like to bring to my conscience all the laws, purify my lips as did the prophets, and touch the hearts of the citizen deputies, because this is the greatest matter that can be presented.

To guarantee freedom of instruction, to convert the promise of the Constitution into truth, is a triumph for human reason, it is an eternal break with backward movement.

Unfortunately, sir, proceeding as we are doing is not the most proper way. We are not in complete agreement with the point of view of the executive, so the addition of an article in which it is stated that the law returns to our scrutiny with the goal that our conscience be tranquil seems very good to me. Why? Because although the Constitution proclaims liberty of instruction, this liberty is thwarted by sad experience.

One says liberty of instruction. That is to say that everyone, wherever and however and in the time that doing so might be possible, in the manner it is convenient, can pick up instruction, and that the state has the duty to respect knowledge that has been obtained in the midst of the occupations of the countryside, in the midst of the roadways, in the midst of the deepest misery, or in the midst of the most majestic mansions.

The hour, the plan, the regulation, this last is a passport so that knowledge might be reaped by any man who has the necessary comprehensions, in a word: be he a stranger to learning, be there obstacles, be it that the knowledge is not for everyone. Thus it is that in this first part, it appears that the intent is to destroy all those obstacles the regulation poses.

There is an individual who has not wished to be tested in anything whatsoever, and who one day wants to acquire the title of lawyer, taking the four or five exams. He must be admitted to examination without anyone having to know where he has acquired the knowledge, whether a village school teacher has taught him, whether an old woman who might have some knowledge. What falls to us is to appraise this knowledge, respect it as it is, and accept all those who might be worthy of the scientific fellowship.

So this entire first part of the report, as we understand it, does not have the necessary features so long as it has not seeped into the hearts of all inhabitants to bear fruit. So long as this is not so, free instruction is an illusion and a lie, and we cannot proceed in agreement, understanding instruction as the light, as the air that the lungs of humanity breathe, and the Ministry of Justice speaking to undermine it, putting obstacles before those who do not have the requirements and knowledge drawn up according to the law.

Thus it is that in this first part there is no greater objection to make than to recall the last suggestion that Citizen Pacheco has made. As for the second section [of the proposed law], I have said that a sad experience has made us distrustful about what would be the result of this second foundation, which says this: "Divide studies into general secondary schools and special secondary schools."

When the discussion between us began, an attempt was made to create an antagonism between those of us who wanted an end to specific hindrances and those who demanded a certain type of knowledge. As Congress will remember, there were some moments in the discussion when, as though in the midst of a storm, things moved uncertainly, bringing one almost to doubt whether the plan was under discussion.

We have wanted one of two systems be followed: either acquire specific knowledge to pursue professional studies, or the other system, which consists of forming a depository of all possible human knowledge so that everyone might have access to it and it be within the reach of all levels of intelligence.

To proceed in this way, we had to keep in mind that, however much in Germany and in England a system of instruction is followed in which special knowledge flows from the first basic principles, however much in Germany there might be another system of instruction leading to the completion of special schools, however much in the United States the success of a system of instruction with political knowledge has been achieved, we seek not a system but a route, a sure direction, with the goal of not going astray with either the principles of encyclopedism or the old exclusivity. The matter of the old exclusivity has been debated since the end of the eighteenth century. It will be remembered that, because of the exigencies of the studies, the advantages of knowledge in men became clear; intelligence to grasp all knowledge, to grasp all the successes, in order to discover all the horizons, in order to let the soul soar into the infinite of its being was made known. But then, after many debates, these two schools have appeared: one that makes the study of mathematics and practical knowledge necessary, and the other that seeks human knowledge in moral science and metaphysics.

Well then, sir, we move away from these two systems. Without taking part ourselves in such a heated discussion about the knowledge that can be called purely scholastic, I would have desired, following the United States for example, that children have the aptitude for being good citizens, that democracy be converted into a reality, that men by means of their wisdom come to fulfill those functions on which the future of nations depends. The child forming his interests in the school, the child acquiring specific practical knowledge, the child acquiring the quality of being and his individual dignity was the republican who later ruled the fate of his *patria;* he was the man who threw away the tailor's shears to grasp the reins of government; he was the man who left the field of the farm to be called Grand, the redeemer of humanity.

Thus we understand the school, and thus we seek specific knowledge in what is called political instruction and in what the beneficent influence of democracy provides. But the way in which the article has been written means this: it means moving backward from what has been called the preparatory school; it means this confusion, this corrupt whirlpool of knowledge.

We do not want, like the father of the family, to have a boy who narrates a fable by memory; nor do we want dilettantes. What we want is that everyone have the human knowledge that is taught, some languages, that all knowledge, all the wealth of human knowledge, be an inexhaustible torrent of enlightenment, and, from this whole, the knowledge indispensable for all careers be extracted. This is what has been desired. We want, for example, what is done in a pharmacy, where every type of medicine is made, and these are applied to different illnesses according to what the makers advise. If there is pain in the side, a medicine is applied, and if there is another type of pain, another type of medicine is applied.

The same happens in a printer's shop; there are periods, commas, and letters distributed among all the cases, and when they are needed, the appropriate types are taken but not all.

If the article is not rewritten and specified in a certain way, an educational institution will be established where all human knowledge is cultivated and where specific knowledge is stipulated for certain careers; as long as the article is not written in this way, we will return to our old disputes, we will return to hearing a clamor against the reactionaries and over whether knowledge is useful.

No one can doubt this; nor can anyone dispute progress or knowledge. We are sufficiently experienced to seek the truth; this is the work of a Congress. So it seems to me that the second of the foundations, if it does not have an application, is in danger of falling again into the unhappiness that the chamber has wished to eliminate for the good of the youth.

Another of the matters that has been put into the present report is the following: secondary education will be free, uniform, and obligatory. Uniformity refers to establishing one or more normal schools for teachers. Here the matter of primary instruction and the matter of secondary instruction are confused, to my way of seeing. Primary instruction is indispensable for the happiness of the people, for democracy, and for the realization of their ideas of liberty. Reference to this primary instruction is made as if by chance, and for me it is of such importance and of such high consequence that the sacrifice of secondary instruction can definitely be made provided primary instruction is spread everywhere. This is so true that, when this subject has been discussed, what has been desired is that instruction be spread everywhere, that no means be omitted, that by means of itinerant teachers, by means of oral classes, in whatever way, instruction be spread.

When the Emperor Iturbide entered triumphant, he understood the importance of instruction, and he designated Dr. Mora for this work, and he said: Doctor, we are going to create instruction because it is necessary. This was said in the year 1824; afterward, when in the year 1853, point of departure for the Reform in the time of Farías and Atilano Sánchez and various others who headed public instruction, these fathers of instruction said: Primers, not guns, is what we have to send to the people.

So our Congress being so diligent, our government being so persevering, we were taking the first steps with respect to primary instruction. I would wish that the conditions for primary instruction might be based on this foundation.

The matter of primary instruction has been raised, the matter that even today has been the object of very special study especially in France when, after the disasters France has suffered, in the midst of the debris of the Commune, crying over ruined buildings, in the midst of these circumstances, eyes have been turned in a very preferential way to public instruction. There has been a man who has dedicated himself to public instruction, who has created a sort of Congress, where the noteworthy personages of the academies of science meet, and in this assembly one deals with the matter of whether the fathers of the family have the specific obligation to provide education to their children in a certain way, providing them with instruction as if it were corporal bread.

But at what point can the government enter into the domestic home? Can it search like the one who remedies an evil, like the one who enters to remove a rotting body, because that is how the man who deprives his children of all social goods must be considered, putting obstacles in the way of the development of their intelligence, like that weight that it is said the Abbot Faria had on one of his feet, which trapped him in the depths of the sea no matter how much of an effort he made to rise?

This is the ignorance of five million men who turn liberty and progress into futility.

How do we conceive of uniformity of instruction? To us it is not important that some learn logic through Balmes and others through Mill. What is important to us is that, in saying that one knows logic, it be true. This is another of the difficulties, and the principal difficulty with oral lessons is the speaking, the preaching of knowledge; oral lessons are principles thrown to all the winds. Those who are greatly enamored of the brilliance of the eloquence of an orator, how is a person going to be examined on oral lessons?

Nothing has been touched upon more thoroughly than tariffs; everyone has put his five senses into this matter, yet it is not possible that there are even three deputies who can take an examination on it.

Oral lessons are publicity for knowledge, creating a revolution regarding history. Oral lessons are Guillaumen giving his doctrines; oral lessons are the wise men seducing with their words, attracting the multitude with their eloquence to the terrain of knowledge. Then one who is moved goes to seek knowledge.

It cannot be done this way with oral lessons. How does one take an examination on oral lessons? In the oral lesson the professor struts about, praises himself for the triumphs he obtains with his word.

Thus it is that oral lessons are given to the entire secular and sacred world so that the light of knowledge might enlighten everyone, dispelling the shadows of ignorance, that everyone might enjoy its beneficent influence, that everyone might feel in his brain the fresh aura of knowledge, that he might sense in his intellect the maternal kiss of scientific education.

Very good, sir, perfectly, but within a college where degrees are going to be issued, where responsibilities are going to be entered into, this cannot be. I beg the committee that it amend its report in the sense we have discussed, and if, by any chance—which I do not expect because the persons who make up the committee are very intelligent—if by any chance, I repeat, it does not accept our suggestions, then we will not follow the committee on the path it has taken.

A final point remains which, because it is troublesome, I have left until last. It is about the matter of the governing board. I will not make allusion to any of the persons who make up the governing board. They are for me very respectable, very beloved persons, so I will not speak about persons. The governing board should be abolished because it is useless, because it is a hindrance, and because, if tomorrow there were not a staff member like the current one, it would be infinitely more harmful for the youth. I say, sir, that it is useless because this board does not deliberate for itself, because this board has to limit its regulations, because this board does not exercise its powers. It is a board that has all the conditions for bad and none for good. It is a board that can regulate; it is a board that can create all kinds of hindrances. Of all the useless bodies, it is a board that does everything such bodies do. These bodies have one standing order to enter the house, another to carry a dress sword, another to take the fork, another to whisper, in short, a body of regulations that has no importance whatsoever because of the nature of the matters, the more so to the degree that it is not made up of legal experts like Justinian, of doctors like Hippocrates, because all their labors are reduced to directing copied communications to you for the consequent ends, and the sessions of the board are useless. So we have ten calluses on the hand and they place on us only five, but they are double in size of the others. Inasmuch as the report the committee presents us is not acceptable, I request the Chamber to declare it without reason to vote. [. . .]

Citizen Prieto: I would have no objection at all to put up against the brief words of the previous citizen speaker if he had not expressed a doubt that absolutely makes it impossible for us to give him this vote of confidence to a certain extent very necessary for the committee.

If the idea is discarded that the report return for the review of the chamber; if we, after relinquishing our powers, do not have any opportunity to see whether we are in agreement with the executive or not, for this the previous citizen speaker will see that it is imperative to insist that the law come back for the review of Congress.

On the other hand, although my observations have been directed especially at specific articles with the objective of fostering amplifications or modifications to these same articles, nonetheless, regarding this it seemed to me more agreeable to make all the observations so that whatever corrections might be necessary be made, or to make seven or eight additions after the law is declared with time to vote. For this reason, it is not possible for me to accept the suggestion that is made to me, notwithstanding his promises that for me carry much weight, and perhaps they will convince me to vote in favor of the report if I have the guarantee that one of the members of the committee has given me.

With much emotion, with genuine sorrow, I am going to make some observations to Citizen Frías y Soto, more as a testimony to respect for his opinions than because I believe mine have more strength than his, he being a person of such talent, and if I insist on the observations I have made previously, it is because in my humble opinion he has distorted what I have said in the heat of his extemporization.

No one spoke here about the first article, absolutely no one, so it is to have such a strong champion in a cause that has absolutely no reason for existing. No one made objections to the first article and consequently to the constitutional article, and if no objections were made with respect to the liberty of professions, it is because there is very advanced work on this subject.

I am sorry to remind Citizen Frías y Soto that the gentlemen Dublán, Saborío, and I are the authors of this plan with the goal of seeking the advancement of youth, that we had as a foundation what the previous citizen speaker just asserted, that it is not possible for human intelligence to encompass all branches of human knowledge in their entirety.

A short time ago, absolutely nothing was known about the life of insects; today, with the discovery of the microscope, this matter has changed completely. A few years ago the twitching of a frog on a railing aroused Galvani's first awareness of galvanism, and with this the *hosanna* to the Lord of the Heavens can be sung in the depths of the waves.

We have not wanted to put a limit on the sciences, we have wanted, in treating of instruction, to respect all human knowledge, and might Citizen Frías y Soto allow us to come to an agreement so that I not be an adversary of a person I esteem.

When I have spoken of primary instruction in Mexico, I have not spoken of examinations but rather of other things, because notwithstanding the keen desire of the municipality, notwithstanding the dedication of the government, notwithstanding that we can say with pride that we spend more than three million pesos, as in the epoch of some administrations, notwithstanding this, there are very great voids, voids that Citizen Frías y Soto knows better than I because my baptismal faith has a much earlier date, to my misfortune. So it is that Citizen Frías y Soto, while he might tell me that the children are educated well and in great numbers, I will say to him that there are schools where there seems to be sufficient room for all the pupils, as in Bitterness Street,[1] where there seems to be room for more than two hundred children, who are not being educated but are only becoming ill in this oven of human flesh that is called school.

There are a multitude of schools like the one I have mentioned, which, because of the latest efforts of Citizen Frías y Soto, have an endowment of twenty-five to thirty pesos.

Citizen Frías y Soto knows that there are schools where the children have to relieve themselves at the entrance to the classrooms, and it seems to me that it is not one of the best examples of morality to offer those

1. In Spanish, *calle de la amargura* ["traer por la calle de la amargura"], according to Christian tradition "Bitterness Street," was the path Jesus walked with the cross during one of the cruelest moments of his passion. Since the Middle Ages it has been common to use the expression to depict figuratively a painful and desperate situation created by the actions of others. (Editor's note)

pictures (*laughter*) to the view of passersby, with a different system of teaching that makes impossible that public instruction have its proper development. And in this, Citizen Frías y Soto must remember that the word "centralization" in dealing with public instruction is a genuine blasphemy, because instruction must be for everyone, and this is a true democracy. This is perfectly underlined by the principle that says the government has no more obligation than to set the conditions for the development of the natural elements of the people.

This is what they have to do. Governments do not educate, neither do governments have heart, nor are governments anything but the conservers of society, which have to provide conditions of life for the development of the elements of society; they must provide peace, justice, order, and liberty, and these are the conditions that the government must have.

In the moment when it is desired that a government support, that a government intrude in everything, liberty is dead, individual initiative is lost, men are minors, they have the liberty of tyranny because they do not know liberty. This is administrative centralization; it is not liberty as democratic peoples have understood it.

In the United States the child is placed in conditions suitable for becoming a citizen. This child has his flag to attend festivities. The day when a great orator speaks, the children go to the chamber to listen to him. They give the history of their country in front of the monuments of Washington.

This is the people, this is liberty, this is democracy; and this liberty, free as the wind, as thought, as God, is not the text; they are not the authors. From the moment there is a text, from the moment a restriction is placed, from this moment the safeguard of liberty of instruction is broken; from this very moment the seeds of the life of man are blunted.

How does intelligence proceed? It proceeds either by hypothesis or by experience. What is the history of human discoveries? Did industry perhaps flourish when men were dominated and reduced to slavery? The same can be asked about commerce and agriculture; advancements do not date from the epoch of oppression.

This is the emancipation of the government. The government guides, develops, protects, but the government does not oppose, because the contrary position is the backwardness of the people, so that what Citi-

zen Frías y Soto has said about this subject of the administrative centralization accords with my ideas.

Citizen Frías y Soto said that I have tried to satisfy what in the matter
of primary instruction in Mexico are precarious conditions because they
do not have their proper fulfillment. When one wants to make obligatory education in some towns that do not have all the elements, one is
following a misconception. In Germany education is obligatory in some
principalities and in others is not.

5

On Freedom to Work. Report on the Speech before Congress on November 5, 1874

Citizen Prieto: Gentlemen, I am going to follow, with the thoroughness that is possible for me, the young orator who has just spoken, making use of his excellent method and with the confidence that is inspired by such a gentlemanly and loyal adversary as he to whom it has fallen to me to oppose.

Let us read the constitutional article. It states:

Every man is free to take on the industry or labor that suits him, being useful and honest, and in order to avail himself its profits. Neither the one nor the other can be prevented, except by judicial ruling when he attacks the rights of a third, or by governmental resolution pronounced in the terms that this law designates when he offends members of society.

To explain this article, the regulation we debate says: "The fact of not working is not a crime," and the present question is limited to this; that is, to discover whether or not vagrancy is a crime.

A crime is the breaking of the law, and this principle is so absolute that there is no crime whatsoever prior to the designation of the law; the crime arises from the law, the law creates it, so that, to begin by judging vagrancy as if it were made by declaration of the law is a flaw in logic that perverts the matter.

We are now are going to make law independently of all tradition and all legislation; nothing of that exists for us. Preliminary to that law is this question: Should we consider vagrancy a crime?

Original title: "Sobre el proyecto de libertad de trabajo" [pronunciado en el Séptimo Congreso Constitucional, durante la sesión del 5 de noviembre de 1874]. Source: *Diario de los debates, Séptimo Congreso Constitucional*, vol. 3 (Mexico: Imprenta F. Díaz de León y Santiago White, 1874).

Which article of the Constitution imposes the obligation or duty to work? Which? None.

So, not working, the simple fact of not working, is not a crime.

The article, in the last analysis, respects the right of choice of work. It respects the free will of man, without which all liberty is chimerical and conscience becomes inconceivable. But the article supposes the will to work; if he does not have that will, his right is respected also, because without those two phases of the will, the existence of liberty is not possible. Why, then, the anathemas for the exercise of a perfect right? Can it not be seen that the ideas of free choice and *obligatory work* are incompatible?

The right in this case is the consecration of full, absolute liberty, as must be in order that it exist complete, without conditions; and that liberty disappears the instant work is imposed by force.

What would we say if we had the liberty to speak but not to keep quiet, to move an arm but not to hold it in repose, to open the eyes but not to close them? Liberty is the suppression of all bonds that are not those that guarantee the liberty of others. Obligation is a link that tightens. To confuse the one with the other is to rush headlong into absurdity.

With the liberty of man consecrated, with man free to choose to work or not, if he does not opt for the first of these, why consider him criminal? How to tell him, first, you are free to choose the road you like, but if you do not choose some road I will punish you? Who would be satisfied when they say to him, you can do what you think, and then awaken him with blows, because *sub pectore* the one who made the proposal kept secret the intention of not letting him sleep?

To enlarge on these ideas as the regulation does is not to confuse them or pervert them or corrupt them; it is to perfect them. In the critical sense, in the literary, the explanation will be redundant but not incongruous. Being explained, the article is strengthened, it is made more practical. At the same time as it breaks with tradition, it recognizes liberty, giving to each person responsibility for his actions.

Not to explain it is to leave its development exposed to the contingencies of tradition; it would inevitably come through persecution of leisure to obligatory work, to the organization of labor, to the right to work, to the national workshop, to socialism; that is to say, to a reactionary revolution, highly disastrous and unconstitutional, to the substitution of force for liberty, of paramount order for individual effort, to the gendarme as an active expedient of social progress instead of nature and the interest in preservation.

Looking over history, although very superficially, we find leisure demanded as a right of the privileged castes of nobles, priests, and warriors; work offended, anathematized, considered degrading and relegated to the plebeian and the slave.

Thus Greek writers of loftiest renown heaped real curses on manual labor: Plato and Xenophon in Greece as well as Cicero in Rome. Even trade entered into that excommunication, and only Carthage seems to defy the universal prejudices.

Greco-Roman civilization is saturated with that spirit, and the slave revolts and mass desertion of the eternal city by the plebeians in order to situate themselves on the Sacred Hill are nothing more than attempts at emancipation, efforts to divorce work from abject slavery.

In the warlike Middle Ages, the slave was little more than a beast. The feudal lord either lived from the booty of the enemy or from the work of his slave or by begging for his subsistence with a sword in his hand.

In those conquests the man who worked for himself was, for the conquistador, like a complete oaf, *vaco vacante,* and this was called vagrant or vagrancy afterward.

The emancipation of the slaves, the affluence of the newcomers who inundated Europe after the Crusades, the woes that these swarms of adventurers produced made the idea of vagrancy adhere indivisibly to bothersome begging and harmful, bad amusement; and so the ideas have since been confounded in history, in the laws, and even in common language. Vagrancy was in fact made blameworthy; it was assumed always to have offended a third person; it included the vagrant, the beggar, and the evildoer in an anathema.

The English demand the stock, or post, on which the vagrant or beggar is tied to expose him to public shame. Other times it passes him from parish to parish. Edward VI condemns them to whippings and death.

In the Spanish town councils, the correctives against vagrancy and false mendacity were centuplicated.

The Ordinance of 1745 attacks vagrants as true criminals; and only in 1775, in the wise Ordinance of Charles III, the order indicates philosophical principles of modern civilization; education, mores, and liberty appear, opening their broad horizons to human activity and making man master of them, endeavoring that he might unfold, dignified, the wings of his free will.

Drinking from these fountains, the law in the old times always characterizes the person who does not work as badly occupied; it always matches the idea of vagrancy, of inaction, with the idea of a vice or a crime.

More philosophical, the administrative law in Spain itself is in the hands of Colmeiro, the Gayóns, Díaz Cerna, and others. They tried to classify willful idleness and forced idleness, temporary idleness and habitual idleness, simple idleness or designated idleness, and doing so calls, in support of the law, questions of legal charity as an appeal to the conscience actually clouded by confused notions about idleness.

Glancing through the *Diccionario de la lengua española,* one reads: "*Vagar.* Wander through various places without specifying place or location or without a special stop anywhere. To wander aimlessly, with neither occupation nor benefice."

What kind of crime is that? What rights are violated in that meaning of the word? What third person comes out harmed by a man wandering from one point to another without offending anyone?

The dictionary says, "One who wanders from one part to another without stopping in any place. The man without a trade and *badly occupied.*"

We see in this sense of the word the relapse into injurious historical interpretation; that is to say, a qualifying evil that has corrupted legislation is resurrected, authorizing arbitrariness; but even so, the man without a trade and occupied badly is now not only the idle man but, moreover, he who employs or occupies himself doing something bad.

If one could use a word to mean "without trade" or "badly occupied," the one would be punishable, the other not, but to draw the inference that a "vagrant" has to be "occupied badly" is outrageous. It is to deduce that he who passes by the mansion conspires or that a pharmacist by virtue of that fact is a poisoner. That is an absurdity.

From what has been explained it follows that, if the article stated the fact that not working is not a crime, it would cause less repugnance than with the introduction of the word "vagrancy," a reason for alarm.

In fact, a friend and not a friend says something different from a friend and an enemy. To know and not to know is not the same as to know and to be ignorant of. A believer and not a believer is not the same as a believer and an impious one. Work and not work is not the same as work and vagrancy, because a twisted meaning is given to this last word that perverts it.

Why, then, is the word preserved? It is preserved precisely to kill the tradition, because that tradition is the root deeply embedded in millions of abuses that still hound us, that corrupt us, and that inexorably eat away at liberty.

The word is preserved because it contains the practical part of the question that everywhere, in the [Federal] District most especially, has the greatest importance.

Here the vagrant, capriciously classified as such because the article of the code lends itself to it, is placed outside the law through corrective punishment. From the vagrant can be made a justification of the levy, of exile, of revenge.

In various parts, vagrancy is the great cause of electoral prostitution. We have seen that law, as a party weapon in some state, dissolve electoral colleges, destroy town councils, and convert the presumed right of persecuting vagrancy into a party weapon.

Who is so shortsighted, who so apathetic about the most sacred rights of the people, that he is satisfied with seeing in this an academic discussion and not the most important of all matters, because nothing is more important than liberty?

Halfway is not possible. The declaration of obligatory work imposes on the state the inevitable obligation of producing work for the one who does not have it, and there you have the state converted into a colossal manager of all branches of human activity, and the tailor without customers, the lawyer without clients, the doctor without ill people, requesting from the government, their protector and agent, an *honest* way of living. That is absurdity, that is socialism in its most absurd and most harmful phase. And such ideas infest and contaminate the people who are said to be more enlightened, who generally say, "The government is not protecting, the government does not provide work." What ideas do such ignorant people have of what government is?

Returning to matters of usefulness and honesty, let us examine this matter under another light.

Utility is everything that serves to meet our needs. It is an idea tightly connected to those needs, so for a being with few or no needs, there are few useful things.

Well now, the Stoics, for example, living on abstractions, feeding themselves very humbly, disdaining the goods of the earth, needed little to meet their physical needs and would have warranted persecution for vagrancy. Christianity disdains what is of this world, paints the present life as transitory, its goal is eternal life; for this, manual work is not needed, poverty is virtue, inactivity leads to ecstasy, prayer is almost meeting with God. Dante called Saint Francis second spouse of poverty. A raven feeds the hermit Saint Onofre. The angels yoked oxen to Saint Sebastian. The nudity of Saint Jerome is praised . . . In a word, it is confirmed in everything that work is the curse of the Lord . . . and, nonetheless, abstention from work is considered so useful that it is for them nothing less than the agent of the sublime perfection of man.

Work is an idea indivisible from the idea of property, and how is this to exist where the renunciation of all terrestrial good is the goal of the beautiful ideal? . . . These are the points of contact of asceticism, communism, and socialism.

Even the physiocrats, precursors of Smith, lost their way because they did not know how to determine the extent of utility and they limited the sphere of work. Smith himself cut short his doctrine with the exclusion of intellectual work.

Yes, sirs, because like work, it is assistance for the production of intelligence and strength. This first part (the intelligence) can escape and, in fact, does escape the inquiry, not only of the authority but also of the entire world. For that reason I have said that, for the police, Homer would have been a vagrant, the same as Columbus, although the stanzas of the one run through the centuries honoring humanity, and the other sublime vagrant had brought to the eyes of science and humanity, with his surprising discovery, the world where we live . . .

Here is stupid preoccupation with regulations in the face of victorious truth.

Were one to begin the assessment of "honest," one would arrive at the ridiculous.

Let us try it out. The dictionary says: "*Honest.* Decent, decorous. Pure, demure."

In these last meanings the universal intelligence has been established.

Armed with these meanings, the police can condemn as not honest work that of the painter and sculptor who copy from the natural, the teacher of swimming who does not require his students to swim clothed, surgeons, teachers of obstetrics . . . folk healers of hospitals . . . Gentlemen, that is the height of the ridiculous, and nonetheless, that is the constant path of regulationism.

Being a matter of good faith, the matter of honesty can only be given the meaning of the legitimate, of the authorized . . . Well then, let us see in this terrain the absurdities of regulationism.

Prostitution of the woman is regulated; it is a licit industry. The pimps of that merchandise cannot be unknown to the authority that created the industry.

The shyster is declared vagrant. The folk healer the same. As among the pimp of love affairs, the executioner (creation of the law), the shyster, and the folk healer, will it be punishment and excommunication for the last ones?

Thus, by driving out the drones of laziness from the beehive of work, this matter has been turned into a moral matter, and that is another absurdity. The article does not say that vagrancy is good; the article says that it is not a crime, which is very different. It will be a sin, but we are not here to sanction Father Ripalda.

That disorder of ideas, that meddling of legislator in the domain of morality, has brought him in all times to tyranny and the inquisition.

At one time he hurled his lightning rays against the innocent child, punishing it as a bastard or sacrilege; he looked into the conjugal mysteries in the sacred home, making atrocious revelations; he, in that meddling of the temporal power with the conscience, ignited the bonfires of the holy office, and it was, for centuries, the ignominy and blemish of humanity.

In the economic terrain, in the social, the matter of salary cannot be considered, for example, unless as the result of a contract, of *I give to you because you give to me* or *I do to you because you do to me;* it is the result of an exchange of two commodities, work for money or money for work.

What will come of this exchange if the most complete liberty does not preside over it? In the matter of the strike, when it is not disorderly, when it is reduced simply to the worker rejecting the rate for his work, why should the authority intervene? What would we say if those workers who used their right to withdraw from the tyranny of the overseer were declared vagrant?

Among our people of the country, the work teams are, without doubt, the most free. Various workers gather together and go where it suits them in search of work; what happens when they do not find it or when the open market is not suitable for their abilities? Do we declare them vagrants?

One bad calculation alone in the export duties of the Mexican railway has brought about the ruin of many property owners, the vagrancy of a multitude of working men, and we have no other remedy to amend the evil produced by us than prison and persecution by the police?

Among free people as in the United States, vagrancy is pursued tenaciously and effectively with education, with customs, with the ennoblement of work, with the ease with which man exercises his liberty, above all, by making him from childhood responsible for his own actions. Without responsibility man is an automaton, man is a chess piece that exists in the square in which the hand of the player places him. How can it be believed that there is liberty when such absurdities are agreed to?

Tutelage, eternal tutelage, the insistence on making ourselves happy even when it be against our will. This is the certainty of tyrannical governments, and for that I call the restriction that my adversaries defend highly reactionary.

Citizen Obregón González, after exhausting his ammunition combating the article, and as if he might surprise vagrancy in flagrante delicto, cites Article 34 of the Constitution, saying that in order to be a citizen one must have an honest means of making a living, and, calling the deprivation of citizenship punishment for idleness, finds the article cited of our pact contradictory to the article we are discussing.

As for the matter in the abstract, what the quote by the previous citizen speaker would prove uniquely is that he did not reflect carefully on the limitation of the article, but no incompatibility exists in the existence of the constitutional articles once the fourth and the fifth were developed, as the committee has done.

Why? Because in the first case, the rights of man are proclaimed; they touch on his being as belonging to the human lineage. Better said, they recognize preexisting rights in every man outside of any pact. The second point treats of the contract, of conditions that, because of the nature of things, are changeable. Thus, for example, a state could order that, to be a citizen of the state, one would have to know how to read and write, but it would not be able to compel such a man to follow a specific religion. Work is a matter of natural law. The laws of citizenship are in the class of positive laws; they are not created by God, because we involve ourselves in the chaos.

And why is the constitutional precautionary measure called punishment and not seen as stimulus to work itself?

Citizen Obregón González, giving proof of the good faith with which he deals with this and all matters that merit the attention of his judgment, explains that he believes simple vagrancy is not a crime but should fall under the rule of the authority as smoking in theaters is prohibited, notwithstanding that it is not a crime to smoke.

My young adversary might remember that the strength of our defense is based on the fact that laziness or vagrancy neither harms nor bothers anyone, because in that case the instigator of the trouble or damage would deserve admonition. And this is exactly what happens with the one who smokes in a theater; he is not prohibited from making use of his liberty except when he assaults the liberty of others, when he infests the air that others breathe.

In this discussion, what undermines the true sense of the article is the preoccupation with which the word is considered. From this comes the accusation that we want impunity for laziness, its reward, its apotheosis, and the article says nothing about that. It simply declares that the man who does not want to be occupied in anything, for that fact alone is not guilty.

I am certain that the article would have approval in these or similar terms: "Man, free to work or not work, is free also, in conformity with Article 4 of the Constitution, to choose the work that suits him."

But be advised that that compromise with retrogression is to compromise with the entire system of backwardness and shame that the colonial system bequeathed us.

In the name, then, of human dignity, highly compromised in this discussion, in the name of the positive progress of our people, above all in the holy name of liberty, I request this chamber to honor with its vote of approval the article that is being discussed.

CONSTITUTIONAL GOVERNMENT OF MEXICO, 1857–1861 (BENITO JUÁREZ, MELCHOR OCAMPO, MANUEL RUIZ, MIGUEL LERDO DE TEJADA)

A new constitution was enacted in 1857, but both the Catholic Church and the conservative faction opposed it. Civil war was imminent. At the end of that year (in spite of the fact that he had sworn to uphold the charter), President Ignacio Comonfort decided not to enforce the constitution and instead called on all factions to discuss a new fundamental law that would be acceptable to all parties.

Conservatives were not satisfied with Comonfort's actions and deposed him, and in 1858 conservative general Félix Zuloaga became president. These events started the Three Years' War. Benito Juárez, who at the time of Comonfort's coup against the new constitution was chief justice, became president in the absence of the executive according to constitutional provisions. Juárez managed to escape from the conservatives, who held Mexico City, and set up his government in the port town of Veracruz. From there he conducted the war effort.

The struggle between liberals and conservatives was bloody and ferocious. No side seemed to have a critical advantage over the other. In mid-1859 the Juárez government issued a set of decrees known as the Laws of Reform that separated church and state. The property of the Catholic Church was to be confiscated and sold; the civil registry was established, and freedom of worship was secured. In 1860 the military standoff was finally broken and the liberal armies defeated the conservatives.

We present a proclamation from the constitutional government signed by Benito Juárez, Melchor Ocampo, Manuel Ruiz, and Miguel Lerdo de Tejada, in which they make the case for the Laws of Reform. This text was written in July 1859, a month after these laws were issued. Likewise, we present the 1860 decree on freedom of worship.

1 The Constitutional Government to the Nation (on the Laws of Reform). Proclamation, Veracruz, July 7, 1859

In the difficult and compromised situation in which the Republic has found itself for the last eighteen months as a consequence of the scandalous insurrection that exploded in Tacubaya at the end of 1857, and in the midst of the confusion and disorder introduced by that outrage, as unjustifiable in its ends as in its means, the public power, which by virtue of the political code of the same year has the imperative duty of preserving legal order in cases like the present, had judged it appropriate to keep silent about the intentions it harbors to treat radically the ills that afflict society. Because once the armed struggle between an immense majority of the nation and those who seek to oppress it was begun, the public power believed, it fulfilled its mission by supporting the rights of the people by the means that were in its scope, secure in that the very goodness of a cause that has reason and justice in its favor and that the repeated disillusions, because of their powerlessness to triumph over that cause, their adversaries had to accept at every step would make them desist from their criminal intent or succumb quickly in such a struggle.

But when, unfortunately, it has not been thus; when, despite the prolonged resistance society is putting up against the triumph of that insurrection the authors of this insurrection continue, determined to sustain it, supported solely by the resolute protection of the high clergy and the strength of the bayonets they have at their service; when, as a result of that disgraceful and criminal stubbornness the Republic seems condemned to continue suffering, even for some time, the disasters and calamities that form the horrible history of such a scandalous rebellion,

Original title: "El gobierno constitucional a la nación [sobre el sentido de las leyes de Reforma]" (7 de julio de 1859). Source: Benito Juárez, *El Gobierno Constitucional, á la Nación* (Veracruz: s.p.i. [unknown editor], 1859).

the government would believe itself failing in one of the primary duties that the very situation imposes on it if it withheld any longer the public declaration of its ideas, not only just about the serious questions being aired today in the sphere of armed events, but also over the course it proposes to follow in the various branches of public administration.

The nation finds itself today in a solemn moment, because its entire future depends on the outcomes of the fierce struggle that the partisans of obscurantism and abuses have stirred up this time against the clearest principles of liberty and social progress. In such a supreme moment, the government has the sacred duty to address itself to the nation and to make heard in it the expression of its most beloved rights and interests, not only because public opinion in the appropriate sense will thereby become more and more uniform, but also because the people will thereby value more the cause of the great sacrifices they are making in fighting with their oppressors, and because, in short, all the civilized nations of the world will thereby see clearly what the true objective of this struggle is that touches the Republic so deeply.

To fulfill this duty today, the government needs to say nothing with respect to its intentions about the political organization of the country, because, being an emanation of the Constitution of 1857 and being considered, moreover, the legitimate representative of the liberal principles set down in it, it must naturally be understood that its aspirations would be directed to ensure that all citizens, without distinction of classes or considerations, enjoy as many rights and guarantees as might be compatible with the good order of society; that rights and guarantees always be made effective through the good administration of justice; that the authorities all faithfully fulfill their duties and obligations without ever extending beyond the circle delimited by the laws; and, finally, that the states of the federation make use of the powers that fall to them to administer their interests freely in such a way as to promote everything leading to their prosperity to the extent that it does not oppose the general rights and interests of the Republic.

But inasmuch as those principles, despite having already been written down at greater or lesser length in the various political codes the country has had since its independence and ultimately in the Constitution of 1857, have not been able nor will be able to take root in the nation as long as, in their social and administrative character, the diverse elements of despotism, hypocrisy, immorality, and disorder that oppose them are preserved, the government believes that, without moving away essentially from the constitutive principles, it is obligated to be engaged very seriously in making those elements disappear, fully convinced now by the extensive experience of everything that has occurred until now, that as long as those elements continue to exist, order and liberty are not possible.

To make order and liberty actual, then, giving unity to the intention of the social reform by means of the measures that produce the solid and complete triumph of the good principles, here are the measures the government intends to carry out.

In the first place, to put a definitive end to that bloody and fratricidal war that a part of the clergy has been fomenting in the nation for some time for the sole reason of preserving the interests and prerogatives it inherited from the colonial system, scandalously abusing the influence that the riches it had in its hands gave it and the exercise of its sacred ministry, and to disarm for once this class of elements that serve as support for its disastrous rule, the government believes it indispensable to:

1. Adopt as a general, invariable rule, the most complete separation of the affairs of state from those that are purely ecclesiastical.

2. Suppress all the bodies of regular clergy of the masculine sex, without any exception whatsoever, secularizing the priests who are currently in them.

3. Destroy uniformly the confraternities, archconfraternities, brotherhoods, and, in general, all the bodies or congregations of this kind that exist.

4. Close the novitiates in the convents of nuns, keeping those who at present live in them with the wealth or dowry that each one might have brought in and with the allowance of what is necessary for the service of worship in their respective churches.

5. Declare that all the property the secular and regular clergy administer today with various titles has belonged and does belong to the nation, as well as the excess that the convents of nuns might have, deducting the amount of their dowries, and selling that property, accepting as payment, for a part of its value, bonds of the public debt and of the capitalization of investments.

6. Declare, finally, that the remuneration the faithful give to the priests both for the administration of the Sacraments and for all the rest of the ecclesiastical services, and whose annual yield, well distributed, is

enough to cover amply the maintenance of worship and its ministers, is the object of free agreements between both, without the civil authority interfering with them at all.

Besides these measures, which, in the judgment of the government are the only ones that can result in the submission of the clergy to the civil power in its temporal affairs, leaving it, nonetheless, with all the means necessary so that it might consecrate itself exclusively, as it should, to the exercise of its sacred ministry, it believes also indispensable the protection of religious liberty in the Republic, with all its authority, this being necessary for its prosperity and expansion, as well as a necessity of current civilization.

In the justice branch, the government understands that one of the most urgent needs of the Republic is the formation of clear and simple codes concerning civil and criminal affairs and concerning procedures, because only in this way will we be able to remove our legislation from the confused labyrinth in which it now finds itself, standardizing it in the entire nation, facilitating the action of the courts and placing knowledge of the laws within reach of everyone; and inasmuch as, for carrying out this important work it will be sufficient that the legal experts to whom it has been entrusted dedicate themselves to it with determination, the government proposes to make an effort that this improvement not be postponed any longer, so that society might begin to enjoy the numerous benefits it will surely produce.

The establishment of de facto jurors for all common crimes is also one of the needs of the nation, and the government will do whatever might be its part to establish such an interesting reform.

Until this innovation is realized and the codes promulgated, the government proposes to facilitate without delay those means it judges pressing to make actual the primary guarantees of the citizens and destroy the errors or abuses that are opposed to the free circulation of public wealth.

With respect to justice being administered free of cost, the Constitution of 1857 has now established this principle as a fundamental precept; but because it is essential that payment of the salaries of the magistrates, judges, and employees of the judicial branch be given very punctually for such a precept to produce the good effects that the legislator proposed, the government proposes to attend to this matter with the priority it merits, because it is convinced that, lacking this circumstance, that precept, instead of good, would cause society great misfortune. On this point the government also proposes to pronounce the ruling it believes most suitable for preventing the multiplication of pleadings to which this important reform can give rise.

On the abolition of class privileges regarding common crimes, the government has nothing to say because this is already expressly prevented in the Constitution, and it will certainly not be the present administration that might ever think of reestablishing such unjust and odious distinctions.

On the subject of public instruction, the government will endeavor, with the greatest determination, to have the number of establishments of free primary public instruction increased, and to have all of them be directed by persons who combine instruction and morality, which are required in order to carry out with success the responsibility of teachers of the young, because it has the conviction that instruction is the first foundation of the prosperity of a people, at the same time the surest means of making impossible the abuses of power.

With that same objective, the general government, on its own and stimulating the individuals of the states, will sponsor and develop the publication and circulation of simple and clear manuals concerning the rights and obligations of man in society as well as those sciences that might most directly contribute to their well-being and enlighten their understanding, arranging for those manuals to be studied even by the children who attend the establishments of primary education, so that from their most tender age they will be acquiring useful basics and forming their ideas in the way that is appropriate to the general good of society. With respect to secondary and higher education, the government proposes creating a new plan of studies, improving the financial position of the teachers who are employed in this area of public instruction as well as the system for public instruction currently followed in the colleges; and, adapting to the principle the Constitution contains regarding this, the system of the broadest liberty with respect to every kind of studies as well as to the exercise of careers or professions that will be created with them will be introduced, so that every individual, national or foreign, once he demonstrates the ability and necessary knowledge in the respective examination, without inquiry into the time and place he might have acquired that knowledge, can dedicate himself to the scientific or literary profession for which he is competent.

With respect to relations of the general government with the individuals of the states, the current administration, far from opposing their interests and just needs, is on the contrary resolved to support them as much as is in its power, aiding them, moreover, in anything that in any way might lead to improving their situation, in order thus to tighten the ties of union that should exist between the localities and the center of the Republic.

One of the first needs of the Republic today is to attend to the security of the roads and population centers, to get rid of the evildoers who are encountered in both, not only for the immense woes that the existence of that scourge causes internally in the nation, paralyzing the movement of its population and wealth and keeping in constant alarm and danger the life and interests of its inhabitants, but also because it discredits the country more and more every day abroad, and it prevents from coming to settle in it the multitude of wealthy and hardworking persons who, for that reason, are going to establish themselves in other places. For such reasons the government is firmly resolved to work tirelessly to remedy this serious woe with all the means that are in its reach.

As for the odious system of demanding passports of travelers or wayfarers, it is useless to say it will be abolished when the Constitution has already done so, and the present government could scarcely think about reestablishing it when its ideas set out specifically to destroy all the obstacles that oppose the free transit of persons and interests in the national territory.

Spreading ideas through the press must be as free as the ability to think is free in man, and the government does not believe it should impose fetters on it other than those that tend solely to prevent the publication of immoral, seditious, or subversive writings, and those that contain calumnies or attacks on private life.

The civil register is, without a doubt, one of the measures our society urgently demands in order to remove from the clergy that compulsory and exclusive interference that it has exercised until now in the principal acts of the lives of citizens, and for this reason the government resolves that that reform be adopted, the great principle that such a measure must have as its objective finally triumphing, that is, establishing that once these acts are entered into before the civil authority, all legal consequences already apply.

With respect to relations of the Republic with friendly nations, the government proposes to cultivate them always with the same pains-taking care, avoiding on its part any reason for disagreement. For this it believes sufficient observing faithfully the treaties concluded with them and the general principles of the law of nations and international right and to abandon, above all, forever, as it has until now, that system of loopholes and moratoriums that, with serious harm to the nation, has been followed frequently in the official dispatch of the affairs of this branch; on the contrary paying attention to every claim in the action that arises with the greatest determination and resolving it without delay, in view of the circumstances of the case, according to the principles of fair justice and mutual convenience that form the solid foundation of friendly relations between civilized peoples of the world.

Also the government believes it will be very appropriate to establish clearly, by a general provision and in agreement with the rules and prac-tices established in other countries, the intervention that foreign consuls and vice consuls in the country might take, as much in the affairs of their respective nationals as in their relations with the authorities, in order to avoid in this way the repetition of problems that have arisen more than once over this point.

As for the appointment of legations in the foreign countries with which relations of friendship link us, the government believes that the current state of these relations with those countries is very far from re-quiring a minister resident in each of them, and its opinion is that, for now, they should be limited to two: one in the United States of America and another in Europe, this last establishing his residence in Paris or London, from where he can be moved, in case of necessity, to the point assigned him. In the remaining capitals of Europe and America, be-cause no business takes place which, by its very seriousness, demands the presence of a minister plenipotentiary, it will be enough that there be consuls general with the standing of chargé d'affaires. These agents, according to the new law that for the purpose must be expedited, will necessarily be born in the Republic.

As for the national treasury, the opinion of the government is that very radical reforms must be made, not only in order to establish a sys-tem of taxes that does not impede the development of wealth and that destroys the serious errors the colonial regime left us, but also to put a definite end to the bankruptcy that the mistakes committed later in all branches of public administration have introduced into it, and above all to create great interests that identify themselves with social reform, contributing effectively to the liberal and progressive advance of the nation.

In the first place, internal duties and customs [*alcabalas*], tolls, and in general all taxes collected in the interior of the Republic on the movement of wealth, persons, and the means of transport that carry both, must be abolished forever, because such taxes are, from any point of view, contrary to the prosperity of the Republic.

In a similar circumstance, although without all the unfortunate consequences, the fees for transfer of possession of rural and urban properties are encountered, and for that reason they must also be abolished completely.

The fees of three percent on gold and silver extracted from mines and the fees of one real per half pound, called *de minería,* are at their base truly unjust and odious taxes, because they do not fall on the earnings of the miner, but rather on the gross product of the mines, which most times represents only a small part of what has gone into these businesses before arriving at the sought-after wealth. For this reason, and because those taxes are genuinely in open contradiction to the protection that, in the present state of the Republic, the government must give to that type of industry, the present administration believes it appropriate to reform them in such a way that speculators in risky mining businesses do not suffer any encumbrances until they begin to receive profits, and with such an objective it can be adopted as established and invariable, the foundation that on the dividends or portion of the profits made in each mining transaction, the government receive what corresponds to two ingots of the twenty-four into which they are divided, conforming to the ordinance, all other encumbrances that weigh on them being abolished.

With respect to foreign trade, the government is resolved to do its part to facilitate the development of this element of wealth and civilization in the Republic, whether simplifying the requirements exacted for it by the laws in force, or whether regulating its current encumbrances. One of the measures it proposes to issue with this very objective is establishing some ports of deposit on the coasts of the Gulf and the Pacific with the authority to reexport merchandise when it is advantageous to the interested parties, as is practiced in all the countries where there are ports of this kind.

The different laws that until now have been issued over the classification of income, to designate which belongs to the states and which to the general government, suffer from the defect of not resting on a secure foundation that clearly marks the separation of the one from the other, because more attention has been paid to proceeds than to the nature of the taxes, which has given rise, moreover, to questions and quarrels that should be avoided between the authorities of the center and the states. For these reasons, and to establish the complete separation of the income of the states and the center on a well-known principle of justice and agreement, the government believes that the concept must be adopted as a fixed base that all direct taxes on persons, properties, establishments of business and industry, professions, and the rest of the taxable items belong to the states, and the indirect to the center. The fundamental reason for this separation cannot be clearer or more perceptible, because it is supported by the obvious principle that only the supreme government, which is the one that focuses on the expenses and obligations of the nation, is also the one that has the right to collect taxes that encumber all its inhabitants in general, while the governments of the states have only the right to encumber those who are in their respective territories, given that those governments focus only on the expenses of those inhabitants. Besides that reason, there are many others of general agreement that without doubt, all who examine the matter thoroughly will understand; and it is also easy to understand that only by adopting this idea will the states see themselves truly free from the power of the center in the matter of resources, which is the foundation of liberty in all other branches of internal administration. By adopting this system, there will no longer be any obligation on the part of the states to contribute a quota of their income toward the expenses of the general government.

One of the most serious ills the treasury of the nation suffers today as a consequence of the measures of the Spanish government during the colonial regime and of the confusion with which subsequently advantage has been taken of them, is that multitude of pensioners from the civil and military branches who seek to live on the public treasury with the titles of retired persons, jobless employees, old-age pensioners, widows, and other denominations. The size to which this ill has progressively grown and the pernicious consequences it is producing at every step demand a prompt remedy, and this can be nothing other than immediately capitalizing those rights, which, acquired properly or improperly, cannot be disavowed as long as they have been granted according to the laws and by qualified authorities. The government, then, proposes to proceed without delay to the capitalization, not only of the rights of whatever pensioners there are in the civil and military branches, but also of the rights of the employees who are redundant by virtue of the new law made in the offices of any branch, and even in those branches that, conforming to the laws in effect before the law of May 1852, might have individuals who remain employed in these offices, in order to stop the ill in this way so that it can never again reappear. This capitalization will be represented by government bonds that will be called "bonds of capitalization," and they will be issued on the bases of and with the circumstances and requirements that a law will establish.

With that measure having suppressed the system of reductions that employees and soldiers bore in their respective salaries with the objective of guaranteeing a pension, almost always illusory, for their old age, or assistance for their family in case of death, all of them will be able in the future to attain that outcome with greater assurance, depositing their savings in savings banks and mutual aids that, without doubt, will be established throughout the Republic, the government making, as it has in effect, the resolution to support those establishments and the funds gathered in them with all the tax exemptions within its capacity. Those establishments, besides being a very effective means of ensuring the inheritance of the families of the employees, like the inheritance of all types of scarce resources, will produce for society immense advantages in other ways, because the capital accumulated successively in them will serve to carry out a multitude of useful enterprises advantageous for the entire nation.

The disposal of the clergy's farms and capital, which, as has already been said in another place, should be declared property of the nation, will be by allowing the payment of three-fifths parts in certificates of capitalization or of internal or foreign public debt without any distinction, and the remaining two-fifths parts in cash, payable in monthly installments over forty months, with the aim that the acquisition of those assets can be made even by those persons least well off, the purchasers or redeemers giving, for the cash part, *promissory notes* to the order of the bearer with a mortgage on the sold farm, or on that farm that the redeemed capital identified, and delivering the share of certificates or bonds in the act of formalizing the contract of sale or redemption.

The vacant or national lands that currently exist in the Republic will also be applied to the amortization of the interior or foreign debt, linking these operations with projects of colonization.

The government believes that, with these two great means of amortization for all pending obligations of the treasury applied practically, a large part of the certificates of capitalization will disappear, as will the public debt in general. With respect to foreign debt and debt that has been arranged by diplomatic conventions, the government will persistently seek their extinction, whether with transfer of national assets or transfer of vacant lands; but if this is not achieved, it will continue respecting, as it does today, what has been agreed with the creditors, delivering punctually the assigned part to the payment of interest and amortization of capital, because it has the conviction that only in this way will the nation be able to recover the credit and good name it has lost by not faithfully observing that conduct.

To complete the most urgent reforms with respect to national finance, and by whatever means it will carry out the desired arrangement of this important branch of public administration for the realization of intentions already indicated, it is indispensable that it also proceed, at the same time, to the arrangement of its offices and employees; and this operation, so full of stumbling blocks in other epochs, will now be facilitated by the capitalization of all redundant employees, whose rights and aspirations created those difficulties. On this point the government has the intention of reducing the number of offices and employees to the purely necessary, neither more nor less, simplifying as much as might be possible the current system of bookkeeping. With respect to personnel, adopting the system of a certain percentage in all the tax-gathering offices is proposed, and in those offices of bookkeeping only, the system of providing employees with salaries in proportion to the general needs of life among our populations, because only in this way will these offices be able to have few and good employees. For the provision of employees, the government will pay attention to, above all, aptitude and honesty, and not to favor or the blind spirit of partisanship, which so unfortunately have been and will always be in the administration of public income.

In the branch of war, the government proposes to regulate the army in such a way that, improved in its personnel and the flaws removed that are noted in its current organization, it can worthily carry out its mission.

The national guard is one of the institutions for which the government will care, because it understands that the national guard is also the support of public liberties, and for this reason it will try with persistence to organize it in the way most appropriate for corresponding completely with its objective.

As for the navy, Mexico, lacking all the elements needed to create it and it already being well demonstrated by experience that expenditures made in this branch constitute a genuine extravagance, the government believes that all our naval forces on both coasts should be reduced for now to some small armed boats, whose primary objective would be serving as protection and maritime postal service.

With respect to the various branches of which the Ministry of Development is charged, inasmuch as they all involve the material progress of society, the current government proposes using all the means it has in its capacity to attend to this part of public administration as it deserves.

The main roads that depend directly on the government require not only that some important works be undertaken right away to put them in good condition, but also constant care to preserve them well in the future. To attain the first of these objectives, the government believes that the system of carrying out those works by agents of the government itself should be abandoned, and that of contracting with specific enterprises be adopted, the government being limited to looking after its punctual fulfillment by the engineers who participate in the works and watch over their execution. As for local roads, although they are under the immediate direction of the governments of the states, the general government will make the commitment that those that currently exist will be improved and that other new ones will be constructed, helping them on its part, as much as it can, to facilitate in this way the increase in new ways of communication that, like arteries in the human body, are what must give life and movement to our uninhabited country.

As for railroads, it must be attempted at all costs that, as quickly as possible, the one now projected from Veracruz to one of the Pacific Ocean ports, passing through Mexico, be constructed; and as this is a work of incalculable importance for the future of the Republic, there is no effort the government is not disposed to make to accelerate its completion and overcome the difficulties put up against it. Moreover, in order to promote effectively the construction of other railroads in various places and to remove these enterprises from the hands of the schemers who have been speculating with the titles or partial concessions made by the government for specific lines, that system of special decrees on this subject will be abandoned, and a law will be issued that serves as a general regulation for all roads of this type that can be constructed in the country, more ample and generous concessions being made in the law in order thus to stimulate national and foreign capitalists to enter into those useful speculations.

Regarding public works of utility and embellishment, the government will endeavor to hasten the conclusion of all those which are already begun and the carrying out of others, because it is convinced that in this way it will fulfill one of the duties every government of a civilized people has today. Among the works ready for completion, it will pay preferential attention to the penitentiaries of Guadalajara, Puebla, and Morelia, abandoned for some time because of political upheavals, and whose completion will influence so effectively the improvement of our penal and prison system, which is one of the great needs of the Republic. In order to pay close attention to the works on the roads and the carrying out of all other public works, a body of civil engineers will be organized in the Ministry of Development who will also serve for all the tasks with which the government charges it.

The immigration of active and industrious men from other countries is without doubt one of the primary needs of the Republic, because on the increase of its population depends not only the progressive development of its wealth and the consequent internal well-being, but also the preservation of its nationality. For these reasons, the government proposes working very tenaciously on making it effective; and so that it be carried out in an advantageous way, more than creating or writing special laws of colonization with sterile offerings of lands and more or less broad exceptions for the colonists, it will take care to overcome the practical difficulties that stand in the way of their entry and stay in the country. These difficulties consist principally in the lack of immediate, lucrative occupation for the new colonists and in the scant security that exists among our own populations. To make this last obstacle disappear, I have already indicated in another place the resolution to organize a good preventive police force and security; and in order to remove the first obstacle, the government by itself, and stimulating wealthy and speculative men, will cause public and private works to be undertaken of the type that, like roads, canals, and others of various nature, require many laborers, in order that a multitude of immigrant persons come to be employed in them who, once established for a certain time in the Republic, will settle down in it to dedicate themselves to some type of occupation or industry; and they will in turn attract, with their example and with their invitations, many other individuals and families from their respective countries. Moreover, arrangements will be made right away with some property owners of vast terrains in the central and most populated part of the Republic by which, for their own interests and for the general good of the nation, they will cede some lands to the immigrants who come to establish themselves on them, entering in effect into mutually advantageous contracts of sale or lease. Only with these and other measures of a similar nature alone, with the consolidation of public peace, with the arrangement of the administration of justice, with liberty of worship, and with the facilities that at the same time the government must provide for moving immigrants to our ports, will our population be augmented and improved quickly; because if it is not done in this way, the business of colonization will continue being, as it has been for thirty-eight years, a cause of empty oratory for all the political traffickers who spring up from our revolutions and who, with the sole objective of deceiving the nation, speak always of its very serious woes without having the intelligence or will required to remedy them.

Another of the great needs of the Republic is the subdivision of the territorial property, and although this operation cannot be made to the extent desired except through the natural stimulus that the progressive improvement our society will continue experiencing might produce as a consequence of the reforms that must be carried out in it as well as improvements in the actual means of communication and the increase in population and consumption, the government will attempt to overcome quickly the great obstacle that the laws that govern mortgages on rural farms present for such subdivision, issuing a new law by which the landowners of these rural farms are empowered to subdivide them into the fractions that suit them for the purpose of facilitating their sale, the value of the mortgage that each farm has being distributed proportionally in these instances among the parts into which it is subdivided. Besides this measure, which will surely contribute effectively to dividing up the territorial property with advantage for the entire nation, the government will also encourage with the current owners of large holdings what, by means of mutually advantageous sales or leases, will improve the situation of farming peoples.

With respect to the businesses with which the general government must deal in agriculture, manufacturing, the arts, commerce, means of transport, and, in general, every type of work or occupation useful to society, the current administration will give to these matters whatever protection is in its reach, working always with the aim of supporting their growth and progressive development, fully convinced that protecting those branches is to work for the prosperity of the nation, supporting and increasing by that means the number of legitimate interests that are identified with the preservation of public order.

In the development of statistics, the general government, working in accord with those of the states, will constantly gather whatever information is possible in order to know fully the true state of the nation in all its branches; and it does not seem necessary to suggest the importance of this work, because no one is unaware that, without such knowledge, it is impossible for a government to proceed with certainty in its determinations. These data will be published periodically through the press, because knowledge of them is not only important to the government, but also to all and each of the individuals in the society.

Such are, in sum, the ideas of the current administration on the course that it is appropriate to follow in order to affirm order and peace in the Republic, guiding it, by the secure path of liberty and progress, to its enhancement and prosperity; and to formulate all its intentions in the way it presents them here, it does not believe it does anything more than interpret faithfully the feelings, desires, and needs of the nation.

In another time, the openness with which the current government declares its ideas for resolving some of the serious questions that for such a long time have disturbed our unfortunate society could perhaps have been considered imprudent; but today, when the rebel faction has brazenly defied the nation, denying the government even the right to improve its situation; today, when that very faction, letting itself be guided solely by its savage instincts in order to preserve the errors and abuses in which it has placed its heritage, has trampled the most sacred rights of the citizens, stifled all discussion of public interests, and despicably misrepresented the intentions of all men who do not offer to respect its brutal domination; today, when that fatal faction has now carried its excesses to an extreme of which no example is found in the annals of the most unrestrained despotism, and which, with an insolent disdain for the serious woes its obstinacy is causing society, its seems resolved to continue its course of crimes and evil deeds, the legal government of the Republic, like the numerous majority of the citizens, whose ideas it represents, can win only by showing clearly, to the face of the entire world, what its intentions and tendencies are.

Thus will it manage to make disappear victoriously the clumsy imputations with which, at each step, its opponents tried to discredit it, attributing to it ideas disruptive of all social order. Thus will it let the entire world see that its intentions regarding all business relating to politics and the public administration set out only to destroy the errors and abuses opposed to the well-being of the nation. And thus it will be demonstrated, finally, that the program of what is entitled the liberal party of the Republic, whose ideas today the government has the honor of representing, is not the standard of one of those splinter groups that, in the midst of internal upheavals, appear in the political arena to work exclusively for the advantage of the individuals who create it, but rather the symbol of reason, order, justice, and civilization, and at the same time is the open and genuine expression of the needs of society.

With the awareness that it proceeds down a good road, the current government proposes issuing, in the sense that it demonstrates now, all those measures that might be most opportune for terminating the bloody struggle that afflicts the Republic today, and to guarantee immediately the solid triumph of good principles. To proceed in this way, it will do so with the blind confidence inspired by a cause as holy as that it is charged with sustaining, and if, to the misfortune of the men who today have the honor of personifying as the government the intention of that very cause, they are not successful in having their efforts result in the triumph that one day must unfailingly succeed, they will be able to console themselves always with the conviction of having done their part in achieving it; and whatever might be the success of their zeal, whatever might be the vicissitudes that must be suffered in the pursuit of their patriotic and humanitarian commitment, they believe at least that they have the right to have their good intentions valued in some way, and that all honest and sincere men who, fortunately, still abound in our unfortunate society, might even say, in remembering them: *Those men desired the good of their country, and they did whatever it was possible for them to do to obtain it.*

Heroic Veracruz, July 7, 1859. —*Benito Juárez.*—*Melchor Ocampo.* —*Manuel Ruiz.*—*Miguel Lerdo de Tejada.*

2

Declaration to the Inhabitants of the United States of Mexico on Freedom of Worship, December 4, 1860

CITIZEN BENITO JUÁREZ, INTERIM
CONSTITUTIONAL PRESIDENT OF THE
MEXICAN UNITED STATES, TO ALL THE
INHABITANTS I DECLARE:

Exercising the comprehensive powers with which I have been invested, I have seen fit to decree the following:

Art. 1. The laws protect the exercise of Catholic worship and of the others established in the country as the expression and result of religious liberty, which, as a natural right of man, has not and cannot have limitations other than the right of another and the requirements of public order. In everything else, the separation between the state, on the one hand, and religious beliefs and practices, on the other, is and will be complete and inviolable. For the implementation of these principles it will be observed what the laws of the Reform and this document have declared and determined.

Art. 2. A church or religious society is formed of the men who have voluntarily desired to be members of it, declaring this decision by themselves or through their parents or guardians whose dependents they are.

Art. 3. Each one of these societies has the liberty to regulate, by itself or by means of its priests, the beliefs and practices of the religion that it professes and to specify the conditions with which it admits men to its association or removes them from it, provided that neither by these measures nor by their application to individual cases that might occur is it influenced by any misdeed or transgression prohibited by the laws, in

Original title: "Bando por el que se decreta la libertad de cultos, 4 de diciembre de 1860." Source: Benito Juárez, *Presidente interino constitucional de los Estados-Unidos mexicanos, á todos sus habitantes, hago saber, que, con acuerdo unánime del consejo de ministros . . .* (Veracruz: s.p.i., 1860).

which case the procedure and verdict that those laws prescribe will take precedence and the general intent be carried out.

Art. 4. The authority of these religious societies and their priests will be purely and absolutely spiritual without any coercion of another kind, whether it be exercised over men faithful to the doctrines, counsels, and rules of a religion, whether over those who, having accepted these things, might later have a change of mind. Popular action is granted to accuse and denounce violators of this article.

Art. 5. In the civil order there is no obligation, punishment, or coercion of any type with respect to purely religious matters, misdeeds, and offenses. As a consequence, no judicial or administrative procedure because of apostasy, schism, heresy, simony, or any other ecclesiastical offenses will take place, even if some church or its directors demand it. But if some misdeed or offense contained in the laws now in force is attached to them and not repealed for this reason, the appropriate public authority will know of the case and will resolve it without taking into consideration its status and quality in the religious order. This same principle will be observed when the indicated misdeeds or offenses might come about from an act judged proper and authorized by any religion whatsoever. As a consequence, the declaration of ideas on religious points and the publication of papal bulls, briefs, rescripts, pastoral letters, commands, and any writings whatsoever that also treat of those matters are things to be enjoyed in complete liberty unless order, peace, or public morality is attacked by them, or private life, or in whatever other way the rights of a third person or when some crime or offense is provoked; for in all these cases, leaving aside the religious element, the laws that prohibit such abuses will be applied irremissibly, keeping in mind what is laid out in Article 23.

Art. 6. In the internal economy of the churches and the administration of the wealth whose acquisition the laws permit to religious societies, these societies will have, in what corresponds to the civil order, all the powers, rights, and obligations of any legitimately established association.

Art. 7. Any recourse to force is abolished. If some church or its directors carries out an individual act reserved to public authority, the author or authors of this illegality will suffer respectively the punishments that the laws impose on those who separately or as a body commit it.

Art. 8. The right of asylum in churches ends, and force can and should be used that is judged necessary to seize and remove from the churches those persons declared or presumed culprits in accordance with the laws, without the ecclesiastical authority being able to intervene in this judgment.

Art. 9. Oaths and their retractions are not the concern of the laws. All rights, obligations, and legal punishments are declared valid and consequent without the need to consider the oath sometimes related to acts of the civil order. Consequently, the inherited obligation ceases of swearing observance of the Constitution, the faithful discharge of public and various professional duties, before entering into their exercise. In the same way, the legal obligation ceases of swearing certain and determinate statements before agents of the public treasury and the pleas, testimonies, opinions of experts, and whatever other declarations and assertions made within or outside the courts. In all these cases and in whatever others in which the laws mandate taking an oath, this will be replaced from now on by the explicit promise to tell the truth in what is witnessed, to fulfill well and loyally the obligations contracted; and the omission, negation, and violation of this promise will cause in the legal order the same results as if it were a question consistent with the pre-existing laws of an oath omitted, negated, or violated.

In the future, the swearing of an oath will have no legal effect on contracts concluded; and never, by virtue of the oath or the promise that replaces it, will an obligation be confirmed of those that previously necessitated swearing of an oath to secure force and consistency.

Art. 10. He who, in a church, insults or ridicules by speech or in another way expressed by external acts the beliefs, practices, or other objects of the religion to which that building was intended, will suffer, according to the situation, the punishment of imprisonment or exile, whose *maximum* will be three months. When, in a church, an injury is inflicted or some other crime is committed in which violence or dishonesty occurs, the punishment of the culprits will be one-half greater than that imposed by the laws on the crime of which it treats, considering that it is committed in a public and frequented place. But this augmentation in punishment will be applied in such a way that, in the secular prison, deportation or forced labor will not be generated for more than ten years.

In these arrangements the old law regarding sacrilege is revised, and the rest of the offenses to which this name is given will be subject to what the laws prescribe for identical cases without the purely religious circumstance.

Art. 11. No solemn religious act will take place outside the churches without written permission granted in each case by the local political authority according to the regulations and orders that the governors of the [Federal] District and states might enact, in agreement with the following requirements:

1a. The preservation of public order, above all, must be secured.

2a. These permissions need not be granted if it is feared they might produce or give occasion to some disorder, either from disrespect for the practices and sacred objects of the religion or for reasons of another nature.

3a. If, because of not harboring fears in this sense, said authority grants a permission of this kind and some disorder on the occasion of a permitted religious act should occur, this will be ordered stopped, and authorizing it in the future outside the churches will not be possible. Failure to obey in these cases will not be punishable except if it degenerates into force or violence.

Art. 12. It is prohibited to establish the spiritual director of the testator as heir or legatee, whatever might be the religious communion to which he belongs.

Art. 13. It is similarly prohibited to name mendicants to beg for and collect alms intended for religious objectives without the express approval of the respective governor, who will grant or deny it in writing as he deems appropriate; and the persons who practice those acts without presenting a certification of approval will be held as vagrants and will answer for the frauds they have committed.

Art. 14. The privilege called obligation [*competencia*] ends, by virtue of which Catholic clerics can hold back with detriment to their creditors a part of their wealth. But if, when sequestration for debt of the priests of whatever religion takes place, there is no other wealth on which distraint should fall in accord with the law except some fixed salary, only a third part of their periodic income can be seized. The books of the interested party will not be considered subject to seizure, nor things he possesses that are considered as belonging to his ministry, nor other goods that as a rule the laws except from sequestration.

Art. 15. The testamentary clauses that stipulate the paying of tithes, perquisites, or pious bequests of whatever type and denomination will be executed solely insofar as they do not go against the obligatory hereditary fee according to the laws, and in no case will the payment be made with property.

Art. 16. The action of the laws will not be exercised over grants of the faithful for maintenance of a religion and its priests unless those consist of real estate, or unless force or deceit intervenes to demand or accept them.

Art. 17. The official title usually given to various ecclesiastical persons and corporations ends.

Art. 18. The use of bells will continue subject to policy regulations.

Art. 19. The priests of all religions will be exempt from the military and from all restrictive personal service, but not from taxes or remunerations that the laws impose for these exemptions.

Art. 20. The public authority will not intervene in the religious rites and practices concerning matrimony. But the contract from which this union arises remains exclusively subject to the laws. Whatever other matrimony might be contracted in the national territory without observing the formalities that the laws themselves prescribe is null and, consequently, incapable of bringing about any of those civil outcomes the law confers only on legitimate marriage. Outside of this punishment, no other will be placed on unions disapproved by this article unless force, adultery, incest, or deceit is involved in them, for in those cases, what the laws mandate relative to these transgressions will be observed.

Art. 21. The governors of the states, district, or territories will take care, in accord with their strictest responsibility, to put into practice the laws issued with respect to cemeteries and mausoleums, and in no circumstance is the dignified interment of bodies forfeit, whatever might be the decision of the priests or their respective churches.

Art. 22. The laws that punish outrages made on bodies and their graves remain in full force.

Art. 23. The minister of a religion who, in the exercise of his functions, orders the carrying out of a crime or exhorts someone to commit it will suffer the punishment of this complicity if the above-mentioned crime is carried out. In the opposite case, the judges will take into account the circumstances in imposing up to half or less of said punishment whenever the laws do not designate a greater punishment.

Art. 24. Although all public functionaries in their status as men will enjoy a religious liberty as broad as all the inhabitants of the country, they will not be able, in an official capacity, to take part in the acts of a religion or of deference to their priests, whatever might be their place in the hierarchy. The standing army is included in the foregoing prohibition.

Therefore, I order it printed, published, circulated, and given the proper fulfillment.

Issued in the palace of the national government in Veracruz, December 4, 1860. — *Benito Juárez* — to C. Juan Antonio de la Fuente, Minister of Justice and Public Instruction.

3

Liberty and Order
1876–1912

JUSTO SIERRA

Justo Sierra (1848–1912), born in Campeche, was a writer, lawyer, politician, and historian. Sierra was one of the "new" liberals influenced by positivism in the second half of the nineteenth century. He started his literary career at a very young age, publishing essays and reviews in newspapers, and eventually became the chief editor of the influential daily *La Libertad*. Some of the key proposals of the new liberals regarding institutional reform were published in this newspaper. He was elected to Congress on several occasions. As a representative, Sierra worked to improve public education in the country. He also wrote important books on political and social history, such as *La evolución política del pueblo mexicano*.

Sierra was a believer in the power of science and in efficient public administration. He was a critic of "metaphysical" liberalism, a form of liberalism that enshrined natural rights. As we shall see, he debated with "doctrinaire," older liberals such as José María Vigil on the true nature of liberalism. He believed in strong but not unlimited government. While Sierra supported Porfirio Díaz (he held high positions in his administration), his support was not unconditional. He strove for important institutional reforms that would limit the power of the president, such as the permanent tenure of the justices of the Supreme Court.

We present some of his newspaper essays and the polemic with Vigil from the years 1878–79.

1

Emilio Castelar and the Program of *La Libertad*

La Libertad, in honoring its columns with the program of *El Globo* of Madrid, has as its principal aim not only to demonstrate its complete adherence to the principal ideas expressed by Mr. Castelar,[1] but also to show the close harmony with which that program and the thinking that governed the creation of our daily newspaper are united. *La Libertad* prides itself in having found such a brilliant expression of its principles, and in the shelter of the most eloquent voice of the modern rostrum it dares to reproduce them in categorical formulas.

We do not have a person as our standard but rather an idea: to rally all those who think that the epoch of wanting to realize their aspirations through revolutionary violence has now passed for our country, all those who believe that the definitive moment has now arrived for organizing a party friendlier to liberty practiced than liberty declaimed, and profoundly convinced that positive progress depends on the normal development of a society, that is to say, on order.

At the end of a half century of painful experiences, it seems to us that the present hour will not repeat itself again in our history. We sense that, if the strengths of men of peace and work are not sufficient in a brief period to make the will of the country triumph over the appetite for anarchy—to deflect, in a word, the direction of our political life and make it take the course not only of right, which ends by being converted

---

Original title: "Emilio Castelar y el programa de *La Libertad.*" Source: *La Libertad,* Mexico, February 14, 1878.

1. Emilio Castelar (1832–99) was a Spanish republican and the first president of the Spanish Republic (1873–74). He advocated establishing a federal republic and abhorred bloodshed and mob rule. He disapproved of military revolts, or *pronunciamientos.* While advocating free popular elections and parliamentary government he also gave due consideration to religious traditions and national unity. This conservative strain did not endear him to the more radical liberals. (Editor's note)

into disturbing protests, but also of duty, whose more elevated political formula is the inviolability of the law—we will cast ourselves down a slope on which, just as we have relinquished the national wealth, we will relinquish, torn asunder and dying, the nationality itself.

More fortunate than the Spanish republicans in arriving at our objective, we do not have to change our institutions, but rather seek them in the sense of their practical realization. For that it is necessary for us to make the foundations of public instruction more rational and extensive every day; to approach steadfastly the truth of the suffrage, seeking the conditions under which it can become rooted in our customs, and accepting these conditions without hesitation even if they might disagree with our ideal conception of democracy; demanding of our moral awareness, as free men, the civic conscience sufficient to make the responsibility of every official and the punishment of every criminal not a legal truth but rather the actual foundation of our political mechanism.

We are individualists in the sense that we put human right above all action of the state, but not because we believe that everything called individual right is absolute; on the contrary, our opinion is that, as society is not a fiction but rather a genuine organism subject to laws more complex than those of individuals, its action can in specific cases serve as the limit to some human rights, like that of property; and we believe that, starting from this foundation, a part of the solution to the social problem can, in conditions of the highest justice, be requested of a legislation that would extend in a prudent and firm manner the disentailment of territorial property. We believe this is the means of pulling the most numerous of our classes from the situation in which it finds itself and of developing, rapidly, the great improvements from which agriculture, industry, and commerce expect a new life.

Mr. Castelar has condensed into a few words the new face of the democratic evolution. We are entering, he says, the scientific and experimental period; the epoch of springlike dreams has passed. Here is what we strive always to keep in mind; these are the words that we try constantly to make the quarrelling factions hear. Will they hear us? Will we ourselves always know how to fulfill our intention with a calm spirit without allowing ourselves to be dragged along by the passions of the moment, the more ardent as the more fleeting?

The future will say. In the meantime, it is clear that, in demonstrating our complete consent to the program of the Spanish democrat, we have not had difficulty in declaring that we desire the creation of a great conservative party, composed of all those elements of order that in our country have sufficient ability to emerge into political life. And this ability is measured by the open and complete acceptance of the foundations of modern society.

Our readers will not insult us by supposing that we have reproduced the words of the great political speaker for the foolish arrogance of showing that his political thought coincides with ours, but rather because we would like to empower our modest ideas with those of Emilio Castelar, who has, without doubt, an irreproachable conscience and an incomparable talent.

2 | Reservations

When we speak of the Constitution, when we demand respect and honor for it, when we assign this as the first of our political duties, we do not claim that constitutional principles should be accepted as articles of faith; nor do we believe they are a perfect work, no. In our judgment, the Constitution of '57 is a fine liberal utopia but destined, by the prodigious amount of political *lyricism* it contains, to be realized only slowly and painfully. The same thing happens with it that has happened with all laws made to transform customs that permeate the social masses, provoking conflicts and incessant struggles, and sometimes society suffers, other times the law is discredited until, when the definitive work of amalgamation has occurred, society and the Constitution are transformed.

The principles of political emancipation, the bright prospects for liberty and regeneration, and more than all that, the destruction of clerical rule, fired up the enthusiasm of our fathers for that code promulgated as a new Decalogue in the name of God. That was yesterday; today, principles, dreams, and theories are coming to the discussion anew. All the precepts of the fundamental law are destined, because of the fatal demands of history, to suffer severe revision before the tribunal of new ideas. This could not be done in a moment of storm and struggle, so it was necessary to affirm, from the stormy summits of the liberal party, our religious dogma (constitutional dogmas are nothing other than that) and point out from the seats of the Constituent [Congress], in the loftiest and purest region of the heavens, our ideal of citizens and men.

Our fathers believed they had made a work profoundly practical because they took our institutions from a practical people, and this idea was radically erroneous. What the practical consists of in American people is not having consigned in the federal code such and such prin-

Original title: "Reservas." Source: *La Libertad,* Mexico, February 23, 1878.

ciples, but rather that those principles are perfectly appropriate to the social medium in which they had to unfold.

We believed that, in copying the principles, we were imitating their practical sense, and this was not true; what we should have done, what would have been true imitation, was to give ourselves institutions that could unfold not in the heart of our corrupted habits, but of those habits that our history, our material necessities, our climate, and even our geographical conformation imposed on us. This examination was impossible, we recognize, in the epoch of passion and combat that was present at the advent of the Constitution.

We do not reason without proof. An induction based on the cruelest experiments can take us gradually to these conclusions, and we claimed those experiments in the saddest hours of our history, from '57 until now. Our fundamental law, created by men of the Latin race who believe that something is certain and realizable to the degree it is logical, who tend to humanize brusquely and through violence any ideal, who pass in one day from the rule of the absolute to that of the relative without transition, without nuances, and wishing to obligate the people to practice what is true in the region of pure reason; these men, we are among them, perhaps, who confuse the heavens with the earth, made us a lofty and noble code of union, but one in which everything tends to differentiation, to individual autonomy carried to its *maximum;* that is to say, to the level at which the action of social duties stops and everything is converted into individual rights.

Thus each one of the political powers tends to include the sphere of action of the others, basing itself on the Constitution; each state tends to weaken, to nullify, the federal bond, based also on the Constitution; it tends to declare its absolute independence from the social group in which it lives. But as, in order to carry out each one of those ideas, we find ourselves with a nation at two or three centuries' distance from the constitutional ideal, everything miscarries into political convulsions, into muffled tremblings of the unsettled society, and into that unconquerable apprehension that puts in the depths of all our consciousnesses I do not know what vague and tenacious skepticism with respect to the next day.

But why, then, do we demand respect for the Constitution? If we do not believe it to be good, why have we made it our standard? Why yesterday in its name have we battled a government that had begun by calling us its friends and today we embrace another government that began by treating us as enemies? Here is the reason: the Constitution is a rule, it is a law, it is the impersonal authority of a precept, supreme guarantee of human liberty; beyond it, there is nothing but arbitrariness, personal despotism, and, in a word, the rule of one man over the others. And as we believe that, given our present mode of being, there is nothing worse than the absence of rule and limits; as we believe that what is established in this way, although it might be a marvel, will remain established on a crumbly base of sand and will be destroyed, not only for our love of liberty—which is, in the last analysis, human dignity—but also for our love of order, a principal factor of progress, we have to maintain that it is necessary to place the Constitution above everything else. It will be a bad law, but it is a law; let us reform it tomorrow; let us obey it always.

3

Liberals and Conservatives

In our country there have been neither liberals nor conservatives, but rather only revolutionaries and reactionaries. This refers to the factions, not the men. The revolutionary faction, to be liberal, has lacked the knowledge that liberty considered as a right cannot be realized outside of the moral development of a people, which is order; and the reactionaries, to be conservatives, lacked even the instinct for progress characteristic of our epoch, outside of which order is only immobility and death. In large part this has not been their fault, and it is absurd to demand of a country born and raised in conditions so unsuitable for social life what people better endowed with long experience and the dissemination of scientific instruction demand today, not always with good success.

Our existence has gravitated toward two extremes. The colonial system based on isolation is one extreme; the other is the constitutional regime based on this dogma: the individual is an absolute sovereign. The first gave us a reality without an ideal; the second offers us an ideal without reality; and this is an error, because it is necessary to be concerned simultaneously with the power of attraction that an idea exercises on a people and with the conditions in which that people live and up to what point those conditions permit the people to approach that ideal.

When our fathers promulgated the Charter of 1857, they believed themselves called to exercise a function more priestly than political; that time has passed. New ideas gain ground every day over the old verbal principles of liberty, and these ideas are inflexible because they are scientific laws. They teach us that the individual and society are two large organic realities that cannot be separated without destroying them. These laws teach us that nothing is definitively improved by revolu-

Original title: "Liberales-Conservadores." Source: *La Libertad,* Mexico, May 10, 1878.

tions because inevitable reactions follow them, and that the result of this oscillation is precisely to attain a progress equal to the progress that would have been obtained by the regular activity of peaceful means. So it is that there is always too much blood shed and vitality wasted.

What is it, then, that we want? To alienate forever from the mind of our country the idea that it can be regenerated by violence; to study the conditions in which we live, the obstacles placed in our advance, with such a desire to arrive at the truth, with such a profound determination to speak it, that we might manage, even at the risk of being victims of the rhetoric of fools, to find what our true needs might be and try to resolve them; thus it might be necessary to pass over a principle in our path or erase an ideal from our heavens.

Liberty! And where is the social force that secures us sufficiently against the violence of others? Democracy! And where are the people who govern, where is the enlightenment that directs their vote? Where is the faithful mandatary who collects it? Is our democracy perhaps something other than a shattered ballot box into which only fraud puts its hand? Who would be able to prevent it? The sovereign. We do not know it. This sovereign is a word. It is not a man. And how will it come to be? With work, with peace, with instruction.

Can this be a living fact, here where individual initiative is null except for the efficient action of the public authority of the state? Can this action be exercised without subjecting the strength of the state's momentum to rules, without giving it the right to do good where today it does evil, because it does it arbitrarily? To this study we consecrate ourselves.

We are young and we arrived at public life yesterday, still filled with dreams. We have been returned to reality by the spectacle of our disgraced country, which, however much it has inscribed beautiful ideas in its laws, continues along as disgraced as always; the spectacle of the other people who, not wishing to lose their prosperity, withdraw into themselves and create what suits them, what is useful to them, without worrying about political dogmas; the voice of science that tells us that nothing absolute is given to man to realize, man being subject irremissibly to the inflexible laws of nature; and the voice of our conscience that compels us to sacrifice a world of illusions in order to obtain an atom of well-being for our country.

We declare, consequently, not to understand liberty if it is not realized within order, and for that we are conservatives; nor order if it is not the normal impulse toward progress, and we are, therefore, liberals.

Immense is the seriousness of our social and political problems. We do not presume to present a solution; certainly, we have the assurance of advancing along the only road by which it can be found.

4

Polemic with José María Vigil

MR. VIGIL AND ARTICLE 5
OF THE CONSTITUTION

The bulletin *El Monitor Republicano*[1] of Thursday is dedicated to a critical examination of the recent interpretations of Article 5 of the Federal Constitution[2] made by the Supreme Court. Its author, Mr. Vigil, takes advantage of the opportunity to add some dark and vigorous brushstrokes to the picture, so many times repeated, of the profound lack of respect for individual rights, the chronic illness of our country.

As a result of these eloquent ideas, the journalist refutes the Court's interpretation by virtue of which legally required public services are not understood in the words "personal labors," of which Article 5 of the fundamental law makes use.

No one respects Mr. Vigil more than we do, and we regret being in disagreement with him. The eminent journalist of *El Monitor,* we are sorry to assert, belongs to the old liberal school that, as the French say, *a fait son temps.*[3] It is what we would call literary literalism, which is more pleased with a sonorous sentence and a well-turned phrase than with one of those straightforward and positive truths that we are condemned

Original title: "Polémica con don José María Vigil." Source: *La Libertad,* Mexico, August 23, 1878; August 30, 1878; September 6, 1878; October 23, 1878; and October 30, 1878.

1. In 1878 the editor in chief of *El Monitor Republicano* was Vicente García Torres, and José María Vigil, an old liberal, was a contributing editor. (Editor's note)

2. Article 5 of the 1857 Constitution states: "No one can be compelled to render personal services [*trabajos*] without due compensation and without his full consent. Law cannot authorize a contract that aims at the loss or irrevocable sacrifice of a man's liberty, be it for work, education, or religious vows. Neither can it authorize compacts in which a man accepts his banishment or exile." (Editor's note)

3. "Has had its day." (Editor's note)

to encounter in the street at any time, and that we trip over, at the risk of injuring ourselves, because we are looking at the sky while walking.

All our authorities have tyrannical instincts, says Mr. Vigil. We ask him, do these authorities fall to us from the clouds? No. They rise up from society and are genuine products of our defective Constitution; they are the scrofula that reveals the destructive poverty of our temperament.

And how to correct the illness? By means of Article 5 interpreted at the gallop of the imagination? Respect for individual rights! But in what tree of our fields does that fruit grow? Does Mr. Vigil not observe the hatred for the different life and the disdain for liberty that every Mexican left to his instincts has? What does it come to, then, to take up the sonorous horn of the revolutionary declamation so as to cry out: Article 5 must be an absolute article because the democratic revolution has won that great principle by virtue of which neither the army nor the municipality nor the penitentiary regime is possible?

No, this is not true; it is not to penetrate into the facts and take notice of them simply and frankly; it is not to put the probe in the wound, but rather to cover it with a veil that hides with the golden warping chain of the academic term the innermost and disgusting evil that is killing us. The violation of guarantees, the insult to right, comes because, when the legal precept does not accord with the needs of life, arbitrariness and despotism are the only possible regime in societies like ours that are barely embryonic.

And then does Mr. Vigil believe that, because he has said that the interpretation of the Court is dangerous, it has already been refuted? Frankly, we have not found any strength in the journalist's reasoning. We would like to see him descend from generalities and approach the fundamentals of the interpretation mentioned under its triple aspect: historical, constitutional, and philosophical. Mr. Vigil believes that the application of Article 16 is useless because slavery has been abolished.[4] Well, it is the coercion of the Indian *constable,* it is the servitude of the

4. "Nobody can be disturbed in his person, family, place of abode, papers, and possessions without a written warrant issued by a competent authority based on legal grounds. When an offense is committed in flagrante delicto, any person can arrest the criminal and his accomplices by placing them without delay in the custody of the nearest authority." (Editor's note)

peon, it is that slave of a piece of ground, the serf of the glebe, as it was called in the Middle Ages, that, like an instrument of redemption, Article 4 intends to rectify.

As was natural, Mr. Vigil recommends to us the example of the United States in organizing its army in the recent civil war. An American would laugh to himself at this charming idea. Precisely by violence, breaking the contracts of the volunteers and compelling them to remain in the encampment, was Sherman able to organize the Army of the Potomac and thus save the cause of the North. And this is because the Saxon, who so much respects individual right, when the hour of social danger sounds, makes the right of the individual yield to everything necessary to counteract the danger.

Mr. Vigil is correct to condemn that horrible abduction of the levy that has drawn the young blood from the veins of our country, and that is one of the causes of our incurable anemia; but let his anathema not move from there if he wants his arrows to go to the target and no further.

LA LIBERTAD AND MR. VIGIL

The journalist of *El Monitor* does us the honor of answering some of the observations we directed to his criticism of a ruling in which the Court of Justice expresses a new interpretation of Article 5 of the fundamental law. It was our objective to stimulate debate over the basics of this interpretation, which Mr. Vigil's bulletin left untouched. We have not succeeded, and we are going to reply for the purpose of making a second attempt on the same point, rescuing, in any case, our respect and sympathy for a writer before whose intellectual and moral worth we have long been accustomed to bow.

We sense that Mr. Vigil might have taken poorly the classification that we make of the school in which the character of his writings places him. In truth, our intention could be only to express a fact: We call that school *old* because in Mexico it tends to be replaced by another so different that, although it might well be considered a historical consequence of the revolutionary school, it is not, nor is it by far its scientific consequence. Let us explain.

The *old liberal school that has passed its time,* as Mr. Vigil says, or has accomplished its mission, as we said, availing ourselves of a French locution, is the school that believes that a society regenerates itself thanks to political dogmas linked with metaphysical dogmas; that without taking into account the truth of the facts, or the experience, or the conditions in which a people lives, it makes factitious laws that are not the product of social needs, but rather that tend by means of false propositions to reduce societies to a specific way of being, which is a scientific error; it is the school that believes that the way to mold the people to those dogmas is violence, that is to say, revolution, which is a moral error; it is the school that believes, with Mr. Vigil, that the men of [17]93 established forgotten or unknown rights on eternal foundations, which is a historical error.

That school, born in disturbance and for disturbance, needed eloquence and rhetoric to stir up the passions of a part of society and hurl it like a formidable battering ram on the other part; from here come its methods, essentially literary and sentimental, which consist in replacing what should be a rigorous scientific proof with a poetic turn of phrase. For example, an impartial man observes that when all sensible Mexicans acknowledge that "only with difficulty can there be a people that lives in more anarchic conditions, in which the authority has lost more of its prestige, in which political passions ferment more actively (?), and that it is necessary to recognize with sadness that our country is very backward" (Mr. Vigil's text), and that observation is followed by this other: Given that Mexico finds itself in that state, how is it that it has a Constitution in which there are one hundred times fewer conservative elements, elements of stability and order, than in the most liberal of the countries that march at the forefront of civilization? How is it that in France, where the men of '93 made the marvels that Mr. Vigil attributes to them, it has been recognized that only an ultraconservative republic is possible? How is it that England, the classical country of self-government, has an aristocratic constitution? How it is that Germany maintains semifeudal institutions? Why in the United States does individual right yield every day, every minute, before society, whether the government represents society confiscating the goods of the Confederate, whether the inhabitants of a town who *lynch* the criminal, setting aside the judge and the Constitution? And here, in a backward and essentially anarchic country, we have a fundamental law that assumes a state of progress ten times superior to that of those peoples?

And this is not talking for the sake of talking. Mr. Vigil, for example, maintains that the article in the Constitution that says, "No one can be compelled to give personal labor," must be understood in an absolute way, the same for private labor as for public service. Mr. Vigil does not linger over this distinction; let us move on. Logic makes terrible demands; what human action does not involve the idea of effort, and what effort is not labor? Then who has the right to compel nothing or nobody in this blessed country? And what Constitution, even be it that of '93, has proclaimed such an enchanting and practical liberty above all? This is the absurdity, Mr. Vigil will say. Well, before this absurdity the majority of the Court has backed down and has sought an interpretation that not only reason authorized, but also that the historical sources of the Constitution demanded, the voice of the Ponciano Arriagas, of the Léon Guzmáns, of the Ignacio Ramírezes, who expressed the spirit of the constituent.

This is, among others, the historical point of view from which we invited the illustrious journalist to study the question. For this study, it was sufficient to appeal to the texts and to reason within everyone's grasp without soaring to abstractions which, being abstractions, had to be unintelligible as Mr. Vigil seems to believe, falling into a banality unworthy of his talent.

Well then, to all those observations, what does literary liberalism answer? Purely and simply that the Constitution is holy, that the people have spilled their blood for it, that to destroy the woes that trouble us it is necessary to observe the Constitution faithfully. The Republic has seen pass through power the whole liberal party in all its faces and nuances; it has seen pass with their partisans branched out throughout the country the Juarista party, guided by an eminently practical citizen; the Lerdista party, presided over by one of the most intelligent men we have known; the Porfirista party, led by a *caudillo* of incorruptible probity; and when, in what day, in what moment, has the Constitution been observed?

Will this not mean that there are impractical things in our political code because it is not in harmony with our social conditions? Between the rigorously inductive argument that can be supported with an infinite series of facts and the deduction of Mr. Vigil, imperfect, without proven foundation, based in simple a priori truths, that is, in dogmas, which is it to be? What is it that reason demands?

Two brief caveats fit here. When we said that our Constitution was flawed, a printing error that consisted of changing a lowercase *c* for an uppercase, Mr. Vigil suggested that we were referring to the Constitution of '57. No, we were speaking, as the other sentence indicated, of the general state of our particular organization, of our aptitude for life. What the esteemed writer has said regarding the matter has therefore been in vain. The second caveat is directed to a willful error of Mr. Vigil. We have not said in absolute terms that arbitrariness and despotism are the only regimes possible in this embryonic society; the writer himself transcribes the proposition that preceded this one: When the legal precept is not in accord with the needs of social life, then arbitrariness is the only possible regime. And this is a truth of such a nature that it is enough to cast a glance around us to be overwhelmed with its proof.

Far from desiring arbitrariness, we are its most convinced enemies; for that reason we want practical legal rules, so that not one single reason for despotism remains alive.

But not for this reason is our disagreement with Mr. Vigil less radical. He believes that when a law like three [burying one's head in the sand] cannot be carried out, it is necessary, to correct the ill, to change the three into ten, but this is a dream, it is an infantile illusion; this is not done, nor has it ever been done. History has never seen such an undertaking realized.

Ay! We are culprits in that offense. So we have spoken in prose and verse until the day when at last we were men, and when the fundamental importance of identifying an ideal with bitter reality was revealed to us in hours of supreme anguish and we took off the old vestments. We understood then that in a country, no matter how strong and great it might be, civil divisions cannot be prolonged indefinitely, and that either the energy of good men imposes silence on the others or foreign domination imposes silence on everybody. In the spirit of helping the good men, we remember those words of a Greek historian from the times in which the civil wars, ignited in the name of liberty and democracy, had put an end to Greece:

"Some will wonder that I speak with this bitterness when it was incumbent on me, more than on any other, to palliate the failings of the Greeks. But I am of the opinion that, in the eyes of sensible persons, the sincere friend is not the one who fears being frank, nor is the good citizen the one who is unfaithful to the truth so as not to hurt some of his contemporaries: he writes not to praise the hated ones but rather to correct evil ways and prevent repetition of the same faults" (Polybius).

OUR PRINCIPLES

We said that the old liberal school based its principles on metaphysical dogmas, and *El Monitor*, in its Tuesday bulletin, takes it upon itself to give us the reason in the most explicit terms. The columnist and colleague declares that he belongs to the radical democratic school, "that he starts from the absolute and returns to it; that he rests on the a priori of certain ideas that do not come from experience; that the radical democratic school is the child of Rousseau; that it originates from the *Social Contract,* etc." *El Monitor* is, then, classified, and, we confess, the category of liberalism in which it places itself surprised us not a little. We did not expect that the defender of absolute individual right would fix on the sect of Rousseau, whose fundamental principles are the existence of a happy primitive state from which the current state is a degeneration, of a "contract" that is the foundation of social relations, which means that society is something purely contractual, and, above all, of the famous dogma of the absolute power of the people to whose right are subordinated those of the individual. This school, which is the one that Madame Staël condemns in the eloquent phrases cited by the journalist, is in poor agreement, truthfully, with the theories of individual supremacy adopted by our colleague.

But Mr. Vigil goes further. Imitating a talented "rhetorician," who is certainly not a radical democrat, he takes on the mission of remaking man immediately on the standard of these three absolutes: the absolute of right, the absolute of equality, and the absolute of liberty.

There the confusion of doctrines; here the war of words and absurdity. What does this thing about the three absolutes mean? The absolute either is one or is not one. To say three absolutes is like saying three infinities, which is a piece of nonsense, given that the idea of plurality and that of limitation are coincident. Absolute right, which arises only from the relationship of individual to individual and which is limited by the right of another; absolute equality (a delirium proven false by everything that can and might exist) when this absolute would be in contradiction with the previous one, given that, in this case, everyone would have right over everything, which is the same thing as denying right; absolute liberty when, just as with society, the individual and in the individual what is called spiritual and what is called material are subject to invariable laws that govern the universe in which they are atoms, man, and society!

The journalist sees that to shape the eminently positive structure of social relations on a metaphysical foundation is like using the sea as a foundation for a pyramid. These dogmas, to which one does not come by experience, are not, cannot be the object of human science; they are the object of faith, which is the most personal that exists beneath the sun, and consequently the most arbitrary, the most variable, the most irreducible there is. How to extract from this immense void the complicated mechanism of a political constitution?

Continuing in pursuit of Mr. Caro and making use of his analysis, intentionally incomplete, the journalist has the kindness to tell us what it is we want and where we are going. "We are aristocrats and we are going to the dictatorship to deliver society to the arbitrary will of a supreme ruler." We appeal to the uprightness of the journalist to show us whether he believes in all conscience to have found in our assertions any that might authorize him to infer such an extraordinary conclusion, or if it is only in the interest of winning that he is led to set us up by so absurd a remark with the goal of providing himself with an easy victory.

If, instead of letting himself be transported by the interested and artificial criticism of the French professor, the journalist had gone to the sources, he would not attribute to us, neither to the masters nor to us the disciples, those bizarre and brutal ideas. The new school, the school of the future, as Mr. Caro ironically calls it, the experimental English school, which cannot be confused with that of Auguste Comte, proceeds in a more serious way and with more forceful methods than the school with which *El Monitor* deals. An example suffices: the radical democratic school declares itself child of the *Social Contract*. We ask, is there any book in which individual right is more systematically disavowed than in this one? The positive school counts, among the best of its productions, the book by [John] Stuart Mill, *On Liberty*. Have individualism and positive liberty been defended anywhere more admirably than in that work? Well then, to compare those two books is almost like comparing the two schools.

But let us proceed to something more concrete. Which are, in their general features, the ideas of that school we believe called to replace the

old liberalism in Mexico? It is necessary to spell them out so that someone else's liabilities do not continue being attributed to us.

1. Society, like all concrete existence, is the product of a development subject to fixed laws. Guiding investigations, in the sense
of knowing these laws and conforming the positive laws to them,
must be the work of the statesman, the legislator, the public writer.
Everything that might be contrary to these laws is artificial, can be
maintained only by physical or moral violence, and is condemned to
perish irremissibly. This violence is, as a general rule, what receives
the name of revolution or reaction. We call the organic development of human groups "the social evolution."
2. Right, not being able to have, outside of metaphysical arbitrariness, a foundation other than the principle of utility with respect to
the progressive interests of the human species, and progress being
the result of the growing activity of each individual, it is the duty of
everyone, expressed in the law, to facilitate the development of this
activity. This is what we understand by "individual right."
3. The function of the state consists in protecting those rights; that
is what we call social justice. But as the state is, whatever might be
its form or legal appearance, a product of the sentiments that prevail in a society, to the degree to which these sentiments are more
antisocial, let us say, the state has to be more conservative, the authority more vigorous, to prevent the dissolution of the national
group; in which case individual right must yield and has yielded and
will always yield in order not to perish.

This is the irrefutable truth sanctioned by all constitutions. For absolute individualists, like the writer we are combating, the constitutional
power to suspend guarantees is a contradiction. Come now, the right
based in the three absolutes can cease to be, even if temporarily? But,
we will repeat it a hundred times, logic makes terrible demands, and
social needs ruin the most sacred dogmas of radical democracy. This
is the reality; all of us are aware of it, except that some of us declare it
and others keep quiet about it in order to flatter we do not know what
ephemeral idol of lies and dementia.

So certain is this that the article writer, in his defense of the Constitution, such as it is, and in his ill will toward the system of friars,

has thrown out individual right. Why can the friars not consociate? Where are, gentlemen knights of the ideal and of eternal and indescribable right, where are your resonant principles here? The most lay of the secularized laypeople could exclaim, "How do you remake man on the standard of absolute liberty, of absolute equality, and prevent us from joining together? Well, perchance are we friars not men? Why do you not permit us to gather even a leftover scrap from that feast of absolutes which your political metaphysics gives us as a gift?" Well then, if *El Monitor* is faithful to its church, neither now nor ever will it give to this reproach an answer worth the trouble.

We have too long continued these notes, but, on the other hand, we have set down some of the cardinal fundamentals of our program, providing our objectors a more extensive and firmer ground for their attacks. What consequences do we extract from these premises? How do we try to reduce them to practice and formulate them into law? It is a question regarding which we will not lack an opportunity to discuss later; probably the illustrious journalist of *El Monitor* will provide us the occasion to do so.

One observation and we will conclude.

Not because we are guided by the facts, not because we deny that there are demonstrable truths other than those that internal or external experience teaches us, do we lack an ideal. We pride ourselves on placing the ideal higher than the revolutionary school. Enough to say that, for us, progress is a necessity, it is an immutable law; that the knowledge of this law permits us to assure that a day will come when the constraint of the moral law in the human spirit will replace all positive laws and the state will be reduced to its functions of protection, that is to say, to administer justice. Democracy is also an ideal for us, not because we see in the government of the greater number anything rational or good in and of itself, but rather because it is what provides greater expanse to individual development.

No, we are not the ones who deny the marvelous power of the idea; it is a principal factor in the improvement of societies. If our worthy colleague had contented himself with showing us the ideal, our disagreement would have been less, perhaps. But faithful in this to the methods of the revolutionary party, he wants that that ideal, that those principles, be forcibly reduced to positive laws, and this happened in the Constitution, and to this we owe the fact that the Constitution is not practiced and that there is in reality another constitution in force, the only one that a people in the conditions of ours can have, but that, because in contradiction with the written law, leaves a wide space for arbitrariness and despotism.

When men have wanted to convert an ideal into reality and impose it by compulsion of law, it opens to nations the era of bonfires of the Inquisition to realize a religious ideal; that of the guillotine to realize a political ideal; that of tarring to realize a social ideal.[5] It was fifty years ago that the radical democratic school and the reactionary school, in order to realize their ideals, opened wide the gates of Mexico to civil battles. Do we deserve the terrible anathemas, those of us who believe the time to close those gates has arrived?

SOME WORDS TO *EL MONITOR*

In his bulletin of yesterday, Mr. Vigil deals with refuting the ideas of *La Libertad* with the same arguments of which he has constantly made use. Nor did Mr. Vigil even think about entering into the editing room of the worthy colleague of the street of Letrán,[6] when *La Libertad* had already explained at length what it understood by the word "conservative," basing its principal attribute on opposition to revolution and its absolute opposition to the word "reactionary." Then we said that, in Mexico, there had not properly been either liberals, because in the hands of these liberty had been a myth, or conservatives, because those who are called thus were radically incapable of shoring up order. There has not been, then, in our country, anything but revolutionaries and reactionaries. It would suffice for us to show this, with regard to the liberals, simply by pointing out, among the opinions of the most sensible and moderate of them, political creeds like that of the radical democracy adopted by Mr. Vigil.

Revolutionaries wish to make progress by ax blows, imposing it by violence, not understanding that progress is not at the mercy of dreamers or made by means of political codes, but rather is brought about

---

5. Tarring was a form of corporal punishment that entailed smearing a person's body with tar. It was sometimes inflicted by a mob on an unpopular or scandalous character. (Editor's note)

6. The offices of *El Monitor Republicano* were in the street of San Juan de Letrán in Mexico City. (Editor's note)

slowly and laboriously. The result is that when, by virtue of a revolution constitutions are drawn up, these float on the surface of the societies like aquatic palms on the currents, without touching bottom with their roots. It happens then that between the written institutions and the natural institutions there is no connection whatsoever; and as they injure and hurt each other mutually, the reality is, as a consequence, that a people lives without institutions and is the plaything of political and social ventures. This is what happens with the Mexican Republic, as we will not tire of repeating, as we will show only too well.

Mr. Vigil sees that he does not have to appeal to "distinctions" with our epithet of conservatives: the literal significance and the political significance are blended for us; for him, "conservative" means conserve the Constitution; for us, it means to conserve the social order, the only means of acclimatizing liberty, exotic plant in our history. And the wonder that this causes Mr. Vigil surprises us; he does not live so distant from the political movement in the modern world to be unaware that the word has been transformed and, without losing its original meaning, has been enriched with first-rate scientific elements. When American conservatives dominate definitively in the United States, and in England the conservative party also dominates; when the young republican generation in France, thanks to political ability acquired in hours of terrible dangers, calls itself conservative and supports an ultraconservative constitution; when Emilio Castelar proclaims, as the only possible one in Spain, a conservative republican constitution also, why is he reproaching us for calling ourselves the same and requesting, not in the name of the divinity in years past, but rather in the name of science and truth, order in a disordered country?

Another mistake Mr. Vigil makes in attempting to show our lack of scientific method is that of saying that our solution to the social problem is provisioning a strong government, that is to say, one capable of preserving order. Not a letter, not a tilde of *La Libertad* authorizes such an assertion. The authors of social panaceas disgust us, and never have those who speak of the prosperity of a people by virtue of infallible means, kept in enchanted bottles, seemed to us anything but charlatans. The problem of the happiness of Mexico is complex in the extreme; we need many things and much time to resolve it. We beg Mr. Vigil to lend us two minutes more of attention.

In reality we have neither institutions nor rights nor guarantees; all this is at the mercy of the revolutionary man. What is the practical way to make this condition disappear? Adapt individual right to the conditions of our existence, invigorate the principle of authority, give us a strong government.

What we want, then, with a strong government, around which the conservative elements of society can assemble, is to combat revolutions, is to make them gradually impossible. From this, peace would come, and that certainly is a condition to realize material improvements, the only path that guides us to the solution to the problem.

Do we have here some sin against the scientific method, that is to say, against experience and reason? Is there a just reason for so much scandal in our affirmation that constitutions that have as their objective, like ours, to do the good of humanity and that begin only by admitting the constitutions that are good for the Italians, for the French, for the Chileans, etc., have ended in all civilized countries? If every country encounters itself in itself and studies its needs and tries to satisfy them, without setting itself to ascertain which are the rights of man and which are not, by what strange misfortune has Mexico been eternally unable to do the same? Why are the doors closed to this healthy and comforting egoism? Does it not seem to *El Monitor* that it is now time that the wisdom tooth might come through?

THE LAST WORD OF *EL MONITOR*

The journalist of *El Monitor* has spoken his last word in the polemic that he began with *La Libertad*. This last word is exactly like the first. We will overlook everything Mr. Vigil insisted on attributing to us, probably applying the art of discussing the scientific method of which he has an idea; thus it is that the journalist insists that our ideal in the matter of national prosperity is a strong government despite the fact that his own reference contradicts it. We have explained that we do not claim to have discovered a panacea or system to cure all the ills of the country, but rather simply that one of our most urgent needs is establishing a robust government, not because in satisfying it our ills will be cured as if by enchantment, but rather because in the midst of a society that every day loses an element of union, that lives as if for a short time, that "is going out," as an ancient said, speaking of the anarchy in a country of the Orient, it is necessary, it is indispensable, it is of an inexpressible importance to form a strong nucleus capable of attracting some powerful interests in their turn and trying to save, in that way, what the constituents considered the supreme objective of their labors: the unity of the *patria.*

Despite the fact that we have been clear and conclusive as much as is possible in the matter, Mr. Vigil responded that we were maintaining vaguenesses. This is a polemical retort, it is not a sincere truth. We do not know what is vague about requesting the establishment of a conservative government.—That is dictatorship, they have said to us.— Calumny, we have responded; dictatorship is arbitrariness and we want order, and as a condition for getting there, the reform of the Constitution, widening the sphere of the authority and arming it, not with the prohibited arms of despotism, of intrigue, and of chicanery, child of an impracticable constitution, but rather with those that put in their hands a law reconciled with our true needs and that would be sufficient to promote the progress of all and look after the right of each one, today at the mercy of force and corruption.

Is this clear? Is this vague?

Ah, no; but Mr. Vigil certainly is a staunch enemy of vagueness; he certainly supports a very clear, very fecund, very precise program, a great practical program. What is the remedy for our ills? Comply with the Constitution. Has nothing clearer been seen? Yes, this is the sun. How could I be cured, Doctor? By curing yourself. Comply with the Constitution! And what does one do to comply with it? Enough of wanting it, Mr. Vigil will tell us; it is purely a matter of good will. Certainly, men of good will would save us; but as there are none here, to judge by the history of the Constitution, it will be necessary to have them made somewhere else.

But we have a classic example of the way in which the journalist understands that the Constitution must be fulfilled. To bring it to mind is to bring to mind also the first word of this polemic. It dealt with Article 5 of the Constitution, which, according to *El Monitor,* must be understood thus: no inhabitant of the Republic is obliged to lend his personal labor to society without his full consent. The article does not say that, according to the interpretation of the highest court of the country; but that is what Mr. Vigil wants it so say, forgetting that the Letter kills.[7]

---

7. "The Letter kills but the spirit gives life" (2 Cor. 3:6). In this context the phrase refers to the fact that under the Old Covenant, the Law/Letter given in Sinai brought condemnation and debt as no one could obey it perfectly and be saved. (Editor's note)

The journalist wants, as we do, that authority be respected; but when it comes to the army, well that is another matter, because from the moment the citizen does not consent to serve, no one can compel him; he wants the democratic institutions to be a fact, but it is necessary to pay the gentlemen councilmen, a very easy thing in the Republic, because the day their full consent is lacking, who can compel them to serve? And the work in the penitentiaries, how will it be demanded? And the tax, how will it be collected? Is not money a representative value of personal labor? Doesn't the taxpayer give a form of personal labor to the state in the form of money? And if he does not wish to give it? Article 5 will protect him.

As one sees, nothing is more positive and nothing can bring the country more benefits than this precept! Will Mr. Vigil not want to reform it in the sense of "increasing liberties"? Because according to his theory, the more a liberty is stretched, the more practical it is. In truth, in France and in England such liberty does not exist; but why be concerned with England and France? Let us be concerned with Mexico; here is where that liberty has been strengthened; here is where it is admirably adequate for what we need. We already have too much order, we have done too much to preserve ourselves. Liberty, lots of liberty. Evohe![8]

But let us descend the resounding steps of enthusiasm, and let us conclude with this humble and pedestrian observation. The Constitution has existed for twenty years and no one has put it into practice. Does our worthy opponent believe that, only because he says no one has wanted to put the Constitution into practice, it is suddenly going to be put into practice? If the illness is in men, does it not seem to him that the illness might spread? Does not Mr. Vigil have in reserve some remedy for this epidemic? And it can happen, not that he recovers virginity for the Constitution, as in Marión Delorme, Victor Hugo, but that he fertilizes it and gives us, finally, the desired child, the Messiah of the social regeneration of Mexico.

---

8. Interjection. The cry of the Bacchae (in Greek mythology, the priestesses of Bacchus) in honor of Dionysius. (Editor's note)

5 | Our Battle Plan

No one is in a better situation than we to choose positions in the face of future events. We have maintained, supported by the good sense of the country (of this we have more conclusive proofs every day), that it was necessary to reform the Constitution in the sense of creating elements of governmental energy in order to preserve social interests. Political events subsequent to our first affirmations have demonstrated that we were right when, in a society that is unsettled, we maintained that it was necessary to strengthen the center of cohesion.

A legitimate consequence of the principles in which we have believed, that every effective attempt at political reconstruction must be supported, has been this, which we hold as an incontrovertible truth: there is nothing to hope from revolutions now; every revolution is essentially antipatriotic and criminal.

Two laws derive from this for us: to support at all costs the present administration against revolutionary attacks; to combat those attacks in whatever form they present themselves. For that reason, we fight at all costs against the candidacy of Mr. Benítez.[1] He was a man who had the unanimous abhorrence of the country; everything that might be done in his favor had to be artificial; to put official resources at his disposal was to solicit boldly an uncontainable revolution, because it gave him, more than a pretext, a reason for being.

Thanks to the good sense shown this time by the president of the Republic, Mr. Benítez has given up his candidacy, and this relinquishment, even though it might not be sincere, the circumstances will make irremediable. The new tendencies that start, if not from the center, certainly from the circle that immediately surrounds it, seem to us to show that

---

Original title: "Nuestro programa de combate." Source: *La Libertad,* Mexico, May 16, 1879.

1. Justo Benítez wanted to be a candidate for the presidency in 1880. (Editor's note)

the idea of creating a candidacy with official means, without the support of opinion, has not been abandoned. We must oppose that tendency with all our strength.

We do not delude ourselves. We know perfectly that the country will not take part in the election; that our parties are not political groups but rather personal factions; that our country needs them to wait on its table; what is necessary, and in this the eternal error of Mexican governments has consisted, is to serve the country a meal it likes. This is the secret: a question of cuisine, like the majority of political questions. For that we have requested in all the annotations of the registry of supplications [*registro deprecatorio*] to the gentleman president, that he settle on one citizen that the country accepts, and he will see how, without appeals to force, the election, or what is called such, deserves the applause of all honorable citizens.

It is not hidden from us that the profound work of decomposition that undermines and wears down this society, not now muffled but rather visibly, necessitates in the crises in which the latent anarchy will rise from the muck heap to the street, men of extreme energy, incapable of tyrannizing but trained to repress. So as much for the country as for the future president, the effective collaboration of General Díaz would be very fortunate, and all these circumstances increase greatly the responsibility of the current leader of the executive. Men have little influence on the current of human events, ruled by inevitable laws; but a man can hold back or hasten the advance of this current, and General Díaz is in that situation.

Our role in the future is, then, very simple. To support the administration; to combat the official efforts on behalf of candidates not accepted by opinion. If these efforts continue, we will contribute with all our strength to the consolidation of a group of unofficial parties that might bring to the electoral field the possible struggle against the forces of the government.

Nonetheless, and even if this is equivalent to the most serious of admissions, subject to making it more explicit in a subsequent article, we declare that, in any case, we will fight against the revolution and we will bow before the resolutions of Congress, be they in agreement with our aspirations or not, because outside of this we do not see salvation.

JOSÉ MARÍA VIGIL

José María Vigil (1829–1909), born in Jalisco, was a professor, writer, and journalist. He belonged to the older generation of liberals who held the 1857 Constitution in high regard. He wrote articles for several newspapers, among them *El Siglo XIX* and *El Monitor Republicano*. Vigil served two terms in Congress after the Republic was restored in 1867 and later became a justice on the Supreme Court. Vigil taught at the Escuela Nacional Preparatoria and was the director of the National Library. He was a critic of positivism, believing that it corrupted the nature of liberalism. In 1878, in the daily *El Monitor Republicano,* Vigil countered Sierra's arguments published in *La Libertad* by criticizing the practice of limiting constitutional rights in order to make the government stronger.

We present some of Vigil's essays as well as his contributions to that polemic.

1 Bulletin of *El Monitor,* August 22, 1878

The great objective of the democratic revolution, for which the Mexican nation has suffered long years of bloody struggles, is the rights the Constitution of '57 set down in section 1 of title 1 and those designated generally by the name of constitutional guarantees. All the rest — the political system that governs us, the form adopted of federative republic — do not intend any end other than the strengthening of those guarantees, the inviolability of those rights, without which not a single step would have been taken on the road of progress and true liberty for the people.

Our society, like French society before the famous revolution of '80, found itself deprived of the greater part of those precious rights set down in our Constitution. The absolute regime that ruled throughout the entire colonial epoch professed doctrines radically opposed to those that dominate today; and it is worth noting that, among the first methods adopted by the revolution of independence, one finds the consecration of certain guarantees that, once Mexico won its national sovereignty, came to be expanded progressively until the year '57, when the nation saw those saving principles of life and liberty included in its fundamental law.

It is sad, nonetheless, to acknowledge that, among the reforms of which the Republic is so proud, the full and absolute respect for individual guarantees cannot be counted. The theories are proclaimed, the principles have been elevated to the category of constitutional prescriptions, it being declared solemnly in Article 1 of the fundamental law that "the rights of man are the foundation and the objective of social institutions." But despite that, the habits of tyranny our ancestors bequeathed us are perpetuated among us in the specter of the ignorance of

Original title: "Boletín del *Monitor,*" 22 de agosto de 1878. Source: *El Monitor Republicano,* August 22, 1878.

the masses with regard to making their rights respected and of the arbitrariness of mandarins, who, putting on airs as liberals, are nothing more than odious petty dictators disposed to abuse, everywhere they can, the poor and the helpless.

The guarantee most frequently violated is the one contained in Article 5 of the Constitution; on the other hand, that guarantee is, perhaps, the most precious, because it has as its objective the person himself, his time, his work, his will, and even his life; that is to say, it is about man in the entire breadth of the word, physically and morally speaking. The number of *amparos*[1] filed for violation of Article 5 is incomparably higher than those lodged for other abuses, without having diminished even up to this time, as would be desired by all of us who are interested in having the observance of the Constitution come to be a genuine practice.

The reason for such a difference is explained by keeping in mind the innumerable quantity of victims that the barbarous system of the levy sacrifices; for the effort of maintaining a growing army that absorbs the greater part of the budget, the ill will that our republican governments profess for the national guard, and that type of systematic forgetfulness to concern itself with the creation of a law of recruitment make it resort to the savage method of uprooting the most helpless class from their homes so they might wield arms with the most enormous detriment to their families and interests.

It is right to add that the Supreme Court has protected, in the majority of cases, those unfortunate people who appeal to it requesting the liberty of which they have been deprived, without our recalling that not once has it permitted condemnation of the levy's odious abuses in the most explicit way. Nonetheless, in these last days, it has introduced in the explanatory part of some sentences certain doctrines that come to be an innovation, in which we would find nothing unusual if, at the same time, we did not see that a door opens slightly, through which abuse and arbitrariness can readily be introduced.

Certainly, the levy continues to be condemned, but not yet for violation of Article 5, because the guarantee of not giving personal labor

1. The writ of *amparo* is filed by persons who claim that their individual rights have been violated by an authority. (Editor's note)

without just compensation and without full consent refers only to person-to-person activities and does not speak of duties to the *patria,* but rather because such a system violates the constitutional requirement that demands proportionality and equity in giving public service to which Article 31² subjects Mexicans. Thus it is that from the obligation that Article 31 imposes on every Mexican to defend the independence, territory, honor, etc., of the *patria* and to contribute to the public expenses of the federation, the state, and the municipality, one deduces that, in a question of public service and taxes, the Mexican can be obliged to give personal labor even without there being just compensation and full consent, "provided only that these services are demanded of him in the proportional and equitable manner that the laws set out."

It occurs to us, of course, that the new interpretation the Supreme Court has thought it wise to give Article 5 is somewhat useless and ridiculous; given that Article 2 abolished slavery, no inhabitant of the Republic has run the risk that his neighbor might compel him to give him some service against his will and without fair compensation. If every man who steps on our territory is free, if no individual has the power to demand forced service from anyone, then Article 5 is totally superfluous in the Constitution, since it was intended to guarantee rights that no one thinks of attacking because the horrible institution of slavery was abolished.

It is said in support that such was the mind of the constituents in approving the article cited. That may be so, but that does not eliminate the fact that the interpretation the Supreme Court had previously adopted is more natural, more in conformity with the written text, and more in the spirit of our institutions. In effect, and here is where we see the danger, it is necessary to keep very much in mind that the primary enemies the Mexican people have with respect to their liberty are, with rare and honorable exceptions, the authorities. From the highest officials to the lowest policemen, from the illustrious young men who command

2. Article 31 of the 1857 Constitution states: "The obligations of Mexicans are (1) to defend the independence, the territory, the honor, the rights, and interests of the homeland; (2) to contribute to the public expenditures of the federation, and the state and municipality in which they reside, in the proportional and equitable manner provided by law." (Editor's note)

the ship of state to the obscure mayor of a village, all seem inspired by the same despotic sentiment for abusing power, oppressing the weak, harassing the helpless, sometimes by the shameless use of brute force, other times by means of chicaneries and subtleties, very ingenious, if you will, but that reveal the complete lack of respect that those who should be faithful guardians of its rights profess to society.

If the abuse ceases to be such simply by coming to be encompassed by certain legal formulas; if man can be deprived of his individual liberty, "even without there being fair compensation and full consent," by means of general measures, it can then be said that the guarantees granted by the Constitution, where they reside mostly as simple theories, have received a death blow, the simplest way having been discovered to perpetuate abuses and tyranny, of which the people have been victims despite the principles attained.

But it is said that those involuntary services cannot be demanded except in a proportional and equitable way; we like the words, except that they have such elasticity that they fit within concepts diametrically opposed to those they express. If those among us who manage to exercise power, almost always by evil means, would be inspired by the desire to act well; if society feels itself completely sure that its will would always be respected and its opinion dutifully paid attention to, some appearance of reason would be conferred on the theory we are combating; but when the complete opposite happens, when we live in the midst of abuse and corruption, to proclaim such a principle, false according to the liberal point of view and of such injurious consequences, seems to us so absurd and dangerous that we harbor the hope that the Supreme Court will retrace its steps and dispense with proclaiming it in similar cases that come before it.

To deduce the new interpretation of the duties imposed by Article 31 seems to us a not-very-clever sophism. From the fact that the Mexican citizen has the obligation to "defend the independence, territory, honor, rights, and interests of his *patria*," one does not logically deduce that someone can be obliged to give personal labor without fair compensation and without his full consent.

Let us suppose an extreme, exceptional case; let us suppose the case of a foreign war. Well, not even so would it be just, rational, or appropriate to appeal to those methods of violence and tyranny. And this is not an opinion exclusively ours; it is the feeling of well-known experts in public law, as it will be easy for us to demonstrate despite the little fondness we have for citing authorities.

"As soon as war is threatened," says Filangieri,

one turns to violence. What a sad spectacle! What an unfortunate omen! Those citizens who have not been able to hide, who have not been able to flee or withdraw themselves with the help of some privilege or with money to despotic recruiters, are bound and dragged before a subdelegate whose functions are always odious and whose sense of probity is always suspect by the public. The parents of those unfortunate ones accompany them; they deliver, trembling, the names of their sons to the subdelegate and await their fate. Then a black ball shoots from the fateful urn and marks the victims whom the prince sacrifices to war. This ceremony, accompanied by the tears of the fathers, the desperation of the mothers, the sobs of the wives, what value can inspire those new combatants for whom everything foretells a certain death?

No, that is not the price with which true soldiers are obtained; it is not thus that the peoples of the North are called to go to war. . . . Such a sad and dismal apparatus did not precede then the horrors of combat, and without doubt, war would not begin today under such terrible auspices if soldiers pledged voluntarily to defend the *patria,* if no violence at all were used against them, and if it were not fate that determined their destiny.

"It is important," says Fritot,

that a forced recruitment, that an odious law of conscription not violently uproot, from their labors and their families, men whose natural inclination distances them from the noble career of bearing arms, and that they not drag them in chains like criminals or slaves beneath the standards of the *patria* and liberty. . . .

In society, those who are not called by a natural vocation to embrace the career of bearing arms can be honorable and useful citizens, industrious artisans, hardworking proprietors, but they will almost always be, in more than one way, bad soldiers.

Men compelled by violence to take on the job of bearing arms, enlisted and led under the standards against their will, are easily persuaded that injustice and force are the only regulators of the world, and they themselves very quickly have no other rule of conduct or rule of law; very soon they breathe nothing more than disorders, wars, conquests and pillages.

One sees, then, how far from being acceptable in good philosophy is that violence the Supreme Court today seems to want to convert into a duty of Mexican citizens. If one wishes to know what a civilized and democratic government does in such emergencies, one should look at the way the United States of the North organized its armies, both in the war of independence and in that of secession. But nothing of the brutal violence that attacks the most sacred personal rights; nothing of those savage practices that tend to enslave free men by nature and by law, because that would be as much as to regress to the darkest epochs of absolutism, eradicating with the stroke of a pen the most precious victories of a democratic revolution. For all these reasons, we hope that the Supreme Court relegates to oblivion the strange theory it has recently proclaimed and continues on this point the practice it had adopted, which is the most fair, most liberal, and most appropriate in every way.

2 | Bulletin of *El Monitor,* August 27, 1878

We have received the following letter that we are publishing, acceding to the wishes of its illustrious author.

Mexico, August 22, 1878.—Mr. José María Vigil, editor of the *El Monitor Republicano.*—My very dear sir: Whereas for some time I have had the pain of maintaining in the press the opposite of what you defend, the great satisfaction falls to me today of congratulating you for your brilliant article of today, with which I agree completely because it contains the ideas I have professed since I have been able to concern myself with politics, which I have maintained and practiced to the extent it has been possible for me and which you explain with every elegance, with every lucidity and a lovely style that corresponds to your well-established literary reputation.

I believe that you will not scorn, because they emanate from me, these expressions of applause and interest, and that you will be kind enough to publish them, because although the voice of approval is humble, it is very much meritorious and very sincere.—*Eduardo F. Arteaga.*

The preceding letter has given us genuine satisfaction, for if once we have disagreed with the opinions of Mr. Licenciado de Arteaga, we have always recognized in our worthy adversary the capable jurist and sincere republican who seeks in observance of the Constitution the natural means for strengthening the peace and liberty of the citizens. Accept then, Mr. de Arteaga, in the present lines, the frank expression of our gratitude for such a spontaneous demonstration that lends valuable sup-

Original title: "Boletín del *Monitor,*" 27 de agosto de 1878. Source: *El Monitor Republicano,* August 27, 1878.

port to the opinions expressed by us in our Bulletin of Thursday, the twenty-second of this month.

We are now going to take on the observations that our worthy colleague, *La Libertad,* has directed to us with respect to the same Bulletin.

Of course, we must confess that we do not know what that old liberal school is that has passed its time, and to which our colleague said, with a certain tone of sorrow, that we belong. If seeking social liberty in securing individual rights, if striving for those rights to be protected from the attacks of the authority by means of respect for the fundamental law of the Republic, is an *old* liberal school, we declare that we belong to it body and soul, and that far from being ashamed, we have pride in professing its principles and dedicating our weak intelligence to rooting it in the country with faith that it might inspire an irrevocable conviction.

It matters very little to us whether these doctrines are old or new; what is relevant to our intention is that they be genuine and beneficial, and as, until now, we have had no reason to believe the contrary, it follows naturally that we are not greatly concerned with counting the years. The label of new development is not sufficient in our eyes to lend prestige to a school and to persuade us of its intrinsic excellence, and we believe, on the contrary, that there are many new things eminently bizarre and ridiculous.

We have said, and it is true, that all our authorities, with rare exceptions, have tyrannical instincts; and our colleague asks us, "Do these authorities fall to us from the clouds?" answering immediately, "No; they rise up from society and are *genuine products of our defective Constitution;* they are the scrofula that reveals the destructive poverty of our temperament."

As to whether these authorities are *genuine products of our defective Constitution,* we deny it categorically, because if such a thing were to happen they would not be tyrannical, because they would proceed from the law and adjust their behavior to it. With respect to the epithet *defective* applied to our fundamental law, we will observe in passing that, without believing that it is a perfect work in every way, it seems to us that it is sufficient to bring about the prosperity of the Mexican people if it is observed faithfully, subject to correcting, by the means it itself indicates, the defects to which experience is pointing.

But it is not observed! And from this *La Libertad* seems to deduce that, far from opinion bending in the sense of keeping the law, far from inculcating that saving principle of a civilized society, it must, on the contrary, put to one side the legal precept because "it does not accord with the needs of life," and in such a case, "arbitrariness and despotism are the only possible regime in societies like ours that are barely embryonic."

Decidedly, our disagreement with *La Libertad* cannot be more radical or more profound. Our colleague establishes the cold bare fact, somewhat exaggerated as we will see later, and, paying attention exclusively to it, considers the demand that the law be carried out as a *revolutionary declamation*. We, reflecting in a different way, recognize the sad truth of the appalling legacy that our ancestors created for us; but instead of conforming ourselves to it, we try to hasten the day the regeneration will be completed. We continue struggling without stopping for a moment to destroy the monstrous system of subjection and servility, and we do not hesitate to take that *sonorous horn* of the democratic revolution in order to cry out in all keys that the authorities that infringe on individual guarantees are tyrannical, that the doctrine that tends to justify the violation of the law that has consecrated the rights of man as foundation of our institutions is tyrannical and antiliberal.

Our colleague, without wanting to, perhaps, is going to place himself in the terrain of the reactionary party, because accepting his theory, it is a blunder to concede superior rights to the general needs of the people, and as, in a society *barely embryonic* as ours, the only possible regime is arbitrariness and despotism, it comes about that "the violation of the guarantees, the insult to right comes because, when the legal precept does not accord with the needs of life," it follows that the best means of avoiding the violation of guarantees and outrage to the law is to suppress the law and the guarantees, because in effect, no one can violate or outrage what does not exist. This is no more, no less the reactionary dogma.

But that doctrine that tends to confine the people to an indefinite status quo, that implicates the democratic revolution in a general anathema, cannot be accepted by the liberal party, and we now understand the disdain with which our colleague treats it in calling it *old*, although, according to all appearances, the ideas he is praising are no less old.

A thousand times the Mexican liberal party has been treated as visionary, utopian, theoretical, etc., etc. But these unjust charges that the conservatives have made at all times regarding the parties that represent a progressive principle are clichés contradicted by the nature of things themselves and by the general advance of human societies. The Christians who rose up against the corruption of ancient Rome were visionaries; visionaries the reformers of the sixteenth century who laid the foundations for modern liberty; visionaries the men of '93 who established, on eternal foundations, forgotten or unknown rights; visionaries the Mexicans who proclaimed the independence of the *patria;* visionaries the liberals who founded the Republic; and visionaries the reformers who ended the preponderance of the privileged classes.

And what! From what, in a society dominated by certain interests and certain corruptions contrary to reason and justice, can be deduced something against the doctrines of the militant parties that are proclaiming precisely the destruction of those interests and those corruptions? The Mexican liberals distinguish themselves in no way from the liberals of the rest of the parties of the world. Party of struggle, party of promise, it cannot conform to palliatives that perpetuate the ills it is trying to eradicate or wait patiently for tyrants to yield good-naturedly the position they usurp and the people to be enjoying rights perfectly understood, both by reason of a slow and impossible evolution. All that will be very beautiful in theory but radically impractical.

Our colleague insults the Mexican people when he notes, *"Every Mexican, left to his instincts, has hatred for the different life and disdain for liberty."* No, that is not true; it is an unsustainable paradox from any point of view to claim that every Mexican might be by instinct murderer and slave, the literal translation of the words we have transcribed.

That demagogic spirit that flatters the people, hiding from it the truth and canonizing its defects, is far from our purpose. We recognize with sadness that our country is very backward, that it is still very far from having eliminated the flawed habits it inherited from the long regime of despotism under which it developed; but to suppose from this that Mexico is a country in full barbarity, in which only feelings of destruction and servility rule, there is an immense distance. If we examine the truth coldly, if we examine the Mexican people without any prejudice—their nature, their tendencies, the circumstances in which they are gathered, the conditions of the country they inhabit, etc.—it will be necessary to acknowledge, against what *La Libertad* claims, that in Mexico a certain sweetness of character, a certain pride and independence dominate, which are very far from the ferocity and servility gratuitously supposed of them.

The narrow limits to which we have to confine ourselves do not permit us to enter into details as we would like, but we will make just one general observation. Only with difficulty can a people present itself that live in more anarchic conditions, in which the authority has lost more of its prestige, in which political passions ferment more actively; and nonetheless only with difficulty also can a people be seen in whom revolutions offer fewer repugnant and bloody episodes, very common, unfortunately, in nations that boast of being more civilized. This simple observation proves sufficiently that the Mexican people are not at all like the figure our colleague sketches of them and that they are worthy for this reason of something more than arbitrariness and despotism.

In sum, we believe the democratic party must not lose sight of the ideal that forms its standard and must work constantly so that it maintains unharmed the rights the Constitution consecrates, for that will be the only way the nation will regenerate itself; that is to say, that it will emerge from that abyss of traditional servility that fortunately is not now so profound, thanks to the constant publicity of the visionaries, as our colleague imagines.

La Libertad wants us to refute the interpretation the Supreme Court has given to Article 5 of the Constitution under the triple historical, constitutional, and philosophical points of view. It seems to us that, without the need to rise to the region of unintelligible abstraction, what we have said before and what we add now clarify our thought, which is limited to the idea that the interpretation cited opens the door to the abuse of authority and that it nullifies, for that reason, a precious guarantee, without which we can say that the conquests of the reformist revolution are worth nothing. Our colleague seems to indicate that the absolute observance of said article makes impossible the army, the municipality, and the penitentiary regime; this last we do not understand, but as for the first, we will say simply that, far from sharing in the opinion stated, we have the opposite opinion, for we harbor the innermost conviction that the day in which Article 5 might be a practiced truth, we will have a genuine army and a genuine municipality. Our colleague will then see if we will sustain the observance faithfully.

We hasten to conclude, because we have expounded at greater length than we had intended. It has seemed to us, nonetheless, that we had to offer the fundamentals of our opinion, making known at the same time those points on which we differ from the colleague who impugns us. We do not know if we will have made a bad interpretation of the ideas of *La Libertad,* but to the degree we believe ourselves to have understood them, it seems to us that we depart from very different points and that it is difficult, for that reason, for us to understand each other. Our program is clear, simple, well specified: to reduce to practice the precepts of the Constitution, to respect without restrictions of any type the rights it consecrates, attacking without respite all tyranny, whether it takes the historical character or whether the scientific. Civilized peoples have secured the liberties they enjoy in the shelter of those principles; this is what we desire for our *patria.*

J. M. Vigil

3

Bulletin of *El Monitor,*
September 3, 1878

Our esteemed colleague at *La Libertad* has replied to the response we made to him, saying that he had as his objective to stimulate this debate over the basics of the new interpretation that the Supreme Court of Justice has given to Article 5, basics we have left intact. We will, of course, give an explication: If it is a matter of discussing the reasons the Supreme Court might have had for its new interpretation, which are found in the explanatory part of the ruling with which we concerned ourselves in our Bulletin of the twenty-second of last month, we believe we have said enough to support our disagreement without, until now, having been attacked directly by *La Libertad* or by any other periodical we know. Consequently, we did not believe nor do we believe it opportune to linger over what we have since then expressed; however, we needed to follow our colleague on the ground he himself had chosen, which, strictly speaking, produces the same result.

The question *La Libertad* has raised is much more important than the one that might have been maintained in the strictly constitutionalist sphere. The discussion of Article 5 comes to be a secondary matter in the face of the critical meaning our colleague develops and that has as its objective the Constitution of '57 itself and even the institutions that govern us. It would be useless, for that reason, to linger over simple details when the debate must rise to a higher sphere into which we will go with enthusiasm, although always having to collide with the narrow limits to which our pen is constrained to confine itself.

La Libertad begins by giving us a description of that *old* liberal school, whose mission, it declares, is worn out; that school is the one that believes . . . but our colleague should excuse us for quoting the following passage from an excellent article by M. E. Caro, inserted in the *Revue de*

Original title: "Boletín del *Monitor,*" 3 de septiembre de 1878. Source: *El Monitor Republicano,* September 3, 1878.

deux Mondes of November 1, 1875,[1] in which, between parentheses, *La Libertad* can find a profound examination of the scientific theories of that new school called to replace, as it is claimed, the old liberalism, and of which it appears to have constituted itself champion. Well, then:

"Radical democracy," says Mr. Caro,

> is essentially rationalist; it is that in its origin, in its history, in its principles; it is an application of pure reason; it goes out from the absolute and returns to it; it rests on the a priori of certain ideas that do not come from experience, of certain axioms whose character and origin it would deny in vain. It is truly the child of Rousseau; it was born with the *Social Contract*. Still today we see it accept, without discussion, the terms in which Jean-Jacques has set forth the problem: "Find a type of association that depends on and protects with all general strength the person and wealth of every member, and for which each one, joining together, does not obey, nonetheless, anything but himself and remains as free as before." If there is a problem of social geometry, this is certainly it. With Rousseau, this school establishes that sovereignty resides in the general will and laws are nothing but the authentic acts of this will. With it is established in principle that the will of all people is infallible, that no portion of it can be delegated or alienated or subjected to another sovereign. With him, it believes in the equivalency of all the members of the city, of their equal right to participate in the expression of the general will. It believes, finally, like him, in the original goodness of man, which cannot desire more than the general good, except in situations in which its reason goes astray from lack of knowledge or prejudices, which it is necessary to combat at all costs and uproot at whatever price from the Republic.

With the fundamental principles known on which rests the old liberalism, declared quite dead and buried by *La Libertad,* let us see what

---

1. Elme-Marie Caro (1826–87), a popular and fashionable philosophy professor, and later a member of the French Academy, was concerned with defending Christianity against modern positivism. Caro saw the rage and despair in which the French Commune ended as the logical result of the moral dissolution and indiscipline that prevailed in French intellectual life during the nineteenth century. (Editor's note)

this other scientific school is that is called to replace it and that rejects with horror the metaphysical dogmas, the laws, artificial, paying attention only to the facts, to experience, etc.

"The social classes," we continue translating Mr. Caro,

have been formed in each society in the same way and by action of the same law as the races in the heart of the species. Who would dare rationally complain about it? . . . By a series of strongly linked deductions, one manages to establish these two fundamental propositions: (1) There is no inequality of right that cannot find its reason in an inequality in fact; there is no social inequality that should not have and does not originally have in its point of departure a natural inequality. (2) Correlatively, all natural inequality produced in an individual, established and perpetuated in a race, must have as a consequence a social inequality, above all when the appearance and establishment of that inequality in the race correspond to a social need, to an *ethnic usefulness* more or less enduring.

This is enough to see that there can be no point of contact between the two schools, and it pleases us that our colleague acknowledges and recognizes it as such. In effect, what can a theory that denies everything the democratic school affirms, "the absolute of right, the absolute of equality, the absolute of liberty, and the need to remake man immediately on the standard of these three absolutes," have in common with the democratic school? For where can a doctrine that proclaims liberty, equality, and right for everyone come into contact with another entirely aristocratic doctrine "that entrusts everything, the integrity of rights, the direction, the initiative, and the highest of all the functions, that of progress, to the privileged classes"?

We understand now the great disdain with which our colleague, from his scientific point of view, regards the Constitution of '57 and the guarantees it sets out. If our people are backward, if they are incapable of practicing the liberties the fundamental law grants them, the remedy is very easy: take those liberties away from them, give them a legislation appropriate to the needs of their backwardness, sacrifice the individual to society, and *lynch* the criminal, "setting aside the judge and the Constitution."

But why are we wasting time on so little? "Logic has terrible requirements"; let us condemn once and for all what those old liberals call victories of the revolution, those to whom the great misfortunes we are suffering must be attributed, let us return to the privileged classes or, if one would prefer, to the colonial epoch. But for a backward, ignorant people like ours, who do not understand liberty nor are capable of practicing it, the most suitable regime is the paternal government of the friars, the humanitarian Laws of the Indies. Are privileged classes desired? There is the clergy that at least had an ideal to offer to the disinherited classes and inspires in us, for that reason, less antipathy than the learned men who aspire to constitute the aristocracy of the future republic. It is necessary not to linger on the road, nor is politics reduced to the arid ground of criticism acceptable.

No one more than us recognizes the deplorable state of our society; but what is the remedy? Take a step backward under the pretext of putting the law into harmony with our practical needs? And on what foundations would such a reaction be brought about? Will we suppress the popular suffrage, which is nothing more than a farce? And then who would govern and with what qualifications? Will we establish a military dictatorship like that of Santa Anna in his last epoch? Will we suppress all the *artificial* rights set out in that Constitution that "has never been observed," and will we deliver society to the arbitrary will of a supreme ruler? It seems to us that a school that proceeds *scientifically* must have specific and categorical solutions for all those problems, and we desire with longing to know them, not so much to satisfy our curiosity as because the nation will be shown the correct road that will lead it to its well-being and on which the very contented people will continue because they will find the means to satisfy their practical needs.

While that happens, we will continue using our rhetoric so that that Constitution that is not observed is practiced; so that the defects observed in it can be reformed, always in the liberal sense; and above all, so that the rights set down in it might be profoundly respected by the petty sultans who exercise authority in the name of the people.

Our colleague considers this an unrealizable dream. We think it is the result we must achieve on pain of death; it is a question of values that time will be charged with confirming. Our colleague gives primary importance to the facts; we subordinate them to the ideal, which is the true reality. Our colleague has understood "that in a country, no matter how strong and great it might be, civil divisions cannot be prolonged indefinitely and that either the energy of good men imposes silence on the others or foreign domination imposes silence on everybody"; we think the same, with the exception that, in order for that energy to be effective, it must be exercised within the limits of the law and justice, because in the contrary case, instead of putting an end to internal discords, it will only prolong them indefinitely, because in the final analysis, every revolution expresses unknown rights that try to realize themselves in facts. In sum, we believe that a state not based in justice, and justice for all, is a building that rests on false foundations that must collapse unfailingly; and that to sacrifice individual right to the common good, according to the theory recommended to us, is the sure means of opening the door to tyranny, for as Madame Staël very correctly stated, when once it has been said that it is necessary to sacrifice right to national interest, it is very close to narrowing from day to day the meaning of the word "nation" and to make of it first its partisans, then its friends, then its family, which is nothing other than an honest term for designating oneself.

4

Bulletin of *El Monitor,* September 6, 1878

Reading an article with the title "Truths," published by our colleague *La Libertad* in its issue the day before yesterday because of the defense we have made of the democratic party and the constitutional order, has caused us profound pain. We say that that article has caused us profound pain not so much because of the question itself, but because we see in it a revelatory symptom of the devastation that, in the spirit of the greater part of our studious youth, certain doctrines have caused, which, with scientific ostentation of very debatable value, tends to extinguish everything there is of greatness and importance in the human soul, reducing us to a brutal materialism, which, to be realizable, would bring us directly to tyranny and barbarism.

It is sad that persons of intelligence and courage like the young author of the cited article, in whom the call of faith and enthusiasm should blaze to signal to society in its days of conflict the dawning of happier days, let themselves be crushed under the weight of a fictitious realism, and instead of maintaining the sacred fire transmitted by the martyrs of democracy and justice, conclude by opening their breasts to the icy inspirations of a pessimistic philosophy, scoffing at the idea of right, treating as dreamers its altruistic champions, and pronouncing these horrible words that surround an impious paradox: "Now we are going to try a little tyranny, but *an honorable tyranny,* to see what results it produces."

We are not surprised, moreover, by this type of moral contagion that makes the best minds ill and debilitates and degrades the noblest characters. This is a common phenomenon of the great social crises that nations suffer in their days of trial. In epochs of disorder, of anarchy, of derangement, in which all ideas are confused, all rights shipwrecked, in which injustice and force take possession as absolute owners of human

Original title: "Boletín del *Monitor,*" 6 de septiembre de 1878. Source: *El Monitor Republicano,* September 6, 1878.

destinies, men like Machiavelli and Hobbes spring up, who proclaim the philosophy of evil, who convert pessimism into a system, and who put at the service of their false and destructive theories all the resources and all the subtleties of their dialectic. It is not surprising, then, we repeat, that when we go through a period of social anxiety and political dissolutions, when we see ineptitude exalted, cynicism deified, corruption and immorality triumphant, somber doctrines like those of Schopenhauer and Hartmann find an echo in generous souls, which, deeply affected by the present ills, see as of the essence what is only a passing accident, and judge as the definitive fate of the people what is nothing more than an episode in its long historical peregrination.

Let us try, nonetheless, by means of our small strengths, to face that new enemy that presents itself and that has, of course, the advantage of being supported by a reality whose ugly nakedness we do not claim to conceal. The matter is worthy of being discussed, and we will need to go into details even at the risk of going on longer than we wanted.

Our colleague begins by stating this maxim which we accept in all its breadth: "There is no greater teacher for nations than experience," and then adds by way of commentary, "whereas no matter how good the teacher might be, his instruction produces no fruit if the student does not wish to learn; thus, experience, as hard as it might be, serves for nothing certain people who pay no attention to the terrible lessons they have received." This observation, true in general, deserves, nonetheless, a small corrective.

It is not accurate that some people stop paying attention to the lessons of experience; for that it would be necessary that they find themselves on a rung lower than the beasts. Between the ill that experience makes evident and the will to remedy it are often interspersed causes that will inevitably develop, no matter what the effort; but from this it cannot be deduced that the people scorn the lessons of experience, nor much less that they follow lovingly the ill that experience has exposed.

Our colleague is surprised at first to see that "after half a century of constantly battling for an ideal that *once realized* has produced only unfortunate consequences for the country, our notable men still insist on putting it into practice . . ." Will our colleague *La Libertad* have the kindness to tell us when and how that beautiful ideal has been realized and how, from its realization alone, the country has harvested unfortunate consequences? Only a few days ago the same periodical told us that the Constitution has never been observed; and if this is so, what is that beautiful ideal that, to the country's misfortune, has been realized? Let us listen a little and perhaps we will learn it.

The surprise of our colleague is changed into profound sadness in seeing that, "with the atrocious wounds that the revolutions and civil war have inflicted on the Mexican Republic still bleeding, the *revolutionary ideal* still finds those who defend it among us, and that writers of worth who, in the course of its existence have witnessed the constant ruin toward which the *patria,* victim of those revolutions, travels, speak as one of those did yesterday in *El Monitor,* of the *rights of the revolution,* unknown rights that attempt to be realized in facts." Here we have to make various explanations and corrections, for our colleague seems not to have understood our thought sufficiently, a result, perhaps, of our not having expressed ourselves with sufficient clarity.

Of course we make a profound differentiation between the great democratic revolution and the insurrections and shameful disturbances that, although they have taken the name of revolution, have served only to dishonor it. We must distinguish, moreover, between the democratic ideal and revolution used as an instrument to destroy the obstacles opposed to the triumph of that ideal. Thus it is that, speaking with precision, there is no revolutionary ideal, because revolution is a means, not an end; nor could we defend the disturbances when, with obstacles overcome and democratic principles achieved, only its taking root and development have been lacking, things that cannot be attained except by means of peace and respect for law.

We have said that every revolution, and we request of our colleague that he watch carefully the meaning we have given, indicates unknown rights that are trying to realize themselves in facts, and we believe we have stated a truth; but that is an idea entirely different from those claimed *rights of the revolution* whose defense is attributed to us, for neither does the revolution have rights, because it is one thing to mean and another to have, nor could we defend such rights, which in the sense that our colleague gives them are for us genuine crimes.

After having brought upon itself such unfortunate confusions, *La Libertad* gives free rein to its eloquence, making a caricature of the rights that the democratic school proclaims and defends, giving itself a bit of permission to identify them with the abuses and crimes that violate them. It speaks to us of the widow whose spouse died on the fields of battle in defense of an ideal he could never understand, of the hacienda owner who saw the property that gave bread to his children set on fire, etc., arguments that, referring to the genuine revolution, have the same value as the reproaches reactionaries have made to insurgents because they did not win independence without shedding blood.

But then is added as an apothegm: "After sixty years of making revolutions, the political and social condition of the Mexican is the same, with slight difference, as it was in the beginning." Yes, in effect, it is the same, with the slight difference of being very distinct. Does our colleague now see how bad we are? Well then, neither he nor we wish to be *as in the beginning,* and the reason for that anyone who takes the trouble of leafing through a little of our history can know.

"None of those rights," continues our worthy adversary, "has been realized in facts"; then the ills we suffer cannot come from those rights, and this luxury of declaiming against a thing that is yet to be realized is useless. "The facts are there in plain sight," continues *La Libertad,* "the complete ruin of the country, the paralysis of all sources of wealth, arbitrariness ruling imperiously under the mask of liberty and right." Magnificent! Our colleagues should exclaim, given that what rules is tyranny, which has all its preferences against that cursed right that causes it such a bad outcome.

"I would like to ask," says our attacker, "those tireless defenders of the right of the revolutions" (this is not directed to us, because we have never defended such a right, nonetheless we will attempt to answer), "if, given that *all* men, *individually,* have the right to sacrifice the *patria* as they please" (we are unaware who has granted to *all, individually,* that barbarous right), "the *patria* would not have in its turn the right to defend itself as best it could against its enemies" (undoubtedly yes, even against tyrants, who, according to the sense of *La Libertad,* seem to be the best friends of the *patria*), "if the good of the majority is not more worthy of being paid attention to than the whim and caprice of a few" (here we must differ from our colleague: provided that those *few* do not belong to the privileged classes), "and if the most brilliant idea lodged in the head of a dreamer is worth more than an hour of well-being of an entire people" (let it be understood that here one is not speaking of pessimistic dreamers but rather of old liberals). "Rights! Society rejects them still; what it wants is bread." Society is quite right since it has been persuaded that bread and rights are incompatible and, as in order to eat bread it is necessary not to have rights, it follows logically, according to our colleague, to reject the second in order to obtain the first . . .

"This singular claim of our dreamers, who want the people to suffer, resigned and even content, all the ills that befall them, in order to have the sweet compensation of being governed by a Constitution that is incapable of satisfying any of their desires . . ." And who are those stupid or evil dreamers who, convinced that the Constitution is the sower of all the ills that befall the people, want the people to suffer resigned? Our colleague has to prove two things: that the Constitution is incompatible with the happiness of the people, and that we liberals want the people to support it despite that fact. Both seem difficult to us but, in the end, we will see.

La Libertad concludes its article with these words which, frankly, we cannot take seriously: "We have now realized an infinity of rights" (keep in mind that earlier it has been said to us that *none of those rights have been realized*) "that produce nothing more than misery and discontent in the society. *Let us now try a bit of tyranny, but* HONORABLE TYRANNY" (this is something like our saying, "honest criminal" or "civilized barbarism"). "It will produce evils" (is it possible? an attempt *in anima vile* can be used by science) "no greater than those our constitutions and our rights have caused the country." (Notice that it speaks of the constitutions that have not been observed and of the rights that have not been realized in facts, although later it says otherwise.)

Decidedly, either our colleague has tried to joke or the blackest misanthrope has confused its clear intelligence. Apart from this, we believe that, from the analysis we have made, it will be seen that our colleague has confused all the ideas, has fallen into the strangest contradictions, and has attributed to us the most singular propositions. We suppose, nonetheless, that this time we will have been more explicit and that, in the future, if the debate continues, it will be on more established foundations and on clearer and more definite ideas. Be that as it may, we can say for now that what *La Libertad* so pompously called *truths* cannot be more than gratuitous affirmations, risky deductions, unsustainable paradoxes, and deplorable forgetfulness of our history and of the legitimate aspirations of Mexican society.

5

Bulletin of *El Monitor,* September 10, 1878

Two of the worthy editors of *La Libertad* have taken as their task opposing us, or better said, refuting the principles of a school beloved by us, this last consideration being the one that makes us continue the polemic begun; for were it only about our person, we would cede the ground with pleasure to such worthy writers, but because this matter deals with an interest of the greatest importance to the country, we consider it a duty on our part to continue along the road our adversaries themselves have set out.

We will have to note, of course, that between the two editors of *La Libertad* to whom we referred, deep contradictions exist that we will not attempt to explain, much less reconcile; but it is indeed necessary to bear in mind in our respective responses because, it being impossible to reduce them to one single point of view, it is inevitable for us to appeal to different categories of reasoning. This, so far as it can be understood, always produces its difficulties and obstacles, but finally we will endeavor, as best we can, to play the double role that has been imposed on us.

In effect, while on the one side tyranny is praised as the loveliest form of government (!) to which we might be able to aspire; on the other it tells us that democracy "is the only possible government, because it is what provides greater expanse to individual development." While, on the one hand, every ideal is condemned, those who harbor it being treated as dreamers; on the other, having a *higher* ideal than the revolutionary school is affirmed, which would signify being more of a dreamer in the language of the former. Finally, on one side, even the *word* "right" is condemned as a sort of satanic invention that has served only to cultivate the misfortunes of the country; on the other, it is prophesied that "a

Original title: "Boletín del *Monitor,*" 10 de septiembre de 1878. Source: *El Monitor Republicano,* September 10, 1878.

431

day will come when the constraint of the moral law in the human spirit will replace all positive laws and the state will be reduced to its functions of protection, that is to say, to administer justice," something that, frankly, seems to us to cross the boundaries of the most fantastic dreams. But in the end, be this as it may, as we said before, once we respond to the *truths* of *La Libertad,* we are now going to say some words about the article that the periodical itself addressed to us on Thursday the sixth of this month.

When we, in answering, made use of Mr. Caro's magnificent article in order to make manifest the profound disagreement within the liberal school, called revolutionary by our colleague, and the new positivist doctrines, it was very far from our intention to turn ourselves into defenders of all and every one of the words of the famous French writer. We wanted to point out the antagonism that exists among the ideas both schools profess, antagonism our colleague has acknowledged, apart from this and disagreeing with its European coreligionist, that in accepting the new creed, they have not renounced the old democratic denomination. We will not linger, then, on "the three absolutes," a phrase which, incidentally, although our colleague may strictly be philosophically right, our colleague is mistaken, nonetheless, in the sense Mr. Caro used it, so that it is neither a war of words nor absurd to speak of three truths with reference to three ideas even when we know very well that, metaphysically speaking, there is no more than one truth.

We can say the same thing of the surprise he shows, imagining that we have enrolled in the sect of Rousseau. To establish that the democratic school is essentially rationalist, that it is the child of the philosopher of Geneva, from whom it has retained many principles, and that it has arisen with the *Social Contract,* is simply to assert a historical truth, without that fact signifying that the school referred to accepts in every way the theories and applications of Rousseau. It would be to go too far, and a subject better of a book than a periodical article, to examine the relationship of the political ideas that form the creed of modern liberalism. It is enough for our purposes to note that even though we are admirers of the French Revolution, and recognizing the immense services that it lent to the liberty of peoples, we are very far from sharing the ideas regarding the state that were dominant at that time. A classical conception derived from the doctrines contained in the *Social Contract,* in which, on the other hand, individual right was not sacrificed so completely, as is seen in these words: "the establishment of liberty would be bought too expensively if it cost the life of one single man." Our colleague, in his hatred for metaphysical principles, which we already know of him, manages even to make a sad commentary on the words of Caro, assuming that the tendency to remake man *on the type* of right, of equality, and of absolute liberty is to wish to establish *absolute* liberty, equality, and right; fashioning on this mistake a series of fantastic rationalizations, he tells us that "these dogmas [he calls thus the principles established a priori] to which one does not come by experience are not, cannot be, the object of *human science; they are the object of faith,* [?] which is the most personal that exists beneath the sun, and consequently the most variable, the most irreducible that there is." That must be a very wise philosophy that nonetheless does not recognize one of the immanent tendencies of the human spirit, the transcendental, which it obeys despite itself, making an obvious contradiction, as we have seen before, and expanding in a thoughtless way the domains of that *faith,* with its personal, variable, and irreducible character.

Coming to something more concrete, *La Libertad* formulates in three paragraphs the foundations of the school which, in its judgment, is called to replace the old liberalism in Mexico. If we are not mistaken, such foundations are just so many other dogmas of faith, following the language of our colleague, because those established laws that lay down rules for the development of society are a purely subjective concept like social evolution, invoked as it seems to suppress all movement of revolution or reaction; and as one does not come to those dogmas through experience, inasmuch as experience demonstrates the complete opposite, it follows that our colleague has given "the sea as a foundation for a pyramid."

According to that doctrine, right has no other foundation "than the principle of *utility* with respect to the progressive interests of the human species, and progress being the result of the growing activity of each individual, it is the *duty* of everyone, expressed in the law, to facilitate the development of this activity." This is what is called *individual right.* Notice that here the utilitarian principle of Bentham seems to be established as the foundation of right; that is, it brings us to the full morality of interest. This means that, fleeing from metaphysical principles, we are going to end in egoism, which, making use of the phrasing of our adversary: "is the most personal that exists beneath the sun, and consequently the most arbitrary, the most variable, the most irreducible there is."

"The function of the state," it continues, "consists in protecting those *rights,* this is what we call social justice. But as the state *is,* whatever might be its form or legal appearance, *a product* of the sentiments that prevail in a society, to the degree to which these sentiments are more antisocial, let us say, the state has to be *more conservative,* the authority more vigorous, to prevent the dissolution of the national group, in which case *individual right must yield,* and has yielded and will always yield in order not to perish."

If we are not mistaken, here it is claimed that, when in a society antisocial sentiments dominate—that is to say, sentiments that do not facilitate the development of individual activity—the state, which is nothing more than the product of those sentiments that thus attack the right of the individual, must be more vigorous in order to repress the very sentiments of which it is the product, in which case it must yield individual right, which, as it appears, it was trying to protect. That doctrine, thus understood, seems to us illogical, and we hope, in order to formulate our judgment, it might be explained to us a bit more.

As we distinguish between the absolute type and its relative realization, we do not understand the contradiction one claims there is in the constitutional power of suspending guarantees. We said much the same with respect to the baseless affirmation by which we defended the Constitution *such as it is.* No, colleague, we acknowledge, and have acknowledged, that our fundamental law has defects, and we maintain for that reason the necessity that it should be reformed, but that this be by the means that it itself indicates and according to the needs experience designates. This will explain to our worthy antagonist that we have not thrown out individual right from ill will toward the system of the friars. The provision to which the colleague refers is of a purely transitory character, which will disappear sooner or later when the institutions no longer have anything to fear from the communities suppressed by the Laws of Reform.

La Libertad assumes that the democratic party, to which it attributes a permanent revolutionary tendency, has wanted to reduce its principles to positive laws by means of violence; that this happened with the Constitution, to which we owe the fact that it is not practiced; "and that there is in reality another Constitution in force, *the only one that a people in the condition of ours can have,* but that, because in contradiction with the written law, it leaves a wide space for arbitrariness and despotism."

In this our colleague proceeds in accordance with the false idea that has been created of the democratic party, a matter over which we will not linger because we have already started to treat it separately. We would certainly like to be told which might be that other constitution in force that conflicts with the written law, and inasmuch as our colleague possesses the secret of the laws that lay down the rules for the development of social groups, we would also like our colleague to explain to us what it is that makes an idea, political or social, able to conquer the obstacles in opposition to it, and which might be the people happy enough that, without need of jolts or revolutions, have effected great reforms by responding only to social evolution.

Very far are we from defending the horrors of the guillotine and tarring; but we can certainly say that pausing to lament the disasters to which humanity is subject without taking into account the wealth produced from these disasters is to be ignorant of the condition of humanity. It is always curious to see the partisans *enragés*[1] of the experience, the untiring detractors of the metaphysical principles putting themselves in opposition to the experience of all the centuries and reforming the world from the depths of their office by reason of laws and formulas discovered through a single rationality, giving in this way "the sea as a foundation for a pyramid."

Finally, we anxiously await the consequences extracted from the premises that have been made known to us, and how it is sought to reduce them to practice and formulate them into law. No one more than we deplores the state in which we find ourselves, and if our colleague has found the way to appease all ambitions, to guarantee all rights, and this with neither shocks nor unrest nor bloodshed, we will be the first to put ourselves at its side, joining our poor efforts to that great work of closing forever the gates of our country to civil struggles. But no tyranny, no dictatorship, no *lynching,* is that not so?

---

1. Fanatics. (Editor's note)

6

Bulletin of *El Monitor,*
September 18, 1878

In the very moment we are writing these lines, cannon shots, music, and rapidly pealing bells announce the celebration of the sixty-eighth anniversary of Mexican independence, an unforgettable date in the annals of liberty because it commemorates the first efforts of a people who, from the depths of the most profound abjection, when everything conspiring to rise up against the established power should be described as foolish, did not weigh the magnitude of the task they were undertaking, but rather, obeying the voice of their conscience, threw themselves into an unequal struggle whose outcome was, nonetheless, the triumph of the patriotic idea proclaimed in the town of Dolores the night of September 15, 1810.

We know well everything that has been said and that continues to be said against that famous movement and its old leader. Unfortunately for Mexico, since the first attempt at its emancipation, the hydra of discord reared its terrible head; the spirits of the sons of this soil were deeply divided, and from that instant it was easy to foresee that the struggle that was begun would then take on a civil character; that is to say, that interests rooted in the new ideas would begin to clash, among which emancipation from the Spanish metropolis was no more than a detail, even though essential and of the highest importance.

The flag hoisted by the powerful arm of Hidalgo hid among its folds an entire world of pleasing promises, an entire future filled with the most agreeable hopes. The people, and we construe this word in the sense of the disinherited classes, glimpsed, without understanding exactly what it meant, the prospect of a way of being unknown by them until then, in which they would enjoy liberties and rights whose possession had been kept constantly remote from them.

Original title: "Boletín del *Monitor,*" 18 de septiembre de 1878." Source: *El Monitor Republicano,* September 18, 1878.

This explains that murky and disorderly impulse that cast numerous and amorphous masses into the vicissitudes of a gigantic battle; at the same time it explains the panic with which the truly conservative interests, grounded in the privileged classes, contemplated such a storm. Those who considered that outburst an imprudent and premature attempt at emancipation, and even more, those who allege for it truly mean reasons, are deplorably mistaken about the significance of those great jolts that arouse societies in solemn epochs like the omens of profound transformations against which no human force can prevail.

The unity of thought that invigorated the Mexican Revolution begun by the venerable parish priest of Dolores appears throughout the years in the entire period that includes our contemporary history. Independence, the Republic, the Reform have been nothing more than so many other steps on the same ladder, stopping points on a single road the Mexican people have traversed in a straight line to arrive at securing those three great ideas synthesized in the idea of their regeneration.

For this reason, the liberal party sees in the insurgents of 1810 their natural direct ancestors, given that they and the constituents of '24 and the reformers of '57 and the defenders of independence in '62 constitute nothing more than a single political entity that, under different names, has been guided by the same idea and inspired the same goals. For the opposite reason, the current enemies of the institutions do not conceal their sympathies for those who, in the first decade of the century, supported the colonial regime with all their strength; who later accepted independence on the condition of perpetuating the predominance of the privileged classes; who, when they could not suppress the republican movement, contented themselves with centralism and military dictatorship; who, nourishing the illusion of establishing a monarchy, did not waver from provoking the most evil of foreign interventions; and who today, reduced to absolute impotence, content themselves with caricaturing the anarchy into which the liberal party has fallen as a consequence of the sordid ambition of some false democrats, and put themselves under the protection of some candidate of bad character who cherishes the crazy idea of creating a personal party that might raise him to the highest magistracy in a country fed up with suffering the results of ineptitude and immorality.

In vain one seeks to make some break in the parallel course followed by the two ideas whose clashes and simultaneous development shape our entire contemporary history. He who today condemns the democratic revolution, pointing to it as the efficient cause of all our misfortunes, he who dreams of a modification in the conservative sense for our institutions, must return to 1810 to condemn as criminal stupidity the undertaking of Hidalgo, Allende, and Abasolo, continued by Morelos and Bravo, by Guerrero and Iturbide, by Pedraza and Gómez Farías, and completed in our days by Juárez, Ocampo, Degollado, Zaragoza, and all the other leaders of the Reform, ultimate consequence of the idea proclaimed at Dolores.

But that anathema necessarily carries with it the complete and unconditional acceptance of the system that Calleja[1] and the high dignitaries of the Church supported and that, preserving deep down the same tendencies, was, with the passage of time, taking on the different shades of centralist, Cuernavaquist,[2] reactionary, interventionist, all names that are understood in the most general epithet of conservative and that, by their historical antecedents and their never-denied doctrines, will never be able to join together and be mistaken for the party that has kept the banner of Hidalgo elevated on high, banner that has always signified all liberties and all rights.

One sees, by what we have just said, that the revolution whose anniversary the Republic celebrates on September 16 has been a work of true social and political regeneration, that in each one of its advances, if it has sown the soil with the debris of some vexatious fear, it has also left a great conquest standing, that in its vitality and robustness has been able to resist the combined forces of its enemies, while these enemies have been abandoning little by little the terrain of which they were previously the absolute possessors.

Apart from this, the liberal party finds itself so closely identified with the existence and future of the Mexican people that its errors, its divisions, and its anarchy are what have brought about the deplorable situation the Republic is in today; that having lost its compass in the midst of the chaos where the mean aspirations of some false democrats have cast it, it sees independence threatened, the social edifice deeply shaken, un-

1. Félix María Calleja was a viceroy of New Spain who fought the insurgents. (Editor's note)

2. In 1834 a revolt was launched in Cuernavaca that ended the rule of the liberal vice president, Valentín Gómez Farías. (Editor's note)

able to perceive in the future anything other than the unleashing of all the evils that accompany great catastrophes.

But if this is a truth, as painful as it might be to acknowledge it, it is not less so that the salvation of the *patria* is based exclusively on the reconstruction of that party on its legitimate foundations, eliminating every spurious element, flinging from its breast those baneful personalities that strive only for their individual aggrandizement, even when to do so might make it necessary to sacrifice all principles and compromise the very existence of the Mexican people.

On this solemn day, when the rejoicing *patria* recalls with pride and gratitude the memory of its liberators and its martyrs, we make a formal appeal to liberals of good faith, to Mexicans in whose soul is preserved intact the love of the people to which they belong, that, whatever might have been the accidental denominations that have divided them in the last years, they unite in a single intention, that of saving the country, that of maintaining national independence, a very holy cause identified with the institutions that govern us, with the liberty they proclaim, with the rights they guarantee. Here is the only saving plank in the midst of the shipwreck that threatens us. Only force of will, energetic and unshakable, to commit itself to that intention of greatest social and political interest will be enough to quell all those criminal and ridiculous ambitions that stop at nothing in order to be satisfied, even at the cost of the ruin of the Republic and the destruction of our race. That effort, we repeat, will make the confidence lost today rise again, and the entire country will willingly accept all the sacrifices the circumstances require of it, because it will know that those efforts will not be made unfruitful by impure hands and base passions. Unification around this saving intention on the part of honorable and sincere liberals is the only way to provide a favorable outcome to the horrible crisis that we are going through and that, in the serious state to which it has come, no longer permits either going back or delaying. The work of Hidalgo will thus remain worthily crowned, and on future anniversaries of independence the liberal party will be justly able to pride itself on having saved, with its selflessness, the cause of the *patria* and of liberty.

7 Bulletin of *El Monitor,* September 27, 1878

One of the facts that has characterized the current administration has been a marked tendency to favor the old reactionary party, summoning many of its men, to whom it has entrusted positions of greater or lesser rank, and even placing them in the legislative bodies and in the tribunals and courts of justice. What is the thinking that has determined that policy? What is the objective the government has put forward in setting out that plan of management? What is the intention of the individuals who enter into the service of an administration that, although in name only, declares ideas diametrically opposed to those that form its politico-religious creed? The question is serious and worth the trouble of being examined, although it might be in the briefest possible way.

We must, of course, show that we are not among those who believe that, in order to be liberal, a necessary condition is not to have religious ideas, and we are so far from thinking that true Christianity is opposed to democratic opinions that, on the contrary, we find in the first the fundamental foundations of the second. In this sense we recall that when it was a matter of constitutional affirmation, we maintained that it did not conflict with the religious beliefs of any person, and we considered as a partisan weapon the great hullabaloo that was raised then by conservative periodicals. Time has proved us completely right, given that today the ecclesiastical authority has permitted the affirmation to the Constitution and Laws of Reform to be accepted, dispelling in this way the scruples that so distressed the timid souls.

We must also show that, considering the conservative group simply as a political party inasmuch as between it and the liberal party we find only disagreements of this nature and not that conflict of religious ideas

Original title: "Boletín del *Monitor,*" 27 de septiembre de 1878. Source: *El Monitor Republicano,* September 27, 1878.

that some attempt to set out, we have not considered it impossible that the conservative group, yielding to the demands of the times, might modify its exaggerated tendencies and accept the constitutional order sanctioning the Reform, the conservative group might renounce the abstention to which it has confined itself since the downfall of the empire and might begin to fight openly on legal ground. Although this has not been completely realized, it does not appear to us that the day is far off when we might see it, given that now a considerable number of old conservatives appear in political posts of greater or lesser importance, which equates to accepting an order based, as it is said, in the Constitution.

We must show, finally, that the liberal party does not belong to the number of those intolerant exclusivists who systematically keep men who profess certain political or religious ideas out of all participation in public matters. Here, nonetheless, we have to make a necessary distinction. In the matter of posts, we find a great difference between those that are tied directly to the development of political ideas that form the program of the government and those that are purely administrative. It is clear that we, professing the principles of the liberal party, will not support for the former posts any but men who have a perfectly clear and defined democratic character, and we will never concede our trust to an enemy of the institutions, even if he is flexible enough to consent to play the role of liberal.

We consider this point so sensitive that, even dealing with the diverse factions of the republican party, we find it neither strange nor reprehensible that governments surround themselves on the first line with men of their circle who inspire in them more confidence because of their intelligence, their honor, and their personal loyalty. To attack a government as exclusivist because the ministries, for example, include individuals identified with the leader of the executive branch in political principles and on the course he proposes to carry out is the worst kind of weapon, which simple common sense condemns.

The same does not happen with respect to other branches of the administration where the political ideas of the persons have no influence. Individual opinions, party commitments, should not in any case be preferred to honesty, ability, industriousness, and education. Good public service, the demands of order and morality, impose on governments the duty of seeking the most suitable persons to occupy the posts without making merit consist of ideas, often purely theoretical, that those who seek to ingratiate themselves profess. We will not say anything about those whose naming is popular in origin, because assuming that they should be perfectly free, that the authorities must not control them in any way, it is understood that both the liberal and the conservative find the way clear to attain them by means of the formalities established by law, and they cannot be the object of censure by an administration that knows how to fulfill its obligations.

These general ideas, which in our judgment are the most acceptable in the matter with which we are dealing, are very far from having been practiced by the current administration. One of its first acts, on the triumph of the revolution,[1] was to dismiss en masse all the old employees, proceeding immediately to fill the vacant posts with individuals who earned its special consideration. The letter of convocation that was immediately issued for the election of authorities, both in the federation and in the states, was so full of restrictions that it could have been summed up in this article alone: "Only Porfirian revolutionaries can elect or be elected." The scandalous pressure that since then has been exercised on the popular vote has ended by demonstrating that the most intolerable exclusivism is the most pronounced feature that, among others, distinguishes the current administration.

One cannot find in a principle of lofty policy, in a noble inspiration of impartiality and resolve for good public service, what it has done in recruiting from the ranks of the old reactionary party the many servants who figure in the Tuxtapecano government. What can be, then, that predilection for the traditional enemies of democratic doctrines? Why that unjust preference with discredit and offense to honorable liberals who have consecrated their entire lives to the defense of the institutions? This, to our way of thinking, has only one explanation, and it is the following:

The enthronement of the circle that dominates today never signified the triumph of any idea or political principle. The partisans themselves of the Plan of Tuxtepec have described it in the end as an unrealizable absurdity, so no one now takes seriously the promises contained in it. Personal interests, poorly veiled with a disguise of liberalism, are the

---

1. The 1876 Revolution of Tuxtepec placed General Porfirio Díaz in power. (Editor's note)

only motive that can be pointed out clearly and resolutely in the midst of the anarchy that envelopes the current administration.

In such circumstances, it is natural that one seeks, not men of strict principles who do not accept violating them easily, but rather those who, enemies of such principles, regard with pleasure their vilification and disparagement and happily cooperate in the ruin of the institutions, because they could not prevail against them fighting them face to face on the field of battle or in the terrain of politics.

No one is more fitting to help in this liberticidal undertaking than the faction traditionally opposed to democracy and the Reform. There the little Caesars can find all the elements necessary to realize their work of regeneration; there the men are who, because of an episcopal permission, have no obstacle to accepting that tremendous affirmation that, not very many years ago, constituted one of the most serious and terrible mortal sins. To produce chaos, systematically undermine the institutions, try to introduce into society the feeling that the Constitution is impractical, that this people is not made for liberty, that democracy is an odious farce, preparing in this way the road to a dictatorship, here is the only idea released in the midst of this confusion and this general unhinging that seems produced deliberately by men who should march with a firm step along the path of the law, securing the glorious conquests of the Mexican Revolution. The congeniality between the current administration and the conservative group does not admit another explanation, given that neither the intolerant exclusivism of the first nor the tenacious intransigence of the second would have permitted them to draw near to one another were it not that a point of contact existed that might link their contact and unite their efforts.

8 | Bulletin of *El Monitor,* October 22, 1878

Our esteemed colleague *La Libertad,* taking personally a paragraph of our bulletin of the sixteenth, pauses to explain its opinions in the article entitled "Idealism," about which we will in turn say some words, having first to offer a little clarification.

La Libertad finds it strange that we have abandoned the field of discussion that we maintained not very long ago; in this there is some inaccuracy. As will be remembered, the polemic was initiated by our colleague because of one of our bulletins; we responded, it replied to us, we responded again, and then it replied to us a second time in two articles by two different editors of said daily, taking the question in two entirely different senses; for our part, we answered the two opposing replies separately, and our double answer received only a single response. We believed it then appropriate to remain silent, both to await the other answer, which has not come, and because in the response it had given us we seemed to notice a certain humorous style that made the polemic truly degenerate, for although the spirit of our rival pleases us greatly, we find it out of place in a question as serious as the one upon which we have touched.

One sees by this that it was not exactly we who abandoned the field of discussion, because if we did not again address *La Libertad,* it was because of the attitude assumed by our attackers. Apart from this, no polemic must cross certain bounds because it would run the risk of becoming interminable; with rationales expressed from both sides, in which each supports its respective opinion, it is appropriate to end the debate, letting the public pass judgment, for otherwise it will only continue to incur innumerable repetitions, making the discussion take on the character of an angry altercation.

Original title: "Boletín del *Monitor,*" 22 de octubre de 1878. Source: *El Monitor Republicano,* October 22, 1878.

Our colleague laments that we have not understood its political ideas, confusing "the aspiration to establish a strong government with conspiracy against public liberties." But what is it that *La Libertad* understands by "strong government"? What sort of political form does it expect when it makes the Constitution, with the rights and guarantees it grants, the constant object of acerbic criticism? Even now it says that "the consciousness of the duties and rights of man and citizen does not exist in the great majority of the people," and further on it adds that a reform of the Constitution in the conservative sense is necessary.

From this one deduces that what *La Libertad* wants is for the government to be strengthened at the expense of the liberties and rights of man and citizen or, what is the same, that those rights and those liberties be reduced to the benefit of the governmental authority, and this is what it calls reforms in the conservative sense. It is claimed nonetheless that in operating in that way, it is because it is desired "that the country acquire the practical use of public liberties," believing that the opposing theories, that is to say the theories of those of us who support maintaining the Constitution, will necessarily lead the country "to an abyss from which it will surely not emerge except to fall into another that is deeper."

Our colleague throws in our face for the hundredth time our empiricism, our absolute lack of practical spirit and scientific method, in sum, our idealism, metaphysical, as it has done in calling the opinions constitutionalist. Might *La Libertad* permit us to say to it that, because of a rare contradiction, it is falling into the very faults that it attributes to its opponents, as it is easy for us to prove in a few words.

To suppose *possible* the reform of the Constitution in the *conservative* sense so that the country might acquire the *practical use* of public liberties is a paradox that good sense rejects and that demonstrates the most complete lack of practical spirit and scientific method. The word "conservative" has a double meaning, the literal and the political; which of them does our colleague take it to be? In the first, we the constitutionalists are the true conservatives because we try to preserve the fundamental law, the political institutions that govern us, and whatever innovation is made to alter these institutions at their foundation cannot properly be called conservative because the ideas of preserving and destroying mutually exclude each other. In the second sense, we have no need to say a word; everyone knows what, among us, the party called conservative wants and claims so that it might be able to reconcile its theories with the practice of public liberties.

On the other hand, to suppress constitutional liberties in order to broaden the sphere of a strong government, and this with the purpose of "the country acquiring the practical use of public liberties," is so contradictory and absurd a theory that the flight of the loftiest metaphysics cannot reach it. To suppress liberty in order to acquire the *practical* use of liberty is to condemn the individual for many years to the most complete inaction so his limbs might be developed and strengthened; it is to enclose him in profound darkness so he might acquire perspicacious sight; it is to deprive him of all instruction so he might become a learned man of the first order. Now we are not surprised by the story of the student who, as Calderón de la Barca tells it, not knowing how to swim threw himself into a pond and, having been on the verge of drowning emerged from there protesting that he would not again go into the water until he knew how to swim.

In the course of such contradictions, which reveal neither a very practical spirit nor a very scientific or logical method, the idea constantly arises that that pitiless mutilation of useless liberties because the people do not know how to make use of them, and that creation of a strong government as if the ilk were unknown to us, have as their objective saving society, putting a brake on anarchy, protecting all legitimate interests profoundly threatened by disorder and immorality. Here indeed appears empiricism in its full development, the complete absence of all practical spirit, of all scientific method, etc.

To entrust the solution to the great problem troubling Mexican society to purely political innovations is absolutely not to see what is in front of our eyes, it is not to live in this world, it is to go off one's rocker.

Let us suppose that the conservative theories of *La Libertad* have been realized; that we now do not have that jumble of useless rights and guarantees; that in place of that shallow prattle of the periodicals, fruit of the useless liberty of the press, we have a gazette of a half sheet each month, as in the time of the viceroys; that the authority can make use at its will of the lives of Mexicans; that all those idle formalities have been set aside that serve only to encourage criminals, and one imprisons and shoots without ceremony; finally, that we have a political regime adequate to the needs of our people as they are depicted. Does our colleague believe that it has now obtained the supreme good of peace and happiness of the nation? Does it believe we have entered into that ideal era of concord and tranquility, leaving everyone content in his place, the entire society gathered around that strong government, venerable model of the familiar father of the peoples, who distributes rewards and punishments to his obedient subjects in accord with his *good will?* If it believes all that, its idealism is incurable and we need to present to it the reality of what would be.

That retrograde evolution, because it cannot have another sense, that *La Libertad* seeks would be the beginning of a period of horrendous calamities for the country, because we would see begin again, in great proportions, the fratricidal struggles that have bloodied our soil, and the only result they would produce would be to precipitate the final dissolution of our unfortunate society. But let us grant for a moment that the new order of things succeeds; what would happen? We would see ignorance and brutal force take possession of the situation, the most opprobrious tyranny would touch the furthest extremes, and we would watch one of those repugnant and ridiculous spectacles, because it is beyond doubt that the men who will play the lead role in the tragicomedy would not have the stature of a Caesar or a Cromwell. Is this what *La Libertad* wants?

Let us acknowledge the truth: the evils we suffer and the still more serious ones that threaten us neither come from political questions, nor can a radical remedy be sought in them. Let us exploit our sources of wealth, let us stimulate work, let us offer a wide field to activity, to honesty and intelligence of all the inhabitants of the country, and we will see change, as if by magic, the scene that surrounds us. Then *politics* will cease being an office that everyone wants to exploit, because it will cease being synonymous with the mania for public employment. Then the authorities will fulfill their duties, because they will not see themselves under constant pressure from those who want to topple them in order to avail themselves of the post into which they enter exclusively and with rare exceptions to make money, because they know that sooner or later they will be put to one side so that others might come to do the same. Then the elections will be free, the selection falling to the most worthy because popular representation will cease being a sinecure for whose fulfillment neither science nor conscience is required. Then, finally, the complete opposite of what happens now will happen, because the social circumstances will have changed, and men, it is necessary not to forget, work according to the circumstances in which they find themselves.

This is what must be done. Toward this end, effort must be directed without provoking conflicts, without occasioning new complications, as would happen irremissibly if in some empirical way one attempts to modify the institutions for the reduction of liberties that are in no way responsible for what is happening. To do otherwise is to yield to the impulses of an ugly and contradictory idealism, because there are also ugly idealisms; it is to be made an instrument of preconceived judgments, seeing evil where it is not, basing the solution where it does not exist.

To conclude, we will say to our esteemed colleague that if it wishes to continue this discussion, we beg it to explain to us the scientific method it has followed to deduce scientifically the conclusion that the ills that oppress Mexican society come from the institutions that now govern, and that the way to end those ills is to destroy said institutions, or, what is the same, to reform them in the conservative sense. For our part we commit ourselves to demonstrate that it is not in the political order that the radical cure of our suffering should be sought, and that, on the contrary, it is to make these sufferings deeper and more injurious, detracting in this way from the questions. We believe that, with the point of the debate reduced in this way, we will be able now to understand each other and will be able to proceed in full knowledge of the issue.

9

Bulletin of *El Monitor,* October 26, 1878

The article in which *La Libertad* responded to our bulletin of the twenty-second has caused us true disappointment because, while we were hoping our colleague would explain to us the scientific method it has followed to deduce scientifically that the ills overwhelming Mexican society stem from the institutions that now govern and that the way to put an end to those ills is to destroy said institutions, all we encounter is the repetition of words and vague concepts that have been expressed to us since the beginning without our moving forward a single step in the debate. We have reason to believe that the discussions should not go beyond certain limits.

The *qualification* we placed on the word "conservative" was not a scholastic pedantry, as *La Libertad* seems to indicate, because in every debate it is highly necessary to establish the significance of words; and so much has that qualification not been useless, that we already know our colleague does not belong to any of the political entities that have existed and exist in the country, for it is not liberal, because in the hands of this party liberty has been a myth, nor conservative either, because those who are called such are incapable of strengthening order; rather it constitutes a third type that goes neither backward nor forward, that likes neither revolutions nor reactions, but rather "to conserve the social order, the only means of acclimatizing liberty."

Our colleague probably believes after this that it has said something; to us it appears that it has said nothing, for the vagueness of its ideas amounts to this. "To conserve the social order, the only means of acclimatizing liberty" is a truism of Perogrullo[1] that nobody denies or places in doubt. For what! Is there some party that has tried to destroy the

---

Original title: "Boletín del *Monitor,*" 26 de octubre de 1878. Source: *El Monitor Republicano,* October 26, 1878.

1. "*Verdad de Perogrullo*": to be patently obvious. (Editor's note)

social order? We do not know of it, at any rate; and from the most re-calcitrant conservative to the most exalted liberal, no one will hesitate to accept our colleague's opinion. One sees, then, that on this point nothing new is said to us, nor have we advanced a single step.

But this is not the issue. "To conserve the social order" is a truth be-yond discussion. What we need is to be told the means of conserving that order. Here is the difficulty, and this is what we have wanted our colleague to specify for us, for the method of our esteemed contradictor is on a par with that of the physician who, called to cure a sick person, declared himself completely satisfied with pronouncing to him the great principle that what he needed was good health.

Let us see, nonetheless, if some effective prescription is furnished to us to "conserve the social order." Before, we were told that the means of attaining that attractive outcome was the creation of a strong govern-ment; now such a thing is denied, and it is affirmed that "neither a letter nor a syllable of *La Libertad* authorizes such an assertion." We have read, nonetheless, in the issue of the seventeenth of this month, "the idea of a *strong government* endowed with abundant means of action, placed by the law itself in a wide sphere of power, does not necessarily presuppose *tyranny*. . . . There, where greater liberty exists, that *force* of public power becomes even more necessary. . . . The idea of a strong government not only does not imply a reactionary spirit, but rather, on the contrary, it can be sustained with success by the sincerest defenders of public liber-ties. . . . There, where the individual can enjoy a great amount of liberty, is exactly where the public power must have greater vigor. . . . Most par-ticularly this can be said of Mexico."

One sees by this that some tittles and bits exist that give license to the assertion that our colleague bases the solution of the problem on the creation of a strong government. Now the opposite is said to us, and the following shot, with which we are in total agreement, is launched at that kind of government: "The authors of social panaceas disgust us, and never have those who speak of the prosperity of a people by virtue of infallible means, kept in enchanted bottles, seemed to us anything but charlatans."

Very good, perfectly good. But then, "what is the practical way to make this condition disappear?" Let us listen to the colleague who has been charged with asking and responding itself, "Adapt individual right to the conditions of our existence, *invigorate the principle of authority,*

GIVE US A STRONG GOVERNMENT. What we want, then, with a strong government, around which the conservative elements of society can assemble, is to combat revolutions, to make them gradually impossible. From this, peace would come, and that certainly is a condition to realize material improvements, the only path that guides us to the solution to the problem." We have, then, the solution already, although it must be understood that it does not belong to social panaceas or to infallible means kept in enchanted bottles, and despite the fact that, some lines above, it has been said to us that neither a word nor a tilde of *La Libertad* authorized the assertion that it might have entrusted the solution of the social problem to the creation of a strong government.

Next, this extraordinary question is put to us: "Do we have here some sin against the scientific method, that is to say, against experience and reason?" Yes, we say, there is a sin, and a very great one, and it consists in that that solution resolves nothing, because to a vagueness, "to conserve the social order," are presented three other vaguenesses: "adapt individual right to the conditions of our existence, invigorate the principle of authority, give us a strong government." All of that will be very good; but we do not find it very scientific to establish commonplaces whose discussion would be entirely useless, making a point that neglects the only one that should be the object of debate: the means by which to realize the great outcomes that are preached.

Let *La Libertad* be aware of the truth: the ground on which it has placed itself is unsustainable. Gratuitous affirmations, general principles, abstract maxims—this is all we have encountered up until now in what can be called its political program.—Constitutions should be appropriate to the needs of the peoples;—no one denies such a truth.—Our Constitution is not made for the people of Mexico;—and from what is such an affirmation deduced? Where are the scientific data on which it rests?

Let us suppose, nonetheless, that that were true; what is offered to us in its place? Where is the Constitution or the scientific regime that presents itself to resolve all problems, to calm all ambitions, to dissipate all errors that have complicated the situation to an unbelievable extreme? A strong government! And what does a strong government mean? A government that does what it feels like doing, that has no law to which to subject itself, that applies its will arbitrarily in the sense that seems best to it? Invigorate the principle of authority! And how to realize that phenomenon when the authority is the first to bring about its own discredit with its ineptitude, its lack of respect for society, its little tricks, and its mean intrigues in which nothing grand or elevated appears.

That kind of compromise, which *La Libertad* dreams of realizing, is a true paradox: between the conservative reaction, with all its old attributes and traditional habits, and constitutionalist liberalism, with its aspirations for progress, there is no middle ground. The first, the conservative reaction, is not now possible; the great interests it defended have been destroyed, the ideas it represented have lost all their influence. There remains, then, only the liberal party, which, if it wants to save the situation and return to its political mission, has to become attached to the Constitution, advance with it, be inspired by its spirit, reform it if desired, but by means that it itself indicates.

We also wish to conserve the social order; we wish to extirpate forever the revolutionary fever that devours us and that no longer has any reason for being. But those exactly are the very powerful motives that make us sustain at all costs support of the fundamental law, because we have the innermost and profound conviction that the first injudicious step taken against it will be the signal for a new civil war that will end by annihilating the few elements that remain to us, by casting shame and infamy on the name Mexican, seriously compromising national independence.

This is what makes us insist tirelessly on sustaining the constitutionalist idea. If, unfortunately, the current government pays attention to the doctrines of *La Libertad* and other periodicals that produce antiliberal propaganda and tries to make a *scientific* attempt to strengthen itself, attempting to adapt the rights of the Mexican people to the needs of their existence calculated by its criteria, we would see the drama in which President Comonfort was the lead actor played out in greater scope, with the difference that the conservatives of today could not offer, to the one who will try to follow in that person's footsteps, either the pecuniary elements or the social and political influence the conservatives of that epoch had. *La Libertad* should study a little our history and our situation rather than being preoccupied with what is being done in France and Spain, for it can very well happen that what might be conservative there would be turned into revolutionary here, and we are sure that it will come to concede scientifically to our side, for as is very well said, it is now time that we arrive at the age of reason, and we should not go amusing ourselves with dangerous games, because it is no less a matter than the public peace and the existence of the nation.

Otherwise, convinced of the uselessness of prolonging any longer the present discussion, which only led us to countless repetitions and rectifications, let us call an end to it, hoping that our colleague will become convinced by the experience that the road it has taken is not the one that can lead to the fulfillment of its desires.

10

Bulletin of *El Monitor,*
October 30, 1878

We have noted that a certain antagonism frequently establishes itself between the guarantees the Constitution grants to all inhabitants of the Republic and the needs of society to ensure citizens the enjoyment of their life and their interests, even managing to attribute to the first some protection of evildoers, in seeking to find the source of the exceptional growth criminality has come to acquire among us. Nothing can be more false or more dangerous than that rationale, as it is easy to become convinced by examining the question a little.

The force of the argument consists in saying that the law protects wicked persons because once the authority has apprehended them, the formulas of a protracted legal action are followed, while the man of good will, who has been the victim of the criminal, has nothing to defend him against the blows of the criminal, who proceeds ceremoniously to commit his misdeeds. It seems, according to this, that the ideal of justice would be for society to adopt with evildoers the very conduct they observe, applying punishment with rapidity and unusual lack of forethought.

Nonetheless, if one pauses to think that the guarantees have been established precisely to protect the man of good will, one will readily see that the argument collapses of its own weight, and that, far from seeking, in the suppression of the protective formulas that should surround all criminal justice, the means of attacking disorder and immorality at its root, it will succeed only in creating a great number of innocent victims, on whom the consequences of unjust proceedings would often weigh heavily.

It is unquestionable that society is highly interested in the suppression of criminal offenses, in their punishment, in their eradication;

Original title: "Boletín del *Monitor,*" 30 de octubre de 1878. Source: *El Monitor Republicano,* October 30, 1878.

but inasmuch as this latter is not possible, all their forces should be directed to seeing that the punishment being administered carries, as far as human weakness permits it, the characteristics of strict justice, so that the guilty one might suffer appropriate punishment for the crime he has committed, because everything that might depart from this principle is to commit a true iniquity, which must be avoided in any country that boasts of being civilized.

But in order to attain that objective, two things are absolutely indispensable: the identification of the person of the offender and the substantiation of the deed imputed to him, with all those circumstances that can increase or diminish his guilt. Well then, this will never be obtained if it is not by means of a series of procedures, more or less drawn out, that our laws, inspired by a lofty philosophical spirit, have established.

The investigation of a criminal deed always presents extraordinary difficulties that cannot be overcome with the speed that would be desired. The individual on whom an accusation of that type weighs tries, as is natural, to defend himself as far as his strengths allow, confusing the inquiries of the judge, mocking his wisdom, trying to erase or corrupt all traces of his crime, with the goal of hindering as much as possible the imposition of the punishment he deserves. In such a case, a singular struggle is entered into between the accused, who appeals to as many means as his intelligence suggests to him, deeply spurred on by an interest so important to him, and the unyielding course of the judge, who follows the trail of the crime, taking advantage of the slightest evidence to establish with precision the deed he is investigating and bring to full light the innocence or guilt of the accused.

Is there in this something to reprove, something to censure, as long as the functionary charged with the lofty mission of administering justice fulfills the very important charge entrusted to him? Definitely not; but will it not be to offer protection to criminals, giving them occasion to avoid the punishment or, at least, not receive the ideal punishment they deserve with the timeliness that the victims and society in general are right to demand? In no way; because as we have said before, the objective of the guarantees is to protect the honorable citizen, who can become implicated in false accusations or be the victim of lamentable errors that would have subjected him to an iniquitous judgment if he did not have all the means necessary to prove his innocence.

It will be said, nonetheless, that the criminal can sometimes go unpunished, that, taking advantage of all the resources the laws grant him and by force of cunning, will possibly free himself from punishment or, at least, that this punishment might be much less than what he justly deserves. It is true, but from this cannot be inferred in any way the need to suppress the protective formulas that accompany justice because of a preoccupation solely with the idea of harming the delinquent, even if by doing this it would be necessary to sacrifice the innocent, for in that alternative, philosophers and experts in public law have not wavered in establishing the principle that it is preferable that a guilty person be saved than that an innocent person perish.

When one pauses to think, on the other hand, about the fallibility of human decisions, when one brings to mind some memorable decisions when, because of a conjunction of fatal circumstances and despite all the scrupulousness that can be applied in the investigation of a crime, innocent persons have been condemned to death, persons whose innocence has come to be proven when it is no longer possible to undo the evil caused, a genuine anguish takes hold of the heart to contemplate the fate that would befall the inhabitants of a rather unfortunate country because, in it, ears will be closed to the wise principles of a rational legislation, making prevail, in the spheres in which only serene and impartial justice should predominate, the savage harshness suitable only to barbarous epochs.

If to this is added the special situation our country has, in which political passions poison everything, availing themselves of the flimsiest pretexts for carrying out terrible revenges, and when we see the disdain with which some authorities regard human life, leaving unpunished the crimes they commit against their political enemies, then one senses with absolute certainty how very cruel, how very dangerous it would be to suppress or even diminish the guarantees that protect the accused and that are violated with such frequency by the very functionaries who should be the first to respect them.

We are far from denying the scandalous increase that criminality has acquired in our country and the widely known urgency for adopting effective means to place a strong restraint on it, reestablishing the confidence with which, in every civilized country, peaceful citizens live in the protective shadow of a foresightful and intelligent government; but these evils we all deplore will not disappear in the way the enemies of constitutional guarantees indicate, but rather, on the contrary, they will assume greater proportions the day one appeals to those absurd and extreme means, leaving society in worse condition than it is now. Expedite at the right time the action of justice by means of speedier procedures, but do not forget the social objective of punishment or the natural means of defense the laws grant.

Everyone knows the causes that have produced the increase in crimes—crimes that deservedly have scandalized and struck fear into the entire Republic, and the only effective means that can be successfully employed to improve the situation are also known; but one will object that those methods are slow, and to cure the evil that exists requires prompt and active remedies. The first is the work of time and reflection, while the second is the urgent need to prevent present dangers, to root out acute ills that seriously threaten the most respectable and sacred social interests. We repeat, for our part, that we do not excuse the magnitude of the evil, but we deny and will always deny that violence can be advantageously substituted for reason and law and that it would be wise to flee from a hidden danger in order to throw oneself into an abyss, as would certainly happen if we managed to suppress completely the beneficial fetters legislation has established so that the punishment of evildoers might provide all its moral effects.

If one examines a little the elements that come together to create the current state of affairs; the sad conditions to which our people find themselves reduced; the multitude of deleterious germs disseminated in our social atmosphere; the ignorance; the abandon; and, above all, the misery in which the destitute classes find themselves, a feeling of sadness and bitterness will replace the indignation caused by the frequency of crimes that today have alarmed society, and will make gazes focus a little higher instead of wanting to impose without mercy the iron and the fire on the cancer that is devouring us. "He who commits a crime to increase his riches," says Mr. Pastore, "and he who, unfortunately, lacking bread for himself, for his wife and his children, determines after long struggles to demand the nourishment without which all will die, have not committed an equally guilty deed. . . . The crimes that arise from corruption are the most vile; those that the passions produce are the most dangerous; those that arise from misery the most excusable."

11

Bulletin of *El Monitor,* December 17, 1878

Knowing a few of the most important facts about our history, their intimate relationship and their social and political significance, one must acknowledge the inevitable necessity for the Reform, as well as the fact that the Reform could not have occurred except in a revolutionary manner.

That the clergy had been the principal obstacle to the nation being constituted in the form of government most appropriate to its circumstances is a fact no one can deny without contradicting the evidence. The conservative party, political incarnation of the clerical idea, was the one that inspired in General Santa Anna the coup d'état of 1834, first offense against the legitimately constituted authorities, that opened the door to the civil war, initiating the most turbulent period of our history.

In reestablishing the Constitution of 1824 in 1846, it was found that that law could no longer satisfy the demands of the situation, for it was understood that it was necessary to move forward, to overcome resolutely the difficulties that prevented consolidation of peace, to enter fully on the road of a radical reform that would nullify forever the elements of the party that had openly declared itself the enemy of the nation's peace and liberty.

From this comes the division in the heart of the liberal party into purists and moderates, for while the first, knowing completely the situation and its demands, wanted to proceed immediately to set about the great work of regeneration, the second, more timid, postponed resolution of the problem, believing that an evolution could be slowly effected, that avoiding disastrous jolts would result in the consolidation of democratic institutions.

Original title: "Boletín del *Monitor,*" 17 de diciembre de 1878. Source: *El Monitor Republicano,* December 17, 1878.

The clergy itself undertook to make evident the chimerical quality of this ideal that left nothing to desire in the field of philosophy but was entirely impractical on the terrain of facts. The audacity of the clerical party in overthrowing the administration of General Arista and creating the despotic dictatorship of Santa Anna persuaded those who were most deluded that conciliation was not in any way possible with a faction that stopped at no means to realize its goals, and from that moment it was necessary to begin a struggle without quarter, leaving clearly established the alternative between reaction and reform, between the clerical and the progressive idea, without middle ground and without any means of negotiation.

Such was the character the struggle assumed until the revolution initiated in Ayutla in the first months of 1854. The provisional administration of General Comonfort, despite the moderate character of that leader, marks a period of transition, very worthy of study, toward the new era that would end with the Reform. Each one of the measures taken in that temporary period shows the general tendencies to the conclusive solution that was in the conscience of all liberals.

The Constituent Congress, meeting in 1856, encouraged very enlightened discussions that touched the entire nation; nonetheless, despite the very advanced principles set down in the Constitution of 1857, the last word has not been spoken, for great events are never brought to completion except through more or less slow preparations that make the opportune moment finally arrive.

It was the clergy itself that took charge of hastening that moment. Trusting in its moral power and wealth, it believed it would be easy for it to destroy its antagonist, and instead of accepting agreements that might have delayed its fall, it rejected with the greatest insolence all those measures that tended to diminish its influence, and while in the press and in the pulpit the most inflammatory protests and the most violent polemics persisted, in Puebla, in San Luis Potosí, and in other parts of the country, threatening insurrections broke out against liberal institutions in which torrents of Mexican blood ran.

In the midst of that immense disturbance, discussion and approval of the Constitution were completed, it being immediately solemnly sanctioned; but the clerical labor continued more actively than ever, managing in the end to ensnare in its nets the chief of the nation himself, who, forgetting the serious obligations he had contracted, executed a coup d'état and delivered to the clerical reactionaries the considerable resources the government had at its disposal.

But the work of the democratic revolution was already too far advanced for retreat to be possible. The states faced the reaction in possession of the capital of the Republic. The national government took refuge in Veracruz and entered into the struggle of three years, during which the clergy exhausted its resources, not sparing any means to destroy its antagonist and subdue the nation.

Then, in the midst of the heat of combat, the Reform pronounced its final word, proclaiming the great principles that would now make possible the existence of a government in Mexico, destroying forever the disorganizing element that had brought so many days of sorrow to the *patria*. The nationalization of ecclesiastical wealth, the separation of church and state, with all its consequences, were the result of that tremendous struggle that, during three years, stained the territory of the Republic with blood.

Can it be said, after this, that the work of the Reform was premature and violent, that it was one of those inopportune convulsions that could occasion ills without number, not bringing in exchange any positive benefit at all for society? Those who say so are either unaware of the history of the country or try to lead opinion astray, driven by base interests.

To criticize, on the other hand, that very important event because it did not provide a use for the ecclesiastical wealth that could have brought the nation one or another advantage in a determinate direction, is not to understand the nature of the revolution in which one sought, above all, to destroy the weapons of a powerful enemy, creating deep interests that can oppose it, and making it impossible for the wealth to be recovered, as would have happened had one kept it entirely.

Nationalization had two objectives, one political and the other economic, and both were attained completely, for at the same time it stripped the clergy of its most powerful weapon, which it had employed so harmfully against the country, nationalization was successful in releasing that immense wealth, putting it under the control of individuals, and consequently making it more productive for the general benefit of the nation.

Apart from this, the Reform so satisfied the most imperative needs of society that, when the foreign intervention took place and the empire was born in its shadow, both devised by the clergy to recover its wealth or influence, the clergy had the most bitter disappointment, for the new order of things, established under such unfavorable auspices, let the Reform remain, protecting it well from coming into contact with the powerful interests it had created.

And this was in the nature of things; the intervention and the empire understood at first sight the essence of the matter, and they could not, if they aspired to create something lasting, reestablish the obstacles that had been destroyed at such cost and against which they would have had to collide if they had managed to establish an administration that would function with complete order. Because, we repeat, the Reform was not a matter of political format, but rather one of those fundamental matters that affected the very existence of society, that above all needed not to live on borrowed time, not to remain subordinate to hostile powers that changed it completely at the hour it suited their interests to do so, not to permit, in sum, that it remain a state within the state, an *independent and disorderly sovereignty* within the great national sovereignty.

What has been said is sufficient so that, historically and politically speaking, the cause of the Reform remains justified, the Reform against which formidable tempests have been raised in vain, not having been able even to touch the very firm base on which it definitively rested from the moment of its appearance. The Reform was not one of those unconsidered and premature steps that compromise the peace of nations for the simple desire of trying absurd theories, but rather the saving measure of the Republic that cut out the cancer that was destroying it and put the "this far and no farther" on the unfortunate power that had erected disobedience and rebellion as a sacred doctrine and that, with its words and its actions, had shown itself to be incompatible with the peace, order, and progress of the Mexican nation.

12 | Bulletin of *El Monitor,*
December 27, 1878

We have seen that the principal author of our public misfortunes, the one that kept the country submerged in civil war and anarchy for many years, the one that slackened every principal of authority, providing the example of contempt for the laws and the functionaries charged with executing them, was the clergy, whose antipatriotic conduct will present it before the tribunal of history as the one greatly responsible for the woes that weigh heavily on Mexico. We have seen also how its unwise conduct precipitated events, ensuring that its power would collapse in the midst of its terrifying cataclysm. Now is the time to examine the effects that such events produced on public morality, so that this will help explain to us the situation in which the country remains and the great amount of work it has still to do in order to get through its difficulty if the instincts for its own preservation rise above, as we expect, the dissolving elements that endlessly fight against it.

To put this matter in its true perspective, it seems to us opportune to remember the astute and wise observations that a Mexican of great talent made in 1836, when the clerical party had just destroyed the institutions, regarding the state of public morality in our country during those times. Those observations constitute a precious revelation that gives us the key to the fundamental problem whose solution we must strive to find at all costs. Here is how Dr. Mora expressed himself on this important topic:

> Among every people in which social duties are confused with religious duties it is almost impossible to establish foundations for

Original title: "Boletín del *Monitor,*" 27 de diciembre de 1878. Source: *El Monitor Republicano,* December 27, 1878.

BULLETIN OF *EL MONITOR*, DECEMBER 27, 1878 : 463

public morality. Sins and crimes are by their very nature things of
different orders, although many or most of man's actions have this
double character at the same time. Society must recognize as crimes
only actions that, properly so-called, are infractions of laws that disturb the social order begun and established by them. Religion considers, and must consider as sins not only actions, but even the most
hidden movements of the soul opposed to divine precepts. Society
must be, as a general rule, inflexible in the punishment of crimes,
even when the repentance of the criminal and his resolve to mend
his ways are clear. In religion, on the other hand, from the moment the sinner sincerely repents, he is pardoned, whatever might
be the evils that have resulted from his sins, which many times will
not be in his own power to repair. The result of these different aspects under which religion and society consider man and his actions
is that the speed and means by which these powerful agents have
an effect on him must be entirely different, and when they are confused, there must necessarily be in one, in the other, or in both, a
disorder very detrimental to the religious and political moral order.

At once the author makes clear that the confusion that had disappeared completely in Europe still existed in Mexico and that the masses
were convinced that political and civil duties received their only force
from religious sanction.
Then he adds:

As, on the other hand, these same masses do not have a fundamental knowledge of the religion they profess nor are capable of dis-
tinguishing the opinions of the clergy from religious duties, they
confuse the ones with the others, they believe themselves obliged to
do blindly whatever the priests or confessors order them, and they
believe themselves dispensed from social duties when a minister of
worship in the public exercise of preaching or in the confessional
gives an opinion on it. From this state of things, it results that the
force of the laws depends on the opinion the clergy forms of them,
and as this can be mistaken sometimes and other times is contrary
to what said laws prescribe, it is clear that, on the one hand, a thousand pernicious errors will be incurred regarding social duties, and,

on the other, society will have to receive its strengths from an alien power that, sometimes with reason and other times without reason, will not be disposed to lend it and it will be negated.

When this happens, men who, in the infraction of civil laws, see only an *offense against God* because the clergymen tell them they are not, in conscience, obligated to carry out the civil laws, nor are such offenses against God in the infraction of civil laws, they become angry at the civil laws and at the legislator who has imposed unjust obligations on them, and then they rise up if they can, and if not they elude civil laws by subterfuges that those who proceed thus in bad faith are accustomed to making. The clergy, it is true, does not establish as a maxim or general principle that it is lawful to disobey the authority or its laws, but in fact it reserves and exercises the power in individual cases of *giving its opinion,* in the classroom and the confessional, on the validity or nullity of such and such a law or on the interpretation of its meaning, and as such, an *opinion* is a true rule of conduct for the one who requests it or receives it; when it is not in conformance with the law or the authority, the law is undermined in its primary principles and authority in its fundamental foundations.

As the clergy is a corporation made up of men, as these men live in society, and as considered individually or as a *civil* corporation they can demand a reform also *civil,* because the force of the laws depends on them, it is clear that, even when the reform is assumed necessary, as it will be and has been many times by the acknowledgment of the men themselves, the government will not have the means to carry out the reform, because the laws that stipulate it will be considered unjust and their execution an act of tyranny.

The clergy, then, will always weaken the action of the government in all its judgments, whether they are adverse or whether indifferent to their interests, just for the fact of being the only creator and regulator of social duties, and because there is no political conscience that, like the religious, establishes the need to carry out those social duties. But not only the government, the individuals will also have to suffer, and a great deal, from this lack of political conscience. Why is this so? Because the clergy will convert into social duties not only *purely* religious precepts but also practices that cannot be considered obligatory even in the *religious* order.

The author then sets out some consequences deduced from such pernicious antecedents, like hatred for dissenters in the *matter* of religion, the double intrigue of the clergy teaching one thing in the classrooms and universities and inculcating in the masses practical errors that have made them confuse religion itself with vain and superstitious beliefs. "With this double intrigue," he adds, "the ravings of the multitude are sustained as religious principles and the discredit that could result to the body from conveying as religious principles those that are only popular errors is avoided. In sum, one is the religion taught in the schools by the books, and the other the one insinuated in practice in the churches."

Directly, we find this observation of profound and incontestable accuracy:

> The principles of morality are always overstated, and through theory or practice they are made to consist of obligations that transcend the common forces of nature; the people become immoral because, breaking the overstated principles, they dispense as easily with those that are not overstated, and the society that easily functions without the overstated principles cannot exist without those principles that are not overstated. For that reason there are no people less law abiding than those that establish more austere principles as a rule of conduct, because the number of violators increases in the same proportion as difficulties presented by their observation arise. Well then, this happens and must happen to all peoples among whom the clergy is the exclusive teacher of morality.

The preceding quotes have seemed important to us for various reasons: because they portray with admirable accuracy the state that public morality had some years after independence; because they show the pernicious influence exercised on the Mexican people by the clergy; and, finally, because it is necessary to know those antecedents in order to form a complete judgment of the current situation. This knowledge provides the explanation for our revolutions and of their inevitable consequences, and it will temper a little the indignation that seethes in some breasts before the spectacle of our woes and that overflows in invectives against the Mexican people.

In effect, when a people like ours has been systematically led astray by those who have the mission to guide and moralize it, it is necessary, to be just, to direct the censure with all its bitterness not on the people who has been the victim, but rather on the teachers of perdition, on the false apostles who, inspired by the spirit of sordid ambitions, did not hesitate to corrupt the religious principle, to poison the fountains of private and public morality. When this is known and seen, feelings of a very different nature have to clear the way, and if there is a place for admiration, it will not be for the many woes that exist among our people, but rather for the few goods that have been able to survive that violent shipwreck of all the wise principles of order and morality that preserve and protect human societies.

EMILIO RABASA

Emilio Rabasa (1856–1930), born in Chiapas, was a jurist, novelist, diplomat, journalist, and historian who opposed the Mexican Revolution. During the Porfirio Díaz era Rabasa was governor of Chiapas. After Díaz fell he supported the coup of Victoriano Huerta (1913) and agreed to enter the diplomatic service. He spent the years 1914–20 in exile but later returned to Mexico. A "new" liberal, Rabasa believed in a liberalism based on scientific politics drawn from positivism and rejected the abstract doctrines of natural rights. His emphasis was on a strong, centralized, yet constitutionally limited authority. Rabasa's main work is *La Constitución y la dictadura,* a theoretical and historical indictment of the 1857 Constitution. He argued that by making governance impossible, the Constitution had condemned the country to de facto dictatorship. While the amount of power concentrated in Juárez's hands had been unsurpassed, Rabasa claimed that he used such power vigorously and successfully to fulfill his high purposes.

We present two chapters from *La Constitución y la dictadura.*

1 | The Election (excerpt)

I

When an adolescent first becomes aware of what a popular election is and the goal it has, the idea presents itself to his spirit in its simplest form; it is like a revelation of justice that seduces him and wins over his will. The idea is annoying mainly because of its simplicity, the simplicity of the immaculate theory. On the eve of the election, each citizen reflects on the individual most suitable for the position with which the election is concerned, rejects some, puts others aside, chooses, and classifies until fixing his preference on that one who combines the greatest talents and offers the most because of his civic and private virtues. How could one not do it in this way, when good judgment affects his own interest and error his own liability? When the hour of action arrives, the citizens file in before the ballot box, depositing their ballots; the inspectors read and count; the president makes the numbers known and proclaims the one elected by the people. Nothing more just, nothing more natural, nothing more simple.

Although this idea assumes a great number of virtues in practice, much greater still is the number its consequences assume. The innocence of the adolescent, developing the theory of government emanating from the people from the theory of election, believes that each elected person, already virtuous in himself, feels the force of public opinion, simultaneously his strength and his menace, and he will be unable to be less than a zealous guardian of general interests and an active promoter of the common good. The man invested with the dignity that election confers on him and elevated by the delegation of popular power, which is the only legitimate power, divests himself of common passions, gets inspi-

Original title: "La elección." Source: Emilio Rabasa, *La Constitución y la dictadura,* chapter 10, in *Estudio sobre la organización política de México* (Mexico: Tipografía de "Revista de Revistas," 1912).

ration from justice, forgets or does not know from the beginning who gave him their vote, who rejected him, and, with only the fulfillment of duty and the subordination of his acts to the laws, he satisfies the broadest program of good in the government and equity in the administration. Thus it has to be; but if it were not thus, if, through an error very remote from the electors, the one designated by the majority should disappoint public confidence, the force of opinion or the action of the law put into practice will dismiss him from the post to replace him with another more worthy.

It is not an innovation that has need of proof that, as the peoples are less cultured, they resemble children more in their way of thinking. Between them they have in common a simple spirit without malice that, in good faith, falls into error and innocently produces failure in the individual and catastrophes in the peoples. Uniformity, for which an embryonic logic is sufficient, seems typical of the state of nature; children conjugate all the verbs as regular, and in new peoples, all political ideas are turned into syllogisms. The former would take us, if we would permit it, to the most solid *Esperanto,* as the latter have gone, whenever they have been able to dominate, to the most disastrous Jacobinism.

The way of conceiving of an election and calculating its consequences that we have shown in the adolescent is also the way of our people, the way of the limited part of the nation capable of perceiving its electoral right, if we deduct from it the very scant number of citizens with specific education who reflect on the problems of our political existence. The summary of this idea is contained in two entirely false suppositions: the first, that popular election is easily realizable; the second, that the actual election will instill order in the whole political organism. And if the number of those who, because exceptional, do not accept the first is very small to begin with, there are still among them many who believe in the extraordinary virtue of the actual election.

The common conception to which we first alluded produces, as a great error, serious consequences. If there is the conviction that citizens will carry out the election with order, with disinterest, and even with wisdom if only the liberty of suffrage is not obstructed, and that such an election certainly produces the public good, every intervention that obstructs that liberty must correctly be considered a criminal offense that has neither extenuations nor other explanation than the despotic egoism of whoever has the elements of force at his disposal. When, from a false premise, a logical inference is made, the legitimacy of the consequence gives to this consequence glints of truth sufficient to dazzle the common people, and the common people are the great majority. Any badly thought out and poorly written newspaper, generally a work of noxious tendencies, makes use of the logic of the consequences applied to principles invoked from the fundamental law in order to acquire, through the voice of anonymous writers on public affairs, because little known, greater prestige among the masses than the most sensible government with the greater proven patriotism. But as the false premise is nothing less than a constitutional precept that bases a right in the democratic system established by the Constitution, the accusations appear legally reasonable, however much satisfying them might bring the country to greater danger.

This situation causes the perpetual conflict between popular aspiration and the action of governments, which must be guided by needs rather than principles, because principles do not obey needs, nor were they inspired by the realities that in the end dominate in spite of all the chimeras. All revolts have invoked electoral right, seeking to base their action in the propensities of the masses and to cause the men in power to lose prestige; but all revolts, in becoming government, have responded to the supreme need for stability and have had to thwart the aspiration of the people, which, realized, would make national life impossible. As long as the people have the right to do what the government has the need to resist, the country will remain in a state of latent revolution, capable of showing itself in any moment of weakness in the organism.

It is useless to attempt the reconciliation of two contradictory extremes. For this reason all effort dedicated to calming the public conscience is wasted, that is to say, all effort to make the only true peace neither by election nor by repression. If, in Mexico, should there be an election realized by universal suffrage, the first concern of the government emanating from it (if it can endure) would be to prevent such a phenomenon from repeating itself, for universal suffrage is necessarily the enemy of all established government, the disorganizer of every ordered mechanism, because of a need that springs from the articles of our Constitution that created the incompatibility. As for repression, it can make peace but not constitute it, because something can be constituted even on a movable sediment provided it is permanent, and repression is a condition but not a substance, and this condition is, if one permits the image, the troubled result of two variable forces.

All the conservative elements of a society are on the side of the government that ensures order because they live from order; they prefer authority to the exercise of rights that, at most, would lead them to the tranquility they now enjoy without the need of securing it or putting it in danger. But the conservative elements, which are always found in the highest strata of the people, if they are excellent with respect to passivity and resistance, they are less than useless in the activity of political struggles, in which they have much to lose and little or nothing to gain. So general is this truth that, among people as intensely democratic and as broadly institutional as the North American, the electoral corruption that perverts the parliament and decays the tribunals is owed principally to the abstention of the higher classes who feign disdain to hide their egoism.

On the other hand, the appeal to right and to absolute truths, which are held out as ideals to arouse the people, move and exalt the conscientious majority, which lives on aspirations because the realities of existence make the impatient ones incline toward a new condition that always assumes better.

Here one discovers a new unhappiness: the social field is divided into two parts that should have the same interests and that do not collide in well-constituted countries, at least regarding the general idea of suffrage as a foundation for the stability of the nation. The remedy consists of making of the election not a threat to the order, but rather the foundation of security. In this way the conservative elements and those who proclaim the right will have a common interest in guaranteeing the suffrage. And as for the governments, they will have relief from duties when, proceeding from the election, they know that, in the popular suffrage, they find the release from many responsibilities and, in the strength of the parties, a solid foundation of support.

II

Far from being easy and simple, the electoral act is the most difficult step for peoples ruled by a system more or less democratic, or that aspires to that government. The honest and simple election we have assumed in the preceding section is impossible in any society, because in any human social unit, great or small, there are distinct interests that soon become antagonistic, fight to prevail, and come inevitably to dispute and struggle. When there are no opposing ideas of government, the interests that act are, at least, tendencies to put authority in favorable hands, and, lacking parties of programs, one arrives at parties of persons, which are fruitless for the good. The struggle of opposing interests does not occur without winning over partisans, convincing, seducing, imposing, and bribing, that is to say, denying to as many as it can the absolute and paradisiacal liberty pure theory gives them. Among the sought after, some resist because they have personal ideas, which are blank ballots in the dispute; others yield; the timid hide; the arrogant abstain; and the few who initiated or took the active and effective part of the movement have thus designed the political parties, although only in a temporary and transitory way. When the repetition of successive electoral events and the results of the government they establish characterize the ideas of both sides and define the limits of their propensities; when, in addition, the directing groups classify themselves and acquire a genuine individuality, each faction is a system and each system an organized party. Having arrived at this point, the ideal liberty of the citizen in the election is reduced practically to the liberty of choosing the party in which he would like to register and to whom he has to submit himself. He preserves the right to vote, but he has lost the right to choose.

The creation of parties is a necessity that arises from the nature of things; it is not an invention of ingenuity, but rather a natural and inevitable product of electoral liberty. For this reason, to invent political parties that are simply electoral, to arrive through them at the liberty of elections, is to claim that nature inverts its processes, and nature does not lend itself to such inversions. If the general principle that necessity creates the organ can still be doubtful, it is not doubtful that there is absurdity in creating the organ to produce the necessity for the function. The invention of the railroad would be impossible if commerce had not existed before; and in the social order, it is useless to create the Central American union, which, nonetheless, would be constituted spontaneously if Colombia or Mexico tried to absorb the five little republics by violence.

The works realized as a result of natural forces are impossible for human effort; the intervention of man is useful, in such cases, only to put natural forces in working condition. Thus, for example, if an elevated temperature is required for two bodies to combine chemically, it is useless to *force* the phenomenon, but this phenomenon will be realized inevitably if the chemist intervenes, heating the flask to make possible the action of the mysterious forces of the atom.

To create a party for electoral purposes in Mexico is pure political *dilettantism*. What is important is making the election possible, suppressing disruptive causes that make impossible the spontaneous action of social forces. These social forces are responsible for producing the parties, creating their mechanism for them, giving them movement, and arming them for the efficacy of their functions. The disruptive causes are in the very Constitution that one is trying to carry out and not in the governments that have always been blamed.

The organization of political parties in democratic countries is very complicated, even in those countries where it seems simpler, only because the weft of the thread is not immediately apparent at a mere glance during the election; and it cannot be otherwise, given that all uniform action of multiple and complex elements suppose subordinations and disciplines that are not acquired except by processes, established rules, recognized sanctions, and they require unity that necessitates directors and even almost renouncing personal ideas.

No organization has been created without an evolutionary process and without it being urgent for the operational need of the parties. Let us take the most characteristic, the one we, for powerful reasons, incline to imitate—that of the North American parties.

It is known that, when Washington retired from public life, the great lines of the two national parties were marked out: the Federalist (today Republican) and the Republican (today Democrat); the first, with Hamilton, aspiring to federal unity to give strength to the nation; the second, with Jefferson, defending local independence against an absorption dangerous to the states and to the lofty right of the individual. It is also known that these two elements, representing the centripetal and centrifugal forces that create balance in the system and that so marvelously served to constitute the nation on its constitutional principles, have managed to blur their differences when the federal equilibrium, definitively established, made them disappear as if by automatic action; but the life of the two parties remained as an integral part of the institutions, and [the parties] are maintained, despite the evolution that has come to blend their dogmas, because of the simple need to renew the power, with the primarily personal aims of their followers, but in the end, and above all, as indispensable wheels of the political machinery. So necessary thus is the establishment of parties for constitutional life!

In 1796 Adams and Jefferson were candidates of both parties by a spontaneous sentiment that did not require express declarations. Four years later, the then Republicans, unanimous in the candidacy of Jefferson, were not unanimous with respect to the designation of vice president, and to agree upon it, the deputies and senators of the party met in the first nominating caucus. This system continued without any great obstacle until 1816. In 1820 the nominating caucus of deputies and senators, which came under attack as usurpers of the right of the people, although it met, did not dare *nominate* a candidate; and in 1824 the one nominated came in third in the polls, which ended up discrediting the system. The system had to change, and so in 1828 the candidacy of Jackson was recommended by the Tennessee legislature and by meetings of the people, giving rise to the practice that, one year before the next election, conventions would meet, composed, for both parties, of delegations from the states; and for the same election, a convention of young people, accepting the nomination of the new national Republicans, adopted ten resolutions that constituted the first party *platform*. In 1836 only the Democratic party had a convention, but in 1840 there was a convention of both parties and the process was regularized. Bryce, whom we follow in this account, adds: "This precedent has been followed in all subsequent contests, so the national nominating conventions of the major parties are today as much a part of the regular political machinery as the rules the Constitution prescribes for the election. The establishment of the system coincides with (and represents) the complete social democratization of politics in the time of Jackson."

Forty-four years were consumed and twelve electoral exercises spent to arrive at the organization of the system that prepares each party and brings it into agreement for the campaign; this for a Saxon people who were preparing themselves for democratic life since before thinking about their independence. One sees, then, in what was just expounded, the complexity of the mechanism, and we have confined ourselves only to the presidential election, assuming the nominating convention created; but for the convention to meet, a mechanism prepared in each party is needed, and as, besides the deputies, the officials of the state, those of the district, those of the county, and those of the city must be elected, all of which put the mechanism into action very frequently, this requires having a permanent committee in every locality and a perfectly defined process, commonly practiced, better known even than the electoral laws of public order, so that the foundation of every election and, consequently, of every nomination of candidates might be the will of the primary electors.

The permanent committee convokes in each case the primary caucus, which in theory is composed of all citizens qualified to vote in the smallest electoral district. The primary caucus selects the candidates of the party as officials of their own locality and names delegates to gather in their delegation at larger electoral district conventions that include delegates of various primaries; this convention of secondary electors must designate candidates for higher posts of the state. But there is still more; the secondary convention has, at times, the task of naming new delegates to a third and higher convention, the national convention, which nominates candidates for the presidency and vice presidency of the Republic. Consider the complexity of this mechanism with all the details each stage requires, and bear in mind that the work begins in the meeting of the primary assembly, in which is discussed the right of each person in attendance to vote, his status as party member, his conduct toward the party in preceding elections, labors that provide occasion for the danger of fraud, bribery, the influence of the professionals to commence from the beginning, and the alienation of men of good faith who do not wish to expose their electoral district to such a game.

This system is not rigorously uniform in the entire country, but the local modifications do not alter its essence. It was not created, but rather was formed over a half century by experiences and efforts at accommodation. It is not an emanation of race, for all that the conditions of race helped its development, but rather a derivation of the vitality of parties. But the parties were started and strengthened because there was, from the beginning, respect for electoral right and a field of free action.

This is where we need to start. When there is confidence in electoral liberty, one will think about going to the polls; one will go to them. It will be necessary to report the misfortunes of the first attempts, which would not be trivial. The parties will be established in the American way because there will be no other, given our form of government, and the parties will rest on a mechanism as complex, difficult, and exposed to fraud and corruption as that of the United States. Democracy and federal government are very difficult. Their fundamental foundation, popular election, is very far from responding to the dream of purity of the adolescent and the childlike people.

III

When liberty in the election is ensured, in the sense that the public power does not restrict it with persecutions or obstruct it with critical influences, citizens go spontaneously to the polls, and soon with growing interest, but with the help of two conditions: that they have an awareness of the purpose of the event, and that they surmise a real value in their vote to the results of the election. Against both conditions, the Constitution established, in deference to French handbooks of democracy, universal suffrage and the indirect vote, the first because all the sons of the country have a right to take part in naming their mandataries, given that all are equal, and the second because Mexican citizens, with that universality, are incapable of electing well, and even of electing poorly.

The Drafting Committee of '57 had not committed such an error; with the good sense that always placed it so much above Congress as a whole, it ended the article that expressed the conditions of citizenship with this sentence: "From the year 1860 forward, besides the conditions expressed, knowing how to read and write will be required." But the deputy Peña y Ramírez "declares himself against the requirement of knowing how to read and write, because it does not seem to him to conform very well with *democratic principles,* and because *the indigent and needy classes* are not to blame, but rather the governments that have overseen public instruction with such carelessness" [Ponciano]. Arriaga, to whom it seems that the continuous attacks of his own coreligionists since the meetings of the commission have cast doubt on his own criteria, responded "that he did not agree to answer the objections of the previous speaker," met with his fellow committee members, and this committee withdrew the final sentence of the article.[1] Thus, so simply and briefly, without awareness of the seriousness of the resolution and by a unanimous vote, Congress closed the doors on possible democracy in the name of theoretical democracy. The government was guilty of the fact that indigents did not know how to read or write—that govern-

1. Zarco, *Historia del congreso constituyente 7,* Session of September 1.

THE ELECTION : 477

ment, which in thirty-five years of independence, revolts, and penury, had not disseminated instruction to all parts—and the exclusion of the illiterate was unanimously seen by the deputies not as a measure of political order but rather as an article of penal code that punished ignorance unjustly.

Suffrage is not simply a right; it is a function, and it requires, as such, conditions of aptitude that society has the right to demand, because the function is nothing less than the primordial function for the ordered life of the Republic. It is as much a function as that of the inhabitant who serves as a juror, and who, within free institutions, has the right to be registered on the lists of judges of the people; but for the task to be given to him, he must meet certain conditions that ensure his suitability. The vote is not exercised to the detriment of the citizen, but rather at the expense of the destiny of the social body, and only an incomprehensible aberration of criteria and common sense can have placed the right of each man above the interests of the nation to oppress it, to stifle it, and to overwhelm it.

Universal suffrage produces in all countries the appearance of *disruptive elements,* that is to say, elements that obstruct the genuine expression of the conscious will in popular election. But in advanced countries, although such elements are harmful, they are dominated by the actively free population, which is the majority, or they cause, in the end, a tolerable misfortune. In the United States the black people and the new and poor immigrants are electors that are won by the bribes of political professionals or by the trickery of the jongleurs at the polls; they are a minority, but all American treatise writers still regard them as very dangerous. In England the influence of the great landowners creates a disruptive element in the tenants and farmers. In France the disruptive element is the workers in the great factories, through the intervention of the well-liked employers. But these subordinate groups do not generally manage to prevail in the election, and therefore they are simply disruptors. For us, seventy percent of illiterates is not a disruptive element in the expression of the will of the people, but rather destroyer of the election itself. If the cities of importance are excepted, which are very few, the rest of the country has electoral districts in which the great majority is unlettered, completely ignorant of the system of government; and it is not venturesome to maintain that, in a fifth of the total electoral districts the greater number of the so-called citizens belong to the indigenous race and do not have the slightest notions of the law, nation, president, Congress, or state. That there be the will of the people, which is the obligatory phrase of all known theorizers, each citizen must have will, and will is impossible without knowledge of the matter that must activate it.

In these conditions, seventy percent of the electors are nothing but material on hand for the violation of the will of the citizens who do actually have a will; and as those citizens are, because of an age-old flaw, submissive and obedient to an authority that commands them from close by, they have been, without exception of place or time, the force with which governments have served themselves in order to avoid free elections and make the election benefit their purposes. The weapon is a double-edged sword: when the central power employs it, it subdues the states; when the local government uses it, the federal government does not have the opinion of its partisans in the state to balance or bring down the aggressive force of the rebellious local power. The election has always been (with very rare exceptions that occur only in revolutionary periods) in the hands of the general government or those of the governor; but still today theories of democracy are invoked to sustain this shameful and lamentable condition; and one blames the power for using such a process, without considering that it is the least unfortunate process that can result from the absurd institution, given that it would be much worse for the country if greedy agitators, always of a mean disposition, replaced the power in the privilege of making and unmaking governments, congresses, and tribunals.

The truly democratic principle of universal suffrage consists of extending the right to vote to the greatest number of members of the social body qualified by their fitness, and without making exclusions by reasons of birth, social or pecuniary condition, or any other that constitutes privilege. As there are no external signs that reveal electoral suitability, and laws must provide general rules, qualities have been sought that presume the probability of fitness, with not only knowledge of the act and its objective being considered within the condition of suitability, but also interest in carrying it out well. In France the general culture and the democratic spirit have extended the law up to the suffrage of all adult men; the limited number of illiterate people cannot appreciably influence the election. In England, which had elections during five centuries before arriving at the nineteenth century in its present democratic state, social status based on income is required; but this is so low that the United Kingdom has around seven million electors. In the United States the constitutional amendment that gave the vote to black people is still considered by native and foreign treatise writers as a grave error that will threaten the great nation with very serious dangers, and has certainly imposed on southern politicians the need to resort to games of intrigue in order to deceive people of color and make a joke of their right to elect.

The requirement of knowing how to read and write does not guarantee knowledge of the electoral act, but it gives probabilities of it and abilities for acquiring it; and at any rate the electors are encouraged and the politicians animated by the assurance that the fight to exclude the ignorant masses, in whom only the action of force can work for carrying out their mechanical function, is possible. When free and possible elections give birth to parties, even if they might be at heart parties of personality, they will be charged with instructing the elector by means of publications that not only bring the elector up to date on the function and its objective, but also bring to him through their discussions, even if exaggerated and intense, information about their purposes, knowledge of their methods, and features of their men.

No restrictive quality more liberal than this to which we refer, given that it can be acquired with ease and in some months; and if we should not expect, in a people apathetic about the existence of political right, that each man would intend to learn to read and write out of eagerness to be an elector, it is not an illusion to suppose that interest in increasing the number of votes might induce the parties to increase the number of schools for adults in the regions where they have followers. The progress of instruction, which in the last twenty years has been notable, will increase the elector body from day to day and will expand the democratic system naturally and spontaneously. Thus it happened in England with the income requirement, much less dependent on the will of the individual: in the fifteenth century, the amount of required annual income was twenty shillings; but the increase of wealth in currency and the development of agriculture and industries lowered the value of money gradually and constantly, and the income of twenty shillings was becoming less significant and ended by being laughable, making the number of electors who were persons of independent means grow notably. English writers maintain that twenty shillings in the fifteenth century meant at that time as much as eighty pounds now.

The expression "universal suffrage" is one of the many hyperboles that political language has invented, to the detriment of the health of democracies; the word "universal" was chosen because another of greater breadth was lacking, and, nonetheless, in all countries, requirements for the elector are established that do not permit, for the suffrage, the less promising adjective of "general." Words like that, like "sovereignty" of the state-divisions within the federal state, make people ill with hallucination, bring them to the disorderly trembling of delirium, and damage the discernment even of the good part of the directing class of the country. The suffrage that democratic principles imply is not *right-of-man* suffrage, attributed to all the inhabitants, nor to all the natives, or even to all the men, or, finally, to all the adult men; but rather *political-right-and-function* suffrage, guarantee of the community, which must be extended to all those, and only those, who have sufficient knowledge of the function to perceive the responsibility of exercising it. To this condition, the restriction of knowing how to read and write, which has the advantage of opening the doors of current citizenship to all who would like to pass through them, approaches the possible; this is not to exclude anyone or to establish a suffrage less universal than that of the most democratic peoples.

The preceding arguments will seem pointless, if they are not seen as foolish, to anyone who might be a stranger to the way our political ideas develop. It will seem unbelievable that it is necessary to discuss exclusion from the polls of men who are, because of their ignorance, as incapable of voting as crazy people and idiots; of men who have not entered into the community of conscious life; for whom there is no epoch; who have no sense of evolution at all, whether or not the government is at fault; that there are, among those, entire peoples who, not knowing the national language, have not yet even been put in contact with the civilized world, and they have today the same notion of a national government as they had in the sixteenth century of the privileges of the crown. And nothing, nonetheless, more urgent than the need for this discussion, because men of government, persons called to exercise influence in the order of political ideas, still declare themselves, either because of Jacobin vices or because of conventional democratism or because of malevolent mumbo-jumbo, maintainers of good faith of universal suffrage, whose modification they see as an outrage on the rights of the people.

Democracy has no worse enemies than men of the upper classes who, courtiers of the errors of the people, court common fears that are the means of trading in applause and obedience. Thus, religious faith has no more harmful enemy than the priest without a conscience, who, to ensure the faith of the humblest followers, nourishes, instead of fighting, the most miserable worries and preaches words he does not believe but that contribute to ensuring him the dull submission he cultivates.

The true citizen should mistrust any public man who fights against, and any government that objects to restriction of, the suffrage. Defense of universality of the vote reveals the underhanded purpose of excluding all people from the public interests.

IV

Succession in the highest power has been the primary problem in constituting peoples, including primitive peoples. Wandering tribes, nomadic peoples, recognize as leader the one who leads them in war and devotes himself to victory; conquered, they submit to the rule of the conquering leader. Succession is determined by the murder of the *caudillo* or by his defeat in the daring rebellion of a conspiratorial group, and then the people have as general and king the murderer or rebel who imposes himself and who is acclaimed because of admiration and fear, and because his very action shows that he meets the conditions of valor and fierceness that are the ones the horde needs in its captain. When the leader arrives at the level of prestige sufficient to elevate himself over his tribes until coming to be seen as of superior lineage, he establishes hereditary succession, which is the first form of peaceful transmission of power; the rebel, to supplant him, kills him and also puts an end to his sons, but by doing so he confirms the right of succession in popular sentiment, because he makes the heirs disappear in order to establish his right, now secondary to ferociousness and strength.

Later nationalities are begun, and the conquering and prestigious leaders link their authority and their right to rule with the religious principle, which gives it a new prestige and a sacred origin. The succession takes place in the laws of the people, and ruling families begin. Rebellions are not now made against a man, nor is disappearance of the direct descendants sufficient; it is necessary to overthrow the dynasty. At any rate, the establishment of political societies has entered a new stage that means an important advance. The succession is legal; the usurper makes use of the law, avails himself of the religious principle, and bases his own dynasty on both. The evolution that operates since with respect to the royal power, until arriving at the limitations of modern monarchies, gives no importance for purposes of succession to the supreme leader, who continues to be merely and purely legal, given that he only obeys preestablished rules to find title to the crown.

In the third and final stage, the supreme power is conferred by popular election and for a determinate period; the law does not provide rules to define on whom the succession of the power falls, but rather to establish by whom and in what form the successor should be designated. The succession enters into a new period that the constitutional system perfects, leading it to secure the advantages of renewal and the stability that public opinion, which has authorized and must sustain him, should give to the leader of the government.

Such has been, in the general movement of the world, the successional evolution of the power, and although human history has many centuries now, the forms of succession are reduced essentially to those that characterize the three great stages: usurpation by force, designation by law, election by the people.

As happens with all general classifications that arise from the analytical observation of history, what has been expounded is not uniform in all epochs or among all the peoples of the world if, in attempting to find the pure type of each stage, it is sought in particular cases. There are in antiquity peoples of elective rule, but incomplete and above all fleeting, and which is lost later, as if in order for the exceptional people to obey the inevitable law of progressive evolution.

In modern times what happens with all the great classifications happens also with the law of progressive evolution: there is hybridization, like that of languages on the borders of peoples who speak different ones; there are shades, like those of the colors in contact with one another; finally, there are confusions between the laws and the practices, between the supposed and the realized, and between the temporary and permanent that mislead the criteria of analysis. Careful and calm observation always discovers the essential character of the stage.

Among the Latin peoples of America, who did not develop spontaneously, but rather were influenced by others more advanced in history and saw themselves subject to an anomalous form of government not produced by their own evolution, forward movement suffered disruptions that still persist after having them break the orderly advance of the model peoples of Europe. During the centuries of the viceroyalty, they did not pass to the second stage, but rather, their growth force nullified, they remained without evolutionary action, and, upon gaining their independence, found themselves filled with the most advanced ideas of the transformed peoples, but lacking the harmonious development that gives strength and equilibrium to whomever has exercised, in the normal struggles of nature, all the muscles of the body and all the psychic faculties. From this arises the fact that the Latin nations of the continent have laws from the last stage and have not yet emerged, for the realization of the succession of the government, from the period of primitive peoples.

Argentina, Brazil, and Chile are barely managing to provide, to their transmission of power, a character less similar to the first stage, because the changes owing to violence are less frequent in the three nations. An abrupt modification, and for that reason little deserving of confidence, has shown in Peru the legitimate succession of recent presidents, not without attempts at revolt that threaten the constitutional order. Only the little republic of Costa Rica, for reasons that for us do not have sufficient explanation, presents an exception that could not be taken into account without studying in depth its history and the internal process of its political practices and customs.

As for Mexico, it is clearly and fully in the first stage. In order not to go to the confusion of the epoch of daily revolutions, let us take the series of governments from [18]55 to now: Santa Anna was thrown out by the Revolution of Ayutla; Comonfort was defeated by the Revolution of Tacubaya; Juárez attacked by the Revolution of the Noria, which failed; Lerdo de Tejada deposed by the Revolution of Tuxtepec; General Díaz deposed by the Revolution of the North. After each triumphant revolution, the leader of the rebellion becomes the president of the Republic. Although the processes have changed during the time that has elapsed since the Christian era, the fact is, at heart, the same that occurred more than twenty centuries ago in the forests of the north of Europe. In the succession of power, the people does not express its will to elect a new president, but rather to depose the one who governs, and expresses it by taking up arms and fighting. Once the victory is obtained, the election is unnecessary because there is no candidate other than the leader of the subversive movement. In these cases the election is free of physical coercion precisely because no one has moral liberty.

The man who assumes power in those cases, not because they give it to him but rather because he takes it, does not come to his rule with strong ideas of democracy, nor less does he think of them as rules of government. The defects of origin continually extend to mentality and conduct, because of the necessity that it appear logical and that only a spirit more than superior, exceptional, capable of infringing laws of human nature can break.

He who overthrows a president and imposes himself in his place does not feel himself to be mandatary or leader of the government; he feels himself master of the laws and leader of the nation, because it is not natural that he would superimpose juridical theories on the deep impression left by the events from which his authority is derived. The imposition having sprung spontaneously from him, he does not tolerate obstacles; limitations irritate him, and, as a consequence, he subordinates to his will all elements that must intervene in managing public affairs, and before long he arrives, if it did not begin with a dictatorship, at a dictatorship so much less benevolent the more resistance is opposed to it. Perpetuity comes right away, which is the highest condition of dictatorial force and, consequently, its necessary company, and with perpetuity established without law, the succession of power can be operated only through violence. Here we are, then, in the first stage of successional theory, condemned to have dictatorship as a form of government, and as an end for each dictatorship a revolution.

We are not trying to deny in an absolute manner the charges made against our race and our education as being the cause of our deplorable and backward political condition. Perhaps it might be true that we put "in the conquest of power the same ardor free of scruples that the companions of Pizarro put into the conquest of gold,"[2] obeying hereditary impulses, but there is less observation and clemency in condemning us without extenuation when we are within the historical laws which the old peoples of Europe have obeyed over long centuries.

We are going to arrive at the third stage of the successional evolution

2. Barthélemy, *Le Rôle du Pouvoir Exécutif dans les républiques modernes*, p. 204.

without having prepared ourselves in the second; it obliges us to force the law of gradual development, and the violation of natural laws has inevitable and harsh sanctions. Every effort of public men of patriotic conscience must be consecrated with loyalty and disinterest to helping the evolutionary movement so that it might be realized in practice, since it is operating in theories and in public sentiment. The perspective of the Republic presents itself in this simple and hard dilemma: *Either election or revolution.*

[...]

2 | Supremacy of Legislative Power

I

The actual election establishes the government but does not regulate it, and precisely in the harmonious operation of the branches created by the Constitution lies the secret of the stability of the government, the guarantee of liberties, and the foundation of the tranquility and success of the nation. The peoples who have already passed their political infancy and have liberated themselves from fear of usurpations, because they have the disposition sufficiently superior not to tolerate them, take up the real problem of government organization, which consists of the balance among the powers that constitute it in order that the superiority of one not come to destroy the others, degenerating into an oppressive power. Each of those peoples has given, to the complex problems of political organization, the solution to which their history, their idiosyncracy, and their needs have led them, in such a way that, if well within the general common principles founded in human nature and analyzed by reason, each has found the special solution it has consecrated in its laws and embodied in its customs. For this reason, no two nations have equal institutions in practice, despite the fact that, besides general common principles, some among them certainly have similar histories and origins, and despite the fact that commerce in ideas and study of foreign experience have also caused reciprocal imitation.

The old classification of systems, which could have had scientific merit one hundred years ago, reveals today only the external appearance of the governments, but it misleads with respect to the intrinsic reality. There is greater similarity between the governments of the North American republic and the German empire than between the

Original title: "Supremacía del poder legislativo." Source: Emilio Rabasa, *La Constitución y la dictadura,* chapter 11, in *Estudio sobre la organización política de México* (Mexico: Tipografía de "Revista de Revistas," 1912).

republics of the United States and Switzerland or between the empires of Germany and Russia. The essence of the classification takes root in the strength and constitution of the executive power, which directs and regulates the community's interior and exterior life, and which varies from absolute rule in Russia to the balance of powers in North America and the almost complete abrogation of powers in Switzerland.

But in order to speak only about the type of government in which the popular element participates by means of the suffrage, a type to which all peoples of the world are tending to accommodate themselves, we focus on the great division between parliamentary governments (the English model) and the balance of powers (North American model). The first is based in the theory that national sovereignty resides in the assembly elected by the people, whose will it represents exclusively; the second rests on the principle of a plurality of powers, to which the people delegates its sovereignty (executive and legislative), giving them jurisdictions that should keep their activities separate and in a balance that guarantees against omnipotence that not even the people themselves should have. European experts in public law attribute great superiority to the parliamentary system, which predominates on the Old Continent, but the grand model of the American type does not permit them to condemn, or even declare the system of the New Continent definitively inferior.

With the intent of speaking about parliamentarianism later, we confine ourselves, in order to limit our subject matter, to the system that, with reference to republics, is now called "presidential."[1]

The presidential system establishes power and national sovereignty in its three departments: legislative, executive, and judicial, with jurisdictions and limitations that ensure their independent, balanced, and harmonious action. The first two represent the will of the people and have authority to interpret it in order to "require" in the name of the constituent and determine according to suggestions of the nation or accord-

---

1. The systems should be called: European the one, which arose in Europe and has spread throughout the entire continent, and American the other, which had its origin in the United States and is the foundation of all the constitutions of this hemisphere. Such designations would have the advantage of avoiding the words of specific connotation that are used today and that are all inappropriate because of this very connotation they have from beforehand.

ing to their own ideas that they have because of ideas from the nation; as a consequence, the officials who represent those agencies must necessarily originate from popular election. The judicial is an organ of the nation that enters into certain elevated functions as a great equalizer of elements, but, limited to applying the law (declaration already made by the will of the people), it cannot "require" in the name of the people because, in the administration of justice, the people itself is inferior to the law and must subject itself to it; consequently, to appoint the holders of this function, public election is not only not necessary, it is not logical.

In every constitution of this system, what is essential and delicate lies in the balance of the two powers that represent the will of the people; the theory of parliamentarianism rejects precisely that double representation of a single and indivisible will. But, leaving to theoretical conceptions the limited value that falls to them in the practical sciences, it is necessary to recognize that the fact of two distinct agencies sharing the representation of the will of the people creates between them an inevitable antagonism and causes the major difficulty of keeping them constantly within established limits. Each one fighting to expand its activity at the expense of the other, the legislative tends toward converting the government into congressional anarchy, and the executive toward taking it to dictatorship; and if neither of the two extremes is reached, at the very least the expansion of one of the two powers deforms the constitution that the country has desired, and always with the danger of going further. The president of the French Senate reproached a member of the chamber, interrupting him with applause from his colleagues, because the member alluded to the constitutional power of the executive to have reconsidered a project voted by the chambers. The allusion seemed to dishonor the sovereignty of the assembly, when in reality it was the Senate that disrespected the constitution. In France the legislative has gained such ground on the executive that, in official acts, the legitimate powers of the executive are not recognized.[2] In the United States the succession of presidents without great character made the constitutional balance vacillate in favor of Congress, in the opinion of Wilson, to the point that the distinguished writer considered that the nation was threatened by parliamentarianism;[3] and later, Barthélemy,

2. Barthélemy, *Le Rôle du pouvoir exécutif dans les républiques modernes,* p. 678.
3. Wilson, *Congressional Government.*

writing in 1906 after the administration of MacKinley [*sic*] and during that of Roosevelt, saw, on the contrary, the already insuperable tendency of the American government toward the personal influence of the holder of the executive. It is certain that, in the events of 1906 until now, neither the American people nor President Taft has permitted the confirmation of this tendency, which seems not to have shown itself except in specific circumstances.

Outside the legal order, the president possesses elements of strength that give him superiority in the struggle with Congress. He has the public force materially at his disposal, has the army of employees who depend on him, has on his side the interest of those who hope for his favors, and generally attracts popular sympathies, which, only in moments of intense unrest, the collective and almost anonymous personality of a legislative assembly gains. But, within the constitutional order, which is what we must take into account in examining the makeup of the government, the superiority of the Congress is unquestionable because of its sole power to prescribe the laws to which the entire nation and even the executive power must submit. The danger, then, of encroachment that alters the stability of the institutions is principally in the abuse Congress can make of its legitimate powers, for all that this seems paradoxical in our country because we have never lived under the constitutional system, and, consequently, the preponderance has been on the side of the executive.

The complete separation of the two powers would not ensure their balance. It would give them an antagonistic independence in which each would exert itself to reach the maximum expanse, and both would become unbearable for the governed. It is required, on the contrary, that one serve as a limitation to the other by means of specific intervention in their activities; and, as the legislative already has as its specific function the great means of prescribing laws in order to regulate the course of public affairs, the attention of the fundamental law directs itself primarily to arming the executive against the encroachments and excesses of the legislative power, strong because of its faculties, immune because of its absolute lack of responsibility, bold because of its nature as representative of the people that it wants exclusively to claim for itself, and impassioned because of its crowdlike nature, which subjects it more to oratorical efforts than to the value of reasoning.

In the form of government the Mexican Constitution adopted, there is another element of complication and another force to take into account for the balance of the whole: the legal status of the independent states, which confers on them a freedom of internal activity to which has been given the improper name of sovereignty, which we use in this specific sense for the sake of brevity. The federal powers are limited, by local independence, to everything that, and to only what concerns the interest of the nation, leaving to the governments of the federal divisions the care and management of the interests of each, which assumes for them the characteristics of an autonomous people. A new distribution of jurisdictions is added to what the division of powers entails and demands, and in this distribution, the fundamental law again seeks the counterweights that might guarantee, of course, the liberty of the federal entities, but in the end, and most important, all the liberties of the people against the tyrannical power and the never-ending tendency to absolutism; because the federal system, if it was created with the goal of preserving their rights for the English colonies that formed the North American Republic, proves to be in every instance excellent for reducing the power of the government, with advantages for the security of public liberties, always in danger before a formidable power.

The legal status of the states is manifest in two forms to limit the omnipotence of the national government. The first is their internal independence, which puts local interests beyond the authority of the national government; the second is their status as political entities, which, on the one hand, gives them the right to constitute a chamber of Congress, with an equal number of representatives for all, and, on the other, gives them the right of voting as units for the highest laws, those that modify the fundamental pact of the nation.

The liberty of action of the states, as electors of the federal chamber and as legislative agency in constitutional matters, depends on their strength and their independence, and it cannot give cause for legal conflicts; not so their liberty of internal rule, which can be violated by laws or acts that encroach upon or restrict it. The agency of equilibrium is, for those situations, the judicial department of the nation, which, without abandoning the forms of procedure appropriate to the administration of justice, without general declarations that would convert it into the omnipotent power it is trying to combat, prevents the execution of every act of violation and defends the independence of the state or division from every threat. If the balance is broken by the state to the detriment of the federal jurisdiction, the judicial agency of the nation reestablishes it by the same procedure, limited to preventing the simple execution of isolated acts.

Such is the coordination of powers and the mechanism of balances on which the American system of government is based, established with simplicity and mastery in the Constitution of Philadelphia, "the most admirable work," according to Gladstone, "that human understanding has produced." From it, our [Constitution] took an organization that our constituents managed to improve on certain points, but that proved to be profoundly modified by the very different criteria it used for the work of adaptation.

Did the modifications made in that work leave the balance that is the goal of the presidential system ensured in our political organization? Certainly not. The elimination of the Senate broke it, as much by increasing the power of the unitary chamber as by depriving the states of their equal representation in an assembly of the legislative power.[4] With the Senate established in a subsequent epoch, some errors remain in the supreme law that, in the free practice of its precepts, will cause serious conflicts among the powers; the preponderance of the legislative over the executive remains, which will result in any of the extremes to which the omnipotence of Congress leads: the submission of the executive, which establishes the dictatorship of an assembly, or the coup d'état, which enthrones the dictatorship of the president. And after any of these dictatorships, revolution again. We do not yet know what the outcome of our Constitution will be in full practice because we have never realized it, and foresight is insufficient for calculating it in the complexity of elements that enters into the physiology of a people that lives by its agencies. The machinery constructed to make a new product is not free from the danger of malfunctioning at the moment of connecting it to the motor that must set all its parts in motion, and only the flying asunder of a part will reveal the error of calculation that must be corrected so that the entire mechanism meets its objective. Our political organization, written in the Charter of '57, needs to be connected to the actual suffrage, which is the force that must set it in motion. Only then will we know which is the work that produces and the effort that provides, but

4. The 1857 Constitution suppressed the Senate, but a constitutional amendment restored it in 1874. (Editor's note)

through the experience of other similar mechanisms we already know what parts are going to fly asunder if they are not adjusted beforehand.

There is also another reason why the Constitution might, for the most part, be an enigma as long as it is not put into free practice, to which it arrives only through the genuinely popular origin of the two powers, which are not possible, neither the interpretation nor the adaptation. The interpretation, which determines the scope that must be granted to each precept, is not possible as long as the constitutional agencies are not free to use their judgment, to discuss with the others their limits of activity, and to establish their sovereignty as an insurmountable barrier to disruptive encroachment.

For the interpretation, the adaptation is made first; but the adaptation is essentially evolutionary and, in our judgment, as inevitable as useful. If two peoples of analogous origins and situations were to adopt identical written constitutions, ten years after putting them into practice with equal liberty, they would have different actual constitutions, and fifty years later, it is probable they would have totally distinct ones. Not only has the English common-law constitution made the admirable evolution from ruling aristocracy to broad democracy in a century without altering the visible organization of its government, but also the inflexible (written) constitutions, have, without modifying their texts, changed their principal ideas through slow transformation. The American Constitution was established on the greatest respect for independence and for the almost real sovereignty of the states, which the states required to accept it. Jefferson, the zealous sustainer of such a principle, dedicated eight years of government to its development, and nonetheless, at the end of the separatist war, the absolute and sole sovereignty of the nation remained the unquestionable foundation of the federal union, and this new principle has produced the effect of giving the central government a preponderance that is neither written in the law nor would have been accepted by the free colonies. The French Constitution of 1875 was voted by a Congress with monarchical tendencies and with the view to a restoration, and it tried to preserve in the president of the Republic the prerogatives that should not be denied a monarch. It was based on the division of powers and on the limitations of balance, and nonetheless, keeping to its texts, it has permitted the transition to the most complete parliamentary government, with a near nullification of the executive under the unlimited sovereignty of the popular assembly.

The persistent action of the social constitution imposes little by little and day by day its characteristic forms and makes the political constitution, which always has much of the artificial and mathematical, yield. The modifications that, in general ideas, produce the changing needs of life, the progress of ideas, and all the forces of national growth do not adjust themselves conveniently to the unchanging mold that a past generation forged, and it is preferable that the mold yield slowly and permit less rectilinear forms than that the mold shatter in pieces under the strength of irresistible forces.

II

To Congress can be applied, in the abstract, the expressions of Wilson, "Congress is the aggressive spirit," and of Bagehot: "Congress is a despot that has unlimited time, that has unlimited vanity, that has or believes it has an unlimited ability, whose pleasure is in action and whose life is work."[5] So that, having faculties superior to those of the other branches of the power, an instinct for attack, and not only capacity but organic need to work, it brings together the most complete conditions for disturbing the harmony of the government and frustrating the best calculated precautionary measures of the fundamental law. But there is more that Bagehot in his phrases, cited and written for comparison with the limitations that fatigue, pleasures, sociability, and his individual psychology impose on the president, should not take into account: the lack of responsibility of the Congress (especially the most numerous chamber) makes it bold and careless; its method of election, in which demagogic elements play more than any other, give it, generally, a majority inferior to the task; individually, its members do not have an opinion on the matters submitted to their vote; together, it lets itself be carried off by the coarse eloquence that fascinates it with greater docility than by the serious reasoning suitable for persuading it.

In the House of Representatives of Washington, the representatives frequently request that, at the moment of the vote, the session be suspended, because they do not know what to do and they need to go to the people best informed about the matter to orient themselves. Their personal opinion is null, the work abundant and rapid, and thus made impossible for the deliberation of a body whose value depends precisely

---

5. W. Wilson, *Congressional Government;* Bagehot, *Principles of Constitutional Law.*

on the fact that it is constituted to deliberate. The discussion, and even the vote of the chamber, has been replaced by the discussion and vote of the permanent committees, about which it should not be said that they give an opinion, but rather that they themselves alone resolve the affairs of state. In each committee the "chairman" who presides over it prevails, and notwithstanding the transcendental importance of his exceptional functions, the "chairmen" are named directly and exclusively by the Speaker of the House, who thus assumes an enormous power in the functions of the state. If we have to speak of being guided by general cases, we must say that the sole serious and reliable function of the House is exercised in the election of the Speaker, which is done through the majority of votes . . . of the party that dominates in the assembly.

Thus we refer to the most learned democracy of those that have adopted the presidential system of government.

Among those subject to the parliamentary system, the most numerous chamber is of a much higher intellectuality because the prominent participation that it takes in the government of the nation makes of the election of the deputies the act of greatest importance for the country, and the subject matter of the participation attracts persons from the serious elements of society and especially of the political world. In the chambers of representatives of England and France are seated many men of the first order, deep thinking in political science, masters of diplomacy, consummate jurists, famous soldiers and sailors, eloquent orators. Personal opinion can be, if not entirely general, in the great majority, but subject to the needs of the party and, within the party, to the group, to the factions, which in France, above all, give to the deliberations of the assembly its particular appearance and to the votes their definite direction. The importance of the vote that in one day changes the government and determines all the acts of the executive—that is to say, all the daily life of the nation—makes the discussion impassioned, intense, more of a dispute than a deliberation, and arrives at the moment of deciding with the "yes" or the "no" of the sovereignty of the people in an atmosphere charged with ill will and threats, that still vibrates with the rude words of the interrupters and the strikes of the president's gavel, and maybe a raised fist agitated in order to slap a face or some inkwells hurled some distance in order to wound.

There is no way to choose between an assembly like the American, which is more or less satisfied by mediocrities and incompetents, in which the custom of speaking is deteriorating more and more, which, subject to the committees, is at the point of completely abdicating its functions as a deliberating body, and another assembly like the French, in which there are representatives of great quality by talent and knowledge, but who are ceaselessly stirred up in the struggle against the government and make of it the preferred, almost only, occupation, turning discussion into a combat of eloquence, at times drowned out by clamors, insults, and affronts. The American nation tolerates and rewards the unhappiness with the strength that it takes from its incomparable and healthy youth, as a well-nourished and vigorous body supports and restores the local illness of a member. The French superimposes its well-being of accumulated wealth, its superior culture, and the patriotism that constitutes its saving virtue upon constant threats from reaction and from international complexities. But neither the one nor the other nation has the assembly conceived by the constituent legislators for the loftiest functions that popular sovereignty confers, and each one on its path follows a course that does not yet give signs of stopping or deviating and that can lead the country to profound alterations in the system of government.

What will be the tendency in Mexico of a Congress freed from controls by the actual election from the electoral districts? What its influence in the specific system of government that will have to arise from the letter of the Constitution combined with our character, our education, and our idiosyncrasy? It is not possible to conjecture correctly in the responses, if what is desired is to determine details with precision or nuances with subtlety, but the most serious dangers can indeed be determined with the certainty of not erring greatly on the side of foreboding, and consequently suggesting the means of preventing the greatest and most certain ills so as to minimize the influence of possible surprises from experience.

The natural reaction the unfortunate effects of a current situation cause in the public spirit make it see poorly the good effects that it also carries with it and incline it completely in favor of a situation diametrically contrary, whose unsuitable aspects it refrains from perceiving. The absolute preponderance of the executive in our political system raises hope in the legislative and fills it with the prejudice of all saviors in waiting. The nation aspires to a system in which Congress predominates, and by shaking the omnipotence from the president of the Republic, it does not fear his nullification, because it does not see it as an evil, nor does it assume the omnipotence of the chambers, of which it has no experience whatsoever. This support of public opinion, which a free Congress would suddenly have, is what makes it most dangerous for the balance of national powers and the stability of institutions.

If the country is lacking electoral agencies, which only the exercise of the suffrage creates and perfects, one cannot expect in the first elections that the conservative elements, which are the masters of wealth, culture, and the good judgment there is in the entire nation, would vigorously take part; but it is even difficult for such agents to be very useful for the good designation of representatives, because in countries of the presidential system interest is in the election of the president, and, as in the United States, the election of deputies is left officially to the politicians, who are generally men of second order if one classifies by learning and patriotism. Our Congresses (the first ones without any doubt) will be made up, in their majority, of men gathered through the spell of small localities or by clever intrigues in which a local competence triumphs; of politicians from the states who usually become confident and seize great opportunities in the broad and favorable medium of the capital; of some experienced in legislative tasks by some previous service, ready to use a liberty they did not have before, and who it is probable owe their credentials to the influence, that will not come to be null, of the governors. A Congress composed of such personalities will probably have qualities of good faith, of interest in the states, and of preferential dedication to their tasks, and it will provide moreover the advantage of bringing to light men who renew the ranks of politics, owing to the spontaneity of the medium, which is the great revealer of characters and talents. On the other hand, even when it has men of note, the common intellectual standard in such assemblies will be very narrow, and the instruction in political science and in the various types of knowledge that enrich and support it, very scarce.

Skeptics will say that this Congress will subject itself to the executive, like the previous ones, through promises or habit; we will not assert the contrary, but in such a case, the assumption of independent chambers would not hold, and we will not have advanced at all in the development of the institutions. No danger, but no progress!

The free Congress is one that takes note of its important role, that studies its faculties, that senses itself the first of the powers and immediately makes itself invader, provoker, and aggressor. If its general culture is low, as in what we have foreseen, hostility is impulsive because it proceeds from erroneous ideas that give it, as its first and even as its only conviction, that of its own omnipotence and the feeling of its lack of responsibility. The resistance of the executive to the invasion of its jurisdictional ground seems to it rebelliousness, and the eloquence of the orators overflows, always convincing for the mute benches. And after some time of burdening itself with excitements of pride, stimulants of greed, it ends up by being persuaded that it must unconditionally subjugate the leader of the executive power or compel him to resign.

In September 1861 the Congress that began meeting in May, which harbored a great number of distinguished men, found it very natural, almost like the exercise of one of its simpler legitimate faculties, to request President Juárez to resign from the government in order to deliver the power to General González Ortega. The form employed had nothing in common with parliamentary processes, for it was done by a petition that fifty-one deputies endorsed. To it was opposed another, signed by fifty-four representatives, which supported the president. So if, of the total, the hostile ones had attained three more adherents, the position of Juárez would have been so weak that the president would have had to resign or attempt a coup d'état. And if one considers that Juárez had just accomplished the triumph of the Constitution and the Reform, worthy of the laurels the nation has not scrimped on giving him, that his recent election was a vote of confidence of the Republic, which should not be proven false by the representatives of the people, and that, on the other hand, the country continued to be in disarray and was still threatened by enemies of the liberal party, it will be seen in this lamentable fact, of what errors of judgment and lack of loyalty and even patriotism the collectivity of men of good and patriotic judgment are capable when the omnipotence of their legislative faculties dazzles them.

If it does not arrive at such extremes, the Congress will not stop claiming the supremacy that its sovereign authority to make the laws from which the nation lives and its influence that the threat of paralyzing the government originates and sustains offers it at such little cost. It will surreptitiously introduce a kind of forced parliamentarianism, made at the expense of the liberty of the executive and thanks to the timid complacencies of the executive or to concessions that the fear of violent clashes between the two powers extracts from him. This degeneration of the established constitutional system has come to be introduced even in the American government, better prepared than ours because of its supreme law and so openly sustained by the people. With what ease would it not prevail in the weak organism of ours, and how much would it not advance in its effort to dominate the executive, even making of it a simple instrument!

Earlier we spoke of the legislative power of the Congress, because the two assemblies that form it take part in the enactment of the laws in exercising almost all the faculties in the scope of their powers. At times the Senate will also be able to be, in its specific faculties, invader and oppressor of the executive, but it is an unalterable fact that the predominance of the Congress is summed up in the specific supremacy of the Chamber of Deputies. In parliamentary governments it is the popular chamber that makes and unmakes governments; the Senate, reduced to the mere status of reviewer, rarely dares to reshape a project the other chamber sent it, and little by little cedes its most important prerogatives. In France the Senate has a first-line role; in England the House of Lords has been ceding the terrain to the democratic advances of the Commons for a century, and recently it surrendered to it, subjected by force, the right of veto in the budgets voted by the lower chamber.

The danger of the single chamber is thus implicated in the predominance of the Congress, threatening by all the evils inherent in it and with the violation of the constitutional system. Perhaps the subordination of the Senate, in the European countries ruled by cabinet governments, depends greatly on the hereditary or less popular origin of their members, but that is not the only nor probably the main reason. The primary cause is that the more numerous a body, the more imprudent, bold, and irresponsible it becomes; the Senate must take refuge in prudence to avoid clashes of serious consequences, and prudence is always on the frontiers of weakness.

4

Against the Current

1930–1989

JORGE CUESTA

Jorge Cuesta (1903–42), born in Veracruz, was a chemist, poet, and writer. He was a friend and collaborator of Aldous Huxley. Although Cuesta was a scientist by training, he was an artist at heart and joined a group of writers in the first half of the twentieth century. The members of this group, among them Xavier Villaurrutia, José Gorostiza, and Gilberto Owen, published a magazine called *Contemporáneos* and came to be known by this name.

In the 1930s a wave of nationalism swept Mexico that had a significant impact on the artistic and cultural currents of the country. Art, it was believed, should reflect national traits. However, as cosmopolitans, the Contemporáneos defied the ruling consensus regarding art and sought to connect with artistic currents outside Mexico. They published and wrote on French poets at a time when there was a vogue for all things Mexican. Cuesta was also an essay writer who published articles on various subjects in the daily press. His pieces on politics are remarkable because he challenged prevailing ideas in ideological matters just as he did in art. In the 1930s collectivism was at its highest point in Mexico and the world. Liberalism seemed outdated and dying. Against this mood Cuesta defended and extolled the liberal tradition and criticized illiberal policies and ideas.

We present three newspaper articles published between 1933 and 1934.

Politics in the University

A few months ago, in two articles published in *El Universal,* I took the liberty of criticizing some ideas that Lic. Don Vicente Lombardo Toledano has about the university, because they are not very academic in that, under the pretext of serving the university, in reality they wish its ruin. Those ideas have had good luck; now not only are they uniquely the ideas of Lic. Lombardo Toledano, they are, in addition, held by other important persons, the official dogma of the university, and, if we consider the recent Congress of University Students, a near philosophy, at least of the sector of university activity of the nation represented there. It seems, then, that my criticism now turns out to be unfounded, given that the university finds its law and its prosperity in the ideas that, according to that criticism, lead it only to its corruption and ruin. I would be disposed to recognize it as such and beg the pardon of Lic. Lombardo Toledano and the authorities who are the echo or the very substance of his voice if the first evidence that today springs to the eyes were not evidence of the university's corruption and ruin.

To judge by the development of the above-mentioned congress, its objective was none other than the political one of having it pronounce that profession of faith, thanks to which, by means of a maneuver that represented its goals as strictly academic, a commitment to the political order is created for the university. That profession of faith, according to the way it reads, is a socialist profession of faith. Its mission is nonetheless exclusively political, but this does not prevent the most serious consequences for the university being expected from it. Without ignoring politics, it is university politics we are interested in bemoaning.

From the point of view of socialism, nothing worse can happen to it for its revolutionary ends than to be turned into the official doctrine of

Original title: "La política en la universidad." Source: *El Universal,* September 21, 1933.

an academy; there, simply, its revolution ends. Nonetheless, if this happens, and it is not possible to know which of the two is showing itself in reality—a corruption of socialism or a corruption of the academy—it would have as its only outcome that of, putting aside its revolutionary sense, killing socialism in the academy by starvation; it would not be so serious, then, if socialism is effectively a vital and revolutionary act of thought, that by going to seek its nourishment somewhere else, it can save itself from the death the university is preparing for it. But if the university remains within itself without nourishment, I do not believe it will find outside any other opportunity for living. Now, certainly, it could perhaps still have the opportunity in some independent schools, but it is absolutely certain that within a few moments the secretary of education will already have gotten rid of them.

That "the ideology of the university" manifests itself at the moment of birth as a political ideology and not as a university ideology is a fact that manifests the total lack of consciousness that the university has regarding its own existence. Its internal symptoms of corruption are already well known, having been made public by the university itself: lack of scholarly discipline, lack of seriousness of studies, ineffectiveness of exams, and, finally, the "lack of a university philosophy." Whoever frequently spends time with university professors, with those who still have a personal consciousness of university responsibility, also finds out about the lamentable fate that this rare responsibility has, preserved by those professors having to divide not only the practice but even the preparation of scholarly programs with a number three times greater than theirs of professors who are absolutely unthinking and irresponsible. As a consequence, each field of study drags along a miserable university life, which already has no other objective than dividing up the budget of the university among anyone who without merit squabbles over it, nor other justification than authorizing the student to dispute other budgets that flourish in the economic world, where in the spiritual sense the university languishes, and even the spirit of the university itself. And it cannot justify more nor can it give to this field of study a reason to perfect itself, as the university itself perceives it with an admirable but wasted playfulness, which this field of study might work to serve the student in his professional life so he might earn a living in an economic system like that of the university; this is to say that it does not even manage to seem philosophical to those benefited, and less to the university, which always has the reasonable impression that it does not benefit the university enough. Without a philosophy, in effect, each one of the university fields of study becomes corrupt, and students and professors desert and defraud it. It is only reasonable that the university seek and adopt a philosophy.

But if their meaning and value come to the sciences and the arts from the philosophy, no political maneuver will provide them with this philosophy, but rather its study. Philosophy means nothing but seriousness. To make philosophical the study of a science and the teaching of an art means only to study and teach it with seriousness. The philosophy cannot be known, that is to say the nature and perfection of a field of study, as long as it is not practiced; of an instruction, as long as it is not performed. University instruction, as the university demands it, lacks a philosophy; but if philosophy of instruction means knowledge of its nature and perfection, what is lacking in university instruction to be philosophical is, exclusively, having a nature and perfection of instruction; it is, solely, to instruct. To seek the philosophy of grammar in a political practice is to end up corrupting the practice of teaching grammar. To seek in a political position, whatever it might be, the sense of the philosophical functions of the university is to complete the corruption of the university.

In effect, the socialist thesis of the university cannot be more absurd or more depraved, for to attribute the university's failure and the lack of philosophy to the existence of a not-very-philosophical economic system, from which the university thinks its norms and its philosophy should come, so that as a consequence the university could benefit from it, is to be unaware of the nature of economic life, the nature of the university, and the nature of philosophy. The university is not unaware that economic life is not the product of a philosophy, of a reflection, but rather of an incalculable diversity of passionate acts; and it cannot be accepted that if the university sees itself incapable of giving philosophical meaning to the reflective acts of its own spirit, it sincerely believes it will be able to give philosophical sense to the unreflective passions that economic life produces and that are beyond its material reach. This university thinking is already little philosophical, is already not the product of a reflection, and, if it is a passion as unreflective as any other of the passions of economic life, let us wonder how the university will have obtained its objective of making that life philosophical when this very objective begins by lacking philosophy and moral conscience.

Nonetheless, it is not so absurd, although from another point of view, that the university might want *its* philosophy to be that of the economic system; for it escapes nobody that what the university means by "economic system" is nothing other than "political system." The university knows, because economic science knows, that the laws—that is to say, that properly economic systems—are the same in a capitalist system as in the purer communist system, and that if they were not the same, economic science would have no meaning, nor would socialist doctrines that derive their deductions of the economy from economic nature have meaning. From one system to another, the nature of the system does not change, but rather the politics. It is absolutely certain that what the university means is that it is not in agreement with the current political regime, perhaps because one of its virtues, which is a lasting glory of Lic. Don Emilio Portes Gil,[1] has been to deliver the university to the regime of its own nature, of its own philosophy, declaring it autonomous. It is altogether explicable that the act of the government that gives it liberty to have a philosophy and personal responsibility now seems to the university little philosophical, when it must admit its inability to achieve it.

When the university was run by the state, it could be explained that the university did not resign itself to suffering over its philosophy, the rule of politics, the rule of the state; it was explained that, in the face of the political demand of directing the university with a philosophy not its own, the university could be abandoned and corrupted, holding only the state responsible for the consequences of acts that were of the state and not of the university. But with the university now autonomous, if it itself creates another political slavery and abandons the philosophy, the nature belonging to it, it is because the university itself wants to be falsified and corrupted. Now the state has no blame at all, even if it is called "economic system" in order to burden it with the blame; now all the blame is the university's. And if the university is now going to continue subjecting itself to a political demand of the state, with the aggravating circumstance that the will that now desires it merits the name of traitor to the state and the university, it follows that the blame is the university's.

A socialist doctrine, whatever might be its origin or source, is a political doctrine. Its ideas are appropriate for anyone who aspires to govern

---

1. Emilio Portes Gil (1890–1978) was president of Mexico in 1928–30. (Editor's note)

and not to instruct or to learn. The sphere in which such persons have a concrete action is the sphere of government, while they are incapable of having any natural influence in the strictly university sphere. The physical sciences are absolutely immune to socialist doctrines. Even in the mind of a socialist physicist, the physical laws do not change their nature if the mind does not change its. Language and literature, like the other belles lettres, precisely because they can serve to express even socialist doctrines, maintain intact their capacity for expression even be it for opposing and different doctrines, because the nature of their language does not change. But politics, on the contrary, is not the same after it becomes socialist as it was before becoming it; in it, socialism certainly has natural consequences that can be felt.

Well then, the university cannot, in accordance with any logic whatsoever, aspire to having politics emanate naturally from the university, that is to say, to be an agency of government, besides which no juridical law authorizes it, very wisely and philosophically. And although it is legitimate that the officials of the university aspire to that other more enviable function of governing, it is immoral that they try to govern from their chair, preserving their role as citizens and compromising, in a political struggle that brings them nothing, their university functions that, in designating a political objective, always betray and corrupt. This immorality is already confirmed in the maneuver we mentioned, that being feigning an academic congress to compromise the university in a political affirmation. And the dignified resignations to congress by Lic. Don Antonio Caso and Lic. Rodolfo Brito, this latter director of the Faculty of Jurisprudence, effectively made that immorality evident, something that honors them greatly and that the university will not be able to thank sufficiently, nor the state to value as their action deserves.

For, on the other hand, university autonomy is also an interest of the state. For the integrity of this latter's authority, and not only because it benefits the university, it suits the state that the university not abandon its learned functions to engage in ignorant politics. It suits it as much, and for the same reason, that the church not engage in politics. And the state has as much right to demand from the two, the university and the church, that they not commit such an outrage against the state as that; because the nation pays them, functions useful to the nation are expected of them, not criminal acts against its sovereignty. And to what point is the political party of the university treason for the state, whatever party it may adopt, when the state pays to maintain the university within the sphere of its usefulness and autonomy; it is conceived in considering the importance of the political maneuver, by means of which, not only is the ruin of the university completed, but that ruin is also blamed on the state, with the result of discrediting it and favoring a change of political regime.

So serious is this political aspect of the question that one does not know how to clear up the confusion that results from the state or, more appropriately, the secretary of education, who is seeming to patronize and protect the act that is making clear its purpose in obtaining, along with that of the university, the ruin and discrediting of the state. Even if this act attempts only to commit an outrage against university autonomy, without immediate political ends, the state ends up, as we already saw, seriously hurt by it. But perhaps that political confusion that is produced now is not different from the confusion one sees in some part of the *Annual Report of the Secretary of Education* of 1932, in the current programs of the Department of Fine Arts of the same secretary and in some speeches of his current citizen secretary, in which generally occurs an idea like the idea of the university, to wit: that the failure of education is owed to the ruling political regime and not to the secretary of education. At any rate, it is not explainable that, although the very ideas of the secretary are used for such a thing, the secretary has not noticed, given that it seems to protect and patronize the university, the discredit that the criticism the university makes of the political regime, from which the secretary of education should not feel himself separate, is hurled at it.

Let us not be concerned for now with clearing up this political confusion. What can always be lamented, as much from the point of view of the state as from the point of view of the university, is that the autonomy of the university is being lost. It does not matter on whose part, whether the state or some political party, that, as a consequence of the political determination of the university, the state might, for its part, suspend its autonomy; it is not improbable that it occur. Once the current citizen secretary of education, Lic. Bassols,[2] informed me personally his ideas regarding university autonomy, which are none other than those that permitted Mussolini to silence the Italian press, to wit: that the autonomy of the university represents a serious danger for the university

2. Narciso Bassols was secretary of education in 1931–34. (Editor's note)

and for the state, because it gives the opportunity for the enemies of the citizen secretary of education to convert that institution into their political rostrum. And as things are presented, it is only very probable that the citizen secretary—who is part of the government, despite his fear and his political and public demonstrations to the contrary—might see himself compelled to consent to the suspension of university autonomy as a task of the government, although now not taking into account his personal ideas, but rather because of political force of circumstance, inasmuch as, on this occasion, the enemies of the university and the government are the friends of the citizen secretary and express nothing but his same ideas.

2

A New Clerical Politics

In two previous articles I have pointed out the political depth that exists in the official tendency to impose a communist dogma on the school, a tendency that, although originating in the heart of the state itself inasmuch as it is systematically supported by the secretary of education, who finds in it the superior standard of his acts, represents also an opposition to the state. In this political contradiction, which pits the state against the state, the rivalry of two politics that vie for the government is manifested only superficially, a rivalry in which the communist alleges a greater right to possess it completely given that, if it is the one with a most certain revolutionary sense, the direction of a state that is or claims to be revolutionary belongs to it. With the question presented in this way, it is logical that a doubt is produced within the state, of which communist doctrines take advantage in order to make themselves felt, at least in educational policy, and that seems to enjoy an official favor, which, nonetheless, is very far from representing a definitive inclination to convert those doctrines into the standard for all national politics. The state has a revolutionary origin and wishes to be revolutionary. It is natural that, in the face of the political trend that claims to govern it and that presents itself with the prestige of the most revolutionary trend, the state might have numerous reasons for hesitating and for not immediately rejecting it; inasmuch as considering itself a philosophical doctrine closer to the field of education than its own field of politics, it leaves in liberty, for the moment, those other objectives of politics, dissembling and softening in this way its dissenting and profoundly oppositional character.

But at heart, the sense of that opposition is very different from a struggle between the revolutionary left and right; its true nature corresponds to the natural opposition between a romantic outlook and a real-

Original title: "Una nueva política clerical." Source: *El Universal,* October 9, 1933.

istic outlook. The communist trend in the school, precisely because it is presented in the school, lacks positive political significance, lacks true political roots; so to speak, it does not represent, for the political life of the country, an "I want to be," but rather barely the "I would like to be" characteristic of vague minds detached from reality, which are a natural product of student life. But if the positive aspect of this outlook lacks reality because of its own nature, the same cannot be said of its negative aspect, for the fact that this outlook is detached from reality is a real fact that has calamitous real consequences. The "I would like to be" of our student spirits does not have a positive reality, but its lack of reality is, in turn, a perfectly tangible and dangerous reality because it does not represent anything other than groundless nonconformity, which does not consist in preferring anything different from what has been rejected, but rather in a pure rejection, in a pure nonconformism and a pure aimless opposition.

This is the aspect of the question that cannot be disavowed, because it is what reveals its true significance to the communist doctrines with which this deals. Communism does not have any importance at all here; it is only the pretext or vessel of the romantic nonconformity of our student spirits. What has real importance, to explain it, is the student nature of this oppositional romanticism. It makes clear that the citizen secretary of education is not dissatisfied with the ruling political regime, and for that reason with his own person, because he is communist; but rather, on the contrary, he is a communist because he is dissatisfied with his own person and with the rest of the national politics. The student nature of oppositional romanticism explains, in the same way, the passionately blind communism of Lic. Vicente Lombardo Toledano.[1] For if the contrary happened, the natural thing would be that the two would not take their oppositionism to the school but rather to politics, and neither the secretary of education nor Lic. Lombardo Toledano would accept—the first to be minister of the regime that does not please him; the second seems to want to be a minister.

I say that this oppositionist outlook has been preferred by the stu-

1. Vicente Lombardo Toledano (1894–1968) was a leftist politician and intellectual who belonged to the revolutionary leadership that ruled Mexico after the revolution. He was the founder, in 1948, of the Mexican socialist party, or Partido Popular Socialista. (Editor's note)

dent spirit of Mexico for many years now, and that the communism in it does not have an essential significance. In effect, everything here is in nonconformity with "the Mexican reality," whose base is absolutely religious, as is the base of all nonconformity with reality; its objective is only to be nonconformist, with the goal of making felt the superiority of the state of things that does not exist over the existing state of things, objective that is the foundation of all clerical politics. It is easy to see that not just now with communism, but rather for many years, a romantic tendency presents itself in the history of Mexico to erect the school in the church of the state, in the church of politics, with the goal of subordinating every kind of authority to the authority of its dogma, with the goal of subordinating politicians to the priests, or holders of the official doctrine. The base of this doctrine has its support in Plato, government by the philosophers, and its tradition in the entire history of the Catholic Church. In its new form it could be called, if it were not a contradiction, scientific clericalism. Perhaps its Mexican roots should be sought in Ignacio Ramírez, who could not distinguish between a clear critical spirit and a confused romantic soul. Perhaps its first ecclesiastical experience presents itself with Gabino Barreda and his positivist religion. But until José Vasconcelos,[2] this new clericalism did not have the threatening proportions it has had since.

Someday we will analyze more thoroughly the responsibility that falls to José Vasconcelos, which is so great that it merits a special chapter; let it be sufficient for us now to observe, in order to have an approximate idea of it, that his cronies in the clericalization of revolutionary politics are nothing but his servile imitators without the least personality. The use of Marx and the communist doctrines, in this respect, is certainly subsequent to Vasconcelos and foreign to him, but we now see that in this clerical movement what has least importance is the internal foundation of the doctrine; the only thing that has a real importance is the will that the school have an ecclesiastical function with respect to politics, or that it be the source, as one is accustomed to say, of "the revolution-

2. José Vasconcelos (1882–1959) was a philosopher, teacher, and politician who served as minister of education in the early revolutionary governments. He sought to enlighten Mexican society by reprinting the basic works of Western civilization and distributing them in the remotest parts of the country. He was the author of a very influential book, *La raza cósmica* (*The Cosmic Race*) (1925). (Editor's note)

ary ideology," with no other objective than making the revolutionaries the unreflective blind and obedient arms of a holy father, whose identity is not yet known: the secretary of education, the rector of the university, or the director of the preparatory school. Without a doubt that would have been Vasconcelos if he had not preferred to pursue a personal adventure,[3] as generally happens with all mystical temperaments to a great degree, and constituting, with respect to the church founded on his word and on his example, a prenatal and admirable heresy.

But whatever might be the fascinating personal destiny of Vasconcelos, his influence in Mexican politics and primarily in the politics of education has not ceased to be ever deeper and ever more nefarious. It does not matter that he condemns it and that he does not recognize himself reflected, as now no one could recognize him, in the miserable student products of his truly demonic thought. It is during the passage of Vasconcelos through the Secretariat of Public Education when this new clerical politics reaches full awareness of itself. Since then the school assumes the Platonic function of giving birth to a perfect state based in wisdom and virtue, nourished by science and philosophy, but with no other objective than being the motive for showing itself in nonconformity with the imperfect states we contemplate, and whose ideal also has the undeniable advantage, for the secretaries of education who worship it, of making the school and the secretaries of education forget the most tangible and immediate commitment to convert it into a better school, because it seems that this better world admits of being it, even if the schools have become worse by then. Rural schools, cultural missions, the university for the people, the university ideology of the Revolution, the propaganda art, the civilizing function of art, the redemption of the Indians, "For My Race the Spirit Will Speak,"[4] etc., all these Vasconcelist notions contain nothing but religious aspirations, which, if in Vasconcelos they could respond to a mystical sentiment, in his cronies are nothing but a will to take over political consciousness by means of the school. On the base of student thinking following Vasconcelos lies

3. As a presidential candidate, Vasconcelos opposed Pascual Ortíz Rubio, the official candidate of the president, Plutarco Elías Calles, in 1929. He lost but later claimed that the election was rigged. (Editor's note)

4. This is the motto, given by Vasconcelos, of the National University of Mexico. (Editor's note)

nothing but this ecclesiastical ambition, which is the same that today, through Lic. Narciso Bassols, current secretary of education, compromises the school in the official adoption of a political-religious faith — the communist — whose nature since its origin has been to join with a false philosophical prestige.

3

Crisis of the Revolution

A notable change has taken place in Mexican political thinking with respect to the epoch immediately following pacification of the Republic. Then, the political horizon was much more expansive than now; the future was rich in prospects, and the activity that flourished in politics was that of the imagination. Today exactly the opposite happens; the political horizon is narrow and shallow; the future is fashioned after a simple outline of an unchanging prospect, and the most prized action is the faithful observation of the facts. The prior epoch gravitated toward the future and was freer; the present epoch begins to gravitate toward the past, linked together. The reign of facts has succeeded the reign of acts. To be successful today in public life, a good memory and no imagination are necessary. That is to say, the young have few opportunities, for youth has almost nothing to remember.

This disheartening phenomenon is not exclusively Mexican; the world has aged uniformly; everywhere one perceives an equal fear of events and the desire to determine them beforehand. Fathers take charge of the future of their sons and rob them of the right to create and govern their own destiny. Political programs and doctrines have the tone and gravity of wills. Everything is an absolute and zealous determination of tomorrow so as to prohibit it from being in any way different from the way it is thought it should be from now on. The idea of changing ideas is detested; one has horror of imagination, and there is something like the proposal to suspend the advance of thought, which is unpredictable and full of surprises. The words that enjoy the favor of the world are "dictatorship," "control," and "plan," the three signifying testament or *last* will. On the other side, liberal ideas no longer know where to hide the embarrassment of their loss of prestige.

It would be interesting to determine the causes of this phenomenon,

Original title: "Crisis de la revolución." Source: *El Universal,* June 25, 1934.

which, fortunately, is exclusive to politics and has no parallel in other aspects of social activity. For example, in science the opposite happens. An even greater liberalism has succeeded the scientific dogmatism of the past century, so that it can be said that, in actuality, the objective of scientific thought is not to establish its conclusions in a definite way in order to determine by them future thought, but rather to grant to this thought the greatest liberty possible, allowing it to be established on its own experimental proofs and to get rid of historical chains. In contemporary art, as long as it is not mixed with politics, a similar liberty is observed. In philosophy also, as long as politics does not confuse it, a radicalism is observed that has not had its equal in the history of the world. Thus, then, political dogmatism is presented as an isolated product, although the most voluminous in modern culture. In other words, politics seems to have been detached from the progress of the culture and, for many years, to have lagged behind. Many social and psychological reasons influence this universal depravity of politics, but surely all can be expressed as a deficiency of selection. Art, science, and philosophy are the products of select minorities, laboriously cultivated. Politics, on the contrary, is the product of improvisation, of vanity,[1] and of violence, and from this comes its intellectual inferiority; from this comes its dogmatic and arrogant character; from this comes its repugnance for liberty; from this its fear that the future might reveal its inability and destroy its feeble structures; from here the fever for "controlling," for "planning," for "rationalizing," for strengthening, finally, from now on, the edifices that it raises and that, abandoned to themselves, would inevitably collapse, owing to their lack of roots in the consciousness of society.

Returning to Mexico, it is interesting to note that the change has taken place in a few years, giving it the strange spectacle that the generation that was liberal in 1917 appears today to be converted into a dogmatic one, so that in 1934 it seems to begin to obtain as political fruit precisely everything contrary to what it was proposing in 1917. But the heart of the phenomenon is even more surprising in that it consists of the gradual penetration the lamentable products of depraved universal politics have made in Mexican politics, a penetration that has taken

1. The Mexican revolutionaries convened a constituent congress in 1916, and a new constitution was enacted in 1917. (Editor's note)

place across the succeeding generations, corrupted by the ease they have found, thanks to the political doctrines in fashion, in eluding the responsibility of constructing the authentic national destiny to which the Revolution aspired.

The political thinking of 1917 knew what it wanted; it had a profound awareness of its responsibility; it had been matured over a long and painful reflection in the midst of an intense struggle that compelled it each day to justify and strengthen itself; it was a thought prepared to confront the most dangerous and unexpected experiences and to become enriched by them. From here it comes that, with the pacification of the country, the political horizon was broad and full of incitements. Youth never had a more admirable opportunity. They counted on it. The creation and enhancement of their future was placed in their hands.

But in vain the young people had unlimited access to power. Youth did not find, in that marvelous liberty the Revolution had so painfully won for it, anything but an authorization to improvise and satisfy its vanity easily. To the profound and sincere revolutionary intuition a false, vain, and fatuous action was returned, more prepared to benefit from the triumph of the Revolution than to make itself worthy of it. But the most disastrous consequence is that, in order to hide its inability and its failure, this action has blamed the liberty itself that it did not know how to use, but rather to corrupt it, claiming immediately that, because liberty is corrupted, the inability and failure have been from the Revolution because it became attached to a *liberal* Constitution.

It is not necessary to seek another purpose in the antiliberalism that currently flourishes in Mexico than that of excusing a political action that has not been able to rise to the height of its responsibility. If in the contemporary prosperity of the antiliberal political doctrines it seems to find a justification and even an opportunity to ennoble itself, presenting itself as the most advanced tendency like the doctrine of the "present moment," it is not impossible to perceive that the antiliberalism of other nations is satisfying the same end of hiding and justifying a similar moral incapacity. For, the absolutely contrary direction contemporary thought in science, art, and philosophy follows is showing what is, when not subject to violence that disfigures it, the true sentiment of advanced ideas. And in any place where political antiliberalism preponderates, the intellectual divorce is observed between politics and the superior culture that has taken hold in Mexico, with the thought of university instruction getting out of touch critically with politics.

The current situation of Mexican political thought is clear; constitutional liberalism is dangerously threatened by this passionate dogmatic attitude of recent origin. This situation has been created and is maintained in the shadow of an intellectual confusion that allows any new liberal trend and the constitution of '17 to be considered reactionary, and the acts that reflect indiscriminately the priesthood of Stalin, the priesthood of Hitler, or the priesthood of Mussolini as revolutionary and advanced. Nonetheless, it is not daring to declare that Mexican liberalism will have to survive the confusion that endangers the authentic radical aspirations of the nation, which have made imperative that the Revolution be considered the legitimate continuation of the Reform and that it not be confused with the backward motion of politics toward unreflecting, sentimental, and primary forms.

ANTONIO CASO

Antonio Caso (1883–1946), born in Mexico City, was a philosopher and university professor. As a young man he became dissatisfied with the prevailing philosophical ideas of his time. Indeed, during the first decade of the twentieth century positivism was the official doctrine supported by the minister of education, Justo Sierra.

Caso joined like-minded luminaries such as José Vasconcelos, Alfonso Reyes, and Pedro Henríquez Ureña and in 1909 founded a literary club called El Ateneo de la Juventud. The group criticized positivism and developed a philosophy based on intuition and emotion that was influenced by the thinking of Henri Bergson.

Caso was president of the National University between 1920 and 1923. In the 1930s he vigorously opposed the project of adopting socialism as the official doctrine of the university and debated the key proponent of this idea, Vicente Lombardo Toledano. Caso defended the role of the university as an institution devoted to the pursuit of truth and knowledge through research and teaching. He argued that teachers should be free to teach what they considered to be true and relevant. Liberty was required to sustain the quest for truth and knowledge. Around that time Caso also wrote on socialism and fascism and on the challenges these doctrines posed to the "human person."

We present a selection from his essay *La persona humana y el estado totalitario,* from the 1940s.

Consciousness
of Liberty

1. THE ATTRIBUTES OF THE CENTURY

Our epoch, which begins with the war of the nations, possesses attributes that differentiate and characterize it. The great industrial development, like the scientific unfolding, does not constitute, certainly, an exclusive attribute of the period of human history to which we refer, because during the entire nineteenth century, the apogee of science and industry—its immediate corollary—was already brought about as a characteristic element of this other period of history.

Nevertheless, the development of the physical sciences has continued in our time, manifesting itself in the elaboration of the electric theory of matter. The great hypotheses of physics have expanded the complexity of scientific knowledge in such a way that it is a problem today for the middle level of instruction, the pedagogy of modern physics. How to make young minds, necessarily lacking in higher mathematical culture, understand the hypothesis of physicists about the constitution of matter? . . . The discovery of radium began the forward movement of the development of contemporary thinking with respect to the structure of the atom. In reality, just as the cell changes into a very complex organism for those who study biology, the atom is converted into a solar system for those who investigate the structure of the universe.

The great names of Einstein and Planck dominate the theories of modern physics, and one comes to think about a certain indeterminacy that rests at the base of reality, so that scientific laws would mean only "a limitation of possibilities" according to the perfect expression of Mach in his book on scientific knowledge.[1]

Original title: "Conciencia de la libertad." Source: Antonio Caso, *La persona humana y el estado totalitario* (Mexico: UNAM, 1941).

1. Ernst Mach (1838–1916) was an Austrian physicist and a philosopher of science. (Editor's note)

Dr. Carrel makes note, in agreement with the opinion of many other scientists, of the lack of proportion that occurs between the progress of the physical sciences and that of the biological and moral sciences. Tolstoy already declared that "modern man resembles a child who plays with dangerous toys of nitroglycerin." In past epochs, man made use only of animal energy and some of the physical forces to put machines into motion. Today he has managed to make use not only of heat and electricity, but also, breaking down matter into its atomic elements, makes use of fabulous energies that he will be able to use someday, without doubt, to economize on his effort, achieving fantastic results. Therefore, one of the differentiating attributes of our century is the incomparable development of the physical sciences.

What can such an extraordinary apogee of science signify in the advance of the culture? . . . Science is the final fruit in the development cycle of cultures. Scientific knowledge prospered in Greece, not in the classical epoch, but rather in the days of Hellenism and Alexandrianism. From the Museum of Alexandria sprang the scientific movement of antiquity. When for centuries letters and history had already flourished, science inaugurated its splendor. This indicates that the great epochs of scientific development do not correspond to the creative moments of humanity, but rather to the twilight instants of decline. Alexandria was the magnificent evening twilight of Greek culture.

Philosophy also achieves in our time an admirable development, and this only confirms the thesis of decline. Because to philosophize is a type of reflection at the second level, a reflection on reflections, a universal meditation on the world and the I already explored in other branches of the culture. The philosopher is also a late fruit. The values he creates can produce only after human meditation has been exercised directly on life and history. Socrates, Plato, and Aristotle are for Nietzsche symptoms of decadence. After the great Greek century of drama and politics, the great Aristotelian synthesis appears, coinciding with the life of Alexander.

Great philosophers, comparable to the most distinguished names of human thought, are Bergson, Husserl, and Scheler. Bergsonianism and phenomenology coincide with Einstein and the theory of relativity. Therefore, at the apogee of philosophical development can be seen, sometimes, another symptom of the great twilight of the European culture. There are neither great lyric nor dramatic poets, nor brilliant artists like those that other centuries begat. What certainly exists and honors our century is the philosophical and scientific meditation, undeniable differentiating attribute of our age.

Finally, politics, unquestionably renewed, brands contemporary life with its creation. Two great struggles are begun between democracy and the totalitarian state, just as between the two types of totalitarian states. The state, the privileged community par excellence, tends to include social life in its fullness. The old liberal individualism is moving away from the European political constitutions; the rights of man, which the French Revolution consecrated, are disrespected today by many theories of law and of the state. It has come to be declared that the world initiates in its advance the episodes of "a new Middle Age." And the conflict is not only between democracy and the totalitarian state, but also the discussion between the Russian and German regimes, between *racism* and *classism.*

A student of political science or of constitutional law of the past century who attended seminars on contemporary politics would see denied all the fundamentals of the science he learned. The individual was conceived then as the final end of civil organization. It was said: the state exists for the individual, to sanction the rights of man. Today it is said: the individual is only an element in the hands of the state. The "transmutation of values" tends to be completed.

How not to see in the contemporary political vicissitudes one of the distinctive attributes of our time? . . . Science and industry—its immediate corollary—again organize people in large groups around the machines. Architecture, which makes use of new industrial resources, is, perhaps, among the liberal arts, the only one that stands out, being able to exercise its aesthetic creation in magnificent constructions that bring to mind the days of Babylon or Memphis. Great masses woven of iron that climb to the sky, formidable structures whose vertebrae machines forge, the incomparably more powerful Cyclops of our industrial and scientific mythology!

The world is transformed into an accelerated political and economic rhythm whose movement marks the hour we arrived, in the haste of our life, constantly agitated and complex, and the anguish of our heart, suffering with the perpetual outbreak of war and the urgent, formidable social revolution.

2. KANT

A singular rhythm guides the forward movement of philosophy, that is to say, of independent thought. The great critical thinker appears first, who proved to be the teacher and founder of a large and illustrious philosophical tradition; afterward the brilliant metaphysician who organizes into a vast synthesis the metaphysical idea; and, finally, the great encyclopedist, who, in harvesting the fruits of his precursors, organizes knowledge and effects in his work a universal definition of the type of a culture.

Greek philosophy before Socrates was, perhaps, the preferred period of speculative creation. Parmenides, Heraclitus, Pythagoras, Democritus, Empedocles, and Anaxagoras created the cosmological ideas of thinking humanity. It seems that in those remote days, the Greek genius contributed to the coming centuries all the ideas that afterward were discussed and appreciated with the effort of the generations.

Socrates refined the critical spirit of his race; he ordered the systematic dialectic and created ethics as a discipline independent of religion. His fine and classical irony, his supreme art of "midwife of souls," taught the fundamentals of morality independent of the will of the gods. For this reason, without hyperbole, Aristotle could call him "the founder of moral science," distinguished title among all philosophical titles!

Plato is the philosopher of the ideational act, the brilliant metaphysician of the Socratic cycle: "What is inherent in man is to understand the general, that is to say, the rational unity in the scattered multiplicity of the sensible." But this is the memory of what our soul beheld in its journey in pursuit of God, when, treating disdainfully what is improperly called reality, it elevates its awareness to what in itself is true. "When man sees beauty on the earth (says the philosopher in *Phaedrus*) he remembers true beauty, takes wing, and burns with the desire to fly toward it."

Perhaps the title of the most profound intelligence of the evolution of thought should be reserved for Plato. His work is one of the keystones of Western civilization. Champion of philosophical paganism and precursor of Christianity, "Father of the Fathers of the Church." After the great critic (Socrates), the great metaphysical creator (Plato), arises the encyclopedist Aristotle. He grounds the Platonic ideas in life and experience. The world of Plato was divine. The Stagirite conserved for him his august divinity but brought him nearer to earth. The *idea* became *form*, and only through abstraction could it be separated from *mat-*

ter. The Aristotelian encyclopedia summed up the teaching of Greece. Hereafter, stoics, epicureans, and skeptics will distribute the immortal inheritance, as the lieutenants of Alexander his ephemeral empire.

In modern times the rhythm of ancient philosophy is repeated. Descartes is the first modern philosopher. He inverted the ends of human certitude. He made of the I the origin of philosophy: *I doubt, therefore I think, therefore I am.* France—said Hegel to Cousin—did enough for philosophy in giving it Descartes. Never before had skepticism been vanquished. Greek thought in the end asserted its topics. According to Descartes, doubt affirms something over all dubitability. Even today, the beginning point of phenomenology is the Cartesian *ego cogitans,* and Husserl calls his own system neo-Cartesianism.

After the great critical thinker, the great independent metaphysicians, Spinoza and Malebranche. They are the Platonic philosophers of the Cartesian cycle. The saintly Benedict Spinoza, intellectual lover of God, is the pride of the modern world. The systematic pantheism of the *Ethics* is still, today, one of the limiting points of speculation. Parmenides revived in the seventeenth century of the Christian era! . . .

Leibniz represents the recovery of spiritual individuality before the vast synthesis of pantheistic and Cartesian rationalism. His work initiates all the contemporary psychological and metaphysical ideas: evolution, the subconscious, the ideality of time and space . . . He is the Aristotle, the encyclopedist, of the Cartesian cycle.

And when another great rectifier of intelligence appeared in the eighteenth century, his *Critique of Pure Reason* came back to repeat the Cartesian position, making it more profound, modifying it, strengthening it. In the evolution of ideas exist, in our opinion, three calm and self-sacrificing founders: Socrates, Descartes, and Kant. They represent the three moments of development of an immortal idea—to wit, that the genuine certitude, the positive seat of the human sciences, cannot come from outside consciousness, but rather must be extracted from the depths of our moral being. The oracle at Delphi said it already, "Know thyself." The words of the oracle of Apollo produced in the course of the centuries three fixed stars of the mind: the Greek, that is to say, Socrates; the French, that is to say, Descartes; and the German, under whose immediate light we live, Kant.

Why is Kant great? . . . Because, to the three great fundamental questions that intelligence posed and that constitute philosophy, he gave an original response. What is knowledge? — human curiosity inquired — and Kant answered: "A synthetic a priori judgment." To know is to synthesize the forms of reason with the matter that experience provides. The judgments that extend and perfect knowledge are those in which the predicate is not yet implicit in the subject. Nonetheless, they are formulated for what has still not occurred, with as much certitude as if it were before the facts that were to come. All science is a synthesis of knowledge, of synthetic a priori judgments. Philosophy also asked, What is beauty? And Kant, founder of aesthetics, answered: A "finality without an end," a necessary and universal disinterestedness. The difference that exists among the useful, the good, and the beautiful rests on the fact that the useful and the good are desired for the good they cause, while the beautiful is sought for itself. The beautiful is disinterested; it signifies a repose amidst the eagerness of desire. This subtle cloudscape that we could not reach is as beautiful as the slight wave that rises to kiss the beach and dies at our feet! The soul stops wanting and desiring when the eye or the ear sees to contemplate or listens to hear.

Philosophy proposes another inquiry as well, the most difficult and frightening of all: What is duty? And Kant teaches: a categorical imperative, that is to say, an unconditional but absolute command, the only absolute command. It is therefore the only categorical imperative. *But duty postulates liberty. Only for free beings does it have meaning. The will is autonomous in doing good, heteronymous in doing evil. As we have to be good, we are free. God is the kingdom of the moral ends that duty imposes.*

In his *Critique of Judgment* Kant says that three attributes distinguish the philosopher: "to think for himself, finding out what others think, without incurring contradiction." The first is characteristic for original and free spirits. Kant was a free and original spirit. The second corresponds to the far-reaching spirits. Kant was a distinguished spirit of breadth. The third is the work of congruent spirits. Few men have thought with greater congruence than the author of the *Critique of Pure Reason*! Moreover, the cosmogonic hypothesis that Laplace conceived mathematically today carries a doubly glorious name: Kant-Laplace. Is it possible to give greater praise to a philosopher? ...

3. GERMAN IDEALISM
Again, the rhythm of independent philosophical thought is repeated in the development of the Kantian cycle. To seek, like Socrates, like Des-

cartes, like Kant, in the knowledge of oneself the unquestionable foundation of a first truth leads necessarily to spiritualism or idealism. Socrates, Descartes, and Husserl are spiritualists. Kant arrives, resolutely, at an idealist position. Socrates did not believe one could have firm knowledge of something in the world. He had, on the other hand, full faith in the knowledge of the spirit. Descartes leaves the solipsism that *cogito ergo sum* imposes, thanks to the ontological argument: existence is a necessary attribute of the perfect being. Kant, who rejects the ontological proof, reduces to the "thing in itself" that which is heterogeneous to the spirit; but he insinuates that this X, this unknown, could very well be found in one's own unexplored consciousness.

His successors, the great idealist metaphysicians. Fichte and Schelling, more intrepid even than the great critic of Königsberg (or less circumspect), address the "thing in itself," the impenetrable unknown, by reducing it to the position that defines idealism. Hegel, the encyclopedist, the Aristotle of the idealist direction inaugurated by Kant, sustains absolute idealism, the immanence of the universe in the idea "everything real is rational."

Kant had declared that "the mysterious unknown that hides behind the sensible phenomena could very well be one's own unknown that resides in ourselves." According to the great philosopher, pure reason creates space and time, and in applying to the phenomena the categories of the relationship, it unites them with the nexus of causation. Reason is the legislator of nature. And from reason arise the ideas of cosmos and God.

If the "thing in itself," if the unknown, is not a reality, if it cannot be conceived, it is nothing, or properly is, like space, time, the categories, and God itself, something identified with the subject of knowledge.

From this arises the philosophy of identity; first Fichte and then Schelling. The supreme principle of Fichte is the I. To philosophize is to be convinced that pure being is nothing. The ought-to-be is everything. *Knowledge is the creation of the I.* The I produces or "creates" the truth. "Theoretical reason," — says Weber, commenting on Fichte, — "is the means or the agent from which practical reason is served in order to realize the ideal." The apotheosis of morality, of the ought-to-be, of the will to good, makes the idealism of Fichte one of the most original and noble philosophical ideas of all time. Kant himself had already insinuated the superior dignity of the ought-to-be over being, in harmony with the moral consciousness of the human genus. The moral idealism of Fichte burst forth as a direct consequence of both *critiques* of *pure reason* and of *practical reason.*

Schelling reaches the apex of the system of identity in his *transcendental idealism.* The life of the culture contains three supreme moments. Through science we intuit the absolute; through art we see the absolute manifest in individuality; in religion the spirit is transformed into absolute reality. Nature and culture: "Everything is one and the same." History is an epic poem in accordance with the spirit of God. It offers two principal parts: one represents the distancing from humanity, from its center until touching the extreme limit; the other represents the return to the primordial center. One is a type of *Iliad,* the other the *Odyssey.* In the first, the direction is centrifugal; in the second, centripetal. The universal point of view is expressed in history. Nature shows the spirit in the law: "Everything is one and the same."

After the great Platonic philosophers of German Idealism comes Hegel, that is to say, the Aristotle of the Kantian cycle. According to the philosopher, everything is immanent in the idea. "Everything real is rational, everything rational is real." Nothing is extrinsic to the idea. Logic, science of the idea, is metaphysics. The world is a universal dialectical process. Hegelianism is method and doctrine, dialectic and system. Each one of the things is linked, necessarily, to other things that precede and follow it. Each one of our thoughts leads to other thoughts and is the fruit of thoughts that led to it. Thoughts originate as things follow one another. This is not a simple coincidence. The real and natural orders are not distinct orders. The order is unique, reality is unique. Existence and truth are identical. The mental process is the real process. The logical unfolding of the idea is the cosmic process.

Each isolated concept is false; it represents only a more or less considerable and imperfect part of the truth; it demands its complement; it converts itself into its negation. Now then, for two negations to exist is impossible. Every idea tends to find, in its superior idea, the affirmation of what it contains of genuine and the negation of what it has of false.

The synthesis is, simultaneously, affirmation and negation of the thesis and of the antithesis. But in its turn, the synthesis—which is an idea like the very ones it resolved—has its opposite, its antithesis, which, together with it is resolved into a superior synthesis, and thus, successively, from the pure being or abstract idea to the absolute idea that encompasses everything. "Becoming" is developed by triads, and, supported by the dialectic method, Hegel can dare to construct the universe, because the "thought of existence" is, according to the sublime phrase of the philosopher, "existence itself that thinks within us."

With reason, Ortega y Gasset has written:

> The block of German Idealism is one of the greatest edifices that has been constructed on the planet. For it alone, it would be enough to justify and consecrate before the universe the existence of the European continent. In that exemplary construction, modern thought reaches its greatest height. Because, in truth, all modern philosophy is idealism. There are only two notable exceptions: Spinoza, who was not European, and materialism, which is not philosophy.

4. VICISSITUDES OF HEGELIANISM

The system of Hegel originated in itself a "center" central to the teaching of the master, a "right" inclined toward misoneism, and a revolutionary "left." The three Hegelian positions have influenced, and continue influencing, the political-social vicissitudes of the world. Here is how:

Hegel himself was the philosopher of monarchy. In his opinion, the state is the organism of morality. Through it the substance of the ethical is made, in general, the ethical substance itself, conscious of itself, because the state creates the organization of the national will. The state is not something artificial, but rather *the politically organized person of the nation* in a given country. The political constitution is an organic product of the spirit of the nation and of its individual history.

> This Hegelian philosophy was made (says Sauer in his *Juridical and Social Philosophy*, page 49 of the Spanish edition) to be converted into "Prussian philosophy of state," justified "the reason of state," then practiced as a national resource that gave a fundamental logic to the patriotic rebirth of this state, deteriorated and again restored, and attributed to the state itself a broad cultural mission, in opposition to Kant, who only saw in it a juridical organization for the protection of individuals.

The state signifies the dominion of the idea, of what is, in truth, universal of the *objective spirit*. The republic does not constitute the most perfect form of government. It rests on the confusion of civil society and the state, it maximizes the importance and significance of the individual. Precisely for having sacrificed the Idea to the individual, the family, and the lineage, the republics of antiquity ended in dictatorships. Greek tyranny and Roman caesarism are the result of the inherent defects in the republican form (democratic or aristocratic). On the other hand, monarchy is the political regime in which the national idea determines its adequate expression. The prince, according to Hegel, is *the state made man,* the general will converted to individual will. Thus the maxim of absolute royalty acquires meaning: "I am the state."

Against this Prussian state erected in *the European state* par excellence, the historic materialism—Hegelianism of the "left"—evokes another, different political social idea. Thus, as the theory of the teacher informed the thought of the Prussian monarchy, the disciples fomented with their social theories the contemporary organization of Bolshevik Russia. The state—according to Marx—is only *the ideological superstructure* of those who command or rule in the bourgeois society. The basis of all "ideology" is economic, and all "ideology" denies, nevertheless, that its ascendancy might be economic. It is evident, nonetheless, that culture (politics, law, religion, art, science, etc.) is based on the economic, according to the Marxist thesis. It is not that Marx denies culture itself (this would be impossible and absurd); what he denies is that the fundamental structure of social life might be of a cultural kind and not economic. As workers enjoy only strict remuneration to live from their labor, wealth is accumulated in the hands of the capitalist. By virtue of this, the state must be converted into "the proletarian state"; or be "the systematic expropriation of those who have inveterately been expropriators." Marx believes that the "administration" will replace the "bourgeois state." The triumphant economy will end up being the apotheosis of the *material,* as the state of Hegel signaled "the advance of *the idea,* that is to say, God, in history" . . .

But in the course of its development, Hegelian philosophy is not summed up only in pure Marxism, but rather it forms the base of another new, different social philosophy: anarchism. Max Stirner, author of the famous book *The Individual and His Property,* is the theoretician of "anarchism" as Marx is of "collectivism" and Hegel of "monarchism."

The divine contemplates God; the human, man; I—says Stirner—am neither divine nor human; I am myself: the unique one; and the world is "my property." This is the absolute thesis of anarchist individualism, with its corresponding social formula, "free association of egoists . . ."

In comparison with the socialist and collectivist "ideologies" Stirner outlines, eloquently, his political system. The divine contemplates God (Stirner is not God). The human relates to man (Stirner is not man). God and man, in his judgment, are abstractions. Stirner is the unique one: "der Einzige." Humanity has been the plaything of abstractions, which Hegel blends into a constant dialectical rhythm. The social relates to society, the collective to the community. Stirner is neither "community" nor "society." He is himself; neither divine nor human nor social nor communal. He denies all these "ideologies"! There can be nothing over the "individual and his property." The I is absolute. Apotheosis!

For Hegel, the absolute is "the state," which indicates the course of God in history; for Marx, the *economy* is the foundation of the cultural "superstructures"; for Stirner, the *I* is the absolute. Here are the distinct Hegelian symbols of right and left! . . .

Our eager curiosity now asks: how could an "official philosophy" be acknowledged if, within a given philosophy (the Hegelian school itself), social and political thought shows itself so fertile in opposing positions? . . .

5. LIBERTY, AUTHORITY, AND LAW

What we are going to say does not constitute a political theory, much less a metaphysical or moral hypothesis that contains the proclamation of a philosophical system. It is only a matter of affirming truths that the conscience of the honest man accepts in its fullness to the degree they are formulated for him with clarity. We could say, repeating the famous expression of Newton, "I make no hypotheses." We also do not make them because the synthesis of the thoughts posed here have been expressed by Kant in his moral philosophy independently of any reference to a metaphysical principle sui generis.

Two elements constitute the ends between which all civil life turns: *liberty and laws. Civil life without liberty is not conceivable, from the moral point of view.* Nor is civil life conceivable without law. Therefore, *all civil life implies the necessary combination of liberty and law.* They are both (law and liberty) indispensable components of the axis around which human solidarity turns.

A society in which law disappears is disturbed in its foundations. To disrespect the law is to destroy the bases of the social order; but to disrespect liberty or exaggerate its radius of action, even provoking libertinism, is also to deny the social order in one of its indeclinable foundations.

There is need, therefore, for something that mediates between liberty and law, which on the one side looks toward the enormous ideal of liberty, and on the other refers to the essential form of the law. This third element must realize the plasticity of the social order, adapting itself to the aspirations of autonomy but being shaped within the form of law. *Being a little liberty and a little law.* This third element, which looks toward liberty and toward law with equanimity and elegance, is power, the authority.

One sees clearly, from the foregoing, that the authority occupies a middle condition; it signifies an intermediate position, it is true, but essential, between liberty and the formula of the law. Authority by itself makes no sense. The meaning that it can have arises from its purpose. Power in itself lacks meaning. The powerful ones, from the social-political point of view, are the means and not the end; *the purpose is liberty within law.* The authority of the one who has power is justified by the ultimate end I have just expressed. If the power is not an end in itself, it is, nonetheless, as essential, when it is ordered by moral reason, as the ultimate end of liberty obtained within the law. In this way are unified in one public intention, which all human units approve and enhance, the authority (full of greatness and distinction if it is adapted to its intrinsic purpose, reprehensible as an abomination if it oversteps its limits consecrated by its own purpose), liberty, and law.

Every transgression, every disturbance of the order I have just described, every inharmonious surmounting of one of the elements over the others, has been defined in pejorative terms by the moral conscience of humanity. These three terms: barbarism, anarchy, and despotism, imply a negative estimation of the moral conscience, an implicit condemnation. Anarchy, like despotism and barbarism, is opposed to the republic, to culture.

It is easy to become fully aware that anarchy, as much as despotism and barbarism, results from combining, in a defective way, power, liberty, and law. Only harmony, social eurythmy of these elements, engenders the cultured republic. Let us propose the definition of anarchy.

Anarchy is nothing other than the apotheosis of chaotic liberty, which denies all power and loathes the law. The anarchic state exaggerates without proportion one of the indeclinable elements of collective life: liberty; and by this exaggeration it engenders chaos. The axis of the law is broken and authority is crushed: this is anarchy.

Despotism constitutes the apotheosis of the power and law, but without liberty. Despots abhor liberty, as the anarchists power; therefore, they constitute another chaotic state, because the law without liberty only engenders a power without authority, without moral sense, without social eurythmy. It is seen clearly how anarchism and despotism are explained by the same reasoning because they suppress an element of their being indispensable for civil life. *The loathing of the power is anarchy; the loathing of liberty, despotism.*

Barbarism suppresses liberty and law; that is to say, it eliminates culture. It is a matter only of blind forces that play within the natural order, realizing the thinking of Spinoza on natural law. "In the state of nature," said the philosopher, "the right of each person is extended until it reaches its power." The elimination of culture is the suppression of what man has added to nature, the elimination of the human, which puts us in the presence of the pure natural laws that govern life and matter. Man is then, as Hobbes expressed, "a wolf to man."

Don Francisco de Quevedo, profound Castilian writer who lived in times of public corruption, left his judgment on liberty and moral culture formulated in this lovely fragment that we cite in its entirety so that it serves us simultaneously as epigraph and epilogue: "*The aspiration we all have is the liberty of all, endeavoring that our subjection be just and not violent; that reason governs us, not caprice; that we are of the one who bequeaths us, not of the one who seizes us; that we are in the care of princes not merchandise; and in the republics, companions and not slaves, members and not things, bodies and not shadow.*" Therefore, here is the noble definition of the cultured republic, according to the noble genius of Kant: "*power with liberty and law.*" All this, we reiterate in concluding, does not constitute a metaphysical hypothesis or a newly arrived theory that can disappear and be annihilated by time in its indefinite development. We are not making a hypothesis, we are simply declaring what the experience of the human species has been able to formulate of true and eternal in the sad but profound instruction of history!

6. DEMOCRACY AS MEANS AND END

> *Man is the indirect being, and the more so, the more cultivated he is.*
> — Simmel

If, instead of putting himself in the service of the spirit, the demagogue tries to dominate it, with his very stance he is obliterated before reason, and he dishonors, corrupting it, the very principle of liberty. This is the great fallacy of all democracies, that their endeavors on behalf of the liberty of the people transgress their own and essential limits: *the confusion of the means with the end.* On occasions the means for attainment of human ends are so admirable that these means are made into ends, and they are then devoid of all possible sense.

In corroboration of the foregoing, we propose the study of the behavior to which man responds in accord with the essential development of culture. There exists a radical difference between the way an animal acts and the conduct of a human being. The animal responds to instinct. It is an active being that cannot imagine distinctly the ends of its action. Man has a conduct, that is to say, a series of coherent actions that responds to ends. Conduct is an order sui generis that is explained, like all order, by the end that governs it. It happens that, as civilization develops, the ends of human activity diversify in a marvelous way. A very clear mirror of this disconcerting diversity, of the intermediate ends that cultural development involves, is the machine. Every machine is a tool, but not every tool is a machine. To the extent that technology develops, the tools that directly serve to achieve the end of the relative action are replaced by machines, which only indirectly actualize the ultimate end for what was intended. And modern factories in the great industrial centers of the world are complex and very varied organizations of exquisite machinery that, most times, engender, only, an element for the production of social wealth.

What happens with the complexity of industrial technology happens also in all orders of social activity. Political and juridical institutions, like the machinery of our industries, do not immediately actualize *the end for which they were conceived, the ultimate end,* which can be nothing different from achieving the happiness of the people with the attainment of the highest values of the culture: truth, beauty, justice, goodness, holiness. Between the final end and the principles of human action, a series of subordinate ends is established, lofty in themselves, noble by their essence, but that cannot be converted into the ultimate ends of the action, and that therefore induce error many times if some political or social theory converts them into the ultimate norms of the activity.

> For primitive man, says Simmel, the will achieves what is intended, taking possession of it in a direct way or using only a scarce number of simple means. The growing multiplicity and complexity the elevation of life brings with it do not permit this trinity of the series: *desire, means, end;* but rather they transform the intermediate member into plurality, in which the precisely effective means turn out to be results produced by other means, and this by another in turn, until that incalculable complexity appears, that chain of practical activity in which the man of mature cultures lives.

That stepwise increase of intermediate ends between the desire and the ultimate end to achieve leads to democracy, which is only a political means for guaranteeing liberty, being converted by some theories into the ultimate end that must supplant the highest values of human culture. Then the democratic sophism appears in all its splendor! Liberty and its corresponding political form (this is the democratic form) are means and not ultimate ends. Anyone who converts elements into highest finalities of human action is victim of an illusion!

Culture without liberty is inconceivable. Only in an environment of liberty can the work of a civilization mature. If the spontaneity of the spiritual center of man is suppressed, his cultural relationships concomitantly dry up, the lushness of creative invention shrivels, the very nature of the producing spirit is crippled. But if, because liberty is a precious gift, an inescapable condition of human perfection, one tries to put the means above the end, subordinating culture to democracy and liberty, one generates the monstrous effect of making Simmel's trinity, *desire, means, and end,* meaningless. What is desired is liberty and democracy for good and for truth, for justice, beauty, and holiness; but the constriction of the highest values within a democracy converted into an ultimate end has no meaning (because it is not what is desired). Democracy for democracy lacks meaning. Liberty for liberty also lacks meaning. On the other hand, the desire and the means harmonize in the final end: culture integrated with the splendor of the supreme values.

How to explain the error of the sophism of democracy by itself and for itself, of liberty by itself and for itself? How to understand the formulas of traditional liberalism that created the apotheosis of the highly celebrated apothegm: "Liberty, Equality, Fraternity, indivisibility of the Republic, or death"? After what was said before, the elucidation of the case becomes obvious. It is that a means, going against the desire that adopted it, has been converted into a final end. It is that, liberty turning out to be so noble, so noble likewise democracy, our elders, fascinated with their nobility, placed the means they judged suitable for the realization of their destinies above the genuine final ends. But this implies a transgression of Simmel's trinity. *The means, unfaithful to the desire, has negated the end.* The solution to the problem appears. The hand has touched the heart of the error.

The contemporary world lacks some ultimate end that organizes all the complex and diverse secondary ends into a luminous sheaf of supreme truths that puts forward beauty and goodness and holiness! It is that contemporary humanity lacks a religion that might save it, a belief that might nourish it, a faith that might redeem it, a hope, finally, that might subordinate all scattered ends into a fundamental affirmation. For this reason our epoch has been compared with the distant days of Roman decadence. *Then also there was no universal ideal; like now, no one understood the supreme finality of the common effort.* Paganism no longer moved people. The pride of the stoic, the indifference of the skeptic, and the "pleasure in repose" of the epicurean suited some sectors of Roman opinion, but they did not manage to form the luminous sheaf of truths that would give meaning to desires and means to action!

The teaching of Saint Paul, apostle of the Gentiles, appeared: "So that if someone is in Christ, he is a new creation; the old things pass, and here everything is made anew."

Might not the remedy for our imperfect democracies depend on their intimate union with Christian truth? *Perhaps, within Christianity, the means, faithful to the desire, will affirm the end.*

7. THE WORD OF ADMONITION

The history of humanity is progress in consciousness of liberty.
— Hegel

In our time, various political systems have arisen over against democracy that would be called the clear negation of the essential postulates of every democracy. Consider that the affirmation of political liberty, within a given democratic regime, constitutes the reiteration of social theories already declining in the development of human history. Nonetheless, Hegel conceived the development of civilization as if it were the very apotheosis of liberty. For this he formulated, in his famous lectures on the *Philosophy of Universal History:* "The history of humanity is progress in the consciousness of liberty." That is to say, the essence of human development, of humanity in man, is constituted by the consciousness of liberty.

Today, another great philosopher, of whom Ortega y Gasset has said that his wealth of ideas is overwhelmed in the splendor of multiple and varied small jewels that spring from his mind, realizing the brevity of his existence, has written: "Liberty, active and personal spontaneity of the spiritual center of man (of man in man), is the first and fundamental condition that makes culture possible." Because Scheler conceives culture as an ontological relationship. To know is to be cultured. The cultured man participates in the being of the things he knows or understands. In the relationship of the understanding, the object determines the attitude of the subject. To know is to observe what is investigated with all the resources of the mind, but without deforming it with prejudgments. And how would this endeavor of understanding be able to actualize this ontological relationship with the object if it did not enjoy liberty in the investigation? How to understand, to know something scientifically, culturally, if, a priori, the guidelines are set out so for knowing the known? In what form, outside an environment of liberty, could criticism, which constitutes the very rhythm of science, be exercised? ...

Therefore, Scheler is right when he demands spontaneity of the spiritual center of man as a condition for the possibility of culture. We are not supporters of just anyone who calls himself "free thinker"; but we certainly believe in every truly free thinker.

Well then, culture is the sublime reason for man. Culture is holiness, goodness, beauty, justice, truth. All the values are integrated into the notion of culture. Human societies are laboratories of the ideal — outstanding laboratories, in which the truth is revealed, in which beauty shows itself, in which justice is realized and attainable holiness works in each historic moment, in human individuals!

Only by one road — asserts Max Scheler — can democracy today save itself from dictatorship and, at the same time, save the goods of culture and science: by limiting itself, putting itself at the service of culture and the spirit instead of trying to dominate them. Otherwise, only one solution remains: an enlightened despotic dictatorship that, without taking into account the feeling of the masses hostile to the culture and of their status as adults, dominates them with the whip, the saber, and the lump of sugar.

The cited text implies various distinct propositions in advance. The first teaches the only road to salvation of democracy, or better, salvation of liberty: limitation of democracy itself, putting itself at the service of culture and the spirit.

Because when it is a matter of liberty and democracy, it is thought, generally, that both constitute an end in themselves by themselves. This specifies the very grave error of accepting that the ultimate end of man and his civilization is liberty and its corresponding political form, democracy. No; liberty is a means and not an end; it can be justified only by putting itself at the service of the goods of culture and science. Liberty for everyone, liberty for all; but provided that it be the means of acquiring the truth, of realizing the good and justice; because we are not born to be free, but rather to be good. Liberty for evil, liberty for error, democracy for crime, totally lack sense; it denies, as Scheler would say, "the active and personal spontaneity of the spiritual center of man." Deny the man in the man! . . . Liberty and democracy as conditions of culture are not only irreproachable, but rather, as we have proved before, only through them can the highest values of existence be realized.

But if—as we have said before—"instead of putting himself in the service of the spirit, the demagogue tries to dominate it, with his very stance he is obliterated in the face of reason, and he dishonors, corrupting it, the very principle of liberty." This is the great fallacy of all democracies, that their endeavors on behalf of the liberty of the people transgress their own and essential limits: *the confusion of the means with the end.* On occasion, the means for attainment of human ends are so admirable that these means are made into ends, and they are then devoid of all possible sense.

The same thing that happens with liberty happens with wealth. What happens with democracy happens with gold. Liberty is good, it is essential, as gold is good for life; but the rich person must serve with his wealth, the same as the free man with his liberty, the superior ends of existence. Over liberty and wealth are truth and the good. No one is free to be evil! No one is rich to be unhappy! Wealth and liberty have their full meaning if they are put in the service of culture and the spirit, if they are judged means and not ends, if they acknowledge that the ultimate end of man must consist only of the harmonious synthesis of eternal true values.

The unavoidable consequence of lack of knowledge of the ends of liberty and democracy leads directly to despotism. This is what the final proposition of Max Scheler's thinking formulates: "Otherwise, only one solution remains: an enlightened despotic dictatorship that, without taking into account the feeling of the masses hostile to the culture and of their status as adults, dominates them with the whip, the saber, and the lump of sugar."

Dictatorships, then, are not absolute goods; they are relative evils. When democracies go too far in the organic exercise of liberties, they appear as defense of an unfit culture, of ridiculed truth; but they cannot have another distinct meaning or another justification, because tyranny goes against the essence of culture, because liberty is the first and fundamental condition that makes it possible. In this way, the diverse ideas to which we have alluded join together in the history of peoples; liberty, democracy, dictatorship, civilization. When the democratic thesis oversteps its essential limits, the antithesis of the dictatorship is produced; but the true synthesis is affirmation and negation of both inadequate, incomplete thoughts; because dictatorships stifle culture in the same way demagogic movements do; and above all, the means figure unfailingly the ends, the indeclinable values: truth, justice, beauty, goodness, holiness! . . . For this reason we can repeat, in closing, the thought of Hegel that serves us as epigraph: "The history of humanity is progress in the consciousness of liberty."

It is characteristic of the great spirits to move forward in life, foreseeing the future action that in their minds is revealed before solidifying, objectively, in tangible historic movements. Science is foresight; that is to say, anticipated vision that infers the near or distant future from the present. To pre-see signifies seeing before having seen. Because intelligence views the object that will be formed, understanding through anticipation, reading with the eyes of the spirit before those of the body, actualize their optical function. But intelligence does not realize its most admirable work through the spirit of prophecy, or by inexistent magical intuitions; but rather it is elevated to the universal, to the eternal and incorruptible essence, and it knows, then, a priori (thanks to its own ideational act), that the future will realize the essential, already perceived from the present. This is not prophecy, certainly, or illusion, or the working of miracles. It is the ordinary act of the powerful intelligence, which, in seeing the universal and concrete essence, knows it will be realized today and always, here and everywhere.

In this way the brilliant thought of Max Scheler continued in confirming that the symptoms of a troubled epoch of coercion and slavery for the human spirit were already vigorously begun. Situated on the threshold of our age, before death put an end, certainly premature, to his independent speculation, the philosopher confirmed, in the midst of his distressed perplexity, the tyranny of a century that prepares itself on the ruins of the decadent individualism of the nineteenth century.

And it is that the contrasts of the diverse political-social dogmas are only that with respect to their subject matter, but the form is identical for the opposing factions. This universal form, this essence, is what Scheler saw, in his ideational act, relative to the characteristics of our age. The *figure* and the *counterfigure,* the positive and the negative, varied in content, but the essence is universal and unique. *It is a matter of both opposing factions denying liberty,* but without liberty there cannot be thought, science, or culture. Because liberty and thought are unified in the human composite, in the human being. *What are the two most noble faculties of the human psyche? How is personality integrated? With which elements is it organized as a true personality? . . . Only by virtue of the narrow relationship that intervenes between the will and the thought, between liberty and the idea. Man thinks freely. This is his total personality, his free thought. Liberty without thought is not conceivable. Nor thought without liberty.*

Animals have neither liberty nor thought. Man has thought and liberty; but he does not have them as differentiated and distant elements, but rather forming a synthetic, indestructible unity. For this reason, all aggression against liberty threatens thought, and all aggression against thought is also that against liberty. Only true thought, which is free thought, can give of itself true thoughts, that is to say, cultural realizations in which the supreme values of culture are integrated.

Let us consider the *figure* and the *counterfigure* of diverse content, but which, together, realize the formal essence of tyranny:

Let us cast a glance—says Max Scheler—on the current world. Russia: an *index liborum prohibitorum*,[2] imitation of that of the medieval Roman Church, in which are included the two Testaments, the Koran, the Talmud, and all the philosophers from Thales to Fichte. No book in which the word "God" figures can pass the border. Only immediately usable sciences, technical, hygienic, and economic, are admitted in accordance with the discredited Marxist and pragmatic theory of the relationship between science and economics. *Marxism, crushed today more than ever by criticism, is ceremoniously exalted to the level of dogma of a great empire.*

In sum, the form is *tyranny,* the essence is exclusion of the liberty of thought. The subject matter constitutes the apotheosis of one doctrine among many, selected to be converted, as the philosopher says, into an intangible dogma of consciousness.

Let us look now at the *counterfigure.* In North America,

a movement that is called *fundamentalism* because it claims to elevate the Bible, in the sense of literal inspiration, to absolute foundation of knowledge and life. Based in this idea, a powerful popular movement that demands nothing less than a legal veto of the teaching of the theory of origins in any of its forms (Lamarkism, Darwinism, vitalism), and all research on it, within establishments sustained by the state.

In some countries, like Mexico, the opposite is sought, even now; throw out every biological theory that might be expressed against transformist scientific theories. But natural science cannot be contained within the limits of any dogmatic affirmation! It is as wrong to exclude without appeal as to concede without disagreement. It is as unfortunate to deny without critical spirit as to affirm without the vitality of liberty of thought. The advance of science passes over Marxism, Lamarkism, and Darwinism because its eternal form cannot be constrained in what a given epoch, a stage of knowledge and culture, grasps as truth. To prohibit or exalt is not characteristic of researchers or of learned people.

2. An index of forbidden books. (Editor's note)

The learned person does not know what, finally, the results of his research will be; and he is always disposed to sacrifice all the ideas in favor of a sole observation, of a sole experiment that negates them.

Before the perspective of essentially common negation arises the perplexity of the philosopher. Why will there be a century like ours, enemy of liberty of conscience? Is it that, in truth, culture is declining? Why do we declare ourselves enemies of what constitutes a fundamental part of human moral being? What malevolent spirit inspires contemporary humanity to make it disown free will, supreme divine gift? How is it that in affirming error one wishes to realize the good? Is it not a pregnant paradox of unforeseen dramatic consequences *to be bent on destroying what is most lofty in the human personality?* Do the nations not seem to be distancing themselves, each time more, from the goods derived from respecting liberty and thought in their essence? . . .

For this reason, the noble spirit of Max Scheler declares its anguish with these moving words, which could be called *the admonition of the man of genius* to the people of his century:

> *A genuine terror takes possession of me in the face of the growing abandonment of liberties and the loss of sensibility, gray and shapeless twilight in which, not only this or that country, but almost the entire civilized world finds itself in serious danger of collapsing, of being slowly drowned, almost without noticing.* And, nonetheless, liberty, active and personal spontaneity of the spiritual center of man — of Man within man — is the first and fundamental condition that makes culture possible, the enlightenment of humanity!

The great admonisher has died; but his word of life and truth resounds over all the sophisms converted into inviolable canons of human thought, because the truth is another eternal essence that no revolution can stop or destroy with its attacks!

OCTAVIO PAZ

Octavio Paz (1914–98) was born in Mexico City. A poet and essayist, Paz is probably the twentieth century's most famous and universally known intellectual from the Spanish-speaking world. He received numerous awards, including the Nobel Prize for Literature in 1990, primarily for his poetry but also for his many essays on culture and politics. He founded important literary magazines, such as *Vuelta*.

In his writings Paz reflected on liberty, modernity, history, art, liberalism, revolution, democracy, and the identity of Mexico and Latin America. Many of his texts dwell on the relation between politics and art. Early on he became disillusioned with communism and thus became a critic of communist regimes.

We present three texts by Paz that examine liberty and liberalism: a speech given on the occasion of receiving the Cervantes Prize (1981), a speech pronounced on the occasion of receiving the Alfonso Reyes Prize (1985), and a speech given on the occasion of receiving the Alexis de Tocqueville Prize (1989).

1 The Liberal Tradition

If I let only my feelings speak, these words would be a long, interminable expression of gratitude. But my emotion is not blind. I know well that the symbolic reality of this act is more real than the fleeting reality of my person. I am barely an episode in the history of our literature, the transitory and accidental incarnation of a moment in the Spanish language. The Cervantes Prize, in selecting this or that writer of our tongue without consideration of nationality, affirms each year the reality of our literature. And what is a literature? It is not a collection of authors and books but rather a society of works. Novels, poems, narratives, comedies, and essays become works through the creative complicity of the readers. The work is a work thanks to the reader. Instantaneous monument, perpetually erected and perpetually demolished, for it is subject to the critique of time: the successive generations of readers. The work springs from the association of author and reader; for this reason literature is a society within society: a community of works that simultaneously create a public of readers and are re-created through those readers.

It is said that ideologies, classes, economic structures, technologies, and the sciences, international by nature, are the basic and determinant realities of history. The subject is as old as historical reflection itself, and I cannot linger over it; I observe, nonetheless, that equally determinant, if not more so, are the languages, the beliefs, the myths, and the customs and traditions of each social group. The Cervantes Prize, justly, reminds us that the language we speak is a reality no less decisive than the ideas we profess or the craft we practice. To say language is to say civilization: community of values, symbols, habits, beliefs, visions, questions regarding the past, the present, the future. In speaking, we do not speak only

Original title: "La tradición liberal." Source: Octavio Paz, *Obras completas,* vol. 3, *Fundación y disidencia* (Mexico: FCE/Círculo de Lectores, 1994), pp. 303–7.

with those who are close by: we speak also with the dead and with those not yet born, with the trees and the cities, the rivers and the ruins, the animals and the objects. We speak with the animate world and with the inanimate, with the visible and with the invisible. We speak with ourselves. To speak is to live together, to live in a world that is this world and its other worlds, this time and the others: a civilization.

Since I was very young, the feeling of belonging to a civilization was very much alive in me. I owe it to my grandfather, Ireneo Paz, lover of books, who managed to assemble a small library in which abounded the great writers of our language. I was eighteen years old when I read the two first series of the *National Episodes,* in which, perhaps, some of the best pages of Pérez Galdós are found. It was an edition in octavo, with golden covers, illustrated by various artists of the time; the ten volumes had been printed between 1881 and 1885 in Madrid by La Guirnalda. This novel-like and novelistic history of modern Spain seemed to me also mine and my country's. When I came to the second series, the figure of Salvador Monsalud captivated me immediately. He was my hero, my archetype. My identification with the young liberal led me to come face to face with his half-brother and adversary, the terrible Carlos Garrote, Carlist partisan. Dualism at the same time real and symbolic: the legitimate son and the bastard, the guard dog of order and the vagabond, the man of the land and the cosmopolite, the conservative and the revolutionary. But Carlos Garrote, as the reader realizes little by little, is not only the adversary who embodies the other Spain, that of *religion and privileges!*[1] but he is also the double of Salvador Monsalud. In the final episode—*One Rebel More and Several Friars Less,* gloomy portrayal of the two Spains and their opposing and symmetrical fanaticisms—we are present at the death of Carlos Garrote and his transformation. He began as the enemy and persecutor of Salvador Monsalud and ends as his brother and protector: they are condemned to live together. Each one is the other and himself. That struggle, no longer private but social, has been the substance of the history of our peoples during the last two centuries. Thus I learned that a civilization is not a fixed essence, always identical with itself: it is a society inhabited by discord and possessed by the desire to restore unity, a mirror in which, in contemplating ourselves we lose ourselves, and in losing ourselves we recover ourselves.

1. *"Religión y privilegios!"* was the motto of the Spanish monarchists. (Editor's note)

Many times I have thought about the Hispano-American parallels of Salvador Monsalud. Although some belong to history and others to the novel, all of them, real or imagined, fought and still fight against obstacles that the hero of Galdós never dreamed. For example, besides meeting face to face with Carlos Garrote, intractable and untamed partisan, embodiment of a sometimes obtuse and sometimes sublime past, the Mexican Salvador Monsaluds have had to combat other realities and exorcise other ghosts: Spain and Mexico have different pasts. In our history appears an element unknown in Spain's: the world of the Indian. It is the dimension at the same time intimate and unfathomable, innermost and unknown, of my country. Without this dimension we would not be what we are. The presence of Islam and Judaism in medieval Spain could give some idea of what the Indian interlocutor signifies in the consciousness of Mexicans. An interlocutor who is not in front of us but rather within. But there is a major difference: Islam and Judaism are, like Christianity, variants of monotheism; by contrast, Mesoamerican civilization was born and grew isolated, with no connection to the Old World. The same can be said of Incan Peru. The world of the Indian was, from the beginning, the *other* world, in the strongest sense of the term. *Otherness* that, for us Mexicans, becomes identity, distance that is closeness.

The appearance of America with its great alien civilizations modified radically the dialogue of Hispanic civilization with its own self. It introduced an element of uncertainty, so to speak, that since then has challenged our imagination and questioned our identity. The Indian interlocutor tells us that man is an unpredictable creature and that he is a double being. In other Hispano-American nations the agents of the dislocation and transformation of the dialogue were the nomads, the blacks, the geography. Instead of *other* history, as in Peru and Mexico, the absence of history. Since its origin, Spain was a land of shifting frontiers, and its last great frontier has been America: through it and in it Spain has a border with the unknown. America or the immensity: the lands without people, the distances without name, the coasts that gaze toward Asia and Oceania, civilizations that did not know Christianity but that had discovered the zero. Diverse forms of the limitless.

The dissimilarity of pasts and interlocutors always induces two opposing temptations: dispersion and centralization. Our peoples have suffered, on one extreme, atomization like that of Central America and the

Antilles; on the other, rigid centralism like those of Castile and Mexico. Dispersion culminates in dissipation; centralization, in petrification. Double threat: we turn into air or we turn into stones. For two centuries we have sought the difficult equilibrium between liberty and authority, centralization and disintegration. The nature of our tradition has not been very favorable to these efforts at reform. The eighteenth century, the century of criticism and the first which, since pagan antiquity, again extolled the intellectual virtues of tolerance, did not have in the Hispanic world the brilliance that the sixteenth and seventeenth had. An example of the persistence of authoritarian attitudes and tendencies, overlaid by liberal opinions, is found precisely in the final pages of Galdós's novel, which I have mentioned before. An important person known for the fervor of his liberal sentiments maintains, without blinking, that "all Spaniards must embrace the standard of liberty and accept the progress of the century . . . and if not everyone wishes to go in by this road, the rebels must be convinced with blows, for which it would be advisable that free men be armed, forming a militia." This curious liberal was a devotee of Rousseau, he of the omnipotence of the "general will," a democratic mask of Jacobin tyranny. Armed with a general theory of liberty, Carlos Garrote enters the twentieth century. He has changed attire, not soul: no longer does he intimidate the adversary with the rusty syllogisms of the scholastic, but rather with the undulations of the dialectic. New chimeras swallow his intelligence, but the odor of blood continues bewitching him. He leapt from the Inquisition to the Committee of Public Safety without changing location.

As soon as liberty becomes an absolute, it ceases to be liberty: its true name is despotism. Liberty is not a system of general explanation of the universe and of man. Neither is it a philosophy: it is an act, at the same time irrevocable and instantaneous, which consists in selecting one possibility from among others. There is not, nor can there be, a general theory of liberty because it is the affirmation of that which, in each one of us, is singular and particular, irreducible to any generalization. Better said: each one of us is a singular and particular creature. Liberty becomes tyranny as soon as we try to impose it on others. When the Bolsheviks dissolved the Russian Constituent Assembly in the name of liberty, Rosa Luxemburg said to them: "Liberty of opinion is always the liberty of that one who does not think like us." Liberty, which begins as the affirmation of my singularity, turns into the knowledge of the other and the others: their liberty is the condition of mine. On his island Robinson is not really free; although he does not experience the will of another, and no one constrains him, his liberty unfolds in the void. The liberty of the solitary one is like the solitude of the despot, populated with specters. To be realized, liberty must embody and come face to face with another consciousness and another will: the other is, simultaneously, the limit and source of my liberty. In one of its extremes, liberty is singularity and exception; in the other, it is plurality and living together. For all of this, although liberty and democracy are not equivalent ends, they are complementary: without liberty, democracy is despotism; without democracy, liberty is a chimera.

The union of liberty and democracy has been the great achievement of modern societies. Precarious achievement, fragile and disfigured by many injustices and horrors; also an extraordinary achievement and one that has something of the accidental or miraculous: other civilizations did not know democracy, and in ours only some peoples, and during limited periods, have enjoyed free institutions. Even now, in the vast spaces of the American continent, many nations of our language suffer under iniquitous powers. Liberty is as precious as water and, like it, if we do not protect it, it spills, escapes us, and disappears. I have alluded to the relative poverty of our eighteenth century, origin of the political philosophy of the modern age. Nonetheless, in our past—the Spanish and the Hispano-American—exist habits, customs, and institutions that are springs of liberty, sometimes buried but still living. In order for liberty truly to take root in our lands, we would have to reconcile these old traditions with modern political thought. Except for some timid and isolated attempts, we have done nothing. I lament it: it is not a task of historical piety, but rather of political imagination.

The word "liberal" appears early in our literature. Not as an idea or a philosophy, but rather as a mood and disposition of mind; more than an ideology, it was a virtue. In saying this, I turn my eyes toward Cervantes, our writer who embodies most completely the different meanings of the word "liberal." With him the modern novel is born, the literary genre of a society that, since its birth, has identified itself and its history with criticism. The *Comedy* of Dante is the reflection of a world ruled by analogy, that is to say, by the correspondence between this world and the other world; the *Quixote* is a work animated by the opposite principle, irony, which is the rupture of the correspondence and which underscores with a smile the crevice between the real and the ideal. With Cervantes begins the criticism of the absolutes: liberty begins. And it begins with a smile, not of pleasure but rather of wisdom. Man is a precarious being, complex, double or triple, inhabited by ghosts, spurred on by instincts, eaten away by desire: a wondrous and lamentable sight. Each man is a singular being and each man is like all the others. Each man is unique and each man is many men he does not know: the I is plural. Cervantes is smiling: to learn to be free is to learn to smile.

2

Literature and the
State (excerpt)

[...]

The Republic of Letters is a nation with an ill-defined territory and shifting frontiers. A constitution rules it whose laws, fanciful and contradictory, are revoked daily in order to proclaim others even more chimerical. An invisible king, without face and without name, governs it; better said, it is a king who continually changes his face and his name: they call him "taste" but he also has other names, almost all ugly and terminating in "ism." The citizens of the Republic of Letters belong to all the sexes, those recognized and those not recognized; the colors of their skin, of their ideas, and of their philosophies are those of the chromatic scale; each one of them claims to speak in a language of his creation, which, nonetheless, he insists on proclaiming universal and comprehensible to everyone. In that country there are many hermits, many magicians, and not a few ecstatics. In the last years the Republic has been devastated by two epidemics: the frenetic epidemic of doctrinaires and the lethal epidemic of scholastics; against both there is only one known remedy: the smile. These learned ones are imaginative and contemplative; also, through astral misfortune, quarrelsome and nitpicky. When they are not occupied with some of their interminable civil wars, they have a passion for more subtle phenomena and for scarcely perceptible realities: the weight of a particle of light on the wing of a butterfly, the color of the shade of the rings of their planet, Saturn. An extraordinary property of the natives of this nation: their illustrious dead converse and live side by side with the living.

The Republic of Letters dwells in the territory of the Republic of Mexico. At times it is larger than the country that contains it, other times it is reduced to the point of being turned into a small, urban ant-

Original title: "La literatura y el estado." Source: Octavio Paz, *Obras completas,* vol. 8, *El peregrino en su patria* (Mexico: FCE/Círculo de Lectores, 1994), pp. 553–58.

hill. The relations between the Republic of Mexico and the Republic of Letters are strained. At times scant cordiality turns into open hostility. It is natural, for Mexican literature is bounded on the east by indifference, on the west by ignorance, on the north by another dialect, and on the south by an abyss. Various stratagems have been devised to break the circle. One of them is called literary prizes. Like everything that exists in that fanciful Republic, literary prizes have provoked great and fierce disputes. I will try to handle this subject with some impartiality.

Opinions on literary prizes are opposed. Some consider them useful and beneficial. They are the just recognition of merits that are not only artistic but also moral; to write is a task that demands something more than dedication and perseverance: the entire life of the writer. Moreover, prizes educate the people; so they are thus at the same time pedagogical enterprises and acts of justice. Others see the prizes as competitions between peacocks, sordid fights for fame and material gain, irrefutable and repeated proofs of the injustice, the stupidity, or the incompetence of the academies and literary guilds. What is worse: the prizes domesticate the independent writer, cut the wings of the inspired, castrate the rebel. Who is right? All of them and none of them. The prizes are good and they are bad: it depends on who awards them, who receives them, and how they are bestowed. In an ideal society there would not be prizes, but there would also not be punishments: both would be unnecessary. Wisdom, goodness, and artistic genius would not be isolated virtues but rather widespread and natural. Each one of us would be an incarnation of rectitude, poetry, and science; every living creature would be a masterwork. But in that society of perfect men and women, constitutions and institutions, governments and courts, the arts and even literature would be superfluous. We write because we lack something or we have too much of something, because of deficiency or because of excess; that is to say, because of an imbalance. We read for the same reason. What we call civilization is the expression of the congenital imbalance among men. I add that this imbalance is creative. Therefore, as long as there are men and societies there will be authors, readers, critics, and crowns of laurel or thorns. Prizes are neither good nor bad: they are necessary.

Some prizes (for example, the Alfonso Reyes Prize) exemplify the relations between the state and literature. In the long history of these relations appear, from the dawn of human society, two extreme situations, to which also correspond two opposing sites: the cell of the prisoner and the antechamber of the prince, the island of the exiled and the drawing room of the courtier. Two types: the rebel and the protégé. The prize introduces a third term, for it is realized in a place of encounter in which, although fleetingly, the government and the writer intersect. The prize is conducive to conversation, I mean, to the dialogue between power and literature. This dialogue can deal with different subjects, many contradictory, but it rests on an implicit agreement: coexistence.[1] It is a relatively new term in our vocabulary (it does not appear, for example, in the *Diccionario de Autoridades,* 1726–39), which presupposes, indirectly, a more civilized idea of human relations. In effect, to coexist is for everyone to live with one another, and it demands, simultaneously, independence and solidarity. Coexistence compels us to reflect on the limits of our liberty and the extent of our rights and obligations. Those limits have many names, but there is one that embraces all: the other, the others. In a moment of that dialogue between the one and the other, certain questions arise: what can the state do in the presence of literature, and what can literature do in the presence of the state?

These questions have had many and very different responses. It would be presumptuous to try to set them out, or even to summarize them. It is not presumptuous to set out, marginally, a few brief reflections. The powers of the state over literature are immense but not unlimited. I will mention some possible and impossible: the state cannot create a literature, but it certainly can suppress it; the state cannot be a literary critic, but certainly censor and inquisitor; the state can and should establish colleges where grammar and the art of reading and writing are taught, but it cannot legislate matters of grammar or dictate laws of aesthetics; the state can support writers, but not too much and without asking anything in return from them; the state can and must teach Mexicans to read, but it must not compel them to read or not read these or those books . . . The list can go on: it would be redundant. It is enough to repeat that the state can neither create nor invent a literature, but it can certainly denaturalize it and, as has occurred in other countries and in

1. The original Spanish word is *convivencia.* English has no exact equivalent for *convivencia,* which means more than just living side by side (in Spanish this is *coexistencia*); *convivencia* refers also to the ability to live peacefully and in an agreeable manner with others. (Translators' note)

different times, strangle it. On the other hand, the state can create the social conditions for the free development of literature. The two words are complementary: "development" means the promotion of the material, intellectual, and legal conditions that permit the production, publication, and circulation of the works; in its turn, development needs, to be truly realized, the freedom to write and publish.

In the presence of the state, the powers of literature are also immense and limited. The writer must choose between literature and power: he cannot govern and write at the same time; neither can the writer be an official, social redeemer, founder of hospitals or houses of refuge for the vulnerable, apostle of repented sinners, hierophant for the worship of the cult of Jupiter Amon, or leader of a band: the writer must choose between collective action, be it philanthropic or messianic, and solitary writing. Naturally, it is good that the writer, at some moment in his life, has known action and the various occupations of men: captain of cavalry, usher, conspirator, ice cream vendor, industrialist, electrician, diplomat, statesman like Milton, or highwayman like Villon. But then, in the moment of his truth, the writer can be only a writer. Although it is not obligatory that he have them, the writer can indeed have moral and political opinions: what he cannot do is exchange literature for action, or propaganda, without ceasing to be a writer. I am not proposing the abolition of criticism; I ask that it not be turned into an admonishment and that it truly be literature. The criticism of customs and ideas, passions and beliefs, institutions and the state, has been and is one of the dominions of modern literature. Many and great literary works are creations that are criticism: Cervantes, Dostoyevsky, Flaubert, Proust, and so many others. Also, sometimes critical thought turns into artistic creation, poem: Nietzsche and Valéry as the nearest examples. Finally, what the writer in the presence of the state can do is, above all and before all, write. I emphasize: write the best that he can.

To write well means to tell his truth. The word of the writer is not the collective word: it is an individual word, unique, singular. If the writer says his truth, his readers will find that this truth belongs also to them. In the individual word of the writer is heard, in its most intense moments, the word of the world. This has been said many times. Among those who have said it is one who did so in such a way that calling it perfect is not an exaggeration: Han Yu, a Chinese poet who lived in the eighth century. He was a public man and a private poet. His words seem as though written today and for us. Nothing better than to conclude with them:

Everything resounds as soon as the equilibrium of things is broken. The trees and the grass are silent; the wind stirs them and they re- sound. The water is quiet: the air moves it and it resounds; the waves roar: something subdues them; the cascade rushes headlong: it lacks ground; the lake seethes: something heats it. Metals and rocks are mute, but if something strikes them, they resound. Thus, man. If he speaks, it is that he cannot hold himself back; if he is moved, he sings; if he suffers, he laments. Everything that comes out of his mouth in the form of a sound is owing to a breach of his equilib- rium . . . The most perfect of the human sounds is the word; litera- ture, in its turn, is the most perfect form of the word. And so, when equilibrium is broken, the heavens choose between men and those who are more sensible, and it makes them resound.

3

Poetry, Myth,
Revolution

La Révolution comfirme, par le sacrifice, la superstition.
— Charles Baudelaire

It is very difficult to express in few and clear words what I feel: emotion, gratitude, surprise. Above all: I have been touched that you, Mr. President, have had the goodness to deliver the Alexis de Tocqueville Prize personally to me. I will never forget your gesture. Your generous words heighten my emotion: I see in them that sign of friendship, precious among all, that sometimes a writer addresses to another of a different tongue, although those tongues might be as close as Spanish and French. My gratitude for this is double: to the man of state and the writer of French, a language whose literature has been my second spiritual land.

My gratitude to the jury of the Alexis de Tocqueville Foundation is mixed with a slight and very agreeable sensation of unreality. When Mr. Alain Peyrefitte had the kindness to announce the decision of the jury to me, my first reaction, I confess, was of astonishment and even incredulity: why me, a poet? Very quickly I suspected the reason: at one time or another, moved as much by the accidents of my life as by the changes and upheavals of the world and of my country, I have participated in public life, and I have written some books on the history and politics of our time. Over and above the doubtful merits of my writings, I imagine that the Foundation has wanted to reward in me, writer from a continent frequently torn between the forced immobility of despotisms and the convulsions of sectarians, a faithfulness. In effect, I have always tried to be faithful to that attitude that the work and person of Alexis

Original title: "Poesía, mito, revolución." Source: Octavio Paz, *Poesía, mito, revolución. Precedido por los discursos de François Mitterrand, Alain Peyrefitte, y Pierre Godefroy* (Mexico: Vuelta, 1989), pp. 47–69.

de Tocqueville exemplifies and that can be summarized thus: my liberty begins with the recognition of the liberty of others. In the dawn of the modern age, before a spectacle that has since been repeated many times: the tyrant disguised as liberator, Chateaubriand wrote these prophetic words:

> La Révolution m'aurait entrâiné . . . mais je vis la première tête portée au bout d'une pique et je reculai. Jamais le meurtre ne sera à mes yeux un argument de libert je ne connais rien de plus servile, de plus lâche, de plus borne qu'un terroiste. N'ai je pas rencontré toute cette race de Brutus au service de César et de sa police?[1]

Since my adolescence I have written poems, and I have not stopped writing them. I wanted to be a poet and nothing more. In my books of prose I intended to serve poetry, justify and defend it, explain it before others and before myself. Soon I discovered that the defense of poetry, undervalued in our century, was inseparable from the defense of liberty. From this my passionate interest in the political and social matters that have shaken our time. After the Second World War I became acquainted with André Breton and his friends. I do not share today many of their philosophical and aesthetic ideas, but I keep intact and alive my admiration. In his writings as much as in his life, liberty and poetry appear with the same fiery face, simultaneously seductive and turbulent. Nor did he, like Chateaubriand at the other extreme, ever confuse the tyrant with the liberator. Liberty is not a philosophy, nor even is it an idea: it is a movement of the conscience that brings us, in certain moments, to pronounce two monosyllables: Yes or No. In its instantaneous brevity, like the light of the lightning flash, the contradictory character of human nature reveals itself.

Throughout the course of history and in the most diverse circumstances, poets have participated in political life. I do not refer to the concept of poetry as an art in the service of a state, a church, or an ideology. We already know that that concept, as old as the political and ideo-

---

1. "The revolution had pulled me along . . . but I saw the first head on the end of a pike, and I drew back. I will never see in murder an argument for liberty; I know nothing more servile, more cowardly, more narrow of mind than a terrorist. Have I not met that entire race of Brutus in the service of Caesar and his police?" (Editor's note)

logical powers, invariably has yielded the same results: states collapse, churches break up or turn to stone, ideologies disappear—but poetry remains. No: I allude to the free participation of the poet in the affairs of the city. Even in societies that did not know political liberty, like ancient China, poets who contributed to the course of public affairs were not rare. Many among them did not hesitate to censure the abuses of the Son of Heaven, and not a few suffered imprisonment, exile, and other punishments for their opinions. In the West this tradition has been very much alive, and I hardly need to evoke the Greek and Roman poets. Two of the greatest poets of our tradition, the Florentine Dante and the Englishman Milton, were also notable political thinkers. We owe to the first the treatise *On Monarchy* and to the second daring defenses on behalf of the emancipation of consciences, such as his famous defense of the right to divorce or his criticism of the censure decreed by Parliament, which he had the courage to make before Parliament itself.

These historical precedents should not conceal from us that there is a major difference between these attitudes and the situation of modern poets. The Chinese poets censured the throne but belonged to the imperial bureaucracy; almost all were high officials, and censure formed part of the Confucian moral and intellectual tradition. Dante and Milton found themselves involved in controversies in which politics was indistinguishable from religion. For both, the foundation of their opinions was in theology. They fought in this world with their eyes fixed on the next and with motives that came from that other world. In the last circle of Hell, at the side of Judas Iscariot, the archtraitor, Dante put two enemies of the empire: Brutus and Cassius. For Dante the reality of this world was an imitation of the more real reality of the other world; for this reason, political offenses were judged in the divine tribunal. In the Greek cities and in the Roman Republic the influence of religion was less; the questions that divided citizens were clearly political and were not tinged by theology. Nonetheless, the similarity with Greco-Roman antiquity is deceptive; a central element is lacking in it, and that is the distinctive mark, the sign of the birth of the modern age: the idea of Revolution. It is an idea that could arise only in our time, for it is heir to Greece and Christianity, that is to say, to philosophy and the yearning for redemption. In no other historical period has the idea of Revolution had that power of magnetic attraction. Other civilizations and societies experienced immense changes—tumults, dynastic falls, fratricidal wars—but only their great religious mutations can be compared with our fascination before Revolution. It is an idea that, during more than two centuries, has hypnotized many consciences and various generations. It has been the North Star that has guided our wanderings and the secret sun that has illuminated and warmed the vigils of many solitary persons. In it have been fused the certainties of reason and the hopes of religious movements.

From the moment in which it appeared on the historical horizon, Revolution was twofold: reason made act and providential act, rational determination and miraculous action, history and myth. Child of reason in its most rigorous and lucid form: criticism, in the image of revolution, is at the same time creator and destroyer; better said: in destroying, it creates. Revolution is that moment in which criticism is transformed into utopia and utopia becomes incarnate in some men and in an action. The descent of reason to earth was a true epiphany, and as such was lived through its protagonists and, later, through its interpreters. Lived and not thought. For almost everybody, the Revolution was a consequence of certain rational postulates and of the general evolution of society; almost no one realized that they were present at a resurrection. Certainly the novelty of the Revolution appears absolute; it breaks with the past and institutes a rational regime, just and radically different from the old. Nonetheless, this absolute novelty was seen and lived as a return to the beginning of the beginning. The Revolution is a return to the time of origin, before injustice, before that moment in which, Rousseau says, in designating the boundaries of a piece of land, a man said: *this is mine.* That day inequality began and, with it, discord and oppression: history. In sum, the Revolution is an eminently historical act and, nonetheless, is an act negating history: the new time that it installs is a restoration of the original time. Child of history and reason, the Revolution is the child of linear, consecutive, and unrepeatable time; child of myth, the Revolution is a moment of cyclical time, like the gyre of the stars and the cycle of the seasons. The nature of the Revolution is dual, but we cannot think of it without separating its two elements and rejecting the mythical as a foreign body . . . and we cannot live it without connecting them. We think of it as a phenomenon that responds to the predictions of reason; we live it as a mystery. In this enigma dwells the secret of its fascination.

The modern age broke the old link that bound poetry to myth but only in order to bind it, immediately afterward, to the idea of Revolution. This idea proclaimed the end of the myths—and thus it was converted into the central myth of modernity. The history of modern poetry, from romanticism to our days, has been nothing but the history of its connections with that myth, clear and coherent as a geometric proof, turbulent as the revelations of the ancient chaos. Connections inflamed and extreme, from the seduction to the horror, from the devotion to the anathema, from the idolatry to the abjuration—the entire gamut of the two great passions: love and religion. The enthusiasm of Hölderlin before the young Bonaparte and the disillusion he feels in seeing him become the emperor Napoleon, the Girondist sympathies of Wordsworth and the abhorrence that Robespierre inspires in him, are just two examples of the vacillations of the German and English Romantics in the face of the French Revolution. Those violent oscillations are repeated throughout the nineteenth century in the face of each revolutionary movement and culminate in the twentieth with the immense and successive waves of contradictory sentiments—again from fanaticism to repulsion—that the prolonged influence of the Bolshevik Revolution stirred up in the world.

The movements of adherence that all revolutions provoke can be explained in the first place by the necessity that we men feel to remedy and put an end to our unhappy condition. There are times in which that need for redemption becomes more intense and urgent because of the disappearance of traditional beliefs. The old divinities, riddled with superstition, vilified by fanaticism, and eaten away by criticism, disintegrate. Amidst the rubble springs up the tribe of the specters: they appear first as radiant ideas but soon are deified and turned into frightening idols. Although there are other explanations for the revolutionary phenomenon—economic, psychological, political—all of them, without being false, essentially depend on this basic fact. A faith that arises from the vacuum that the old beliefs have left and that is nourished, jointly, by the consciousness of our misery and the geometries of reason, is coriaceous and resistant; it closes its eyes with obstinacy equally to the incoherencies of its doctrine and to the atrocities of its leaders. In this, revolutionary faith is like religious faith: neither the slaughters of September 1792 nor the butchery of Saint Bartholomew nor the concentration camps of Stalin made the convictions of the faithful waver. Nonetheless, there is a difference: revolutionary beliefs are subject to the proof of time, while religious beliefs are registered in another world, untouched by time and its changes. Revolutions are historical phenomena, that is to say, temporal. The criticism of time is irrefutable because it is the criticism of reality: showing without demonstrating. And what shows is that the Revolution begins as a promise, dissipates in frenzied agitations, and congeals in bloody dictatorships that are the negation of the impulse that caused it to arise. In all revolutionary movements, the sacred time of myth is inexorably transformed into the profane time of history.

Hope is reborn after each failure. The enthusiasm of Shelley refutes the disenchantment of Coleridge, and Heine writes *Of Germany* in order to respond to Madame de Staël and heap ridicule on the poets of the previous generation, who had initially shown sympathies for the French Revolution but who ended by being its enemies. The circle of adhesion–negation–adhesion is repeated during more than two centuries, first in Europe and afterwards in the entire world. The poetic word has been simultaneously prophecy, anathema, and elegy of modern revolutions. Although the differences and contrasts between the two great revolutionary prototypes (the French Revolution of 1789 and the Russian Revolution of 1917) are greater and more profound than the similarities, the feelings they provoked obeyed the same emotional rhythm of attraction and repulsion. Despite the fact that the religious function of modern revolutions has invariably been broken by the eminently historical nature of those movements, the result has been the rebirth, in the following generation, of similar aspirations and chimeras. Or the adoption of personal mythologies. Here appears another of the differences between modern poetry and that of yesterday: for Dante, the Sacred Scriptures, axis of the universal analogy, were the key to his poem; Blake, by contrast, created a mythology with remnants of gnosticism and the hermetic tradition. Many poets arrived at the same solution, and I have hardly to bring to mind the beliefs of Nerval or of Hugo and, already in the twentieth century, the theosophy of Yeats or the occultism of Breton. The reason for this apparent paradox lies in the following: the public religion of modernity has been the Revolution, and poetry its private religion.

The criticism of revolutions has been made by those nostalgic for the old order and by the liberals (in the broad sense of the term liberal: more than a doctrine, a philosophical and political disposition). Contrary to reactionary criticism, liberal criticism has been effective: it dismantled the ideological constructions of the revolutions, it pulled away the religious mask from them, and it showed them in their historical, profane nakedness. Liberalism did not intend to replace those constructions with others; the very nature of this intellectual tradition, essentially critical, has prohibited it from proposing, like the other great political philosophies, a metahistory. Earlier, this had been the domain of religions; liberalism offered nothing in exchange and confined religion to the private sphere. It established liberty on the only base that can sustain it: the autonomy of the conscience and the acknowledgment of the autonomy of other persons' consciences. It was admirable and also terrible: it locked us into a solipsism, broke the bridge that joined the I and the you and both to the third person: the other, the others. Between liberty and fraternity there is no contradiction, but rather distance — a distance that liberalism has not been able to erase. What would be the foundation for fraternity? Inspired by the ancients, Robespierre and Saint-Just wanted to establish the solidarity of the citizens in virtue. Except, what can be the foundation for virtue? The Jacobins, as later their descendants, the Bolsheviks, did not ask themselves this question. Better said: their response was virtue by decree, the Terror. But the Terror can engender only two irreconcilable fraternities: that of the executioners and that of the victims.

Democratic liberalism is a civilized way of living together. For me it is the best among all those that political philosophy has conceived. Nonetheless, it leaves without answer half the questions that we men ask ourselves: fraternity, the question of the origin and purpose, the question of the meaning and value of existence. The modern age has exalted individualism and has been, thus, the period of the dispersion of consciences. Poets have been particularly sensitive to this vacuum. Around 1851 Baudelaire writes in a notebook:

> Le monde va finir. . . . Je ne dis pas que le monde sera réduit au desordre bouffon des républiques du Sud Amérique ou que peutêtre nous retournerons à l'état sauvage. . . . Non, la mécanique nous'aura tellement américanisés, le progrès aura si bien atrophié en nous toute la partie spirituelle, que rien parmi les rêveries sanguinaires des utopistes ne pourra être comparé à ses resultats positifs . . . mais ce n'est pas par des institutions politiques que se manifes-

tera la ruine universelle (ou le progrès universel, car peu m'importe le nom). Se sera par l'avilissement des coeurs.[2]

Ninety years later, as if continuing the reflections of Baudelaire, in one of his *Four Quartets,* Eliot sees our world, which we consider moved by progress, as the interminable fall from the vacant into the vacant:

O dark dark dark. They all go into the dark,
The vacant interstellar spaces, the vacant into the vacant,
The captains, merchants, bankers, eminent men of letters,
The generous patrons of art, the statesmen and the rulers,
Distinguished civil servants, chairmen of many committees,
Industrial lords and petty contractors, all go into the dark,
And dark the Sun and Moon, and the Allmanach [*sic*] of Gotha
And the Stock Exchange Gazette, the Directory of Directors,
And cold the sense and lost the motive of action.
And we all go with them, into the silent funeral,
Nobody's funeral, for there is no one to bury.[3]

I could add other testimonies, but it seems to me that the two I have cited are sufficient to illustrate the state of spirit of the poets in the face of the disasters of modernity. The reflections of Baudelaire and the verses of Eliot are a gloomy counterpoint to the enthusiastic hymns of Whitman and Victor Hugo. Both are examples of the schisms; better said, of the rent in modern poetry. That rent is the mark that distinguishes it from the poetry of other times and civilizations. Suspended between the hands of time, between myth and history, modern poetry consecrates a distinct and much older fraternity than that of the reli-

2. The world is going to end. . . . I am not saying it will be reduced to the buffoonish disorder of the South American republics, or that perhaps we will be returned to the state of savagery. . . . No, the mechanism will have Americanized us so much, progress will have atrophied our spiritual faculties so completely, that nothing among the bloody dreams of the utopians will be comparable to their excellent results . . . but it is not through political institutions that universal ruin will be manifest (or universal progress, because the name is not important to me). This will be through the degradation of hearts. (Editor's note)

3. This passage is in English in the original. (Editor's note)

gions and philosophies, a fraternity born of the same feeling of solitude the primitive had in the middle of an alien and hostile nature. The difference is that now we live that solitude not only facing the cosmos but also before our neighbors. Nonetheless, we all know, each one in his room, that we are not really alone: fraternity over the vacant.

After a long period of political deadlock, always on the brink of the precipice, always in the presence of the specter of a new total war and the threat of the annihilation of humankind, we have been witnesses, during the last twenty years, to a series of changes, portents of a new era, which, perhaps, is dawning. First, the sunset of the revolutionary myth in the very place of its birth, Western Europe, today recovered from the war, prosperous and, in each one of the countries of the Community, the liberal democratic regime secured. Following this, the return to democracy in Latin America, although still wavering between the specters of populist demagoguery and militarism—its two endemic diseases—the iron shackle of debt around its neck. Finally, the changes in the Soviet Union, in China, and other totalitarian regimes. Whatever might be the scope of those reforms, it is clear that they signify the end of the myth of authoritarian socialism. These changes are a self-criticism and equivalent to a confession. For this reason I have spoken of the end of an era: we are present at the twilight of the idea of Revolution in its last unfortunate incarnation, the Bolshevik version. It is an idea that survives only in some regions on the periphery and among insane sects like that of the Peruvian terrorists. We do not know what the future holds for us: virulent nationalisms, ecological catastrophes, rebirth of buried mythologies, new fanaticisms, but also discoveries and creations: history and its entourage of horrors and wonders. Nor do we know if the peoples of the Soviet Union will become acquainted with new forms of oppression or an original and Slavic version of democracy. In any case, the revolutionary myth is dying. Will it come back to life? I do not believe so. A Holy Alliance is not killing it: it is dying a natural death.

Joyce said that history is a nightmare. He was wrong: nightmares disappear with the light of dawn whereas history will conclude only toward the end of our species. We are men through it and in it; if it ceases to exist, we will cease to be men. But the end of the revolutionary myth perhaps will permit us to think anew about the principles that have established our society and about their deficiencies and lacunas. Relieved, finally, of the struggle against totalitarian superstition, we can now reflect more freely on our tradition. Thus, the subject of the *virtue* of citizens reappears. It is a subject that comes from Classical Antiquity; it preoccupied Machiavelli as well as Montesquieu, and today it has a painful actuality in many countries, among them the Anglo-American democracy based on the Puritan ethic. Kant taught us that morality cannot be based on history: it flows without ceasing, and we do not even know if some law or plan rules its unpredictable passing. We know also that the metahistoric constructions—be they religious or metaphysical, conservative or revolutionary—strangle liberty and end by corrupting fraternity. The thought of the era that is beginning—if an era is really beginning—will have to find the point of convergence between liberty and fraternity. We must rethink our tradition, renew it, and seek the reconciliation of the two great political traditions of modernity, liberalism and socialism. I venture to say, paraphrasing Ortega y Gasset, that this is "the subject of our time." It seems to me that our days are auspicious for an endeavor of this significance; in some contemporaneous works—for example in that of Cornelio Castoriadis—I already note the beginning of a response.

What can be the contribution of poetry to the reconstitution of a new political thought? No new ideas but rather something more precious and fragile: memory. Each generation of poets rediscovers the terrible antiquity and the no-less-terrible youth of the passions. In the schools and faculties where the so-called political sciences are taught, the reading of Esquilo and Shakespeare should be obligatory. Poets nourished the thought of Hobbes and Locke, of Marx and Tocqueville. Through the mouth of the poet speaks—I emphasize: *speaks,* not writes—the *other* voice. It is the voice of the tragic poet and that of the buffoon, that of the melancholy solitary person and that of the fiesta, it is the guffaw and the sigh, that of the embrace of lovers and that of Hamlet before the skull, the voice of silence and that of tumult, insane wisdom and wise insanity, whisper of confidence in the bedroom and surge of the multitude in the plaza. To hear that voice is to hear time itself, the time that passes and that, nevertheless, returns transformed in a few crystalline syllables.

Index

This book is set in Espinosa for the text type, with Klavika
Medium and Regular for the display. Klavika was designed by
Eric Olson in 2004. Espinosa was designed by Cristóbal Henestrosa
in 2010. The face is based on type used by Antonio de Espinosa,
a sixteenth-century Mexican printer. He is thought to have been
the first punch cutter in the Americas.

This book is printed on paper that is acid-free and meets the
requirements of the American National Standard for Permanence
of Paper for Printed Library Materials, z39.48-1992. ♾

Book design by Richard Hendel,
Chapel Hill, North Carolina

Typography by Tseng Information Systems, Inc.,
Durham, North Carolina

Printed and bound by Sheridan Books, Inc.,
Ann Arbor, Michigan